21st-Century Africa

Scan the QR code to see all the titles in the
Africa Flagships collection.

21st-Century Africa

Governance and Growth

Edited by
Chorching Goh

WORLD BANK GROUP

ISBN (paper): 978-1-4648-2186-8
ISBN (electronic): 978-1-4648-2187-5
DOI: 10.1596/978-1-4648-2186-8

Cover photos: Clockwise from top: © insta_kenya / iStock; © Charday Penn / iStock; © ThamKC / iStock; © Sabrina Bracher / Shutterstock.
Cover design: Jihane El Khoury Roederer, Global Corporate Solutions, World Bank.

Library of Congress Control Number: 2025902042

Contents

FIGURES

TABLES

Foreword

Will the 21st century witness a major push by African countries to catch up with their peers? Or will the continent, overall, continue to lag other regions? A flagship report published by the World Bank in 2000, *Can Africa Claim the 21st Century?,* provided a blueprint for Africa to claim the new century. Twenty-five years later, Africa's aggregate progress reveals some advancements. Yet some of the endeavors identified as pivotal to accelerate progress at the century's outset have fallen short. Much more needs to be done to mitigate conflicts, invest in people, bolster economic competitiveness, and reduce dependence on external financing.

What will it take to reshape Africa's trajectory, not only for the few countries that have made notable advancements but also for current and future generations across the continent? The goal of fostering inclusive green growth remains pertinent today, yet its attainment is increasingly daunting. The growth model—based on labor-intensive, polluting industrialization that once brought wealth elsewhere—faces headwinds as automation expands, trade patterns shift, and climate pressures mount. Amid rapid population growth, achieving social and economic inclusion becomes more demanding. Moreover, sustainability is threatened by pollution, resource overextraction, and the exacerbating impacts of climate change.

Nevertheless, promising instances and hopeful examples in numerous African countries demonstrate that no inherent barriers prevent Africa from accelerating development and narrowing the gaps with other world regions. To achieve this goal, countries must intensify efforts to address three crucial enablers of development:

1. Governance with accountable leadership, widespread public engagement, and a competent and committed state. Without such elements, progress on any aspect of development is unattainable.

2. Africans equipped with skills, technology, and access to quality health care, enabling them to engage in society and the economy, particularly given the influx of individuals joining the workforce.

3. Robust, well-functioning market systems that cultivate growth, foster opportunities, and generate productive employment.

This sequel report analyzes past achievements, enduring obstacles, and potential policy alternatives. The chapters in this report outline strategies for governments to enhance support for inclusive green growth. They delve into ways the continent can empower its expansive, young labor force with the requisite skills and resources for a modern, productive economy. Moreover, they explore how trade in goods and services can distribute economic gains across what historically has been the most fragmented world region. The chapters also address how countries can bolster resilience against climate change and capitalize on the energy transition to foster inclusive productivity growth and welfare enhancements.

This sequel report argues that replicating the development paths of today's industrialized nations will not suffice to make the 21st century Africa's century. Instead countries should focus on using the continent's inherent potential to gain from a growing population, credible states, and an integrated market. They need to chart their own paths in a climate-resilient framework toward higher incomes and widespread prosperity.

Ousmane Diagana
Vice President
Western and Central Africa
World Bank

Victoria Kwakwa
Vice President
Eastern and Southern Africa
World Bank

Acknowledgments

This report was prepared under the guidance and supervision of the Chief Economist for the World Bank Group's Africa Region: Andrew Dabalen (since July 2022) and Albert Zeufack (before July 2022). The team expresses its gratitude for strategic counsel and support from the Vice President for Eastern and Southern Africa, Hafez Ghanem (January–June 2022) and Victoria Kwakwa (since July 2022); the Vice President for Western and Central Africa, Ousmane Diagana; the Director of Strategy for Eastern and Southern Africa, Amit Dar; and the Director of Strategy for Western and Central Africa, Elisabeth Huybens.

This team is grateful to peer reviewers Abebe Adugna, Haroon Bhorat, Ibrahim Elbadawi, William Maloney, and Stephen O'Connell. The team also thanks the report's advisory panel of experts for their valuable insights and suggestions. The panel consists of Elizabeth Asiedu (Howard University), Robert Bates (Harvard University), Haroon Bhorat (University of Cape Town), Paul Collier (University of Oxford), Ibrahim Elbadawi (Economic Research Forum, Arab Republic of Egypt), Bernadette Kamgnia (Center of Economic Research, Côte d'Ivoire), Pierre Nguimkeu (Georgia State University), Stephen O'Connell (Swarthmore College), and Michael Ross (University of California, Los Angeles). The distinguished experts provided written comments on earlier drafts, held discussions with chapter teams during virtual meetings, and contributed background papers to ensure that frontier knowledge was brought to bear in the report.

The core team consists of Chorching Goh (task team leader), Beatrice Berman, Abrah Desiree Brahima, Flore Martinant de Preneuf, Uwe Deichmann, Kenneth Omondi, Rose-Claire Pakabomba, and Fan Yang. Fan Yang also provided excellent research assistance and effective coordination. Roberta Bensky skillfully edited the report. Jewel McFadden and Mark McClure provided superb support throughout the publication process. The chapters were authored by Debbie Isser, Gael Raballand, Michael Watts, and Diane Zovighian (chapter 1); Kanta Kumari Rigaud and Anna Gayatri Singh (chapter 2); Cesar Calderon and Ayan Qu (chapter 3); Cristina Constantinescu, Mathilde Lebrand, and Gianluca Santoni (chapter 4); Leila Aghabarari, Ricardo David De Castro Martins, Justice Tei Mensah, Vincent Palmade, and Volker Treichel (chapter 5); Kaleb Abreha, Woubet Kassa, and Pierre Nguimkeu (chapter 6); Montserrat Pallares-Miralles, Yevgeniya Savchenko, and Anita Schwarz (chapter 7); Izak Atiyas and Mark Dutz (chapter 8); and Abdoulkadre Ado and Josephine Ofori Adofo (chapter 9). The team is grateful for the contributions from Jean-François Arvis, Monica Beuran, Mathieu Cloutier, Alvaro Espitia, Lionel Fontagné, Bene Wende Anicet Kabre, Hoyoung Kwon,

Yujin Lee, Jean Michel Marchat, Siobhan Murray, Jinhwan Oh, Ibrahim Okumu, Emir Sfaxi, Jisun Song, Daria Ulybina, and Quentin Wodon during the drafting stage.

Throughout the report's production, the World Bank's Africa Region Chief Economist, Andrew Dabalen, and the report team consulted widely on the continent and elsewhere to ensure that the report's analyses and narratives are anchored in country-specific policy debates. Individual chapter teams and the overall report narratives were presented during academic conferences, policy-based events, learning forums, and bilateral meetings with policy makers and scholars. The report team gratefully acknowledges constructive suggestions and invaluable feedback received from the following consultations and discussions: Secretariat for the Africa Continental Free Trade Area (March 2022, February 2023); African Economic Research Consortium (April 2022, July 2022, February 2023); University of Ottawa (April 2022, June 2023, November 2023); Chief Economists of Government Networks (May 2022, June 2023); regional high-level meetings (Cotonou, Benin, May 2022); United Nations Economic Commission for Africa (May 2022); African Development Bank (Annual Meetings, October 2022; Spring Meetings, April 2023, June 2023); African Union (Annual Meetings, October 2022; African Union headquarters, January 2023); international forum (Niamey, Niger, November 2022); African Economic Forum (Mauritius, December 2022); Centre d'Etudes Prospectives et d'Informations Internationales (CEPII) Seminars (February 2023); Kenya's Partnership for Economic Policy (Spring 2023); Global Trade Analysis Project (GTAP) Annual Conference (June 2023); Telfer School of Management and University of Cape Town (June 2023); and African Center for Economic Transformation (Accra, Ghana, July 2023).

Main Messages

Africa's progress despite persistent challenges

Over the past 25 years, Africa has achieved notable progress (refer to figure M.1). Mortality rates have fallen, with life expectancy rising from 50 years in 1998 to 61 years in 2022. School attendance has improved, with primary school enrollment increasing from 80 percent in 1999 to 99 percent in 2022 and secondary school enrollment increasing from 26 percent to 45 percent over the same period. The early 2000s saw strong economic growth fueled by high commodity prices. China emerged as a trade and investment partner, and the continent experienced a massive inflow of foreign capital from 17.6 percent of gross domestic product (GDP) in 1998 to 38.1 percent in 2018. Consequently, African countries have shown significant growth performances: from 2000 to 2019, 7 of the world's 10 fastest-growing economies were in Africa. Aid dependence has declined, tax revenues have increased, and the median poverty rate fell by about 10 percentage points to about 43 percent.

Despite such hopeful signs, Africa remains the world's biggest development challenge for several reasons. First, the continent faces the following structural economic challenges:

- *Persistent poverty.* By 2030, 90 percent of the world's extremely poor population will live in Africa.

- *Economic stagnation.* Sub-Saharan Africa's share of the global economy remains at 2 percent, with minimal change in the region's merchandise exports.

- *Investment levels.* Private investment remains low, with the informal economy accounting for 59 percent of total nonagricultural employment.

- *Limited growth.* The reliance on smallholder agriculture limits economic growth due to low investment and productivity.

- *Electricity access.* Only 51 percent of the African population has access to electricity, compared to the global average of 91 percent.

Second, Africa has experienced a shift in trade partners and development assistance. Trade with China has risen sharply, while the US trade share has dropped. Recent years have seen increases from Asia, focusing on economic infrastructure, whereas Western aid focuses more on social infrastructure.

FIGURE M.1 Africa's challenges and opportunities

Despite corruption and conflict, civic engagement offers hope.

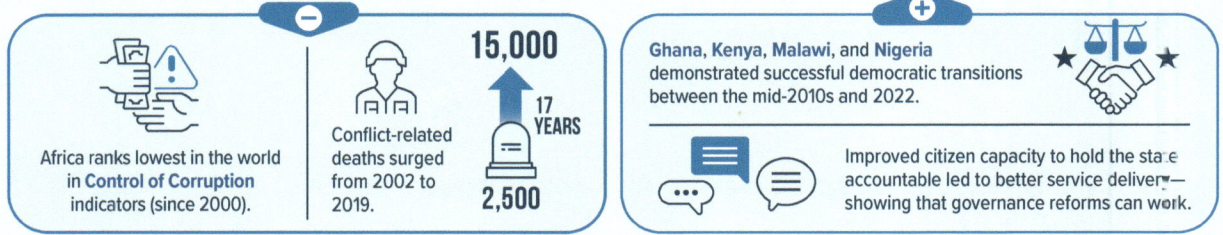

Africa ranks lowest in the world in **Control of Corruption** indicators (since 2000).

Conflict-related deaths surged from 2002 to 2019.

15,000
17 YEARS
2,500

Ghana, Kenya, Malawi, and **Nigeria** demonstrated successful democratic transitions between the mid-2010s and 2022.

Improved citizen capacity to hold the state accountable led to better service delivery—showing that governance reforms can work.

Restoring trust in institutions and improving governance will do the following:

Transform Africa's economic future

1990 — Africa's income level per capita would be **40%** higher if it had grown at the global average since 1990.

Nearly **83%** of Africa's employment is informal.

Africa's exports to the world rose from US$136 billion in 2002 to **US$662 BILLION** in 2022.

Private investment as a share of GDP is rising.
8.5% (1990s) — 9.5% (2010s)

Africa's economy faces challenges, but trade and investment drive transformative progress.

Raise Africa's human capital

86% of 10-year-olds in Africa can't read and understand a simple paragraph.

Only **45%** of youth enroll in secondary school.

Just **10%** complete tertiary education.

92 IN 2000
49 IN 2022
Infant mortality rates have declined from 92 (2000) to 49 (2022) per 1,000 live births.

Countries like **Côte d'Ivoire** (89%) and **Ethiopia** (52%) have made significant literacy gains in the past two decades.
20 YEARS

Africa's human capital gaps are substantial, but health and education investments can yield positive results.

Foster sustainable growth

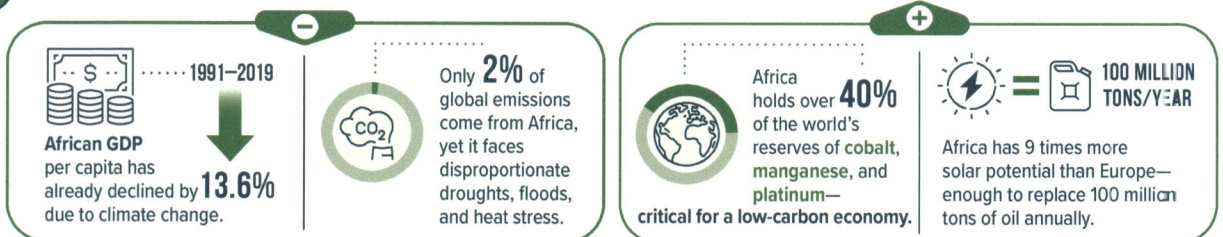

1991–2019
African GDP per capita has already declined by **13.6%** due to climate change.

Only **2%** of global emissions come from Africa, yet it faces disproportionate droughts, floods, and heat stress.

Africa holds over **40%** of the world's reserves of **cobalt**, **manganese**, and **platinum**—critical for a low-carbon economy.

= 100 MILLION TONS/YEAR
Africa has 9 times more solar potential than Europe—enough to replace 100 million tons of oil annually.

Africa's natural environment is vulnerable, but the green energy revolution can sustain its future.

Source: World Bank.

Third, the continent faces significant and disproportionate effects from climate change:

- *Minimal contribution, maximum vulnerability.* Africa has contributed only about 2 percent of global emissions but suffers disproportionately from climate change.

- *Reduced economic gains.* Since 1991, increments in Africa's average GDP per capita were 14 percent lower than they would have been in a world without climate change.

Finally, Africa suffers from political instability and governance difficulties:

- *Political upheaval.* Violent conflicts increased eightfold between 2000 and 2023 throughout the continent, leading to increases in conflict-related deaths and the number of internally displaced people.

- *Governance challenges.* The issues of corruption, political instability, and a lack of trust in government and institutions persist.

Investing in people is the path to Africa's transformation

Africa's development challenges point to the following opportunities for improvement by investing in people. Achieving sustainable development, however, will require restoring trust and continuing improvements in governance.

- *Demographic dividend.* While many of the world's economies suffer from a declining workforce, Africa has the world's youngest population, a trend that is expected to grow. If productive opportunities exist, Africa's demographic dividend can create a large skilled population.

- *Clean energy.* Africa enjoys significant solar potential, nine times greater than that of Europe. Africa's abundance of minerals vital to the low-carbon economy—including 40 percent of global reserves of cobalt, manganese, and platinum—positions it as a critical player in the transition to clean energy.

- *Health and education.* Investments in people have driven progress in health and education outcomes across Africa. Between 2000 and 2022, infant mortality rates declined from 92 to 49 deaths per 1,000 live births, and the maternal mortality rate decreased from 870 to 536 deaths per 100,000 live births in 2020. Immunization rates increased overall by 21 percentage points, and stunting dropped by 27 percent. Under-five mortality rates fell by 22 percent, from 128 deaths per 1,000 newborns in 1998 to 100 in 2021. These trends must be sustained and expanded.

- *Internet access.* The share of the population covered by internet-enabled networks (third and fourth generation) has increased, a key driver for labor productivity. The availability of third-generation (3G) coverage reached 96 percent in North Africa and 84 percent in Sub-Saharan Africa in 2023. From 2010 to 2023, internet subscriptions in Sub-Saharan Africa increased by 24 percent. Africa needs to accelerate these trends to become a truly connected continent.

- *Restored trust in governance.* Despite the increasing political instability throughout the region, since the mid-2010s Ghana, Liberia, Nigeria, and Sierra Leone have experienced peaceful regime change through elections, demonstrating democratic resilience. Both Kenya and Malawi have weathered successful constitutional challenges to fraudulent elections. Between 2000 and 2010, improvements in civil capacity were a strong predictor of increased quantity and inclusiveness of public goods and services. Empowered civil societies are better able to bargain with the state for stronger outcomes.

Without improving governance, however, countries will not be able to make the most of these opportunities. Achieving this improvement will require both substantial investments to enhance public sector capability and transformative policy change to address the underlying social dynamics influencing political behavior. The most remarkable development is the proliferation of popular social movements across the continent that engage in sustained collective action for change. It is essential for African governments and policy makers to prioritize restoring trust in state institutions, because that trust is crucial for effective governance and sustainable development.

By focusing on the aforementioned opportunities, Africa can overcome its challenges and progress to a brighter future.

Navigating the Report

In 2000, the World Bank published *Can Africa Claim the 21st Century?* Twenty-five years later, most of the world's poor live in Sub-Saharan Africa. This sequel report, *21st-Century Africa*, reexamines persistent barriers to development and explores emerging opportunities for the continent. It discusses policies that can help countries sustain inclusive green growth.

The report begins with a critical examination of institutions. Governance remains a priority because without a committed and capable government, progress in all policy areas will remain elusive. The population of internally displaced due to conflict (26.7 million in 2023) is at an all-time high and rising in the region. Political violence, spreading from the Sahel to the Horn of Africa, increased sixfold between 2000 and 2020. Mass demonstrations and protests in the region have grown by more than twice the global average. Building state capabilities is a domestic process in which outsiders can play only a supportive role. Chapter 1 offers a diagnosis of the state of Africa's governance, examining its multiple dimensions and highlighting the factors that have enabled pockets of state effectiveness.

Chapter 2 focuses on climate resilience and environmental sustainability in growth. It discusses policies to achieve universal electrification without compromising inclusive green goals, explores ways to reduce damage from climate change, and identifies opportunities for Africa as part of the global solutions for climate change. Although Sub-Saharan Africa bears the least responsibility for climate change, it bears the brunt of the consequences. Accounting for only 2 to 3 percent of the world's carbon dioxide emissions, African countries nevertheless have already paid a sizable growth penalty as a result of anthropogenic climate change.

The next four chapters are about economic efficiency in growth. They analyze options for raising productivity, which is indispensable for achieving competitiveness, higher living standards, and societal well-being. Throughout history, no country has achieved higher income status without sustained, inclusive productivity growth. The four chapters tackle pertinent questions in the areas of sectoral and input productivity, trade, private sector investments, and industrialization. They discuss topics such as the drivers behind trade performance, strategies for integration into global value chains, and ways to optimize investments and attract new industries. One hopeful development is the establishment of the Pan-Africa Continental Free Trade Area, a pan-African commitment with the potential to encourage broader regional integration and cooperation. For example, African countries successfully collaborated during the COVID-19 pandemic, particularly in vaccine distribution.

Following the discussion of economic efficiency as a generator of jobs, chapters 7 and 8 highlight skill formation and technology, respectively. These themes are closely related because the large number of young workers entering Africa's labor markets must be well-suited to perform tasks reliant on rapid adoption and adaptation of new technologies to local contexts. The chapters discuss the need to equip Africa's burgeoning population with the skills, knowledge, and other complementary capabilities to take advantage of economic opportunities. The chapters also underscore the role of digitalization in enhancing workforce readiness and competitiveness. Whether Africa can harness the demographic dividend in a changing global economic landscape rests critically on the extent to which its population is equipped with adequate human capital.

The report concludes with a discussion of leveraging Africa's economic partnerships with the rest of the world to advance inclusive productivity growth. Notably, in 2000, only three African countries—Benin, the Democratic Republic of Congo, and the Seychelles—had an Asian country as their top trade partner. By 2021, Asia had emerged as the major trade partner for 33 African countries, indicative of evolving global dynamics. Furthermore, an increasing number of Africans are graduating from universities in China, India, Türkiye, and the Middle East, fostering deeper business engagement with these locations. This final chapter explores avenues for nurturing African entrepreneurship and expanding commercial links around the world. It also scrutinizes strategies to effectively harness external cooperation to promote Africa's private sector investments, optimize Africa's trade patterns, and accelerate economic diversification.

Abbreviations

3G, 4G, 5G	third-, fourth-, fifth-generation (of mobile cellular network)
ACLED	Armed Conflict Location & Event Data
AfCFTA	African Continental Free Trade Area
AI	artificial intelligence
ASYCUDA	Automated System for Customs Data
BIM	building information modeling
BRI	Belt and Road Initiative
Cat DDO	Catastrophe Deferred Drawdown Option
CCDR	Country Climate and Development Report
CO_2	carbon dioxide
CPIA	Country Policy and Institutional Assessment
CPSD	Country Private Sector Diagnostic
CRDC	Climate Resilient Debt Clause
CS-PIM	Climate-Smart Public Investment Management
DT	digital technology
EU	European Union
FAT	Firm-level Adoption of Technology (survey)
FCPF	Forest Carbon Partnership Facility
FCS	fragile and conflict-affected situations
FCV	fragility, conflict, and violence
FDI	foreign direct investment
GBF	general business function
GDP	gross domestic product
GHG	greenhouse gas
GIS	Geographic Information System
GVC	global value chain
HBF	Health Basket Fund (Tanzania)
HCI	Human Capital Index
ICT	information and communication technology
IFC	International Finance Corporation
ISIS	Islamic State of Iraq and Syria

ISP	internet service provider
ITS	Intelligent Transport System
LFTZ	Lekki Free Trade Zone
LPI	Logistics Performance Index
MFN	most favored nation
MNO	mobile network operator
MSMEs	micro, small, and medium enterprises
MW	megawatt
NEET	not in employment, education, or training
ODA	official development assistance
OSBP	One-Stop Border Post
PBC	performance-based contract
PCG	partial credit guarantee
PFM	public financial management
PIDA	Program for Infrastructure Development in Africa
POS	point-of-sale
PPP	public-private partnership
PTA	preferential trade agreement
RIA	Research ICT Africa (survey)
RTA	regional trade agreement
SDGs	Sustainable Development Goals
SEZ	special economic zone
SMEs	small and medium enterprises
SOE	state-owned enterprise
STEM	science, technology, engineering, and mathematics
TFP	total factor productivity
TFPR	revenue total factor productivity
TVET	technical and vocational education and training
UNCTAD	United Nations Trade and Development
WTO	World Trade Organization

Note: This report uses "Africa" to refer to the continent generally. It uses "Sub-Saharan Africa" for specific data or statistics that apply to the region, because there is no readily available aggregate for the entire continent.

CHAPTER 1

Governance

Debbie Isser, Gael Raballand, Michael Watts, and Diane Zovighian

Summary

Almost 25 five years after publication of the report *Can Africa Claim the 21st Century?* (World Bank 2000), Africa's development trajectory underscores the continued relevance of improving governance and resolving conflict as a priority area for sustainable and equitable growth. The continent's mixed track record of limited progress, reversals, and marked failures demonstrates the difficulty of achieving governance objectives. Empirical analysis from the governance sector points to four key trends:

1. *Effective state institutions capable of maintaining peace, fostering growth, and delivering services have developed unevenly.* Despite some progress on fundamentals such as revenue mobilization and public financial management (PFM), overall public administration, rule-based governance, and regulatory capacities have stagnated, with particular challenges in fragile and resource-rich countries. This lack of progress underlies the persistence of corruption and the low performance of public service delivery.

2. *Progress made to enhance the inclusiveness and accountability of institutions remains constrained by weak checks and balances, and by persistent patterns of centralized and exclusive power arrangements.* Repeated multiparty elections across the continent have introduced some level of electoral accountability, but checks and balances on executive power tend to be weak, transparency is limited, and access to political and economic power remains highly unequal.

3. *Civil capacity has risen considerably, but the inability of institutions to respond to social expectations threatens to turn liberal civic engagement into distrust, populism, and radicalization.* In spite of an exponential increase in mass demonstrations and protests as a means of contesting failing social contracts, with a considerable acceleration since the early 2010s, civic mobilization has not been met with state responsiveness.

4. *The combination of these three trends contributes to the rise of political instability and violence, which poses a major threat to sustainable and inclusive growth.* Citizens'

This chapter includes contributions by Monica Beuran and Mathieu Cloutier.

disappointment in the ability of states to deliver basic services, weak institutional channels for accountability, and high levels of distrust point to the fragility of the social contract. The region has experienced a sharp uptick in violent events since 2015, with insecurity spreading across the Sahel region to the Horn of Africa as evidenced by eight successful military coups since 2020.

In the face of an uncertain national and global stage, the ability of Africa to claim the 21st century will require efforts to identify innovative ways to invest in institutions and forge social contracts capable of addressing questions of poverty, inclusion, equity, and justice. Successful strategies will not always correspond to standard models of best practice, nor will they emerge as a result of conventional reform templates. They will require looking beyond technical policies to understand how power dynamics and citizen-state relations can be reshaped to generate mutual accountabilities. This chapter points to three overarching principles that should guide the way to more effective and responsive governance:

1. *Exploit opportunities to strengthen the fiscal contract.* Increased and more progressive domestic resource mobilization is a priority for Africa; however, without commitment to demonstrably improve services and pro-poor interventions, increased taxes exacerbate distrust and foment unrest.

2. *Safeguard civic space and democratic forms of governance.* Because of widespread erosion of trust in state actors and institutions across Africa, governments will need to (re)gain trust to break the cycles of low expectations, low development, and high instability. Although transitions to democracy can be volatile, ultimately democracies tend to be better governed and able to sustain inclusive growth.

3. *Effective national governance requires that the international community address critical constraints at global and regional levels.* Climate change, violent extremism, natural resource exploitation, geopolitical rivalries, and global financial markets all play a significant role in shaping country-level policy making and (in)security. Unless these constraints are addressed as global public goods, Africa will struggle to achieve its potential.

Context

The 2000 report highlighted the nexus of governance, conflict management, and poverty as "the most difficult" yet "the most fundamental" for faster development (World Bank 2000). The report argued that the fundamental goals of promoting peace and security and improving economic management demand effective and inclusive institutions. Rather than prescribe specific technical solutions, it emphasized the need to strengthen processes and enablers of demand- and supply-side "good governance"; that is, state capacity[1] to regulate the economy and deliver services demands an empowered citizenry to channel demands and hold the state to account.

The messages and policy foci of that earlier report were shaped by the particular historical circumstances on the continent in the wake of the end of the Cold War. A release of political enthusiasm was witnessed in the proliferation of nongovernmental and civic organizations, and in the wave of democratic transitions across the continent. The worst of the political violence of the 1980s and 1990s had seemingly subsided, and use of the term "Africa rising" reflected the optimism of the time. A post–Cold War political and economic order offered the possibility of new resources and opportunities for Africa.

There is still a strong academic and policy consensus that governance matters for development. Evidence shows that development trajectories are largely shaped by the presence—or absence—of an effective state monopoly on the use of violence; stable and predictable rules and institutions that regulate economic relations, enforce contracts and regulations, and promote economic investments; and open and inclusive political institutions that ensure the representation of plural economic interests and create political incentives to level the economic playing field (Acemoglu and Robinson 2012; Centeno, Kohli, and Yashar 2017; North 1990; Rodrik, Subramanian, and Trebbi 2004; Vom Hau 2012). Figures 1.1–1.3 illustrate the positive correlation between governance determinants (political stability, rule of law, and voice and accountability) and growth in Sub-Saharan Africa. They also hint, however, at the many conundrums of institutional and economic development—including the uneasy relation between natural resources, governance, and growth—as well as the wide variations in economic performance of countries situated in the "messy middle" of the governance spectrum. Refer also to box 1.1 for a definition of governance.

Empirical data lead to an emerging consensus about what matters for governance. First, the aspirations set out in 2000 are still highly relevant—that inclusive, representative, and accountable governance is a prerequisite to sustainable and equitable growth. Second, no clear linear pathway or set of institutional forms exists to achieve these goals. Governance is shaped by configurations of power, norms, and structural dynamics that in turn shape the legitimacy of forms of public authority, and the transparency and accountability of civic and governmental institutions. Effective strategies must address power asymmetries and incentives in ways that enable institutional functions needed for policy implementation. These strategies need to consider that governance is not the exclusive domain of national governments but is also shaped by local and transnational factors (World Bank 2017). In short, good governance is necessary for development, but getting there involves complex negotiations between a wide range of actors with diverse interests and different capabilities.

What is the quality of governance on the continent, and how does it shape development? What can we learn from the governance trajectory of African countries since the beginning of the 21st century? The first decade of the millennium saw promising growth and poverty reduction on much of the continent. Violence and fatalities dropped significantly as major conflicts in Liberia, Sierra Leone, and the

FIGURE 1.1 **Political stability and economic development in Sub-Saharan Africa, 2021**

Log GDP per capita (PPP)

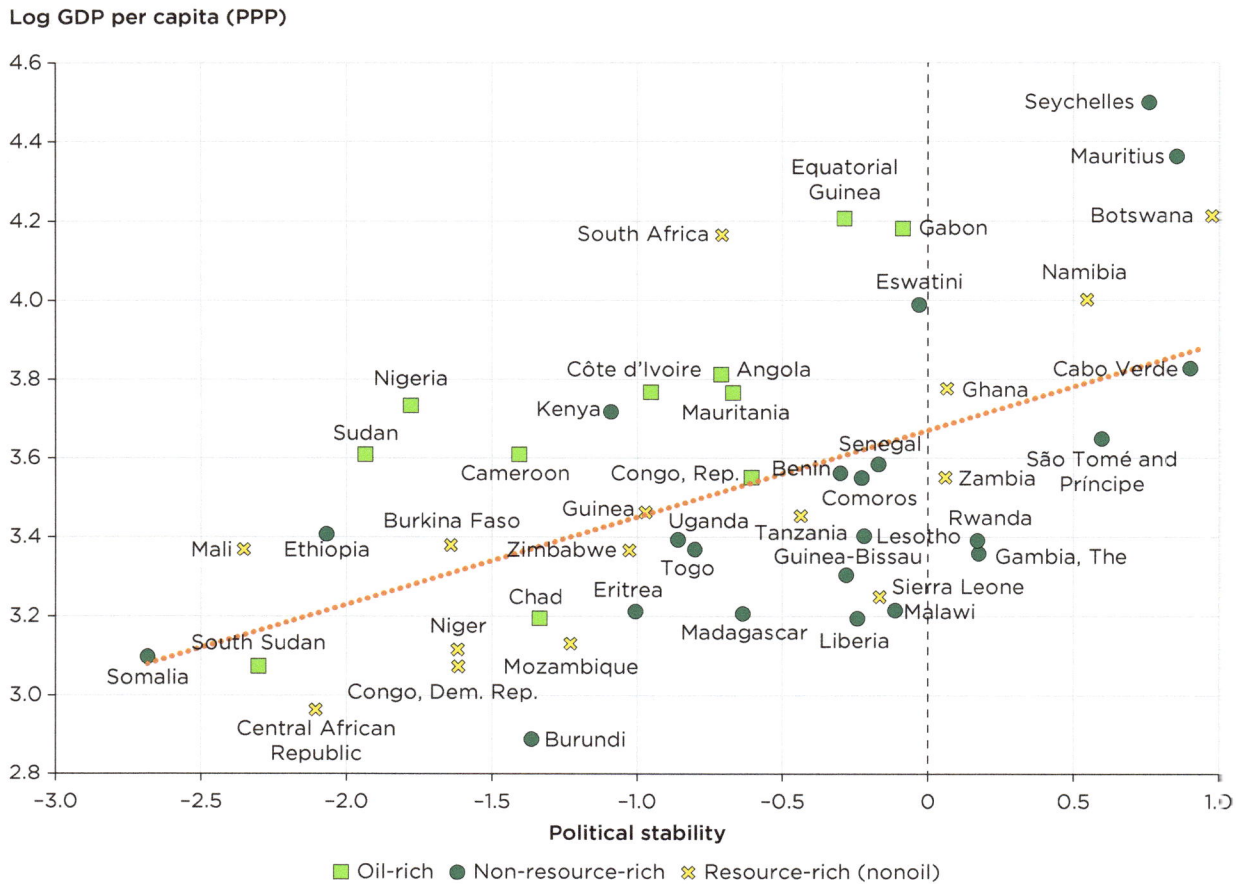

Sources: World Bank, Worldwide Governance Indicators database for political stability indicator, https://databank
.worldbank.org/source/worldwide-governance-indicators; World Bank, World Development Indicators database for
GDP per capita, https://data.worldbank.org/indicator/NY.GDP.PCAP.CD.
Note: The x axis represents the Worldwide Governance Indicator on political stability. The higher the value, the
greater the stability. The data are the latest available (2021). PPP = purchasing power parity.

Great Lakes region were brought if not under full control at least to new states of
stability. Anecdotal evidence and country case studies point to (sometimes unexpected)
governance wins: Rwanda, a postconflict country, has managed to reform its public
administration to improve service delivery, especially for health; Madagascar, a fragile
state, has made progress on building institutions for revenue generation at customs; and
other countries, such as Botswana, have managed to safeguard their stability for
decades and have built on this conducive environment to push forward selected
financial management and regulatory reforms. In addition, the continent has witnessed
many peaceful electoral transitions to opposition parties, including in places such as
Nigeria with legacies of authoritarian rule and civil conflict, even if the elections
themselves pointed to the existence of ballot rigging, intimidation, and fraud.

FIGURE 1.2 Rule of law and economic development in Sub-Saharan Africa, 2021

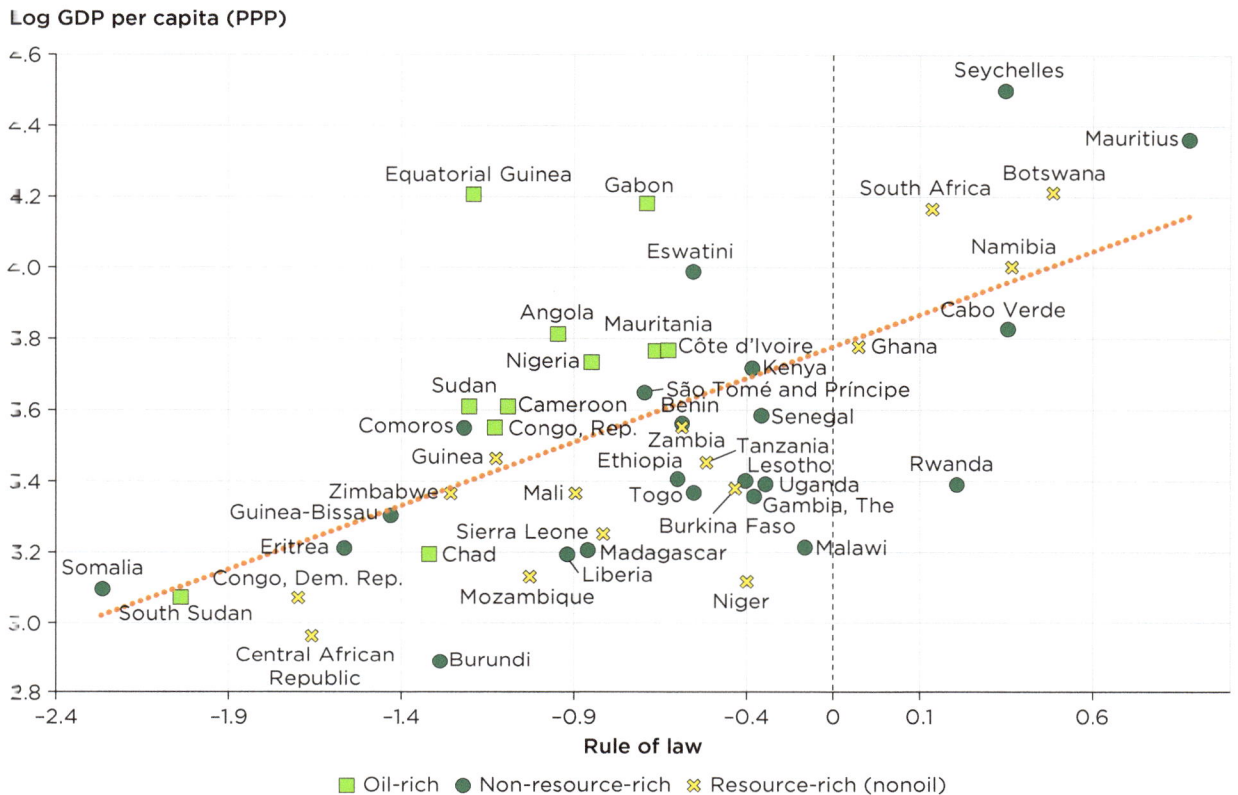

Log GDP per capita (PPP)

Sources: World Bank, Worldwide Governance Indicators database for rule of law indicator, https://databank .worldbank.org/source/worldwide-governance-indicators; World Bank, World Development Indicators database for GDP per capita, https://data.worldbank.org/indicator/NY.GDP.PCAP.CD.
Note: The x axis represents the Worldwide Governance Indicators on rule of law. The higher the value, the stronger the adherence to the rule of law. The data are the latest available (2021). PPP = purchasing power parity.

Along with these wins, Sub-Saharan Africa has also experienced a stream of governance reform failures and policy reversals, and many countries continue to suffer from the consequences of poor governance. Since about 2015, a series of crises with mostly external origins—plunging commodity markets, the spread of insecurity and religious extremism, the COVID-19 pandemic, a rise in authoritarian forms of populism, and a major shift in the geopolitical landscape—have revealed the underlying weakness of democratic institutions and state capacity on much of the continent. Because of a possibly overly optimistic vision in 2000 (due to the current context at that time), many African countries, relying on the commodities supercycle between the late 1990s and 2008, and not having undertaken the necessary governance reforms, started to suffer from growing debt and economic imbalances that contributed to states' inability to respond to growing demands and dissatisfaction from their citizens (Blas 2023). Conflict and violence have increased sharply, fueled by extremist groups capitalizing on locally based grievances such as political marginalization (Dowd 2015) across the Sahel, the Horn of Africa, Mozambique, and elsewhere (Boly and Kéré 2023).

FIGURE 1.3 Voice and accountability and economic development in Sub-Saharan Africa, 2021

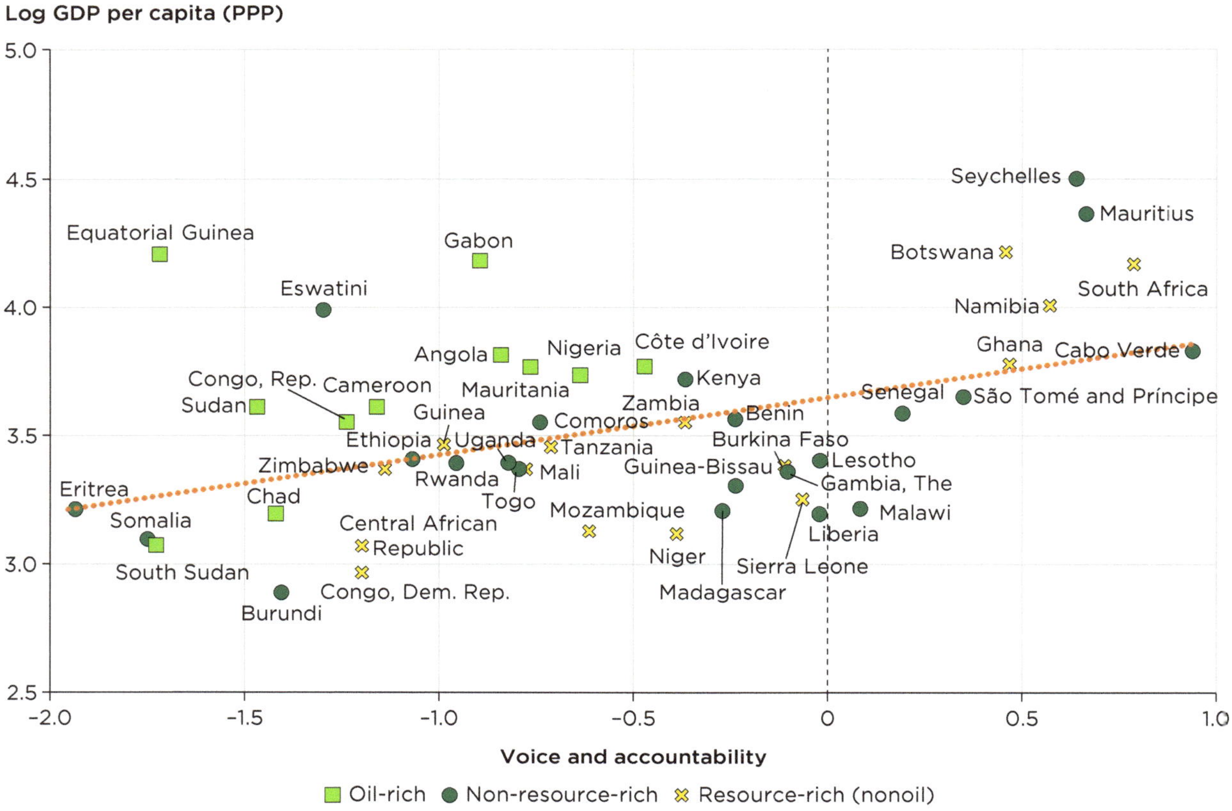

Log GDP per capita (PPP)

Voice and accountability

☐ Oil-rich   ● Non-resource-rich   ✖ Resource-rich (nonoil)

Sources: World Bank, Worldwide Governance Indicators database for voice and accountability indicator, https://databank.worldbank.org/source/worldwide-governance-indicators; World Bank, World Development Indicators database for GDP per capita, https://data.worldbank.org/indicator/NY.GDP.PCAP.CD.
Note: The x axis represents the Worldwide Governance Indicator on voice and accountability. The higher the value, the better the ability of citizens to express their views and hold their government accountable. The data are the latest available (2021). PPP = purchasing power parity.

Despite increased military spending, national security forces have been in decay (Bagayoko 2022; Dwyer 2017) and African states have not been able to respond to the security demands of their citizens. State effectiveness is hindered by political interference in recruitments and promotions, inefficient public spending, and chronic poor or understaffed administrations due to low revenue collection. Moreover, a global backlash against liberal institutions, coupled with the rise of populism and facilitated by social media and pressure on traditional media, has also contributed to broken social contracts. High levels of corruption, including illicit financial flows, have resulted in falling levels of citizen trust in political authorities and state institutions. Populations are fed up with the failure of governments to provide basic public services, including security, as evidenced by the surge in social protests and low levels of trust in government.

In some African countries, a failing social contract and the rise of nonstate armed groups have gone hand in hand with the return of coups and the militarization of politics, further fueling political instability. Although a common occurrence in the postindependence era, coups decreased substantially from the 2000s. The decade before 2021 had on average only one successful coup per year. Since 2020, however, the continent has seen the resurgence of military coups in countries such as Burkina Faso, Chad, Gabon, Guinea, Mali, Niger, and Sudan. The context of these coups varies substantially, but there are reliable coup predictors, including failing social contracts, insecurity, and the militarization of politics. In several countries, these contexts have resulted in social protests and, in the initial phases at least, popular support for military coups and military governance, despite citizens' strong expressed preferences for democratic forms of government. Most countries have also experienced coups partly as a by-product of the imbalanced aggrandizement of their armed forces in the face of serious security threats—whether from domestic insurgencies, organized crime, or the spread of militancy related to the global war on terror or insecurity contagion from failing neighboring states (Opalo 2023). The strongest predictor of future instability is past instability. Some countries, such as Burkina Faso in recent years, already show signs of being at risk of getting stuck in a coup trap, whereby the militarization of politics and intra-elite factional infighting lead to repeated countercoups and prolonged instability.

This chapter explores the dynamics of governance reform on the continent and attempts to make sense of the heterogeneity of African governance trajectories. The "Facts" and "Analysis" sections identify long-term trends and lay out some of the reform wins and some of the areas that lag behind. Although the analysis inevitably relies on aggregated data for generalizations and on imperfect benchmarks for comparisons, it also, when possible, attempts to provide nuanced and fine-grained country perspectives. Using this evidence, the "Policies" section reflects on strategies that countries might deploy to enhance governance in ways that create the space for much-needed policy reforms.

Facts

The continent has a mixed track record on building effective and accountable governance institutions capable of managing conflict and driving inclusive growth. Overall, however, it has not matched the (arguably excessive) expectations of the early 2000s.

The state of governance in Africa: An overview of status and trends

Analysis of the state of governance in Africa since 2000 points to four key trends. First, effective state institutions capable of maintaining peace, fostering growth, and delivering services have developed unevenly. Despite some progress in reforming state institutions, including on fundamentals such as revenue mobilization and PFM in selected countries, overall progress on building strong and effective state institutions, including public administration and regulatory capacities, has stagnated. Reformers have had to contend with repeated reform failures and reversals, particularly in fragile and resource-rich countries. This subpar progress on institutional development underlies the persistence of petty and grand corruption and low performance of public service delivery.

Second, progress made on enhancing the inclusiveness and accountability of institutions remains constrained by weak checks and balances and persistent patterns of centralized and exclusive power arrangements. Although multiparty elections across the continent have introduced some levels of electoral accountability, checks and balances on executive power tend to be weak, transparency is limited, and access to political and economic power remains highly unequal. In this context, countries in democratic transitions have struggled to deliver on their development promises, and many are stuck in a stable equilibrium of extractive political and economic institutions.

Third, civil capacity has risen considerably, but the inability of institutions to respond to social expectations and political mobilization threatens to turn liberal civic engagement into distrust, populism, and radicalization. Democratic development at the turn of the century opened a window of opportunity and created pressure for more public transparency and space for social mobilization, but civic mobilization has not been matched by complementary state responsiveness in service delivery, security, or public integrity. This mismatch comes with high risks of instability and could open the door to social demands for less liberal forms of governance, especially with the increased presence of China and the Russian Federation, which provide alternative models.

Finally, these three trends combined contribute to the rise of political instability, which constitutes a major threat to the continent's ability to claim the 21st century. Citizens' disappointment in the ability of states to deliver basic services, weak institutional channels for accountability, and high levels of distrust point to the fragility of the social contract. Interstate wars have declined since the turn of the millennium, but the region has experienced a sharp uptick in violent events since 2015, with insecurity spreading across the Sahel region to the Horn of Africa. Eight successful military coups have taken place since August 2020. Such instability and violence are core binding constraints to growth on the continent: instability creates policy volatility, shortens policy horizons leading to suboptimal macroeconomic policy decisions, and decreases investors' confidence, with negative effects on economic performance. African democracies are more likely to invest in pro-poor growth, spending more on education and health, whereas autocratic regimes invest more in military expenditures (Ndayikeza 2021). Fang et al. (2020) estimate that in Sub-Saharan Africa annual growth in countries in conflict is about 2.5 percentage points lower on average, and that the impact on gross domestic product (GDP) per capita is cumulative and increases over time. Despite the potential volatility of transitions to democracy, ultimately democracies tend to be better governed and able to sustain inclusive growth.

Lessons learned from African countries' governance trajectory since 2000

Although the messages set out in the 2000 report are still highly relevant—inclusive, representative, and accountable governance remains a prerequisite to sustainable and equitable growth—it has become clear that there is no linear pathway to achieving these goals. This chapter's journey through two decades of governance development offers four insights that, taken together, call for more careful and nuanced thinking around governance reform in Africa.

First, the governance trajectories of African countries show that institution building is a slow, protracted, and deeply political process. As Andrews, Pritchett, and Woolcock (2017) demonstrate, if history is any indication, it takes decades or even centuries for developing countries to develop strong state capabilities. The *World Development Report 2017: Governance and the Law* states that the interests and incentives of key players shape their political commitment to the adoption and implementation of critical governance reforms (World Bank 2017). Such interests and incentives include economic rents and interests, electoral and other political incentives, and popular pressure. Thus, institutions are shaped by the distribution of power and tend to replicate the interests of those making the decisions. These strong feedback loops favor the persistence of power asymmetries and path dependencies.[2] Fundamental change in the quality of institutions requires more than reforming rules and forms on paper; it requires real shifts in the relative power or interests of those in a position to make, implement, and enforce policy.

Second, the vast heterogeneity of African experiences shows that the factors of success and failure are highly context-dependent and conjunctural. The aggregate picture of the state of African governance belies the considerable heterogeneity and dynamism across the continent and even within states (across subnational entities or across institutions). Because institutions are embedded in and the product of the local political economy, they are responsive to context. Institutional shifts may develop over time from incremental change or in response to a major shock or crisis, or they may emerge in particular spaces and moments as a result of the confluence of contextual factors. One example is in countries with significant natural resource endowments: oil, minerals, and other extractives are associated with higher levels of corruption, lower incentives to develop robust tax systems, and overall lower institutional quality.[3] The challenge is acute in Sub-Saharan Africa, where the contribution of natural resource rents,[4] especially oil and mineral rents, to GDP is much higher on average than in the rest of the world. Sub-Saharan Africa lags behind only the Middle East and North Africa region, as exemplified by the poor governance track record of resource-rich African countries such as Angola, the Democratic Republic of Congo, and Nigeria. Even these countries, however, experience areas of progress and pockets of effectiveness. Although the public sector can be dysfunctional, some parts of the state may be endowed with the capacity and autonomy needed to achieve results (Hickey 2023). Crafting effective governance reforms will therefore require a great deal of contextual knowledge, as well as strategic opportunism.

Third, the pathway to democratic and effective governance is not linear. Among other things, the widely held assumption in the early 2000s that democratic transition on the continent would go hand in hand with better governance has not systematically passed empirical tests. Although democracy tends to be good for governance, the *transition* toward a democratic system is a time of high institutional vulnerability. Country experience shows, for example, that both grand and petty corruption can increase during transition times, and that the introduction of elections can initially reinforce clientelist behavior among electoral competitors, shorten policy makers' policy horizons, and decrease incentives for long-term public investment.

These considerations should not be understood as a call to reconsider support to democratic transition or to promote autocratic governance. Although countries with top-down, authoritarian models of governance, such as Ethiopia and Rwanda, have at different times managed to successfully introduce select governance reforms, these reforms have come at the cost of limited political opening and accountability, which create mid- to long-term risks to political stability and development. Ethiopia is a case in point: autocratic governance backfired into civil conflict, ultimately undermining reform progress and the country's development.

Finally, and related to all of the preceding insights, reformers must confront politics. This necessity holds true for governments and donors alike. Successful reform has hinged on the ability of policy makers to harness politics in their favor. Many of the failures of the good governance agenda, which international development agencies have promoted since the 1990s, can be traced back to an attempt to replicate "best practices" that have tended to ignore, bracket, or underplay the social and political context in which institutions are located, as opposed to developing the best fit that takes into account the country's context and the power struggles at play in governance reforms (Grindle 2004; World Bank 2017; refer also to Andrews, Pritchett, and Woolcock 2012). The uneven impact of donor support for governance reforms results, to a large extent, from the inadequate consideration of local politics and power relations. Recent recognition of the limits of donor support has pushed development practice further toward confronting power and politics. Analyses offered in the 2017 *World Development Report* view the gap between policy adoption and implementation (and its resolution) in relation to "power asymmetries" and "political settlements" (World Bank 2017). Such an approach calls for unpacking policy makers' interests, incentives, and influence—and the process through which they contest, negotiate, or coordinate policy decisions—to understand how political will for reform can emerge or break.

Analysis

A high-level look at governance data suggests that change in Sub-Saharan Africa has been slow over the past 20 years and that governance in the region still lags behind other world regions. Aggregate Worldwide Governance Indicators illustrate those macrotrends. The three aggregate variables presented in figures 1.4–1.6 measure key dimensions of governance: government effectiveness; voice and accountability; and political stability. They show that Sub-Saharan Africa slightly improved its percentile rank for voice and accountability but deteriorated on government effectiveness and political stability. On indicators related to voice and accountability and political stability, Sub-Saharan Africa tends to perform worse than other world regions except the Middle East and North Africa. It lags behind all other world regions in terms of government effectiveness, and its position appears to have slightly deteriorated since the early 2000s.

FIGURE 1.4 **Government effectiveness, by world region, 2000–20**

Percentile rank (0–100)

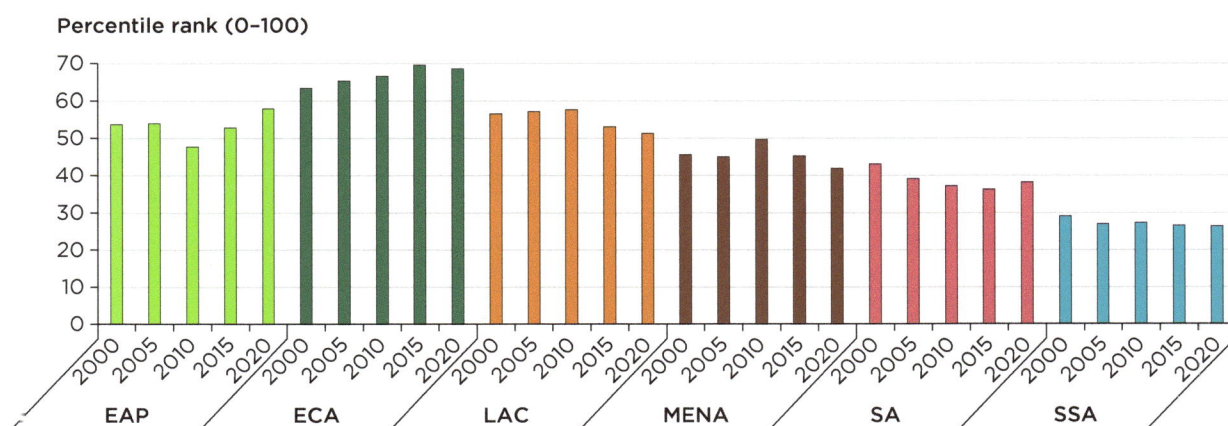

Source: World Bank, Worldwide Governance Indicators, https://www.worldbank.org/en/publication/worldwide
-governance-indicators.
Note: Percentile rank ranges from 0 (lowest) to 100 (highest). EAP = East Asia and Pacific; ECA = Europe and Central Asia; LAC = Latin America and the Caribbean; MENA = Middle East and North Africa; SA = South Asia; SSA = Sub-Saharan Africa.

FIGURE 1.5 Voice and accountability, by world region, 2000–20

Percentile rank (0–100)

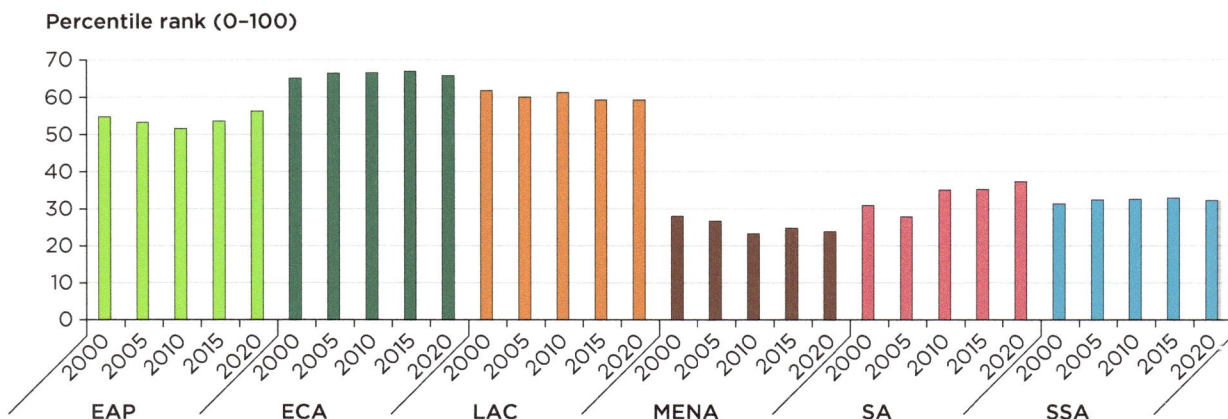

Source: World Bank, Worldwide Governance Indicators, https://www.worldbank.org/en/publication/worldwide-governance-indicators.
Note: Percentile rank ranges from 0 (lowest) to 100 (highest). EAP = East Asia and Pacific; ECA = Europe and Central Asia; LAC = Latin America and the Caribbean; MENA = Middle East and North Africa; SA = South Asia; SSA = Sub-Saharan Africa.

FIGURE 1.6 Political stability, by world region, 2000–20

Percentile rank (0–100)

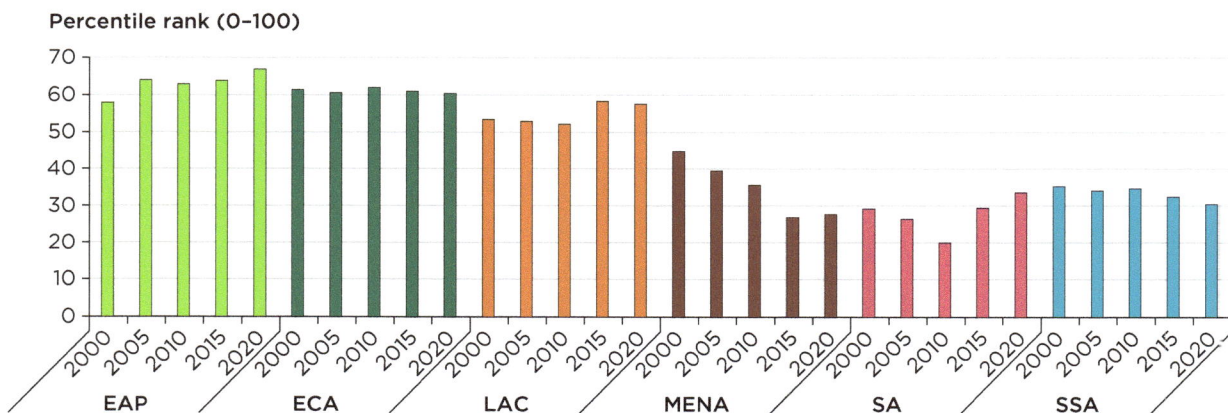

Source: World Bank, Worldwide Governance Indicators, https://www.worldbank.org/en/publication/worldwide-governance-indicators.
Note: Percentile rank ranges from 0 (lowest) to 100 (highest). EAP = East Asia and Pacific; ECA = Europe and Central Asia; LAC = Latin America and the Caribbean; MENA = Middle East and North Africa; SA = South Asia; SSA = Sub-Saharan Africa.

The next subsections dive more deeply into Africa's governance record. They look at four building blocks of inclusive and effective governance: state effectiveness and capability, inclusive and accountable political institutions, civil capacity, and political stability. More disaggregated data provide some nuance to the governance diagnostic and help identify some positive trends hidden by aggregate variables, such as progress made on selected fundamentals of government effectiveness (including PFM and revenue generation), the durability of democratic (and electoral) processes, and the decline in interstate wars. The data also show that, despite these advances, progress has often been subject to reversals and stagnation, and many areas of governance continue to lag.

State effectiveness and state capacity trends

Long-term trend 1: Effective state institutions, capable of maintaining peace, fostering growth, and delivering services, have developed unevenly since 2000.

Despite some progress in reforming state institutions, including on fundamentals such as PFM or revenue mobilization in selected countries, overall progress on building strong and effective state institutions, including public administration and regulatory capacity implementation, has stagnated. Reformers have had to contend with repeated reform failures and reversals, particularly in fragile and resource-rich countries. This subpar progress on institutional development underlies the persistence of petty and grand corruption, and the low performance of public service delivery.

Overall progress on state effectiveness and capacity has stagnated since the early 2000s. On the whole, the region has performed poorly on public sector management and institutions in the World Bank Country Policy and Institutional Assessment (CPIA)—refer to figure 1.7.[5] Data indicate marginal to no progress on these critical dimensions, including the quality of public administration, property rights, and rule-based governance.[6] Better understanding the trends on public sector management and institutions, however, requires putting them in historical and comparative perspective. As illustrated by Andrews, Pritchett, and Woolcock in their 2017 book, *Building State Capability: Evidence, Analysis, Action*, institutional development has historically been an extremely slow-moving process that unfolds over decades, or even centuries. Rather than being an anomaly, slow institutional development that is also subject to reversals appears to be the norm and warrants more realistic and gradual policy prescriptions for governance reform.

FIGURE 1.7 Trends in Country Policy and Institutional Assessment governance indicators, Sub-Saharan Africa, 2005–21

CPIA governance indicators

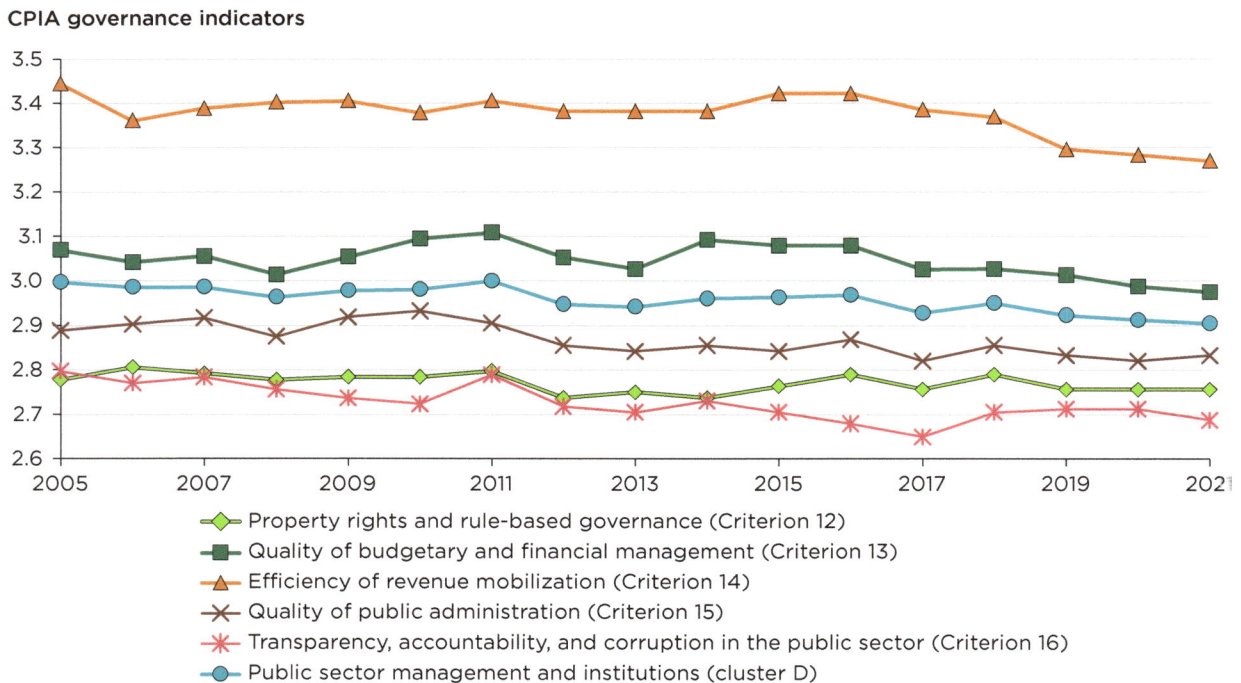

- ◆ Property rights and rule-based governance (Criterion 12)
- ■ Quality of budgetary and financial management (Criterion 13)
- ▲ Efficiency of revenue mobilization (Criterion 14)
- ✕ Quality of public administration (Criterion 15)
- ✳ Transparency, accountability, and corruption in the public sector (Criterion 16)
- ● Public sector management and institutions (cluster D)

Source: World Bank, DataBank, "Country Policy and Institutional Assessment," https://databank.worldbank.org /source/country-policy-and-institutional-assessment (accessed 2022).
Note: Country Policy and Institutional Assessment (CPIA) values range from 1 (low) to 6 (high).

Variations occur across dimensions of state effectiveness in the region: on average, countries have higher scores on selected fundamentals such as revenue mobilization or budgetary and financial management (figure 1.7). This relative performance points to the power of incentives in state building. Faced with high fiscal deficits and pressure from citizens to deliver public services (refer to the subsection "Patterns of contestation and resilience"), governments have strong incentives to build state capacities that allow them to raise more revenues and manage their limited resources more efficiently. Areas that are strategic for governments appear to see more progress, with notable improvements in the adoption of some good practices in budget management and transparency, establishment of anticorruption and accountability agencies, and even increasing public service delivery, such as school enrollment. In contrast, other public sector dimensions remain low—rule-based governance, characterized by clear contract and property rights, and a strong legal and judicial system to enforce them—with deleterious effects on economic activity. The quality of public administration also remains low overall, with some exceptions (box 1.2): national and subnational core administrations in African countries tend to perform poorly, including in managing their own operations or ensuring quality in policy implementation and regulatory management.

BOX 1.2
Public administration reform in Rwanda

Rwanda came out of the civil war with a bloated and underskilled civil service that was ripe with patronage. As early as 1998, however, the country introduced a series of reforms to build an effective civil service and strengthen administrative capacity, both of which were seen as critical to improve service delivery and strengthen political legitimacy in the postwar context.

The first reform plan downsized the civil service, decentralized its personnel, and introduced transparent and merit-based recruitment to improve the quality of civil servants. Four downsizing and voluntary departure programs were implemented between 1999 and 2009, resulting in a leaner civil service. New selection criteria and procedures also shifted the profile of civil servants and led to a substantial increase in the share of civil servants with university degrees, from 6 percent in 1998 to 79 percent in 2005 (Hausman 2011).

The Rwandan government also introduced new management tools to improve the performance of the civil service: Imihigo performance contracts were first signed in 2006 between district council mayors and the president to push local governments to articulate more systematically and clearly their objectives and strategies. Such contracts have since become annual undertakings. Imihigo instilled a culture of results and strengthened the vertical accountability of civil servants and local governments to central ministries and the presidency, resulting in an improvement in the quality of the public administration.

The Rwandan experience points to the importance of political dialogue around potentially contentious reforms; reforms to the recruitment processes were embedded in the Urugwiro consultative dialogue, which emphasized the importance of transparent and merit-based recruitment (as opposed to favoritism and patronage, which fed social tensions in the pre-genocide era). The country's experience also highlights the importance of context-specific solutions: Imihigo is a Rwandan management tool that builds on homegrown approaches to performance management.

Some ambivalence exists as to the effects of the political reforms in Rwanda. The government's capacity to push reforms and deliver results has been attributed to its authoritarian governance, including top-down decision-making by a presidential strongman. The capacity for reforms, therefore, has been indissociable from the broader context of limited pluralism and repressive politics. This context raises questions about the transparency of results, as well as about the long-term effects on reform sustainability from sidelining key accountability mechanisms, including checks and balances from the judiciary or citizen participation.

Source: For more details on the Rwandan experience, refer to World Bank 2019a.

Crises in recent years, including the COVID-19 pandemic, have strongly tested state effectiveness and capacity. The COVID-19 crisis was associated with a decline in the quality of public sector management and institutions, which suffered from the combined pressure of high debt levels, stretched fiscal resources, and increased demands for government interventions. Figure 1.8 illustrates the impact of the COVID-19 pandemic on revenue mobilization, with a drop in total taxes (as percent of GDP) following the crisis.

FIGURE 1.8 Trends in taxation, by world region, 2000–21

Total taxes as % of GDP

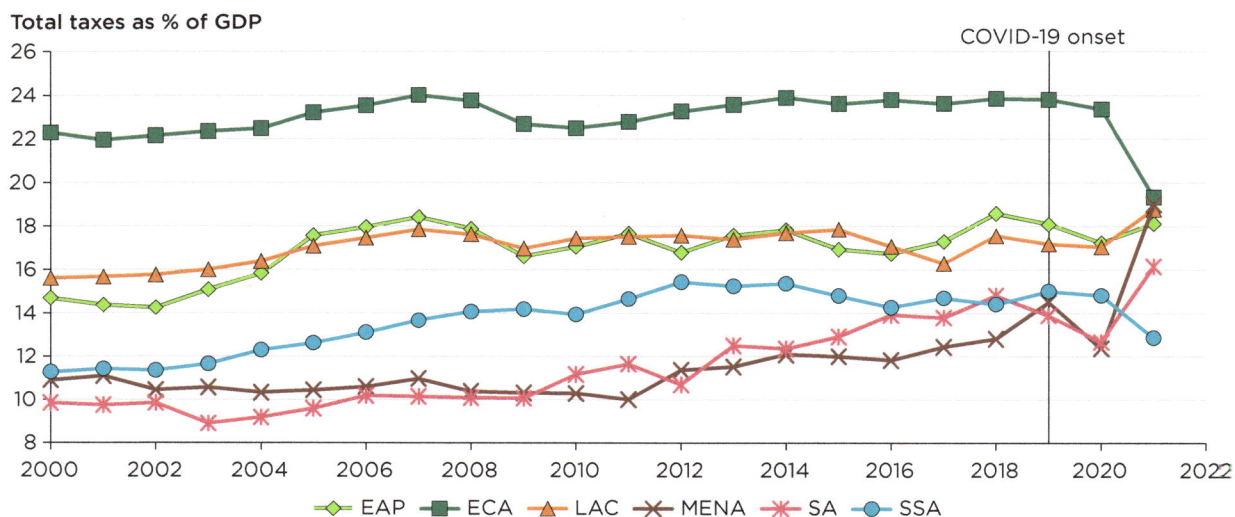

Source: Government Revenue Dataset, United Nations University World Institute for Development Economics Research, https://www.wider.unu.edu/project/grd-government-revenue-dataset.

Note: EAP = East Asia and Pacific; ECA = Europe and Central Asia; LAC = Latin America and the Caribbean; MENA = Middle East and North Africa; SA = South Asia; SSA = Sub-Saharan Africa.

Overall, efforts to build institutional capacities for revenue mobilization have translated into higher levels of taxation. Notwithstanding the negative impact of the COVID-19 crisis, the level of taxation in Sub-Saharan Africa has improved slightly over the past 20 years, with total taxes reaching 14.8 percent of GDP in 2020 (figure 1.8).

Regional-level analysis hides considerable country heterogeneity, with public sector performance varying substantially across countries (table 1.1). The scores show that a small subset of countries stands out; for example, Cabo Verde and Rwanda have been among the better-performing countries in terms of public sector performance for more than a decade. Similar trends emerge when zooming into budget and PFM performance: Public Expenditure and Financial Accountability assessments of budget execution, for example, show that some countries, such as Ghana, Rwanda, and Zambia, outperform their regional neighbors in the level of predictability and control over budget execution (figure 1.9).

TABLE 1.1 Governance performance, selected African countries, 2021 and trends since 2005

Trend	Countries
Top-five performers (2021)	Cabo Verde, Rwanda, Kenya, Senegal, Ghana
Bottom-five performers (2021)	South Sudan, Somalia, Sudan, Guinea-Bissau, Central African Republic
Most positive trend since 2005 (≥0.5 point)	Zimbabwe, Togo, Côte d'Ivoire, Rwanda
Most negative trend since 2005 (≤−0.5 point)	Sudan, Tanzania, Mali, Madagascar, Guinea-Bissau, Eritrea
No change since 2005	Niger, Nigeria, Senegal

Source: World Bank 2022.

FIGURE 1.9 Predictability and control in budget execution: Variations across countries in Sub-Saharan Africa

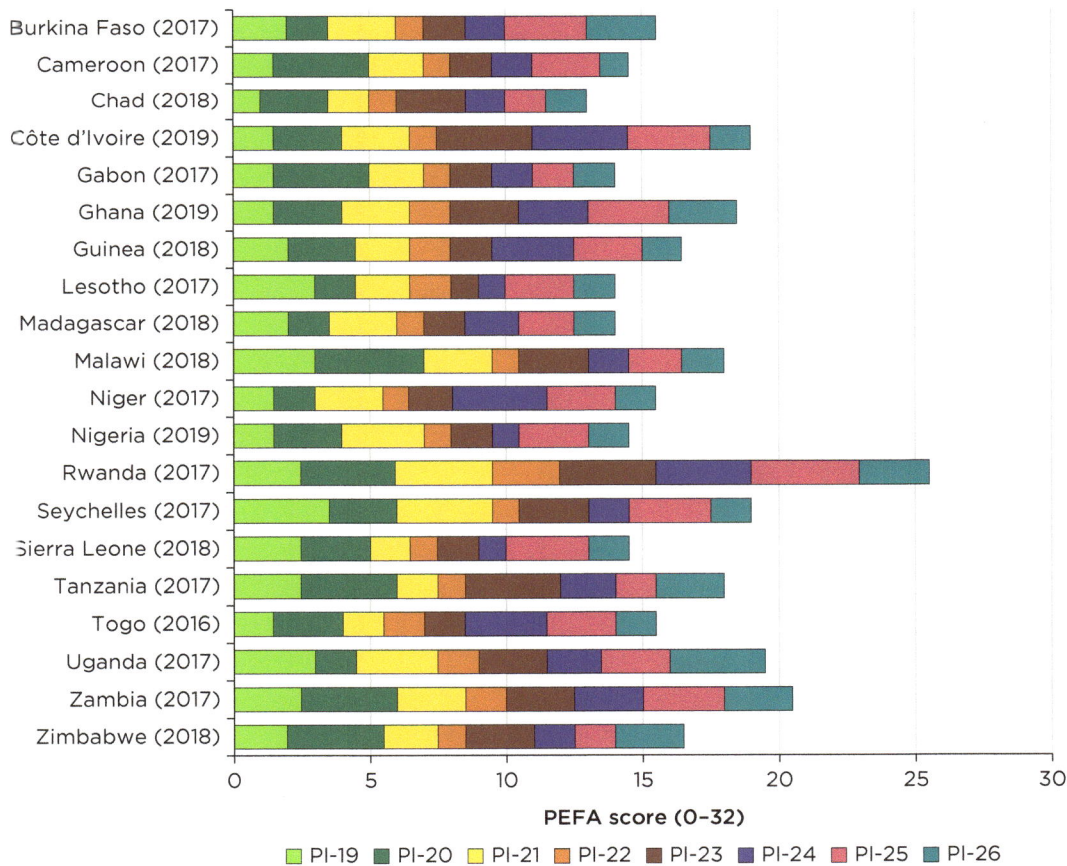

PEFA score (0–32)

PI-19 PI-20 PI-21 PI-22 PI-23 PI-24 PI-25 PI-26

Source: PEFA 2020.
Note: The PEFA pillar on predictability and control in budget execution has eight indicators and covers revenue administration, cash management, expenditure control, procurement, and internal audit. PEFA = Public Expenditure and Financial Accountability; PI = pillar indicator.

Fragility[7] tends to correlate with governance performance, even for the previously mentioned state fundamentals. On average, countries affected by fragility, conflict, and violence (FCV) systematically rank lower on the quality of budgetary and financial management and the efficiency of revenue mobilization (figure 1.10), and appear to be stuck in a low-capability equilibrium—whereby low capacity coexists with little to no progress on capacity development. This self-sustaining equilibrium points to a particularly acute need for financial and technical assistance, and also often reflects an unfavorable political economy environment for reform.

The same holds for resource-rich countries. Among others, resource-rich countries in Africa tend to have poorer fiscal and financial management performance: their capacities for budget and financial management and their ability to raise revenues appear to be systematically lower than other African countries (figures 1.10 and 1.11). This challenge illustrates a persistent *natural resource curse*, whereby governments benefiting from resource rents have fewer incentives to develop fiscal capacities and a fiscal contract with their citizens (Isham et al. 2005; Sala-i-Martin and Subramanian 2003).

FIGURE 1.10 **The role of fragility and natural resources in budget and PFM reforms, 2005–21**

a. Quality of budgetary and financial management, by fragility status

b. Quality of budgetary and financial management, by natural resource status

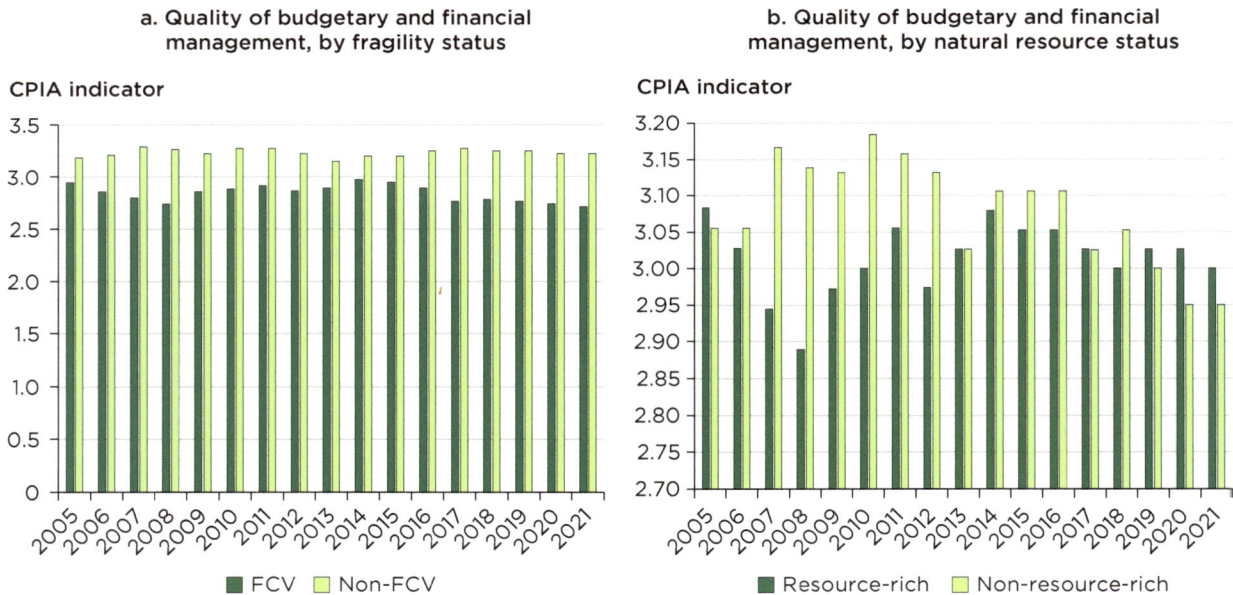

Source: World Bank 2022.
Note: CPIA = Country Policy and Institutional Assessment (World Bank); FCV = fragility, conflict, and violence; PFM = public financial management.

FIGURE 1.11 The role of fragility and natural resources in domestic resource mobilization reforms, 2005–21

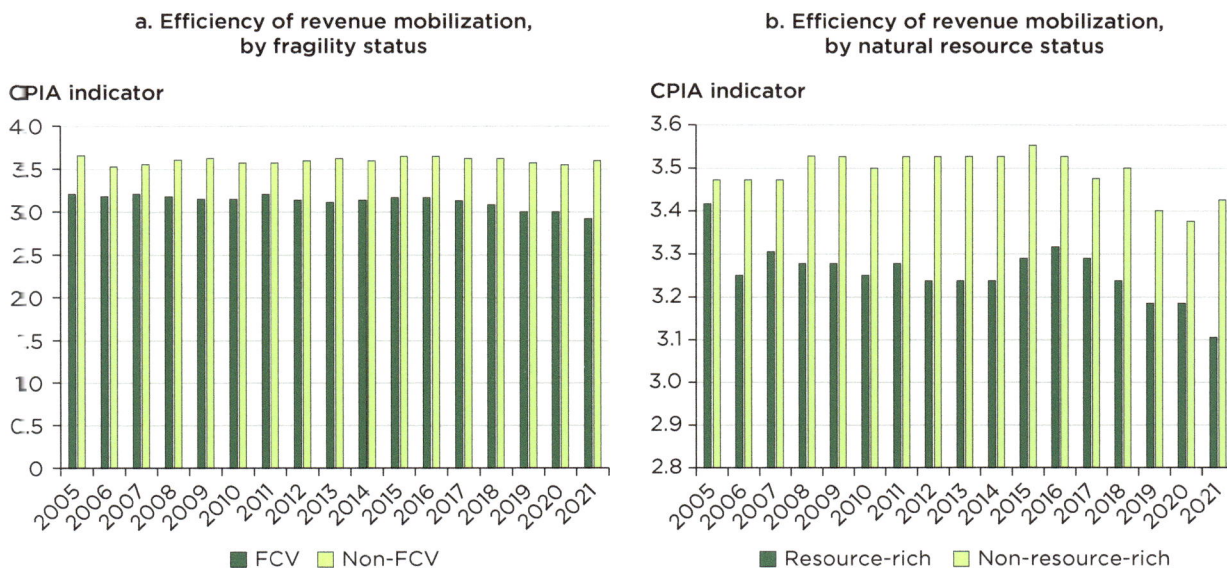

a. Efficiency of revenue mobilization, by fragility status

b. Efficiency of revenue mobilization, by natural resource status

FCV   Non-FCV

Resource-rich   Non-resource-rich

Source: World Bank 2022.
Note: CPIA = Country Policy and Institutional Assessment (World Bank); FCV = fragility, conflict, and violence.

Resources need not be a curse, however. Cross-country research shows that countries with political arrangements that limit rulers' discretion over the management of natural resource revenues are able to mitigate the negative effect of natural resources on fiscal and institutional capacities (Masi, Savoia, and Sen 2020). Botswana presents a case in point: a country rich in diamonds, it has escaped the resource curse with a political economy environment conducive to elite cooperation around resource management, and accountable relations between political elites and citizens. In addition, even within states that are marked as fragile or resource cursed, certain conditions can produce pockets of state capacity. These capacities may inhere in particular institutions or sectors. For example, in Nigeria, a country rich in natural resources and with a complex federal system, the public sector is constituted, especially at the federal level, by a vast array of institutions of various caliber and markedly different standards of efficiency. Some Nigerian institutions, in particular sectors, states, or organizations, work much better than others. Over the past two decades, at various times the Supreme Court and the Economic and Financial Crimes Commission have exhibited (if not consistently) some significant examples of independence and autonomy.

In this overall context of poor governance, corruption remains high in Africa, with little improvement in the past 20 years. Since 2000, the region has consistently ranked at the bottom of world regions on the Worldwide Governance Indicator on control of corruption, a composite indicator that captures perceptions of the extent to which public power is exercised for private gain, including both petty and grand forms of corruption, as well as state capture[8] by elites and private interests (figure 1.12). The indicator appears to have stabilized at low levels, in contrast with other regions that have witnessed improvements, such as East Asia and Pacific or Europe and Central Asia. Recent survey data on citizens' corruption perceptions also point to the resilience of corruption in Africa: according to the 2019 Global Corruption Barometer for 35 countries in Africa, more than 50 percent of respondents reported a perception that corruption was on the rise, and 59 percent of respondents believed that their government was doing a bad job of tackling corruption (Transparency International 2019).

Petty corruption is quite prevalent in public administration and services, and it negatively affects the quality of and access to public services. According to the 2019 Global Corruption Barometer, one in four Africans surveyed had paid a bribe in the previous year for access to public services, such as health care or education; in practice, this proportion means that about 130 million people were likely to have paid money or provided favors in exchange for access to services (Transparency International 2019). Petty corruption skews incentives for politicians and bureaucrats to deliver public services and is associated with poorer management and lower quality of services (World Bank 2004).[9] Petty corruption also has regressive effects: poor users pay a larger share of their incomes on bribes, discouraging them from seeking public services (refer to, for example, Kaufmann, Montoriol-Garriga, and Recanatini 2008). The Global Corruption Barometer also indicates that the poorest are twice as likely to pay a bribe as the richest,

FIGURE 1.12 Trends in control of corruption, by world region, 2000–20

Percentile rank (0–100)

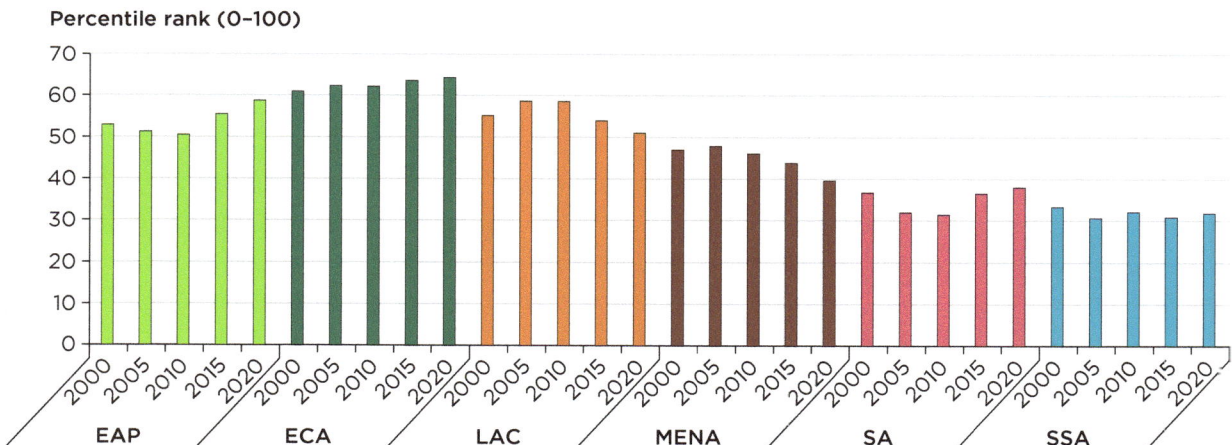

Source: World Bank, Worldwide Governance Indicators, https://www.worldbank.org/en/publication/worldwide -governance-indicators.
Note: Percentile rank ranges from 0 (lowest) to 100 (highest). EAP = East Asia and Pacific; ECA = Europe and Central Asia; LAC = Latin America and the Caribbean; MENA = Middle East and North Africa; SA = South Asia; SSA = Sub-Saharan Africa.

which is particularly delegitimizing when such corruption is embedded in security agencies, such as the police and military, because it represents a failure of basic security, the very basis of any social contract.

Although state capture in Sub-Saharan Africa remains difficult to measure, corruption scandals, selected audits and investigations, and anecdotal evidence confirm its scope and patterns. State capture takes many forms, from embezzlement to rent seeking and patronage. It plays out through the privileged access of politically connected elites to state resources, public employment, and policy decisions, including privileged access to permits and licenses, land, public contracts, grants and subsidies, or tax breaks (Fiebelkorn 2019). For example, external audits and investigations of the 2014 Ebola crisis revealed the misuse of large sums of Red Cross funds in Guinea, Liberia, and Sierra Leone, amounting to up to US$2.7 million in Liberia. Another stark example was the relationship between Jacob Zuma—South Africa's former president and leader of the African National Congress—and the Gupta brothers. Over several years, the parasitic relationship between the president and donors resulted in widespread looting and state capture with which the country is still coming to grips (Budhram 2019; Chipkin et al. 2018).

Perhaps one of the most daunting challenges faced by African countries is capital flight, a large share of which is estimated to be financial flows. Capital flight occurs when financial flows are either illegally earned or used (for example, embezzlement or inflated payments through fraudulent invoices) or illegally moved or diverted (for example, to evade taxes).[10] Empirical evidence about the relations between offshore centers, African elites, and capital flow remains limited; but the release of the Pandora Papers, among others, shows a robust African connection (refer to OECD 2023).[11] Estimates of capital flight from 30 African countries over the period 1970–2018 show that these countries lost a combined US$2 trillion (in 2018 dollars), representing 94 percent of their total combined GDP in 2018 (Boyce and Ndikumana 2022). More worryingly, the estimates show that capital flight from African countries has increased steadily since the turn of the century. Aid is at risk of being diverted by such forms of corruption. As documented by Andersen, Johannesen, and Rijkers (2020), aid disbursements to highly aid-dependent countries coincide with sharp increases in bank deposits in offshore financial centers, but not in other financial centers.

Grand corruption has dramatic fiscal and macroeconomic implications. An example of state capture whereby politically connected firms are granted preferential access to land, subsidies, public contracts, or tax exemptions has a demonstrated negative impact on productivity, job creation, and growth in developing countries (Diwan, Malik, and Atiyas 2019). Grand corruption also has distortive redistributive effects: patronage dynamics translate, for example, into misallocation of public funds and inefficient public investments that benefit narrow political constituencies over the welfare of the general population (Canen and Wantchekon 2022). In addition, the flow of corruption proceeds to offshore centers represents a substantial loss in revenues from African treasuries, at a time when the burdens of debt and debt service in the wake of COVID-19 are especially debilitating,[12] and arguably hampers the development of a fiscal contract between states and citizens.

Resource-rich Sub-Saharan African countries are disproportionately vulnerable to grand corruption, and progress on the transparency agenda in the extractives sector remains limited. Resource-rich countries are more prone to elite rent seeking and corruption, with negative effects on institutional development (Masi, Savoia, and Sen 2020; Sala-i-Martin and Subramanian 2003). As illustrated in figure 1.2 at the beginning of this chapter, the rule of law in Africa tends to be below average in resource-rich countries, especially for countries endowed with oil resources. Countries endowed with natural resources also appear to be substantially more exposed to capital flight than others: Boyce and Ndikumana (2022) show that 6 of the top-10 African countries with the highest amount of capital flight are oil exporters, and that the problem of capital flight also afflicts countries rich in primary commodities such as minerals and agricultural commodities (for example, Côte d'Ivoire and Zambia). Assessments of transparency and accountability instruments in the extractives sector in resource-dependent states show that such instruments have had relatively limited effect. Disclosure and transparency in state-owned and public energy and mining enterprises have left relatively untouched the connections between political elites, transnational corporations and global trading houses, and offshore financial centers (OECD 2016, 2023).

Anticorruption reform remains challenging, but some African countries have successfully experimented with localized, sector-based approaches. Experience in Sub-Saharan Africa and other world regions has shown that, although much-needed, development of an anticorruption ecosystem comprising anticorruption legislation, anticorruption agencies, and strong audit and justice institutions is a protracted and challenging process, especially in low-governance environments (World Bank 2020). The nature of corruption flows and the role of offshore centers in sustaining corruption also point out the need to take seriously the links between local and global governance, and to tackle the role of offshore centers, including through more transparent beneficial ownership—a complex enterprise (box 1.3). In contrast, more targeted sector-based approaches that address the institutional and political factors that enable corruption appear to have delivered more tangible results. For example, in Madagascar, customs malpractice and fraud led to considerable losses in revenue generation. In 2016, performance contracts were introduced in the country's main port, Toamasina, to incentivize customs inspectors to prevent tariff evasion. These incentives, coupled with information technology systems to improve monitoring of inspectors' performance, helped increase fraud detection, decrease processing times, and increase customs revenue.

The globalized nature of corruption

Illicit financial flows illustrate the globalized nature of corruption, particularly the interconnections between the national and global scales. Offshore centers usually originate in the strategies of some Organisation for Economic Co-operation and Development countries, corporations, wealthy individuals, and financial sectors and have thrived in many regions across the world. In absolute terms, the flow of capital and business through offshore centers originates disproportionately from high-income and middle-income economies. The strategies of tax avoidance or evasion, outward financial flows, and corruption enabled by the offshore world have affected Africa to an unusual extent (Soares de Oliveira 2022). According to the United Nations Conference on Trade and Development (UNCTAD 2020), in Africa, on average, extractive export underinvoicing was equivalent to 16 percent of merchandise exports of commodities from 2000 to 2015.

The regulation and curtailment of offshore world practices, a complex and frustrating enterprise even for large and powerful states, is extremely challenging for African states, despite some stirrings of collective action through organizations such as the African Union (OECD 2023). The difficulty shows that governance is not the exclusive domain of countries but is, rather, a process of policy making and implementation that happens simultaneously at multiple scales from the local to the transnational. Improving governance in ways that produce desirable outcomes requires an appreciation of how multiscalar power structures intersect.

Access to health and education services has increased and education and health outcomes improved in Africa over the past 20 years. Literacy improved from 57 percent to 67 percent, and life expectancy at birth rose from 50 to 60 years. In the education sector, countries have made substantial strides toward achieving universal primary education. In 2000, about 33 percent of primary-school-age children and 40 percent of lower-secondary-school-age children were out of school, compared with 17 percent and 33 percent, respectively, by the end of the 2010s (UNICEF and African Union Commission 2021). This progress is the result of policy commitments to create enabling legal frameworks for free and compulsory education in over half of African countries (UNICEF and African Union Commission 2021); support from the international community, including through global multistakeholder partnerships and funding, such as the Global Partnership for Education; and an increase in public spending on education (the average education expenditure in Africa rose during the first two decades of the 2000s, both in absolute terms and as a percentage of GDP) (UNICEF Africa 2022).

Despite those improvements, trends in service *equality* lag behind. The regional average measures of education and health equality[13] show the Africa region lagging on health equality, above only South Asia. These relatively stable averages hide high levels of variation at the country level. Scores have decreased for some countries—Burundi, Eritrea, and Namibia—and have increased for others—Gabon, Liberia, the Republic of Congo, and Tanzania. To some extent, these subpar outcomes can be traced back to financing challenges. Although spending on social services has increased, it remains close to the lower end of international benchmarks: for example, African countries spend on average 4.1 percent of their GDP on education, compared with a global average of 4.3 percent. The levels of government education expenditure vary widely across countries, ranging from about 1 percent of GDP in the Central African Republic to 8 percent in Sierra Leone (UNICEF and African Union Commission 2021). This challenge is compounded by a bias toward recurrent expenditure to finance salaries, versus capital expenditure to which countries devote on average only 13 percent of total education expenditure. Beyond financing, improvements in health and education hinge on governance challenges, including poor management of teachers and health workers, and a lack of autonomy and accountability of education and health organizations, which negatively affect the quality of service delivery.

In the past two decades, some African countries have experimented with civil service management reforms to improve service delivery, including in health and education. In particular, countries have tested reforms to increase the autonomy of public workers and performance-based pay, with varying levels of success. Rasul and Rogger (2016) and Rasul, Rogger, and Williams (2018) show that in Ghana and Nigeria reforms to management practices correlate with project completion rates, although not necessarily as predicted. Whereas increases in autonomy for bureaucrats enhance project completion rates, the use of incentive and performance monitoring systems decreases project completion rates,[14] suggesting that management reforms in service delivery need to be properly calibrated to the context. In the education sector, several African countries have tested pay for performance, with existing studies calling for nuanced assessment of the impact on the quality of education. For example, in Rwanda, pay for performance did not appear to affect the quality of recruited teachers, but it did contribute positively to the performance of teachers as measured by the quality of pupil learning (Leaver et al. 2020). In Tanzania, some evidence shows the positive effect of performance-based incentive schemes for teachers, although the effect is larger when additional incentives are coupled with the allocation of additional financial resources to schools (Mbiti et al. 2019). Additional evidence from Tanzania confirms that performance incentives for teachers can lead to modest average improvements in student learning, and that these improvements can be sustained once incentives are withdrawn. There is also evidence that incentives may have exacerbated learning inequality within and across schools, because increases in learning were concentrated among better-performing schools and students (Filmer, Habyarimana, and Sabarwal 2020).

Reforms to decentralize public services and increase the autonomy of schools or health facilities have also received substantial attention in the past two decades. Here again, the evidence is mixed and largely contingent on other country characteristics

(Channa and Faguet 2016). In the case of school-based management and autonomy, Duflo, Dupas, and Kremer (2007) provide evidence of a positive impact of increased school autonomy and resources to hire teachers and monitor their performance on student learning in Kenya. However, Glewwe and Maiga (2011) find that experimentation with increased resources and autonomy at the district and school levels in Madagascar did not have a discernible effect on test scores, possibly because of the short-lived nature of the intervention. Experiments in The Gambia also point to the importance of reform timing and sustainability (Blimpo, Evans, and Lahire 2020). The evaluation of a four-year, large-scale experiment to provide grants and training to principals, teachers, and community representatives shows that, taken together, grants and training led to a substantial reduction in student and teacher absenteeism three to four years into the program. It also highlights that the effect of decentralization reforms depends greatly on the context: although on average the program had no effect on learning outcomes, villages with high levels of baseline local capacity (for example, high literacy) showed a positive impact on learning outcomes, pointing to potential trade-offs between decentralization and equality in public service provision.

New digital technologies have generated considerable optimism, both in and outside the governance sector. E-governance, for example, is seen to be a relatively cheap and easy way to improve revenue generation, enhance PFM in the public sector, or improve public service delivery.[15] Since the 2000s, African countries have introduced a wide range of technological solutions, such as e-procurement platforms, financial management information systems, digital registries, e-filing, and digital public services. Such solutions, however, have had uneven effectiveness and impact on the quality of institutional processes and service delivery. In Africa and elsewhere, evidence suggests that a large digital divide persists, that digital technologies are not necessarily an easy path to leapfrogging in governance, and, more generally, that the task of building robust governance institutions is a long and arduous slog that differs in character from digital reforms in other sectors, such as providing high-yielding varieties to farmers or cell phones to slum dwellers. In governance there are no easy shortcuts to robust, capable, and democratic rules of the game, and digital solutions are only as good as the analog systems they complement (World Bank 2016)—refer to box 1.4.

BOX 1.4
Opportunities and pitfalls of new technologies in customs reforms

The modernization of border operations is important, notably the use of information technology systems or new expensive equipment. Modernization is often at the core of customs reforms projects. There is evidence that the introduction of information and communication technology systems, such as the Automated System for Customs Data (ASYCUDA), has been accompanied by increased revenues (Cantens, Raballand, and Bilangna 2010), as well as by decreased trade costs (Moïsé and Sorescu 2013).

(continued)

Opportunities and pitfalls of new technologies in customs reforms *(continued)*

It is rather easy to fall into the trap of unwarranted modernization and equipment. Countries often seek systems upgrades, for example, from ASYCUDA ++ to ASYCUDA World. Advances seen in neighboring places and computerization often become an end instead of a tool in many tax and customs administrations (Barbone et al. 1999). The first question to ask is whether the current system is used effectively and, if not, why not. In Cameroon's experience, for instance, automation-related gains could not be sustained as stakeholders learned the system's loopholes (Cantens, Raballand, and Bilangna 2010). A similar experience from Ghanaian Customs shows that information technology configurations in the early stages and related organizational processes can be co-opted by vested interests, thus leading to new forms of corruption, as well as having limited effects on petty corruption (Addo and Avgerou 2021). Ultimately, capacity and incentives are the two core parameters to take into consideration before engaging with new information and communication technology.

Source: Arvanitis and Raballand 2023.

Climate change creates new challenges and pressure for public sector reform. Climate-related increases in food insecurity, diminishing livelihoods in rural areas, and increases in droughts and floods, among others, put pressures on public finances and open debates on the information, capacity, and institutional arrangements required to manage climate and disaster risks. Several African countries are undertaking governance reforms to respond to these new challenges. One area that has received attention is climate-smart public investment management, which provides an opportunity for public investment to facilitate the transition to a green economy. A recent World Bank study shows that, out of 12 African countries surveyed, 6 had conducted countrywide vulnerability studies and established dedicated agencies to collect data and information to forecast the strengths and frequencies of disasters and hazards (Kim, Le, and Glenday 2022). The impact of these studies and agencies is constrained, however, by weak cross-agency collaboration and a disconnect between the hazard data collected and the key stages of public investment management (design, appraisal, and financing of resilient infrastructure projects).

Quality of political institutions

Long-term trend 2: African countries have made progress on enhancing the inclusiveness and accountability of institutions, but their progress remains constrained by weak checks and balances and persistent patterns of centralized and exclusive power arrangements.

Political space opened in African countries at the beginning of the 21st century. The electoral democracies that emerged during the third wave of democratization in the 1990s have, to some extent, demonstrated their relative durability: elections are regularly contested; peaceful turnovers are becoming common, including in large democracies such as Nigeria; and there has been progress (although uneven and fragile) on freedom of expression and of the press. Although democracy scores in the region improved for the period 2000–23, democratic development has been more volatile in countries affected by fragility and conflict, even experiencing a decline beginning in 2015.

African electoral democracies show signs of durability, but elections remain vulnerable to manipulation.[16] Since the mid-2010s, several countries—including Ghana, Liberia, Nigeria, and Sierra Leone—have reached the significant milestone of peaceful regime change through elections. Kenya and Malawi have weathered successful constitutional challenges to fraudulent elections. Many African states, however, remain trapped in a state of "competitive authoritarianism" (Posner and Young 2007; Riedl 2014), with regularly held elections often marked by political thuggery and intimidation (Cheeseman 2018).

Constitutional provisions protecting electoral democracy are threatened by autocratic reversals, as evidenced by modifications to term limits and the recent return of military coups. Term limits were institutionalized in the 1990s to counter the legacy of executive power concentration. According to Siegle and Cook (2021), as of May 2021, only 6 out of 49 Sub-Saharan African countries had not instituted a two-term constitutional limit for presidents.[17] In African countries that do have them, term limits have been regularly threatened: out of 19 attempts to modify or eliminate presidential term limits in African countries since 2000, 14 have been successful. In recent years, attempted or successful coups have taken place in a number of African countries, particularly in the Sahel region. Successful coups in Burkina Faso, Gabon, Guinea, Mali, and Nigeria have brought the military back to power, fueling a renewed trend of militarization, a specter that dominated African politics in the 1970s (the section on political stability further explores recent trends in coups and instability).

The exercise of power remains largely unchecked, making political accountability a major issue across the continent. After an initial improvement in checks and balances in the 1990s, the level of constraints of judicial, legislative, and constitutional counterpowers has stagnated (figure 1.13). In this context, the exercise of power and the working of institutions remain vulnerable to opacity and extractive behavior.

Nonelectoral forms of participation have a mixed record. African countries continue to score low on indicators of freedom of expression and freedom of religion. FCV countries display the lowest levels of freedom of expression, but civil society mobilization has been increasing in Africa. Across the continent, laws and regulations are manipulated to curtail civil liberties, with cybersecurity legislation that violates privacy and antiterrorism laws used to limit free association. Countries such as Eswatini, Uganda, and Zimbabwe have passed laws curtailing civil society participation (Freedom House 2022). Over half of African countries have legislation on access to information, yet the quality of these laws and their level of enforcement vary considerably. Afrobarometer survey data indicate that about two-thirds of African citizens think that it is "not at all" or "not very likely" that they will be able to access information from their governments on, for example, local development plans and budgets, or procedures to register a new business (Asunka and Logan 2021).

FIGURE 1.13 Unaccountable institutions: Stagnating levels of checks and balances, Africa, 1990–2022

Codebook category

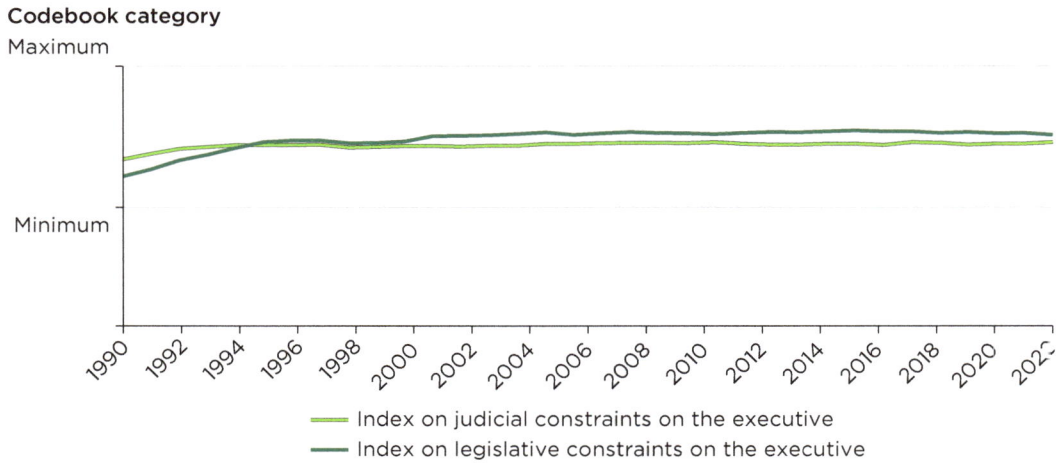

— Index on judicial constraints on the executive
— Index on legislative constraints on the executive

Source: Varieties of Democracy Project, V-Dem Dataset, https://www.v-dem.net/data/dataset-archive/.

Note: The index on legislative constraints on the executive measures on a 0–1 scale the extent to which the legislature and government agencies such as the controller general, the ombudsman, or the general prosecutor are capable of questioning, investigating, and exercising oversight over the executive. The index on judicial constraints on the executive measures on a 0–1 scale the extent to which the executive respects the constitution and complies with court rulings and the extent to which the judiciary is able to act in an independent fashion.

Authoritarian politics weigh heavily on the quality of growth. The economic successes of some African closed political regimes have fed the myth of autocratic stability and growth. Some of these systems have delivered short-term stability and growth, and have even experienced growth acceleration episodes. They have been helped in part by a centralized and top-down governance that can facilitate innovation shocks through a capacity to impose contentious reforms in the short run, as for Robert Mugabe in Zimbabwe in the early years of his rule. However, empirical evidence has shown that, in the long run, democratic systems are better able to sustain growth (Persson and Tabellini 2009). In fact, although authoritarian regimes in African countries are behind some of the successes in developing countries, they are also behind many of the biggest failures. Authoritarian regimes carry mid- and long-term risks to political stability and are less able to sustain growth. Ethiopia is a case in point: autocratic governance backfired into civil conflict, ultimately undermining progress in reform and in the country's development. These detrimental dynamics play out through various channels. State capture and resistance to competition in authoritarian systems nurture exclusion of large market segments generating instability, which harms growth.[18] Captured states are also costly and characterized by high debt levels, misappropriation, and inefficient public investment, all of which undermine the fiscal health of governments and their ability to invest in and implement policies that support productivity and innovation. These types of results make it clear that economic growth in developing countries must rest on a foundation of healthy governance and that stability alone is not enough.

Although democracy provides incentives for inclusive development, democratic transitions in Sub-Saharan Africa have not yet fully delivered on their development promises. The governance and development payoffs of democratic transitions can be slow to materialize for several reasons. First, many transition countries tend to be highly unstable in the short term, in part because of conflicts around the renegotiation of access to economic resources and opportunities between the ruling coalition and excluded segments of the population. Such political instability negatively correlates with growth, because it tends to create policy volatility, shorten policy horizons, and decrease investors' confidence. Second, electoral competition during times of transition can create perverse incentives for economic performance, whereby officials are better off concentrating on easy, visible tasks with clientelist payoffs (for example, building roads with a ribbon-cutting effect for popularity) (Tanzi and Davoodi 1998) rather than engaging in more complex and challenging economic reforms. Third, the introduction of electoral politics in Africa has tended to breed clientelism and patronage, including the strategic allocation of public positions to key political supporters (Cheeseman 2015, 2018; Van de Walle 2012). This tendency may result in bloated executive cabinets, often associated with higher public expenditure and lower quality of public governance (Canen and Wantchekon 2022; Wehner and Mills 2020).

Access to political and economic power tends to remain highly unequal in transition countries. Semidemocratic countries tend to have suboptimal levels of political inclusion, playing out along identity lines, with some social groups having limited access to power. These patterns of power distribution have development correlates: political institutions with limited levels of inclusion tend to go hand in hand with inequitable or exclusive economic institutions (box 1.5).

BOX 1.5
Why do inclusive political institutions matter for development?

Both political and economic institutions matter for inclusive growth. Extractive political institutions tend to go hand in hand with extractive economic institutions that benefit a narrow elite, rather than generating shared prosperity. By comparison, inclusive political institutions create interests and incentives for the design of inclusive economic institutions, which can generate sustained and pro-poor growth. Causality goes both ways: inclusive economic institutions allow for more equitable resource distribution and more plural societies. The interplay between political and economic institutions can therefore create feedback effects, potentially leading to both negative ("vicious cycle") and positive ("virtuous cycle") feedback effects (figure B1.5.1).

(continued)

Why do inclusive political institutions matter for development? *(continued)*

FIGURE B1.5.1 The interplay between political and economic institutions:
Vicious and virtuous cycles

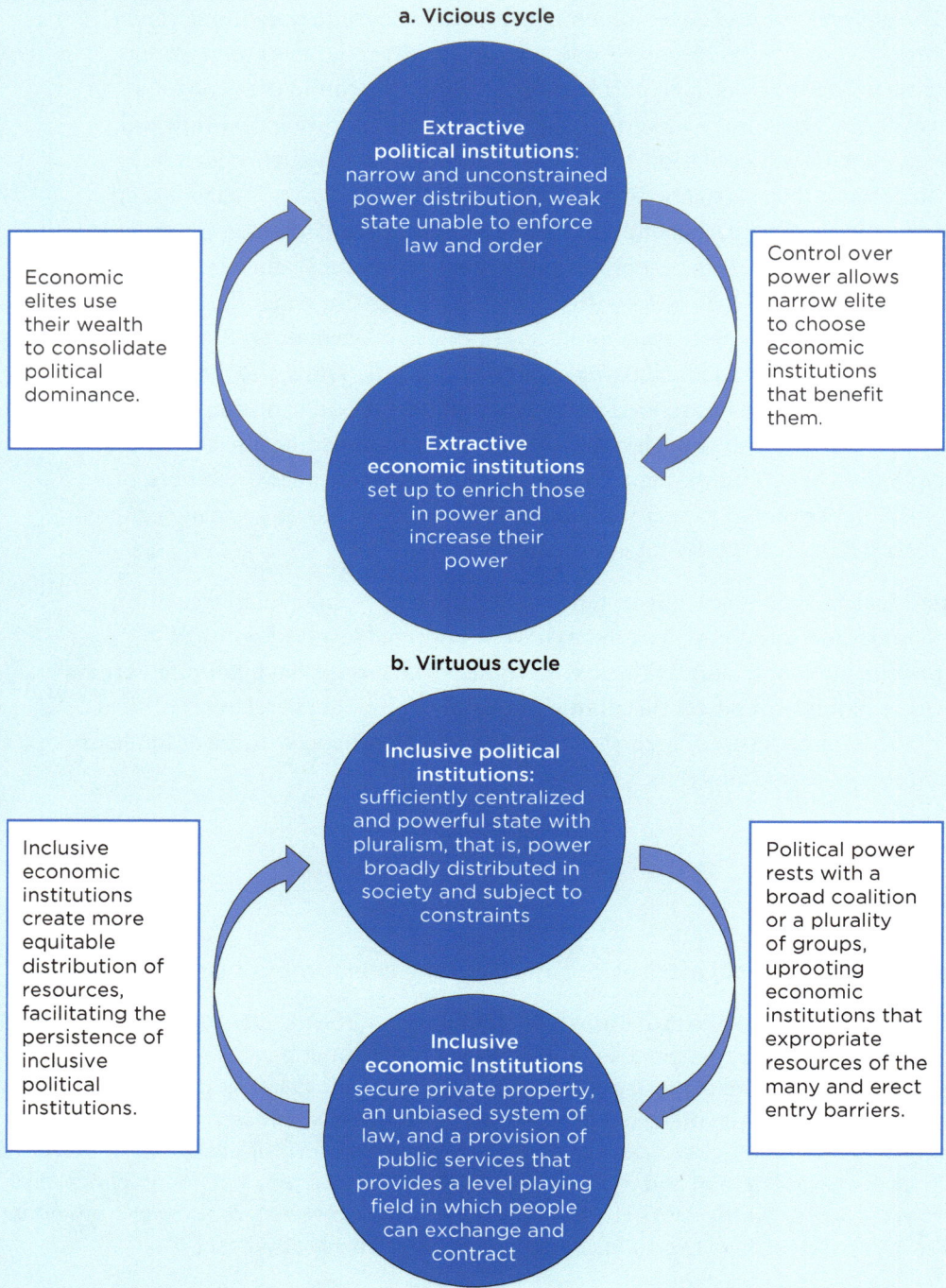

a. Vicious cycle

Extractive political institutions: narrow and unconstrained power distribution, weak state unable to enforce law and order

Economic elites use their wealth to consolidate political dominance.

Control over power allows narrow elite to choose economic institutions that benefit them.

Extractive economic institutions set up to enrich those in power and increase their power

b. Virtuous cycle

Inclusive political institutions: sufficiently centralized and powerful state with pluralism, that is, power broadly distributed in society and subject to constraints

Inclusive economic institutions create more equitable distribution of resources, facilitating the persistence of inclusive political institutions.

Political power rests with a broad coalition or a plurality of groups, uprooting economic institutions that expropriate resources of the many and erect entry barriers.

Inclusive economic Institutions secure private property, an unbiased system of law, and a provision of public services that provides a level playing field in which people can exchange and contract

Source: Adapted from Acemoglu and Robinson 2012.

In practice, this relationship between economic and political institutions sustains the persistence of crony capitalism. The continued predominance of state capture and rent seeking by elites and social groups connected to the executive in place is illustrated in map 1.1, which shows that patterns of access to state business opportunities remain largely in the hands of well-off groups in many African countries. Although still developing in most African countries, the private sector tends to feature private enterprises with substantial economic and political power, able to influence economic and tax policy in ways that serve corporate interests, arguably to the detriment of economic regulation and competition. Analysis of the private sector in Africa shows a highly noncompetitive environment with a few large businesses controlling large market segments. Such dominant market players tend to be well connected to political decision-makers, enabling them to leverage their influence to shape regulation in their favor, avoid accountability when they violate market rules (including integrity or competition rules), access public contracts, or evade taxes (Canen and Wantchekon 2022).

MAP 1.1 Access to state business opportunities, by socioeconomic position, 2025

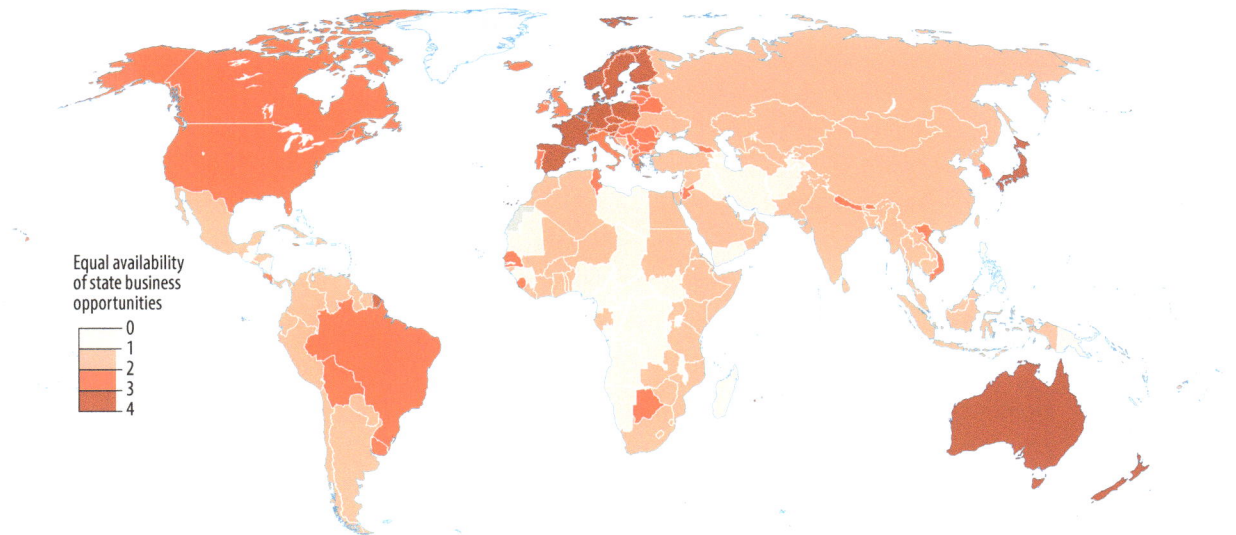

IBRD 48774 | APRIL 2025

Source: Varieties of Democracy Project, V-Dem Dataset v15, https://www.v-dem.net/data/dataset-archive/.
Note: The indicator measures on a scale of 0 (extremely unequal) to 4 (equal) whether state business opportunities are equally available to qualified individuals regardless of socioeconomic position. State business opportunities refer to public procurement contracts, public-private partnerships, and so on. Socioeconomic position refers to attributes of wealth, occupation, or other economic circumstances such as owning property.

Electoral politics are expensive, and party financing creates significant risks of policy distortion and corruption (Canen and Wantchekon 2022), with some countries starting to address this problem through the provision of public funding to political parties. In an attempt to curb reliance on opportunistic private donations and illicit sources, 71 percent of African countries provide direct public funding to parties (Achu Check et al. 2019, 16). However, this funding is not commensurate with the rise in electoral competition and costs, leading political parties to source funding from public, private, and illicit sources. Inherent in this practice are risks of collusion between political parties and opportunistic campaign donors (through the exchange of campaign finance and postelection favors, including, for example, preferential access to public contracts). The clientelist structures of African parties create pressure during campaigns to provide material inducements to voters (Sigman 2023).

Patterns of contestation and resilience

Long-term trend 3: Civil capacity has risen considerably: the opening of politics since the 2000s has led to a surge in collective action, with positive spillovers for development; however, the inability of institutions to respond to social expectations and political mobilization threatens to turn liberal civic engagement into distrust, populism, and radicalization.

In contrast to the 1990s, popular mobilization and pressures exerted by street protests have become recurrent features of the political landscape in Africa. A significant trend over the past 20 years has been an exponential increase in mass demonstrations and protests as a means of contesting failing social contracts. This trend has accelerated considerably since the early 2010s (figure 1.14). Armed Conflict Location & Event Data (ACLED) show a fourfold increase in violent demonstrations between 2012 and 2022. Africa witnessed the largest increases in antigovernment protests in the world since 2012, increasing by 23.8 percent each year (more than twice the global average).[19] Since 2000, most demonstrations and protests have been unarmed and peaceful, but they can turn violent in response to state crackdowns.

Particularly large and enduring mobilizations have occurred across the continent since 2019. Mobilizations have rocked countries at various levels of economic development and with different political regime types, such as Burkina Faso, Cameroon, the Democratic Republic of Congo, Ethiopia, Kenya, Nigeria, South Africa, and Sudan. In previous decades, demonstrations typically endured for days or weeks; however, in recent cases such as in Guinea, Malawi, Sudan, and Togo, they have continued for many months. Election times tend to be propitious for social mobilization. Highly contested elections saw widespread protests in the Democratic Republic of Congo, Gabon, and Uganda, and even in countries such as Angola, Chad, and Zimbabwe, which have tightly regulated public and political spheres. Protests in Malawi against the reelection of the incumbent president in May 2019 led the Constitutional Court to order a rerun, only the second time judges have done so in African history (the first time was in Kenya in 2017)

FIGURE 1.14 Protests and demonstrations in Africa, by type of event and subregion, 2000–22

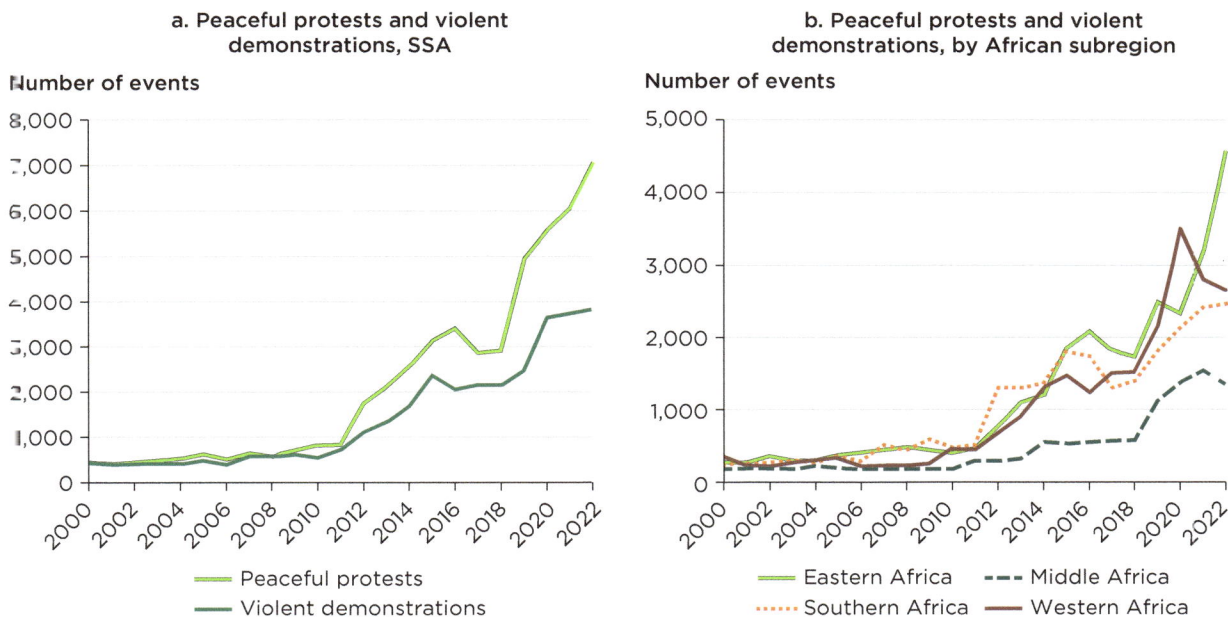

a. Peaceful protests and violent demonstrations, SSA

Number of events

b. Peaceful protests and violent demonstrations, by African subregion

Number of events

Peaceful protests
Violent demonstrations

Eastern Africa · · · · Middle Africa
· · · · · Southern Africa — Western Africa

Source: Armed Conflict Location & Event Data (ACLED), https://www.acleddata.com.
Note: SSA = Sub-Saharan Africa.

The growth of information and communication technology, including mobile phones and social media, can facilitate collective action, but manipulations and restrictions can also backfire against civil protests. In many instances across the continent, social media has played a role in organizing and amplifying the impact of social protests, as illustrated by the #EndSARS protest in Nigeria calling for the dissolution of the Special Anti-Robbery Squad notorious for police brutality, or the #StopGBV campaign against gender-based violence in South Africa. Recent research provides empirical evidence on mobile phones and civic participation: using data from African countries over 15 years, Manacorda and Tesei (2020) find that in periods of economic downturn, when grievances surge and the cost of participation falls, "mobile phones are instrumental to mass mobilization" because they increase individuals' access to information about economic conditions and about their neighbors' participation in protests. In many countries, however, the role of social media remains largely constrained by restrictive regulations and outright repression. In addition, the visibility of social media campaigns should not obscure the important inter- and intracountry digital divides: on average in Africa, 36 percent of individuals use the internet, with a variation from 2 percent in Somalia to 82 percent in the Seychelles, and important gaps persist between rural and urban areas.[20]

Dramatic improvements in data availability and transparency, made possible largely by pressure from civil society and the international community, have transformed the political landscape in the past two decades, opening opportunities for civil society to engage in evidence-based policy debates and hold governments to account. Transparency, accountability, and participation instruments and multistakeholder initiatives have been central to the good governance agenda and widely adopted in Africa, especially in extractive and financial management. As the case of the Extractive Industries Transparency Initiative reveals, however, the theory of change in transparency policies—that information disclosure can trigger reforms and enhance state capacity—often turns out to be shallow and performative (Brockmeyer and Fox 2015) even though some successes have been recorded (Kinda and Thiombiano 2024).

Although protests tend be highly localized events, they share common driving forces. Underlying various movements lie the larger issues of what full citizenship should entail and the validity of the prevailing social contract (refer to Bussolo et al. 2018; McKinsey Global Institute 2020; World Bank 2019b). Protests question the legitimacy and authority of the social contract's tacit and common agreements on what citizens expect from the state and the state's capacity and willingness to deliver on these expectations. In practice, mobilization has tended to emerge from citizens' deep dissatisfaction with their livelihoods—including living costs and access to public services—which protesters have regularly attributed to their country's poor governance, including government corruption and inability to deliver on distributive mandates. South Africa, for example, has been the site of repeated episodes of social mobilization. In 2019, large-scale and persistent student unrest on virtually all campuses over fees, hiring, and curriculum significantly disrupted the academic year. More recently, in 2023, the country witnessed protests about the electricity crisis and repeated power cuts. In Sudan, youth-led demonstrations in 2019 resulted in the removal of President Omar al-Bashir.

Protest and social mobilization can trigger positive change, with a positive correlation seen between improvements in civil capacity and in the quality of public services. Civil capacity is understood here as the political or bargaining power of the average citizen.[21] For the period 2000–10, increased civil capacity was a strong predictor of increased quantity and inclusiveness of public goods and services. This effect is indicative of a social contract dynamic, in which strengthened civil capacity to bargain with the state can yield stronger outcomes (box 1.6). Civil capacity remains statistically significant when controlling for democratization, economic growth, and state capacity.

BOX 1.6
Insights from a social contract approach

The 2021 World Bank report *Social Contracts for Development: Bargaining, Contention, and Social Inclusion in Sub-Saharan Africa* built on the framework of the 2017 *World Development Report* to examine how the citizen-state bargaining process shapes governance (Cloutier et al. 2021; World Bank 2017). *Social contracts* can be understood as a dynamic agreement between state and society on their mutual roles and responsibilities. Social contracts can be evaluated on the basis of three

(continued)

BOX 1.6
Insights from a social contract approach *(continued)*

"compasses": (1) process, or how formal and informal bargaining mechanisms mediate civil and state interests and capabilities; (2) outcomes, or the extent to which social contracts deliver inclusive developmental policies and outcomes; and (3) resilience, or the extent to which social contracts are responsive to and aligned with citizen expectations.

Countries that have sustainable and equitable growth paths are those that have inclusive, responsive, and resilient social contracts. By contrast, those with large imbalances of power generate social contracts that serve the few and may give rise to deep grievance and possibly conflict. These three aspects interact through feedback loops and self-reinforcing cycles, as illustrated in figure B1.6.1.

The report highlights the ways that citizen collective action in Sub-Saharan Africa is hampered by low levels of trust, appeals to identity politics, and layers of mediated authorities. The state, in turn, tends to invest capacity in maintaining bargains among the elite while appeasing citizens with populist policies, such as subsidies. When citizen capacity and expectations outpace what the state offers, it can result in realigning the social contract. When the interests and capabilities of the state cannot accommodate such changes, however, it can result in deeper mistrust and even conflict.

FIGURE B1.6.1 A social contract framework

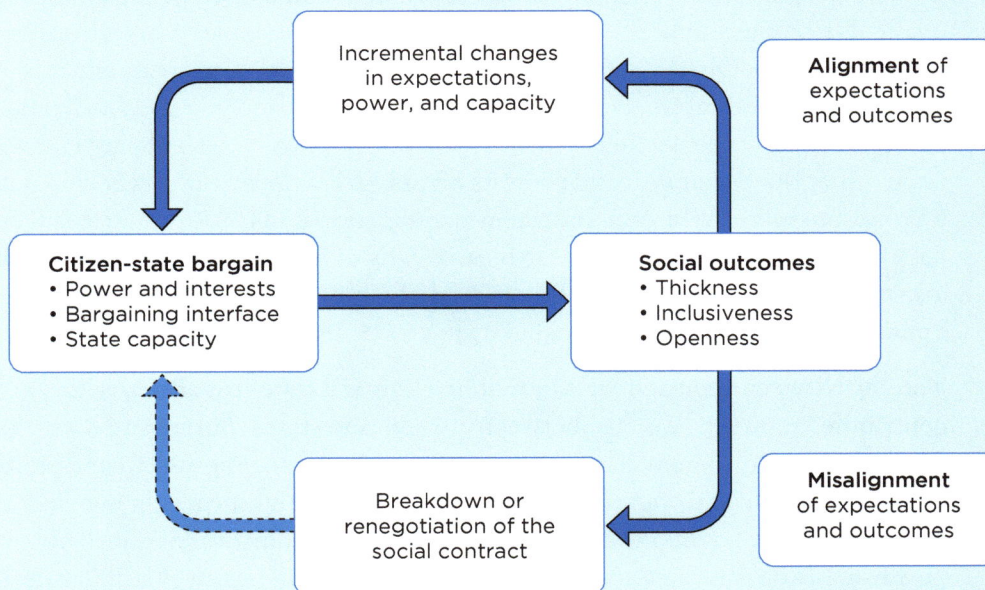

Source: Cloutier et al. 2021.

Protests reflect the broader attachment of African citizens to democratic values. Many protests have in common the defense of existing forms of democracy, however flawed, and a strong commitment to democratic norms and forms, particularly the right of expression. Analysis of Afrobarometer survey data across 39 countries surveyed in 2021–23 shows that 68 percent of African citizens surveyed prefer democracy over any other form of government. The figure is higher when respondents are presented with specific alternatives: 83 percent reject one-person rule; 79 percent reject one-party rule; and 68 percent reject military rule (Gyimah-Boadi, Logan, and Sanny 2021).[22] As noted in the title of an Afrobarometer Network (2023) policy paper, "Africans Want More Democracy, but Their Leaders Still Aren't Listening." Although many protests turn on the legitimacy of public authority, dissent and perceived illegitimacy can also propel popular support for the military, and even for coups. Notably, the extent of citizens' opposition to military rule has declined by 10 percentage points over the past decade, and 53 percent of respondents were willing to endorse military interventions if elected leaders abuse their power.

African citizens' dissatisfaction with the "supply" of democracy arguably goes hand in hand with a steady decline in their trust in representative institutions, particularly for the executive (Gyimah-Boadi, Logan, and Sanny 2021)—refer to figure 1.15. A healthy dose of critical trust is needed to generate positive spillovers for development (Norris, Jennings, and Stoker 2019; Zmerli and Van Der Meer 2017). Such trust requires public transparency and access to information to critically evaluate policies, and institutional channels to contest policies and hold government accountable. When citizens perceive transparency and institutionalized accountability as limited, mistrust can turn into distrust. This crisis of trust can have deleterious effects, including radicalization of social protests, to the detriment of sociopolitical stability.[23] It is indicative, in that regard, that the rise of peaceful protests across Africa since 2019 has been paralleled by a significant increase in violent demonstrations (figure 1.14). Declining trust could also harm development prospects. An extensive body of literature shows that economic growth, social cohesion, and well-being are highly contingent on citizens' trust in political institutions (Algan 2018; Fukuyama 1995; Zak and Knack 2001).

The gap between civic demands or mobilization and state response has likely contributed to fueling distrust between citizens and states (Börzel and Risse 2016). Many protest movements have had to contend with strong repression and political backlashes. In several countries, social protests had initial success in making their demands heard and toppling autocratic rulers. A lack of institutionalized opposition, however, has complicated the task of alternance, and the legacy of military involvement in politics has, in places such as Burkina Faso and Sudan, opened space for military coups and civil conflict.

FIGURE 1.15 **Trends in citizens' trust in executive institutions, selected African countries, 2005–21**

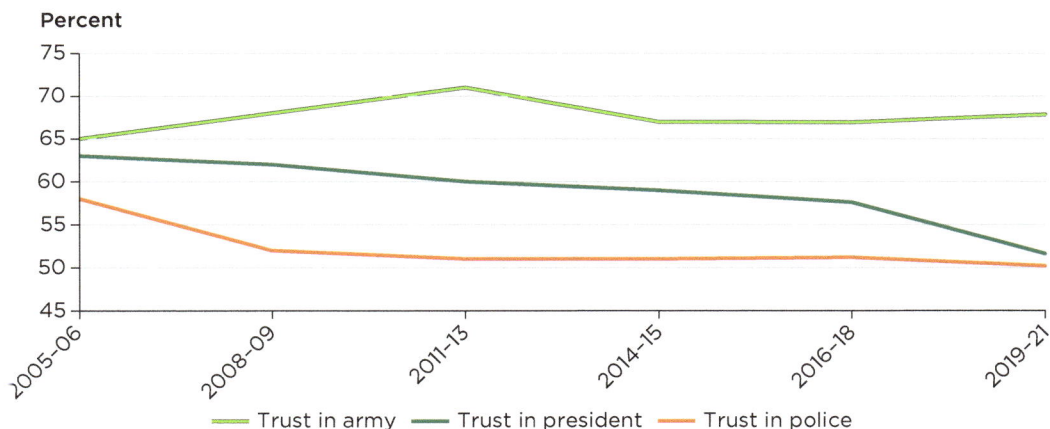

Source: Afrobarometer database, https://www.afrobarometer.org/online-data-analysis.
Note: Sample of 16 countries: Benin, Botswana, Cabo Verde, Ghana, Kenya, Lesotho, Madagascar (except missing data in 2019–21), Malawi, Mali, Namibia, Nigeria, Senegal, Tanzania, Uganda, Zambia, and Zimbabwe.

Political stability

Long-term trend 4: Political instability is on the rise in Africa and constitutes a major threat to the continent's ability to claim the 21st century.

Political violence is at a historical high in Africa, and the continent fares poorly compared to other regions. As illustrated in figure 1.16, after a short-lived decrease in the early 2000s, violence has reached new highs in the past decade. This violence is likely the product of long-term trends identified earlier, the fractured nature of the social contract, and the challenge of ensuring state control over the territory, particularly in fragile states with weak institutions. Violence remains a core binding constraint to growth on the continent: instability creates policy volatility; shortens policy horizons, leading to suboptimal macroeconomic policy decisions; and decreases investors' confidence. Estimates of the cost of conflict in Nigeria alone in 2021 were US$15 billion, and total costs between 2008 and 2021 were US$113 billion. Fang et al. (2020) estimate that in Sub-Saharan Africa annual growth in countries in conflict is about 2.5 percentage points lower on average, and that the impact on per capita GDP is cumulative and increases over time. They also show that conflict negatively affects public finances, including by lowering revenue and raising military spending, and incentivizes a shift in resources away from social spending.

FIGURE 1.16 Armed conflict, by world region, 1946–2021

Number of conflicts

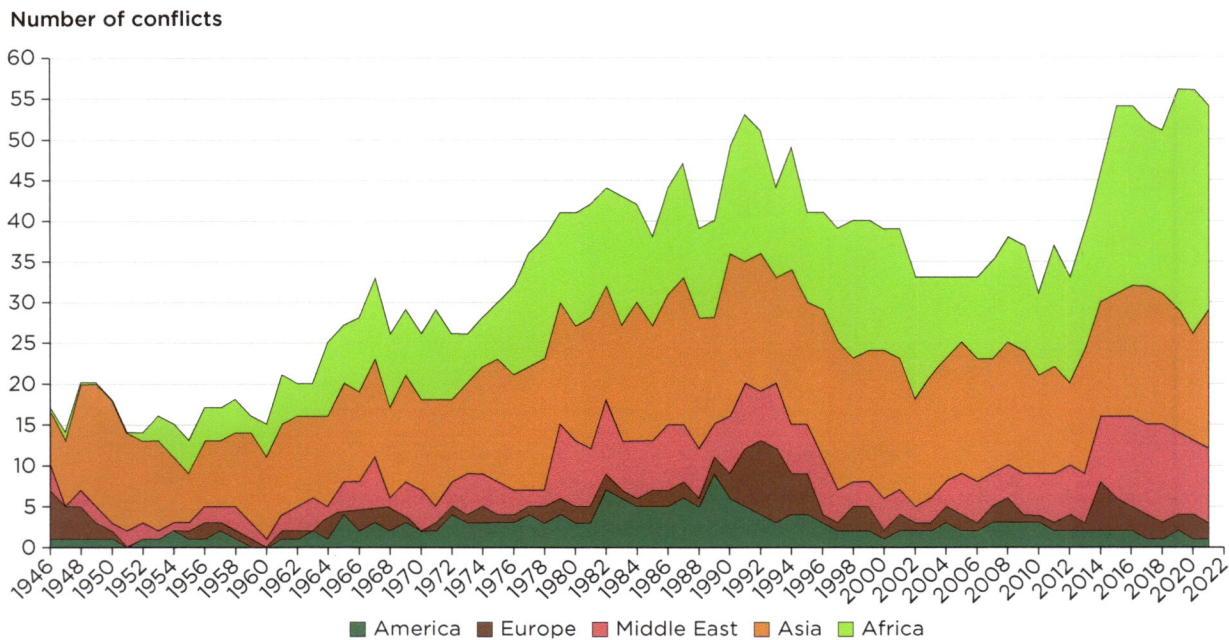

Source: Uppsala Conflict Data Program (UCDP) data set 22.1, https://ucdp.uu.se/downloads/.
Note: Regions are defined according to UCDP classifications.

Since the 2000s, violence has shifted in significant ways: whereas interstate violence has decreased, intrastate violence associated with the presence of nonstate armed groups and transnational terror groups has risen. The region has experienced a sharp increase in violent events since 2015, with insecurity spreading across the Sahel region to the Horn of Africa. A recent stream of coups points to the fragility of political settlements. Trends in fatalities are largely driven by violence against civilians, battles, and forms of remote violence (figure 1.17). Most of these fatalities occur in countries classified by the World Bank as FCV; it is noteworthy that the number of fatalities in FCV countries has drastically increased since 2020, in large part driven by the bloody conflict in Ethiopia and multiple forms of conflict in Nigeria.

World Development Report 2011: Conflict, Security, and Development (World Bank 2011) pointed to a new and worrisome landscape of violence and fragility involving terrorist groups, criminal networks, vigilantism, ethnic militias, and insurgency.[24] In the past two decades, interstate and civil wars have continued to decrease worldwide, including in Africa.[25] Although more localized today, African conflicts have a transnational feature. As illustrated in OECD and SWAC (2020), the number of regions experiencing a local intensification of political violence has increased significantly and faster than other types of conflicts. Burkina Faso, the Democratic Republic of Congo, Ethiopia, Mali, and Nigeria[26] are examples of rapidly increasing conflict and violence in subregions with cross-border spillovers (figure 1.18). In the Sahel, political violence is highly concentrated in bordering regions, with more than 40 percent of violent events and fatalities occurring within 100 kilometers of a land border. With conflicts largely localized, violent events are more likely to occur near one another (OECD and SWAC 2020).

FIGURE 1.17 **Number of conflict fatalities in Sub-Saharan Africa, by type of event and country classification, 2000–22**

a. Type of event

b. Country classification

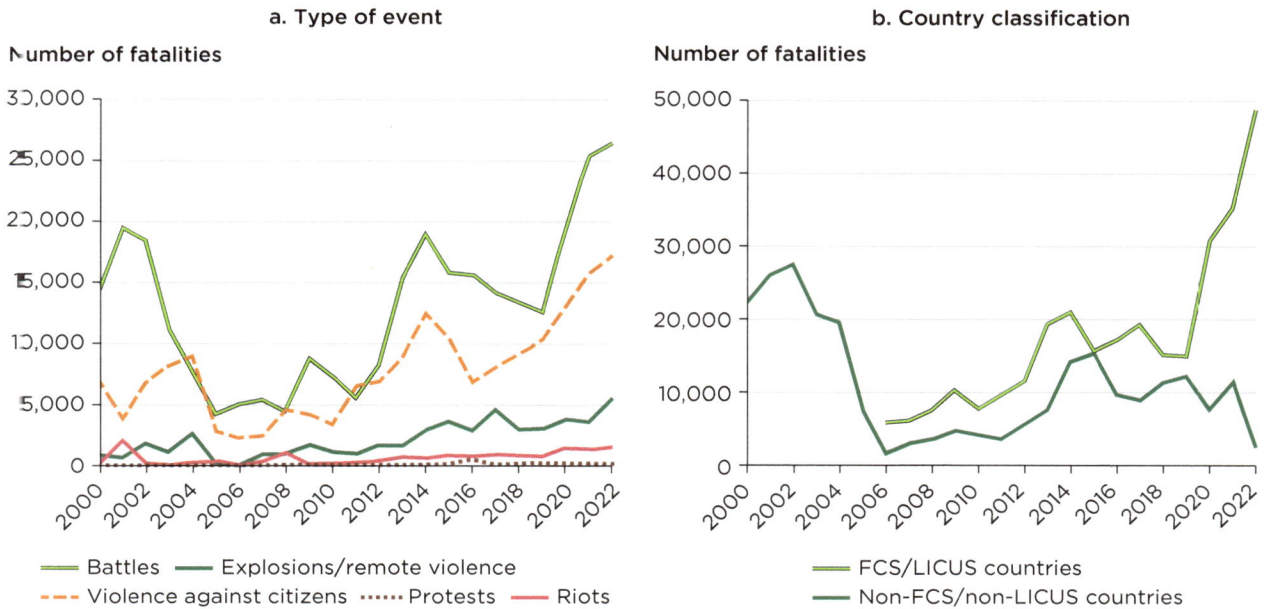

Source: Armed Conflict Location & Event Data (ACLED), https://www.acleddata.com.
Note: FCS = fragile and conflict-affected situations; LICUS = low-income countries under stress.

FIGURE 1.18 **Number of conflict fatalities, selected African countries, 2000–22**

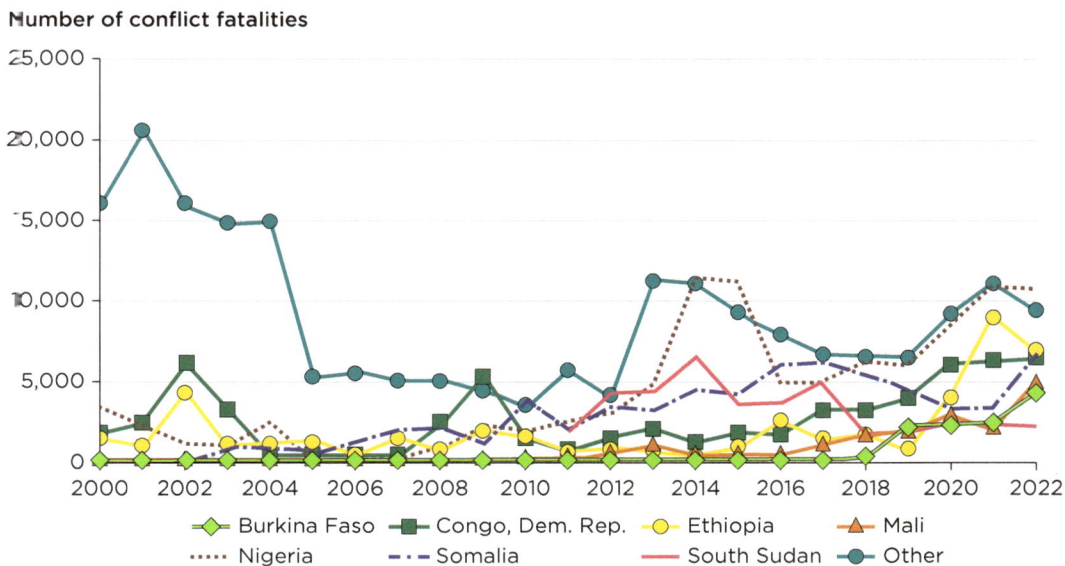

Source: Armed Conflict Location & Event Data (ACLED), https://acleddata.com/data/.

In striking contrast to 2000, some parts of the continent are now in the midst of encompassing regional instabilities driven by transnational networks. Militants linked to the Islamic State of Iraq and Syria (ISIS), particularly from the Islamic State West Africa Province, have made headway across much of the Sahel; its counterpart, ISIS Central Africa Province, has joined hands with militants in the Democratic Republic of Congo. The black flag of ISIS now flies over the Mozambique province of Cabo Delgado. The Sahel presents an especially troubling case (refer to Devermont 2020; Pye 2021; Raleigh, Nsaibia, and Dowd 2020; Thurston 2020). The crisis that enveloped Mali in 2012 has since escalated into a protracted and widespread crisis across the Sahel, now extending from Senegal to the Horn of Africa.

The rise of nonstate armed groups and violence is almost, by definition, a marker of a fractured or broken social contract.[27] The question of fragility, resilience, and endemic conflict—which encompasses everything from civil wars to the rise of militias, transnational gangs, and terror groups[28]—centers on the legitimacy of states and the limits to their powers (or lack thereof). It is obvious that economic and poverty factors play a role in the conflict in the region.[29] However, experts on conflict in Africa also emphasize the gap between the state and the people, as in the case of Mali (Thiam 2017).[30] A weak social contract between the elite and the people in Somalia shows how the robustness of social contracts varies across scales (Cloutier et al. 2021). Multiple and overlapping social contract relationships exist in Somalia, with the strongest tending to be at the most local level, primarily within a clan. The strength of the contract within the clan is based upon the extent of the clan's capacity to use informal tax collection to keep its residents safe (and solve some conflicts). At the federal level, Somalia's social contract is characterized by a weak bargaining mechanism. On the state capacity side, Somalia has some of the lowest measures of state efficiency compared with its regional neighbors. Citizen capacity in terms of cohesion and collective action is weak and indirect. Given the extremely limited capacity of the federal government and federal member states to provide services, it is not surprising that the social contract between the state and citizens is weak.[31] The chronic political instability and insecurity that characterize Somalia are deeply rooted in short-term and exclusionary aspects of the social contract.

Policies

This chapter's journey through two decades of governance reform in Sub-Saharan Africa leaves no doubt that empowering citizens and developing inclusive, representative, and accountable governance are prerequisites to sustainable and equitable growth. It also demonstrates how demanding and difficult these efforts have proven to be, and how the record since the beginning of the 21st century has been mixed, at best, with limited progress on some fronts, reversals in fundamental respects, and some cases of outright failures. The agenda described in the 2000 World Bank report *Can Africa Claim the 21st Century?* is still relevant. Promoting a sustained positive development trajectory will require effective and resilient governance, especially because the continent confronts an increasing set of challenges: the effects of global climate change, a fast-increasing population, postcarbon transitions, new theaters of war and multipolar geopolitical tensions, and expanded offshoring and financialization, to name a few.

This chapter's subsection "Context" shows that the important gains in technologies for governance and institutionalizing key ingredients of political inclusion, including regular elections and increased civil society capabilities for collective action, have not yet led to a fundamental shift in the primacy of elite interests. Significant aid and investment in the good governance agenda, with a focus on both supply-side interventions in the PFM cycle—political and administrative decentralization, and civil service reform—and demand-side engagement on the transparency, accountability, and participation agenda, have accounted for some improvement on indicators. Such aid and investment have helped enable certain gains in development that are amenable to technical inputs and basic capabilities. For example, countries have made notable improvements in adopting good budget management and transparency practices, establishing anticorruption and accountability agencies, and even increasing school enrollment.

Improvements in the credibility of budgets, accountability of processes and actors, and quality of education services require a different, and arguably more complex and taxing, set of governance capabilities that can overcome vested interests, coordinate different actors, balance autonomy with accountability, and provide effective incentives. It is important to bear in mind the words of Andrew Natsios (2010, 1): "Development programs that are most precisely and easily measured are the least transformational, and those programs that are most transformational are the least measurable." More directly, the development literature has put power and politics front and center (Carothers and de Gramont 2013).

Governance in Sub-Saharan Africa is, for the most part, not yet to the point at which episodes of growth have been able to change the logic of elite interests. Technical inputs have not yet transformed incentives, and transitional democratic institutions cannot yet really forge positive accountability loops and developmental social contracts. In short, the selective use of state capacity where it aligns with elite interests combined with shallow forms of citizen-state bargaining mechanisms and low expectations from the citizenry have produced weak social contracts. Some African countries have been described as being stuck in a low-level equilibrium of limited state effectiveness and low expectations, leading to minimal structural transformation; those countries' citizens able to do so "opt out" by seeking services in the private sector or abroad (Risse and Stollenwerk 2018). Other countries, however, show clear cracks in the social contract. Some have experienced opportunities to renegotiate the social contract, some successfully and some less so. For example, constitutional reforms have sought to rebalance power constructively through decentralization in Kenya and Nigeria, or through federalism in Somalia; and, following mass protests in Malawi, the judiciary stepped in to avoid autocratic tendencies to end term limits.[32] In other countries, economic shocks, anger over corruption, and ethnic exclusion have triggered large-scale protests and demands for deeper change, sometimes succeeding in ousting heads of state but sometimes installing military regimes, seen by many to hold the promise of addressing security threats despite their poor track record in bringing peace and development.

What should be the main policy recommendations for governance going forward? Fully addressing this question requires an understanding of how power dynamics and citizen-state relations can be reshaped to generate mutual accountabilities. Successful strategies will not always correspond to standard models of best practice, nor will they emerge as a result of conventional reform strategies. Often, they arise from particular political arrangements or settlements in which elite interests align with certain reform directions. This discussion focuses on three types of actors—development leaders, civil society, and nonstate actors—and the actions they can take toward more effective and responsive governance.

Development leaders

Development leaders should work with the grain (Levy 2014) to push forward governance reforms that break patterns of extraction and exclusion. The political environment in which they operate constrains the ability of development leaders to achieve significant governance reforms. Tackling capture and corruption head-on may not be politically feasible, may have perverse effects, and may be short-lived. But strategies that focus on selective areas of reform where traction is possible and that, over time, can change incentives to enable additional reforms, can be successful. Such strategies might have some of the following characteristics.

Considering the importance of the fiscal contract and tax equity. It has been demonstrated that voluntary tax compliance in developing countries mostly depends on the perceptions that tax receipts will not be (too) diverted and will generate public services (Dom et al. 2022; Prichard 2015). Citizens will be less reluctant to pay their taxes if they are satisfied with what they receive in return and if they feel like they have influence over how taxes are used. Taxation thus generates incentives for explicit and implicit "tax bargaining" between citizens and states, as increased tax collection is exchanged for greater responsiveness and accountability (Cloutier et al. 2021). This finding also shows why the concepts of tax fairness and equity are so important. In most cases, the focus is on how much is collected, but Moore, Prichard, and Fjeldstad (2018) demonstrate that how taxpayers are taxed matters even more. Taxpayers who are victims of extortion or who feel that rich people do not pay their fair share will be more reluctant to pay taxes—an increasingly important consideration for states facing higher levels of public debt.

Pockets of effectiveness.[33] Development leaders would do better to invest in improving performance in specific sectors and institutions, or around particular issues, than to embark on wholesale public service reform. Several countries have adopted comprehensive plans for public service reform; however, because public service tends to be a vehicle of patronage and vested interests, these plans are difficult to implement. Nevertheless, development trajectories in many African countries include the emergence at certain times of relatively effective public organizations and development outcomes. For example, in Ghana, Kenya, Rwanda, Uganda, and Zambia, institutions of economic management—central banks, ministries of finance, and tax authorities—have experienced periods of relatively high performance underpinned by merit-based human resource management and performance targets (Hickey 2023). Within countries, patterns of governance vary greatly across scales, with these variations even more evident in complex federal systems, such as Ethiopia, Nigeria, and South Africa, which show very substantial variations across subnational entities, even at the level of local governments (Iddawela, Lee, and Rodríguez-Pose 2021). Research shows that pockets of effectiveness are rarely due to isolation from the broader context but, rather, are products of political settlements that allow for an alignment between the interests of the powerful and an effective discharge of the mandate, and the development of a trusted relationship between bureaucratic and political rulers (Hickey 2023).

Smart bets to reduce corruption. Corruption, both petty and grand, has a corrosive effect on growth, equity, and security, and is one of the biggest causes of trust deficits—with a direct impact on social contracts. Political campaigns often run on an anticorruption platform, and new governments often feature renewed energy for investigations and prosecutions. This priority is often limited in time and scope, however, as crackdowns align narrowly with the political interests of those in power. In countries with low levels of diversification and competitiveness, elites have few incentives to enforce the rule of law, because doing so would mean confronting powerful vested interests. The generally poor results of systemic anticorruption efforts point to the need for a different approach. "In contexts where levels of development and political arrangements do not yet allow the effective enforcement of formal rules, anti-corruption strategies should *sequentially attack corruption at critical points where anti-corruption is both feasible and has a high impact on development*" (Khan, Andreoni, and Roy 2016, 3; italics in original). In other words, development leaders should support targeted efforts to reduce particular forms of corruption that do not directly confront powerful interests, such as efforts that are in the interest of a critical mass with sufficient bargaining power to support reforms, and efforts that have potential to contribute to inclusive development and, over time, shift incentives in favor of the rule of law.

The potential of digital dividends to tackle governance. E-governance is seen to be a relatively cheap and easy way to enhance PFM or control corruption in the public sector. The advent of new technologies, ranging from big data analysis to web scraping and machine learning, expands frontiers for data transparency and use.

This development is likely to further transform the dialectic between demand and supply for data and information in the next decade. Evidence shows, however, that a large digital divide remains and that digital technologies do not offer a straightforward path to leapfrogging in governance. In governance there are no shortcuts—technological or otherwise—to robust, capable, and democratic rules of the game.

Civil society

There is a need to safeguard and invest in spaces for collective action and constructive contestation to leverage the reformist potential of civil society. Democratic gains need to be safeguarded and built upon, and the context is challenging, if not adverse. At the global level, the rise in populism and support from dominant global players to autocratic rulers weaken the legitimacy and popular support of democratic systems. Financing of political campaigns largely distorts incentives toward short-term horizons and relations between politicians and businesses, which go against long-term governance reforms. At the regional level, the stream of coups and the return of military politics across many Sahel countries threaten to derail hard-won political breakthroughs. In that context, the years ahead will require sustained and proactive efforts from civic-minded reformers—across government, civil society, and the international community—to safeguard and expand civil liberties and political freedoms. Overcoming elite resistance to political reforms and popular disillusion with the development payoffs of democratic regimes will require not only cross-interest and cross-class collective action but also efforts to reinject trust in democratic institutions, including by increasing public integrity and policy credibility. Whereas governments can and should do their part to re-enchant democratic governance, particularly to address perceptions of corruption and policy inefficiencies, civil society also has a role to play in creating space for policy debates to nurture the emergence of an informed and politically engaged citizenry, and continuing to monitor and advocate for more transparent, accountable, and effective governance.

The road to government accountability is through the empowerment of civil society and the institutionalization of checks and balances. For example, safeguarding constitutional provisions such as term limits against autocratic reversals will require both civil protests and strong counterpowers in the form of an established and autonomous judiciary. In the elections sphere, electoral integrity is best preserved when the engagement of civil society organizations in election monitoring is buttressed and legitimized by strong and independent electoral commissions able to set, implement, and monitor electoral rules. In the fight against corruption, whistleblowers and anticorruption advocates can only benefit from a strong and autonomous justice system or anticorruption agencies able to investigate and prosecute cases of corruption. Several countries have started to put in place mechanisms of asset declarations, but data are usually not analyzed or are analyzed with limited transparency to the public, despite strong demands from the citizenry.

Civil society is at the forefront of the reform agenda on digital inclusion and digital rights, and these efforts should be supported and sustained. Although access to the internet and social media has dramatically expanded since the 2000s, the continent still regularly witnesses internet and social media disruptions and shutdowns, especially during times of political crisis and protests. Poor regulation, malfeasance, and political manipulation also expose internet users to a range of risks, from cyberattacks to identity theft and surveillance. More and better regulation is needed in the digital sphere, including protection of digital rights; regulatory frameworks on data protection, privacy, and security; and regulatory authorities, such as independent data protection agencies.

International community

The international community should tackle the continent's biggest governance challenges at the supranational level. Looming crises need transnational governance and commitment mechanisms. The past decades have shown that governance on the continent is increasingly influenced at supranational levels—for example by regional groups such as the African Union or by international bodies such as the United Nations and World Trade Organization. Issues such as security, terrorism, illicit financial flows, transfer pricing, or gold smuggling all go beyond nation states and need to be addressed at the regional or global level. Responses at the national level are suboptimal.

Developed and developing countries should seriously tackle illicit financial flows, which account for a huge loss of revenues for African economies as debt distress is growing and public spending appears increasingly important. To address illicit financial flows, countries should prioritize transparency and regulation in extractive industries, multilateral cooperation in stolen asset recovery, financial investigations, and dealing with corruption cases (UNCTAD 2020).

In conclusion, in the face of an increasingly precarious and uncertain national and global stage, the ability of Africa to claim the 21st century will require deliberate efforts to step out of business as usual. Africa will need innovative ways to invest in institutions, and strategies that forge social contracts capable of addressing not only questions of poverty, inclusion, equity, and justice but also economic growth and accumulation. It is paramount for African governments and the broader community of policy makers to tackle the widespread erosion of trust in state actors and institutions across the continent.

Notes

1. State capacity is the government's ability to raise taxes, maintain order, and provide public goods (Lindsey 2021).

2. For a theoretical discussion on path dependence in politics, understood as the conception that "preceding steps in a particular direction induce further movement in the same direction," refer to Pierson (2000, 252). It can be argued that, in African countries, historical legacies include the long-term impact of decisions related to sectoral policies, public investments, and organizational capabilities taken in the colonial and immediate postindependence period, or during other critical historical junctures. These policy, budget, and organizational decisions made in the past put countries in a path-dependent policy process, whereby historical decisions and their outcomes (rather than current conditions) constrain the range of policy options available in the present.

3. For an overview of the resource curse literature, refer to Ross (2015).

4. "Total natural resources rents are the sum of oil rents, natural gas rents, coal rents (hard and soft), mineral rents, and forest rents," according to the World Bank's World Development Indicators, table 3.14, https://wdi.worldbank.org/table/3.14.

5. For more information, refer to World Bank, DataBank, "Country Policy and Institutional Assessment," https://databank.worldbank.org/source/country-policy-and-institutional-assessment.

6. Notably, other CPIA clusters have behaved differently. The overall CPIA score has been relatively stable over time, hiding conflicting trends across clusters (refer to figure 1.7): CPIA cluster scores show a clear regression on economic management but an improvement on social inclusion. Whereas the "Social inclusion" cluster experienced continuous improvement over the 2000–19 period, the "Economic management" cluster's trend has had a steady decline from 2012. The "Structural policies" cluster and "Public sector management and institutions" cluster, by contrast, have been relatively stable over the observed period, but with lower levels for the latter.

7. The definition of "fragility" lacks consensus. In most cases, this term describes a fundamental failure of the state to perform functions necessary to meet citizens' basic needs and expectations.

8. State capture is perpetrated by interconnected corrupt economic and political actors targeting state assets and (ab)using weak institutions for their private benefit (Raballand and Rijkers 2021).

9. In a similar vein, vote buying tends to be associated with lower levels of investments in public services (Khemani 2015).

10. Note that not all illicit financial flows proceed from corruption; some may proceed from criminal activity (for example, mafia extortions).

11. Soares de Oliveira (2022) identifies a number of key themes, about which we know very little: the politics of finance and banking, the extractive industries and commodity trading, the political economy of metropolitan service providers, the engagement of African elites with the offshore world, and the increased salience of Asian financial centers in Africa's global offshore links (refer also to Oppong, Patey, and Soares de Oliveira 2020).

12. Signé, Sow, and Madden (2020) also make this point, estimating that between 1980 and 2018 Sub-Saharan Africa emitted over US$1 trillion in illicit financial flows and comparing that amount with the levels of foreign direct investment and official development assistance, which stood at about US$2 trillion.

13. The V-Dem Institute at the University of Gothenburg defines "public service equality" as the extent to which high-quality service is guaranteed to all and is sufficient to enable adult citizens to exercise basic political rights, https://www.v-dem.net/data/the-v-dem-dataset/.

14. Rasul and Rogger (2016, 414) provide an explanation for this counterintuitive finding: they advance that bureaucrats operate in a multitasking environment, and that the incentive and monitoring management practices "pick up elements of subjective performance evaluation that lead to other dysfunctional responses" among bureaucrats. In this case, the increased use of mistargeted incentives and key performance indicators may incite bureaucrats to reallocate efforts toward nonproductive tasks, thus reducing project completion rates.

15. One of the areas in which technology has had a significant impact on the lives of the poor is in mobile banking. Innovations have made it possible for millions of poor Africans to have access to financial services through their mobile phones.

16. The V-Dem Institute identified Benin, Ethiopia, and Mauritius as African instances of a wider global trend toward autocracy: the percentage of the world's population living in "autocratizing" countries increased sixfold between 2010 and 2020 (refer to V-Dem Institute 2021).

17. Those six countries were Eritrea, Eswatini, Ethiopia, The Gambia, Lesotho, and Somalia.

18. Similarly, Bueno de Mesquita and Smith (2012) argue that the elite pact needs to grow and that for dictators it tends to shrink and become increasingly exclusive.

19. ACLED data confirm that the general trend of falling fatality rates also holds for all forms of political activity, including armed rebellion and insurgency. Adjusting total fatalities for Africa's rapid population growth to represent the ratio of fatalities per million people in the population makes it clear that the fatality rate has slowly come down over long-time horizons.

20. World Bank, DataBank, World Development Indicators, https://databank.worldbank.org/source /world-development-indicators (accessed 2021).

21. Civil capacity—a concept introduced in Guiso, Sapienza, and Zingales (2016) and developed in Cloutier et al. (2021)—is meant to represent the political power or bargaining power of the average citizen. It comes mostly from citizens' capacity to be politically engaged, to cooperate, and to organize to resolve the collective action problem and hold the state accountable.

22. Afrobarometer, "Analyse Online," https://www.afrobarometer.org/online-data-analysis/.

23. In this regard, Cheeseman and Peiffer (2023) show that, in Nigeria, anticorruption messages raise awareness of corruption risks and lead to reduced tax collection because of concerns that taxes will be wasted. Their finding demonstrates the unintended consequences of interventions aimed at increased transparency of government failures.

24. A recent report by the Escola de Cultura de Pau (2021) summarizes the Africa situation as follows: almost half of the world's 34 armed conflicts in Africa exhibited a significant increase in high-intensity armed conflicts.

25. Uppsala Conflict Data Program, https://ucdp.uu.se.

26. Curiel, Walther, and O'Cleary (2020) demonstrate that Boko Haram is highly fragmented, with between 50 and 60 cells operating over a large part of the territory.

27. As mentioned in the World Bank strategy for West and Central Africa, "the social contract is breaking down and violent conflict is increasing. Citizens have lost trust in states that fail to protect, render justice, or deliver services to them. Violent conflict is also growing, as states fail to resolve community conflicts, which, in turn, further undermines trust in governments. Eleven of the 22 countries in the region are now affected by fragility, conflict, and violence (FCV)" (World Bank 2021, 11).

28. In this regard, Thurston (2020) describes well the jihadist movements in the Sahel and in North Africa.

29. These factors go along with a very limited state presence and underadministered populations, as demonstrated by the number of civil servants per population (refer to the World Bank's Worldwide Bureaucracy Indicators, https://datacatalog.worldbank.org/search/dataset/0038132).

30. "Le déterminisme économique n'explique pas tout. [...] S'y ajoute [...] le fossé Etat-administrés devenu la source de crispations identitaires et de récriminations multiples" [Economic determinism does not explain everything. [...] Added to this is the gap between the state and the governed, which has become a source of identity-based tensions and multiple grievances] (Thiam 2017, 5).

31. According to Leonard (2013), bargains exist only so long as they produce immediate benefits for all parties, which makes them particularly unstable in countries affected by fragility, conflict, and violence. In such countries, the most important expectation from individuals is an allegiance to a community or state in exchange for protection.

32. Since 2020, 14 African states have successfully modified or eliminated term limits.

33. Various terms are used to describe pockets of effectiveness, such as "islands of effectiveness" or "pockets of efficiency." They are public institutions that deliver public services relatively effectively in the context of a largely ineffective government.

References

Acemoglu, Daron, and James Robinson. 2012. *Why Nations Fail: The Origins of Power, Prosperity and Poverty*. New York: Crown Business.

Achu Check, Nicasius, Tsholofelo Madise, Nkululeko Majozi, and Yukihiko Hamada. 2019. "The Integrity of Political Finance Systems in Africa: Tackling Political Corruption." International IDEA Policy Paper No. 20, International Institute for Democracy and Electoral Assistance, Stockholm, and the Africa Institute of South Africa, Pretoria.

Addo, Atta, and Chrisanthi Avgerou. 2021. "Information Technology and Government Corruption in Developing Countries: Evidence from Ghana Customs." *MIS Quarterly* 45 (4): 1833–62.

Afrobarometer Network. 2023. "Africans Want More Democracy, but Their Leaders Still Aren't Listening." Afrobarometer Policy Paper 85, Afrobarometer.

Algan, Yann. 2018. "Trust and Social Capital." In *For Good Measure: Advancing Research on Well-Being Metrics beyond GDP*, edited by Joseph E. Stiglitz, Jean-Paul Fitoussi, and Martine Durand, 283–320. Paris: OECD Publishing.

Andersen, Jorgen Juel, Niels Johannesen, and Bob Rijkers. 2020. "Elite Capture of Foreign Aid: Evidence from Offshore Bank Accounts." Policy Research Working Paper 9150, World Bank, Washington, DC.

Andrews, Matt, Lant Pritchett, and Michael Woolcock. 2012. "Escaping Capability Traps through Problem-Driven Iterative Adaptation (PDIA)." CGD Working Paper No. 299, Center for Global Development, Washington, DC.

Andrews, Matt, Lant Pritchett, and Michael Woolcock. 2017. *Building State Capability: Evidence, Analysis, Action*. Oxford, UK: Oxford University Press.

Arvanitis, Yannis, and Gael Raballand. 2023. "Customs Reform in Developing Countries—Time for a Rethink?" Equitable Growth, Finance & Institutions Notes, World Bank, Washington, DC.

Asunka, Joseph, and Carolyn Logan. 2021. "Access Denied: Freedom of Information in Africa Falls Short of Public Expectations." Afrobarometer Dispatch No. 452, Afrobarometer.

Bagayoko, Niagalé. 2022. "Explaining the Failure of Internationally-Supported Defence and Security Reforms in Sahelian States." *Conflict, Security & Development* 22 (3): 243–69.

Barbone, Luca, Arindam Das-Gupta, Luc de Wulf, and Anna Hansson. 1999. "Reforming Tax Systems: The World Bank Record in the 1990s." Policy Research Working Paper 2237, World Bank, Washington, DC.

Blas, Javier. 2023. "What Happened to Africa Rising? It's Been Another Lost Decade." *Bloomberg Opinion*, September 12, 2023. https://www.bloomberg.com/opinion/features/2023-09-12/africa-s-lost-decade-economic-pain-underlies-sub-saharan-coups.

Blimpo, Moussa Pouguinimpo, David Evans, and Nathalie Lahire. 2020. "Parental Human Capital and Effective School Management: Evidence from The Gambia." Policy Research Working Paper 7238, World Bank, Washington, DC.

Boly, Ahmadou, and Eric Kéré. 2023. "Terrorism and Military Expenditure in Africa: An Analysis of Spillover Effects." AfDB Working Paper 368, African Development Bank, Abidjan.

Börzel, Tanja A., and Thomas Risse. 2016. "Dysfunctional State Institutions, Trust, and Governance in Areas of Limited Statehood." *Regulation & Governance* 10 (2): 149–60.

Boyce, James K., and Léonce Ndikumana. 2022. "Conclusions: Capital Flight in the World Economy." Chapter 7 in *On the Trail of Capital Flight from Africa: The Takers and the Enablers*, edited by Léonce Ndikumana and James K. Boyce. Oxford, UK: Oxford University Press.

Brockmeyer, Brandon, and Jonathan Fox. 2015. *Assessing the Evidence: The Effectiveness and Impact of Public Governance-Oriented Multi-Stakeholder Initiatives*. London: Transparency & Accountability Initiative.

Budhram, Trevor. 2019. "Political Corruption and State Capture in South Africa." In *Political Corruption in Africa*, edited by Inge Amundsen, 155–74. Cheltenham, UK: Edward Elgar Publishing.

Bueno de Mesquita, Bruce, and Alastair Smith. 2012. *The Dictator's Handbook*. New York: Public Affairs.

Bussolo, Maurizio, Maria E. Davalos, Vito Peragine, and Ramya Sundaram. 2018. *Toward a New Social Contract: Taking on Distributional Tensions in Europe and Central Asia*. Europe and Central Asia Studies. Washington, DC: World Bank.

Canen, Nathan, and Leonard Wantchekon. 2022. "Political Distortions, State Capture, and Economic Development in Africa." *Journal of Economic Perspectives* 36 (1): 101–24.

Cantens, Thomas, Gaël Raballand, and Samson Bilangna. 2010. "Reforming Customs by Measuring Performance: A Cameroon Case Study." *World Customs Journal* 4 (2): 55–74.

Carothers, Thomas, and Diane De Gramont. 2013. *Development Aid Confronts Politics: The Almost Revolution*. Washington, DC: Carnegie Endowment for International Peace.

Centeno, Miguel A., Atul Kohli, and Debra J. Yashar, eds. 2017. *States in the Developing World*. Cambridge, UK: Cambridge University Press.

Channa, Anila, and Jean-Paul Faguet. 2016. "Decentralization of Health and Education in Developing Countries: A Quality-Adjusted Review of the Empirical Literature." *World Bank Research Observer* 31 (2): 199–241.

Cheeseman, Nic. 2015. *Democracy in Africa: Successes, Failures, and the Struggle for Political Reform*. New York: Cambridge University Press.

Cheeseman, Nic, ed. 2018. *Institutions and Democracy in Africa*. Cambridge, UK: Cambridge University Press.

Cheeseman, Nic, and Caryn Peiffer. 2023. "Why Efforts to Fight Corruption Can Undermine the Social Contract: Lessons from a Survey Experiment in Nigeria." *Governance* 36 (4): 1045–61.

Chipkin, Ivor, Mark Swilling, Haroon Bhorat, Mzukisi Qobo, Sikhulekile Duma, Lumkile Mondi, Camaren Peter, et al. 2018. *Shadow State: The Politics of State Capture*. Johannesburg: Wits University Press.

Cloutier, Mathieu, Bernard Harborne, Deborah Hannah Isser, Indhira Vanessa Santos, and Michael Watts. 2021. *Social Contracts for Development: Bargaining, Contention, and Social Inclusion in Sub-Saharan Africa*. Africa Development Forum. Washington, DC: World Bank.

Curiel, Rafael, Olivier Walther, and Neave O'Cleary. 2020. "Uncovering the Internal Structure of Boko Haram through Its Mobility Patterns." *Applied Network Science* 5: 28.

Devermont, Judd. 2020. *Politics at the Heart of the Crisis in the Sahel*. CSIS Brief. Washington, DC: Center for Strategic and International Studies.

Diwan, Ishac, Adeel Malik, and Izak Atiyas, eds. 2019. *Crony Capitalism in the Middle East: Business and Politics from Liberalization to the Arab Spring*. Oxford, UK: Oxford University Press.

Dom, Roel, Anna Custers, Stephen R. Davenport, and Wilson Prichard. 2022. *Innovations in Tax Compliance: Building Trust, Navigating Politics, and Tailoring Reform*. Washington, DC: World Bank.

Dowd, Caitriona. 2015. "Grievances, Governance and Islamist Violence in Sub-Saharan Africa." *Journal of Modern African Studies* 53 (4): 505–31.

Duflo, Esther, Pascaline Dupas, and Michael Kremer. 2007. "Peer Effects, Pupil-Teacher Ratios, and Teacher Incentives: Evidence from a Randomized Evaluation in Kenya." Working paper, MIT Poverty Action Lab. https://scholar.google.com/citations?view_op=view_citation&hl=en&user=yhDMl8AAAAAJ&cstart=400&pagesize=100&sortby=pubdate&citation_for_view=yhDMl8AAAAAJ:qUcmZB5y_30C.

Dwyer, Maggie. 2017. "Situating Soldiers' Demands: Mutinies and Protests in Burkina Faso." *Third World Quarterly* 38 (1): 219–34.

Escola de Cultura de Pau. 2021. *Alert 2021! Report on Conflicts, Human Rights and Peacebuilding*. Barcelona: Icaria.

Fang, Xiangming, Siddharth Khotari, Cameron McLoughlin, and Mustafa Yenice. 2020. "The Economic Consequences of Conflict in Sub-Saharan Africa." IMF Working Paper 2020/221, International Monetary Fund, Washington, DC.

Fiebelkorn, Andreas. 2019. "State Capture Analysis: How to Quantitatively Analyze the Regulatory Abuse by Business-State Relationships." Governance Discussion Paper No. 2, World Bank, Washington, DC.

Filmer, Deon, James Habyarimana, and Shwetlana Sabarwal. 2020. "Teacher Performance-Based Incentives and Learning Inequality." Policy Research Working Paper 9382, World Bank, Washington, DC.

Freedom House. 2022. "How African Democracies Can Rise and Thrive amid Instability, Militarization, and Interference." *Freedom House Perspectives*, September 1, 2022. https://freedomhouse.org/article/how-african-democracies-can-rise-and-thrive-amid-instability.

Fukuyama, Francis. 1995. *Trust: The Social Virtues and the Creation of Prosperity*. New York: Free Press.

Glewwe, Paul, and Eugenie W. H. Maiga. 2011. "The Impacts of School Management Reforms in Madagascar: Do the Impacts Vary by Teacher Type?" *Journal of Development Effectiveness* 3 (4): 435–69.

Grindle, Merilee S. 2004. "Good Enough Governance: Poverty Reduction and Reform in Developing Countries." *Governance* 17 (4): 525–48.

Guiso, Luigi, Paola Sapienza, and Luigi Zingales. 2016. "Long-Term Persistence." *Journal of the European Economic Association* 14 (6): 1401–36.

Gyimah-Boadi, Emmanuel, Carolyn Logan, and Josephine Sanny. 2021. "Africans' Durable Demand for Democracy." *Journal of Democracy* 32 (3): 136–51.

Hausman, David. 2011. "Rebuilding the Civil Service after War: Rwanda after the Genocide, 1998–2009." Innovations for Successful Societies, Princeton University. https://successfulsocieties .princeton.edu/sites/g/files/toruqf5601/files/Policy_Note_ID163.pdf.

Hickey, Sam. 2023. *Pockets of Effectiveness and the Politics of State-Building and Development in Africa*. Oxford, UK: Oxford University Press.

Iddawela, Yohan, Neil Lee, and Andrés Rodríguez-Pose. 2021. "Quality of Subnational Government and Regional Development in Africa." *Journal of Development Studies* 57 (8): 1282–302.

Isham, Jonathan, Michael Woolcock, Lant Pritchett, and Gwen Busby. 2005. "The Varieties of the Resource Experience: How Natural Resource Export Structures Affect the Political Economy of Economic Growth." *World Bank Economic Review* 19 (2): 141–74.

Kaufmann, Daniel, Judit Montoriol-Garriga, and Francesca Recanatini. 2008. "How Does Bribery Affect Public Service Delivery? Micro-Evidence from Service Users and Public Officials in Peru." Policy Research Working Paper 4492, World Bank, Washington, DC.

Khan, Mushtaq, Antonio Andreoni, and Pallavi Roy. 2016. *Anti-Corruption in Adverse Contexts: A Strategic Approach*. London: School of Oriental and African Studies, University of London. https://eprints.soas.ac.uk/23495/.

Khemani, Stuti. 2015. "Buying Votes versus Supplying Public Services: Political Incentives to Under-Invest in Pro-Poor Policies." *Journal of Development Economics* 117: 84–93.

Kim, Jay-Hyung, Tuan Minh Le, and Graham Glenday. 2022. "Stocktaking Survey on Climate-Smart Public Investment Management in Africa: What Did We Learn?" Equitable Growth, Finance & Institutions Notes, World Bank, Washington, DC.

Kinda, Harouna, and Noel Thiombiano. 2024. "Does Transparency Matter? Evaluating the Impacts of the Extractive Industries Transparency Initiative (EITI) on Deforestation in Resource-Rich Developing Countries." *World Development* 173: 106431.

Leaver, Clare, Owen Ozier, Pieter Serneels, and Andrew Zeitlin. 2020. "Recruitment, Effort, and Retention Effects of Performance Contracts for Civil Servants: Experimental Evidence from Rwandan Primary Schools." Policy Research Working Paper 9395, World Bank, Washington, DC.

Leonard, David K. 2013. "Social Contracts, Networks and Security in Tropical Africa Conflict States: An Overview." *IDS Bulletin* 44 (1): 1–14.

Levy, Brian. 2014. *Working with the Grain: Integrating Governance and Growth in Development Strategies*. Oxford, UK: Oxford University Press.

Lindsey, Brink. 2021. *State Capacity: What Is It, How We Lost It, and How to Get It Back*. Washington, DC: Niskanen Center.

Manacorda, Marco, and Andrea Tesei. 2020. "Liberation Technology: Mobile Phones and Political Mobilization in Africa." *Econometrica* 88 (2): 533–67.

Masi, Tania, Antonio Savoia, and Kunal Sen. 2020. "Is There a Fiscal Resource Curse? Resource Rents, Fiscal Capacity, and Political Institutions in Developing Economies." WIDER Working Paper 2020/10, UNU-WIDER, Helsinki.

Mbiti, Isaac, Karthik Muralidharan, Mauricio Romero, Youdi Schipper, Constantine Manda, and Rakesh Rajani. 2019. "Inputs, Incentives, and Complementarities in Education: Experimental Evidence from Tanzania." *Quarterly Journal of Economics* 134 (3): 1627–73.

McKinsey Global Institute. 2020. *The Social Contract in the 21st Century: Outcomes So Far for Workers, Consumers, and Savers in Advanced Economies*. New York: McKinsey Global Institute.

Moïsé, E., and S. Sorescu. 2013. "Trade Facilitation Indicators: The Potential Impact of Trade Facilitation on Developing Countries' Trade." OECD Trade Policy Paper 144, OECD Publishing, Paris. https://doi.org/10.1787/5k4bw6kg6ws2-en.

Moore, Mick, Wilson Prichard, and Odd-Helge Fjeldstad. 2018. *Taxing Africa: Coercion, Reform and Development*. London: Zed Books.

Natsios, Andrew. 2010. *The Clash of the Counter-Bureaucracy and Development*. CGD Essay. Washington, DC: Center for Global Development.

Ndayikeza, Michel Armel. 2021. "Government Expenditure and Longevity of African Leaders." *Scientific African* 13: e00929.

Norris, Pippa, William Jennings, and Graham Stoker. 2019. "In Praise of Scepticism: Trust but Verify." Trustgov Working Paper Series, no. 2 (September). https://www.dropbox.com/scl/fi/qslx77 hica5uylttnoyaa/WAPOR2019-Paper-Trust-by-Verify.pdf?rlkey=5l6k38eauplk2yalqwgx 915rs&e=2&dl=0.

North, Douglass C. 1990. *Institutions, Institutional Change and Economic Performance*. New York: Cambridge University Press.

OECD (Organisation for Economic Co-operation and Development). 2016. *Corruption in the Extractive Value Chain: Typology of Risks, Mitigation Measures and Incentives*. OECD Development Policy Tools. Paris: OECD Publishing.

OECD (Organisation for Economic Co-operation and Development). 2023. *Governing through Transparency: Corruption, Accountability and Illicit Financial Flows in Oil Trading*. OECD Development Perspectives. Paris: OECD Publishing.

OECD (Organisation for Economic Co-operation and Development) and SWAC (Sahel and West Africa Club Secretariat). 2020. *The Geography of Conflict in North and West Africa*. West African Studies. Paris: OECD Publishing. https://doi.org/10.1787/02181039-en.

Opalo, Ken. 2023. "Putting the Recent Coups in the Sahel in Broader Perspective." *An Africanist Perspective* (blog), August 3, 2023. https://www.africanistperspective.com/p/putting-the -recent-coups-in-the-sahel.

Oppong, Nelson, Luke Patey, and Ricardo Soares de Oliveira. 2020. "Governing African Oil and Gas: Boom-Era Political and Institutional Innovation." *Extractive Industries and Society* 7 (4): 1163–70.

PEFA (Public Expenditure and Financial Accountability). 2020. "2020 Global Report on Public Financial Management." PEFA. https://www.pefa.org/global-report-2020/en/.

Persson, Torsten, and Guido Tabellini. 2009. "Democratic Capital: The Nexus of Political and Economic Change." *American Economic Journal: Macroeconomics* 1 (2): 88–126.

Pierson, Paul. 2000. "Increasing Returns, Path Dependence, and the Study of Politics." *American Political Science Review* 94 (2): 251–67.

Posner, Daniel N., and Daniel J. Young. 2007. "The Institutionalization of Political Power in Africa." *Journal of Democracy* 18 (3): 126–40.

Prichard, Wilson. 2015. *Taxation, Responsiveness and Accountability in Sub-Saharan Africa: The Dynamics of Tax Bargaining*. Cambridge, UK: Cambridge University Press.

Pye, Kathryn. 2021. *The Sahel: Europe's Forever War?* London: Center for European Reform.

Raballand, Gael, and Bob Rijkers. 2021. "State Capture Analysis: A How to Guide for Practitioners." Equitable Growth, Finance and Institutions Notes, World Bank, Washington, DC.

Raleigh, Clionadh, Héni Nsaibia, and Caitriona Dowd. 2020. "The Sahel Crisis since 2012." *African Affairs* 120 (478): 123–43.

Rasul, Imran, and Daniel Rogger. 2016. "Management of Bureaucrats and Public Service Delivery: Evidence from the Nigerian Civil Service." *Economic Journal* 128 (608): 413–46.

Rasul, Imran, Daniel Rogger, and Martin J. Williams. 2018. "Management and Bureaucratic Effectiveness: Evidence from the Ghanaian Civil Service." Policy Research Working Paper 8595, World Bank, Washington, DC.

Riedl, Rachel Beatty. 2014. *Authoritarian Origins of Democratic Party Systems in Africa*. New York: Cambridge University Press.

Risse, Thomas, and Eric Stollenwerk. 2018. "Legitimacy in Areas of Limited Statehood." *Annual Review of Political Science* 21: 403–18.

Rodrik, Dani, Arvind Subramanian, and Francesco Trebbi. 2004. "Institutions Rule: The Primacy of Institutions over Geography and Integration in Economic Development." *Journal of Economic Growth* 9 (2): 131–65.

Ross, Michael L. 2015. "What Have We Learned about the Resource Curse?" *Annual Review of Political Science* 18: 239–59.

Sala-i-Martin, Xavier, and Arvind Subramanian. 2003. "Addressing the Natural Resource Curse: An Illustration from Nigeria." IMF Working Paper 2003/139, International Monetary Fund, Washington, DC.

Siegle, Joseph, and Candace Cook. 2021. "Circumvention of Term Limits Weakens Governance in Africa." Infographic, Africa Center for Strategic Studies, Washington, DC.

Sigman, Rachel. 2023. *Parties, Political Finance, and Governance in Africa: Extracting Money and Shaping States in Benin and Ghana*. Cambridge, UK: Cambridge University Press.

Signé, Landry, Mariama Sow, and Payce Madden. 2020. "Illicit Financial Flows in Africa: Drivers, Destinations, and Policy Options." Africa Growth Initiative Policy Brief, Brookings Institution, Washington, DC.

Soares de Oliveira, Ricardo. 2022. "Researching Africa and the Offshore World." *Journal of Modern African Studies* 60 (3): 265–96.

Tanzi, Vito, and Hamid Davoodi. 1998. *Roads to Nowhere: How Corruption in Public Investment Hurts Growth*. Washington, DC: International Monetary Fund.

Thiam, Adam. 2017. *Centre du Mali: enjeux et dangers d'une crise négligée*. Bamako: Centre pour le dialogue humanitaire.

Thurston, Alexander. 2020. *Jihadists of North Africa and the Sahel*. Cambridge, UK: Cambridge University Press.

Transparency International. 2019. *Global Corruption Barometer: Africa 2019*. Berlin: Transparency International.

UNCTAD (United Nations Conference on Trade and Development). 2020. *Tackling Illicit Financial Flows for Sustainable Development in Africa*. Geneva: United Nations.

UNICEF (United Nations Children's Fund) and African Union Commission. 2021. "Transforming Education in Africa: An Evidence-Based Overview and Recommendations for Long-Term Improvements." United Nations, New York.

UNICEF (United Nations Children's Fund) Africa. 2022. "The Impacts of COVID-19 on Education Spending in Africa and Possible Recovery Pathways." Education and Social Policy Working Paper, UNICEF, Eastern and Southern Africa, West and Central Africa, and Middle East and North Africa Regional Offices.

V-Dem Institute. 2021. "Democracy Report 2021: Autocratization Turns Viral." V-Dem Institute, University of Gothenburg, Sweden.

Van de Walle, Nicolas. 2012. "The Path from Neopatrimonialism: Democracy and Clientelism in Africa Today." Chapter 8 in *Neopatrimonialism in Africa and Beyond*, edited by Daniel Bach and Mamoudou Gazibo. New York: Routledge.

Vom Hau, Matthias. 2012. "State Capacity and Inclusive Development: New Challenges and Directions." ESID Working Paper 2, Effective States and Inclusive Development Research Centre, School of Environment and Development, University of Manchester, Manchester, UK.

Wehner, Joachim, and Linnea Mills. 2020. "Cabinet Size and Governance in Sub-Saharan Africa." Policy Research Working Paper 9232, World Bank, Washington, DC.

World Bank. 2000. *Can Africa Claim the 21st Century?* Washington, DC: World Bank.

World Bank. 2004. *World Development Report 2004: Making Services Work for Poor People.* Washington, DC: World Bank.

World Bank. 2011. *World Development Report 2011: Conflict, Security, and Development.* Washington, DC: World Bank.

World Bank. 2016. *World Development Report 2016: Digital Dividends.* Washington, DC: World Bank.

World Bank. 2017. *World Development Report 2017: Governance and the Law.* Washington, DC: World Bank.

World Bank. 2019a. *Future Drivers of Growth in Rwanda: Innovation, Integration, Agglomeration, and Competition.* Washington, DC: World Bank.

World Bank. 2019b. *Social Contracts and World Bank Country Engagements: Lessons from Emerging Practices.* IEG Meso Evaluation. Independent Evaluation Group. Washington, DC: World Bank.

World Bank. 2020. *Enhancing Government Effectiveness and Transparency: The Fight against Corruption.* Washington, DC: World Bank.

World Bank. 2021. *Supporting a Resilient Recovery.* Washington, DC: World Bank.

World Bank. 2022. "CPIA Africa, October 2022: Assessing Africa's Policies and Institutions." World Bank, Washington, DC. https://openknowledge.worldbank.org/entities/publication/9dc0b081 -20a8-5b7a-ac29-81f77a85419e.

Zak, Paul, and Stephen Knack. 2001. "Trust and Growth." *Economic Journal* 111 (470): 295–321.

Zmerli, Sonja, and Tom W. G. Van Der Meer. 2017. *Handbook of Political Trust.* Cheltenham, UK: Edward Elgar Publishing.

CHAPTER 2

Climate and Environment

Kanta Kumari Rigaud and Anna Gayatri Singh

Summary

Africa sits at the crossroads of readiness for transformation to climate action or a downward spiral that amplifies poverty, instability, and conflict, with large-scale impacts on economies and communities. Transformation at scale will require urgent, bold action. A focus on the following five game-changing actions could put countries well on track to achieving green, resilient, and inclusive development that is underpinned by robust and sustainable growth pathways.

1 Adopt targeted solutions focused on protection and disaster prevention to protect people and economies from extreme events and promote responses that ensure resilience. Shifting to inclusive, cost-effective, and far-sighted responses that draw on financial mechanisms, such as Catastrophe Deferred Drawdown Options, and social safety nets, such as the Urban Productive Safety Net Project in Ethiopia, are key to building resilience.

2 Urgently accelerate universal access to affordable energy, which represents the cornerstone of climate adaptation in Africa. Universal energy access is adaptation at its best and is crucial for the region. Evidence shows significant potential for developing diversified energy pathways that are clean, efficient, and renewable to realize universal energy access. Universal energy access will also unleash a multitude of benefits including productive economies in Africa—through improved livelihood and job opportunities for the rapidly growing population.

3 Exploit the abundance of natural resources in Africa to develop a "new climate solution." Doing so will require that countries reimagine the use and management of these resources to harness fully their value proposition as local, national, and global public goods. Africa has two pathways to new climate solution opportunities: carbon markets and green minerals.

4. Prioritize systematic and sustained investments in capacity and dedicated skills in countries backed by strong policy, regulatory, and institutional frameworks to drive far-sighted, integrative climate-smart action and structural reforms. Institutions can facilitate mainstreaming climate considerations into sectoral frameworks as a means to enhance capacity and scale up readiness to better anticipate and respond to climate change.

5. Urgently mobilize financing from the public and private sectors to address substantial climate financing gaps, weak macrofiscal landscapes, and indebtedness in several countries in Africa. For Africa to meet its financing needs, countries need to engage all stakeholders to leverage a range of financing instruments, including concessional financing, grants, loans, guarantees, disaster risk management instruments, green bonds, debt for climate swaps, and public-private partnerships.

These five transformative and game-changing climate solutions are efficient, effective, just, and urgent. These feasible solutions will put Africa in good stead to claim the 21st century for its people and economies in the face of a changing climate. They will not benefit just Africa; they will also support more globally the goals of the Paris Agreement. Coordinating continental and regional efforts and ensuring their coherence within a multilevel governance system are key to driving forward effective, efficient, and ambitious climate actions. In addition, achieving Africa's climate-resilient development agenda will require inclusive multistakeholder partnerships and broad-based collaboration through locally led climate action.

Context

This chapter applies a climate lens to overarching solutions that can propel Africa into claiming the 21st century. Climate change will accelerate alongside other megatrends— population growth, urbanization, and biodiversity loss—and will amplify the potential for violating tipping points in the coming decades. The sheer pervasiveness of its impacts means that climate change cannot be addressed in isolation. The discussion in this chapter intersects with other chapters on governance, trade, productivity, and human capital, among others. This chapter considers game-changing climate solutions that Africa must fast-track to secure low-carbon, climate-resilient trajectories that are fundamental to lay early claim to the 21st century.

One-fourth of the century has passed, and increasing global emissions and escalating climate impacts are now on a collision course. Immediate and second-order climate impacts pose economywide risks that could lead to double-digit gross domestic product (GDP) losses by 2050 (World Bank Group 2024). Coping with and responding to single and recurrent climate crises will not be adequate. Africa urgently needs an enduring multidecade, climate-safe pathway that moves its economies and populations up the ladder of resilience, with improved welfare and growth that are productive and sustainable. African countries can leverage their natural resources for sustainable development throughout the region, enabling leapfrogging into low-carbon pathways.

Africa accounts for only about 3 percent of the world's carbon dioxide (CO_2) emissions from energy and industrial sources, but total global emissions disproportionately affect Sub-Saharan Africa. Brazil, China, the European Union 27,[1] India, the Russian Federation, and the United States remained the world's largest greenhouse gas (GHG) emitters in 2022, releasing 61.6 percent of total global GHG emissions (Crippa et al. 2023). African countries continue to warm at an average rate of +0.1°C faster than the rest of the world, which presents a challenge for African economies and communities (WMO 2023a). Climate change is widespread, rapid, and intensifying throughout the continent, with more frequent and extreme weather events exposing millions of people to acute food insecurity, reduced water security, and intensifying climate shocks. For example, more than 147 million people in Sub-Saharan Africa faced food insecurity in 2022 because of conditions such as drought in the Horn of Africa, erratic rainfall in southern Africa, and flooding in the west of Africa (FSIN and Global Network against Food Crises 2023).

Breaching the 1.5°C threshold will have detrimental and far-reaching impacts on livelihoods and economies across the continent. The World Bank Country Climate and Development Reports (CCDRs) have started to highlight the impacts of future climate change projections. In the Group of Five for the Sahel countries (Burkina Faso, Chad, Mali, Mauritania, and Niger), climate change could increase the poverty rate from 27 percent to 34 percent under different scenarios, pushing an additional 4.1 million to 13.5 million people into poverty by 2050 (World Bank 2022d). The CCDR for Rwanda estimates expected annual damage to capital from extreme weather events at between 0.19 percent and 0.74 percent (World Bank 2022h). In Angola, economic losses in the agricultural sector due to climate change may rise from US$100 million per year in 2022 to more than US$700 million per year by 2100 (World Bank 2022a). Regardless of geographical variances, no country in Africa will escape the escalating impacts of climate change in all sectors and aspects of life.

Readiness to face the "new climate normal" is crucial for Africa's future. Africa must address climate challenges and opportunities proactively and at scale to enable inclusive productive growth and resilient economies while transforming into clean energy pathways. Africa's unique context—low-baseline development, preexisting climate vulnerabilities, limited energy access, high reliance on climate-sensitive sectors, and abundant but degrading natural capital—represents a compelling set of challenges in countering climate risks. A lack of sustained resilience of countries' economies and people has already caused backsliding of development gains and heightened vulnerability to climate change, which unfolds through multiplier impacts across the region. Early warning systems cover only 40 percent of Africa's population. A mere 10 percent of the African population has access to social safety nets, leaving the vast majority of the population vulnerable, with little capacity to anticipate and respond to climate shocks (Beegle, Coudouel, and Monsalve 2018; UNDRR and WMO 2022).

Addressing near-term financial, technological, and economic constraints is critical to overcome the physical risks posed by climate change and support countries to leapfrog into clean energy transitions as a crucial part of achieving universal energy access. With the right set of policies, structural transformations, and accelerated climate-smart actions—and harnessing technological advancement in digital innovations and clean energy transition minerals—the continent can attain clean universal energy access and at the same time keep emissions to below 3.5 percent (IEA 2022).

Africa has some of the fastest-growing economies, with real GDP growth projected to exceed the global average in 2023. Such growth supported by climate-informed policy could influence a green growth trajectory (AfDB 2023). Africa could produce the first generation of truly clean, green economies to achieve the Sustainable Development Goals (SDGs) for a resilient future, assuming it has the right mix of policies, action, and finance. This achievement will yield dividends globally; the world has no viable pathway to solving the climate problem without Africa, in view of the continent's population, which will reach 2.3 billion by 2050 (UN DESA 2019). Africa's youthful human capital base, with 830 million youth by 2050, contrasts with other regions' aging populations and positions the continent to be at the forefront of green growth opportunities (AfDB 2023; World Bank 2020a).

By 2050, the transition from fossil fuels to clean energy will likely create demand for 3 billion tons of the minerals and metals needed to deploy solar, wind, and geothermal energy, many of which Sub-Saharan Africa has in abundance. Any framing for Africa to claim the 21st century in the face of accelerating climate change must consider the national, regional, and global contexts, and must set out finite near- and long-term transitions and sequencing, centered around equity and efficiency considerations of the climate reality.

Facts

The projected impacts of climate change have become more certain in the last several years. Clearly, climate change negatively affects Sub-Saharan Africa and has widespread and severe consequences for key sectors, livelihoods, and economies. The intersection of climate change with other megatrends compounds existing risks for the region and threatens resilient and sustainable development outcomes. However, the trajectory of Sub-Saharan Africa is not set in stone. Urgent and intentional actions taken today can propel the region into a more prosperous, equitable, and resilient future. Africa is unique in that the challenges facing the region are counterbalanced by solutions. The region has opportunities it can harness to shift its current trajectory; when paired with strategic policy design and targeted interventions, these opportunities can allow the region to claim the rest of the 21st century.

Fact 1: The biophysical impacts of climate change are manifesting in widespread and compounding ways throughout Sub-Saharan Africa, with escalating impacts in recent years. Africa heated up at an average rate of +0.3°C per decade between 1991 and 2022, faster than the global average of +0.2°C per decade (WMO 2023a). Climate change has been amplified in Africa, with heat waves and droughts, and a twofold increase in the likelihood of marine heat waves in African waters (Trisos et al. 2022).

If global warming reaches between 1.5°C and 2°C with limited and only gradual adaptation efforts, the negative consequences are expected to spread extensively and become severe, with impacts including diminished food production, hindered economic growth, heightened inequality and poverty, loss of biodiversity, and increased illness and mortality rates among humans (Trisos et al. 2022). By 2050, projections highlight potentially dire consequences of climate change: rising sea levels of 16–46 centimeters, diminished crop yields of 11–25 percent, decreased coastal fishery yields of up to 26 percent, decreased river flow of up to 22 percent, more than 30 percent loss of population in all species, and increased heat-related fatalities of 50–180 deaths per 100,000 people annually under a 2.5°C increase (Trisos et al. 2022; USAID 2018).

Fact 2: Global emissions remain on an upward trajectory positioned to exceed the goals of the Paris Agreement and increase the risk of surpassing planetary tipping points. According to recent assessments, the international community is not on track to meet the goals of the Paris Agreement based on countries' nationally determined contributions (figure 2.1). The Conference of the Parties of the Climate Change Convention reaffirmed the guardrail of 1.5°C as the threshold for safe and just boundaries, which accounts for Earth system resilience and human well-being (Rockström et al. 2023). Because of insufficient efforts to limit global temperature rise to 1.5°C by 2100, global temperatures are expected to overshoot the 1.5°C threshold as early as 2027 (WMO 2023b). There is an increased risk that tipping elements of the climate system will surpass crucial thresholds, resulting in a chain reaction of impacts that reverberate through interconnected climate, ecological, and social systems (OECD 2022). Key tipping points include the collapse of the West Antarctic and Greenland ice sheets, the melting of the Arctic permafrost, and the dieback of the Amazon rainforest (OECD 2022). In Africa, Garcin et al. (2022) find that the Congo Basin peatlands may lie close to a climatically driven drought threshold which would trigger the release of further carbon from peat to the atmosphere, but more research is warranted. Reaching this threshold could disrupt key ecosystem services that the Congo Basin provides, including regulating rainfall patterns and providing food, water, and shelter for more than 75 million people in the region (Tyukavina et al. 2018). On a global scale, these cascading effects have the potential to trigger additional tipping elements, culminating in a "hothouse" global climate that may become less suitable for human existence (OECD 2022). Crossing these critical thresholds within the climate system could cause severe regional or local hazards, including extreme temperatures, more frequent droughts, forest fires, and unprecedented weather events (OECD 2022).

Fact 3: Adaptation is the cornerstone of climate action, particularly in Sub-Saharan Africa, where many countries have high levels of vulnerability and low levels of readiness. Because Africa contributes only about 3 percent of global carbon emissions, it needs adaptation strategies that reduce the impacts of climate change on people. These strategies include building resilience to lift people out of poverty, reduce hunger, raise incomes, and reduce the tensions that lead to conflict (GCA 2021).

FIGURE 2.1 Comparison of scenarios with projected total and per capita global emissions, according to nationally determined contributions, 2010–60

GHG emissions (GtCO$_2$ eq/year using GWP-100 from the AR6)

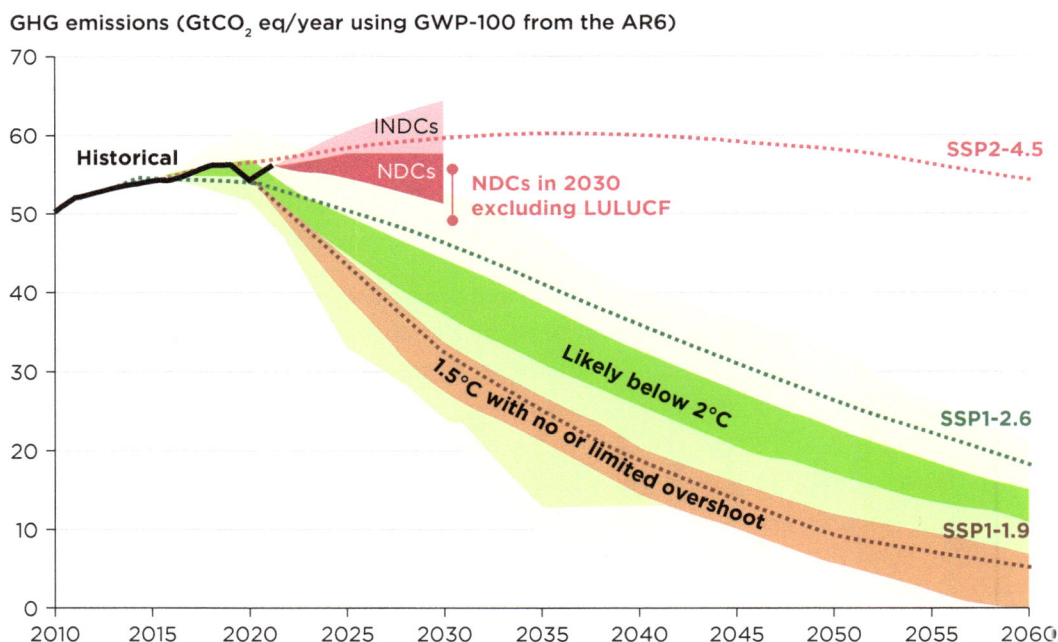

Source: United Nations Framework Convention on Climate Change 2022, https://www.ipcc.ch /assessment-report/ar6/.
Note: AR6 = Sixth Assessment Report of the Intergovernmental Panel on Climate Change (IPCC); eq = equivalent; GHG = greenhouse gas; GtCO$_2$ = gigatons of carbon dioxide; GWP = global warming potential; INDCs = intended nationally determined contributions; LULUCF = land use, land use change, and forestry; NDCs = nationally determined contributions; SSP = Shared Socioeconomic Pathway (scenarios used in climate modeling to explore future global socioeconomic developments and their impact on climate change).

Of the 48 countries that make up Sub-Saharan Africa, 43 (90 percent) rank in the bottom 50 percent of the Notre Dame Global Adaptation Initiative Country Index for readiness,[2] which suggests that the region is largely unprepared to cope with the increasing impacts of climate change. According to the Human Capital Index, Sub-Saharan Africa has attained only 40 percent of its productive potential (Brixi, Rawlings, and Koechlein 2021). In addition, the African continent is only halfway to achieving the SDGs and targets by 2030 (UNECA et al. 2020). A lack of rapid, inclusive, and climate-informed development could push an additional 43 million people in Sub-Saharan Africa below the poverty line by 2030 (Hallegatte et al. 2016).

Fact 4: Sub-Saharan Africa has contributed the least to global climate change, and Africa could be the first continent to leapfrog into renewable options and contribute in an efficient way to reducing GHG emissions—but only if this priority is addressed quickly, to avoid countries being locked into traditional energy sources. Sub-Saharan Africa has some of the lowest historical GHG emissions responsible for human-induced climate change and currently has the lowest per capita GHG emissions of all regions. About 43 percent of the African continent, or 600 million people, still lacked access to electricity in 2022 (World Bank 2023b). Achieving universal access to affordable electricity by 2030 will require tripling the current rate of electrification (IEA 2022). In this context, the Mission 300 initiative of the World Bank and the African Development Bank to connect 300 million people to electricity in Sub-Saharan Africa by 2030 seeks to fill this gap.[3] Despite holding about 60 percent of global solar resources, Africa has only about 1 percent of installed solar photovoltaic capacity (IEA 2022). The cost of solar photovoltaic decreased by 88 percent between 2010 and 2021, making it the fastest-growing renewable energy source in Africa (IRENA 2022)—refer to figure 2.2. Investments in solar photovoltaic increased from 2 percent in 2011 to 62 percent in 2021, but four countries—the Arab Republic of Egypt, Kenya, Morocco, and South Africa—were responsible for attracting 75 percent of total investments in renewable energy between 2010 and 2020 because of their strong enabling policies and financial mechanisms (IRENA and AfDB 2022). Thus, in order for Sub-Saharan Africa to leapfrog into renewable options, countries must build capacity and strengthen enabling factors to reduce financial and operational risks.

Fact 5: Sub-Saharan African countries with fossil fuels as engines of growth need urgently to pursue a "just transition" by diversifying their economies to avoid lock-in of expensive investments and stranded assets. Angola and Nigeria remain key oil producers, and Mozambique and South Africa key coal producers (Mutezo and Mulopo 2021). Sub-Saharan Africa represents about 50 percent of global major petroleum discoveries since 2000, more than any other region, with large oil and gas discoveries in Angola, Côte d'Ivoire, Mozambique, and Senegal, among other countries

FIGURE 2.2 African population with access to off-grid renewable power, 2009–19

Population (million)

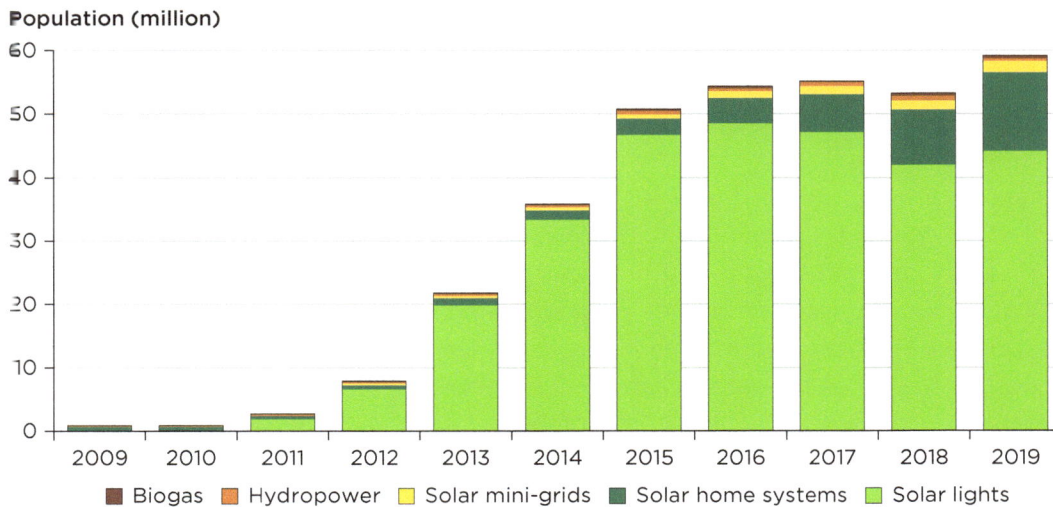

Source: IRENA and AfDB 2022.

(Cust, Mihalyi, and Rivera-Ballesteros 2021). Sub-Saharan Africa's net oil exports fell by 40 percent in the 2010s, a downward trend expected to continue over the next 10–30 years (Cust and Zeufack 2023; IEA 2022). As the cost of renewable energy continues to decline, countries that depend heavily on fossil fuels will be left with stranded assets if they fail to adapt to new market conditions and foster economic diversification (Cust and Zeufack 2023; KFW, GIZ, and IRENA 2021). Natural gas can act as a transition fuel to aid in the shift away from fossil fuels and toward expanded electrification and renewable energy. Switching to natural gas, paired with scaling up renewable energy sources, has already helped limit increases in global emissions since 2010 and can reduce emissions by up to 50 percent (IEA 2019).

Fact 6: Sub-Saharan Africa has the minerals for the clean energy transition readily available. The clean energy transition is projected to create global demand for 3 billion tons of minerals and metals that are needed to deploy solar, wind, and geothermal energy by 2050 (Hund et al. 2020). The African continent already hosts a large proportion of the world's mineral resources that will be particularly important for the low-carbon transition, including cobalt (75 percent), manganese (68 percent), graphite (59 percent), and undeveloped resources of lithium (Cust and Zeufack 2023). Africa's mineral resources were valued at US$290 billion in 2018; however, African countries primarily export raw materials with little local value addition, thus limiting their role in global value chains (AfDB 2023). Processing capacity for minerals remains limited because of skills shortages, insufficient infrastructure, and a lack of adequate financial, technical, and human capital (Cust and Zeufack 2023). Capitalizing on mineral wealth will require creating value on the continent, expanding intra-African trade, and designing tax policies that generate revenue that countries can reinvest in productive capital and in building transparency in institutions. Botswana, for example, has implemented a Sustainable Budget Index that has enabled the country to effectively monitor if mineral revenue is being saved or spent on investments to bolster capacity (AfDB 2023). As in Botswana, good governance and stewardship of mineral wealth will be key for attracting and scaling investments and generating wealth at the country level.

Fact 7: Africa's natural capital, including the Congo Basin forests, is critical for regulating the global climate. The Congo Basin contains about 314 million hectares (1.2 million square miles) of primary rainforest, the world's second largest; and it sequesters about 1.2 billion tons of CO_2 annually, approximately 4 percent of global emissions (Mo Ibrahim Foundation 2022). Compared to Amazonian forests, Congo Basin forests provided six times as much net carbon removal between 2000 and 2019 (Harris et al. 2021). At current rates of deforestation, all of Africa's primary forests will be gone by 2100 (Mo Ibrahim Foundation 2022). The Congo Basin plays a critical role in regulating the global climate and has direct impacts on livelihoods. In Cameroon alone, tropical forests cover almost 40 percent of the country and provide 8 million people with food, fuel, medicines, and construction materials (World Bank 2022b). Depletion of the Congo Basin forests risks not only disrupting global carbon emissions but also pushing millions of people into poverty, increasing their risk of famine.

Fact 8: Sub-Saharan Africa needs massive amounts of financing to successfully and sustainably adapt to and mitigate the impacts of climate change. The African continent needs a total of US$190 billion per year until 2030 to meet its mitigation needs, and US$50 billion per year by 2050 for adaptation (IMF 2023). In 2020, Sub-Saharan Africa received US$15.7 billion in concessional climate flows, which, although short of the needs of the region, amounted to up to 70 percent of total climate flows (IMF 2023)—refer to figure 2.3. Concessional finance itself is inadequate to meet Sub-Saharan Africa's transition and adaptation needs. Meeting African countries' nationally determined contributions alone would require additional funding of US$41.3 billion each year through 2030 from current levels of financing (GCA 2021). African countries urgently need to draw on financial instruments that will enable them to finance activities and implement programs that bolster resilience. Such instruments include green bonds, debt swap programs, disaster risk financing and insurance, and Catastrophe Deferred Drawdown Options. African heads of state and governments recently called on the global community to "establish a new financing architecture responsive to Africa's needs including debt restructuring and relief" and to honor the commitment made by developed countries at the 2009 Copenhagen Climate Change Conference to provide US$100 billion in annual climate finance to less-developed countries.[4]

FIGURE 2.3 **Climate finance flows to Sub-Saharan Africa, 2020**

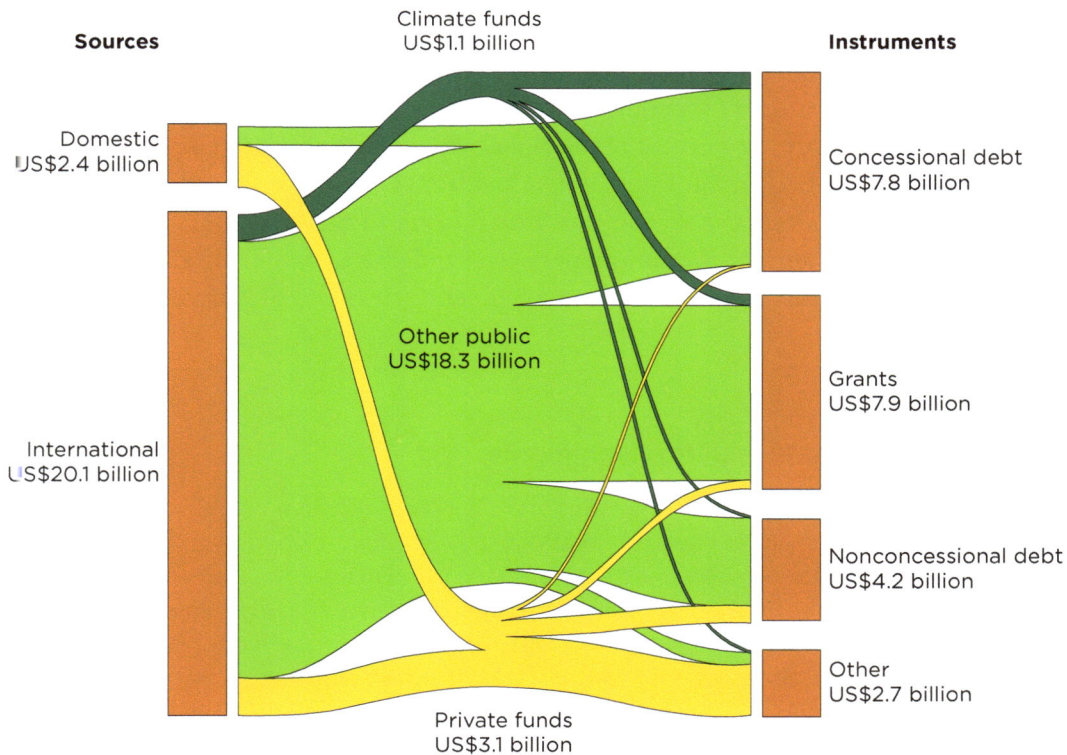

Source: CPI 2022.

Analysis

This section focuses on opportunities that Africa can harness to claim the remainder of the 21st century, and the challenges that impede the continent's ability to enhance resilience. Although climate change is a global phenomenon, its impacts and challenges play out at the local, national, and regional levels and require urgent and far-sighted action at multiple levels, including the international community. Other megatrends—demographics and urbanization—are particularly relevant in the climate context, as are governance and digitalization (refer to chapters 1 and 8). This section draws on the World Bank CCDRs (box 2.1) to contextualize climate challenges at the country level and showcase areas where action is being taken that could be applied to other countries in the region.

Climate shocks and disasters

Climate disasters are increasing in frequency and intensity. The pervasiveness of climate impacts, coupled with the reality of low-baseline development and preexisting climate vulnerabilities, means that inadequate or delayed action will not only unravel development gains or push countries into more vulnerability but also lead to increased poverty, instability, and insecurity. These outcomes will jeopardize the achievement of countries' SDGs and any claim to the 21st century. Addressing the climate-fragility-conflict nexus is key to building social resilience and cohesion to secure the social contract and achieve inclusive growth as a foundation for Africa to claim the 21st century.

The African continent is the most vulnerable to the impacts of climate-induced natural disasters (map 2.1). In 2022 alone, drought affected 88.9 million people in six African countries,[5] and the continent accounted for 16.4 percent of disaster-induced deaths globally, higher than the 3.8 percent of the global share in the previous two decades (CRED 2023). In particular, 2,465 deaths resulted from a drought-induced famine in Uganda, making this event the second-deadliest disaster in Africa in 2022 (CRED 2023). An onslaught of disasters hit the continent in 2021 and 2022, with floods affecting Mali, Niger, South Sudan, and Sudan; drought affecting the Horn of Africa; and three

---

BOX 2.1

Introducing the Country Climate and Development Reports

The World Bank Country Climate and Development Reports (CCDRs) are a core diagnostic tool integrating climate change and development considerations to help countries prioritize the actions that have the most impact on reducing greenhouse gas emissions and increasing adaptation, while delivering on broader development goals. CCDRs build on data and research to identify pathways to reduce climate vulnerabilities, highlighting their costs, challenges, benefits, and opportunities. CCDRs suggest priority actions to support a low-carbon, resilient transition that can be implemented over the next 10 years. The "Analysis" section in the main text uses CCDRs to illustrate pathways to meet low-carbon and resilient development, as well as countries' economic growth trajectories. (Refer also to World Bank Group 2024.)

MAP 2.1 Worldwide vulnerability to climate change–induced natural disasters, 2022

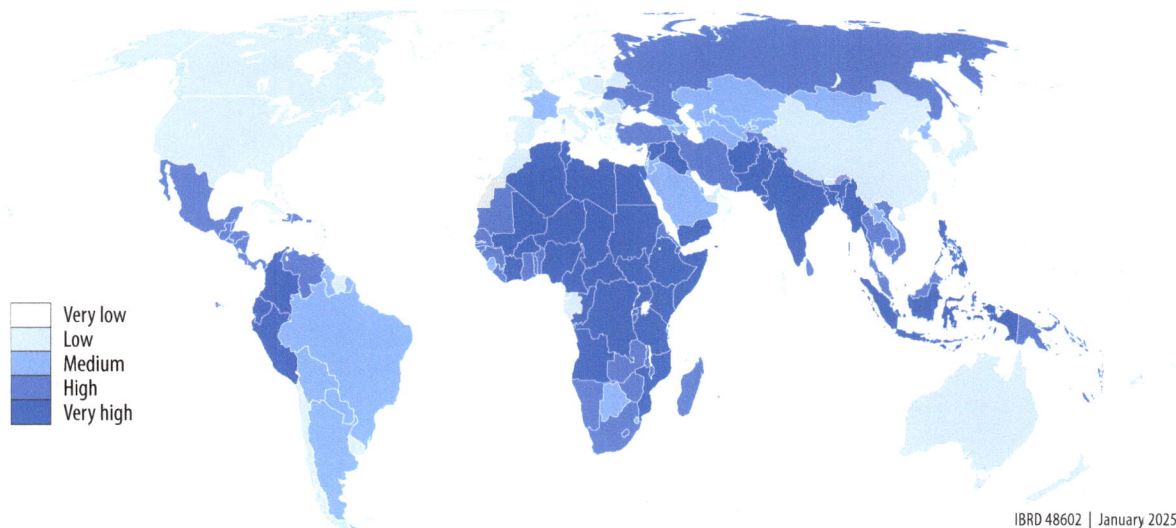

Legend:
- Very low
- Low
- Medium
- High
- Very high

IBRD 48602 | January 2025

Source: Bari and Dessus 2022.
Note: Vulnerability comprises susceptibility, lack of coping capacities, and lack of adaptation capacities. It refers to social, physical, economic, and environmental factors that make people or systems vulnerable to the effects of natural hazards, the negative impacts of climate change, or other processes of change. Vulnerability also considers the capacities of people or systems to cope with and adapt to adverse impacts of natural hazards.

major tropical cyclones making landfall in Mozambique and other southern African countries (GCA 2021). The severity and accelerated frequency of disasters in the region are further compounded by countries' limited adaptive capacity and strained ability to bounce back after disaster strikes (Bari and Dessus 2022).

Disasters contribute to sizable economic losses that compound regional macrofiscal instability. The economic loss and damage from disasters affect resources, goods, and services, including damage to critical infrastructure and supply chain disruptions (Bhandari et al. 2024). The impacts of more severe and frequent disasters translate into higher overall costs for maintenance and repair of infrastructure, and disruption of the supply chain (GCA 2021). For example, Cyclone Idai in 2019 caused flooding in Malawi, Mozambique, and Zimbabwe, resulting in landslides that destroyed houses and left hundreds of thousands of people displaced; damaged roads, bridges, and schools; and washed away crops and livestock, worsening an already precarious food security situation (Mutasa 2022; Trisos et al. 2022). Total damages from Cyclone Idai amounted to more than US$2 billion and affected more than 3 million people (Mutasa 2022). Similarly, Cyclone Ana, which hit Malawi in January 2022, induced damages estimated at between US$126 million and US$192 million, equivalent to between 1.5 percent and 2.7 percent of Malawi's GDP (World Bank 2022f). The damages to infrastructure alone were estimated at US$57 million to US$136 million because of the significant damage to the Kapichira Hydroelectric Power Station, which is responsible for 30 percent of Malawi's electricity generation capacity (World Bank 2022f). In Nigeria, floods in 2022 had an estimated economic cost of US$4.2 billion (CRED 2023). The high costs of recovering from these disasters further strain the limited fiscal space of governments in the region, thereby making it more difficult to allocate sufficient funds to essential development sectors (IMF 2023).

Sub-Saharan Africa lacks the institutional and fiscal capacity not only to respond to these disasters but also to prepare for them before they happen. Responding to disasters pushes countries into further debt, leaving them with little means to get ahead of the curve in preparing for disaster. African countries are largely inadequately insured against climate risk, with limited insurance penetration throughout the region (Trisos et al. 2022). In 2018, the insurance market was valued at US$68 billion with 80 percent of premiums concentrated in South Africa, suggesting that most African countries either are underinsured or lack insurance altogether (GCA 2021). Further, Sub-Saharan Africa's public debt ratio—56 percent of GDP in 2022—has reached high levels last seen in the early 2000s (IMF 2023). In 2022, 19 of Sub-Saharan Africa's 35 low-income countries were already facing debt distress or were at high risk of debt distress, which raises concerns about debt sustainability (IMF 2023). In addition to heightened levels of debt, social safety nets cover only about 10 percent of Africa's population, making people extremely vulnerable to climate shocks (Beegle, Coudouel, and Monsalve 2018). Africa's constrained macrofiscal landscape, paired with the high vulnerability and low readiness of countries in the region, will require a far-sighted, inclusive, and cost-effective response that draws on financial mechanisms to build adaptive capacity.

Pervasiveness of climate impacts

Climate change in Africa affects almost all aspects of the region's economy, environment, and society, exacerbating existing challenges at a faster rate than in the rest of the world. Climate change is pushing Africa to the brink of several tipping points that could disrupt ecological systems and destabilize communities and countries (Rockström et al. 2023). Crossing critical climate thresholds is projected to result in cascading impacts through interlinked climate, ecological, and social systems, leading to severe local and regional hazards such as unprecedented weather events and climate extremes (OECD 2022). The global community is not on track to meet the goals of the Paris Agreement, and efforts remain insufficient to limit global temperature rise to the 1.5°C threshold by 2100. New research expects that, globally, temperatures are more likely than not to breach this threshold at least once by 2027 (WMO 2023b). As noted earlier, a recent assessment of safe and just boundaries that account for Earth system resilience and human well-being reaffirms the guardrail of 1.5°C (Rockström et al. 2023).

The devastating effects of climate change, already manifesting through extreme weather events and escalated warming, amplify people's vulnerability and have negative impacts on human capital and livelihoods. Africans already disproportionately experience the negative effects of climate change, including water stress, reduced food production, increased frequency of extreme weather events, and lower economic growth, fueling mass migration and regional instability (IEA 2022). Africa alone accounts for more than one-third of global extreme weather events since 1970 (WMO 2021). These events, particularly droughts and floods, affect all of Africa (map 2.2). Ethiopia, Kenya, and Somalia experienced some of the worst droughts on record, triggering movement of 2.1 million people in 2022 and millions more facing severe hunger. Disasters in Sub-Saharan Africa in 2022 displaced a total of 7.4 million people—the highest number ever recorded for the region—with a further 9.4 million displaced because of violence and conflicts (IDMC 2023). A growing body of research indicates that adverse climatic events increase the risk of violence and conflict at both interpersonal and intergroup levels (Burke, Hsiang, and Miguel 2015). Climate shocks, as captured through weather shocks, increase the likelihood of domestic conflicts by up to 38 percent (Diallo and Tapsoba 2022).

Key development sectors have already experienced widespread loss including water shortages, biodiversity loss, and reduced food production. The Intergovernmental Panel on Climate Change estimates with high confidence that, with global warming between 1.5°C and 2°C, the negative impacts of climate change will become more widespread and severe, resulting in reduced economic growth and food production, increased inequality and poverty, and increased morbidity and mortality (Trisos et al. 2022). Economic welfare in the agricultural sector is projected to decline by 5 percent at 2°C warming and by 10 percent at 3°C warming, compared with the period between 1995 and 2005 (Trisos et al. 2022). Maize yields have already decreased 5.8 percent on average between 1974 and 2008; without adaptation measures, median yields are projected to decrease further—by 9 percent at 1.5°C warming and by 41 percent at 4°C. Further, above 1.5°C global warming, projections are that half of all assessed species in Africa will lose more than 30 percent of their population or area of suitable habitat, with losses increasing to more than 40 percent under more than 2°C warming (Trisos et al. 2022). Heat-related deaths are also expected to rise sharply with an additional 15 deaths per 100,000 people annually under a 1.5°C warming scenario, and 50 to 180 deaths per 100,000 people annually under a 2.5°C warming scenario (Trisos et al. 2022).

From the Sahel to the Horn of Africa, to the south of the continent and the small island nations, all regions are experiencing the devastating effects of more extreme weather patterns and slow-onset changes. Unfolding alongside the COVID-19 crisis, unusual weather conditions exacerbated by climate change have resulted in locust outbreaks, adding to food insecurity across Africa, with East Africa at the epicenter (Kray and Shetty 2020). Increased levels of warming will have widespread and detrimental consequences for Africa's economic growth. Diffenbaugh and Burke (2019) find that GDP per capita is on average 13.6 percent lower for African countries as a result of anthropogenic climate change since 1991, contributing to increased global inequality. At current rates of warming, projections suggest that African countries could suffer a 20 percent drop in GDP by 2050 and a 64 percent reduction in GDP by 2100 (Pearce 2022).

MAP 2.2
 Number of people affected by climate hazards, by type of hazard, Africa, 2010–20

a. Climate hazards, by type

- Droughts
- Convective storms
- Floods
- Tropical cyclones
- Heat waves

b. Number of deaths from droughts

- 0–150,000
- 150,000–2,000,000
- 2,000,000–10,000,000

c. Number of people affected by convective storms

- 0–150,000
- 150,000–2,000,000
- 2,000,000–10,000,000

d. Number of people affected by floods

- 0–150,000
- 150,000–2,000,000
- 2,000,000–10,000,000

e. Number of deaths from tropical cyclones

- 0–150,000
- 150,000–2,000,000
- 2,000,000–10,000,000

f. Number of people affected by heat waves

- 0–150,000
- 150,000–2,000,000
- 2,000,000–10,000,000

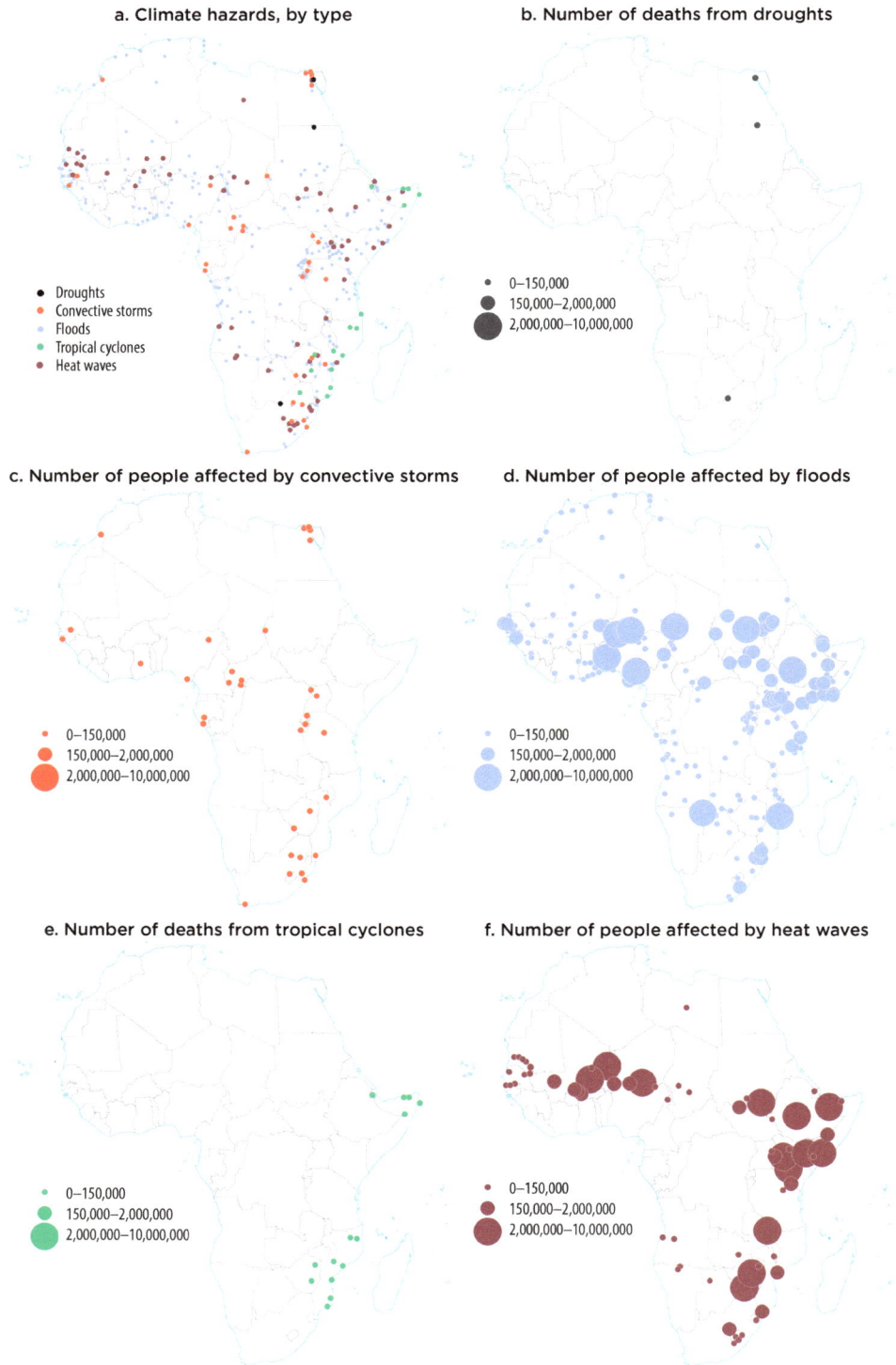

IBRD 48605 | January 2025

Source: Trisos et al. 2022.

Historically, Africa has already faced declining GDP per capita due to climate-related impacts (map 2.3, panel a). Limiting warming could reduce impacts on GDP per capita and generate substantial economic benefits with greater certainty (map 2.3, panels b–d). Even considering only a subset of impact categories and without exploring the larger impacts of warming expected beyond 2050, the impact of climate change on GDP is expected to be significant, with lower-income countries experiencing higher climate change impacts relative to their GDP (World Bank Group 2024). Containing the worst impacts of climate change will require upscaled climate action on adaptation in Africa and deep cuts in emissions as a global community.

MAP 2.3 **Observed aggregated economic impacts and projected risks from climate change in Africa**

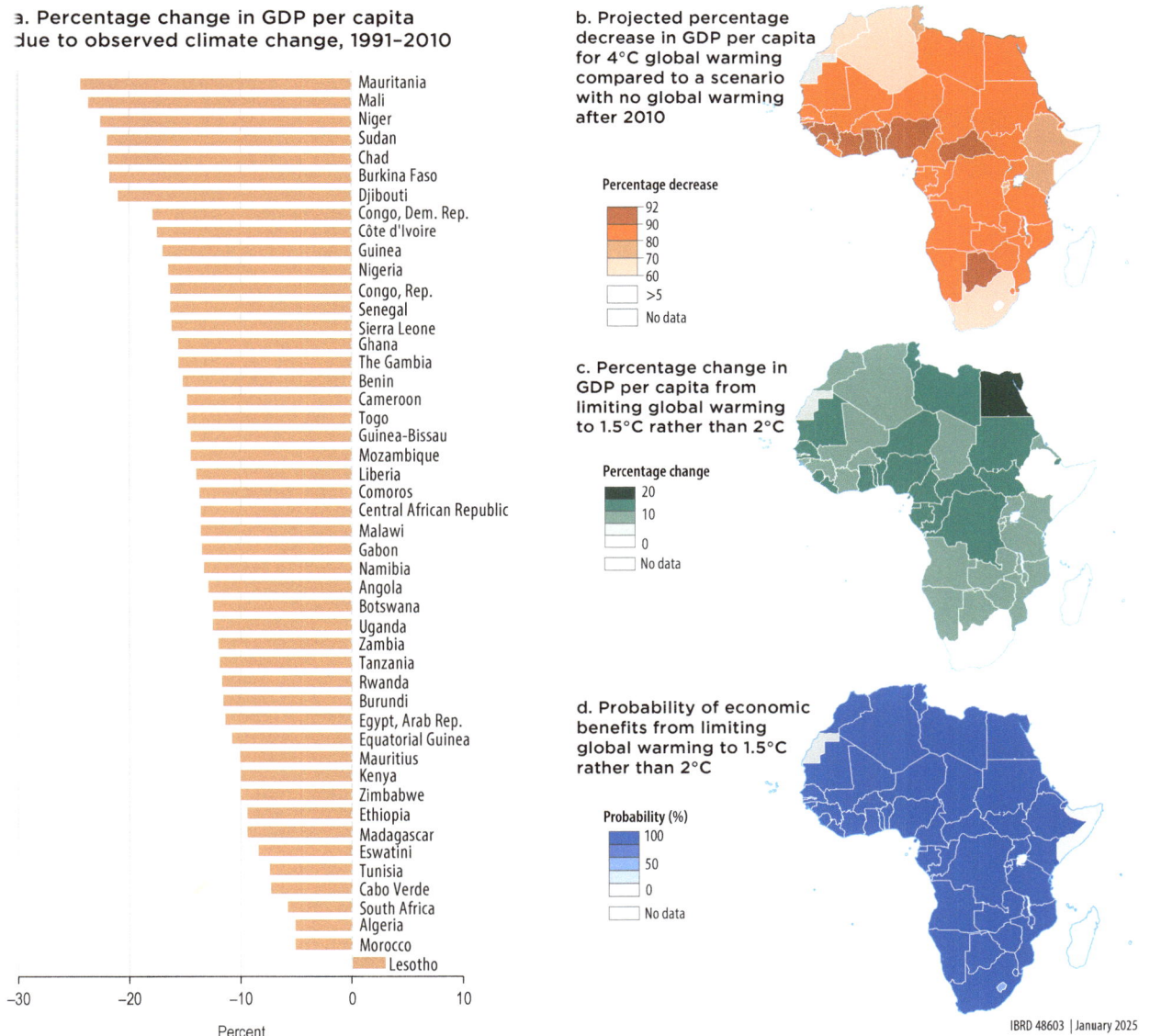

a. Percentage change in GDP per capita due to observed climate change, 1991–2010

b. Projected percentage decrease in GDP per capita for 4°C global warming compared to a scenario with no global warming after 2010

c. Percentage change in GDP per capita from limiting global warming to 1.5°C rather than 2°C

d. Probability of economic benefits from limiting global warming to 1.5°C rather than 2°C

IBRD 48603 | January 2025

Source: Trisos et al. 2022.

Poorer countries, and the poorest and marginalized populations, face greater risks from climate change because they have less ability to adapt to its impacts (figure 2.4). The countries most frequently exposed to droughts, floods, heat waves, and sea-level rise tend to have competing development needs, making it more difficult to invest in resilient growth. Research from the IMF (2021) indicates that a single drought in Sub-Saharan Africa can lower an African country's medium-term economic growth potential by 1 percentage point. Of greater concern, recent empirical results show that climate change vulnerability has adverse effects on income inequality, with an increase of 1 percentage point in climate vulnerability leading to an increase of 1.5 percent in income inequality (Cevik and Jalles 2022).

FIGURE 2.4 **Unequal costs of climate change and links with inequality**

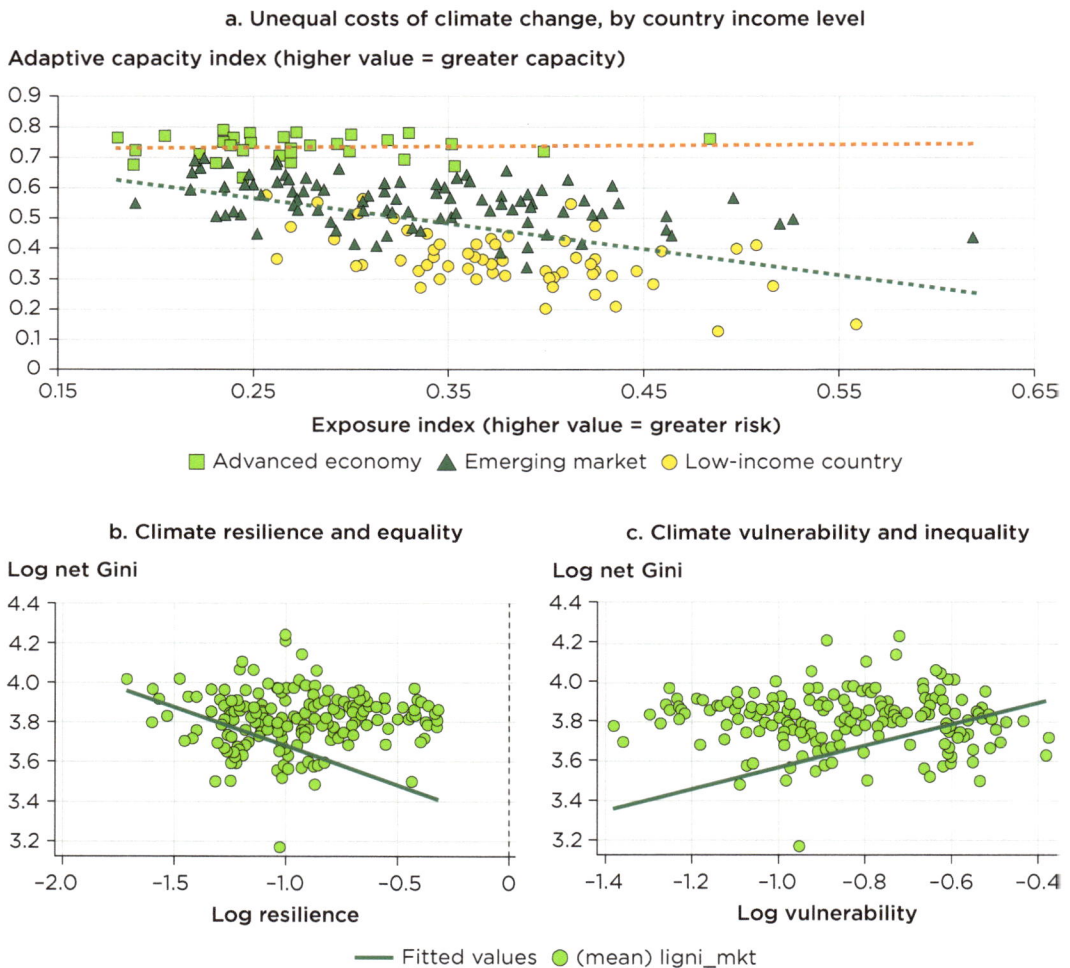

a. Unequal costs of climate change, by country income level

b. Climate resilience and equality

c. Climate vulnerability and inequality

Sources: Georgieva, Gaspar, and Pazarbasioglu 2022 (panel a); Notre Dame Global Adaptation Initiative, Standardized World Income Inequality Database, and World Bank calculations (panels b and c).
Note: In panel a, dotted lines show estimated linear relationships for advanced economies (orange dotted line), and for emerging market and low-income economies combined (green dotted line). Panels b and c present the climate resilience and vulnerability indexes with a linear fit and not adjusted for the level of real GDP per capita (Cevik and Jalles 2022).

The economic impacts of climate change will hit households hard. The coefficient on climate change vulnerability is seven times greater and statistically highly significant in developing countries, largely because of weaker capacity for climate change adaptation and mitigation (IMF 2021). Reporting on the impacts of climate change on poverty, Hallegatte et al. (2016) find that poor households tend to have more frequent exposure than wealthy ones to climatic shocks and that the shocks hit them harder relative to their income or wealth. Droughts and floods increase the poverty rate by 14 percentage points; for those individual with a primary education or less, that increase goes up to 28 percentage points, on average (World Bank 2022c). Shocks include lower agricultural yields due to flooding, drought, or extreme heat; natural disasters that destroy capital, such as homes or roads; and climate-influenced health shocks, such as malaria, that can reduce work or school days. Global crop yields may decline by about 5 percent in 2030 and 30 percent by 2080, reducing income streams for agropastoralists (Biewald et al. 2014; Havlík et al. 2015). Food prices will also likely go up, with extreme poverty estimated to rise by 1.8 percentage points from climate-induced price increases alone.

The nexus between climate change, conflict, and migration: Securing social resilience and cohesion

Climate change is a driver of fragility and a threat multiplier, amplifying risks in the context of emerging megatrends such as demographic change, migration, ecosystem collapse, and environmental degradation. The impacts of climate shocks and crisis deepen preexisting fragility and increase the vulnerability of poor populations in fragile and conflict-prone areas. These outcomes constitute a growing concern for Africa. Projections indicate that by 2030 most of the extreme poor will live in fragile and conflict-affected countries (World Bank 2020b). Without concrete climate and development action, factors like protracted water stress, loss in crop productivity, and sea-level rise could result in as many as 85 million internal climate migrants by 2050 (figure 2.5), and the emergence and spread of hot spots of climate in- and out-migration (Rigaud et al. 2018). A deeper and more granular analysis conducted for countries in West Africa and the Lake Victoria Basin, and that included additional climate variables (ecosystem productivity and floods) and nonclimate variables (conflict), shows the emergence of hot spots as early as 2030, which will continue to spread and intensify, emphasizing the need for early climate adaptation and resilience measures (maps 2.4 and 2.5).

Singular and recurrent climate shocks cause wide-ranging social and economic disruptions that can multiply quickly with intergenerational consequences (Winsemius et al. 2018). Climate impacts on the poor include loss of life and livelihoods, damage to essential infrastructure, disruption of services, malnutrition and poor health, and escalation of distress-driven migration. Poor feeding as a result of droughts during the first 1,000 days of a child's life can lead to child malnutrition, which can have long-lasting effects, including on female reproductive prospects and offspring (Bodewig 2019). Climate impacts can also exacerbate health shocks through, for example, pandemics and disease outbreaks.

FIGURE 2.5 Projected number of internal climate migrants by 2050, by world region

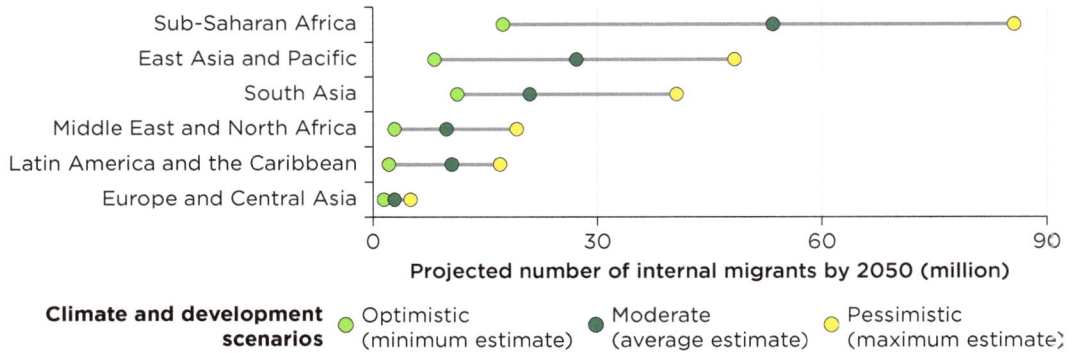

Source: Clement et al. 2021.
Note: Optimistic scenario: more climate-friendly (lower global emissions combined with unequal development), SSP4 and RCP 2.6. Moderate scenario: more inclusive development (high emissions but with improved development pathways), SSP2 and RCP 8.5. Pessimistic scenario: reference scenario (high greenhouse gas emissions combined with unequal development pathways), SSP4 and RCP 8.5. RCP = Representative Concentration Pathway; SSP = Shared Socioeconomic Pathway (scenarios used in climate modeling to explore future global socioeconomic developments and their impact on climate change).

Climate change acting as a stress on natural and social systems can amplify conflict, especially in fragile situations, and governments have limited coping capacities and means to help their populations adapt. Globally, conflicts drive 80 percent of all humanitarian needs. Conflicts can reduce GDP growth by 2 to 8 percent per year on average. The Cameroon CCDR notes that, if current conflicts last through 2025, the national GDP could be 9 percent lower than otherwise expected (World Bank 2022b). A growing body of research indicates that adverse climatic events increase the risk of violence and conflict at both the interpersonal and intergroup levels (Burke, Hsiang, and Miguel 2015). Climate change can increase the likelihood of violence through pressures on natural resources, particularly land and water, and through natural disasters and migration. Overall, 65 percent of present conflicts have a significant land dimension, and conflicts around fresh water are increasing, particularly at the subnational level, as that resource becomes scarcer (World Bank 2020a). In parts of Africa, tensions between pastoralists and agriculturists over access to land and water have escalated to violence.

Damage from climate change of essential infrastructure systems—water, power, sanitation, telecommunications, and roads—will affect the well-being of urban and rural households, and the productivity of businesses (Hallegatte, Rentschler, and Rozenberg 2019). Resilient mobility is an important component of overall societal resilience because it allows relief supplies to reach a stricken area, or evacuees to reach safety. Urban flooding, a significant driver of disrupted traffic flows, has affected the connectivity between firms and supply chains in several Sub-Saharan African cities (Hallegatte, Rentschler, and Rozenberg 2019). Disruption of transportation links due to climate-related failures of roads or bridges has substantial economic consequences for

MAP 2.4 Projected hot spots of climate in- and out-migration by 2050, West Africa

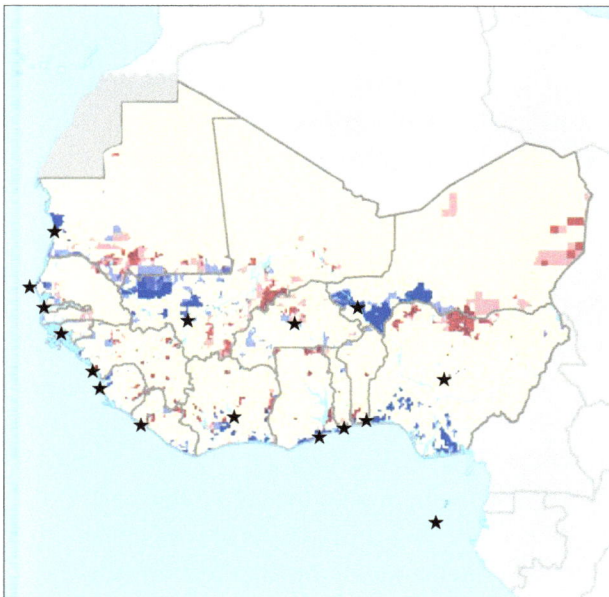

In-migration

- High certainty in high levels of climate in-migration
- Moderate certainty in high levels of climate in-migration
- Low certainty in high levels of climate in-migration

Out-migration

- High certainty in high levels of climate out-migration
- Moderate certainty in high levels of climate out-migration
- Low certainty in high levels of climate out-migration

Source: Rigaud et al. 2021b.
Note: High, moderate, and low certainty reflect agreement across all four, three, and two scenarios modeled, respectively. In- and out-migration hot spots are thus areas in which at least two scenarios concur on density changes. Data are based on a compilation of West African country results between the climate and no-climate impact scenarios by country for the top and bottom fifth percentile differences in density distribution for climate in- and out-migration, respectively.

MAP 2.5 Projected hot spots of climate in- and out-migration by 2050, Lake Victoria Basin countries

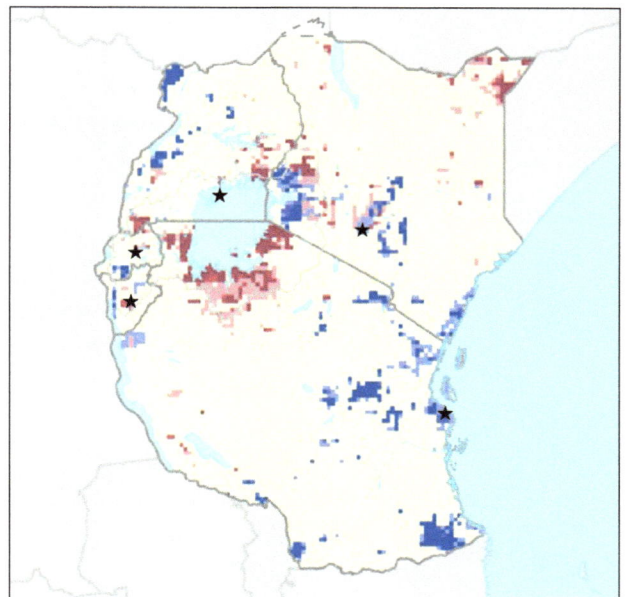

In-migration

- High certainty in high levels of climate in-migration
- Moderate certainty in high levels of climate in-migration
- Low certainty in high levels of climate in-migration

Out-migration

- High certainty in high levels of climate out-migration
- Moderate certainty in high levels of climate out-migration
- Low certainty in high levels of climate out-migration

Source: Rigaud et al. 2021a.
Note: High, moderate, and low certainty reflect agreement across all four, three, and two scenarios modeled, respectively. In- and out-migration hot spots are thus areas in which at least two scenarios concur on density changes. Data are based on a compilation of Lake Victoria Basin country results between the climate and no-climate impact scenarios by country for the top and bottom fifth percentile differences in density distribution for climate in- and out-migration, respectively.

African countries. The situation is predicted to worsen substantially with climate change (Cervigni et al. 2017). A 1 percent increase in electricity outages would account for a loss in firm total factor productivity of 3.5 percent, on average (Mensah 2018).

With the growing numbers of people living in extreme poverty in Sub-Saharan Africa, it is critical to act to reduce the exposure to and impact of climate-induced shocks on the poorest. The number of the bottom 40 percent of people living in extreme poverty increased from 278 million in 1990 to 416 million in 2015. Climate change is predicted to reduce incomes by more than 8 percent by 2030, further constraining the ability of the poorest to respond to climate shocks and to adapt to climate change.

Climate change remains a significant threat multiplier in Africa, spurring conflict and fragility and contributing to local and regional instability. Climate change is pervasive and cross-cutting in nature, with cascading impacts on food security, poverty, human mobility, and political instability (Ahmadnia et al. 2022; Rüttinger et al. 2015). In this context, much debate exists on the extent to which climate change itself is a deterministic or direct driver. Ample evidence suggests that the occurrence of climate change in conflict-inducing conditions can escalate and exacerbate conflict, fragility, and insecurity (Detges et al. 2020; Kosec, Laderach, and Ruckstuhl 2023; Mustasilta 2021). The role of climate change as a threat multiplier raises particular concerns in Africa, where livelihoods are highly dependent on natural resources. The interaction between climate stressors and socioeconomic and political factors poses a severe threat to human security on the continent (Naidoo and Gulati 2022). Climate shocks can contribute to coping failures, or breakdowns of systems, in responding to shocks, and to failures of adaptive capacities, both of which can contribute to mounting risks of conflict or fueling escalation of violence (Mustasilta 2021). Fragile states in particular struggle to handle climate shocks, because these states must, at the same time, manage shocks caused by conflict.

Conflict and violence are continuing to rise throughout Sub-Saharan Africa, and the more frequent and intense impacts of climate shocks compound the effects of this increase. Nonstate violence has generally been increasing since the 1990s. Whereas land-related conflicts represented about 10 percent of all nonstate conflicts in the mid-1990s, they represented almost 30 percent in 2011 (Mustasilta 2021). In 2022, conflict-induced displacement continued to rise across Sub-Saharan Africa, with the highest number of people worldwide living in displacement because of conflict and violence (IDMC 2023). In 2022, 28 million people were internally displaced by conflict and violence, 45 percent of the global total, and 3.7 million people were internally displaced by disasters (IDMC 2023). These high numbers can partially be attributed to drought fueling competition over natural resources and to disrupted seasonal migration trends (IDMC 2023). These internal migration trends are expected to continue in the future as competition for resources becomes more strained (Detges et al. 2020).

Parts of Sub-Saharan Africa are unraveling as they become hot spots of conflict and instability. Conflict hot spots, emerging largely in West Africa and the Horn of Africa (map 2.6), may reflect transboundary conflicts. The Lake Chad Basin, the Tigray region of Ethiopia, the northern tip of Mozambique, and the eastern part of the Democratic Republic of Congo stand out as transboundary conflict hot spots (Palik, Obermeier, and Rustad 2022). In the central Sahel and the Lake Chad Basin, numerous armed groups are perpetrating violent attacks on civilians and engaging in clashes with military forces. These conflicts have extended to the Liptako Gourma region—which comprises Burkina Faso, Mali, and Niger—making the region a hot spot of conflict (Tarif 2023).

MAP 2.6 Conflict events and conflict countries, Africa, 2021

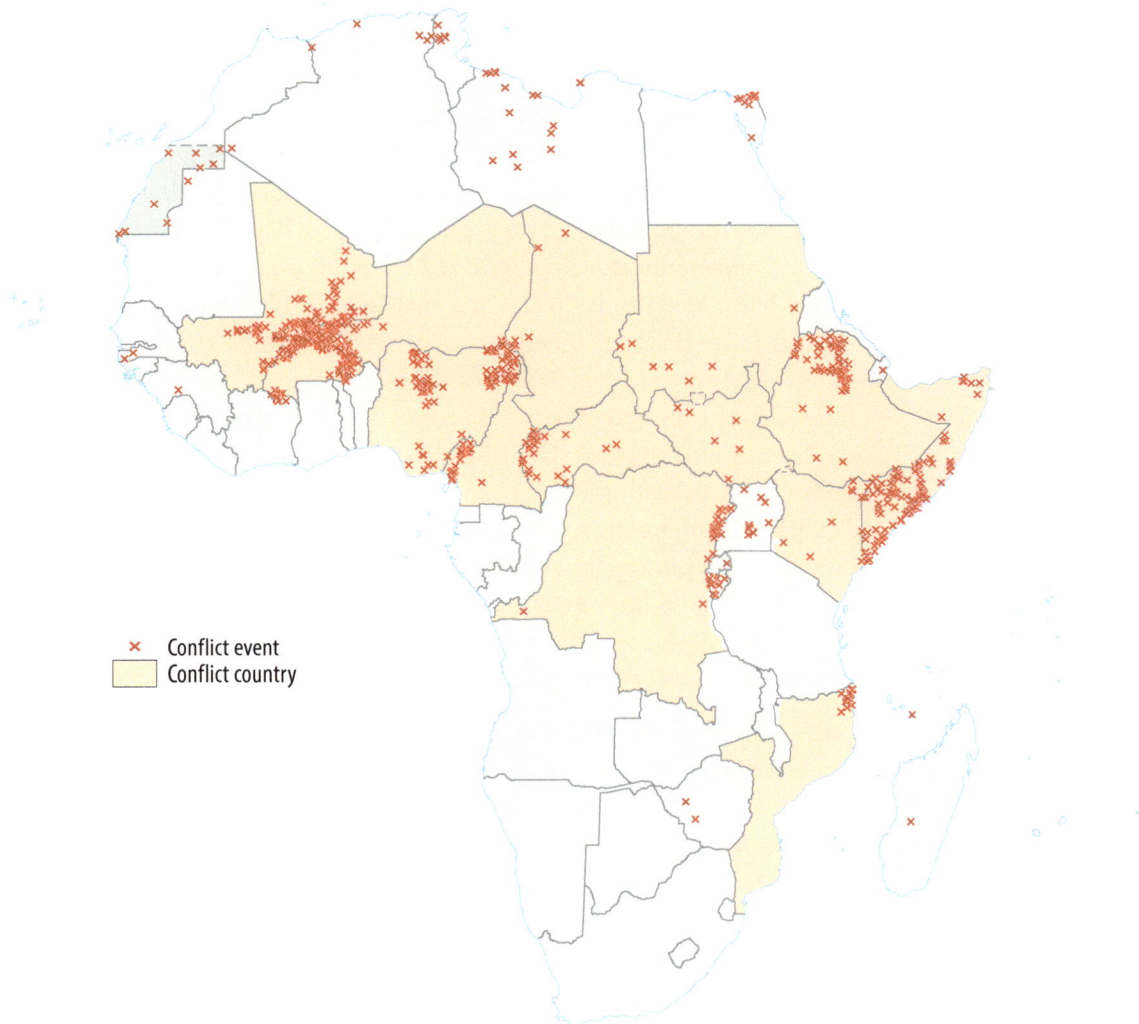

Legend:
× Conflict event
▢ Conflict country

IBRD 48604 | January 2025

Source: Palik, Obermeier, and Rustad 2022.

The underlying factors driving these conflicts include competition over natural resources, politicized indigenous-foreigner tensions, poor drought management, limited political representation, uneven implementation of environmental laws, and the adverse effects of climate change (Amakrane et al. 2023; Tarif 2023). The reduced size of the Lake Chad Basin, which provides livelihoods to 30 million people, has increased competition for depleting resources and led to an increased number of farmer-pastoralist conflicts (Naidoo and Gulati 2022). Further, the Horn of Africa remains one of the most conflict-affected regions globally, with climate shocks compounding the impacts of conflict. The dual impacts of conflict and climate change left more than 7 million Somalis in need of humanitarian assistance in 2022 alone because of increased food insecurity and overall instability in the region (Kurtzer, Ballard, and Fatima Abdullah 2022).

The widespread spheres of influence cast on Africa by increased conflict and crises threaten to roll back development gains and position the continent on the edge of a downward spiral. A study conducted by the International Monetary Fund indicates that countries engaged in intense conflict have 2.5 percent lower annual growth on average, with the cumulative impact on per capita GDP increasing over time (Fang et al. 2020). In addition to its impacts on GDP, conflict strains public finances and shifts resources away from spending on socioeconomic development, reducing the assets that support resilience in the face of shocks (Ahmadnia et al. 2022; Fang et al. 2020; UNECA 2016). As Mustasilta (2021) notes, once an active conflict emerges, climate change and its impacts become more difficult to address because security issues often take precedence. In 2021, net official development assistance and official aid received for Sub-Saharan Africa totaled US$62.29 billion, lower than the region's all-time high of US$66.89 billion in 2020.[6] Although it is not possible to distinguish how much aid went to addressing conflict, countries need substantial financing to adequately respond to conflict and climate-induced shocks. The conflict in Darfur cost the government of Sudan an estimated US$24 billion, or 162 percent of the country's GDP. In order for Africa to claim the 21st century, the issues of conflict, peace, and security require more focused attention and financing to prevent development from suffering because of recurrent and ongoing shocks.

The increasing intensity and frequency of disasters translates into high costs in terms of maintenance and repairs of infrastructure, and supply chain disruptions. As noted earlier, Cyclone Idai—which hit Malawi, Mozambique, and Zimbabwe in March 2019—caused an estimated US$2 billion in damages, and floods in Nigeria in 2022 caused an estimated US$4.2 billion in damages (CRED 2023; Mutasa 2022). The cost of responding to these disasters strains the already limited fiscal space of governments and detracts from funding sectors that are key for development. Initiatives like the West Africa Coastal Areas Management Program support physical coastal protection in nine West African countries to mitigate the impacts of climate shocks by restoring wetlands and mangroves, and building seawalls and dikes. The program also supports seven regional institutions to develop cross-border solutions for coastal management and policy harmonization to deliver impact at scale. Having already reduced the exposure to flooding of 14,368 households in Benin, São Tomé and Príncipe, and Togo, the program is expected to save 2,555,319 tons of CO_2 equivalent by the end of the project cycle (Desramaut 2023). In addition, the lack of institutional and fiscal capacity to respond to these climate shocks pushes countries further into debt, thereby undermining macrofiscal stability. The Urban Productive Safety Net Project supports financial inclusion, encourages savings, and provides skills to more than 600,000 beneficiaries, enabling the opening of bank accounts and providing financial literacy training, all of which are key for building resilience. These safety nets enable people to access funds in times of crisis and to recover more quickly after disaster has struck.

Energy transformation and energy transitions

Universal energy access in Africa deployed through available low-cost and low-carbon options could represent the first at-scale energy transformation globally. This transition must be accelerated to unleash the triple benefits of improving economic productivity, lowering emissions, and increasing resilience. Clean cooking for all Africans represents a "quick win" that must be embraced head-on. With the projected decrease in demand for fossil fuels, a key part of Sub-Saharan Africa's energy landscape, over the coming decades, the region needs to manage an orderly transition away from fossil fuels by fostering economic diversification and leveraging natural gas as a transition fuel.

Ironically, with 20 percent of the world's population, Africa's low level of global carbon emissions of less than 3 percent has not served it (IEA 2022), in large part because low electrification rates in Africa have curtailed a host of opportunities and potential. Electrification throughout the continent remains low: 600 million people, or 43 percent of the continent, lacked access to electricity in 2022 (World Bank 2023b)—figure 2.6. Nearly 450 million people gained electricity access over the past several years, increasing the regional access rate from 39 percent in 2015 to 44 percent in 2017 (IEA 2019). IEA (2019) notes, however, that 530 million will remain without electricity in 2030 given current policies and the pace of electrification. Consequently, of the global population without electricity, 90 percent will be in Africa.

FIGURE 2.6 Population without access to modern energy services, by African subregion, 2000–21

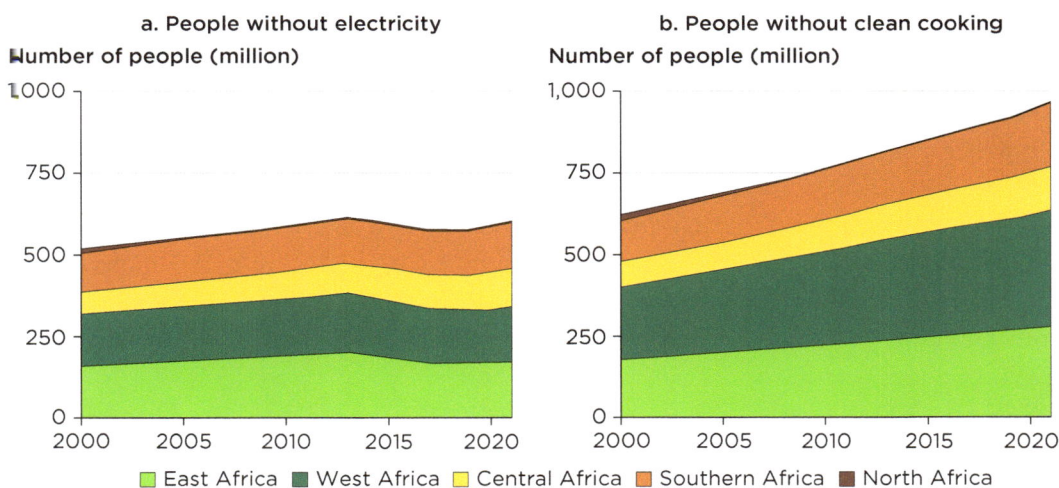

a. People without electricity
Number of people (million)

b. People without clean cooking
Number of people (million)

East Africa   West Africa   Central Africa   Southern Africa   North Africa

Source: IEA 2022.

Recognizing that the lack of access to reliable electricity has acted as a significant barrier to development in Sub-Saharan Africa, regional governments are striving to achieve universal access to energy. The region aims to deliver affordable, reliable, sustainable, and modern energy services—electricity and clean cooking—for all by 2030. Many countries have adopted ambitious access expansion goals and electrification plans; some countries, such as Ethiopia, Kenya, Senegal, and South Africa, aim to achieve universal access to electricity before 2030. The World Bank Group is partnering with the African Development Bank and others on Mission 300 to fill this gap by accelerating the pace of electrification in Sub-Saharan Africa while ensuring that the transition to more diversified and cleaner sources of energy meets growing demand, brings economic growth, and creates jobs. This initiative seeks to connect 300 million people to electricity in Sub-Saharan Africa by 2030.

Universal access to energy does not carry an exorbitant cost, and the urgency for access must be matched with immediate action. For Africa to claim the 21st century, expanded energy access remains an imperative and must be driven by near-term targets. Grid and off-grid solutions offer viable pathways to achieving this goal in rural and urban areas, with solar photovoltaic offering the most cost-effective and promising solution (figure 2.2). Unlike other regions that already invest in carbon-intensive energy sources, Sub-Saharan Africa has yet to make the most of the investments required to meet its energy needs. Despite holding about 60 percent of global solar resources, Africa has only about 1 percent of installed solar photovoltaic capacity (IEA 2022). Tripling the rate of electrification to achieve universal access to affordable electricity by 2030 would cost US$25 billion per year, the cost equivalent of building only one liquefied natural gas terminal (IEA 2022). This amount suggests that the goal of universal energy access is within reach and can be realistically attained with the right strategies and enabling financial mechanisms. Stimulating the necessary investment requires international support aided by stronger national institutions on the ground.

Clean cooking solutions for the continent offer a potential game changer that gets to the core of the environment-climate-poverty nexus. More than 80 percent of people in Sub-Saharan Africa use charcoal, kerosene, or firewood to cook. Achieving universal access to clean cooking fuels and technologies by 2030 requires shifting 130 million people away from these dirty cooking fuels each year (IEA 2022). Shifts to clean cooking would reduce the pressure on forests, which are essential to buffer climate shocks; drastically cut time spent gathering fuel for cooking, allowing millions of women to pursue education, employment, and civic involvement; and reduce premature deaths by about 500,000 a year by 2030.

Despite a reasonable financing gap of US$1.8 billion—an amount significantly lower than for electricity—progress on this front has been elusive (IEA 2018). Most Sub-Saharan African countries have no comprehensive clean-cooking strategy, whereas others have poorly financed strategies. For example, the government of Ghana is developing a National Clean Cooking Strategy to increase the availability of improved charcoal stoves, but this initiative has limited scope in terms of the number of households it will reach, thereby limiting the strategy's impact (World Bank 2022e). Thus, national poverty alleviation and health strategies should include policies and financing for clean cooking, and a buildup of domestic capacity and outreach to facilitate delivering impact at scale (IEA 2018). The gender component is critical to the strategy, and its role extends from awareness campaigns to engaging women as entrepreneurs and champions.

Sustaining electrification and modern cooking must be monitored closely to avert a rollback in gains made. Estimates suggest that, at the beginning of 2022, 10 million Sub-Saharan Africans who had recently gained access to basic electricity service could no longer pay for the service and that about 5 million could no longer afford modern cooking fuels such as liquefied petroleum gas (LPG). With spiking LPG prices, the latter number was expected to have reached up to 30 million as of the end of 2022 (IEA 2022).

Universal energy access, the cornerstone of climate action in Africa, represents a key enabler of resilience and climate adaptation. Leapfrogging into low-carbon strategies is within reach and will yield multiplier benefits across the development landscape. The emergence of renewable, off-grid solutions will enable a new approach for electricity access, even in fragile, conflict-affected, and vulnerable countries and subnational regions, where security concerns, limited governance, and weak utilities make grid-based electricity access challenging. Countries and people deprived of access to electricity are also often the most vulnerable to climate change. Thus, access to modern energy services brings tangible benefits that empower communities and make them more resilient to climate shocks, such as through the use of communication devices, solar-based water pumping to mitigate drought impacts, increased access to electricity for the storage of agricultural products, and cooling technologies to cope with extreme heat (World Bank 2020a).

Sub-Saharan Africa presents a complex energy landscape still underpinned by fossil fuels. In spite of increasing diversification of the region's energy supply through the use of renewable energy sources, fossil fuels continue to make up about 40 percent of the region's overall energy mix, with countries including Algeria, Nigeria, and South Africa heavily dependent on fossil fuels (Mutezo and Mulopo 2021). Fossil fuels comprise the largest share of installed electricity generation capacities in western, southern, and northern African countries, whereas renewable energy sources dominate in the eastern and central parts of Africa (KfW, GIZ, and IRENA 2021).

Renewables have great potential in Sub-Saharan Africa, but meeting this potential will require increased uptake. Twenty-two African countries have more than 50 percent of their electricity generated from renewable sources (Mo Ibrahim Foundation 2022). South Africa, Uganda, and Zambia already hold renewable energy auctions that have attracted private investors and achieved competitive prices (Schwerhoff and Sy 2020). The declining costs of renewables represents an opportunity for expansion of renewables in the region: between 2010 and 2021, the cost of solar photovoltaic plummeted by 88 percent and the cost of wind dropped between 60 percent and 68 percent (IRENA 2022). Even as the price of renewables continues to drop, countries still need technological and financial support to leapfrog into these pathways.

In Cameroon, for example, hydropower is currently the sole renewable source, but opportunities for solar, wind, biomass, and off-grid solutions—if managed well and sufficiently supported—can increase the share of renewables in the country's energy mix from less than 1 percent to 25 percent by 2035 (World Bank 2022b). In Kenya, 67 percent of the country's energy supply comes from bioenergy; by 2040, up to 50 percent of the country's power generation could come from geothermal production (IEA 2019).

Fossil fuels remain a major engine of growth in countries that are rich in nonrenewable resources. Angola and Nigeria remain key oil producers; Mozambique and South Africa are rich in coal, and natural gas is most prevalent in northern and western Africa (Mutezo and Mulopo 2021). Since 2000, about 50 percent of global major petroleum discoveries occurred in Sub-Saharan Africa, more than any other region, with large oil and gas discoveries in countries such as Angola, Côte d'Ivoire, Mozambique, and Senegal (figure 2.7) (Cust, Mihalyi, and Rivera-Ballesteros 2021). Subsoil assets such as oil, gas, and minerals are vital sources of government revenue and contribute to the export earnings and economic development potential in many African countries (Cust and Zeufack 2023). In resource-rich countries such as Chad, the Republic of Congo, and Gabon, oil has at times been responsible for more than 30 percent of total wealth (World Bank 2021b). Despite a commodity price boom experienced in the region between 2004 and 2014, however, most Sub-Saharan African countries have been unable to convert that wealth into broader economic prosperity, thus contributing to an uptick in regional poverty rates (Cust and Zeufack 2023). Although oil and gas prices remain high, the global trend toward decarbonization and the growing commitment of oil companies to reduce their carbon footprint present challenges for the long-term demand of fossil fuels and associated impacts in Sub-Saharan African countries (World Bank Group 2024).

FIGURE 2.7 Estimated oil and natural gas reserves, Sub-Saharan Africa, 1980–2018

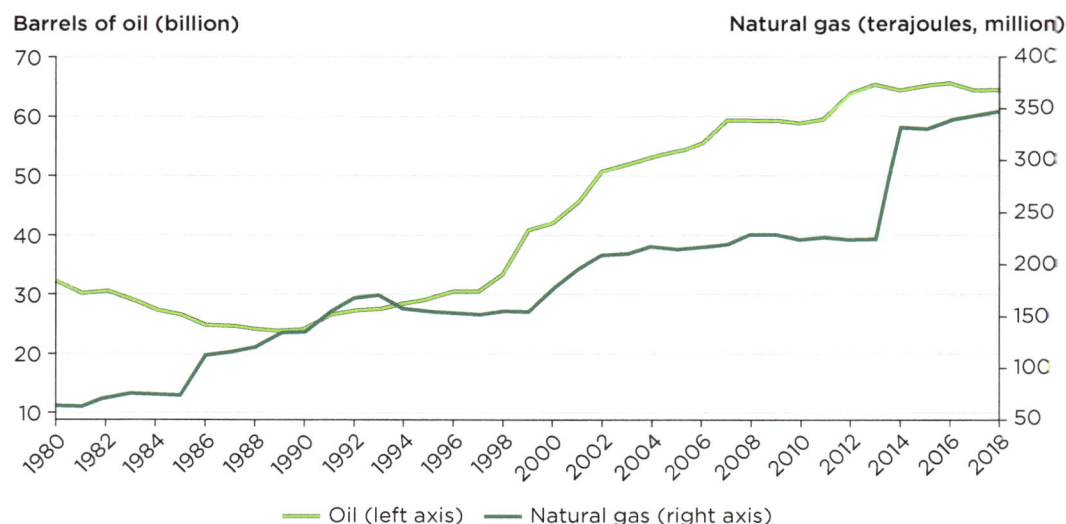

Source: Cust and Zeufack 2023.

Fossil fuel–based economies in Sub-Saharan Africa must guard against stranded assets and lock-ins in light of the global energy transition and projected declining demand for fossil fuel resources. In the 2010s, Sub-Saharan Africa's net oil exports fell by 40 percent (IEA 2022). This downward trend is expected to continue with a sharp projected decline in demand for fossil fuels over the next 10–30 years, with the region positioned to become a net importer of oil by the mid-2030s (Cust and Zeufack 2023; IEA 2022). Given this projected decline in demand for oil and gas, African countries need to adapt to new market conditions and manage an orderly transition away from fossil fuels, using revenues to foster economic diversification (Cust and Zeufack 2023). Otherwise, Sub-Saharan African countries risk developing stranded assets and becoming stranded nations (Cust, Manley, and Cecchinato 2017; IEA 2022; World Bank 2022c). Some African countries are currently investing in and developing fossil fuel infrastructure, such as coal power plants, that will have an economic lifetime that far exceeds 2050 (KfW, GIZ, and IRENA 2021). Large investments in fossil fuel production present risks because, as renewable energy continues to decline in cost and become more widespread, such investments will leave countries with stranded assets (KfW, GIZ, and IRENA 2021). Further, Sub-Saharan African countries that depend on oil and gas exports could experience significant harm as countries outside of the continent begin to implement carbon pricing and taxes, such as the European Union's Carbon Border Adjustment Mechanism (Leke, Gaius-Obaseki, and Onyekweli 2022; World Bank 2022c).

Supporting Sub-Saharan Africa through the renewable energy transition must be well managed to build readiness throughout the region. Most African countries are highly vulnerable to the risks posed by the global energy transition because their economies depend on oil and gas revenues (Cust and Zeufack 2023; Leke, Gaius-Obaseki, and Onyekweli 2022; World Bank 2022c). Given the precariousness of the transition for the region, the transition should leverage existing revenues to spur economic diversification throughout Sub-Saharan Africa (Cust and Zeufack 2023). For example, a key development priority for Angola is to use revenues from its diminishing oil wealth to diversify its economy and reduce the country's overall dependency on the petroleum industry to create opportunities for sustainable growth (World Bank 2022a). In the absence of strong domestic markets for fossil fuels, African countries will require support from the international community to attract and mobilize the financing they need to invest in a renewable energy transformation for the continent (World Bank 2022c).

Natural gas has the potential to serve as a critical transition fuel for Sub-Saharan Africa in the short term. As countries begin the process of economic diversification, the use of natural gas can help displace oil products while allowing the region to meet growing energy demands by complementing the uptake of renewable energy (IEA 2022). When replacing more-polluting fuels, natural gas can reduce air pollution and limit CO_2 emissions (IEA 2019). Natural gas, arguably the cleanest-burning fossil fuel, produces less emission per unit of energy than do oil and coal (Mo Ibrahim Foundation 2022). Research finds that switching to natural gas has already helped limit increases in global emissions since 2010 when paired with the scaling up of renewable energy sources, and it can reduce emissions by up to 50 percent (IEA 2019).

Sub-Saharan African countries can use natural gas as a transition fuel to bridge the gap between the use of intensive fossil fuels and renewable energy as renewable sources of energy are being developed and scaled up throughout the region (Matola et al. 2023). Mozambique, for example, has 100 trillion cubic feet of natural gas reserves, 40 percent larger than the reserves of Canada, which is the world's fifth-largest natural gas producer (Mo Ibrahim Foundation 2022). Leveraging natural gas as a transition fuel can provide African countries with the time they need to establish appropriate policies and financial mechanisms to implement the energy transition (Matola et al. 2023). Although not a long-term solution to climate change, the uptake of natural gas in the short term can lower emissions and spur the renewable energy transition (Gürsan and de Gooyert 2021). Ultimately, a just transition for Africa will depend on successfully harnessing the economic benefits from oil, gas, and mineral resources, including good governance and sound macrofiscal management of resource revenues, while also preparing for a low-carbon future (World Bank 2023b).

Urgent shifts to climate-smart trajectories in infrastructure, agriculture, health, water, and landscapes cannot be achieved at scale through fragmented and slow-paced electrification of the continent. Pooling resources and national grids can unlock the potential of regional power markets to expand access to reliable sources of energy at a reduced cost (UNCTAD 2023). The Southern African Power Pool facilitates the delivery of a surplus of more than 1,000 megawatts, generated mostly from hydropower in the north of Angola, to the south of the country that relies on costly diesel generators (UNCTAD 2023). This scheme allows more households in Angola to be reached with an affordable and reliable source of energy and sets the foundation for cross-border trade with neighboring countries. Further, clean cooking represents a "quick win" that countries should embrace head-on. De-risking investment in renewable energy, facilitating partnerships between the public and private sectors and governments, and leveraging financing will be key to achieving universal affordable energy access.

Emerging economies: Natural resources and green minerals

If managed efficiently and transparently with strong governance and institutional tracking systems, renewable and nonrenewable natural resources, notably forests and minerals, can harness results-based financing and carbon markets, and better capture of resource rents, to unlock the full economic and environmental potential of these resources through transparent and inclusive approaches.

Renewable natural resources: Forests and carbon markets

Africa has abundant natural resources, renewable and nonrenewable, but it needs to manage them in a way that can harness the opportunities as local, national, and global public goods. This natural capital wealth can play a central role in transforming Africa's economic future. The fiscal revenues available from resource extraction can create the fiscal space needed to invest in human and produced capital, and for policies that improve resilience and help reduce poverty (World Bank 2023b). Restoration of degraded landscapes and preservation of native forests provide invaluable ecosystem services, including carbon sequestration, and avoid a breach of tipping points.

Climate change, however, threatens Africa's renewable natural capital, crucial for bolstering adaptation and building climate resilience in people, assets, and economies at large. By area, Africa has one-sixth of the world's forests, many of which have been subject to rapid deforestation in recent years, with Sub-Saharan Africa losing 4.4 million hectares of forest annually between 2015 and 2020 (Mansourian and Berrahmouni 2021). Countries that include land use, land-use change, and forestry in their nationally determined contributions contain more than 99 percent of Africa's current forests (IEA 2022). Unfortunately, wealth per capita has declined over time in many countries with the depletion and degradation of natural assets, in part because of the exclusion of natural capital from national accounts (figure 2.8). Continuing widespread deforestation, including degradation of drylands in Sub-Saharan Africa, not only exacerbates climate change and its impacts but also reduces the adaptive capacity of local communities to respond to climate threats (World Bank 2021a).

FIGURE 2.8 **Change in renewable wealth, selected world regions and African subregions, 1995–2018**

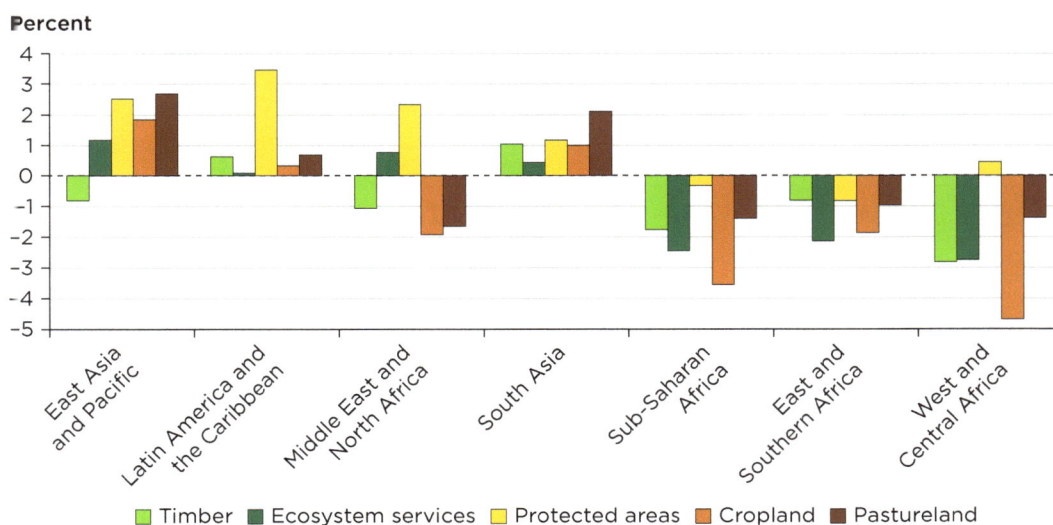

Source: World Bank 2021a, figure 2.7, panel b.

Climate change can leverage the role of natural capital and the blue economy[7] as a pillar of resilience that supports economic prosperity and growth in Sub-Saharan Africa. Nature-based solutions in particular can reduce the impact of storm surges, decrease climate vulnerability, and increase resilience. From reforestation initiatives to wetland restoration projects, nature-based solutions promote sustainable land management, preserve biodiversity, and mitigate climate change impacts, while providing socioeconomic benefits to local communities. They offer integral and cost-effective solutions: for example, green infrastructure can be up to 50 percent cheaper than traditional infrastructure (Oliver and Marsters 2022). Further, Africa's blue economy has the potential to drive the continent's economic growth. The blue economy is estimated to grow to US$576 billion by 2063 and generate 78 million jobs (AU-IBAR 2019). By harnessing the power of nature-based solutions, Sub-Saharan Africa can simultaneously enhance its resilience against climate change and unlock economic opportunities, making natural capital a driving force for sustainable prosperity and growth in the region.

Climate financing for nature conservation and forest management in Africa lags behind that of other regions. Despite critical contributions as the world's largest carbon sink and major regional biodiversity storehouse, the Congo Basin forests have received less climate financing for nature conservation and sustainable forest management compared with forests in the Amazon and Southeast Asia. Constituting about 70 percent of Africa's forest cover, the Congo Basin forests provide crucial values and services—food, fresh water, and shelter—for more than 75 million people (Abernethy, Maisels, and White 2016; Megevand 2013; Tyukavina et al. 2018). The forests also regulate rainfall patterns by recycling more than 50 percent of moisture and are the major source of rainfall for the region and beyond (Sorí et al. 2017; van der Ent et al. 2010).

Carbon markets provide an unprecedented opportunity for resource mobilization, but Africa has had limited participation up to now. Globally, the carbon credit issuances from forestry and land use projects increased 159 percent and accounted for more than 33 percent of total credit issuances in 2021; however, about 70 percent of these credits were generated in Asia, with most of the remainder generated in Latin America (World Bank 2022g). African carbon credit potential is estimated at about 2,400 megatons of CO_2 in 2030, with a value of up to US$50 billion (AfDB 2023). African countries must learn from the missed opportunities to leverage financing in the Kyoto Protocol Clean Development Mechanism. Despite its lion's share of carbon sink, the Congo Basin forests have not received a meaningful share of traded forest and land use credits. In fact, most of these credits come from projects to reduce emissions from deforestation and land use conversion; remove atmospheric emissions, including afforestation; and improve forest management and carbon sequestration in agriculture Standing stocks of forest in high-forest, low-deforestation areas as in the Congo Basin will not benefit from the compliance carbon markets under the Paris Agreement.

There is a growing call for fair compensation for countries' conservation efforts and for fostering a sustainable economy that prioritizes renewable resources over nonrenewable exports.

Minerals for the green energy transition

Sub-Saharan Africa's wealth of minerals can be used to capture resource rents as part of the global transition to clean energy (table 2.1). As noted earlier, a just transition for Africa will depend on successfully harnessing the economic benefits from these mineral resources (and oil and gas), including good governance and sound macrofiscal management of resource revenues, while also preparing for a low-carbon future. Otherwise, by 2030 more than 80 percent of the world's poor will be in the Africa region, and almost 75 percent of the world's poor will live in resource-rich countries (Cust and Zeufack 2023). The export market for nonrenewable natural resources in Sub-Saharan Africa increased from US$56 billion in 2002 to US$288 billion in 2012 (World Bank 2013), but this increase did not generate economywide benefits. Overcoming the much dreaded "resource curse" tragedy will require optimizing resource rent capture in an equitable, transparent, and efficient manner. The African Continental Free Trade Area (AfCFTA) agreement offers an unprecedented opportunity to develop a mine-to-market value chain on the continent.

TABLE 2.1 **Minerals and metals required for various clean energy technologies**

Mineral/metal	Wind	Solar photovoltaic	Concentrated solar power	Hydropower	Geothermal	Energy storage	Nuclear	Gas	Carbon capture and storage
Cobalt	●	●	●	●	●	●	●	●	●
Raw copper						●		●	●
Raw aluminum	●	●				●	●	●	
Chromium ore		●		●	●	●	●	●	●
Graphite						●			
Manganese	●			●	●	●	●	●	●
Raw nickel	●	●		●	●	●	●	●	●
Zinc ore	●	●		●	●	●	●		
Titanium ore				●	●			●	
Lithium						●			

Source: World Bank 2017.
Note: Green cells indicate an important role for these minerals and metals in each low-carbon technology.

Demand for Africa's metals that are so vital to the clean energy revolution will rise dramatically in the coming years. The transition toward the low-carbon economy is irreversible and will be intensive in minerals that are abundant in many countries in the region (figure 2.9). Africa accounts for more than 40 percent of global reserves of cobalt, manganese, and platinum, all key minerals for batteries and hydrogen technologies (IEA 2022). It exports nearly all the world's cobalt, the only commodity used for every form of energy. The clean energy transformation is likely to create demand for 3 billion tons of minerals and metals for solar, wind, and geothermal energy by 2050 (Cust and Zeufack 2023). As major producers of cobalt, copper, and platinum, countries such as the Democratic Republic of Congo, South Africa, and Zambia are already key players in the low-carbon transition. For such countries that are rich in metals and minerals, the longer-term prospects may be better than for the fossil fuel producers.

In sum, first, carbon markets can secure and stabilize the multitude of ecosystem services, reverse environmental degradation and biodiversity loss, and secure livelihoods. Ghana and Mozambique have already started receiving payments totaling US$11.2 million for carbon sequestration efforts, and these efforts can be replicated and scaled up in the ecologically rich Congo Basin and Upper Guinea forests. Second, Africa's nonrenewable natural resources, such as cobalt and copper, so vital to the clean energy revolution, must be managed efficiently by optimizing their rent capture in an equitable, transparent, and efficient manner to overcome and avert the "resource curse" tragedy of the past. South Africa has the existing infrastructure and partnerships necessary to leverage green minerals and add value to capture resource rents that can be used as an entry point into the market.

FIGURE 2.9 Estimates of selected metal and mineral resources, Sub-Saharan Africa

Indexed reserves (2014 = 100)

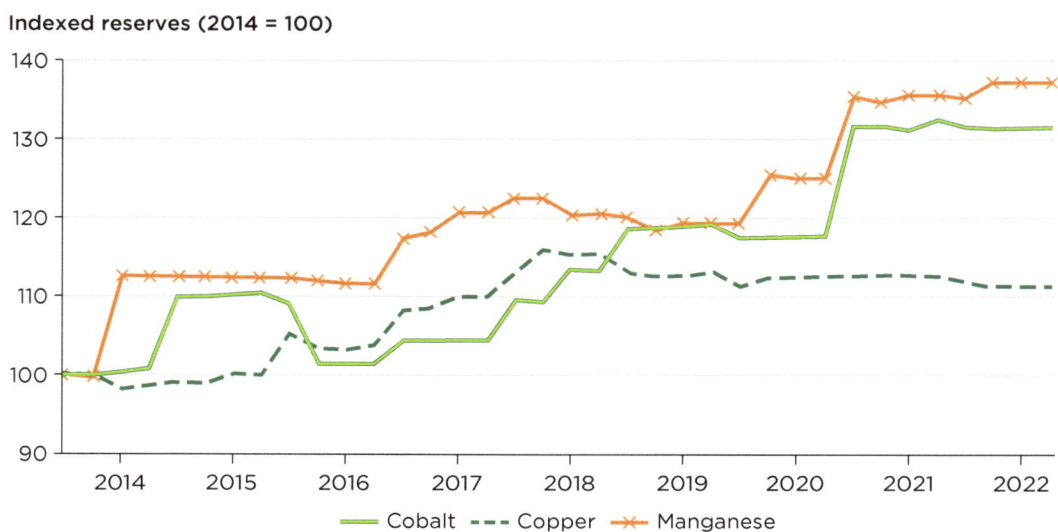

Source: Cust and Zeufack 2023, 7.

Institutional readiness and climate-smart pathways

Countries must adopt climate-smart and informed trajectories that include road maps as blueprints for holistic farsighted action. They should underpin these road maps with a sequence of structural reforms, policies, and actions, using inclusive and knowledge-based approaches and strong attention on human capital development, to secure a sustainable future and enhanced quality of life. Project-by-project climate action, and iterative crises responses, will not be enough for Africa to claim the 21st century.

Broad supporting policies and strong, effective institutions are critical to create the necessary enabling environment for successful design and implementation of climate-smart trajectories. Climate resilience can deliver high cost-benefit ratios ranging from 2:1 to 10:1 (Global Commission on Adaptation 2019). The existence of and progress on implementing national climate initiatives such as climate change policies, national adaptation plans, and climate change adaptation strategies demonstrate a country's readiness for driving policy and investments on climate action. National policy frameworks are often underpinned by further sector-specific initiatives, such as Climate Smart Agriculture Investment Plans. These initiatives can help countries to realize their climate goals and targets—for example, by establishing the necessary legal framework or allocating resources to capacity building. Rwanda's Strategic Plan for Agriculture Transformation emphasizes reducing losses from climate change and extreme weather events through specific interventions such as establishing a comprehensive agricultural ecosystem financing program that includes lease financing and insurance with a focus on priority value chains (World Bank 2022h). The existence of such climate change financing frameworks can catalyze, mobilize, and target finance to help achieve a country's strategic climate goals.

Embedding climate resilience in key sectors such as urbanization, agriculture, energy, water, and health is fundamental to the long-term success of people and economies. In terms of urbanization, low-carbon city development and the viability of cities with burgeoning populations will require climate-smart spatial planning (World Bank 2020a). Niger, for example, developed a legal framework in 2017 to guide the urbanization process, which puts areas that are highly exposed to flooding off-limits to construction (World Bank 2022d). In the case of disaster preparedness, rapid responses must be complemented with far-sighted planning and inclusive approaches to foster social cohesion, including through bottom-up citizen engagement. Climate-smart development applied to key export sectors can also bring positive gains to the economy and growth pathways.

The government of Rwanda, for example, developed a Checklist for Environment and Climate Change Mainstreaming that integrates more than 60 percent of key environmental and climate indicators into sectoral action plans

(World Bank 2022h). Vocational skills development and competency-based training along focused value chains—like agricultural transformation and green mobility-enabling infrastructure—can also drive climate-smart action to scale and instigate sustained behavioral change. Using trainings to connect with the wealth of risk management knowledge of communities and indigenous communities as partners will be invaluable.

Strong alignment of climate action and national development priorities and plans can accelerate action and uptake, compared with driving stand-alone climate responses. Mali, for example, continues to integrate climate change into its policies and planning processes through its implementation of sector strategies and Mali Vision 2040, the Strategic Framework for Economic Recovery and Sustainable Development, the National Environmental Protection Policy, and the National Policy on Climate Change (World Bank 2022d). A joint focus on policy planning and climate risks enables the creation of comprehensive adaptation strategies that help countries reach their socioeconomic objectives and confront any trade-offs, all while enhancing their climate resilience. This alignment between climate action and socioeconomic development is often championed in high-level policy forums, such as the African Ministerial Conference on the Environment and the United Nations Environment Assembly.

Climate change uncertainty is a key issue to consider when developing and designing climate-smart investments, particularly infrastructure projects, in Sub-Saharan Africa because it will severely affect existing and planned infrastructure in many countries. Madagascar and Mozambique, for example, are exposed to extreme weather events such as cyclones and floods that will become more frequent with climate change, and most of the subcontinent is vulnerable to more severe flooding events. In 2019, floods in Burkina Faso cost firms US$92 million, or 1.1 percent of the country's GDP (World Bank 2022d). By 2050, climate change is likely to result in a 60–160 percent increase in maintenance costs for Africa's existing road network (World Bank 2022d). With two-thirds of infrastructure yet to be built in Africa, achieving such resilience to climate shocks in the design of infrastructure projects (such as hydroelectric generation) is not trivial. Regional drought, for example, has resulted in major power shortages with significant economic impacts in hydropower-dependent countries like Ethiopia and Zambia. Diversifying the generation mix with other utility-scale renewable generations, such as solar, wind, and geothermal, will help mitigate such risk. Scaling regional power trade is another measure to mitigate such impacts and uncertainty. Decision-making under uncertainty needs to be part of policy making, as does incorporating variable conditions in project evaluation through grounded methodologies by mobilizing the best data.

Getting to climate-smart trajectories for jobs, quality of life, and vibrant economies must be accompanied by human capital development. Human capital remains critically low in many African countries, with the average Human Capital Index[8] score for the region reaching a mere 0.40 in comparison to the global average of 0.57. Education, training, and job creation—critical ingredients for success in driving climate-smart trajectories—cannot be delivered without an increase in human capital in the region. By 2050, Africa's population is projected to reach 2.3 billion people, of whom 830 million will be youth between 15 and 35 years of age. Without timely and strategic intervention, only about 100 million youth will be able to find stable employment opportunities by 2035 (World Bank 2017). For African cities to become engines of growth, they will require a skilled workforce, which can be achieved by providing education, training, and jobs to the youth population as an avenue to power green growth.

Sub-Saharan Africa's demographic trends have far-reaching implications for the region's socioeconomic development and poverty reduction. Between 2022 and 2050, Sub-Saharan Africa's population is expected to nearly double, with the region surpassing 2 billion inhabitants by the late 2040s (UN DESA 2022). Projections also indicate that Sub-Saharan Africa will account for more than half of the world's population between 2022 and 2050, with population growth at an annual rate of 2.5 percent, more than three times the global average (UN DESA 2022). Further, poverty rates in Africa have not fallen fast enough to keep pace with population growth. Although the share of the African population in extreme poverty declined from 57 percent in 1990 to 43 percent in 2021, the number of people living in extreme poverty increased by more than 100 million because of rapid population growth (Beegle et al. 2016). Africa also has the world's youngest population, a trend that is expected to continue and that will allow the continent to reap the demographic dividend created by shifts in age distribution of the population (Yingi 2023). The youth bulge can create a large skilled population that, if met with an economy that has real job opportunities, can accelerate development (Weny, Snow, and Zhang 2017; Yingi 2023). If not accompanied by adequate job opportunities and educational opportunities, however, the youth bulge may pose significant challenges to peace and security in the region (Yingi 2023).

Regional strategies for climate change in Africa are of critical importance to address the unique climate challenges faced by the continent. The AfCFTA provides a framework for regional cooperation and presents a valuable opportunity to integrate climate action into economic development plans. Through the AfCFTA, African countries can collaborate on climate-resilient infrastructure projects, promote renewable energy investments, and establish common standards for sustainable practices across borders. Additionally, regional strategies can facilitate the sharing of climate-related data and knowledge, enabling evidence-based decision-making and fostering innovation in climate adaptation and mitigation efforts for transboundary resources. Further, implementing regional frameworks for collaborative and responsible mining of the minerals essential for renewable technologies is crucial for the continent's future.

Climate-induced migration will compound the rapidly growing rural-to-urban migration rates in Sub-Saharan Africa, requiring far-sighted planning (Rigaud et al. 2018). Between 1950 and 2015, Africa's urban population increased by 2,000 percent; by 2050, African cities are expected to grow by 950 million people (OECD and Sahel and West Africa Club 2020). Currently, an estimated 143 cities in Africa have populations of more than 500,000 people. This number is expected to increase to 245 cities by 2035, with most growth anticipated in western Africa (Cities Alliance and AfDB 2022). Secondary cities, also heavily populated, comprise 12.5 to 15.0 percent of the total urban population of Africa, with an estimated 180 to 200 million people living in these areas (Cities Alliance and AfDB 2022). Secondary cities are frequently home to refugees from conflict zones, which places increased pressures on countries such as the Democratic Republic of Congo, Kenya, Somalia, and South Sudan (Cities Alliance and AfDB 2022; World Bank 2023e). In addition to population growth, movement among the growing population is also expected to increase along particular corridors, from Burkina Faso to Côte d'Ivoire, and to regional economic poles, such as Nigeria and South Africa (World Bank 2023e). Responding effectively and sustainably to a growing population and migration trends linked to climate will require a scale-up of readiness and increased resilience.

Policies

Claiming the 21st century in the face of rapidly and accelerating climate change will require bold and far-sighted climate policies across the continent, at local, national, and regional levels. The pervasiveness of climate impacts, coupled with the reality of low-baseline development and preexisting climate vulnerabilities, means that inadequate or delayed action will not only unravel development gains or push countries into more vulnerability but also lead to greater impoverishment, instability, and insecurity. This situation will jeopardize countries' achievement of the SDGs and any claim to the 21st century. Emboldened, urgent action and transformation at scale must be underpinned by the unique characteristics of the region and, more specifically, by country context. The interplay of climate and development and the far-reaching nature of climate impacts across spatial and temporal scales along with asymmetrical distributions of vulnerability between populations call for attention to adopting climate-smart trajectories and building social resilience. Countries must adopt climate-smart policies underpinned by strong diagnostics and informed trajectories to drive holistic and far-sighted action. These trajectories should be implemented by a sequence of structural reforms, policies, and actions, through inclusive and knowledge-based approaches, with a strong focus on human capital development to secure a sustainable future and enhanced quality of life. Project-by-project climate action, and iterative crises responses will not suffice to claim the 21st century for Africa.

Scaling up resilience to manage climate shocks

Addressing the climate-fragility-conflict nexus is key to improving social resilience and cohesion, rebuilding the social contract, and achieving inclusive growth as a foundation for Africa to claim the 21st century. The breakdown of communities' resilience and cohesion, and of the social contract—particularly for the poorest marginalized communities—can undermine any efforts to attain sustainable development outcomes and any claim to the 21st century. Addressing social resilience and cohesion in the context of climate migration and displacements should be placed at the intersection of humanitarian, development, and peace partnerships, working with regional, national, and local stakeholders for end-to-end solutions. To support countries in taking holistic action across the mobility continuum will require greater cooperation, information sharing, and action between the development, humanitarian, security, and disaster risk reduction communities. Strong regional and national institutions are essential to address the multidimensional challenges (Opitz-Stapleton et al. 2021). Locally led approaches working with civil society and community actors are critical to generate inclusive, participatory, and empowering solutions.

Response to climate shocks and crises must be combined with proactive and holistic approaches to secure sustained and durable development outcomes that build on a systematic understanding of the underlying drivers of vulnerability and fragility. Doing so will require mobilizing actors across different sectors and levels, including governments, indigenous groups, communities, civil society, and the private sector. Policies to promote low-carbon growth and climate adaptation must be pro-poor and must guard against any blowback that drives inequity and inadvertent consequences. They must also protect and meaningfully engage those who face a higher risk from climate shocks, or those who—because of social, political, or economic marginalization—have limited ability to benefit from development or resilience investments.

Social safety nets, traditionally developed as national programs to provide basic living support to the extreme poor, have increasingly been adapted to respond to emergencies and crises, including climate shocks. Although countries have often designed safety nets after a crisis or disaster has occurred, or as one-off emergency support in case of a disaster, countries' adaptive social protection strategies are increasingly integrating readiness measures to increase the climate (and overall) resilience of communities and subsequent scale-up efforts. For instance, Ethiopia successfully expanded its Productive Safety Net Program during the Horn of Africa drought in 2011, protecting an additional 3.1 million people from the worst impacts of the drought and enabling them to recover more quickly after the shock (Beegle, Coudouel, and Monsalve 2018). With less than a decade left for African countries to achieve their SDGs, and manage the impact of escalating and intensifying climate change on economies, countries will need to focus on at-scale resilience-building activities that can drive change in development trajectories in the African context. A systematic focus on social resilience and cohesion must be advanced, including through the following:

- Targeted, people-centered, community-led, customized solutions and delivery mechanisms for climate actions that strengthen the ability of the poorest and most vulnerable to recover quickly and more effectively from climate (and other) shocks.

- Strengthened and enhanced information systems for early warning and decision support that reach the poorest and most vulnerable.

- Improved institutional, risk-financing, and macrofiscal policy to prepare and respond to climate shocks (and pandemics).

- Prioritizing readiness to drive far-sighted integrative climate-smart action and structural reforms that will require systematic and sustained investments in capacity and dedicated skills backed by strong policy, regulatory, and institutional frameworks.

Universal affordable energy access

Universal energy access in Africa deployed through available low-cost and low-carbon options can be the first at-scale energy transformation globally. It must be accelerated to unleash the triple benefits of improving economic productivity, lowering emissions, and increasing resilience. Despite the plunging cost of renewables in recent years, barriers including unclear policy and regulatory frameworks, and financing constraints continue to impede the proliferation of renewable energy throughout the region. Supporting renewable and low-carbon development will require reforms in the energy sector, such as improving operational performance of electricity companies, adopting payment discipline for electricity bills, and implementing cost-recovery tariffs (World Bank Group 2024). Further, African governments can generate revenue for renewable energy projects by phasing out subsidies for fossil fuels, estimated to account for 5.6 percent of Sub-Saharan African GDP (Schwerhoff and Sy 2020). As investor confidence increases, governments can also develop consistent procurement practices and policies to unlock renewable energy investment flows. For example, after a pilot auction unraveled in 2013 because the government made retroactive changes to the bid site capacity, Namibia held successful auctions in 2017 and 2019, through which the country has added 90 megawatts of renewables to the grid, with a total of 500 megawatts expected by 2025 (Bloomberg Philanthropies 2022).

De-risking investment and facilitating partnerships between the public and private sectors and governments will be key to unlocking the finance necessary and implementing the technical solutions available to facilitate the renewable energy transition. The Sustainable Energy Fund for Africa, a multidonor fund managed by the African Development Bank, has de-risked investments in the energy sector by providing technical assistance and concessional and catalytic financing to countries including Burkina Faso and the Democratic Republic of Congo (Ireri and Shirley 2021). By de-risking investment in the region, the fund catalyzes blended finance initiatives, such as the Africa Renewable Energy Fund. The Sustainable Energy Fund has catalyzed private sector funding of more than US$1.8 billion, leading to the creation of 45 renewable energy projects with a total capacity of more than 750 megawatts across Sub-Saharan Africa (Ireri and Shirley 2021). In rural areas the World Bank is supporting performance-based grants to enable the development of 14 solar-hybrid mini-grids. Other countries such as Burkina Faso, Ethiopia, Mali, and Togo have followed this model to successfully implement similar funding schemes, suggesting that this approach can be effectively scaled up to achieve widespread uptake of renewables (Bloomberg Philanthropies 2022).

The integration of clean cooking strategies into national strategies, with a focus on community engagement and unlocking financing, is fundamental to building capacity and delivering impact at scale. Collaboration between donors, the private sector, and governments, and the implementation of national policies that support clean cooking, has improved uptake, with successful national programs in place in Burkina Faso, Ethiopia, Malawi, Nigeria, Rwanda, Senegal, and Uganda (World Bank 2014). Programs that support the uptake of clean cooking solutions have had the most success when product design accommodates user practices, preferences, and behaviors—highlighting the importance of community engagement for sustained use and widespread dissemination of clean cooking products (World Bank 2014). Further, using small subsidies that have a clear phase-out plan at the early stages of implementation have proven effective in increasing uptake of clean cooking solutions, particularly in the most marginalized and often rural communities, where benefits of clean cooking are significant but the up-front costs are prohibitive (World Bank 2014). This approach was successful for Kenya's ceramic jiko stove technology, which began with subsidies from donors and the government, later transitioned to market-based distribution, and now reaches more than 25 million people in 14 countries in Sub-Saharan Africa (World Bank 2014). Starting with small subsidies and then transitioning to market-based solutions can help to build capacity and deliver impact at scale.

Leveraging new climate solutions from natural resources

Renewable and nonrenewable natural resources can, if managed efficiently and transparently with strong governance and institutional tracking systems, harness results-based financing and carbon markets, and better capture resource rents, to unlock their full economic and environmental potential. South Africa, for example, is primed to benefit from the region's natural resources. The country has an established export infrastructure, an abundant supply of renewable energy resources, and access to mining firms that extract minerals in the area (World Bank 2022i). With preexisting infrastructure and access, South Africa could become a value-addition and export hub for green technology commodities that will be increasingly in demand from the renewable energy transition (World Bank 2022i). However, this process requires strong governance to ensure the capture of resource rents and to ensure that, with an inclusive approach, the value generated from the minerals delivers economic benefits to the community.

Both readiness to engage in carbon markets and results-based climate finance must be prioritized, with attention to end-to-end capacity and institutional strengthening. Article 6 of the Paris Agreement provides better opportunities for African countries to participate in the global carbon market by setting out how they can pursue voluntary cooperation to reach their emissions reduction targets as stipulated in their nationally determined contributions through international transfer (trading) of carbon offsets. Country assessments should examine institutional and governance (policy) frameworks and monitoring systems, and identify existing gaps and capacity needs to enhance readiness for the forest carbon market and the flow of financial streams for forest ecosystem conservation. Carbon credits and results-based financing can also extend to infrastructure investments that pursue green low-carbon strategies.

A select few African countries have begun to receive payments for emissions reductions. If scaled up, these emissions reductions programs can provide countries with a revenue source of rewards for efforts to mitigate climate change. In 2021, Mozambique became the first country to receive payment from the World Bank's Forest Carbon Partnership Facility (FCPF) for reducing emissions. The country received US$6.4 million for reducing 1.28 million tons of carbon emissions since 2019, achieving emissions reductions through strategies promoting sustainable agriculture practices, monitoring use of forest resources, and restoring degraded land. Ghana also received US$4.8 million from the FCPF for reducing more than 900,000 tons of carbon emissions since 2019. Both countries implemented a benefit-sharing plan to ensure that local stakeholders and communities receive most of the monetary benefits from their conservation efforts. Under the countries' Emission Reductions Payment Agreements with the FCPF, Ghana and Mozambique could each receive up to US$50 million for reducing up to 10 million tons of carbon emissions by 2024. Scaling up programs such as the FCPF could enable more African countries, particularly those in the Congo Basin, to harness carbon markets in an economically beneficial and socially inclusive way.

Readiness and transitions to climate-smart pathways

Prioritizing readiness to drive far-sighted integrative climate-smart action and structural reforms will require systematic and sustained investments in capacity and dedicated skills backed by strong policy, regulatory, and institutional frameworks. Enhancing readiness and ensuring just transitions can address key drivers of low-carbon, resilient, and sustainable development. A staggering 43 out of 48 Sub-Saharan African countries are in the bottom 50 percent of the Notre Dame Global Adaptation Initiative readiness ranking. The region is generally unprepared to cope with and address the mounting impacts of climate change. Further, Sub-Saharan Africa has attained only 40 percent of its productive potential as measured by the Human Capital Index (Brixi, Rawlings, and Koechlein 2021). In addition, the African continent is only halfway to achieving the 2030 SDGs and targets (UNECA et al. 2020).

Africa's historical and impending role as a low contributor to the climate crisis and its significant potential to act as a global solution demand urgent attention if these dividends are to deliver benefits all around. The importance of leapfrogging and transforming at scale has never been clearer, and the urgency for climate action has never been more profound. Because African countries are all at different levels of income and development, readiness has to be better tailored and targeted. Critical lessons are emerging on the importance of end-to-end preparedness; the need for systemwide readiness involving all sectors and all peoples (households, institutions, communities, national governments, and international stakeholders); and the imperative for proactive and anticipatory strategies, including flexible macroeconomic policies to face borderless challenges such as pandemics and climate change. Whereas the pandemic and the Ukraine crisis represent somewhat unanticipated shocks, the same cannot be said of climate change. The nature, scale, and pervasiveness of climate impacts mean that solutions cannot be fragmented but must be comprehensive, inclusive, and holistic.

Governance and institutional capacity remain limited throughout the region, impeding the ability of countries to develop and scale up readiness strategies. A running theme throughout the first round of CCDRs is the need to strengthen institutional capacity of countries through better planning, delivery, and management of human, natural, and physical assets in order to address climate change.

Climate-Smart Public Investment Management (CS-PIM) offers strategies that can improve readiness at the national and local levels in Sub-Saharan Africa. CS-PIM refers to the processes and procedures used by the public sector to integrate climate-smart public investment policy in national and strategic planning (World Bank 2022g). Specific CS-PIM interventions can include establishing and implementing climate-informed disaster resilience standards for infrastructure, risk management of infrastructure assets, and leveraging insurance products (World Bank 2022g). These strategies aim to integrate climate change adaptation and mitigation into planning, legal frameworks, and development objectives at the national and local levels, thereby strongly positioning a country to address climate shocks (World Bank 2022g).

Effective early warning systems are a critical tool for enhancing the readiness of communities and their resilience to climate shocks. Early warning systems can enable the integration of climate change adaptation and disaster risk reduction strategies into development planning by leveraging impact-based forecasting and hydrometeorological service delivery systems. The application of the early warning system can strengthen a country's disaster risk management and allowed at-risk communities to plan before disaster struck, thereby enhancing readiness. Scaling up early warning systems throughout Sub-Saharan Africa offers a reliable and cost-effective way of protecting communities from climate-induced natural hazards.

Scaling up climate finance

Substantial climate financing gaps, coupled with weak macrofiscal landscapes and indebtedness of several countries in Africa, raise the urgency for channeling concessional financing to unlock private sector financing. African countries urgently need access to finance to adapt to climate change and shift to a low-carbon growth path. Climate financing pledges have been slow to materialize, leading to a growing urgency to fill this gap. Although the World Bank remains the largest financier of climate action in the region, climate financing is not keeping pace with the large and growing demand.[3] Sub-Saharan Africa received US$15.7 billion in concessional climate finance in 2020, yet the continent needs a total of US$190 billion per year until 2030 to meet its mitigation needs and US$50 billion per year by 2050 for adaptation (figure 2.10). The continent needs trillions of dollars to fund mitigation and adaptation measures, and meeting these pressing needs requires collective global action. Financing adaptation strategies in key development sectors will be more cost-effective than financing increasingly frequent and severe crisis response, disaster relief, and recovery pathways. Overall, progress on implementation of the Paris Agreement remains slow, and African countries must go beyond green pledges to meet climate goals, notably through stronger institutions and policies and greater regional cooperation. More financing from private and public sources is needed to accelerate implementation, but barriers to accessing quality finance to support the delivery of climate action and sustainable development remain, despite the increase in climate finance.

In the near term, concessional financing must prevail and must be used to expand access and connect to public and private capital. Accelerating high-priority public projects can unlock subsequent private investment by creating opportunities for risk-sharing arrangements that address the key concerns of risk-averse investors. Concessional finance can lift investment and close the gap between resources and needs. Because of the significant gaps in financing for adaptation and mitigation, concessional finance alone is unlikely to meet the region's transition and adaptation needs. Sub-Saharan Africa urgently needs new ways of connecting public, private, and concessional finance to lift investment and close the gap between resources and needs.

FIGURE 2.10 Africa's estimated climate finance adaptation and mitigation needs

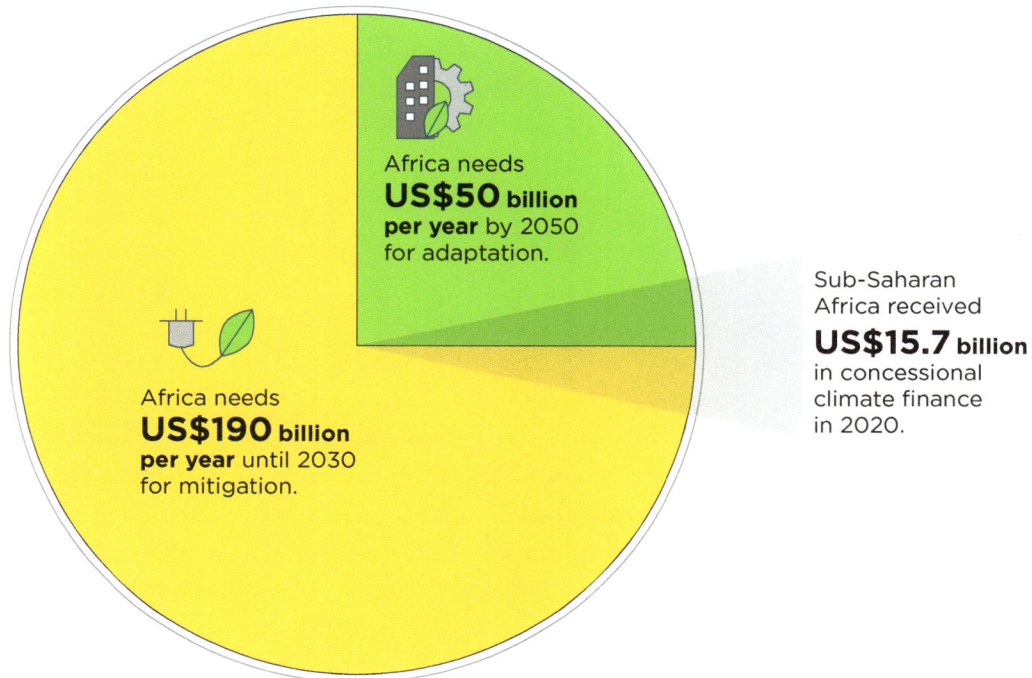

Africa needs
US$50 billion per year by 2050 for adaptation.

Africa needs
US$190 billion per year until 2030 for mitigation.

Sub-Saharan Africa received
US$15.7 billion in concessional climate finance in 2020.

Source: IMF 2023.

The cost of inaction is expected to be extremely high. The CCDRs estimate that, by 2050, climate change could induce GDP annual losses ranging between 2 percent and 15 percent.[10] Consequently, the reports underscore the importance of taking a people-centered approach to climate action and bolstering countries' capacity to seize opportunities in low-carbon economic activities and buffer the impacts of climate risks and green transitions. Transitioning from fossil fuels, expanding access to renewable energy, and promoting e-mobility represent fundamental shifts for ensuring that development in Africa has a low-carbon footprint and is based on increasing total factor productivity.

The 29th United Nations Climate Change Conference, held in Baku, Azerbaijan, in 2024, agreed on a new collective quantified goal to mobilize US$300 billion in climate finance annually by 2035 for developing countries. The agreement also calls on nations to work toward reaching a US$1.3 trillion climate financing goal by 2035. The earlier goal to provide US$100 billion by 2020, reached in full only in 2022, expires in 2025. The multilateral development banks represent important partners for urgently addressing global climate change, development, and poverty through their investment and programs. The International Monetary Fund's Resilience and Sustainability Facility is a new financing instrument that will help Sub-Saharan Africa address longer-term structural challenges, including climate change, and act as a catalyst for climate finance (IMF 2021).

Solving the challenges of financing climate change requires a transdisciplinary approach that draws on a variety of financing mechanisms and instruments. Such approaches include greening public budgets; climate proofing public expenditures; mobilizing private sector financing; implementing regulatory provisions; engaging in credit guarantee schemes, green bonds, and debt swap programs; and ensuring financing from multilateral development banks and climate funds (figures 2.11 and 2.12) (GCA 2021).

Grants, a vital source of financing for many Sub-Saharan African countries, make up 1 to 2 percent of GDP in countries such as Burkina Faso, Chad, Mali, and Mauritania, and 7 percent of GDP in Niger (World Bank 2022d). Market-based financial solutions can complement informal mechanisms and are more effective when they are part of a comprehensive risk management strategy (World Bank 2023c). Integrated financial services based on risk profiles are essential, with savings, credit, credit-linked insurance, and guarantees working together to provide comprehensive financial protection for farmers and rural households (World Bank 2023c). The limited fiscal space of most African states to adapt and build resilience necessitates private sector solutions, including blended finance resources, and the involvement of institutional investors such as pension funds, sovereign wealth funds, and insurance companies in scaling up

FIGURE 2.11 Informal risk management mechanisms and market-based solutions

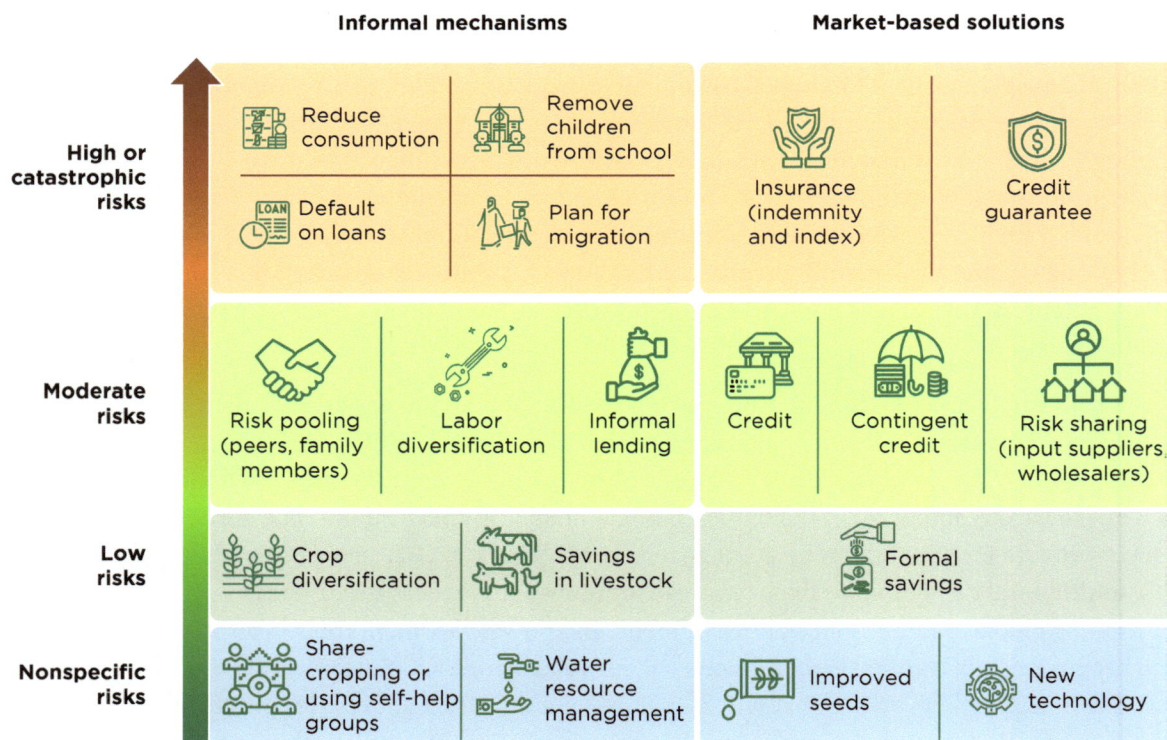

Source: World Bank 2023c.

FIGURE 2.12 Climate finance options

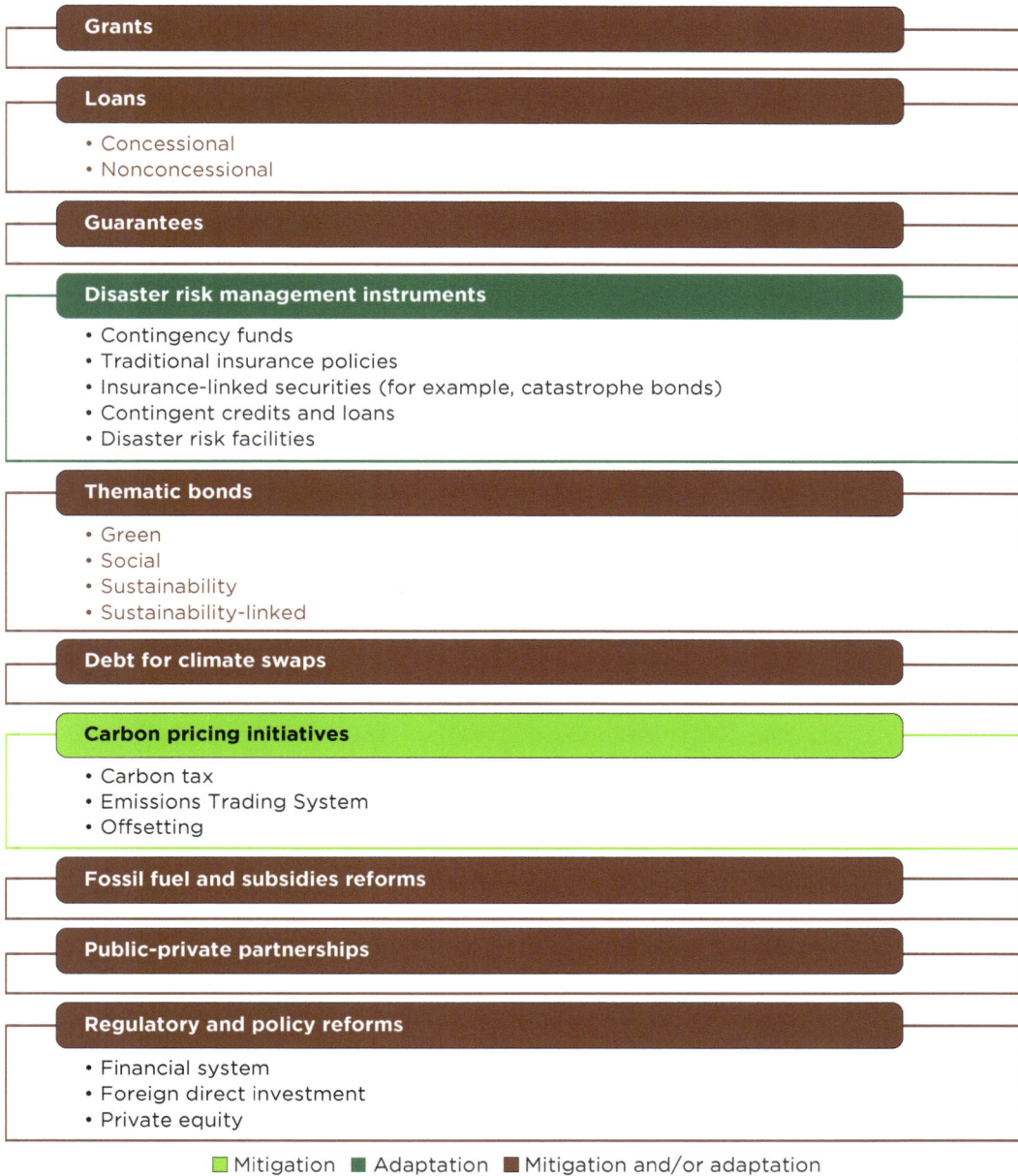

Grants	

Loans	
• Concessional	
• Nonconcessional	

Guarantees	

Disaster risk management instruments	
• Contingency funds	
• Traditional insurance policies	
• Insurance-linked securities (for example, catastrophe bonds)	
• Contingent credits and loans	
• Disaster risk facilities	

Thematic bonds	
• Green	
• Social	
• Sustainability	
• Sustainability-linked	

Debt for climate swaps	

Carbon pricing initiatives	
• Carbon tax	
• Emissions Trading System	
• Offsetting	

Fossil fuel and subsidies reforms	

Public-private partnerships	

Regulatory and policy reforms	
• Financial system	
• Foreign direct investment	
• Private equity	

■ Mitigation ■ Adaptation ■ Mitigation and/or adaptation

Source: World Bank.

climate finance on the continent (GCA 2021). Debt swaps, which convert debt servicing payments into domestic investments, offer an innovative financial tool for securing funding for adaptation projects (GCA 2021). Thematic bonds can also provide an innovative way to support resilience. For example, South Africa has pioneered a US$150 million five-year Wildlife Conservation Bond that will allow the country to protect black rhinos and support local communities without increasing national debt.

Disaster risk financing and insurance constitute another key instrument that can increase the financial resilience of rural households and businesses. Aligning disaster risk policy frameworks with climate adaptation institutions and frameworks is crucial, particularly for African countries most affected by climate-related disasters (GCA 2021). Limited capacity and expertise in designing effective programs pose challenges, yet the World Bank has successfully implemented the Africa Disaster Risk Financing Initiative of the Organisation of African, Caribbean, and Pacific States (World Bank 2023c). Financed by the European Union and implemented by the Global Facility for Disaster Reduction and Recovery, the initiative has supported more than 20 African countries in developing national risk-financing tools and strategies that can reduce disaster losses, speed recovery, and build resilience to natural hazards (GFDRR 2019). It has leveraged an additional US$516.27 million from the World Bank and other donors to build disaster resilience by supporting governments in strengthening their capacity to implement risk-financing policies at the local, national, and regional levels (GFDRR 2019).

Catastrophe Deferred Drawdown Options (Cat DDOs) increasingly offer a contingent financing line that provides immediate liquidity to address shocks related to natural disasters. Cat DDOs enhance countries' adaptive capacity to plan for and manage crises by securing financing before an extreme event (World Bank 2024b). For example, the World Bank provided US$200 million to Kenya in the form of a Disaster Risk Management Development Policy Credit with a Cat DDO that provided assistance to the country in response to severe flooding from extreme rainfall in 2019 and the COVID-19 pandemic. The Cat DDO advanced Kenya's efforts to build resilience to climate shocks and helped the government better manage the impacts of disasters through the development of a National Disaster Risk Financing Strategy. Although leveraged in times of crisis, Cat DDOs can be used to develop strategies that enable enhanced response to future climate shocks.

Preventing further impoverishment of already macrofiscally constrained African countries will require countering increased indebtedness that can arise from responding to climate shocks. Recurrent damages from extreme climate shocks increase debt and point to the need for climate-informed finance mechanisms and fiscal policies. Independent of the action taken to build resilience and expand electricity access, exploring and leveraging climate finance instruments will be essential for addressing the climate agenda and preventing countries from getting into a downward spiral of indebtedness. Acknowledging this need, the World Bank has introduced Climate Resilient Debt Clauses (CRDCs) that, in the event of natural disasters, defer principal and interest payments, and other loan charges to the International Bank for Reconstruction and Development Flexible Loan and International Development Association credits (World Bank 2024a). The deferment of interest payments through the CRDCs will free up government resources to finance disaster response and recovery efforts. Further, the fees associated with the CRDCs can be covered by concessional financing, such as the Livable Planet Fund, or potentially through the loss and damage fund (World Bank 2023d). This coverage of fees will help countries offset the costs of delivering the benefits of the CRDCs and increase resilience without further pressuring already macrofiscally constrained economies.

Conclusion

Four key messages and policy recommendations represent achievable game-changing solutions that will put Africa in a favorable position to claim the 21st century for its people and its economies in the face of a changing climate. First, prioritizing resilience and readiness to drive far-sighted integrative climate-smart action and structural reforms will require systematic and sustained investments in capacity and dedicated skills backed by strong policy, regulatory, and institutional frameworks. Second, accelerating universal affordable energy access is the cornerstone of climate adaptation in Africa. Third, the "new climate solution" opportunities presented by Africa's abundant natural resources call for countries to reimagine management of these resources to fully harness their value proposition as local, national, and global public goods. Fourth, urgently channeling concessional financing to unlock private sector financing including through carbon markets and results-based financing is important to fill the substantial climate financing gaps and weak macrofiscal landscapes and indebtedness of several countries in Africa. In addition to their benefits for Africa, these efficient, effective, just, and urgent recommendations will support the world in its mission to reach the goals of the Paris Agreement. However, the world must also support Africa. Even as the world is locked into some level of warming, the scale and intensity of impacts in Africa, and globally, will be significantly less than the 1.5°C guardrail if large emitters make significant reductions to their greenhouse gas emissions.

The world has no viable solution to its climate problem without Africa for the following reasons:

- Africa must, as an imperative, have the readiness, instruments, and technology (including early warning systems) to develop anticipatory and targeted solutions to counter climate shocks, to secure inclusive solutions for disaster prevention, and to secure resilience of households, communities, and firms.

- Africa's vast resources of minerals are critical for multiple clean energy technologies and for the global transition from fossil fuels to clean energy, beyond national and regional borders. For their part, the global community and external partners must raise the stakes to avoid the repeat outcomes of a resource curse.

- Africa could yield the first generation of "clean green economies" to achieve their SDGs for a resilient future with the right mix of policies, action, and finance. This achievement will yield dividends globally.

- Africa can act as a solution to support the global public good by making the most of the region's natural capital, and stabilizing global CO_2 levels, by timely leveraging of carbon markets. With the support of the global community, the region's countries will need to translate their natural capital assets into revenue streams locally, nationally, and globally through a fair deal. The Congo Basin represents one example of a critical strategic line of defense against climate change.

Africa's pursuit of low-carbon climate-resilient outcomes in support of sustainable development outcomes and pathways will contribute to meeting the goals of the Paris Agreement. The converse could have dire consequences of instability and insecurity, with spillover consequences across borders and within countries.

Notes

1. The European Union 27 consist of Austria, Belgium, Bulgaria, Croatia, Cyprus, the Czech Republic, Denmark, Estonia, Finland, France, Germany, Greece, Hungary, Ireland, Italy, Latvia, Lithuania, Luxembourg, Malta, the Netherlands, Poland, Portugal, Romania, the Slovak Republic, Slovenia, Spain, and Sweden.

2. For more on the Country Index, refer to Notre Dame Global Adaptation Initiative, https://gain.nd .edu/our-work/country-index/.

3. World Bank, "Mission 300 Is Powering Africa," www.worldbank.org/en/programs/energizing-africa

4. African Union, The African Leaders Nairobi Declaration on Climate and Call to Action, https:// www.afdb.org/sites/default/files/2023/09/08/the_african_leaders_nairobi_declaration_on _climate_change-rev-eng.pdf.

5. Those countries were Burkina Faso, the Democratic Republic of Congo, Ethiopia, Niger, Nigeria, and Sudan.

6. World Bank DataBank, "Net Official Development Assistance and Official Aid Received (Current US$)—Sub-Saharan Africa," https://data.worldbank.org/indicator/DT.ODA.ALLD .CD?contextual=aggregate&end=2021&locations=ZG&start=1960&view=chart.

7. The *blue economy* refers to sustainable use of ocean resources for economic growth, improved livelihoods and jobs, and ocean ecosystem health.

8. The Human Capital Index calculates the contributions of health and education to worker productivity. The final index score ranges from zero to one and measures the productivity as a future worker of a child born today relative to the benchmark of full health and complete education.

9. The total of climate action (climate co-benefit total) for fiscal year 2022 for East Africa, West Africa, and North Africa was US$12.34 billion.

10. The analysis used a different modeling exercise for every country and country grouping, and implemented different scenarios. CCDRs estimated annual impacts of climate change on GDP: Angola (3–6 percent); Cameroon (4–10 percent); Ghana (5–7 percent); Malawi (6–15 percent); Mozambique (4–9 percent); Rwanda (5–7 percent); the Group of Five Sahel countries (2–12 percent); and the Middle East and North Africa region (6–14 percent).

References

Abernethy, Katharine, Fiona Maisels, and Lee J. T. White. 2016. "Environmental Issues in Central Africa." *Annual Review of Environment and Resources* 41 (1): 1–33.

AfDB (African Development Bank Group). 2023. *African Economic Outlook 2023: Mobilizing Private Sector Financing for Climate and Green Growth in Africa*. Abidjan, Côte d'Ivoire: AfDB.

Ahmadnia, Shaadee J., Agathe M. Christien, Phoebe G. Spencer, Tracy Hart, and Caio Cesar De Araujo Barbosa. 2022. "Defueling Conflict Environment and Natural Resource Management as a Pathway to Peace." World Bank, Washington, DC.

Amakrane, Kamal, Sarah Rosengaertner, Nicholas P. Simpson, Alex de Sherbinin, Jane Linekar, Chris Horwood, Bryan Jones, Fabien Cottier, Susana Adamo, Briar Mills, Greg Yetman, Tricia Chai-Onn, John Squires, Jacob Schewe, Bram Frouws, and Roberto Forin. 2023. "African Shifts: The Africa Climate Mobility Report: Addressing Climate-Forced Migration and Displacement." Africa Climate Mobility Initiative and Global Centre for Climate Mobility, New York. https://africa.climatemobility.org/report.

AU-IBAR (African Union-Inter-African Bureau for Animal Resources). 2019. *Africa Blue Economy Strategy*. Nairobi: African Union. https://osf.io/3vy94?view_only=ea6924dc03bd4f728f5635e81ee6bfc6.

Bari, Mounir, and Sébastian Dessus. 2022. "Adapting to Natural Disasters in Africa: What's in It for the Private Sector?" Working paper, International Finance Corporation and World Bank Group. https://documents1.worldbank.org/curated/en/099420411182286754/pdf/IDU05618da110fa1f04bb80a3d90a4527408220e.pdf.

Beegle, Kathleen, Luc Christiaensen, Andrew Dabalen, and Isis Gaddis. 2016. *Poverty in a Rising Africa*. Washington, DC: World Bank. http://hdl.handle.net/10986/22575.

Beegle, Kathleen, Aline Coudouel, and Emma Monsalve, eds. 2018. *Realizing the Full Potential of Social Safety Nets in Africa*. Africa Development Forum. Washington, DC: World Bank. http://hdl.handle.net/10986/29789.

Bhandari, Preety, Nate Warszawski, Deirder Cogan, and Rhys Gerholdt. 2024. "What Is 'Loss and Damage' from Climate Change? 8 Key Questions, Answered." *WRI Insights,* November 4, 2024. https://www.wri.org/insights/loss-damage-climate-change?utm_campaign=wriclimate&utm_source=climatedigest-2023-6-6&utm_medium=email&utm_content=content#:~:text=Loss%20and%20damage%20can%20result,degradation%2C%20ocean%20acidification%20and%20salinization.?.

Biewald, Anne, Hermann Lotze-Campen, Ilona M. Otto, Nils Brinckmann, Benjamin Leon Bodirsky, Isabelle Weindl, Alexander Popp, and Hans Joachim Schellnhuber. 2014. "The Impact of Climate Change on Costs of Food and People Exposed to Hunger at Subnational Scale." PIK Report 128, Potsdam Institute for Climate Impact Research, Potsdam, Germany. https://www.researchgate.net/publication/283836922_The_impact_of_climate_change_on_costs_of_food_and_people_exposed_to_hunger_at_subnational_scale.

Bloomberg Philanthropies. 2022. *Scaling Up Renewable Energy in Africa: A NetZero Pathfinders Report*. Bloomberg Finance L.P. https://assets.bbhub.io/professional/sites/24/BNEF-Scaling-Up-Renewable-Energy-in-Africa-A-NetZero-Pathfinders-report_FINAL.pdf.

Bodewig, Christian. 2019. "Climate Change in the Sahel: How Can Cash Transfers Help Protect the Poor?" *Brookings* (blog), December 4, 2019. https://www.brookings.edu/articles/climate-change-in-the-sahel-how-can-cash-transfers-help-protect-the-poor/.

Brixi, Hana, Laura B. Rawlings, and Elizabeth Koechlein. 2021. "Unleashing Women and Girls' Human Capital: A Game Changer for Africa." *Finance & Development Magazine*, December. https://www.imf.org/en/Publications/fandd/issues/2021/12/Africa-Unleashing-Women-Girls-Human-Capital.

Burke, Marshall, Solomon M. Hsiang, and Edward Miguel. 2015. "Global Non-linear Effect of Temperature on Economic Production." *Nature* 527: 235–39.

Cervigni, Raffaello, Andrew Losos, Paul Chinowsky, and James E. Neumann, eds. 2017. *Enhancing the Climate Resilience of Africa's Infrastructure: The Roads and Bridges Sector*. Africa Development Forum series. Washington, DC: World Bank. http://documents.worldbank.org/curated/en/270671478809724744/Enhancing-the-climate-resilience-of-Africa-s-Infrastructure-the-roads-and-bridges-sector.

Cevik, Serhan, and João T. Jalles. 2022. "For Whom the Bell Tolls: Climate Change and Income Inequality." IMF Working Paper WP/22/103, International Monetary Fund, Washington, DC. https://www.imf.org/-/media/Files/Publications/WP/2022/English/wpiea2022103-print-pdf.ashx.

Cities Alliance and AfDB (African Development Bank). 2022. *The Dynamics of Systems of Secondary Cities in Africa: Urbanisation, Migration and Development*. Brussels: Cities Alliance and AfDB. https://www.citiesalliance.org/resources/publications/book/dynamics-systems-secondary-cities-africa.

Clement, Viviane, Kanta Kumari Rigaud, Alex de Sherbinin, Bryan Jones, Susana Adamo, Jacob Schewe, Nian Sadiq, and Elam Shabahat. 2021. "Groundswell Part 2: Acting on Internal Climate Migration." World Bank, Washington, DC. https://hdl.handle.net/10986/36248.

CPI (Climate Policy Initiative). 2022. *Landscape of Climate Finance in Africa*. CPI. https://www.climatepolicyinitiative.org/wp-content/uploads/2022/09/Landscape-of-Climate-Finance-in-Africa.pdf.

CRED (Centre for Research on the Epidemiology of Disasters). 2023. *2022 Disasters in Numbers: Climate in Action*. Brussels: CRED. https://cred.be/sites/default/files/2022_EMDAT_report.pdf.

Crippa, M., D. Guizzardi, F. Pagani, M. Banja, M. Muntean, E. Schaaf, W. Becker, F. Monforti-Ferrario, R. Quadrelli, A. Risquez Martin, P. Taghavi-Moharamli, J. Köykkä, G. Grassi, S. Rossi, J. Brandao De Melo, D. Oom, A. Branco, J. San-Miguel, and E. Vignati. 2023. *GHG Emissions of All World Countries*. Luxembourg: Publications Office of the European Union. https://doi.org/10.2760/953322.

Cust, James, David Manley, and Giorgia Cecchinato. 2017. "Unburnable Wealth of Nations." *Finance and Development* 54 (1): 46–9. https://www.imf.org/external/pubs/ft/fandd/2017/03/cust.htm.

Cust, James, David Mihalyi, and Alexis Rivera-Ballesteros. 2021. "The Economic Effects of Giant Oil and Gas Discoveries." In *Giant Fields of the Decade: 2010–2020*, edited by Charles Sternback, Robert K. Merrill, and John C. Dolson, 21–36. American Association of Petroleum Geologists.

Cust, James, and Albert G. Zeufack, eds. 2023. *Africa's Resource Future: Harnessing Natural Resources for Economic Transformation during the Low-Carbon Transition*. Africa Development Forum. Washington, DC: World Bank. http://hdl.handle.net/10986/39599.

Desramaut, Nicolas Benjamin Claude. 2023. *Disclosable Version of the ISR—West Africa Coastal Areas Resilience Investment Project—P162337—Sequence No: 08 (English)*. Washington, DC: World Bank Group. http://documents.worldbank.org/curated/en/099175503102352733/P16233709e3fd707908ce4014a8e151a6e3.

Detges, Adrien, Daniel Klingenfeld, Christian König, Benjamin Pohl, Lukas Rüttinger, Jacob Schewe, Barbora Sedova, and Janani Vivekananda. 2020. "10 Insights on Climate Impacts and Peace: A Summary of What We Know." Adelphi Research Gemeinnützige GmbH, Berlin. https://publications.pik-potsdam.de/pubman/faces/ViewItemFullPage.jsp?itemId=item_24841_1.

Diallo, Yoro, and René Tapsoba. 2022. "Climate Shocks and Domestic Conflicts in Africa." IMF Working Paper WR/22/250, International Monetary Fund, Washington, DC. https://www.imf.org/en/Publications/WP/Issues/2022/12/16/Climate-Shocks-and-Domestic-Conflicts-in-Africa-527038.

Diffenbaugh, Noah S., and Marshall Burke. 2019. "Global Warming Has Increased Global Economic Inequality." *Proceedings of the National Academy of Sciences (PNAS)* 116 (20): 9808–13. https://doi.org/10.1073/pnas.1816020116.

Fang, Xiangming, Siddharth Kothari, Cameron McLoughlin, and M. Yenice. 2020. "The Economic Consequences of Conflict in Sub-Saharan Africa." IMF Working Paper WP/20/221, International Monetary Fund, Washington, DC. https://www.imf.org/en/Publications/WP/Issues/2020/10/30/The-Economic-Consequences-of-Conflict-in-Sub-Saharan-Africa-49834.

FSIN (Food Security Information Network) and Global Network against Food Crises. 2023. *Global Report of Food Crises 2023: Joint Analysis for Better Decisions*. Rome: FSIN. https://www.fsinplatform.org/global-report-food-crises-2023.

Garcin, Yannick, Enno Schefuß, Greta C. Dargie, Donna Hawthorne, Ian T. Lawson, David Sebag, George E. Biddulph, et al. 2022. "Hydroclimatic Vulnerability of Peat Carbon in the Central Congo Basin." *Nature* 612: 277–82. https://doi.org/10.1038/s41586-022-05389-3.

GCA (Global Center on Adaptation). 2021. *State and Trends in Adaptation Report: How Adaptation Can Make Africa Safer, Greener and More Prosperous in a Warming World*. Rotterdam, the Netherlands: GCA. https://gca.org/wp-content/uploads/2022/07/GCA_STA_2021_Complete_low-res.pdf.

Georgieva, Kristalina, Vitor Gaspar, and Ceyla Pazarbasioglu. 2022. "Poor and Vulnerable Countries Need Support to Adapt to Climate Change." *IMF Blog*, March 23, 2022. https://www.imf.org/en/Blogs/Articles/2022/03/23/blog032322-poor-and-vulnerable-countris-need-support-to-adapt-to-climate-change.

GFDRR (Global Facility for Disaster Reduction and Recovery). 2019. *Result Area 5 Africa Disaster Risk Financing Initiative: Activity Report 2018–2019*. Building Disaster Resilience in Sub-Saharan Africa Program. Washington, DC: GFDRR. https://www.gfdrr.org/en/publication/africa-disaster-risk-financing-initiative-activity-report-2018-2019.

Global Commission on Adaptation. 2019. *Adapt Now: A Global Call for Leadership on Climate Resilience*. Rotterdam, the Netherlands: Global Center on Adaptation. https://gca.org/wp-content/uploads/2019/09/GlobalCommission_Report_FINAL.pdf.

Gürsan, C., and V. de Gooyert. 2021. "The Systemic Impact of a Transition Fuel: Does Natural Gas Help or Hinder the Energy Transition?" *Renewable and Sustainable Energy Reviews* 138: 110552. https://doi.org/10.1016/j.rser.2020.110552.

Hallegatte, Stephane, Mook Bangalore, Laura Bonzanigo, Marianne Fay, Tamaro Kane, Ulf Narloch, Julie Rozenberg, David Treguer, and Adrien Vogt-Schilb. 2016. *Shock Waves: Managing the Impacts of Climate Change on Poverty*. Climate Change and Development Series. Washington, DC: World Bank. https://hdl.handle.net/10986/22787.

Hallegatte, Stéphane, Jun Rentschler, and Julie Rozenberg. 2019. *Lifelines: The Resilient Infrastructure Opportunity*. Sustainable Infrastructure Series. Washington, DC: World Bank. https://doi.org/10.1596/978-1-4648-1430-3.

Harris, Nancy L., David A. Gibbs, Alessandro Baccini, Richard A. Birdsey, Sytze de Bruin, Mary Farina, Lola Fatoyinba, et al. 2021. "Global Maps of Twenty-First Century Forest Carbon Fluxes." *Nature Climate Change* 11: 234–40. https://doi.org/10.1038/s41558-020-00976-6.

Havlík, Petr, Hugo Valin, Mykola Gusti, Erwin Schmid, David Leclère, Nicklas Forsell, Mario Herrero, et al. 2015. "Climate Change Impacts and Mitigation in the Developing World: An Integrated Assessment of the Agriculture and Forestry Sectors." Policy Research Working Paper 7477, World Bank, Washington, DC. http://hdl.handle.net/10986/23441.

Hund, Kirsten, Daniele La Porta, Thao P. Fabregas, Tim Laing, and John Drexhage. 2020. *Minerals for Climate Action: The Mineral Intensity of the Clean Energy Transition*. Washington, DC: World Bank. https://pubdocs.worldbank.org/en/961711588875536384/Minerals-for-Climate-Action-The-Mineral-Intensity-of-the-Clean-Energy-Transition.pdf.

IDMC (Internal Displacement Monitoring Centre). 2023. *2023 Global Report on Internal Displacement*. Geneva: IDMC. https://www.internal-displacement.org/global-report/grid2023/.

IEA (International Energy Agency). 2018. *World Energy Outlook 2018*. Paris: IEA. https://www.iea.org/reports/world-energy-outlook-2018.

IEA (International Energy Agency). 2019. *The Role of Gas in Today's Energy Transitions*. Paris: IEA. https://www.iea.org/reports/the-role-of-gas-in-todays-energy-transitions.

IEA (International Energy Agency). 2022. *Africa Energy Outlook 2022*. Paris: IEA. https://www.iea.org/reports/africa-energy-outlook-2022.

IMF (International Monetary Fund). 2021. "Private Finance for Development: Wishful Thinking or Thinking Out of the Box?" IMF Departmental Paper 2021/011, IMF, Washington, DC. https://www.imf.org/en/Publications/Departmental-Papers-Policy-Papers/Issues/2021/05/14/Private-Finance-for-Development-50157.

IMF (International Monetary Fund). 2023. *Regional Economic Outlook: Sub-Saharan Africa: The Big Funding Squeeze*. Washington, DC: IMF. https://www.imf.org/en/Publications/REO/SSA/Issues/2023/04/14/regional-economic-outlook-for-sub-saharan-africa-april-2023.

IRENA (International Renewable Energy Agency). 2022. *Renewable Power Generation Costs in 2021*. Abu Dhabi: IRENA. https://www.irena.org/publications/2022/Jul/Renewable-Power-Generation-Costs-in-2021.

IRENA (International Renewable Energy Agency) and AfDB (African Development Bank). 2022. *Renewable Energy Market Analysis: Africa and Its Regions*. Abu Dhabi: IRENA and AfDB. https://www.irena.org/publications/2022/Jan/Renewable-Energy-Market-Analysis-Africa.

Ireri, Benson, and Rebekah Shirley. 2021. "Powering Growth." *Finance & Development Magazine*, September 2021. https://www.imf.org/en/Publications/fandd/issues/2021/09/fighting-climate-change-in-Africa-ireri.

KfW (KfW Development Bank), GIZ (Deutsche Gesellschaft für Internationale Zusammenarbeit), and IRENA (International Renewable Energy Agency). 2021. "The Renewable Energy Transition in Africa." KfW, Frankfurt am Main; GIZ, Eschborn; IRENA, Abu Dhabi. https://www.irena.org/Publications/2021/March/The-Renewable-Energy-Transition-in-Africa.

Kosec, Katrina, Peter Laderach, and Sandra Ruckstuhl. 2023. *Fragility, Conflict, and Migration*. Washington, DC: CGIAR System Organization. https://hdl.handle.net/10568/130336.

Kray, Holger, and Shobha Shetty. 2020. "The Locust Plague: Fighting a Crisis within a Crisis." *Voices* (blog), April 14, 2020. https://blogs.worldbank.org/voices/locust-plague-fighting-crisis-within-crisis.

Kurtzer, Jacob, Sierra Ballard, and Hareem Fatima Abdullah. 2022. *Concurrent Crises in the Horn of Africa*. Washington, DC: Center for Strategic and International Studies. https://www.csis.org/analysis/concurrent-crises-horn-africa.

Leke, Acha, Peter Gaius-Obaseki, and Oliver Onyekweli. 2022. "The Future of African Oil and Gas: Positioning for the Energy Transition." McKinsey & Company. https://www.mckinsey.com/industries/oil-and-gas/our-insights/the-future-of-african-oil-and-gas-positioning-for-the-energy-transition#/.

Mansourian, Stephanie, and Nora Berrahmouni. 2021. *Review of Forest and Landscape Restoration in Africa*. Accra: Food and Agriculture Organization of the United Nations and AUDA-NEPAD. https://doi.org/10.4060/cb6111en.

Matola, Joseph U., Olufunso Somorin, Alex Benkenstein, Romy Chevallier, and Adrian Joseph. 2023. "Bridge or Cul-de-Sac? The Role of Africa's Natural Gas Resources in the Green Transition." *T20 Policy Brief*, June. https://www.orfonline.org/wp-content/uploads/2023/06/T20_PolicyBrief_TF4_Africa-Natural-Gas.pdf.

Megevand, Carole. 2013. *Deforestation Trends in the Congo Basin: Reconciling Economic Growth and Forest Protection*. Washington, DC: World Bank.

Mensah, Justice T. 2018. "Jobs! Electricity Shortages and Unemployment in Africa." Policy Research Working Paper 8415, World Bank, Washington, DC.

Mo Ibrahim Foundation. 2022. *The Road to COP27: Making Africa's Case in the Global Climate Debate*. Forum Report. London: Mo Ibrahim Foundation. https://mo.ibrahim.foundation/sites/default /files/2022-07/2022-forum-report.pdf.

Mustasilta, Katariina. 2021. "The Future of Conflict Prevention: Preparing for a Hotter, Increasingly Digital and Fragmented 2030." Chaillot Paper 167, EU Institute for Security Studies, Paris. https://www.iss.europa.eu/sites/default/files/EUISSFiles/CP_167_0.pdf.

Mutasa, Colleen. 2022. "Chapter 11—Revisiting the Impacts of Tropical Cyclone Idai in Southern Africa." In *Climate Impacts on Extreme Weather*, edited by Victor Ongoma and Hossein Tabari, 175–89. Amsterdam: Elsevier. https://doi.org/10.1016/B978-0-323-88456-3.00012-5.

Mutezo, G., and J. Mulopo. 2021. "A Review of Africa's Transition from Fossil Fuels to Renewable Energy Using Circular Economy Principles." *Renewable and Sustainable Energy Reviews* 137: 110609. https://doi.org/10.1016/j.rser.2020.110609.

Naidoo, Dhesigen, and Manisha Gulati. 2022. "Understanding Africa's Climate and Human Security Risks." Policy Brief, Institute for Security Studies. https://issafrica.org/research/policy-brief /understanding-africas-climate-and-human-security-risks.

OECD (Organisation for Economic Co-operation and Development). 2022. *Climate Tipping Points: Insights for Effective Policy Action*. Paris: OECD Publishing. https://doi.org/10.1787 /abc5a69e-en.

OECD (Organisation for Economic Co-operation and Development) and Sahel and West Africa Club. 2020. *Africa's Urbanisation Dynamics 2020: Africapolis, Mapping a New Urban Geography*. West African Studies. Paris: OECD Publishing. https://doi.org/10.1787/b6bccb81-en.

Oliver, Emmie, and Lizzie Marsters. 2022. "Nature-Based Solutions in Sub-Saharan Africa for Climate and Water Resilience: A Methodology for Evaluating the Regional Status of Investments in Nature-Based Solutions from a Scan of Multilateral Development Bank Portfolios." Technical Note, World Resources Institute, Washington, DC. https://www.gfdrr .org/en/publication/nature-based-solutions-sub-saharan-africa-climate-and-water -resilience#:~:text=Nature%2DBased%20Solutions%20(NBS),to%20water%20and%20 climate%20risks.

Opitz-Stapleton, Sarah, Laura Cramer, Fatima Kaba, Leah Gichuki, Olena Borodyna, Todd Crane, Sidi Diabang, Sanjana Bahadur, Aliou Diouf, and Emmanuel Seck. 2021. "Transboundary Climate and Adaptation Risks in Africa: Perceptions from 2021." Supporting Pastoralism and Agriculture in Recurrent and Protracted Crises. https://www.sparc-knowledge.org/resources/transboundary -climate-and-adaptation-risks-africa-perceptions-2021.

Palik, Júlia, Anna Marie Obermeier, and Siri A. Rustad. 2022. "Conflict Trends in Africa, 1989–2021." PRIO Paper, Peace Research Institute Oslo, Oslo.

Pearce, Oliver. 2022. "The Cost to Africa: Drastic Economic Damage from Climate Change." Christian Aid. https://www.christianaid.org.uk/sites/default/files/2022-11/the-cost-to -africa.pdf.

Rigaud, Kanta Kumari, Alex de Sherbinin, Bryan Jones, Susana Adamo, David Maleki, Nathalie E. Abu-Ata, Anna Taeko Casals Fernandez, Anmol Arora, Tricia Chai-Onn, and Briar Mills. 2021a. "Groundswell Africa: Internal Climate Migration in the Lake Victoria Basin Countries." World Bank, Washington, DC. http://hdl.handle.net/10986/36403.

Rigaud, Kanta Kumari, Alex de Sherbinin, Bryan Jones, Susana Adamo, David Maleki, Nathalie E. Abu-Ata, Anna Taeko Casals Fernandez, Anmol Arora, Tricia Chai-Onn, and Briar Mills. 2021b. "Groundswell Africa: Internal Climate Migration in West African Countries." World Bank, Washington, DC. http://hdl.handle.net/10986/36404.

Rigaud, Kanta Kumari, Alex de Sherbinin, Bryan Jones, Jonas Bergmann, Viviane Clement, Kayly Ober, Jacob Schewe, Susana Adamo, Brent McCusker, Silke Heuser, and Amelia Midgley. 2018. "Groundswell: Preparing for Internal Climate Migration." World Bank, Washington, DC. http://hdl.handle.net/10986/29461.

Rockström, Johan, Joyeeta Gupta, Dahe Qin, Steven J. Lade, Jesse F. Abrams, Lauren S. Andersen, David I. Armstrong McKay, et al. 2023. "Safe and Just Earth System Boundaries." *Nature* 619: 102–11. https://doi.org/10.1038/s41586-023-06083-8.

Rüttinger, Lukas, Gerald Stang, Dan Smith, Dennis Tänzler, and Janani Vivekananda. 2015. *A New Climate for Peace—Taking Action on Climate and Fragility Risks.* Berlin: Adelphi consult GmbH. https://adelphi.de/en/publications/a-new-climate-for-peace-taking-action-on-climate-and-fragility-risks.

Schwerhoff, Gregor, and Mouhamadou Sy. 2020. "Where the Sun Shines." *Finance & Development Magazine*, March. https://www.imf.org/en/Publications/fandd/issues/2020/03/powering-Africa-with-solar-energy-sy.

Sorí, Rogert, Raquel Nieto, Sergio M. Vicente-Serrano, Anita Drumond, and Luis Gimeno. 2017. "A Lagrangian Perspective of the Hydrological Cycle in the Congo River Basin." *Earth System Dynamics* 8 (3): 653–75. https://doi.org/10.5194/esd-8-653-2017.

Tarif, Kheira. 2023. *Climate Change and Security in West Africa: Regional Perspectives on Addressing Climate-Related Security Risks.* Stockholm: Stockholm International Peace Research Institute. https://www.sipri.org/publications/2023/partner-publications/climate-change-and-security-west-africa-regional-perspectives-addressing-climate-related-security.

Trisos, Christopher H., Ibidun O. Adelekan, Edmond Totin, Ayansina Ayanlade, Jackson Efitre, Adugna Gemeda, Kanungwe Kalaba, Christopher Lennard, Catherine Masao, Yunus Mgaya, Grace Ngaruiya, Daniel Olago, Nicholas P. Simpson, and Sumaya Zakieldeen. 2022. "Africa." In *Climate Change 2022: Impacts, Adaptation and Vulnerability. Contribution of Working Group II to the Sixth Assessment Report of the Intergovernmental Panel on Climate Change*, edited by Hans-Otto Pörtner, Debrad C. Roberts, Melinda Tignor, Elvira S. Poloczanska, Katja Mintenbeck, Andrés Alegría, Marlies Craig, Stefanie Langsdorf, Sina Löschke, Vincent Möller, Andrew Okem, and Bardhyl Rama, 1285–455. Cambridge, UK: Cambridge University Press. https://doi.org/10.1017/9781009325844.011.

Tyukavina, Alexandra, Matthew C. Hansen, Peter Potapov, Diana Parker, Chima Okpa, Stephen V. Stehman, and Svetlana Turubanova. 2018. "Congo Basin Forest Loss Dominated by Increasing Smallholder Clearing." *Science Advances* 4 (11): eaat2993. https://doi.org/10.1126/sciadv.aat2993.

UNCTAD (United Nations Conference on Trade and Development). 2023. *Commodities at a Glance: Special Issue on Access to Energy in Sub-Saharan Africa.* No. 17. UNCTAD/DITC/COM/2023/1. New York: United Nations. https://unctad.org/publication/commodities-glance-special-issue-access-energy-sub-saharan-africa.

UN DESA (United Nations Department of Economic and Social Affairs). 2019. *World Population Prospects 2019: Highlights.* ST/ESA/SER.A/423. New York: United Nations. https://population.un.org/wpp/assets/Files/WPP2019_Highlights.pdf.

UN DESA (United Nations Department of Economic and Social Affairs). 2022. *World Population Prospects 2022: Summary of Results.* UN DESA/POP/2022/TR/NO. 3. New York: United Nations.

UNDRR (United Nations Office for Disaster Risk Reduction), and WMO (World Meteorological Organization). 2022. "Global Status of Multi-Hazard Early Warning Systems: Target G." UNDRR, Geneva. https://www.undrr.org/publication/global-status-multi-hazard-early-warning-systems -target-g.

UNECA (United Nations Economic Commission for Africa). 2016. *Human and Economic Cost of Conflict in the Horn of Africa: Implications for a Transformative and Inclusive Post-Conflict Development*. Addis Ababa: UNECA. https://repository.uneca.org/handle/10855/23726.

UNECA (United Nations Economic Commission for Africa), African Union Commission, United Nations Development Programme, and African Development Bank. 2020. *2020 Africa Sustainable Development Report: Towards Recovery and Sustainable Development in the Decade of Action*. Addis Ababa: UNECA. https://repository.uneca.org/handle/10855/47554.

USAID (United States Agency for International Development). 2018. "Climate Risk Profile: West Africa." USAID Fact Sheet, December 6. https://www.climatelinks.org/resources/climate -risk-profile-west-africa.

Van der Ent, Rudi J., Hubert H. G. Savenije, Bettina Schaefli, and Susan C. Steele-Dunne. 2010. "Origin and Fate of Atmospheric Moisture over Continents." *Water Resources Research* 46 (9): W09525. https://doi.org/10.1029/2010WR009127.

Weny, Kathrin, Rachel Snow, and Sainan Zhang. 2017. *The Demographic Dividend Atlas for Africa: Tracking the Potential for a Demographic Dividend*. New York: United Nations Population Fund. https://www.unfpa.org/resources/demographic-dividend-atlas-africa-tracking-potential -demographic-dividend.

Winsemius, Hessel C., Brenden Jongman, Ted I. E. Veldkamp, Stephane Hallegatte, Mook Bangalore, and Philip J. Ward. 2018. "Disaster Risk, Climate Change, and Poverty: Assessing the Global Exposure of Poor People to Floods and Droughts." *Environment and Development Economics* 23 (3): 328–48. https://doi.org/10.1017/S1355770X17000444.

WMO (World Meteorological Organization). 2021. *WMO Atlas of Mortality and Economic Losses from Weather, Climate and Water Extremes (1970–2019)*. WMO-No. 1267. Geneva: WMO. https://library .wmo.int/idurl/4/57564.

WMO (World Meteorological Organization). 2023a. *State of the Climate in Africa 2022*. WMO-No. 1330. Geneva: WMO. https://library.wmo.int/idurl/4/67761.

WMO (World Meteorological Organization). 2023b. *WMO Global Annual to Decadal Climate Update (Target Years: 2023 and 2023–2027)*. Geneva: WMO. https://library.wmo.int/idurl/4/66224.

World Bank. 2013. "Africa's Pulse, October 2013: An Analysis of Issues Shaping Africa's Economic Future." World Bank, Washington, DC. http://hdl.handle.net/10986/20237.

World Bank. 2014. "Clean and Improved Cooking in Sub-Saharan Africa: A Landscape Report." World Bank, Washington, DC. http://hdl.handle.net/10986/22521.

World Bank. 2017. *The Africa Competitiveness Report 2017—Addressing Africa's Demographic Dividend*. Africa Competitiveness Reports. Washington, DC: World Bank. http://documents.worldbank.org /curated/en/733321493793700840/The-Africa-competitiveness-report-2017-Addressing -Africa-s-demographic-dividend.

World Bank. 2020a. "The Next Generation Africa Climate Business Plan: Ramping Up Development-Centered Climate Action." World Bank, Washington, DC. http://hdl.handle.net/10986/34098.

World Bank. 2020b. "World Bank Group Strategy for Fragility, Conflict, and Violence 2020–2025." World Bank, Washington, DC. http://documents.worldbank.org/curated/en/844591582815510521 /World-Bank-Group-Strategy-for-Fragility-Conflict-and-Violence-2020-2025.

World Bank. 2021a. *Africa's Pulse, No. 24, October 2021: Climate Change Adaptation and Economic Transformation in Sub-Saharan Africa*. Washington, DC: World Bank. https://openknowledge .worldbank.org/server/api/core/bitstreams/34f98cfe-b27b-58ad-a0cb-99568577e730/content.

World Bank. 2021b. *The Changing Wealth of Nations 2021: Managing Assets for the Future*. Washington, DC: World Bank. http://hdl.handle.net/10986/36400.

World Bank. 2022a. *Angola Country Climate and Development Report*. CCDR Series. Washington, DC: World Bank. http://hdl.handle.net/10986/38361.

World Bank. 2022b. *Cameroon Country Climate and Development Report*. CCDR Series. Washington, DC: World Bank. http://hdl.handle.net/10986/38242.

World Bank. 2022c. *Climate and Development: An Agenda for Action—Emerging Insights from World Bank Group 2021–22 Country Climate and Development Reports*. Washington, DC: World Bank. http://hdl.handle.net/10986/38220.

World Bank. 2022d. *G5 Sahel Region Country Climate and Development Report*. CCDR Series. Washington, DC: World Bank. http://hdl.handle.net/10986/37620.

World Bank. 2022e. *Ghana Country Climate and Development Report*. CCDR Series. Washington, DC: World Bank. http://hdl.handle.net/10986/38209.

World Bank. 2022f. *Malawi Country Climate and Development Report*. CCDR Series. Washington, DC: World Bank. http://hdl.handle.net/10986/38217.

World Bank. 2022g. "Reference Guide for Climate-Smart Public Investment." Climate Governance Papers, World Bank, Washington, DC. https://documents1.worldbank.org/curated/en/099455012 062224218/pdf/P1725690cd27300c30b5f101fd728276fe7.pdf.

World Bank. 2022h. *Rwanda Country Climate and Development Report*. CCDR Series. Washington, DC: World Bank. http://hdl.handle.net/10986/38067.

World Bank. 2022i. *South Africa Country Climate and Development Report*. CCDR Series. Washington, DC: World Bank. http://hdl.handle.net/10986/38216.

World Bank. 2023a. "Early Warning System Saves Lives in Mozambique." World Bank Feature Story, September 11, 2023. https://www.worldbank.org/en/news/feature/2023/09/11/early-warning -system-saves-lives-in-afe-mozambique.

World Bank. 2023b. "Leveraging Resource Wealth during the Low Carbon Transition." *Africa's Pulse*, No. 27 (April). World Bank, Washington, DC. http://hdl.handle.net/10986/39615.

World Bank. 2023c. "Strengthening Financial Resilience in Agriculture." Fact Sheet, Knowledge Exchange Series Part 2: Disaster Risk Financing Solutions for Climate-Resilient Livelihoods in the Agricultural Sector, World Bank, Washington, DC. https://www.financialprotectionforum.org /sites/default/files/Agri%20DRF%202%20-%20Webinar%201_Fact%20Sheet.pdf.

World Bank. 2023d. "World Bank Extends New Lifeline for Countries Hit by Natural Disasters." Fact Sheet, World Bank, Washington, DC. https://www.worldbank.org/en/news/factsheet/2023/12/01 /world-bank-extends-new-lifeline-for-countries-hit-by-natural-disasters.

World Bank. 2023e. *World Development Report 2023: Migrants, Refugees, and Societies*. Washington, DC: World Bank. doi:10.1596/978-1-4648-1941-4.

World Bank. 2024a. "Climate Resilient Debt Clause (CRDC)." Product Note, World Bank, Washington, DC. https://thedocs.worldbank.org/en/doc/6857abe91ef32973cfab7f689e9f00fe-0340012023 /original/CRDC-Product-note-EN.pdf.

World Bank. 2024b. "IBRD Catastrophe Deferred Drawdown Option (Cat DDO)." Product Note, World Bank, Washington, DC. https://thedocs.worldbank.org/en/doc/1820b53ad5cba038ff885cc 3758ba59f-0340012021/original/Cat-DDO-IBRD-Product-Note.pdf.

World Bank Group. 2024. *People in a Changing Climate: From Vulnerability to Action—Insights from World Bank Group Country Climate and Development Reports Covering 72 Economies.* Washington, DC: World Bank. http://hdl.handle.net/10986/42395.

Yingi, E. 2023. "Youth Bulge as a Peacebuilding Opportunity for Africa: The Case of Zimbabwe's Youth Empowerment Programmes." *Journal of Asian and African Studies*, May 16. https://journals.sagepub.com/doi/10.1177/00219096231173392.

CHAPTER 3

Productivity

Cesar Calderon and Ayan Qu

Summary

Labor productivity trends in Sub-Saharan Africa reveal that the region has lost ground relative to aspirational and global efficiency benchmarks over the past decades; however, it has the potential of a turnaround in the 21st century as seen during the region's latest growth spell for the period 2000–14. The persistence of the productivity gap is attributed to relatively lower endowments of physical and human capital relative to the region's population (or labor force), and inefficiencies in the use of the factors of production attributed to misallocation of these resources or barriers to within-firm productivity growth. In other words, the problems of inefficient allocation and restrictions to firms' growth compound the problem of slow accumulation of physical and human capital in Africa.

At the macro level, allocative inefficiencies result from policies and institutions that introduce distortions in the decision-making process of individuals. Underdeveloped financial markets, for instance, pose challenges to occupational choices (entrepreneurial versus nonentrepreneurial jobs), access to education, and participation in the formal sector. At the micro level, within-firm inefficiencies can also arise that restrict adoption of best practices in technology and management, including lack of finance to invest in new products and technologies, and lack of information or awareness among firms about new production technologies (information barriers).

This chapter presents facts on the evolution of productivity and its components, analyzes factors constraining productivity growth, and argues that policies that eliminate distortions to resource allocation and barriers to frontier knowledge can boost productivity and aggregate output. Top priorities for policy makers include investing in human capital that builds fundamental skills and meets the demand of the evolving labor market; expanding infrastructure including energy, transportation, and digital communications for inclusive growth; and leveraging technologies to empower workers and expand production frontiers.

Context

The sluggish growth performance of Sub-Saharan Africa over the past decades has led to a widening gap relative to an aspirational benchmark (the East Asia and

Pacific region) and the global efficiency benchmark (the United States) (Calderón 2021). The widening gap in labor productivity in Sub-Saharan Africa is attributed to both disparities in factor endowments (as well as the pace of accumulation) and increasing disparities in total factor productivity, or TFP (refer to, for example, Caselli 2005; Hsieh and Klenow 2010; Jones 2016; Klenow and Rodriguez-Clare 1997). This productivity gap implies that, on average, countries in the region tend to produce less than the aspirational and efficiency benchmarks with the same amount of inputs (labor, human and physical capital, land, and intermediate inputs, among others).

Growth in real economic activity accelerated over the past decades to an annual average rate of 4.9 percent during 2000–14, from 1.8 percent during 1978–99. Following the plunge in commodity prices and before the COVID-19 pandemic, however, growth in the region slowed to 2.4 percent per year during 2015–19. Furthermore, the region has less than stellar growth performance when accounting for its rising population: from –1 percent during 1978–99, real gross domestic product (GDP) per capita grew at an annual average rate of 2 percent during 2000–14. Recent growth forecasts point to a contraction in real growth per capita in Sub-Saharan Africa over the period 2015–25 (at an annual rate of –0.1 percent), thus marking a lost decade of growth (World Bank 2023).

When compared with the average living standards of the rest of the world, GDP per capita in Sub-Saharan Africa has declined over the past three decades. During the period 1990–2022, three distinct periods can be identified in the evolution of Sub-Saharan Africa's real GDP per capita (figure 3.1): a declining trend during 1990–2000 (from 30 percent to 25 percent of the world average), stagnant GDP per capita relative to the world during 2000–14 (fluctuating around 25 percent), and a declining trend from 2014 to 2022 (from 25 percent to 22 percent of the world average).[1] The region's lack of convergence in living standards with the rest of the world largely results from its inability to sustain growth over time. If Sub-Saharan Africa had grown (in per capita terms) at the same pace as the global economy since 1990, its level of income per capita in 2022 would have been more than 40 percent higher than its actual level. If it had grown at the same pace as emerging East Asia, the region's income per capita would have been nearly three times its 2022 level.

The rapid growth of the Sub-Saharan African region in 2000–14, propelled by the supercycle of commodity prices and supported by sound macroeconomic policies before the global financial crisis, failed to be sustained over a longer period amid multiple shocks. At the onset of the 2014–15 plunge in commodity prices, GDP per capita of the region (as well as in the Eastern and Southern Africa and the Western and Central Africa subregions) resumed the downward trajectory that may not stop along the forecasting horizon. The economic fallout from the different covariate shocks affecting the global economy—the COVID-19 pandemic, climate shocks, the Russian Federation's invasion of Ukraine, and global inflation—is partly deactivating the global growth engine for African economies, thus limiting the region's growth prospects over the near future.[2]

FIGURE 3.1 GDP per capita in African subregions relative to the world, 1990–2025

GDP per capita (% of world average)

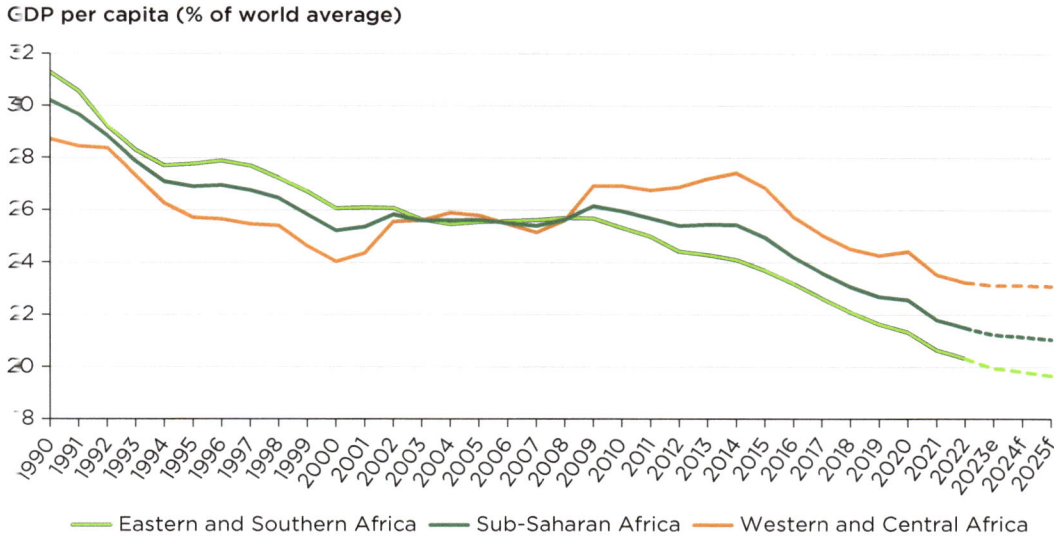

— Eastern and Southern Africa   — Sub-Saharan Africa   — Western and Central Africa

Source: World Bank, World Development Indicators, https://data.worldbank.org/indicator/NY.GDP .PCAP.CD.
Note: Percentage for 2023 is estimated; percentages for 2024 and 2025 are forecasted.

The performance of economic activity (in per capita terms and relative to the world) has been insufficient to contribute to significant poverty reduction. In fact, poverty rates have declined at a significantly slower pace than in other world regions while the (absolute) number of poor people in the region has increased. The percentage of the population living on less than US$2.15 a day was expected to decline from a peak of 37.9 percent in 2020 to 36.5 percent in 2024. Given the region's demographics, however, this decrease translates into an increase in the number of extreme poor—from 437 million in 2020 to 464 million in 2024. The slow reduction of extreme poverty in the region reflects not only the poor growth performance of the region but also its low conversion of growth into poverty reduction (relative to other regions).[3]

Boosting productivity is essential to sustain economic growth in the region (refer to Kim and Loayza 2019 and references therein). Throughout economic history, economic policies to foster sustained and inclusive growth have commonly included a focus on productivity. Improving productivity has been associated with creative destruction and enterprise renewal during high-income countries' recovery since the Great Depression (Hicks 1939; Schumpeter 1942). Productivity has also been linked to the structural transformation of developing countries that have reallocated factors of production from less to more productive sectors of the economy (Chenery 1960; Herrendorf, Rogerson, and Valentinyi 2014; Lewis 1954). The series of megatrends and covariate shocks affecting the global economy have significantly raised interest in understanding the sources of growth and productivity (refer to Ben-David and Papell 1998; Jones 2016; Jones and Romer 2010; Jorgenson, Ho, and Stiroh 2008, among others). Creating resilience to global shocks (for example, financial crises, climate change, or pandemics) while leveraging megatrends (globalization and free trade in Africa, the digital revolution, and the economic emergence of Asia in the global economy) can help African economies significantly raise their productivity, incomes, and standards of living.

Sources of productivity growth

Productivity growth can help countries allocate resources more efficiently to produce along their own production possibility frontier or to expand that frontier (refer to Cusolito and Maloney 2018 for more details). In this context, economic policies to boost productivity operate through (at least one of the following) three different channels (figure 3.2):

1. *Within-firm productivity growth* accounts for improved productivity of individual firms. It depends on changes in the efficiency and intensity with which inputs are used in production (that is, to upgrade firms) owing to increased firm capabilities, including improved managerial skills, labor skills, innovation, and technology adoption capacity.

2. *Between-firm productivity growth* reflects the role of factor reallocation across firms and sectors in determining aggregate productivity growth. An increase of this component implies that the most productive firms would command the largest amount of resources (capital, land, intermediate inputs, and labor, among others), resulting in sizeable output and productivity gains.[4] Optimally, the resources would be reallocated from the least to the most productive production units, thus enabling maximization of output. A strand of the literature argues that allocative inefficiencies at the firm or sector level can hold back productivity and may result from market imperfections (for example, regarding credit and land), preferential trade policies, size-dependent taxation policies, and informality, among other causes (refer to Calderón 2021; Restuccia and Rogerson 2017, as well as the references therein).

3. *Net entry of firms* accounts for productivity gains arising from the entry of high-productivity firms (relative to the industry average) and the exit of low-productivity firms (relative to the industry average). It captures the aggregate effect of firm churning (or turnover) on productivity growth. Understanding this component involves examining the drivers that affect the entry of high-productivity firms and the exit of low-productivity ones—that is, analyzing the determinants of entrepreneurship, including business climate, and social norms.

FIGURE 3.2 Main sources of productivity growth across firms and sectors

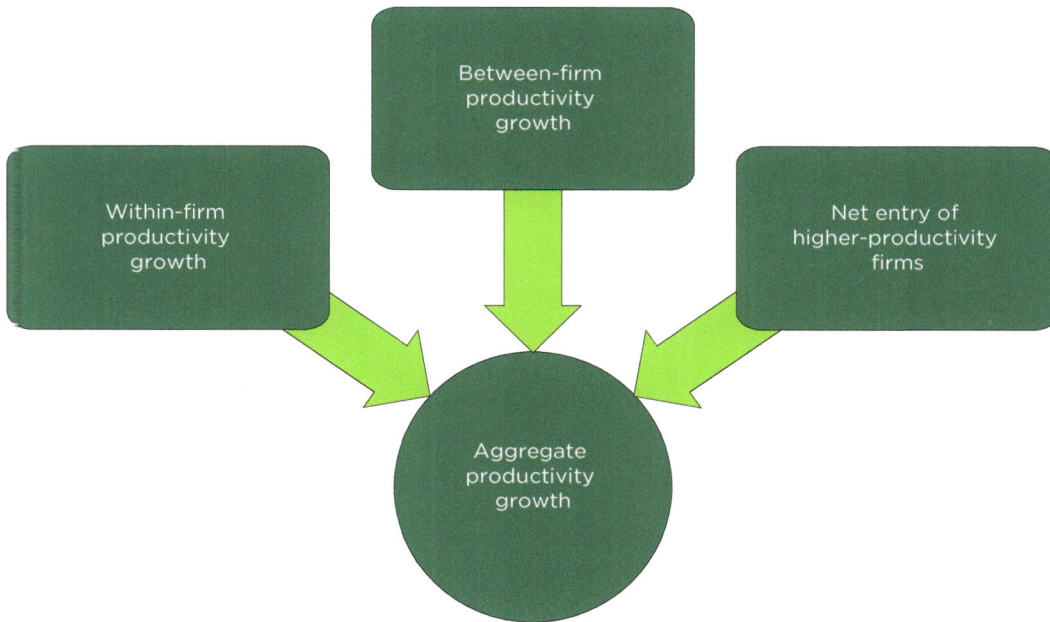

Source: Cusolito and Maloney 2018.

Narrowing the productivity gap in Sub-Saharan Africa in relation to aspirational and world frontier benchmarks will require implementing economic policies that operate through these complementary and interrelated channels. To sum up, boosting productivity in the region will require actionable policies that (1) accelerate the speed of diffusion and adaptation of technology as well as the adoption of best production organization and management practices (Bloom et al. 2013; Bloom and Van Reenen 2007; Parente and Prescott 2005); and (2) improve the allocation of productive resources across firms and across sectors, including the exit of low-productivity firms from the industry and the emergence of new high-productivity firms (Foster, Haltiwanger, and Krizan 2001; Hsieh and Klenow 2009; Restuccia and Rogerson 2008, 2017).

Engineering a steady postpandemic growth recovery will require an agenda that promotes sustained productivity-driven growth that creates more and better-quality jobs, especially for lower-income, less skilled people.[5] The growth experienced in Sub-Saharan Africa over the past decades has not contributed significantly to the creation of high-quality jobs for more people. Despite growing at an annual rate of 2.8 percent during its 2000–14 growth spell, the region experienced only a modest increase in the share of working-age individuals with wage jobs, from 14 percent to 16 percent. Recent estimates show that, on average, for an additional percentage point increase in growth among Sub-Saharan African countries, the proportion of workers with wage jobs increases by 0.04 percent. This disappointing translation of growth into jobs is specific to the region: East Asian countries produce roughly twice the number of waged jobs for a similar increase in growth (World Bank 2023).

Facts

Labor productivity trends in Sub-Saharan Africa reveal that the region has lost ground relative to the rest of the world. More specifically, the sluggish growth of output per worker in Sub-Saharan Africa has led to a widening gap in labor productivity relative to two familiar benchmarks: an aspirational development benchmark constituted by the East Asia and Pacific region, and a global efficiency benchmark proxied by the United States. On average, output per worker in Sub-Saharan Africa relative to the United States declined from 10.5 percent in 1960 to 7.7 percent in 2019, although its downward trend was not monotonic (figure 3.3). It reveals the low and stagnant levels of labor productivity in the region over the past decades and the inability of the region to sustain growth over time and relative to other regions in the world. Unlike in Sub-Saharan Africa, relative labor productivity in the East Asia and Pacific region increased monotonically over the past six decades. On average, its real output per worker compared with that in the United States climbed from 5.5 percent in 1960 to 21 percent in 2019.

A closer look at figure 3.3 shows that Sub-Saharan Africa exhibits long swings in real income per capita compared to its Asian counterparts, but also that it has lost its edge over them in the past decades. People engaged in employment in Sub-Saharan Africa were nearly twice as productive as those in the East Asia and Pacific region in 1960: specifically, they were 10 percent more productive than people in Indonesia and the Republic of Korea, and about twice as productive as the Thai labor force. By 2021, East Asian workers were nearly three times as productive as those in Sub-Saharan Africa

FIGURE 3.3 **Labor productivity in Sub-Saharan Africa compared with benchmark groups, 1960–2019**

% relative to the United States

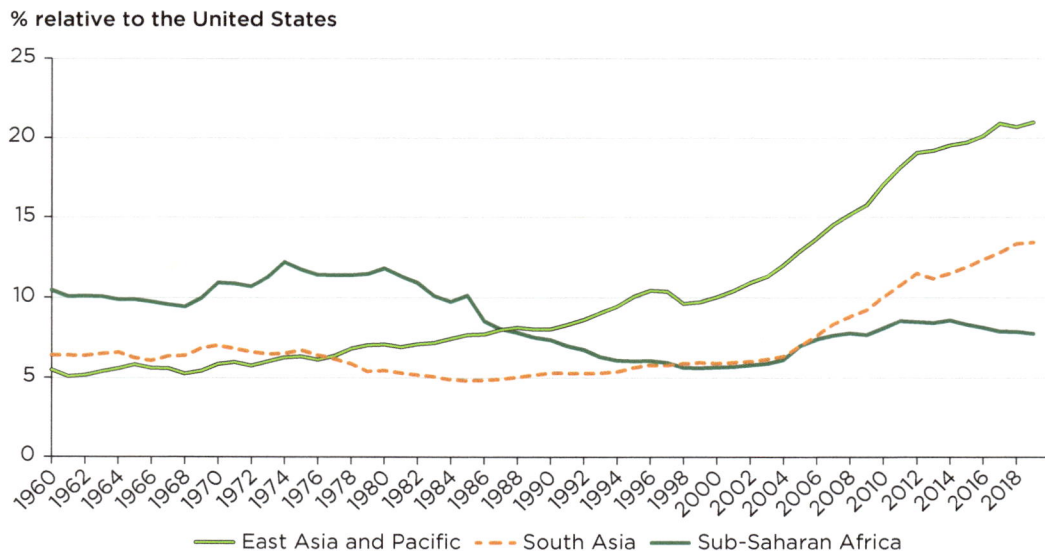

Source: Based on data from Penn World Table version 10.01, https://www.rug.nl/ggdc/productivity/pwt/?lang=en.

and, notably, workers in Korea and Singapore were on average more than eight times as productive as those in the region, whereas laborers in Thailand were more than three times as productive. The contrasting evolution of labor productivity in Sub-Saharan Africa and East Asia indicates not only differences in the pace of human and physical capital accumulation but also a growing divergence in TFP between the two regions.

Looking at the evolution of labor productivity for the region as a whole fails to account for the heterogeneity of country growth experiences in Sub-Saharan Africa over the past 50 years (figure 3.4). Nearly 40 percent of the countries in the region had greater relative labor productivity in 2019 than in 1970. Real output per worker relative to the United States increased by 70 percent over the past five decades in Ethiopia, almost doubled in Mali, and increased about sevenfold in Botswana.[6] In contrast, labor productivity declined relative to aspirational and global efficiency benchmarks for most Sub-Saharan African countries during 1970–2019 (23 out of 37 countries with available data). The countries that lost more ground in relation to these benchmarks include the Central African Republic, the Democratic Republic of Congo, Liberia, and Niger. Relative labor productivity in the Democratic Republic of Congo and Liberia in 2019 was about one-fourth of that in 1970, whereas relative labor productivity in the Central African Republic and Niger in 2019 was one-third of the levels in 1970 (figure 3.4). The question that emerges from these facts is "What explains the dismal performance on labor productivity in some countries of Sub-Saharan Africa compared with the rest of the world?"

FIGURE 3.4 **Real GDP per worker, selected countries in Sub-Saharan Africa, 1970 and 2019**

Real GDP per worker (United States = 1.0)

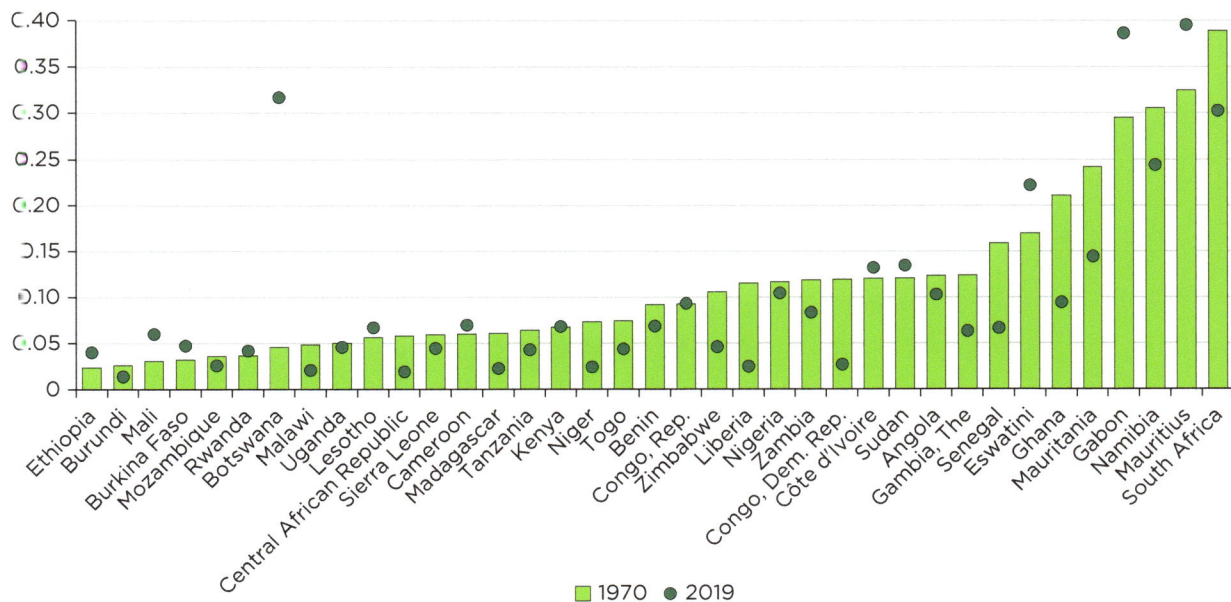

Source: Based on data from Penn World Table version 10.01, https://www.rug.nl/ggdc/productivity/pwt/?lang=en.

What explains the productivity gap in Africa? A development accounting analysis

The development accounting approach suggests that differences in the level of relative output per worker between Sub-Saharan Africa and global efficiency benchmarks (for example, the United States) can be attributed to the fact that the region has relatively lower amounts (endowments) of factors of production—physical and human capital, among others—other than raw labor, and that the region combines these factors of production in a less efficient manner. Assuming a constant returns to scale Cobb-Douglas technology, the gap in labor productivity compared with the global efficiency benchmark can be expressed as

$$\frac{y_t}{y_t^*} = \frac{A_t}{A_t^*} \left(\frac{k_t}{k_t^*} \right)^{\frac{\alpha}{1-\alpha}} \frac{h_t}{h_t^*} = \frac{A_t}{A_t^*} \frac{F_t}{F_t^*} \tag{3.1}$$

where y_t is labor productivity, k_t is the capital-output ratio, h_t is the index of human capital, and A_t denotes the TFP measured in labor-augmenting units. Note that variables with a superscript "*" denote the global efficiency benchmark (the United States). Note also that $\frac{F_t}{F_t^*}$ denotes the differences in factor endowments, whereas $\frac{A_t}{A_t^*}$ represents the differences in the efficient use of these factors.

Development accounting conducted for countries around the world shows the following (Jones 2016):

- The contribution of differences in physical capital to differences in labor productivity across countries is small. In fact, differences in capital-output ratio across countries explain about 8 percent of the labor productivity gap in relation to the United States in 2019, and this share is slightly lower when it comes to differences in relative capital-output ratio across Sub-Saharan African countries (7 percent). This finding could be attributed to the fact that cross-country differences in the marginal product of capital—which, under certain assumptions, is proportional to the capital-output ratio—are not statistically significant.[7] The literature corroborates the weak correlation between real GDP per worker and the capital-output ratio (Feenstra, Inklaar, and Timmer 2015).

- The contribution of human capital is larger than that of capital-output ratios in explaining the productivity gap across countries but remains modest at best. Cross-country differences in relative endowments of human capital account for 17 percent of the labor productivity gap in relation to the United States in 2019, a share comparable to that of differences across Sub-Saharan African countries (16 percent). The region could see its labor productivity gap reduced by a factor of 2 with increased educational attainment, out of an overall 13-fold gap in relation to the United States. Narrowing the gap in educational attainment can reduce the labor productivity gap in relation to the United States by a factor as small as 1.3 (Botswana) and as large as 3.1 (Mozambique).

- The preceding two findings imply that differences in TFP are the largest contributor to labor productivity differences. On average, differences in TFP across countries in the world can help explain 75 percent of the gap in labor productivity in relation to the United States in 2019, a comparable share to that of Sub-Saharan African economies (77 percent) and other developing countries (74 percent). Figure 3.5 plots the relative GDP per worker against the relative TFP for 135 countries in 2019—including 37 Sub-Saharan African countries. Relative labor productivity and TFP are highly correlated (0.91), and the differences in TFP are very large. For instance, labor productivity in the United States is 38 times the level of Mozambique in 2019, but US TFP is 27 times greater. In the case of Kenya, US labor productivity is 15 times greater and US TFP is 7 times greater by 2019. Finally, the fact that relative TFP among African countries is larger than that of relative output per worker indicates the relative scarcity of production inputs (human and physical capital).

FIGURE 3.5 **Total factor productivity and distance to the frontier, 2019**

TFP (United States = 1.0)

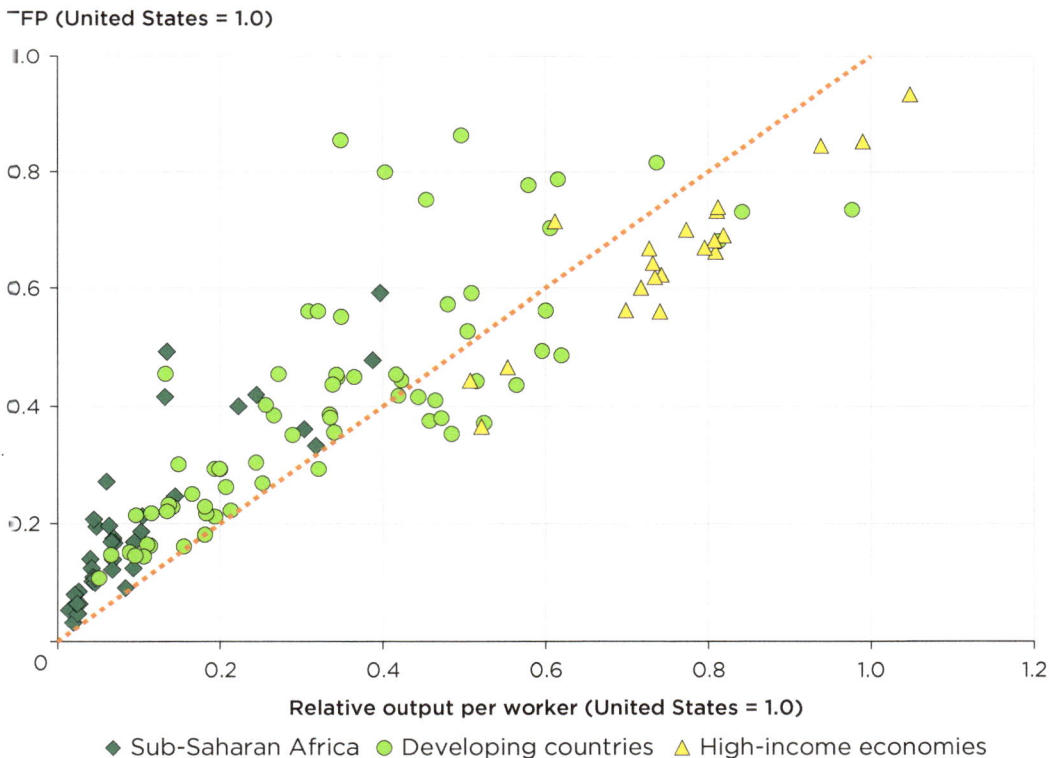

Relative output per worker (United States = 1.0)

◆ Sub-Saharan Africa ● Developing countries △ High-income economies

Source: Based on data from Penn World Table version 10.01, https://www.rug.nl/ggdc/productivity /pwt/?lang=en.
Note: GDP per worker and TFP levels are expressed in terms of the corresponding values of the different indicators in the United States (United States = 1.0). TFP = total factor productivity.

Trends in relative factor endowments of Sub-Saharan Africa

A closer look at the trends in the ratio of capital to output (k/k^*) and in human capital (h/h^*) relative to the United States reveals that (1) the relative capital-output ratio of Sub-Saharan African countries in relation to the United States has declined gradually over time since the end of the 1990s, and physical capital in the region has increased at a slower pace than the population in the same time period (figure 3.6, panel a); and (2) the index of human capital relative to that of the United States has increased since the 1980s, as enrollment and years of schooling have gradually increased in the region (figure 3.6, panel b). Finally, physical and human capital endowment have increased at a slower pace than that of East Asia and a group of large emerging markets such as Brazil, China, and India.

FIGURE 3.6 **Trends in relative capital-output ratio and in human capital, 1960–2019**

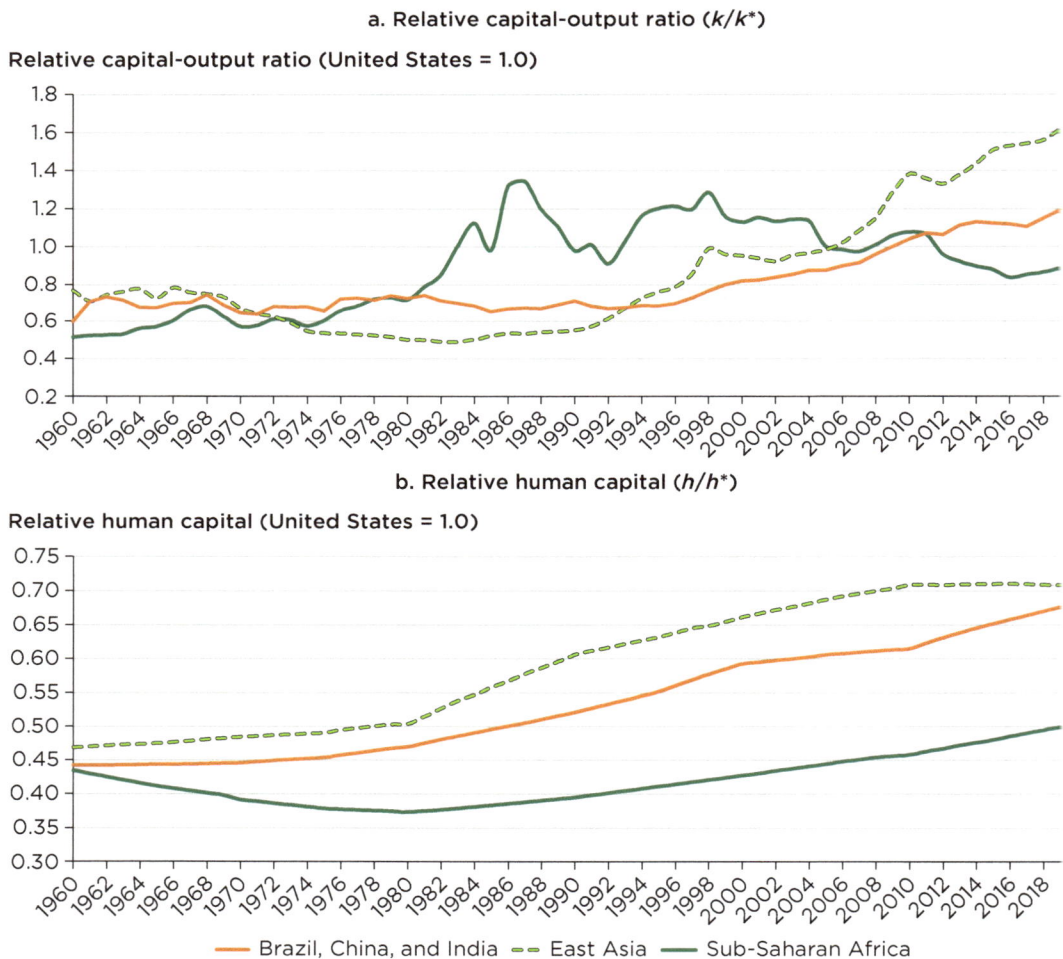

a. Relative capital-output ratio (k/k^*)

b. Relative human capital (h/h^*)

Legend: Brazil, China, and India — East Asia — Sub-Saharan Africa

Source: Based on data from Penn World Table version 10.01, https://www.rug.nl/ggdc/productivity/pwt/?lang=en.
Note: All trends presented in this figure are relative to the corresponding values of the different indicators in the United States (note that, in this case, United States = 1.0).

The importance of total factor productivity

As shown earlier in figure 3.3, for the period 1960–2019, labor productivity in Sub-Saharan Africa relative to the United States exhibited long swings ranging from 5 percent to 12 percent. After hitting a peak of 12 percent in the 1970s, relative labor productivity reached a trough of 5 percent in the 1990s and increased to 8 percent in the 2010s. Not only has labor productivity been unable to sustain growth at the levels of the global efficiency benchmark, but it has also lost ground sharply over the past five decades. By 2019, relative labor productivity was more than a third below its peak level in 1974. In terms of the relative TFP, a protracted decline began in the early 70s, followed by a mild recovery since the early 2000s (figure 3.7, panel a). Still, what drives these persistent differences in output per worker remains a burning question.

The development accounting exercise conducted for Sub-Saharan Africa over the past decades shows the following:

- The gap in output per worker between Sub-Saharan Africa and the United States is primarily driven by lower relative endowments (physical and human) capital (per worker) from the 1960s to the mid-1980s (figure 3.7, panel b). On average, more than half of the gap in relative output per worker in Sub-Saharan Africa was attributed to differences in the relative endowment of factors in relation to the United States from 1960 to 1985.

- Since the 1990s, the gap in relative endowment of factors still plays a role in explaining the differences in relative labor productivity; however, the gap in the efficiency with which Sub-Saharan Africa combines its factors of production has become increasingly relevant in explaining relative productivity gaps (figure 3.7, panel b). The share of TFP explaining relative labor productivity differences has increased from 46 percent in 1985 to 77 percent in 2019. Note that this proportion is comparable to that of other developing countries (74 percent) and of East Asian countries (75 percent).

Figure 3.8, panel a, depicts the relationship between the relative productivity gap in relation to the United States and the share of TFP explaining this gap across countries in the world in 2019. It shows a systematic pattern: countries that are the farthest from the (global efficiency) frontier have the largest share of differences in TFP explaining the labor productivity gap. In other words, as the distance to the frontier narrows, and countries start to catch up with the United States, the share of TFP in development accounting tends to decline. For instance, the median share of TFP is 75 percent for developing countries (including Sub-Saharan Africa) and about 40 percent for high-income countries (figure 3.8, panel a).

FIGURE 3.7 Relative output per worker across Sub-Saharan African countries, 1960–2019

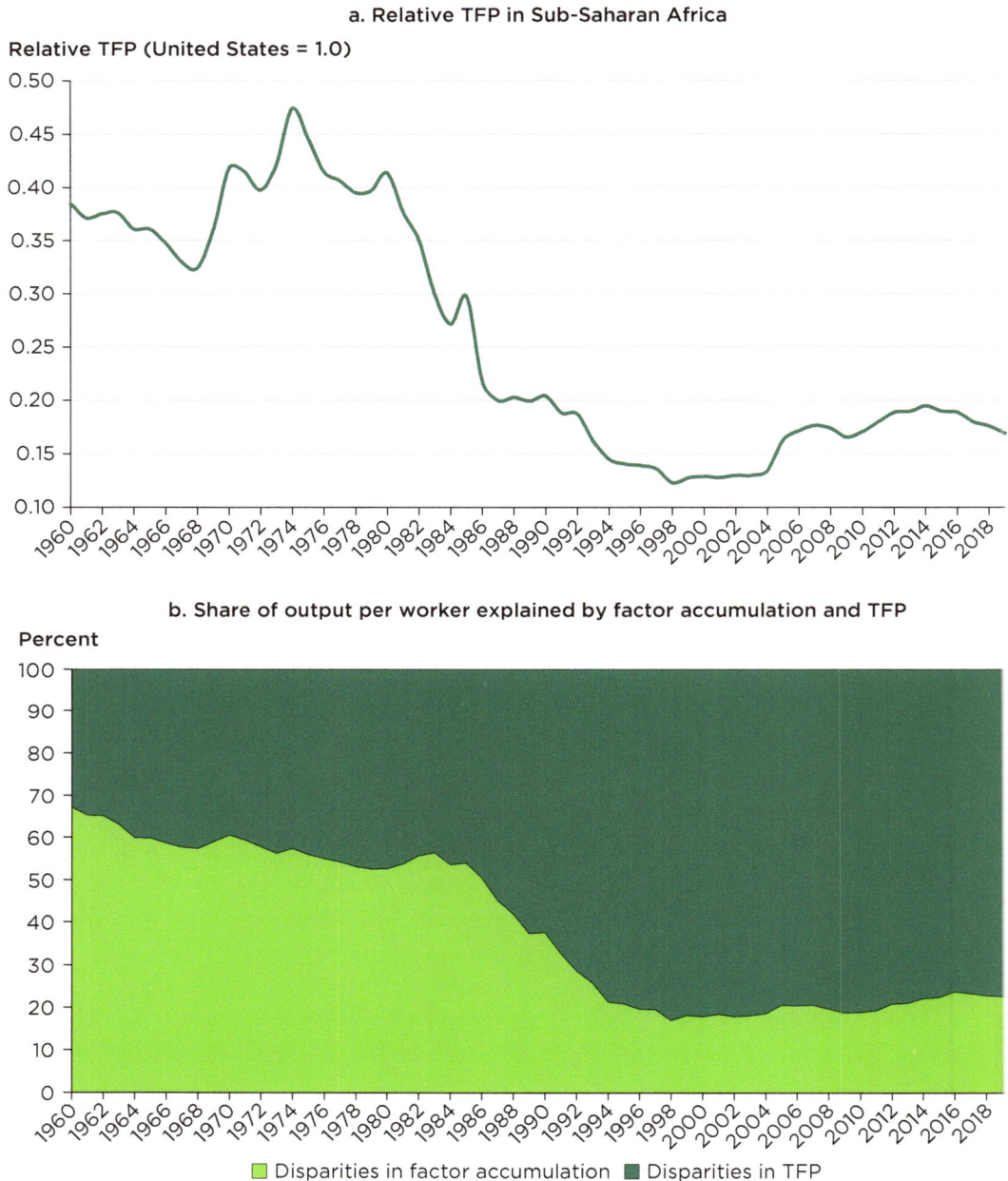

a. Relative TFP in Sub-Saharan Africa

Relative TFP (United States = 1.0)

b. Share of output per worker explained by factor accumulation and TFP

Percent

■ Disparities in factor accumulation ■ Disparities in TFP

Source: Based on data from Penn World Table version 10.01, https://www.rug.nl/ggdc/productivity/pwt/?lang=en.

Note: Panel a shows the employment-weighted average of the relative real output per worker for countries in Sub-Saharan Africa. Panel b shows the proportion of the differences in output per worker that are attributed to either factor accumulation or TFP differences. TFP = total factor productivity.

Over time, the contribution of TFP differences to development accounting has increased across countries in the world—particularly, across Sub-Saharan African countries. Figure 3.8, panel b, shows that all countries in the region are above the 45-degree line, thus, implying that, for the 37 countries in the region with available data, TFP differences account for a larger share of labor productivity differences over time. The median share of TFP across Sub-Saharan African countries increased from 39 percent in 1970 to 76 percent in 2019 (figure 3.8, panel b). Countries in the region with the largest increase in the share of TFP during the period 1970–2019 include the Democratic Republic of Congo, Gabon, The Gambia, Madagascar, Malawi, and Zimbabwe.

These findings suggest that TFP differences account for the bulk of income differences across countries and over time. In other words, the narrative of greater inefficiency in technology use—which could be attributed to, among other things, resource misallocation—plays a critical role in explaining the differences in real output per worker in Sub-Saharan Africa in relation to aspirational and efficiency benchmarks.

FIGURE 3.8 The larger role of total factor productivity in explaining labor productivity gaps relative to output per worker, Sub-Saharan African countries, 1970–2019

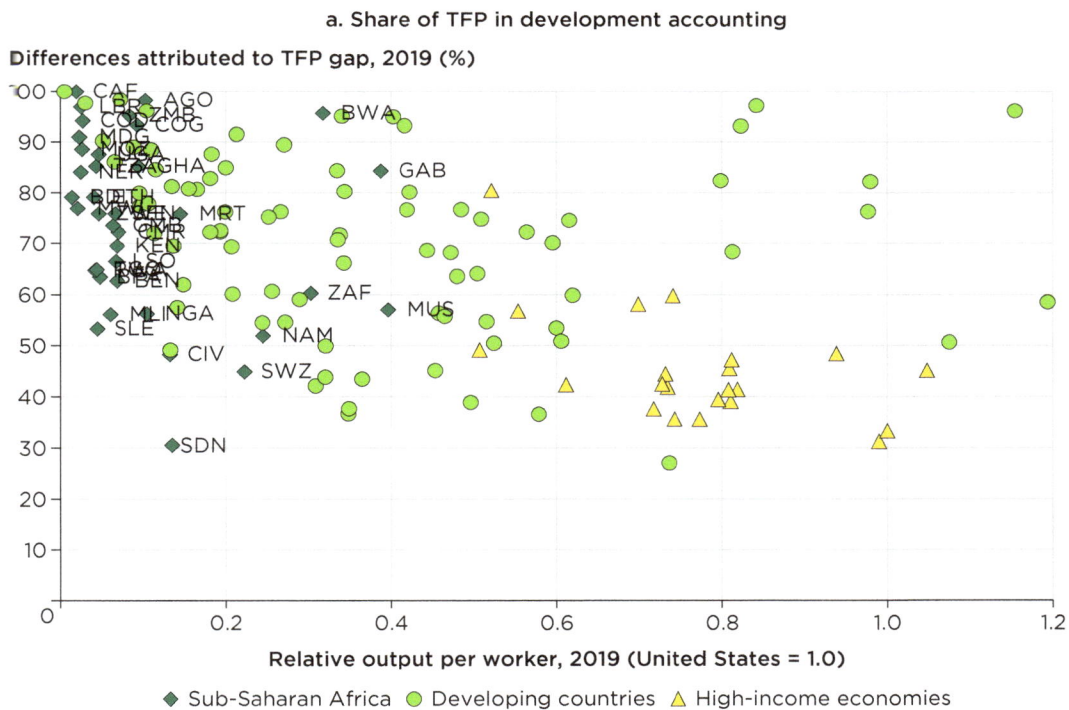

a. Share of TFP in development accounting

(continued)

FIGURE 3.8 The larger role of total factor productivity in explaining labor productivity gaps relative to output per worker, Sub-Saharan African countries, 1970–2019 *(continued)*

b. Share of labor productivity disparities due to lower relative TFP

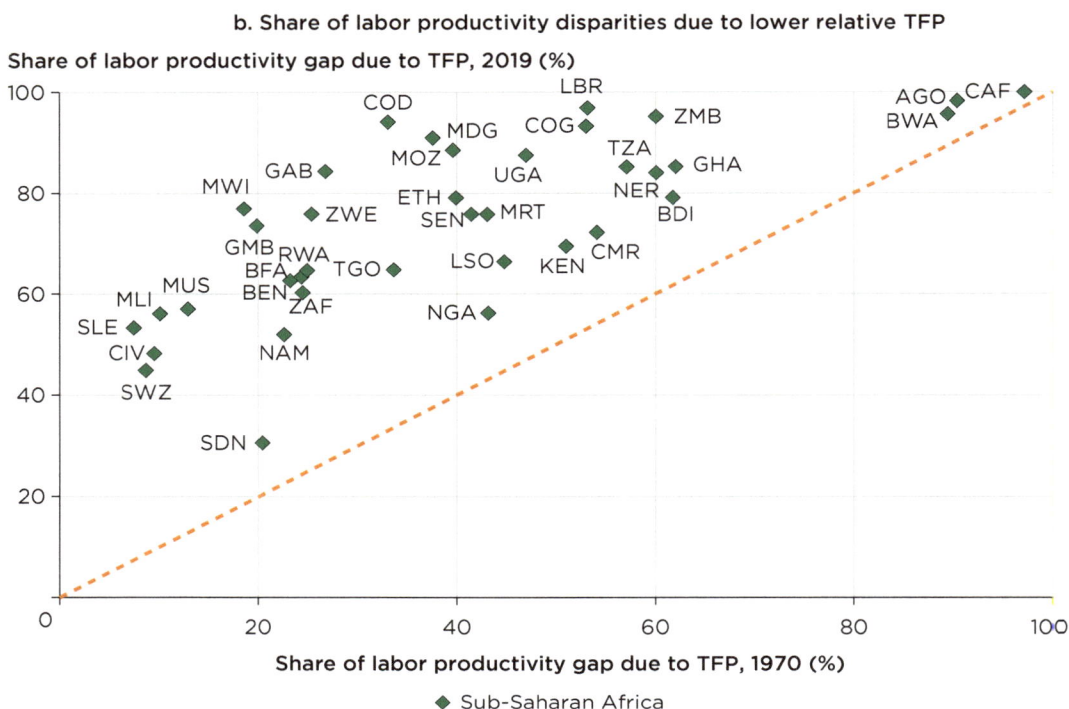

Source: Based on data from Penn World Table version 10.01, https://www.rug.nl/ggdc/productivity/pwt/?lang=en.

Note: Panel a (y-axis) and panel b depict the contribution of relative TFP to the gap in labor productivity in relation to the United States for all countries in the world—particularly, Sub-Saharan African countries. For country abbreviations, refer to International Organization for Standardization (ISO), https://www.iso.org/obp/ui/#search. TFP = total factor productivity.

Figure 3.9 depicts the relative output per worker in relation to the United States for each Sub-Saharan African country as well as the contribution of the different factors of production (physical capital and human capital) and TFP in explaining the productivity gap. In 1970, differences in relative factor endowments accounted for 60 percent of the labor productivity differences on average (28 percent due to differences in the capital-output ratio and 32 percent due to human capital). For 25 of 37 countries in the region, differences in the factors of production explained more than half of the labor productivity differences relative to the global efficiency benchmark. By 2019, differences in relative factor endowments accounted on average for one-quarter of real output per worker differences (10 percent due to differences in the capital-output ratio and 15 percent due to human capital) with approximately three-quarters attributed to TFP differences. For about 90 percent of the countries in the region (34 of 37), differences in TFP explained more than half of real output per worker differences in relation to the global efficiency benchmark.

FIGURE 3.9 Development accounting across Sub-Saharan African countries, 1970 and 2019

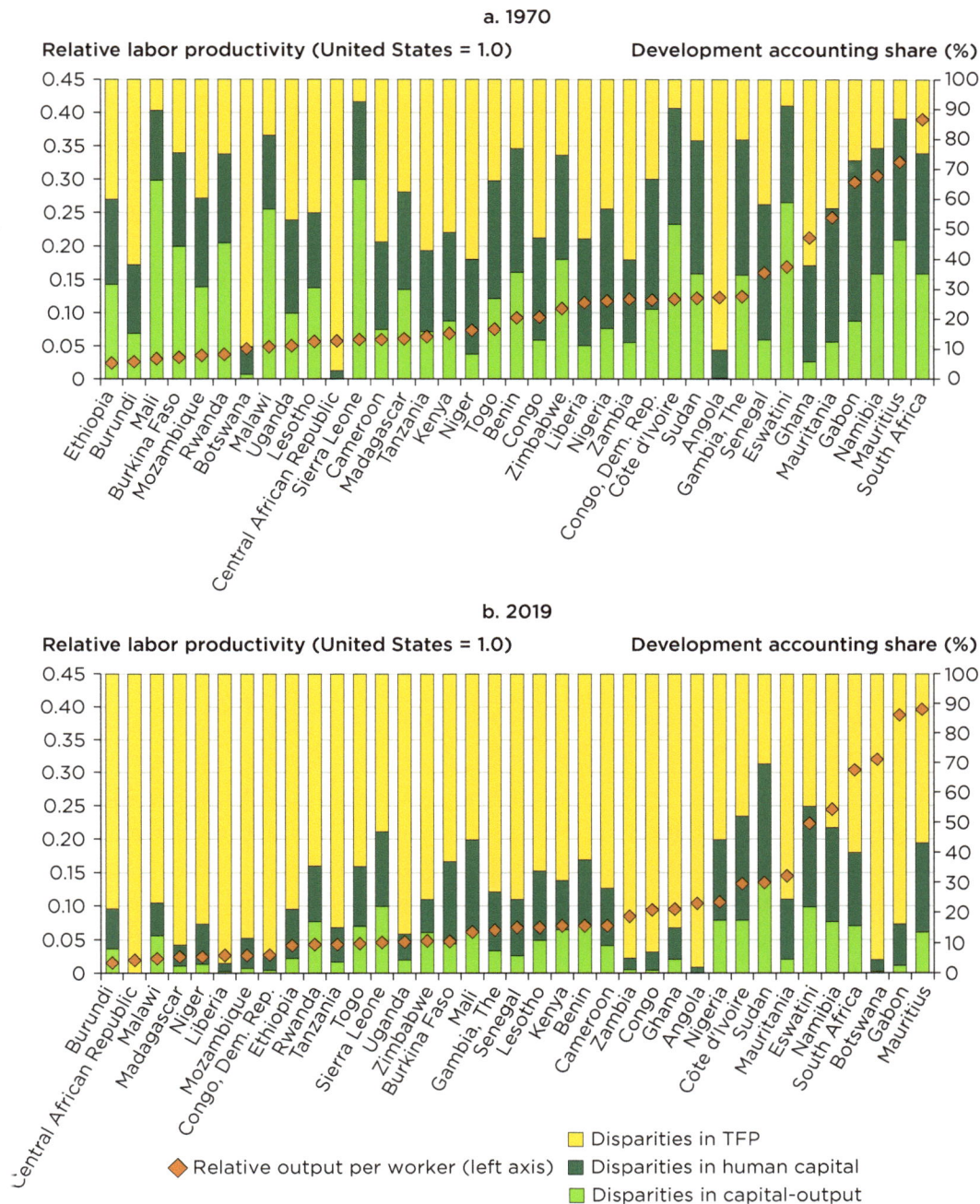

a. 1970

Relative labor productivity (United States = 1.0)   Development accounting share (%)

b. 2019

Relative labor productivity (United States = 1.0)   Development accounting share (%)

- ☐ Disparities in TFP
- ◆ Relative output per worker (left axis)
- ■ Disparities in human capital
- ☐ Disparities in capital-output

Source: Based on data from Penn World Table version 10.01, https://www.rug.nl/ggdc/productivity /pwt/?lang=en.

Note: Panels a and b depict the labor productivity gap of each Sub-Saharan African country in relation to the United States (left y axis) and the contribution of factor endowments and TFP to explain these labor productivity differences (right y axis). TFP = total factor productivity.

In sum, a number of stylized facts emerge from the assessment of productivity trends in Sub-Saharan Africa over the past decades:

- Sub-Saharan Africa has been unable to catch up relative to aspirational and efficiency benchmarks (the East Asia and Pacific region and the United States, respectively) over time. In fact, most African countries lost ground relative to the United States over the past 50 years.

- The persistence of the labor productivity gap relative to these benchmarks can be attributed to the slow accumulation of physical and human capital relative to the region's growing population and the poor allocation of these resources, the latter of which plays an increasingly important role.

How can African countries boost productivity? This chapter argues that institutions and policies that reduce the misallocation of physical capital and human capital are essential. Alleviating financial frictions (for example, overcoming collateral problems and lack of credit history), removing macroeconomic distortions (for example, interest rates and exchange rates reflecting market forces), and fostering the development of complementary infrastructure may help improve the allocation of capital. Improving access to finance (such as through digital financial services) can help alleviate the constraints to entrepreneurial choices (and, more broadly, occupational choices) and provide a path to formality.

Structural change in Sub-Saharan Africa

Differences in labor productivity across countries and regions—in levels and in growth rates—might be due to significant differences in the patterns of structural change. Evidence points to structural change as accounting for the bulk of the differences in the economic performance of successful and unsuccessful countries (McMillan and Rodrik 2011; McMillan, Rodrik, and Verduzco-Gallo 2014). The evidence points to an expansion of high-productivity employment opportunities among Asian economies, including China and India, with a significant contribution of structural change to overall labor productivity growth (McMillan, Rodrik, and Verduzco-Gallo 2014). Furthermore, recent growth acceleration episodes were driven by either rapid within-sector labor productivity growth (Latin America and the Caribbean) or growth-increasing structural change (Africa) (Diao, McMillan, and Rodrik 2017). Estimates of the decomposition of productivity growth in Sub-Saharan Africa show a marked difference in the contribution of structural change over the past three decades (figure 3.10).

FIGURE 3.10 Decomposition of productivity growth, Sub-Saharan Africa and selected subgroups, 1990–2018

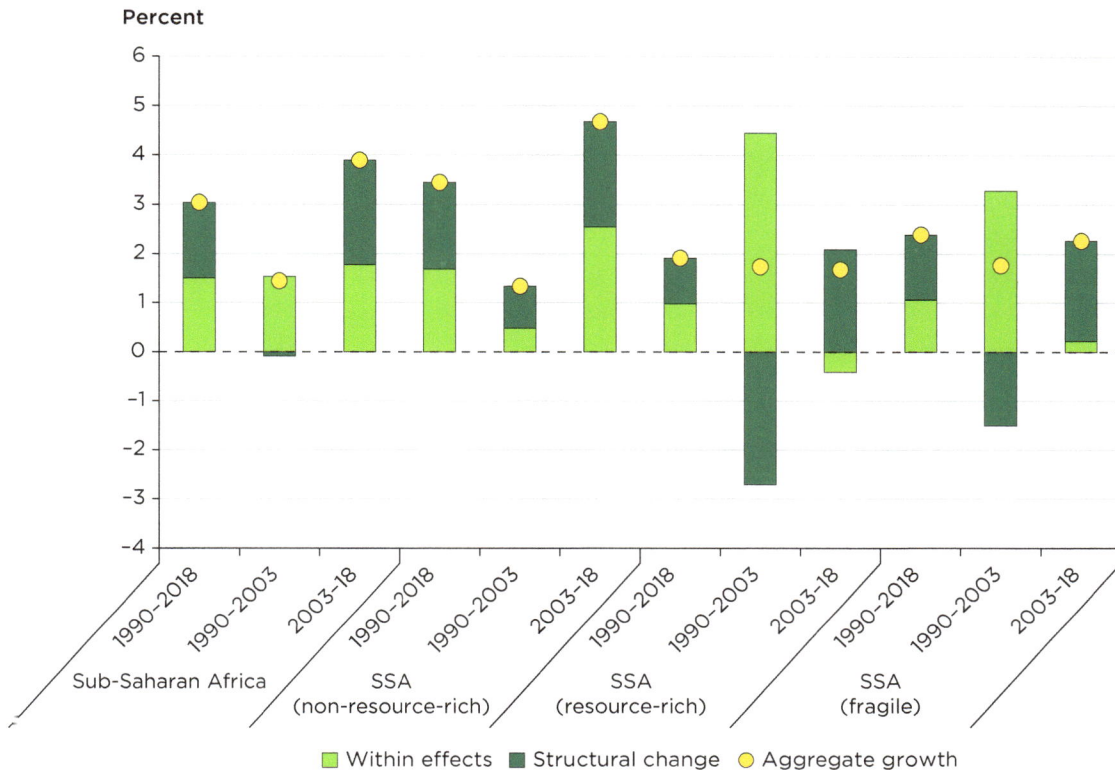

Source: World Bank, based on Groningen Growth and Development Center database, https://www.rug.nl /ggdc/structuralchange/etd-transition-economies.

Note: Regional and group figures are (employment-)weighted average. Within effects refer to productivity increase of workers who remain within the same sector. Structural change effects refer to productivity change due to labor movement across the primary, secondary, and tertiary sectors. SSA = Sub-Saharan Africa.

First, the contribution of structural change to labor productivity growth in the region is negligible from 1990 to 2003. During this period, structural change accounted for more than 60 percent of productivity growth among non-resource-abundant countries in the region. This share was more than offset by growth-reducing structural change experienced by resource-abundant and fragile countries in the region. Second, structural change had a positive contribution to productivity growth in the region and other country subgroups from 2003 to 2018. Not only was labor productivity higher in the second period (3.9 percent per year in 2003–18 from 1.4 percent in 1990–2003), but structural change contributes to more than half of that performance. Although labor productivity growth among resource-rich countries is smaller than that of non-resource-rich countries (1.7 percent versus 4.7 percent per year, respectively), growth in the former was entirely driven by structural change (figure 3.10).

Sectoral structure and long-term growth in Sub-Saharan Africa are characterized by a considerable lag in structural transformation. Many people still work and make a living from agriculture across countries in the region. Furthermore, the region's employment share in agriculture is still high and has been declining at a slower pace than in other world regions (figure 3.11). In 1991, the region's (median) share of agricultural employment was about 60 percent, higher than in high-income countries or developing countries outside of the region. By 2021, this (median) share had declined to only 46 percent, still substantially higher than that of high-income countries (2.5 percent) and developing countries outside Sub-Saharan Africa (15 percent). Although the average share of agricultural employment still exceeded 45 percent in 2021, countries in the region varied greatly in the proportion of people engaged in agricultural activities. Agricultural employment represents more than half of total employment in 44 percent of Sub-Saharan African countries (19 out of 43).[8] The evidence suggests that countries with a higher share of agricultural employment tend to exhibit low levels of agricultural productivity (Duarte and Restuccia 2010, 2018; Herrendorf, Rogerson, and Valentinyi 2014).

The region's (median) share of industry employment remains modest, although it has increased slightly from 12 percent in 1991 to 14 percent in 2021. About one-third of the countries in the region (14 of 43) have a share of employment in industry below 10 percent, most notably, Burkina Faso, Burundi, the Central African Republic, and Guinea.[9] Employment in services increased from a median share of 29 percent in 1991 to 40 percent in 2021 in Sub-Saharan Africa. This increasing trend holds for most countries across the region regardless of their income level, although at different

FIGURE 3.11 **Sectoral shares in total employment, Sub-Saharan Africa and comparators, 1991 and 2021**

Share in total employment (%)

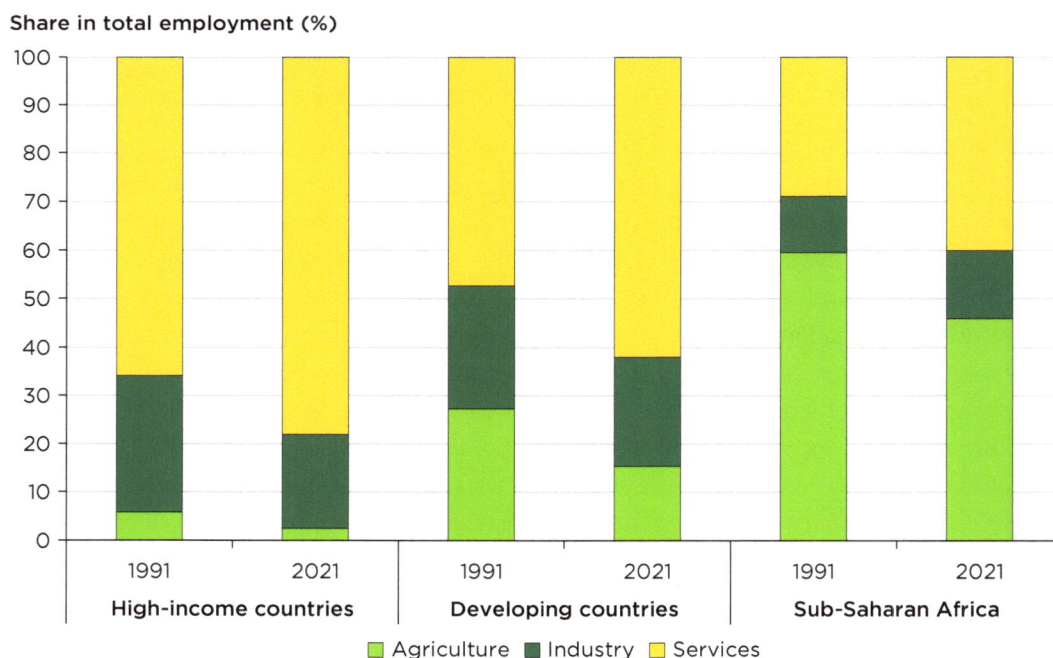

Source: World Bank, World Development Indicators, https://data.worldbank.org/indicator/.

speeds. Only three countries have an employment share in services below 20 percent: Burkina Faso, Burundi, and Madagascar. Overall, Sub-Saharan Africa is experiencing a rapid shift of workers from agriculture to services (figure 3.11).

Recent evidence shows that sectoral labor productivity exhibits large swings over time in most Sub-Saharan African countries; however, labor productivity has improved across most countries and sectors in the region since the mid-1990s (Calderón 2021). Labor productivity in agriculture grew at an annual average rate of 3.22 percent during 2000–10, whereas manufacturing productivity per worker increased at a rate of 1.93 percent per year. Labor productivity growth in services was less dynamic, with an annual average growth rate of 1.89 percent. Despite its faster growth, the level of labor productivity in agriculture is lower than in nonagricultural activities in the region. By 2021, the value added per worker in nonagriculture was about six times that of agriculture, a higher ratio than in high-income countries (1.7) and developing countries outside of Sub-Saharan Africa (3.8). Finally, the productivity gap between nonagricultural and agricultural sectors has remained high and has declined at a sluggish pace over the past three decades (figure 3.12).

The findings here corroborate the growth experience in Sub-Saharan Africa: the large productivity gap relative to aspirational and efficiency benchmarks remains very large and needs to be reduced further. The structural transformation experienced so far in

FIGURE 3.12 **Ratio of nonagricultural to agricultural labor productivity, 1991–2021**

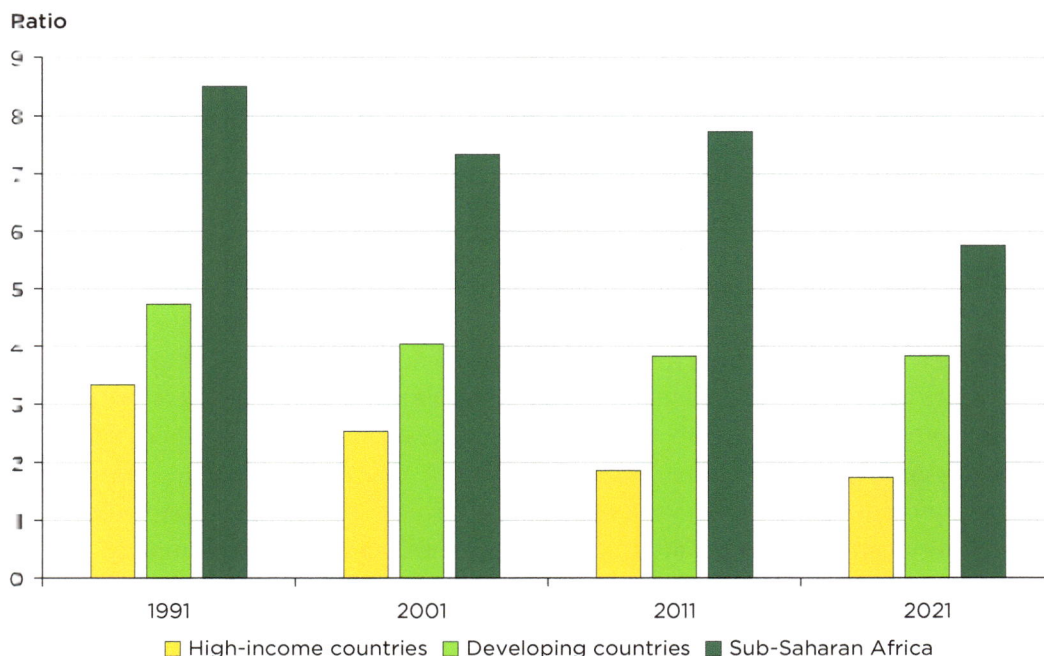

Source: Calculations based on World Bank, World Development Indicators, https://data.worldbank.org/indicator/.

Productivity

the region has contributed to reducing productivity gaps across sectors, although the progress has been slow relative to other regions. The speed of growth-enhancing structural change in the region is likely hindered by policies and institutions that distort the allocation of resources.

Analysis

The poor performance of the African region relative to regional, aspirational, and global benchmarks over the past decades (figure 3.3) can be largely attributed to

- Policy distortions and institutions that led to misallocation of productive resources across firms and sectors, including financial frictions, size-dependent policies, barriers to entry in the industry, and customary land tenure systems; and

- Factors constraining within-firm productivity that include barriers to technology diffusion and restrictions to adopt best practices in production organization or management practices.

This section reviews the empirical literature on the drivers of labor productivity at the production unit level, with emphasis on resource misallocation and within-firm productivity.

Resource misallocation

The low productivity levels of African economies can be attributed to resource misallocation across heterogeneous producers (such as firms or farms) that face idiosyncratic distortions. In turn, these distortions are the outcome of policies and institutions that affect aggregate output and productivity through three interrelated channels (Restuccia and Rogerson 2017): technology, as reflected in the level of productivity of each producer; selection (choice of producers that would operate in the industry given the entry costs and their level of productivity); and misallocation (allocation of capital and labor among operating producers).[10]

Resource misallocation in agriculture

Three stylized facts highlight the role of agriculture in understanding the lack of convergence in output per worker across countries in the region in relation to aspirational and frontier benchmarks: Sub-Saharan African countries exhibit large and persistent differences in labor productivity relative to benchmarks; African countries, on average, tend to allocate most of their labor in agriculture (in relation to other regions); and agricultural productivity tends to be lower than that of nonagricultural activities when compared with higher-income economies (refer to Adamopoulos and Restuccia 2014; Duarte and Restuccia 2010, 2018; Herrendorf, Rogerson, and Valentinyi 2014; Restuccia, Yang, and Zhu 2008).

Evidence shows that the low productivity of agriculture in Sub-Saharan Africa is attributed to inefficiencies in the use of resources rather than poor agronomic conditions (low land quality and unfavorable weather). Spatial productivity growth accounting in agriculture conducted for select countries in the region points to large benefits from closing the actual-potential yield gap of the various crops in the region under different scenarios of input use (low versus high) and water supply (rainfed versus irrigation).[11] Simulations show that aggregate yield gains are larger if agricultural production becomes more sophisticated, although productivity gains vary greatly across countries. For instance, agriculture yields nearly double for the Democratic Republic of Congo in the presence of high input use and rainfed cultivation, and these gains are significantly smaller than those of farmers in Ethiopia, Kenya, and Tanzania. The contribution of irrigation to farmers' productivity is limited once intermediate inputs are used at their highest level. If farmers were to raise their input use from low to high (holding constant the nature of water supply), their potential productivity gains would increase between 7 and 11 times for Ethiopia, Kenya, and Tanzania. If the cultivation method were to shift from rainfed to irrigation (while holding the input use at high), the potential gains are significantly lower. For instance, the marginal yield gains of using irrigation fluctuate from a paltry 14 percent (the Democratic Republic of Congo) to 95 percent (Tanzania). Overall, changes in input use appear to play a greater role than the nature of water supply when explaining agricultural productivity improvements in Sub-Saharan African countries (Sinha and Xi 2018).

The role of land governance

A strand of the empirical literature argues that the underdevelopment of land market institutions is one of the potential drivers of resource misallocation in agriculture across Sub-Saharan African countries. At the farm level, there is strong evidence of misallocation of capital and land in the agricultural sectors (refer to Chen, Restuccia, and Santaeulalia-Llopis 2022 for Ethiopia; Restuccia and Santaeulalia-Llopis 2017 for Malawi). In turn, institutions governing land allocation mechanisms appear to be connected to this severe misallocation of resources across farms in Sub-Saharan Africa and limit the growth in size of farms among the most productive farmers (Restuccia and Santaeulalia-Llopis 2017).

Distortions in farm size can adversely affect agricultural productivity and discourage uptake of modern technologies. These distortions result from a variety of institutions and farm-level policies, particularly in low-income countries. For example, some countries (Bangladesh, Ethiopia, and the Philippines) have imposed ceilings for land holdings and partitioned farms in excess of that ceiling, whereas others (Indonesia and Zimbabwe) have established maximum and minimum size constraints. Several countries, including Malawi, Tanzania, and Zambia, have provided generous input subsidies to smallholder farmers. Others, such as Namibia and Zimbabwe, have imposed higher taxes on larger farms than on small farms (Restuccia 2016).

Land allocation mechanisms are closely associated with inheritance norms and redistribution. They tend to restrict access to land amid underdeveloped rental and sale markets. Insecure property rights on land or inefficient mechanisms of land allocation may lead not only to resource misallocation but also to distorted incentives of technological adoption (Aragon and Rud 2018; Chen, Restuccia, and Santaeulalia-Llopis 2022) and to distorted individual occupational choices between farming and nonfarming activities, as individuals opting to work in the nonagricultural sector may have to forfeit their untitled land (Chen, Restuccia, and Santaeulalia-Llopis 2022).

Evidence at the household-farm level shows that output gains from eliminating distortions in land allocation would be larger in farms operating in nonmarketed lands. In Ethiopia, efficiency gains from reallocation for farmers are larger for those who do not rent land than for those who do (Chen, Restuccia, and Santaeulalia-Llopis 2022). An analogous result is found for farms in Malawi: output gains of farms without marketed land (about 84 percent of the sample) would be 4.2-fold as compared with the 3.6-fold output gains for the entire sample of farmers in Malawi (Restuccia and Santaeulalia-Llopis 2017).

Resource misallocation in manufacturing

An understanding of allocative inefficiencies across manufacturing firms is essential to understand underdevelopment: resource misallocation accounts for up to 60 percent of aggregate TFP differences between poor and rich countries (Bartelsman, Haltiwanger, and Scarpetta 2013; Hsieh and Klenow 2009; Restuccia and Rogerson 2008). Firm-level evidence from select Sub-Saharan African countries shows substantial misallocation of capital, as reflected in a greater dispersion in marginal products of capital, as well as domestic interest rates (Kalemli-Ozcan and Sorensen 2016). In this context, smaller firms tend to display the largest degree of misallocation, which might be tied to their higher cost of capital relative to medium and large firms.

More broadly, there is severe misallocation of resources across manufacturing firms, as resources shift from more productive firms to less productive ones. This misallocation implies the coexistence of a few productive firms with a large number of low-productivity ones. In this context, dispersion in revenue total factor productivity (TFPR) signals resource misallocation, which in turn can be attributed to distortions in output and capital.[12] Evidence from firm-level manufacturing census data for Côte d'Ivoire (2003–12), Ethiopia (2011), Ghana (2003), and Kenya (2010) shows pervasive misallocation of resources across Sub-Saharan African manufacturing firms. TFPR dispersion across manufacturing firms in the region is larger than that in more productive benchmarks (for example, the United States). The magnitude of this productivity dispersion is particularly striking in Kenya: less productive firms coexist with a few very productive ones. Kenyan firms in the top decile of quantity productivity are 290 percent more productive than firms in the bottom decile. The gap between the most and the least productive firms is about 87 percent in Ghana, 39 percent in Ethiopia, and 26 percent in Côte d'Ivoire (Cirera, Fattal-Jaef, and Maemir 2020).

The role of financial frictions
Financial market imperfections can affect aggregate productivity through different channels: they generate differences in the returns to capital across individual producers;

and they introduce distortions to entry, and technology adoption decisions as well as occupational choices.

In other words, financial frictions have an impact on TFP at the extensive margin by affecting the number and composition of entrepreneurs; by contrast, at the intensive margin, they inefficiently allocate capital among active entrepreneurs as their marginal products become unequal.

African countries typically exhibit low levels of financial development, restricted access to formal financial services, and limited access to external finance compared with high-income economies and other emerging markets (Čihák et al. 2013; Lane and Milesi-Ferretti 2017). In a frictionless economy, funds are liquid and can flow to the most profitable project. Productive agents hold most of the productive capital and issue claims to less productive individuals. In the presence of financial frictions, however, liquidity considerations and wealth distribution are essential. External funding is often more expensive than internal funding. Incentives problems indicate that productive agents issue debt claims because they ensure that the borrowers exert sufficient effort to make projects profitable and repay their loans. However, adverse shocks can sharply reduce the borrowers' network and limit their capacity to bear risk in the future (Brunnermeier, Eisenbach, and Sannikov 2013).

Financial frictions tend to have sizeable effects on labor productivity, aggregate and sector-level TFP, and capital-output ratios. Model simulations suggest that financial frictions explain a decline in aggregate TFP of 20–30 percent (Buera and Shin 2013). Nearly two-fifths of the TFP reduction comes from the intensive-margin misallocation of capital among entrepreneurs, with the remainder attributed to reduced entrepreneurship rates (Midrigan and Xu 2014). Additionally, differences in output per worker are overwhelmingly accounted for by lower TFP in economies with underdeveloped financial markets. For instance, the aggregate TFP of a country with low levels of financial development is about 40 percent below that of the United States (Buera, Kaboski, and Shin 2011). At the extensive margin, the evidence points to a large extent of capital misallocation across incumbent firms in Sub-Saharan African countries.[13] For instance, the dispersion of marginal product of capital across Sub-Saharan African firms is, on average, 40 percent higher than that in high-income economies. Across firm types in the region, large firms tend to have higher capital-labor ratios and pay lower interest rates, especially in the case of listed and exporting firms. The degree of capital misallocation is also lower among large firms and, notably, among listed firms and exporting firms.[14]

Alleviating financial constraints has dynamic effects on entrepreneurship rates and aggregate TFP. For instance, quadrupling the access to financial services in Thailand increases entrepreneurship rates by 4 percentage points (Giné and Townsend 2004). Consequently, financial deepening accounted for 70 percent of the overall TFP growth in Thailand from 1976 to 1996 (Jeong and Townsend 2007). Simulations also show that relaxing financial frictions will tend to complement the impact of other growth-enhancing reforms (Buera and Shin 2013). Furthermore, improving technologies to monitor loan activity can help increase financial intermediation and contribute significantly to growth. For instance, Uganda could raise its output level by 116 percent if it were to adopt the world's best practices in the financial sector. However, this effect amounts to only 29 percent of the gap between the country's potential and actual output (Greenwood, Sanchez, and Wang 2013). In sum, improving financial market development would ensure that capital is channeled toward those firms that are more productive and whose survival is highly dependent on the availability of finance—which should, in turn, increase aggregate productivity.

Misallocation of talent

Policies and institutions can also lower aggregate productivity by introducing distortions in the occupational choice of individuals (talent misallocation). For instance, these distortions can lead talented individuals to become rent-seekers rather than entrepreneurs, or high-productivity entrepreneurs unable to join the formal sector. A series of frictions—such as financial, institutional, and land frictions—and their interplay would allocate human capital inefficiently, thus lowering aggregate output and productivity.

In the presence of credit constraints, individuals with low income and high entrepreneurial skills may become workers if their firm has an inefficiently small operational scale. In contrast, people with lower managerial skills may operate in the industry if they are sufficiently wealthy. Thus, the presence of financial frictions affects the decision to become an entrepreneur. Entrepreneurship is critical to fostering growth, thanks to its potential to create jobs, improve operating technology, and boost productivity. However, the coexistence of a sizable informal sector with a formal one poses challenges to formulating policies that foster entrepreneurship. Informal, noncompliant firms are typically less productive than formal, tax-compliant ones. For instance, the value added per worker of informal firms in the median country sample of the World Bank Enterprise Surveys is 80 percent lower than that of formal firms (La Porta and Shleifer 2014). Informal firms may entirely avoid paying taxes or partially pay in the event of underreported revenues (Kanbur and Keen 2014). The value of avoided tax payments and other nonremitted contributions is one of the main benefits of informality (Besley and Persson 2014). Informal firms are important for job generation and incubators for business potential among developing countries and, notably, African economies (Cano-Urbina 2015).

Choosing to become an entrepreneur (either formal or informal) or to work in nonentrepreneurial jobs depends on the individual's personal characteristics (for example, skills and initial wealth endowment) and institutional factors (for example, entry costs, taxation enforcement, and financial frictions). The institutional environment of African countries is typically characterized by onerous registration costs, imperfect credit markets, and low enforcement in tax collection. Occupational choice models typically assume that formal entrepreneurs pay registration costs, with formality implying that they pay taxes and have better access to credit. Informal entrepreneurs evade tax payments and are more likely to face borrowing constraints (Nguimkeu 2015).

Taxation and registration costs create a barrier to joining the formal sector. Models typically predict that these costs induce lower entry of entrepreneurs into the formal sector and a greater number of unproductive firms in the informal sector. Counterfactual policy simulations from these models reveal the likely impact of policies that facilitate firm registration, taxation compliance, and business training programs.[15] The choice of becoming an entrepreneur is also influenced by education. Informal entrepreneurs with rising education levels will find it attractive to join the formal sector beyond a certain threshold of education. Additionally, parents' occupation influences entrepreneurial choices; for instance, more than 40 percent of formal entrepreneurs are offspring of entrepreneurs. Thus, informal business training received at home may lead to entrepreneurial success.

High entry registration costs also undermine the selection of individuals into formal entrepreneurship. Simulations for Cameroon show that lowering registration costs (for example, halving such costs) doubles the share of formal enterprises through greater formalization of informal firms and new entrants to the industry (figure 3.13, panel a). Cutting registration costs also increases aggregate income by 15 percent, and total net revenues more than double the current amount collected by the government (figure 3.13, panel b). Overall, the counterfactual exercises for Cameroon show that an efficient allocation of skills and significant income gains can be obtained from reducing registration costs and selecting the optimal tax rate while fostering entrepreneurial skills and enterprise creation through business training and alleviation of financial frictions by, for example, improving access to credit.

Financial frictions are also likely to lead to individual and aggregate poverty traps by distorting entrepreneurs' entry decisions. For instance, if only a few individuals can afford the fixed cost to become entrepreneurs, the equilibrium wage will be low. In turn, lower wages will lead to higher profits, perpetuating inequality and low output (Banerjee and Newman 1993).[16] Poverty traps are driven not only by lower input prices from constrained entrepreneurial borrowing but also by the initial wealth of the potential (self-financing) entrepreneurs.[17]

Productivity losses and poverty traps resulting from financial frictions have led to a series of antipoverty policy interventions. For instance, asset grant programs to the poor can help identify high-growth entrepreneurs and facilitate their growth. For example, the Youth Enterprise with Innovation in Nigeria (YouWIN!) competition attracted 24,000 applicants who wanted to start a new business or expand an existing one. Top applicants were selected for a four-day business plan training course, and each winner was awarded, on average, US$50,000. Grants were provided to new and existing firms. After three years, grants sharply increased entrepreneurial activity, including entry, survival, employment, and profits. New firm applicant winners were 37 percentage

FIGURE 3.13 Impact of firm registration reform on occupational choice and income, Cameroon

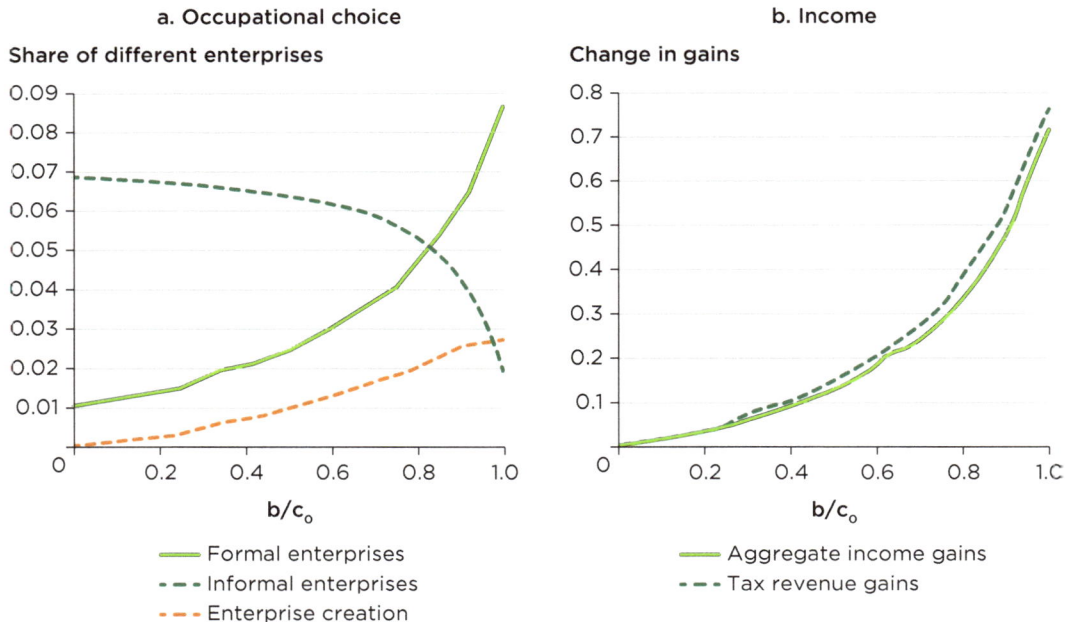

a. Occupational choice

Share of different enterprises

b. Income

Change in gains

x axis: b/c_0

Legend (a):
- Formal enterprises
- Informal enterprises
- Enterprise creation

Legend (b):
- Aggregate income gains
- Tax revenue gains

Source: Nguimkeu 2015.
Note: On the x axis, b represents the reduction of the entry cost implied by the reform, and c_0 is the fixed entry cost for the entrepreneur to join the formal sector.

points more likely to be operating a business and 23 percentage points more likely to have a firm with 10 or more workers. Existing firm winners were 20 percentage points more likely to have survived and 21 percentage points more likely to have a firm with 10 or more workers. Winners tended to innovate more and earned higher sales and profits. Substantial effects persisted more than three years after all grant payments, but with smaller magnitudes. Grants allowed firms to acquire more inputs (capital and labor) without changes in business networks, mentors, self-efficacy, or uses of other sources of finance (McKenzie 2017).

Within-firm or sector productivity growth

Wasoko, a business-to-business e-commerce company headquartered in Kenya, more than doubled its revenue every year shortly after its establishment in 2016. This company helps manufacturers access inventory through more efficient supply chains. Technology application and its operating model are probably at the core of this company's success. Daniel Yu, its founder, was a software developer who saw pain points in the distribution chains and built a digital platform as a solution. The company was not an immediate success in its first attempt, which provided only the system. Yu's team realized that the company needed to shift its operations by stepping in to organize the logistics as well. The founder also owes the company's success to the digital infrastructure and business environment in Nairobi, where mobile money transaction is the norm and the company could easily find the young talent it needs (Ndege 2022).

Wasoko is just one example of how a firm can grow its productivity impressively, and more successful stories like this could help lift the productivity of an industry or a country. In fact, more than 400 companies in Africa earn annual revenues of US$1 billion or more, and these companies are growing fast and are more profitable than peers in other regions (Leke, Chironga, and Desvaux 2018). About 100 companies with revenues of more than US$1.5 million grew at a compound annual growth rate of more than 8 percent between 2018 and 2021, based on the *Financial Times*' ranking of Africa's fastest growing companies 2023 (using data from Pilling 2023). That said, the region has more stagnant firms that are small and struggling to produce, and this section of the chapter focuses on how to improve the within-firm productivity of the laggards.

Aside from shifts of employment across firms and sectors, within-firm labor productivity growth underpins economywide productivity growth. The within-firm effect is estimated to account for at least half of the efficiency growth in more than half of the countries studied.[18] The startling differences in productivity between firms, even those operating in the same environment, imply huge potential for improving a country's productivity if less productive firms could catch up with firms closer to the global technological frontier. Even in the United States, an economy with fewer market frictions, the output of the most productive firms (at the 90th percentile) is twice as high as that of the least productive firms (at the 10th percentile) using the same inputs (Syverson 2004). The wide dispersion of firm productivity is found in virtually all countries where data are available, and is greater in the developing world (Bloom, Sadun, and Van Reenen 2017). Moreover, productivity is seen to grow faster among firms closer to the global technological frontier than among nonfrontier firms; if this trend continues, it will lead to an ever-increasing gap of within-firm productivity (OECD 2016). Besides being large and ubiquitous, within-firm productivity differences are also shown to be persistent (Syverson 2011).

The potential to improve firm productivity is particularly huge in Sub-Saharan Africa. Among world regions, Sub-Saharan Africa has the lowest rate of real growth of firm labor productivity, on average, according to the latest World Bank Enterprise Survey. Besides having lower aggregate value, the region also features the widest dispersion in productivity growth across countries. Sub-Saharan Africa has half of the world's top 10 countries with the highest productivity growth, as well as the bottom 6 countries with the sharpest decline, according to the World Bank Enterprise Survey.[19] Additionally, wide dispersion of firm productivity within an African country has been documented, which also turns out to be persistent. Distributions of firm-level TFPR and physical TFP for four Sub-Saharan African countries, as presented in Cirera, Fattal-Jaef, and Maemir (2020), show various shapes: some feature long tails, whereas others are negatively skewed. Van Biesebroeck (2005) and Diao et al. (2021) studied manufacturing firms in selected Sub-Saharan African countries and found that dispersion of firm productivity either changes very little over time or increases, thus suggesting that convergence is slow if not stagnant.

Despite the manifold causes of within-firm productivity differences, management practices and technology adoption have emerged as two of the main, and sometimes intertwined, drivers. For some, managerial quality, the efficiency in combining and transforming resources such as labor and capital into output, is synonymous with productivity, which, in turn, induces movement of resources (Lucas 1978). Although managerial quality might be abstract, it is possible to measure management practices such as managers' decisions and actions that affect how an enterprise and its staff produce and operate. Technology is also an enabler of firms' productivity growth, and a plethora of technologies linking to various business functions have been identified and measured (Comin, Cirera, and Cruz 2022). Development accounting exercises show that cross-firm variation in technology accounts for one-third of cross-firm differences in productivity (Cirera et al. 2020). Meanwhile, management practices and technology adoption could reinforce each other. Managers decide which technology to adopt and how to better leverage that technology, while management practices could also be considered as technology in the sense that they can be endogenously improved (Bloom, Sadun, and Van Reenen 2017). All in all, both management practices and technology are closely associated with productivity both in concept and as demonstrated in empirical evidence.

To offer constructive recommendations, this chapter looks at what management practices and technologies have been demonstrated to have led to firm productivity improvement. Bloom and Van Reenen (2007) pioneered the measurement of managerial capability and compiled a composite management score that summarizes multiple management practices that are proven to positively affect various performance indicators. These management practices concentrate in four areas: operations (lean manufacturing techniques and documentation of process improvements); monitoring (tracking and monitoring of staff performance); targets (setting realistic, transparent, and interconnected targets); and incentives (rewarding staff on the basis of ability and effort). Improving management practices can raise firms' output and productivity. For instance, a management consulting intervention in textile firms in India raised firms' productivity by 11 percent. Additionally, good management practices are found to improve the use of technology to facilitate data collection and analysis (Bloom et al. 2013). In another study, Neneh and van Zyl (2012) found that marketing, strategic planning, human resource management, risk management, performance management, and teamwork all have significantly positive effects on performance in small and medium enterprises in South Africa. Practices that almost always improved performance include collecting information before making decisions and not promoting incompetent employees to senior positions (Bloom, Sadun, and Van Reenen 2017).

Despite the plethora of technologies developed in the world, much of Sub-Saharan Africa still has not adopted general-purpose technologies. The pace of technological adoption is shown to be slower among firms further away from the frontier (Comin and Hobijn 2010, 2011), a similar pattern found for the overall firm productivity growth. A recent firm-level study in Senegal, for example, found that adoption of computers, internet, and cloud computing for business purposes is still low and that most firms continue to rely on predigital or manual methods to perform critical production tasks (Cirera et al. 2021). Basic digital technologies (DTs) such as emails and websites are estimated to have more positive impact on productivity than exporting or managerial experience in selected developing countries (Cusolito, Lederman, and Peña 2020). As firms grow more sophisticated, they face a wider choice of technologies, and managerial talent becomes important for choosing the right technology that fits business production. Bloom, Sadun, and Van Reenen (2017) also find that, although managerial practices on average explain about 30 percent of TFP differences across 34 countries in the world (including 7 in Sub-Saharan Africa), the portion is higher in more developed economies. Other factors, including technologies, might contribute more to productivity in less developed regions. Comin and Hobijn (2010) found that cross-country variation in adopting technologies accounts for at least 25 percent of per capita income differences.

Beyond firm-specific factors, the external operating environment—where policy makers could make a difference—also affects within-firm productivity. Policy makers should enable an environment in which firms are incentivized and capable of improving their productivity. At least two channels are at play that project external forces on within-firm productivity: (1) selection or competition effect that incentivizes firms to improve and frees up resources from failing firms could strengthen productivity growth of surviving firms; and (2) spillover effects that spread practices from best performers could enhance productivity growth of catching up firms. Reducing market frictions so that resources—people, capital, and information—can flow across firms has the potential to strengthen both channels if the right balance is struck. Access to the global market and knowledge, in addition, has the potential to lift firm productivity across the board.

Policies

After a lost decade of stagnant progress on per capita growth, implementing policies to boost productivity-driven and inclusive growth from 2024 and onward will be critical. At the firm level, greater productivity largely relies on entrepreneurs' capabilities—including leadership and management, effective adoption of technologies, active learning, and analysis. These capabilities could be complemented with policies that enhance firms' productivity growth or remove barriers to firms' growth. As a precondition for sustained and inclusive growth, a sound macroeconomic policy framework with key prices, including exchange rates and interest rates, reflecting market forces is essential for resource allocation. Investments in human capital and building skills for an evolving labor market are fundamental for enhancing competitiveness and increasing productivity in the future. Policies that deliver reliable electricity, including seizing opportunities from the green transition, can power structural transformation in the region. Improving the transportation network increases the connectivity of people to jobs and markets. Finally, reforms that facilitate the adoption of analog and digital technologies, address digital infrastructure gaps, and make the digital economy more affordable are critical for improving connectivity, boosting technology adoption, and supporting more and better jobs for men and women.

Investing in human capital

Boosting educational attainment and outcomes could secure more high-quality jobs, reduce poverty, and accelerate inclusive growth. Transforming education systems in Sub-Saharan Africa requires (1) building a strong foundation of basic numeracy and literacy skills for all children, and (2) equipping youth and the workforce with skills that are relevant to an ever-evolving labor market. Furthermore, investments in tertiary education are critical in driving innovation and competitiveness. Higher education institutions in the region should put emphasis on research and entrepreneurship. Investing in quality education—particularly in science, technology, engineering, and mathematics fields—is critical to adopt technologies that create the conditions for productivity improvement. Africa has invested in poles of excellence to promote regional collaboration among universities and best-practice partners to increase the quantity and quality of science, technology, engineering, and mathematics graduates and professionals. These measures are expected to increase knowledge production that should create knowledge-based competitive advantages.

Although education serves as a foundation for cultivating effective entrepreneurs, managers, and workers, special focus should be devoted to facilitating people's transition into the workplace and progression into managerial roles. The government could fund or facilitate the development of vocational and skills training programs that can adapt to changes in demand of the labor market. Germany, among other high-income economies, is known for subsidizing vocational training programs and working closely with industries to ensure that the skills taught align with labor market needs. On-the-job trainings largely rely on practices at the firm level, although cultivating a conducive culture that promotes learning and exchanges of good practices such as through trade associations could be helpful. Good managerial practices, including evidence-based decision-making and merit-based promotional systems, could be learned through links with international cooperations and communities.

Expanding infrastructure

Inadequate infrastructure, particularly that of energy and transportation, represents a key barrier to entry for new firms, impeding productivity growth through three main channels: barriers to firm entry, high operating costs, and lack of export competitiveness. Africa faces a significant challenge to meet its universal, high-quality energy access goals. About 600 million people in Africa, or 43 percent of the continent, lacked access to electricity in 2022; however, Africa's resource base and associated investments could help accelerate progress by developing diverse energy sources. Because many natural resource projects are located in remote and rural communities, the scale-up of green energy investments and regional infrastructure could be leveraged to alleviate rural poverty and promote productivity gains. Expanding the grid is critical to enhance access to electricity, but alternative solutions are often more affordable and fit for purpose in rural, low-income, or microcommercial markets. Decentralized solutions—particularly minigrids—can be cost-efficient ways to attain universal access, although popular approaches, such as solar home systems, may fail to deliver the quality electricity access necessary to meet development ambitions. These complementary solutions can be deployed judiciously where grid connection is infeasible and costly.

Expanding road access may help induce structural change by shifting employment out of agriculture and into services and manufacturing. Expanding and upgrading the transportation system (including roads, airports, and ports) are key to boosting connectivity within the country and economic integration in the region. Doing so will require accounting for the impact on the road system of climate stressors, such as rising temperatures or flooding. Cost-effective measures include adequate road maintenance and investments in pavement improvements. Further interventions may require assessing the broader impact of road disruption to decide whether adaption is economically sound. Building up financial, technical, and institutional capacity for road asset management is critical. Additional evidence suggests that bundling investments with complementary infrastructure such as roads and electricity amplify their impact on productivity, thus highlighting the role of complementarities in enhancing the impact of infrastructure on economic outcomes.

Leveraging technology

Removing barriers to technological adoption has a positive impact on productivity and job creation in African firms. Recent evidence shows that technology adoption plays a bigger role in improving productivity for firms that are further away from the frontier. Technologies used by firms can be general business functions, which are common tasks that apply to all firms, and sector-specific business functions, which differ across sectors and are linked to core production functions. Technology adoption can accompany employment growth. Employment growth in Senegal, for instance, tends to be higher among firms with better technology regardless of the type of technology—general or sector-specific business function technologies—and the different margins (extensive relative to intensive). Thus, firms with better technologies tend to be more productive and benefit from opportunities to expand, leading to increased employment. The positive co-movement between the level of technology and employment growth is even greater at the intensive margin than at the extensive one, specifically when it involves general business functions.

DTs can also boost productivity through different mechanisms: (1) fostering market transparency by alleviating informational frictions and increasing the capacity to access market information; (2) raising the demand for systems that deliver high-quality information on inputs, better business practices, and technology transfer; and

(3) reducing logistics costs in different stages of the supply chain—including platforms that connect buyers and sellers along the production chain, coordinate product delivery, and facilitate secure payments. Despite the benefits of DTs on growth and job creation, African firms still have low productive use of these technologies. The poor penetration of smartphones, computers, and more sophisticated DTs in a few countries is attributed to affordability problems and digital literacy. Increasing the productive use of network and data infrastructure will require policies to ensure their affordability and availability. Access to credit, targeted regulations, and market-induced price reductions can improve affordability. Creating apps tailored to African entrepreneurs (across different sectors and for the many languages spoken in the continent) can also drive greater adoption of these technologies. Complementary investments in electricity, education, and skills are also critical to boost DT adoption.

Notes

1. Moreover, looking at the evolution of the living standards in Eastern and Southern Africa and Western and Central Africa reveals some slight differences. Despite some convergence of Western and Central Africa's GDP to average world GDP per capita during 2000–14, it remained flat before the global financial crisis and protractedly declined since then (figure 3.1).

2. This situation implies that the region must increasingly rely on its own domestic policy space to deepen the reforms that foster inclusive growth and seize the opportunities from regional integration.

3. Recent research shows that a weaker relationship between GDP and household welfare growth in Sub-Saharan Africa appears to drive this lower elasticity—thus suggesting that African countries need to achieve higher growth per capita to achieve similar improvements in average living standards as households in other regions (Wu et al. 2024).

4. At the firm level, the microstructure of production establishments in different economic sectors can help explain productivity differences across countries (Hsieh and Klenow 2009; Restuccia and Rogerson 2008).

5. Most people in the region live in rural areas (82 percent), earning their living primarily from subsistence farming. Informal labor makes up 75 percent of total employment.

6. Botswana gained significant ground relative to the aspirational and global efficiency benchmarks. Its output per worker relative to that of the United States jumped from 4.6 percent in 1970 to 31.8 percent in 2019.

7. This result is consistent with the findings of Caselli and Feyrer (2007).

8. Twenty percent of countries in the region (8 of 43) employ less than one-quarter of workers in agriculture.

9. By contrast, 10 countries in the region have a share of employment in industry that exceeds 20 percent in 2021.

10. The effects of distortions on aggregate productivity may result from the interplay of these three channels. For instance, policies that may induce distortions in the allocation of resources across producers may potentially generate additional effects through the selection and technology channels.

11. These five countries jointly account for just under half of the region's population, and agriculture is an important activity in terms of both employment and value added.

12. In the presence of multiple factors of production, including intermediate inputs, the efficient allocation of resources is attained when revenue productivity (TFPR) is equal across firms. In other words, there is no dispersion of TFPR in the efficient equilibrium.

13. The analysis was conducted on 4,039 manufacturing firms across 10 countries in the region (Botswana, Burundi, Ghana, Kenya, Nigeria, Senegal, South Africa, Tanzania, Uganda, and Zambia) with information on sales, capital stock, labor, and other intermediate inputs for at least 35 firms as well as data on nominal interest rates. They are benchmarked against a larger sample of high-income and emerging economies (Kalemli-Ozcan and Sorensen 2016).

14. Capital misallocation is measured by the standard deviation of the marginal product of capital as well as the dispersion of (nominal and real) interest rates. For more details on these findings, refer to Kalemli-Ozcan and Sorensen 2016.

15. The implications of the model were tested using data from Cameroon—where the informal sector accounts for nearly 33 percent of gross national product and where 90 percent of the labor force is informal (Nguimkeu 2015).

16. Note that it has also been argued that low interest rates—resulting from an excess supply of capital from a few wealthy entrepreneurs and a constrained demand—can limit individuals' ability to save their way out of poverty over time (Aghion and Bolton 1997).

17. In low-interest-rate environments, individuals with no intention of becoming entrepreneurs would prefer to dissave (Banerjee and Moll 2010).

18. The evidence shows that within-firm productivity contributed about 60 percent of overall productivity growth in China and Ethiopia from 2000 to 2007 (Cusolito and Maloney 2018).

19. According to the World Bank Enterprise Survey, the top-five countries with the highest real labor productivity growth are Angola, the Central African Republic, Sudan, the Democratic Republic of Congo, and Gabon; and the bottom six are South Sudan, Cabo Verde, Uganda, Tanzania, South Africa, and Burundi. Note that, because the surveys were conducted across countries in different years, mostly from 2010 to 2020, cross-country comparisons may not be valid.

References

Adamopoulos, T., and D. Restuccia. 2014. "The Size Distribution of Farms and International Productivity Differences." *American Economic Review* 104 (6): 1667–97.

Aghion, P., and P. Bolton. 1997. "A Theory of Trickle-Down Growth and Development." *Review of Economic Studies* 64: 151–72.

Aragón, Fernando M., and Juan Pablo Rud. 2018. "Weather, Productivity and Factor Misallocation: Evidence from Ugandan Farmers." Unpublished manuscript, Royal Holloway College, University of London, UK.

Banerjee, A. V., and B. Moll. 2010. "Why Does Misallocation Persist?" *American Economic Journal: Macroeconomics* 2 (1): 189–206.

Banerjee, A. V., and A. F. Newman. 1993. "Occupational Choice and the Process of Development." *Journal of Political Economy* 101: 274–98.

Bartelsman, E., J. Haltiwanger, and S. Scarpetta. 2013. "Cross-Country Differences in Productivity: The Role of Allocation and Selection. *American Economic Review* 103 (1): 305–34.

Ben-David, D., and D. H. Papell. 1998. "Slowdowns and Meltdowns: Postwar Growth Evidence from 74 Countries." *Review of Economics and Statistics* 80 (4): 561–71.

Besley, T., and T. Persson. 2014. "Why Do Developing Countries Tax So Little?" *Journal of Economic Perspectives* 28 (4): 99–120.

Bloom, N., B. Eifert, A. Mahajan, D. McKenzie, and J. Roberts. 2013. "Does Management Matter? Evidence from India." *Quarterly Journal of Economics* 128 (1): 1–51.

Bloom, N., R. Sadun, and J. Van Reenen. 2017. "Management as a Technology?" NBER Working Paper 22327, National Bureau of Economic Research, Cambridge, MA.

Bloom, N., and J. Van Reenen. 2007. "Measuring and Explaining Management Practices across Firms and Countries." *Quarterly Journal of Economics* 122 (4): 1351–408.

Brunnermeier, M. K., T. Eisenbach, and Y. Sannikov. 2013. "Macroeconomics with Financial Frictions: A Survey." In *Advances in Economics and Econometrics, Tenth World Congress of the Econometric Society, Vol. II: Applied Economics*, edited by D. Acemoglu, M. Arellano, and E. Dekel, 4–94. New York: Cambridge University Press.

Buera, F. J., J. P. Kaboski, and Y. Shin. 2011. "Finance and Development: A Tale of Two Sectors." *American Economic Review* 101 (5): 1964–2002.

Buera, F. J., and Y. Shin. 2013. "Financial Frictions and the Persistence of History: A Quantitative Exploration." *Journal of Political Economy* 121: 221–72.

Calderón, C. 2021. *Boosting Productivity in Sub-Saharan Africa: Policies and Institutions to Promote Efficiency*. Washington, DC: World Bank.

Cano-Urbina, J. 2015. "The Role of the Informal Sector in the Early Careers of Less-Educated Workers." *Journal of Development Economics* 112: 33–55.

Caselli, F. 2005. "Accounting for Cross-Country Income Differences." In *Handbook of Economic Growth*, Volume 1, Part A, edited by P. Aghion and S. Durlauf, 679–741. Elsevier.

Caselli, F., and J. Feyrer. 2007. "The Marginal Product of Capital." *Quarterly Journal of Economics* 122 (2): 535–68.

Chen, C., D. Restuccia, and R. Santaeulàlia-Llopis. 2022. "The Effects of Land Markets on Resource Allocation and Agricultural Productivity." *Review of Economic Dynamics* 45: 41–54.

Chenery, H. B. 1960. "Patterns of Industrial Growth." *American Economic Review* 50 (4): 624–54.

Čihák, M., A. Demirgüç-Kunt, E. Feyen, and R. Levine. 2013. "Financial Development in 205 Economies, 1960 to 2010." NBER Working Paper 18946, National Bureau of Economic Research, Cambridge, MA.

Cirera, X., D. A. Comin, M. Cruz, and K. M. Lee. 2020. "Technology Within and Across Firms." NBER Working Paper 28080, National Bureau of Economic Research, Cambridge, MA.

Cirera, X., D. A. Comin, M. Cruz, and K. M. Lee. 2021. "Firm-Level Adoption of Technologies in Senegal." Policy Research Working Paper 9657, World Bank, Washington, DC.

Cirera, X., R. Fattal-Jaef, and H. Maemir. 2020. "Taxing the Good? Distortions, Misallocation, and Productivity in Sub-Saharan Africa." *World Bank Economic Review* 34 (1): 75–100.

Comin, D., X. Cirera, and M. Cruz. 2022. *Bridging the Technological Divide: Technology Adoption by Firms in Developing Countries*. The World Bank Productivity Project. Washington, DC: World Bank.

Comin, D., and B. Hobijn. 2010. "An Exploration of Technology Diffusion." *American Economic Review* 100 (5): 2031–59.

Comin, D., and B. Hobijn. 2011. "Technology Diffusion and Postwar Growth." *NBER Macroeconomics Annual* 25 (1): 209–46.

Cusolito, A. P., D. Lederman, and J. Peña. 2020. "The Effects of Digital-Technology Adoption on Productivity and Factor Demand: Firm-Level Evidence from Developing Countries." Policy Research Working Paper 9333, World Bank, Washington, DC.

Cusolito, A. P., and W. F. Maloney. 2018. *Productivity Revisited: Shifting Paradigms in Analysis and Policy*. Washington, DC: World Bank.

Liao, X., M. Ellis, M. S. McMillan, and D. Rodrik. 2021. "Africa's Manufacturing Puzzle: Evidence from Tanzanian and Ethiopian Firms." NBER Working Paper 28344, National Bureau of Economic Research, Cambridge, MA.

Liao, X., M. McMillan, and D. Rodrik. 2017. "The Recent Growth Boom in Developing Economies: A Structural Change Perspective." NBER Working Paper 23132, National Bureau of Economic Research, Cambridge, MA.

Duarte, M., and D. Restuccia. 2010. "The Role of the Structural Transformation in Aggregate Productivity." *Quarterly Journal of Economics* 125 (1): 129–73.

Duarte, M., and D. Restuccia. 2018. "Structural Transformation and Productivity in Sub-Saharan Africa." Background paper prepared for the World Bank project Boosting Productivity in Sub-Saharan Africa, University of Toronto.

Feenstra, R. C., R. Inklaar, and M. P. Timmer. 2015. "The Next Generation of the Penn World Table." *American Economic Review* 105 (10): 3150–82.

Foster, L., J. C. Haltiwanger, and C. J. Krizan. 2001. "Aggregate Productivity Growth: Lessons from Microeconomic Evidence." In *New Developments in Productivity Analysis*, edited by C. R. Hulten, E. R. Dean, and M. J. Harper, 303–72. Chicago: University of Chicago Press.

Giné, X., and R. M. Townsend. 2004. "Evaluation of Financial Liberalization: A General Equilibrium Model with Constrained Occupation Choice." *Journal of Development Economics* 74 (2): 269–307.

Greenwood, J., J. M. Sanchez, and C. Wang. 2013. "Quantifying the Impact of Financial Development on Economic Development." *Review of Economic Dynamics* 16 (1): 194–215.

Herrendorf, B., R. Rogerson, and A. Valentinyi. 2014. "Growth and Structural Transformation." *Handbook of Economic Growth* 2: 855–941.

Hicks, J. R. 1939. "The Foundations of Welfare Economics." *Economic Journal* 49 (196): 696–712.

Hsieh, C., and P. J. Klenow. 2009. "Misallocation and Manufacturing TFP in China and India." *Quarterly Journal of Economics* 124 (4): 1403–48.

Hsieh, C., and P. J. Klenow. 2010. "Development Accounting." *American Economic Journal: Macroeconomics* 2: 207–23.

Jeong, H., and R. M. Townsend. 2007. "Sources of TFP Growth: Occupational Choice and Financial Deepening." *Economic Theory* 32 (1): 179–221.

Jones, C. I. 2016. "The Facts of Economic Growth." In *Handbook of Macroeconomics*, edited by J. B. Taylor and H. Uhlig, Vol. 2A, 3–69. Amsterdam: Elsevier.

Jones, C. I., and P. M. Romer. 2010. "The New Kaldor Facts: Ideas, Institutions, Population, and Human Capital." *American Economic Journal: Macroeconomics* 2 (1): 224–45.

Jorgenson, D. W., M. S. Ho, and K. J. Stiroh. 2008. "A Retrospective Look at the US Productivity Growth Resurgence." *Journal of Economic Perspectives* 22 (1): 3–24.

Kalemli-Ozcan, S., and B. E. Sorensen. 2016. "Misallocation, Property Rights, and Access to Finance: Evidence from Within and Across Africa." In *African Successes, Volume III: Modernization and Development*, edited by S. Edwards, S. Johnson, and D. N. Weil, 183–211. Chicago: University of Chicago Press for the National Bureau of Economic Research.

Kanbur, R., and M. Keen. 2014. "Thresholds, Informality, and Partitions of Compliance." *International Tax and Public Finance* 21: 536–59.

Kim, Y. E., and N. V. Loayza. 2019. "Productivity Growth: Patterns and Determinants across the World." Policy Research Working Paper 8852, World Bank, Washington, DC.

Klenow, P. J., and A. Rodriguez-Clare. 1997. "The Neoclassical Revival in Growth Economics: Has It Gone Too Far?" In *NBER Macroeconomics Annual 1997*, edited by B. S. Bernanke and J. J. Rotemberg, 73–103. Cambridge, MA: MIT Press.

La Porta, R., and A. Shleifer. 2014. "Informality and Development." *Journal of Economic Perspectives* 28 (3): 109–26.

Lane, M. P. R., and M. G. M. Milesi-Ferretti. 2017. *International Financial Integration in the Aftermath of the Global Financial Crisis*. IMF Working Paper 2017/115, International Monetary Fund, Washington, DC.

Leke, A., M. Chironga, and G. Desvaux. 2018. *Africa's Business Revolution: How to Succeed in the World's Next Big Growth Market*. Boston: Harvard Business Review Press.

Lewis, W. A. 1954. "Economic Development with Unlimited Supplies of Labour." *Manchester School* 22 (2): 139–91.

Lucas, R. 1978. "On the Size Distribution of Business Firms." *Bell Journal of Economics* 9 (2): 508–23.

McKenzie, D. J. 2017. "Identifying and Spurring High-Growth Entrepreneurship: Experimental Evidence from a Business Plan Competition." *American Economic Review* 107 (8): 2278–307.

McMillan, M. S., and D. Rodrik. 2011. "Globalization, Structural Change and Productivity Growth." NBER Working Paper 17143, National Bureau of Economic Research, Cambridge, MA.

McMillan, M. S., D. Rodrik, and Í. Verduzco-Gallo. 2014. "Globalization, Structural Change, and Productivity Growth, with an Update on Africa." *World Development* 63: 11–32.

Midrigan, V., and D. Y. Xu. 2014. "Finance and Misallocation: Evidence from Plant-Level Data." *American Economic Review* 104 (2): 422–58.

Ndege, A. 2022. "Wasako Founder on Building Africa's Fastest Growing Company in Nairobi." *Business Daily*, November 25. https://www.businessdailyafrica.com/bd/corporate/boss-talk /daniel-yu-on-building-africa-s-fastest-growing-company--4032190.

Neneh, N. B., and J. H. van Zyl. 2012. "Achieving Optimal Business Performance through Business Practices: Evidence from SMEs in Selected Areas in South Africa." *Southern African Business Review* 16 (3): 118–44.

Nguimkeu, P. 2015. "An Estimated Model of Informality with Constrained Entrepreneurship." Georgia State University working paper, Georgia State University, Atlanta.

OECD (Organisation for Economic Co-operation and Development). 2016. *The Productivity-Inclusiveness Nexus*. Paris: OECD Publishing.

Parente, S. L., and E. C. Prescott. 2005. "A Unified Theory of the Evolution of International Income Levels." In *Handbook of Economic Growth 1B*, edited by P. Aghion and S. Durlauf, 1371–416. Amsterdam: Elsevier.

Pilling, D. 2023. "FT Ranking: Africa's Fastest Growing Companies 2023." *Financial Times*, May 2. https://www.ft.com/africas-fastest-growing-companies-2023.

Restuccia, D. 2016. "Resource Allocation and Productivity in Agriculture." Working paper, University of Toronto. https://www.economics.utoronto.ca/diegor/research/Restuccia_ResAlloc_Oxford.pdf.

Restuccia, D., and R. Rogerson. 2008. "Policy Distortions and Aggregate Productivity with Heterogeneous Establishments." *Review of Economic Dynamics* 11 (4): 707–20.

Restuccia, D., and R. Rogerson. 2017. "The Causes and Costs of Misallocation." *Journal of Economic Perspectives* 31 (3): 151–74.

Restuccia, D., and R. Santaeulalia-Llopis. 2017. "Land Misallocation and Productivity." NBER Working Paper 23128, National Bureau of Economic Research, Cambridge, MA.

Restuccia, D., D. T. Yang, and X. Zhu. 2008. "Agriculture and Aggregate Productivity: A Quantitative Cross-Country Analysis." *Journal of Monetary Economics* 55 (2): 234–50.

Schumpeter, J. 1942. *Capitalism, Socialism, and Democracy*. New York: Harper & Brothers.

Sinha, R., and X. Xi. 2018. "Agronomic Endowment, Crop Choice and Agricultural Productivity." Background paper prepared for the World Bank project Boosting Productivity in Sub-Saharan Africa, World Bank, Washington, DC.

Syverson, C. 2004. "Product Substitutability and Productivity Dispersion." *Review of Economics and Statistics* 86 (2): 534–50.

Syverson, C. 2011. "What Determines Productivity?" *Journal of Economic Literature* 49 (2): 326–65.

Van Biesebroeck, J. 2005. "Firm Size Matters: Growth and Productivity Growth in African Manufacturing." *Economic Development and Cultural Change* 53 (3): 545–83.

Wu, H., A. Atamanov, T. Bundervoet, and P. Paci. 2024. "Is Economic Growth Less Welfare Enhancing in Africa? Evidence from the Last Forty Years." *World Development* 184: 106759.

World Bank. 2023. *Africa's Pulse, No. 28, October 2023: Delivering Growth to People through Better Jobs*. Washington, DC: World Bank.

CHAPTER 4

Trade and Integration

Cristina Constantinescu, Mathilde Lebrand, and Gianluca Santoni

Summary

This chapter examines market fragmentation in Africa, focusing on the importance of regional integration and transportation infrastructure in promoting international trade and economic growth. In order to make substantial progress and claim the 21st century, Africa must prioritize these two key areas. Doing so can help overcome market fragmentation, unlock Africa's vast economic potential, and promote inclusive, sustainable growth.

Despite some progress, Sub-Saharan Africa remains one of the least integrated regions in the world. High trade costs and poor trade performance present major challenges. Trade and transportation reforms, as well as improved connectivity, can help reduce trade costs and promote the integration of African economies among themselves and with the rest of the world. The African Continental Free Trade Area (AfCFTA) and the Program for Infrastructure Development in Africa offer significant opportunities for African countries to boost trade and economic growth.

Trade simulations using a general equilibrium model show that implementing the AfCFTA agreement and increasing intra-African trade could lead to significant gains for the continent, with gross domestic product (GDP) potentially rising by up to 2.27 percent. This potential underscores the importance of regional integration and intra-African trade in creating larger markets and promoting economic diversification.

Based on the analysis, several key messages and policy recommendations emerge for policy makers, civil society, investors, and development partners:

- Combine transportation infrastructure investments and trade reforms, because they complement each other and should be pursued simultaneously.

- Pursue deep integration, which involves combining tariff reforms with trade facilitation improvements and behind-the-border reforms in domestic regulations.

This chapter includes contributions by Jean-François Arvis, Alvaro Espitia, Lionel Fontagné, Siobhan Murray, and Daria Ulybina.

- Focus on specific policy instruments and priority actions, such as addressing nontariff barriers, streamlining border procedures, and modernizing transportation infrastructure.

- Promote open regionalism, allowing African economies to continue opening up to the rest of the world, further supporting economic growth and fostering more inclusive and sustainable regional integration.

In conclusion, African countries can address high trade costs and seize regional integration opportunities by considering these general policy recommendations and focusing on specific policy instruments and priority actions. This approach can contribute to promoting inclusive productivity growth and pursuing development goals in terms of economic efficiency, social inclusion, and environmental sustainability. By doing so, Africa may unleash its immense economic potential and gradually assert itself as an influential player in the global economy.

Context

This chapter examines the issue of market fragmentation in Africa and explores how trade institutions and transportation infrastructure can mitigate this challenge and promote international trade and economic growth. To claim the 21st century and make substantial progress, Africa must focus on two key areas: regional integration and transportation infrastructure. Major progress in regional integration means achieving a level of integration comparable to that of the European Union (EU) or the Association of Southeast Asian Nations Economic Community, characterized by the free movement of goods, services, and people.

Meanwhile, significant improvements in logistics infrastructure would entail the development of efficient, well-connected transportation networks—including roads, railways, and ports—that facilitate the movement of goods across borders. Inclusive productivity growth serves as the common thread linking these two priority areas, contributing to the development goals of economic efficiency, social inclusion, and environmental sustainability.

On the one hand, regional integration can lead to economic efficiency through economies of scale, reduced trade costs, and increased competition. At the same time, it promotes social inclusion by creating jobs and reducing poverty. Logistics infrastructure, on the other hand, can reduce the environmental impact of transportation and improve supply chain resilience. By focusing on regional integration and logistics infrastructure, Africa can address market fragmentation, unlock its vast economic potential, and drive inclusive, sustainable growth.

Africa's markets are highly fragmented. One measure of this fragmentation is the "thickness" of borders (or border effect), that describes the additional costs of trading between two countries compared with within countries.[1] Trade costs include barriers at border crossings, such as tariffs and border delays; "behind-the-border" costs that affect international trade, such as those associated with different rules and institutions; and poor transportation infrastructure, distribution, and logistics networks. Of the 10 thickest borders in the world, 6 are in Africa.[2]

Trade reforms and improved connectivity can help reduce trade costs between countries. World Bank research has shown that "deeper" trade agreements—for example, agreements that go beyond tariffs to include a broader range of border and behind-the-border issues such as investment, competition, and regulatory cooperation—lead to significant increases in trade between countries by reducing trade costs among members, and between members and nonmembers (Mattoo, Mulabdic, and Ruta 2017). Similarly, improvements in transportation infrastructure and logistics networks, and reductions in border delays that reduce travel times, are associated with significant reductions in trade costs between countries and have the potential to boost integration (de Soyres et al. 2019). Reforms to reduce trade costs have particular relevance as developing economies recover from the COVID-19 pandemic (World Bank 2021).

The chapter builds on recent studies of trade integration in Africa (Coulibaly, Kassa, and Zeufack 2022) and recent sources of trade and trade policy data (Mattoo, Rocha, and Ruta 2020) to characterize how the integration of African countries among themselves and with the rest of the world has evolved since 2000. In addition, the chapter provides new estimates of the impact of trade agreements in Africa and of the change in transit times associated with new transportation infrastructure planned under the Program for Infrastructure Development in Africa. This information is used in a general equilibrium model to quantify the impact of trade and transportation reforms on trade and growth in African countries.

Three main messages emerge from this analysis:

1. Despite some progress, Sub-Saharan Africa remains one of the least integrated regions in the world. In 2019, Sub-Saharan Africa accounted for only 1.8 percent of global trade in goods and services, less than any other region. Moreover, Sub-Saharan Africa's share of world trade, which had been rising in the 2000s, has been on a downward trajectory since 2010 as the price of commodities—a major source of exports for many countries in Africa—has declined.[3] Whereas African economies have gradually increased their trade with new partners such as China, intraregional trade has lost some of the momentum it gained in the 2000s over the past decade. At the same time, diversification away from commodity exports has made limited progress, trade in services remains concentrated in traditional services, and participation in global value chains (GVCs) occurs mainly in commodities and limited manufacturing.

2. High trade costs help explain the poor trade performance of African economies. Over the past two decades, the cost of intra-African cross-border trade has declined

by 11.5 percent. Although this decline is in line with the global decline in cross-border trade costs, Africa—which has most of the world's thickest borders—has a much higher level of trade costs. Tariffs in Sub-Saharan Africa have declined slightly over the past two decades, from an average most favored nations rate of 9.8 percent in 2000 to 8.7 percent in 2018, but they remain high compared with other regions. In contrast, South Asia and Latin America and the Caribbean significantly reduced their trade-weighted most favored nations rates over the same period, from 21.4 percent and 13.3 percent, respectively, to 6.6 percent. At the same time, other regions—such as Europe and Central Asia, East Asia and Pacific, and North America—have maintained lower most favored nations rates, at 4.1 percent, 3.9 percent, and 3.2 percent, respectively, in 2018 (refer to figures 4.10 and 4.11 later in this chapter for details on the weighted tariffs by country).

3. African countries have been more active in signing trade agreements during this period. With few exceptions, however, these agreements have tended to be shallow in terms of policy areas covered and substantive commitments. The AfCFTA represents a significant departure in this regard. Finally, the cost of moving goods within and between countries in Africa is high because of a combination of poor transportation infrastructure and logistics networks and excessive delays at borders: average delays at land borders in Africa are 90 hours, with peaks of more than 250 hours.

Trade and transportation reforms can help reverse these trends and promote the integration of African economies among themselves and with the rest of the world. In simulations using a general equilibrium model of trade, Fontagné, Lebrand, et al. (2023)[4] show that a deep trade agreement linking all African countries, such as the AfCFTA, would increase African countries' exports by 3.41 percent and GDP by 0.64 percent per year relative to the baseline scenario; that implementing transportation infrastructure projects and trade facilitation reforms related to the Program for Infrastructure Development in Africa, such as the completion of One-Stop Border Posts, would increase exports by 9.6 percent and GDP by 1.46 percent per year relative to the baseline; and that the combination of deeper trade agreements, transportation infrastructure improvements, and trade facilitation reforms would increase total African exports by 14.80 percent (and increase intra-African trade by 88.2 percent) and GDP by 2.27 percent per year relative to the baseline.

A World Bank assessment (2020a) confirms the significant impact of the AfCFTA on intra-African trade when combined with trade facilitation measures. Intra-African trade could increase by about 81 percent over a 15-year horizon in a simulation that includes not only tariffs and nontariff barriers but also trade facilitation. Although these results are based on a slightly different model and, more important, include dynamic adjustments over a medium- to long-term horizon, they are consistent with the results presented here. This alignment becomes particularly evident when assessing the more ambitious regional integration scenario that combines trade policy with infrastructure connectivity (including key trade facilitation measures such as the One-Stop Border Post).

In conclusion, trade and infrastructure integration are critical to unlocking Africa's economic potential and to making the continent fit for the 21st century. Achieving major progress in regional integration and logistics infrastructure, while promoting inclusive productivity growth, can help Africa achieve its development goals and become a key player in the global economy. It is important to note the common thread of inclusive productivity growth that links the themes of this chapter to the development goals of economic efficiency, social inclusion, and environmental sustainability. By prioritizing infrastructure investments that promote inclusive growth, African countries can boost economic development while ensuring that marginalized communities benefit from this progress.

Facts

Over the past 25 years, Sub-Saharan Africa has experienced both successes and challenges in its economic landscape.

What has gone right:

- During the 2000s, growth in the value of trade outpaced the world average: from 2000 to 2010, exports from Sub-Saharan Africa grew at a rate of 13.1 percent, compared with a growth rate of 9.2 percent for global exports.

- Intraregional trade increased, fostering regional cooperation: intraregional trade increased from 10.8 percent of total trade in 2000 to 19 percent in 2010, before decreasing slightly to 17.3 percent in 2019.

- Participation in GVCs increased for some countries, leading to improved productivity, employment growth, and poverty reduction in some areas: between the 1990s and the 2000s, participation in GVCs increased by 10 percentage points in Ethiopia, Kenya, South Africa, and Tanzania.

- African countries have increased participation in preferential trade agreements (PTAs), with 30 PTAs in place by 2017: the Arab Republic of Egypt and Morocco led in the number of PTAs, with 7 each.

- The signing of the AfCFTA agreement in 2018 could have a transformative effect on economic integration in Africa.

What went wrong:

- Trade has been stagnant and declining since 2010, and the region has lost global market share: during the period 2010–19, export growth in Sub-Saharan Africa stagnated at −0.2 percent, whereas global exports grew at an average rate of 3.6 percent.

- Diversification has been limited with heavy reliance on commodities: in 2019, minerals constituted 40.4 percent of total exports, followed by stone and glass, which accounted for 21 percent.

- Trade is costly with thick borders, high tariffs, and poor infrastructure.

- PTAs in African countries are generally shallow, with limited enforceable policy areas and few country exceptions: Mozambique has the most enforceable policy areas in its 12 PTAs, followed by Tanzania with 11, and Ghana and Morocco with 10 each.

- WTO-X provisions are policy areas not covered by World Trade Organization agreements, such as investment, capital account, and government procurement. They not common in trade agreements with countries outside the region and even less common among African countries.

- Logistics Performance Index scores are low for most African countries, with the lowest infrastructure quality found in West Africa: on a scale from 1 to 5, Sub-Saharan Africa has the lowest score (2.2), compared with 2.3 in South Asia, 2.5 in Latin America and the Caribbean, 3.1 in Europe and Central Asia, 3.9 in North America, and the global average of 2.7.

To scale up successes and address underperformance, African countries should reduce trade costs, strengthen regional integration, and expand their participation in PTAs with other regions and developed economies. They should also invest in transportation infrastructure, continue to implement One-Stop Border Posts to reduce border delays, and implement reforms to improve trade facilitation, including reducing border and port delays, streamlining customs procedures, and modernizing logistics services.

Trade and integration in Africa

Sub-Saharan Africa remains one of the least integrated regions in the world. Home to almost 15 percent of the world's population and more than a fifth of the world's countries, Sub-Saharan Africa contributed less than any other world region to global trade in 2019, accounting for only 1.8 percent of world goods and services trade (figure 4.1, panel a). For context, the EU alone accounts for about 30 percent of world trade, with intra-EU trade contributing 17.1 percent and extra-EU trade adding another 13 percent. Meanwhile, the East Asia and Pacific region accounts for 29.7 percent of world trade. Sub-Saharan Africa's contribution to global GDP is also limited, barely exceeding 2 percent (current US dollars) in 2019. The export intensity of most countries in Sub-Saharan Africa, as measured by the share of exports in GDP, is among the lowest in the world. Reflecting their lower GDP levels, when export intensity is correlated with GDP per capita, these countries all tend to cluster at the lower end of the distribution, with some even exporting less than would be expected given their GDP levels (figure 4.1, panel b). Furthermore, Sub-Saharan Africa's share in global trade has been on a declining path since 2010, losing about 0.4 percentage point between 2010 and 2019. This dynamic reflects the fact that the region's trade values, which grew steadily in the 2000s, slowed in the 2010s (figure 4.1, panel c). Although trade volumes (constant US dollars) continued to grow throughout the 2010s, they did so at a reduced pace compared with the 2000s and the world average.

FIGURE 4.1 Sub-Saharan Africa's aggregate goods and services trade

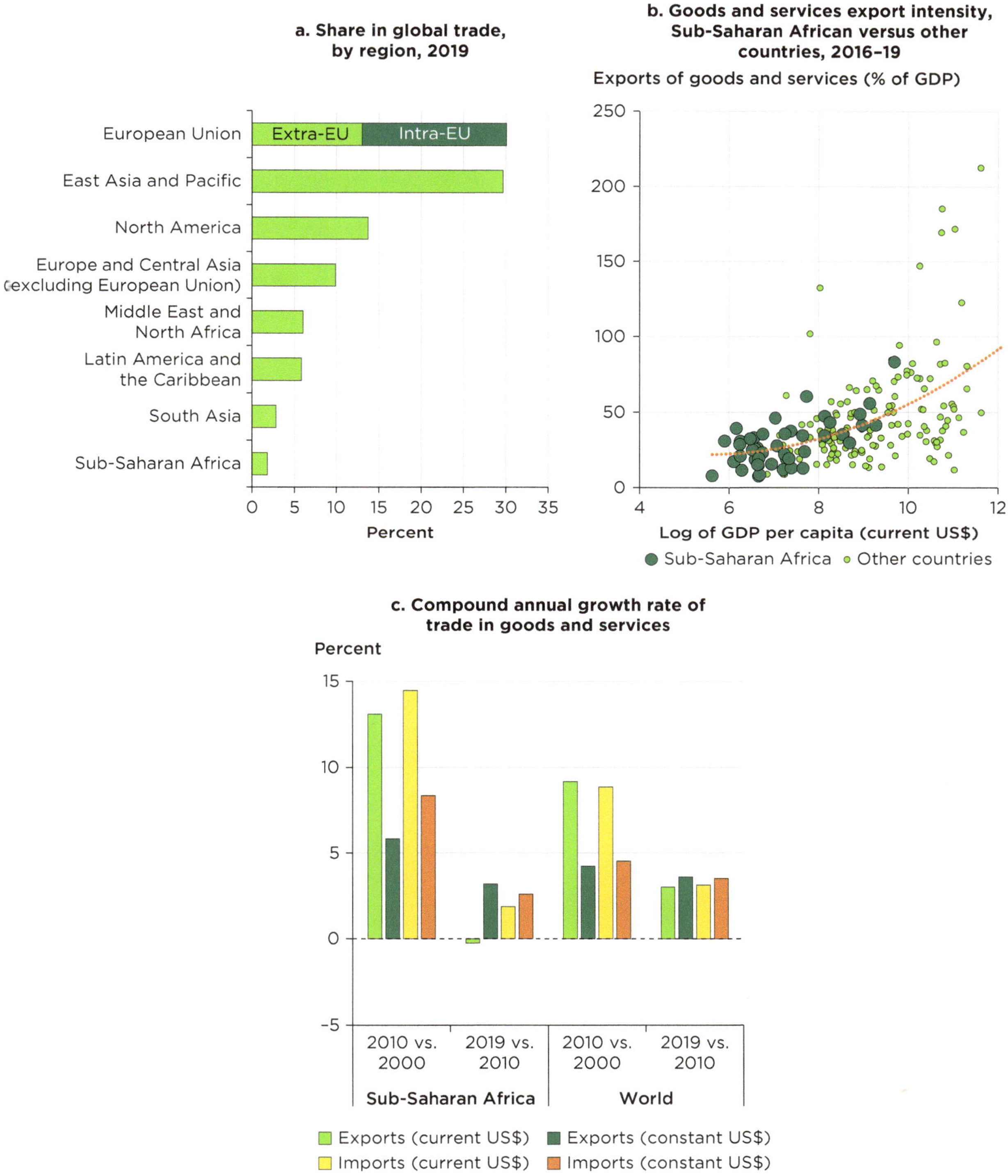

a. Share in global trade, by region, 2019
European Union
Extra-EU
Intra-EU
East Asia and Pacific
North America
Europe and Central Asia (excluding European Union)
Middle East and North Africa
Latin America and the Caribbean
South Asia
Sub-Saharan Africa
0
5
10
15
20
25
30
35
Percent
b. Goods and services export intensity, Sub-Saharan African versus other countries, 2016–19
Exports of goods and services (% of GDP)
250
200
150
100
50
0
4
6
8
10
12
Log of GDP per capita (current US$)
Sub-Saharan Africa
Other countries
c. Compound annual growth rate of trade in goods and services
Percent
15
10
5
0
-5
2010 vs. 2000
2019 vs. 2010
2010 vs. 2000
2019 vs. 2010
Sub-Saharan Africa
World
Exports (current US$)
Exports (constant US$)
Imports (current US$)
Imports (constant US$)

Sources: CEPII BACI International Trade database, https://www.cepii.fr/CEPII/en/bdd_modele/bdd_modele_item.asp?id=37; World Bank, World Development Indicators, https://data.worldbank.org/indicator/.

Note: In panel a, the share of intra-EU trade is estimated on the basis of bilateral goods trade. EU = European Union.

A close look at Sub-Saharan Africa's trade patterns highlights several features that underlie the aggregate trade dynamics in the past 20 years. These features are related to the aggregate trade trends in Sub-Saharan Africa by geographical region, composition of the export basket for goods and services, trading partners, intraregional trade, and participation in GVCs. The following subsections discuss each in turn.

Common trade trends

Different subregions contributed differently to the growth in Sub-Saharan Africa's goods and services trade values, yet they all shared a common trade dynamic. Trade values of all subregions grew robustly in the 2000s, at average rates that exceeded global averages (figure 4.2, panel a). This momentum changed in the 2010s: all four subregions ended the decade at lower annual exports than they started with (figure 4.2, panel b). The Central Africa subregion stands out for the largest declines in both exports and imports during the 2010s, whereas imports of Eastern and Western Africa continued to grow. The trend synchronicity of the Sub-Saharan Africa subregions speaks of common trade boosters and common stumbling blocks in the past two decades.

Sub-Saharan Africa's export basket

With Sub-Saharan Africa's goods export basket still heavily tilted toward commodities, diversification is progressing slowly in the region. In 2019, minerals, stones, metals, and agricultural products accounted for 82 percent of the region's exports, an increase of 8 percentage points since 2002 (figure 4.3, panel a, and annex figure 4A.1).[5] After more than a decade of strong growth, mineral exports, represented primarily by crude oil from Central and Western Africa, saw their share in Sub-Saharan Africa's export basket

FIGURE 4.2 Contributions to growth in goods and services exports, by Sub-Saharan Africa subregion

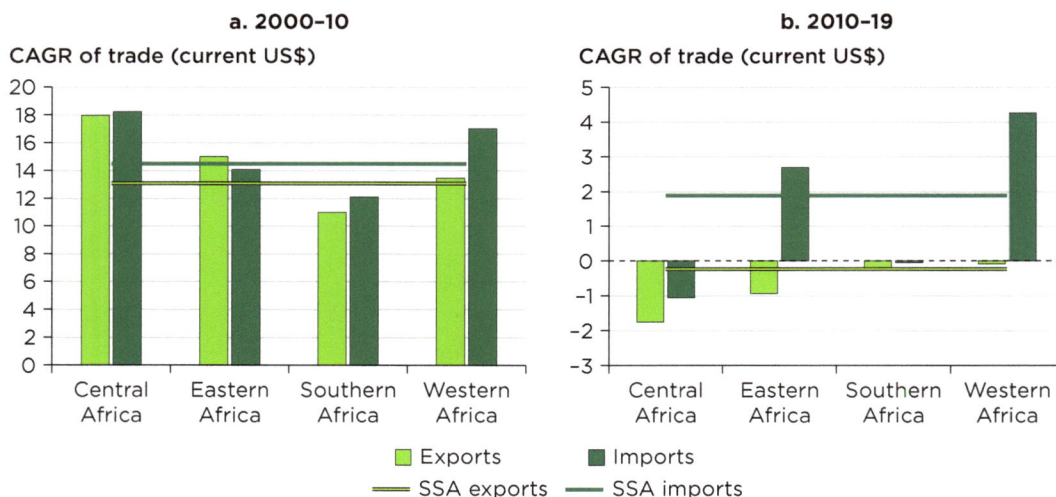

Source: World Bank, World Development Indicators, https://data.worldbank.org/indicator/.
Note: CAGR = compound annual growth rate; SSA = Sub-Saharan Africa.

drop sharply in the mid-2010s, on the back of rapidly deteriorating terms of trade. At the same time, stone exports from Central and Western Africa as well as Eastern Africa experienced an increase in their share. By contrast with Sub-Saharan Africa's exports, which remain focused on extractive and low-end manufacturing industries, the region's imports include mainly complex manufactured goods such as machinery, transportation equipment, and chemicals (figure 4.3, panel b). Moreover, consumer goods represent 20 percent of Sub-Saharan Africa's imports, higher than in the East Asia and Pacific (15 percent) and South Asia (6 percent) regions (figure 4.3, panel c).

FIGURE 4.3 **Composition of Sub-Saharan Africa's exports and imports, 2002–19**

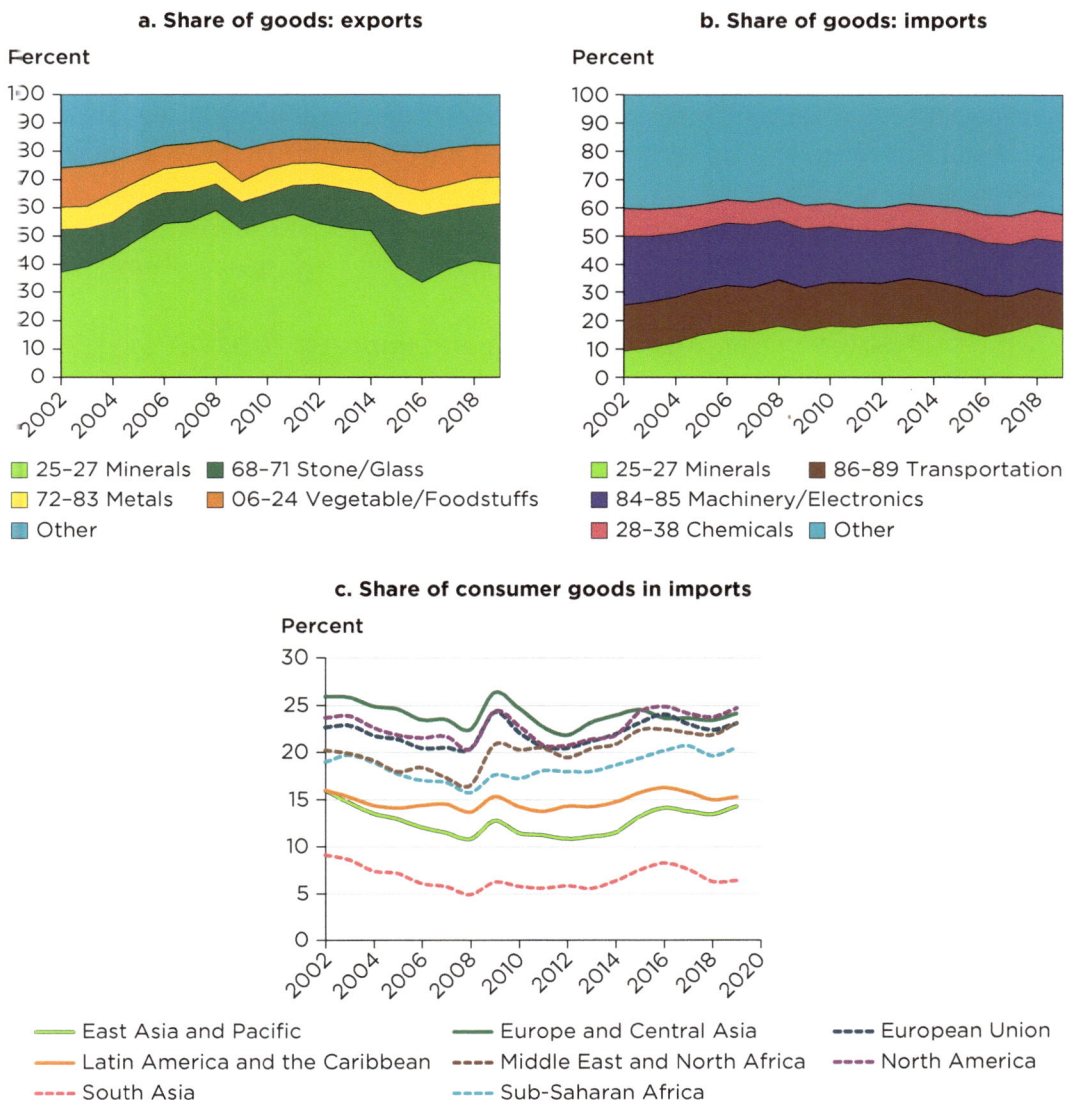

a. Share of goods: exports

Legend:
- 25–27 Minerals
- 72–83 Metals
- Other
- 68–71 Stone/Glass
- 06–24 Vegetable/Foodstuffs

b. Share of goods: imports

Legend:
- 25–27 Minerals
- 84–85 Machinery/Electronics
- 28–38 Chemicals
- 86–89 Transportation
- Other

c. Share of consumer goods in imports

Legend:
- East Asia and Pacific
- Latin America and the Caribbean
- South Asia
- Europe and Central Asia
- Middle East and North Africa
- Sub-Saharan Africa
- European Union
- North America

Source: CEPII BACI International Trade database, https://www.cepii.fr/CEPII/en/bdd_modele/bdd _modele_item.asp?id=37.

The continued focus on commodity exports perpetuates the continent's vulnerability to global demand downturns and sudden price changes. Commodities helped boost Sub-Saharan Africa's goods export values during the 2000s, when China's demand for commodities pushed up global prices, but left the region at a disadvantage in the 2010s, when the upward trends in global prices reversed as China prioritized the rebalancing of its economy from investment to consumption.

Changing structure of trading partners

The structure of Sub-Saharan Africa's export destinations and import origins changed significantly over time. The three most striking developments to export destinations included the sharp drop in the share of North America from 19 percent in 2010 to only 6 percent in 2019, the steady rise of China from only 5 percent in 2002 to 19 percent in 2019, and the rise of the continent's intraregional trade in the 2000s from 8 percent in 2002 to 18 percent by 2010 (figure 4.4, panel a). The top export destinations in 2019 remained the EU, despite a 14-percentage-point loss in the share from 2002 to 2019. China and Sub-Saharan Africa became the second and third most significant destinations in 2019, replacing North America and other non-EU countries in the Europe and Central Asia region that had occupied the respective places in 2002. Exports to South Asia and the Middle East and North Africa regions also grew over time, and their share overtook

FIGURE 4.4 Sub-Saharan Africa's exports and imports, 2002–19

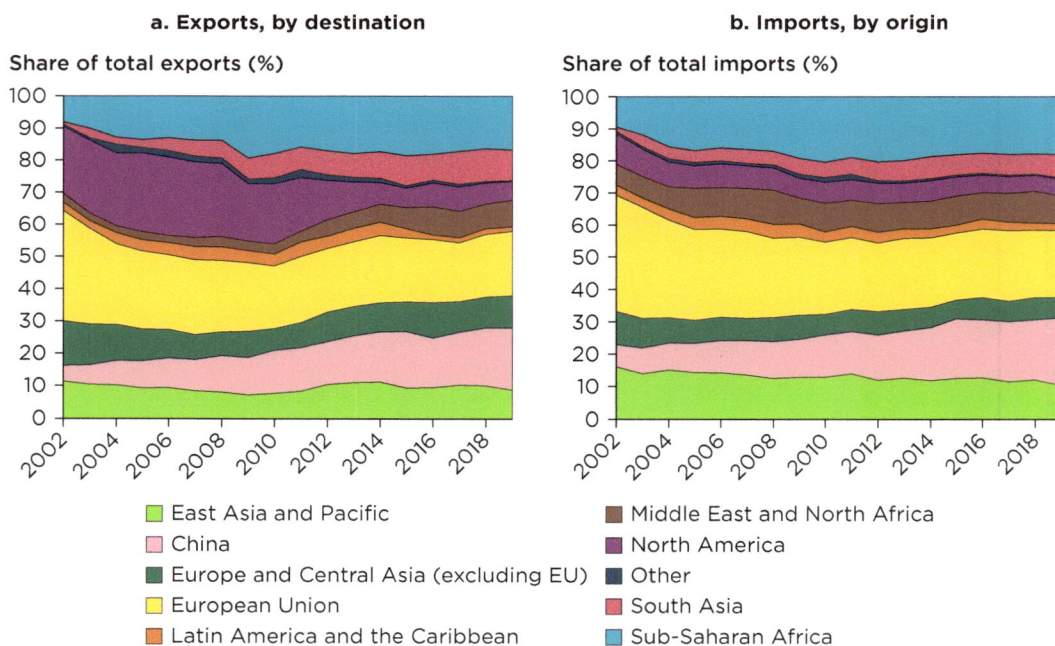

a. Exports, by destination

Share of total exports (%)

b. Imports, by origin

Share of total imports (%)

Legend:
- East Asia and Pacific
- China
- Europe and Central Asia (excluding EU)
- European Union
- Latin America and the Caribbean
- Middle East and North Africa
- North America
- Other
- South Asia
- Sub-Saharan Africa

Source: CEPII BACI International Trade database, https://www.cepii.fr/CEPII/en/bdd_modele/bdd_modele_item.asp?id=37.

Note: The United States is driving the trends shown for North America, accounting, on average, for 90 percent of the data shown in the charts. North America includes the United States, Canada, and Bermuda. Mexico is included in Latin America and the Caribbean. EU = European Union.

that of non-EU Europe and Central Asia by 2020. In the context of the structure of import origin, notable developments included a rise in China's share from 7 percent in 2002 to 21 percent in 2019, the gradual decline in the EU share from 36 percent in 2002 to 21 percent in 2019, and the increase in the Sub-Saharan African countries' share from 9 percent in 2002 to 18 percent in 2019 (figure 4.4, panel b).

Sub-Saharan Africa's subregions vary in their structure of trade by trading partners (figure 4.5). For example, in the case of exports, the largest rise in China's share and the

FIGURE 4.5 **Sub-Saharan Africa's trade dynamics, by subregion, 2002–19**

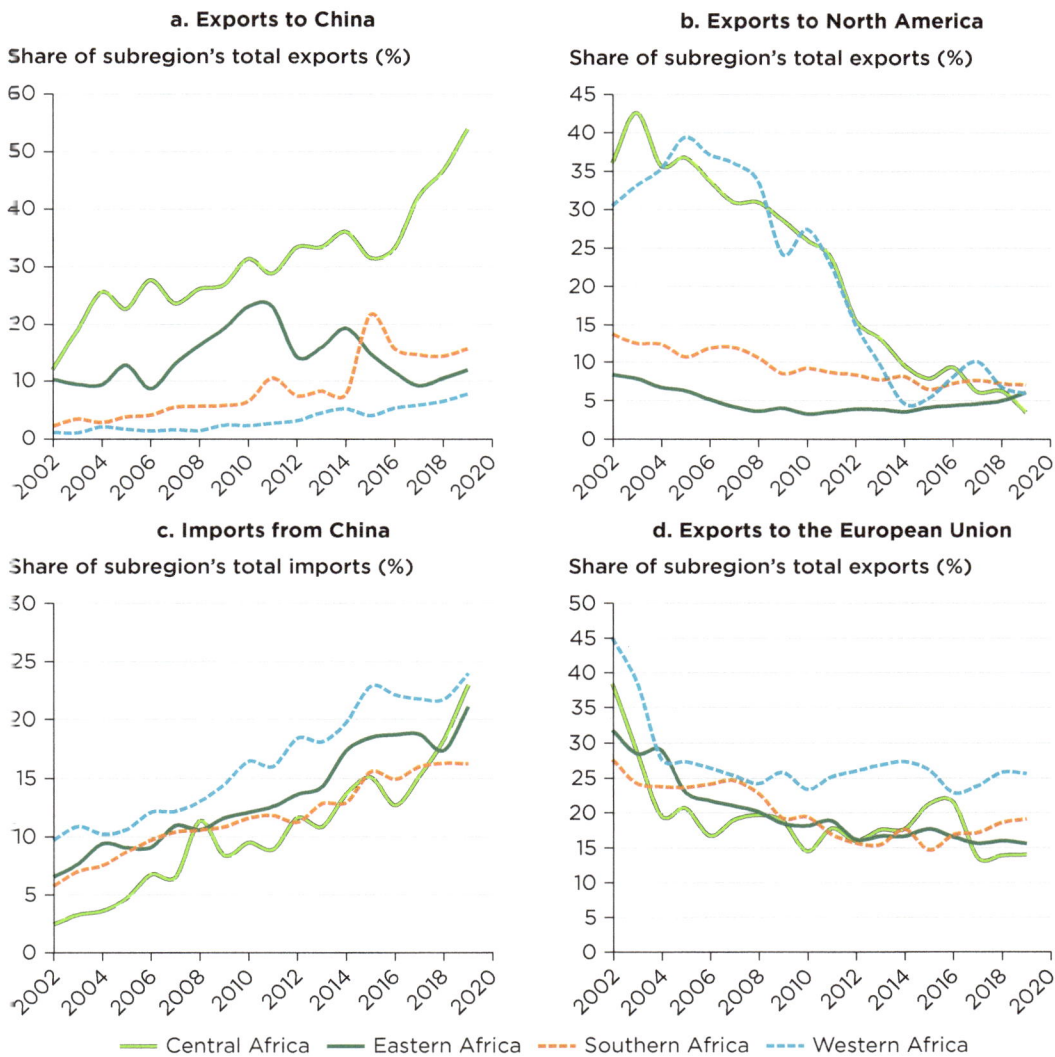

a. Exports to China

Share of subregion's total exports (%)

b. Exports to North America

Share of subregion's total exports (%)

c. Imports from China

Share of subregion's total imports (%)

d. Exports to the European Union

Share of subregion's total exports (%)

Central Africa — Eastern Africa — Southern Africa — Western Africa

Source: CEPII BACI International Trade database, https://www.cepii.fr/CEPII/en/bdd_modele/bdd_modele_item.asp?id=37.
Note: Panels a and b show uneven dynamics in trading partners' shares across subregions; panels c and d show similar dynamics in those shares. The United States is driving the trends shown for North America in panel b. North America includes the United States, Canada, and Bermuda. Mexico is included in Latin America and the Caribbean.

largest decline in North America's share have occurred in Central Africa: by 2019, China's share in Central Africa's exports exceeded 50 percent, whereas North America's share dropped to less than 5 percent, from more than 40 percent in 2003. Underlying this dynamic were declining exports of crude oil to the United States (annex figure 4A.2) from countries such as Angola and Gabon. Western Africa also saw a large decline in North America's share as an export destination, due primarily to Nigeria's declining exports of crude oil. By contrast, the rise of China in the region's imports and the decline in the EU in the region's exports and imports have been gradual across the four subregions.

Stagnating intraregional trade

Although in line with that of other developing countries (except East Asia), the degree of regional trade integration in Sub-Saharan Africa has stagnated in recent years. Intraregional trade accounted for almost 20 percent of Sub-Saharan Africa's trade in 2019 (figure 4.6, panel a).[6] This share is significantly less than the 50 percent observed for the East Asia and Pacific region, but above that of South Asia and in line with the shares of other regions that include developing countries. During the 2000s, Sub-Saharan Africa experienced faster growth than other regions in its share of intraregional trade; however, after peaking at 19.3 percent in 2009, this growth plateaued. By 2019, the share of intraregional trade had leveled off at 17.3 percent.

Minerals, especially crude oil, account for 26.6 percent of Sub-Saharan Africa's intraregional trade, followed by metals at 11.4 percent and transportation equipment at 9.7 percent (figure 4.6, panel b). The variety of the intraregional trade basket and its share of relatively complex products (transportation, machinery/electronics, and chemicals) contrasts with the focus on commodities of the region's overall goods export basket. This focus may reflect the presence in intraregional trade of goods produced outside the region but that cross multiple borders to reach landlocked destination countries (re-exports), as well as of manufactures produced locally in Africa that are competitive regionally but not globally because of high trade costs (for example, matches and plastic pipes).

The aggregate picture hides considerable variation at the subregional level. During the 2000s, all subregions experienced an increase in integration, measured as the share of intraregional trade in total trade, although the pace of integration has slowed in the last decade (figure 4.7). Eastern Africa and Southern Africa are the most integrated in both exports and imports. Central Africa is the least integrated when it comes to exports, and its importance as an export destination for other Sub-Saharan African countries has declined over time. Intraregional trade includes several major trade corridors—such as intra-Southern and Southern-Eastern—and their shares of total intraregional trade have proven remarkably stable in the past decade (annex figure 4A.3).

FIGURE 4.6 Sub-Saharan Africa's intraregional trade, 2002–19

a. Relative to other regions

Intraregional trade as share of total trade (%)

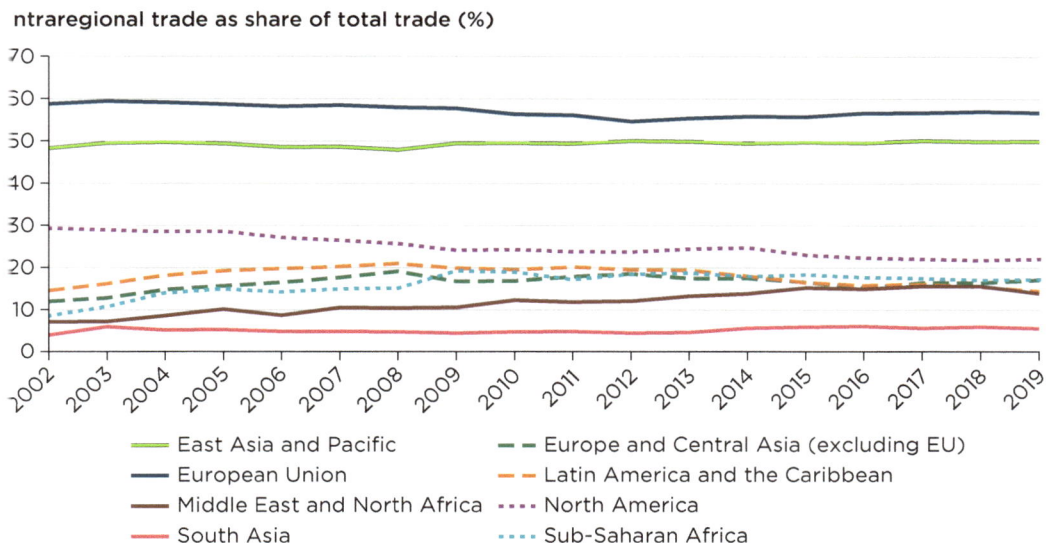

Legend:
— East Asia and Pacific
— — Europe and Central Asia (excluding EU)
— European Union
— — Latin America and the Caribbean
— Middle East and North Africa
···· North America
— South Asia
···· Sub-Saharan Africa

b. By product group

Share of intraregional trade (%)

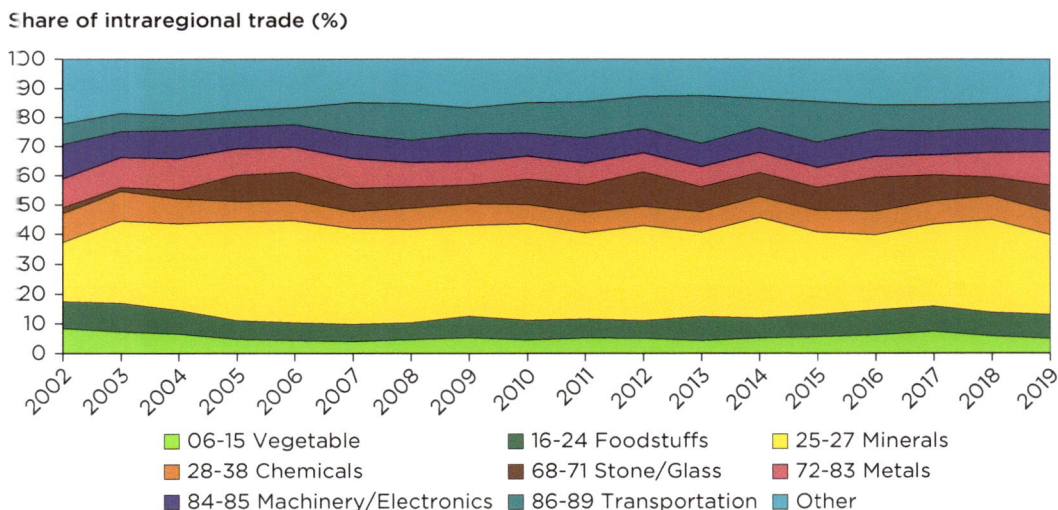

Legend:
■ 06-15 Vegetable
■ 16-24 Foodstuffs
■ 25-27 Minerals
■ 28-38 Chemicals
■ 68-71 Stone/Glass
■ 72-83 Metals
■ 84-85 Machinery/Electronics
■ 86-89 Transportation
■ Other

Source: CEPII BACI International Trade database, https://www.cepii.fr/CEPII/en/bdd_modele/bdd _modele_item.asp?id=37.
Note: EU = European Union.

FIGURE 4.7 Share of Sub-Saharan Africa destinations (origins) in Sub-Saharan Africa exports (imports), 2002–19

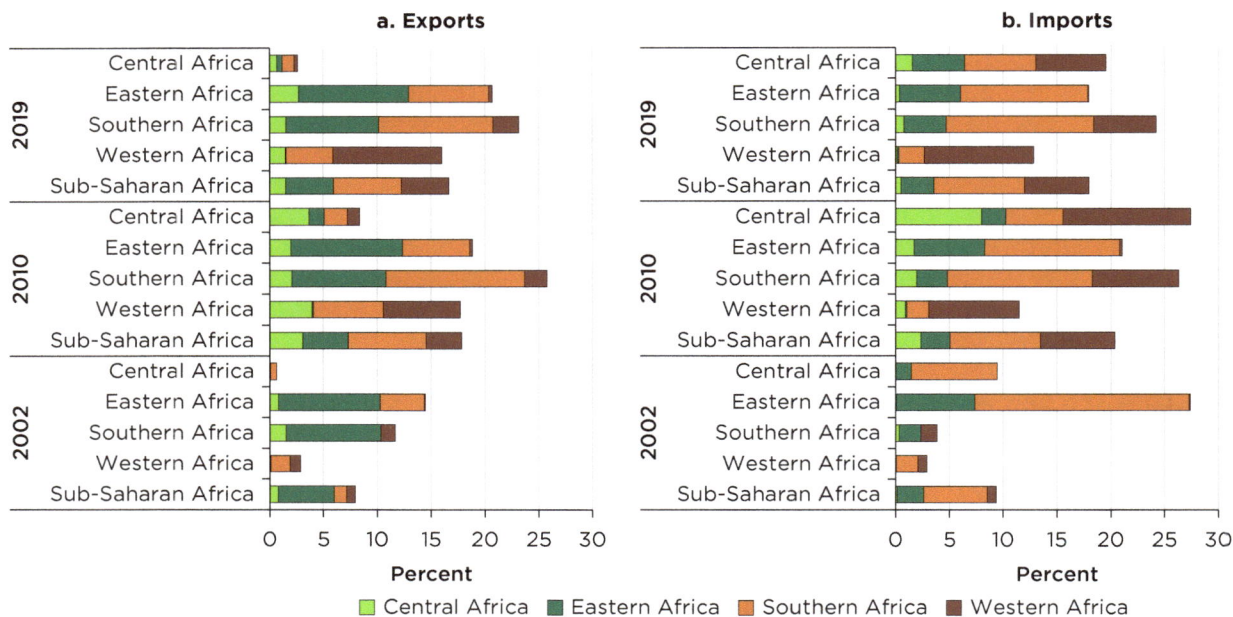

Source: CEPII BACI International Trade database, https://www.cepii.fr/CEPII/en/bdd_modele/bdd_modele_item.asp?id=37.

Services trade

Services trade of Sub-Saharan Africa accounts for less than 2 percent of the world's trade in services. The region's services share has declined in the past decade (figure 4.8, panel a). Sub-Saharan Africa exports about half as much in services as it imports, and traditional services account for most of its services exports. Thus, in the past two decades, travel and transportation services represented approximately 75 percent of Sub-Saharan Africa's services exports (figure 4.8, panel b). The share of "Other" services, including mostly technical, trade-related, and other business services, has increased since the mid-2010s.[7] Various subregions contribute differently to Sub-Saharan Africa's services exports: Eastern and Southern Africa are the largest exporters and Central Africa the smallest, whereas the share of Western Africa picked up in recent years (figure 4.8, panel c).

GVC engagement

Sub-Saharan Africa's engagement in GVCs is primarily as a commodity supplier (map 4.1).[8] According to the 2020 *World Development Report*, most Sub-Saharan African countries produce commodities (oil and other natural resources) for further processing in other countries (World Bank 2020b). Nevertheless, a handful of Sub-Saharan African countries (Eswatini, Ethiopia, Kenya, Namibia, South Africa, and Tanzania) also assume limited manufacturing tasks, sourcing foreign inputs for export-oriented business in sectors such as apparel, agribusiness, and automotives. Morocco and Tunisia also engage in limited manufacturing. In recent years, GVC participation in some Sub-Saharan African countries (Ethiopia, Kenya, South Africa, and Tanzania) grew by 10 percentage points, a dynamic also shared by Poland and Viet Nam in the 1990s and 2000s.

FIGURE 4.8 **Sub-Saharan Africa's services trade, 2005–19**

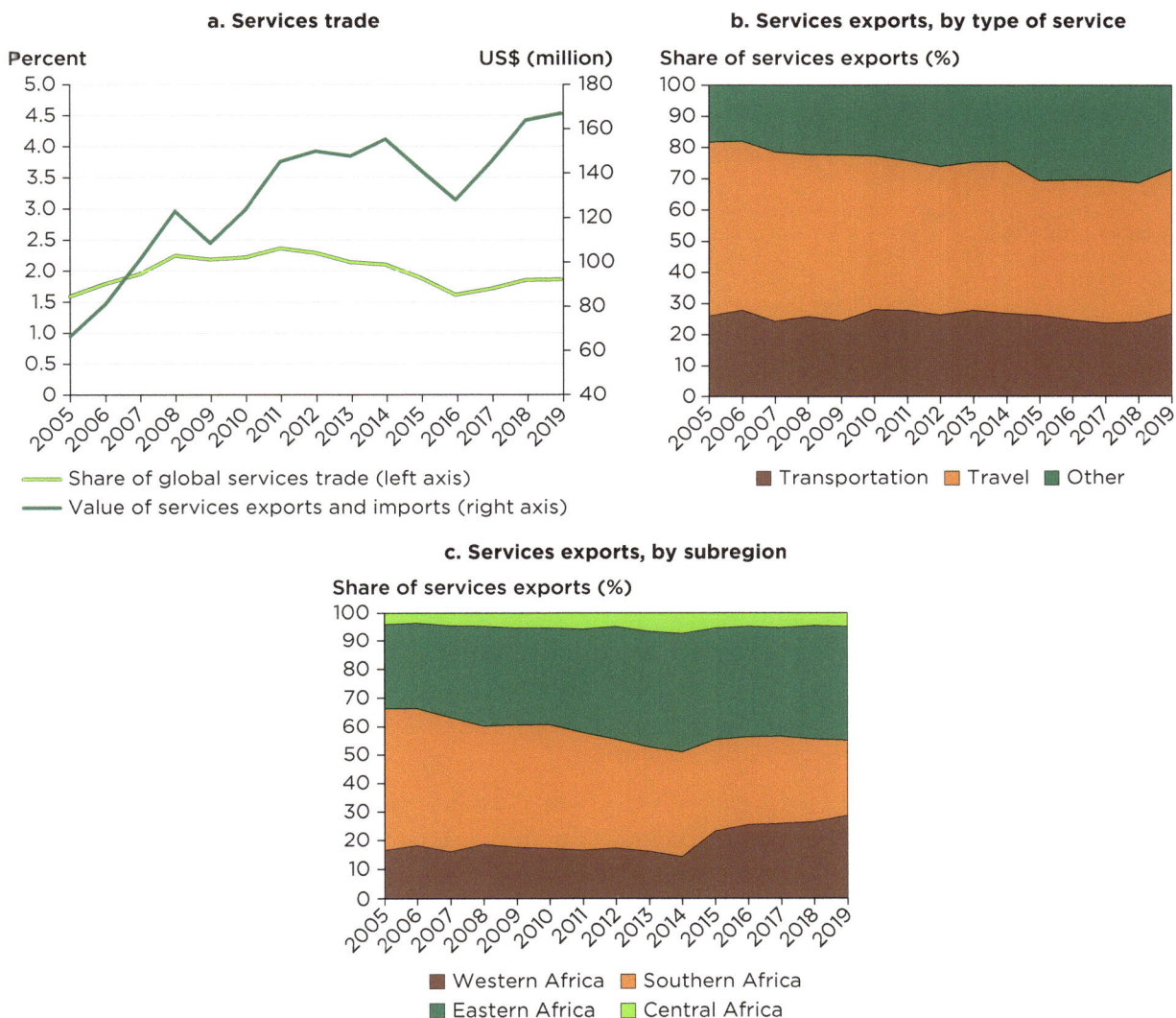

a. Services trade

b. Services exports, by type of service

c. Services exports, by subregion

Source: World Trade Organization data, https://www.wto.org/english/res_e/statis_e/services_trade_data_hub_e.htm.

Sub-Saharan African countries can potentially reap significant benefits from participating in GVCs. By promoting hyperspecialization and durable firm-to-firm relationships, GVCs can help boost incomes, create better jobs, and reduce poverty (World Bank 2020b). Empirical analysis suggests that the biggest growth spurt occurs when countries transition out of exporting commodities and into exporting basic manufactured products such as garments. Sub-Saharan African countries that have transitioned to limited manufacturing are already seeing benefits accruing from GVC participation. A notable example is that of Ethiopia, where firms participating in GVCs have proven twice as productive as firms that participate in standard trade, and have seen faster-growing employment and greater declines in markups (World Bank 2020b).[9]

MAP 4.1 Global value chain participation worldwide, by country, 2015

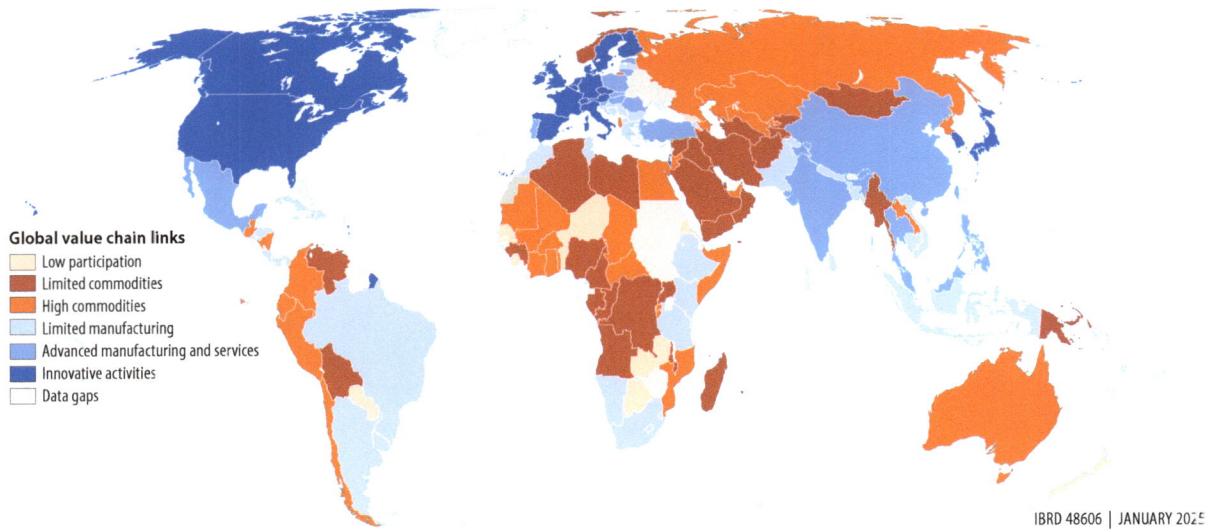

Source: World Bank 2020b.

Policy and connectivity gaps

This section looks at the thickness of borders in the context of trade policies and agreements in Africa.

Border thickness and trade costs

The *thickness* of a border (or border effect) describes the additional cost to trade between two contiguous countries, as compared to trade within countries. In other words, trade costs are the frictions of trade. They come from poor physical and service connectivity between neighbors; impediments encountered at border crossing points, such as tariffs and border delays, as well as logistics and regulatory barriers; trade finance; and insurance costs. In many instances, cross-border safety concerns contribute to reduced trade between neighbors. Finally, trade costs also come from "behind-the-border" effects that affect international trade, such as those associated with communicating in different languages or marketing to different consumer preferences, as well as the lack of integration of production, distribution, and logistics networks. In sum, the thickness of borders provides an indirect measure of the economic fragmentation of the continent.

This chapter relies on the ESCAP–World Bank Trade Cost Database that tracks the costs of trade between pairs of countries since 1995. The bilateral cost of trade is calculated as the ad valorem equivalent "wedge" between international trade and domestic commerce.[10] These estimates use the gravity model of trade, which predicts flows based on the sizes of the economies and the cost of trade between the two partners. Border thickness refers hereafter to the cross-border bilateral trade costs between a pair of contiguous countries. The ESCAP–World Bank Trade Cost Database includes 226 land borders, 57 of which are in Sub-Saharan Africa (refer to annex table 4A.1 for the "thickest" and "thinnest" bilateral borders). Border thickness is significantly higher in low-income regions than in high-income and closely integrated economies, such as the EU or North America: from less than 30 percent to more than 200 percent ad valorem equivalent.

Focusing on border thickness in Africa using the most recent data (map 4.2) shows that, of the 10 thickest borders, 6 are in Africa. Although these estimates reflect the costs of trade, each individual value must be interpreted with care and does not necessarily reflect physical or administrative barriers to trade. As noted earlier, the estimates capture additional variables not directly tied to the physical borders. For example,

MAP 4.2 Bilateral border thickness, Africa, 2015–18 average

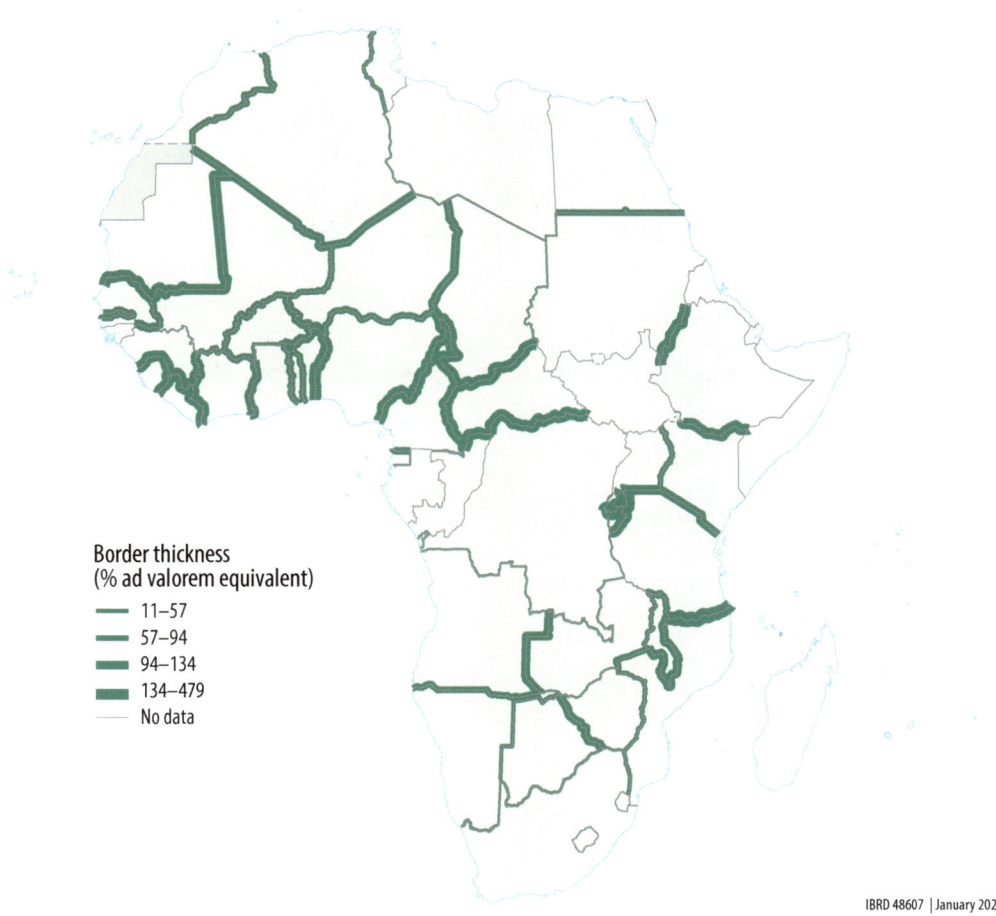

Border thickness
(% ad valorem equivalent)
— 11–57
— 57–94
— 94–134
— 134–479
— No data

IBRD 48607 | January 2025

Source: Calculated using data from the ESCAP–World Bank Trade Cost Database, https://www
.unescap.org/resources/escap-world-bank-trade-cost-database.
Note: Border thickness, which refers to the cross-border bilateral trade costs between neighboring countries, is calculated as the ad valorem equivalent "wedge" between international and domestic trade. It encompasses all friction sources, including intangible ones, and not just actual monetary expenditures like transportation or tariffs. The gravity model of trade is used to estimate these costs, predicting trade flows based on the sizes of economies and the cost of trade between partners.

the thickest border, between Chad and Niger, is estimated to be 479 percent of the value of the goods traded. This border is remote and unsecure. At the other extreme, some subregions, such as Southern Africa, have comparatively moderate cross-border costs of trade because goods can move more smoothly between these countries, with significant integration of logistics and distribution networks from South Africa. In general, free trade agreements help reduce trade costs between countries.[11]

Comparing cross-border trade costs in Africa and other world regions between two periods, spanning two decades, table 4.1 reports the change in trade costs between the periods 1997–2000 and 2015–18, the most recent years with extensive coverage.[12] The main finding is that, globally, cross-border trade costs have decreased slightly over the two decades—a 9.3 percent reduction, on average. Sub-Saharan Africa's internal border costs declined by 11.5 percent, on average, in line with the reduction at the global level. The reduction of trade costs shows some dispersion, with a bell curve distribution (figure 4.9); however, no clear subregional patterns appear within Africa (annex table 4A.2). Interpretation of changes at specific borders must be done cautiously. The numbers may not necessarily reflect policy changes but eventually serendipitous changes tied to the appearance or disappearance of a bilateral activity that may affect the statistics of relatively small trade flows. Many large changes are related to changes in bilateral relationships or to security issues.

TABLE 4.1 Percentage change in bilateral trade costs, by world region, 1997–2000 and 2015–18

Region	East Asia and Pacific	Europe and Central Asia	High-income countries	Latin America and the Caribbean	Middle East and North Africa	South Asia	Sub-Saharan Africa
East Asia and Pacific	−15.6	−6.4	11.5	—	—	−24.5	—
Europe and Central Asia	−6.4	−10.2	−7.3	—	−0.5	—	—
High-income countries	11.5	−7.3	−10.2	−12.0	4.3	—	—
Latin America and the Caribbean	—	—	−12.0	−5.9	—	—	—
Middle East and North Africa	—	−0.5	4.3	—	17.8	—	−5.9
South Asia	−24.5	—	—	—	—	−15.4	—
Sub-Saharan Africa	—	—	—	—	−5.9	—	−11.5

Source: Calculations based on ESCAP–World Bank Trade Cost Database, https://www.unescap.org/resources/escap-world-bank-trade-cost-database.
Note: — = not available.

FIGURE 4.9 Distribution of changes in bilateral trade costs, Sub-Saharan Africa and rest of world, 1997–2000 and 2015–18

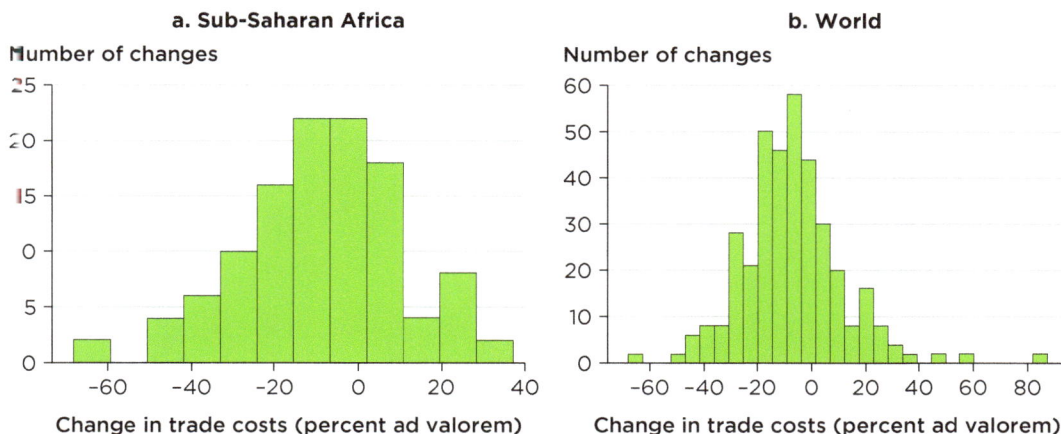

a. Sub-Saharan Africa

Number of changes

Change in trade costs (percent ad valorem)

b. World

Number of changes

Change in trade costs (percent ad valorem)

Source: ESCAP–World Bank Trade Cost Database, https://www.unescap.org/resources /escap-world-bank-trade-cost-database.

Trade policies and trade agreements

At the global level, tariffs have progressively fallen since the establishment of the General Agreement on Tariffs and Trade in 1948. Unilateral liberalization and eight rounds of multilateral trade negotiations have significantly reduced tariffs applied by World Trade Organization (WTO) members. World trade-weighted nondiscriminatory (most favored nation [MFN]) tariffs fell from 11.1 percent in 2000 to 8.1 percent in 2018. Despite progress made in recent years, however, the Middle East and North Africa and Sub-Saharan Africa remain the regions with the highest trade-weighted MFN rates: 11.5 percent and 8.7 percent in 2018 from 14.5 percent and 9.8 percent in 2000, respectively. During the same period, the South Asia and Latin America and the Caribbean regions decreased their trade-weighted MFN rates from 21.4 percent and 13.3 percent to 6.6 percent and 6.6 percent, respectively. By contrast, regions such as Europe and Central Asia, East Asia and Pacific, and North America imposed relative lower MFN rates during 2018 of 4.1 percent, 3.9 percent, and 3.2 percent, respectively.

The extent of preferential liberalization varies across African countries. About 27 percent of countries in the region have reduced their applied trade-weighted average tariffs to less than 5 percent (figure 4.10). For Botswana, Burundi, Eswatini, Lesotho, and Morocco, trade-weighted applied tariffs are more than 6 percentage points lower than their trade-weighted MFN rates. By contrast, for countries such as Djibouti, Gabon, and The Gambia, applied trade-weighted preferential tariffs are more than 14 percent and equal to their trade-weighted MFN rates.

FIGURE 4.10 Trade-weighted average tariffs imposed, by country, 2018

Trade-weighted average tariff (%)

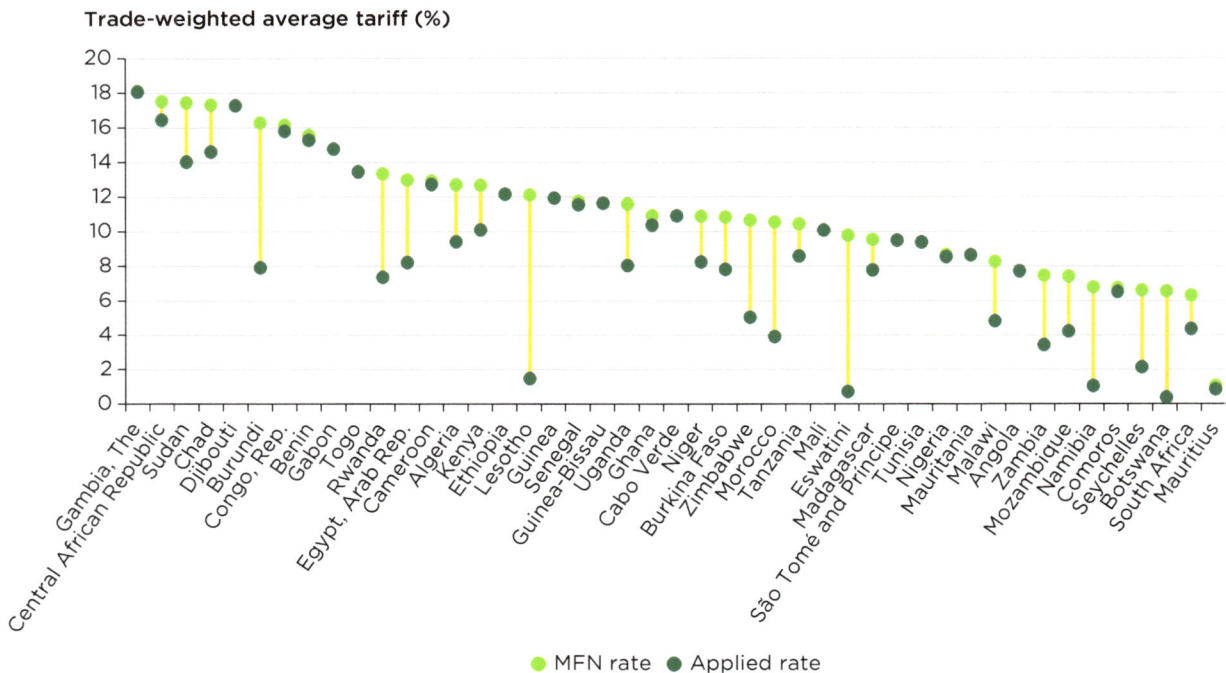

● MFN rate ● Applied rate

Source: World Bank, World Integrated Trade Solution, https://wits.worldbank.org/default.aspx.
Note: Most recent data for Algeria (2017), Cabo Verde (2015), Cameroon (2014), Central African Republic (2017), Chad (1995), the Comoros (2013), the Republic of Congo (2014), Djibouti (2009), Eswatini (2017), Ethiopia (2015), Gabon (2009), Guinea (2008), Guinea-Bissau (2005), Lesotho (2017), Malawi (2016), Mali (2017), Mauritania (2014), Morocco (2017), Niger (2016), Nigeria (2016), Rwanda (2016), Sudan (2017), Togo (2017), Tunisia (2016), and Zimbabwe (2016). MFN = most favored nation.

The type of preferential liberalization that African governments have made in trade agreements varies by origin of the signatories, with greater opening in relation to regional partners. Trade-weighted preferential margins applied to imports from African countries are 8.3 percent, whereas those applied to extraregional partners are 3.1 percent (figure 4.11). In other words, whereas the trade-weighted preferential tariff applied to imports from African partners is 1.8 percent—8.3 percentage points lower than the trade-weighted MFN rate—imports from a partner outside of the region face a trade-weighted preferential tariff of 6.9 percent—3.1 percentage points lower than the 10.0 percent trade-weighted MFN rate (annex table 4A.3).

Beyond tariffs: The evolution of trade agreements in Africa

Starting at the end of the 1990s, more and more countries signed bilateral and regional PTAs that went beyond simple market access. Modern trade agreements are increasingly "deep" because they cover a wide-ranging set of border and behind-the-border policy areas regulating customs procedures, services trade, technical barriers to trade, sanitary and phytosanitary measures, rules on investment, intellectual property

FIGURE 4.11 Trade-weighted average tariffs, by type of trading partner

Percent

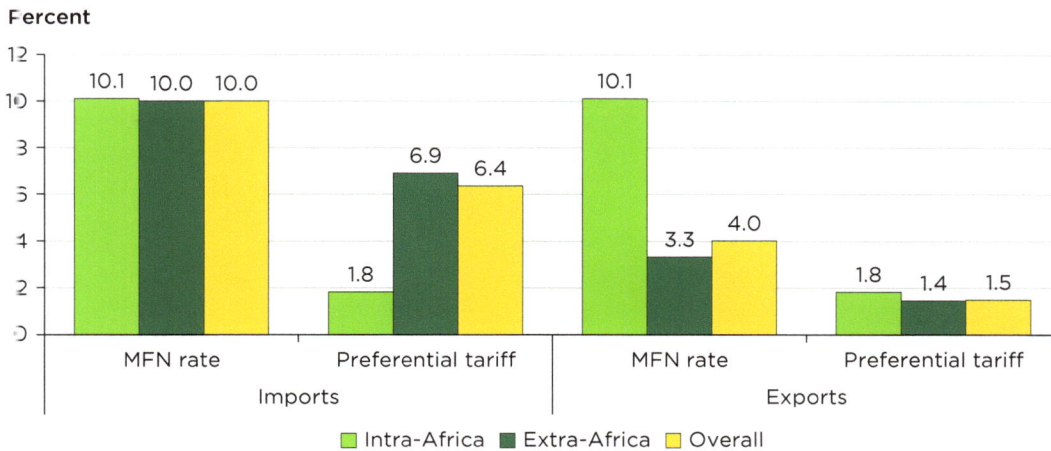

Sources: Mattoo, Rocha, and Ruta 2020; World Bank, Deep Trade Agreements database, Https://datatopics.worldbank.org/dta/table.html.
Note: MFN = most favored nation.

rights protection, competition policy, labor and environmental standards, and so forth. Some of these policy areas aim to promote integration in goods, services, or factor markets. Others aim to limit government actions that can undo these rights, for instance through regulatory protectionism. Yet other policy areas aim to improve efficiency, such as competition rules, or have broader societal objectives as in the case of environmental standards (Mattoo, Rocha, and Ruta 2020).

The African region has increased its participation in PTAs, but the level of integration varies widely across African countries. PTA participation has in general accelerated over time, with African countries taking part in 30 agreements, a 10th of the total agreements in force by 2017. Egypt and Morocco have the highest number of agreements with seven, followed by Mauritius, Tanzania, and Tunisia as members of six agreements. Botswana, Eswatini, Lesotho, Madagascar, Mozambique, Namibia, the Seychelles, South Africa, and Zimbabwe are members of five agreements. In terms of country partners with whom agreements are signed, more than half of African countries have so far not participated in agreements with other regions, nor with any high-income economy. In contrast, Egypt, Morocco, and Tunisia have integrated mainly with high-income economies (annex table 4A.4).

With a few exceptions, PTAs in African countries are shallow on average.[13] Agreements signed by countries in the region include 17 policy areas on average, of which 7 are legally enforceable. Map 4.3 presents the average depth for all countries in the world as measured by the number of enforceable policy areas included in a country's trade agreements.[14] Within Africa, countries with the largest number of enforceable policy areas are Mozambique (12), Tanzania (11), Morocco (10), and Ghana (10). Southern Africa countries, such as Botswana, Lesotho, and South Africa, include on average 9 enforceable policy areas.

MAP 4.3 Average depth of active trade agreements worldwide, 2019

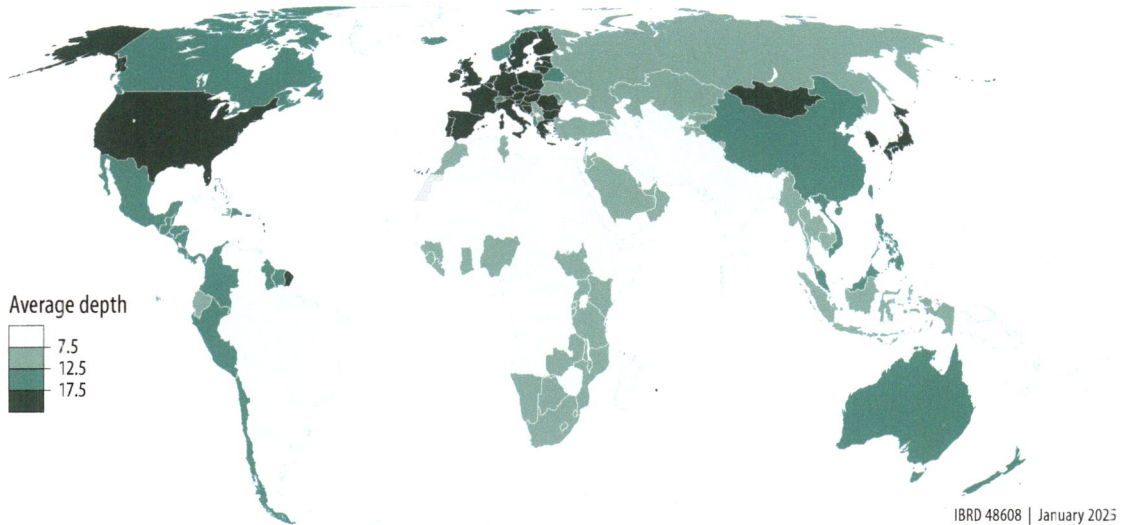

Average depth
- 7.5
- 12.5
- 17.5

IBRD 48608 | January 2025

Sources: Hofmann, Osnago, and Ruta 2017; World Bank, Deep Trade Agreements database, https://datatopics .worldbank.org/dta/table.html.
Note: The depth is measured as the average number of legally enforceable policy areas included in a country's trade agreements.

Trade agreements among African countries usually include policy areas that currently fall into the mandate of the WTO (referred to as WTO+ provisions). These policy areas encompass tariff reductions on industrial and agricultural goods, customs and trade facilitation, technical barriers to trade, sanitary and phytosanitary measures, anti-dumping, countervailing measures, export taxes, and areas covered by the WTO in terms of trade in services. Other policy areas that go beyond the WTO mandate (WTO-X provisions) such as investment, movement of capital, and public procurement are not common in trade agreements with countries outside the region and are even less frequent among African countries (table 4.2). In addition, there is significant variability in the detailed content of these policy areas and in how they translate into reforms in national laws.

The AfCFTA agreement, signed in March 2018, could be transformational by promoting economic integration in Africa in two ways:

- First, it includes policy areas that have largely not been covered in Africa's subregional PTAs: intellectual property rights (covered in only one subregional PTA, the East African Community) and state trading enterprises (not covered by any subregional PTA).

- Second, in the policy areas already covered by subregional PTAs, the AfCFTA agreement will offer a common regulatory framework, thereby providing a uniform set of rules for the continent, reducing market fragmentation created by different sets of rules (World Bank 2020a).

TABLE 4.2 Most common policy areas included in subregional African trade agreements

Discipline	Common Market for Eastern and Southern Africa (COMESA)	East African Community (EAC)	South African Development Community (SADC)	Economic and Monetary Community of Central Africa (CEMAC)	Economic Community of West African States (ECOWAS)	West African Economic and Monetary Union (WAEMU)	South African Customs Union (SACU)	African Continental Free Trade Area (AfCFTA)
Tariffs on manufacturing goods	✓	✓	✓	✓	✓	✓	✓	✓
Tariffs on agricultural goods	✓	✓	✓	✓	✓	✓	✓	✓
Competition policy	✓	✓	✓	✓	✗	✓	✓	✓
GATS	✓	✓	✓	✗	✓	✓	✗	✓
Customs	✓	✓	✓	✓	✓	✓	✓	✓
TBTs	✓	✓	✓	✓	✗	✗	✓	✓
SPS measures	✓	✓	✓	✓	✗	✗	✗	✓
Movement of capital	✓	✓	✗	✓	✓	✓	✓	✓
Export taxes	✓	✗	✓	✓	✗	✗	✗	✓
Anti-dumping	✓	✗	✓	✗	✓	✗	✗	✗
State aid	✓	✓	✓	✓	✓	✓	✗	✓
Investment	✓	✓	✓	✓	✗	✗	✗	✗
Environmental laws	✓	✗	✗	✓	✓	✗	✗	✓
Countervailing measures	✓	✗	✓	✗	✗	✗	✗	✗
IPRs	✗	✓	✗	✗	✗	✗	✗	✓
Labor market regulations	✓	✗	✗	✗	✗	✗	✗	✗
STEs	✗	✗	✗	✗	✗	✗	✗	✓
Public procurement	✗	✓	✗	✗	✗	✗	✗	✗

Sources: Hofmann, Osnago, and Ruta 2017; World Bank, Deep Trade Agreements database, https://datatopics.worldbank.org/dta/table.html.

Note: Green ✓ refers to policy areas that are covered; red ✗ refers to policy areas not covered. GATS = General Agreement on Trade in Services; IPRs = intellectual property rights; SPS = sanitary and phytosanitary; STEs = state trading enterprises; TBTs = technical barriers to trade.

Agreements that African economies sign with countries outside the region have increased in number and include more commitments. The number of extraregional trade agreements has expanded since 2000, accompanied by an increase in the number of policy commitments (figure 4.12).[15] Although in 2000 only four extraregional PTAs were in force,[16] by 2017 there were nine intraregional compared with 21 extraregional agreements (refer to annex table 4A.4 for the complete list of agreements considered). The number of intraregional agreements has increased mainly because of accessions to regional communities. Figure 4.12 shows how the coverage ratio—the share of provisions contained in a given agreement relative to the maximum number of provisions—has changed over time. With only a few exceptions, most new PTAs signed after 2000 have a coverage ratio higher than 10 percent.

In terms of depth of commitments, extra-African agreements tend to include a higher number of provisions compared with agreements signed within the region. These provisions comprise a set of substantive commitments, such as opening of services or investment markets, and supporting regulations covering procedures, transparency, and enforcement, that are complementary to achieving the substantive commitments. As shown in figure 4.13, agreements between African countries and countries in other regions on average tend to have a higher share of provisions in supporting and substantive commitments. In other words, intraregional integration tends to be shallower in terms of the nature of the commitments signed by countries.

FIGURE 4.12 **Number of African trade agreements over time compared with coverage ratio**

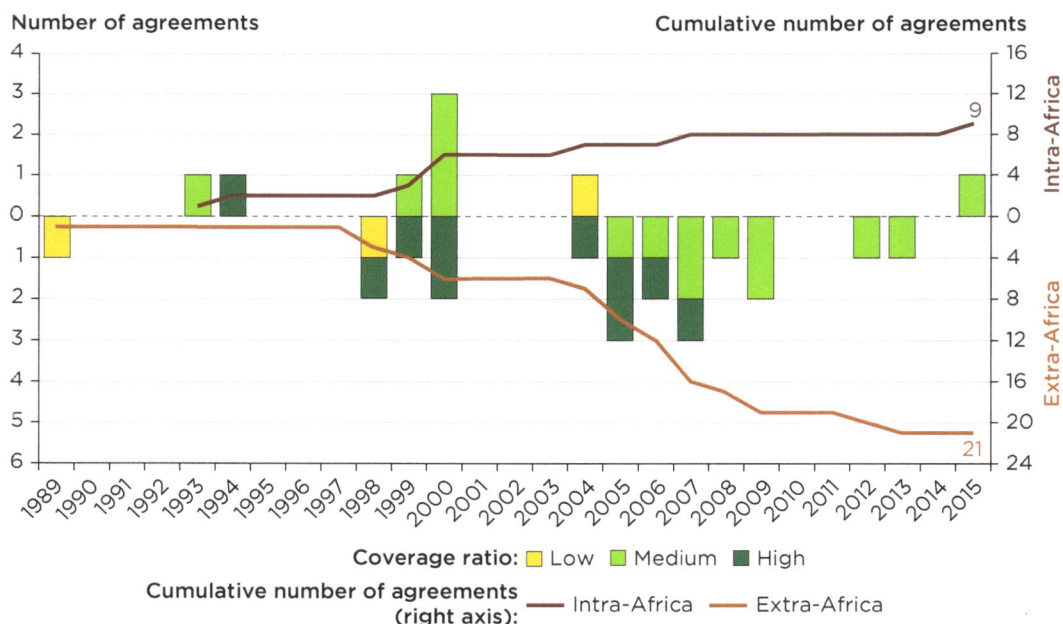

Sources: Mattoo, Rocha, and Ruta 2020; World Bank, Deep Trade Agreements database, https://datatopics.worldbank.org/dta/table.html.
Note: Coverage ratio refers to the share of provisions contained in a given agreement relative to the maximum number of provisions.

FIGURE 4.13 Substantive provisions and a breakdown of nonsubstantive provisions in African preferential trade agreements

Share of total provisions (%)

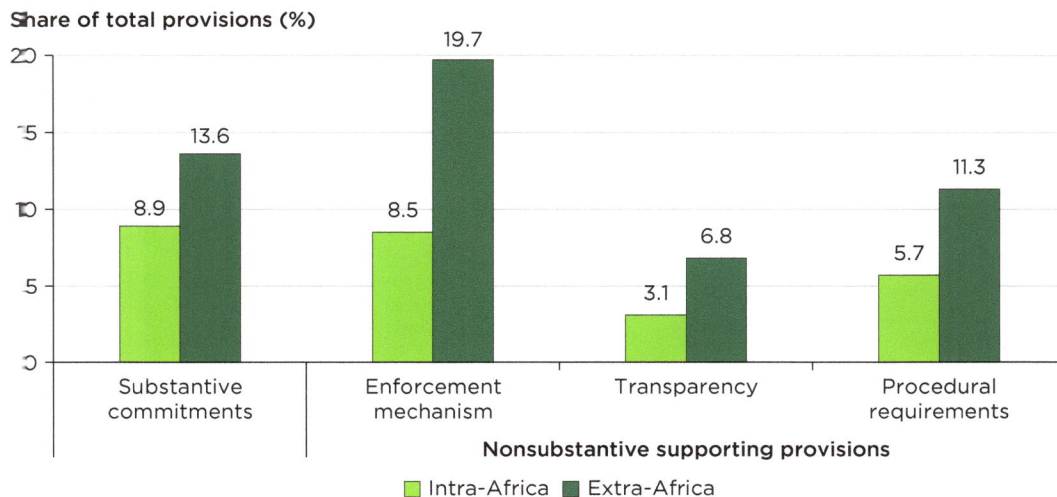

Sources: Mattoo, Rocha, and Ruta 2020; World Bank, Deep Trade Agreements database, https://datatopics.worldbank.org/dta/table.html.
Note: The figure shows only essential provisions.

Transportation infrastructure and border delays

The costs of moving goods within and across countries are generally higher in developing countries than in the rest of the world, and this situation is especially true in much of Africa. In some areas of Africa, transportation costs due to poor infrastructure and limited services may constitute a higher trade barrier than import tariffs or other trade restrictions. Transportation in Africa is often unpredictable and unreliable, with transportation infrastructure perceived as very low quality when compared with other regions in the world (figure 4.14). The Logistics Performance Index (LPI) measures the perceived quality of transportation infrastructure on a scale of 1–5. Sub-Saharan Africa has an average score of 2.2, the lowest compared with 2.3 in South Asia, 2.5 in Latin America and the Caribbean, 2.8 in the Middle East and North Africa, 3.0 in East Asia and Pacific, 3.1 in Europe and Central Asia, and 3.9 in North America (the world average is 2.7).

Most African countries have LPI scores below those of other regions, and the countries with the lowest infrastructure quality in the world are in Western Africa. The median infrastructure quality of all African regions, with the exception of Southern Sub-Saharan Africa, is significantly lower than the quality in East Asia and Pacific, Europe and Central Asia, North America, and the Middle East (figure 4.15). Within Africa, the quality of transportation infrastructure across countries varies significantly (figure 4.16). Only a limited number of countries on the continent meet or exceed the global average on the LPI. In Sub-Saharan Africa, these countries are Côte d'Ivoire, Mauritius, and South Africa; in North Africa, Egypt is the only country to do so. Furthermore, of the 35 African countries for which 2010 data are available, 11 saw their

FIGURE 4.14 Average LPI score of perceived quality of transportation infrastructure, by region, 2018

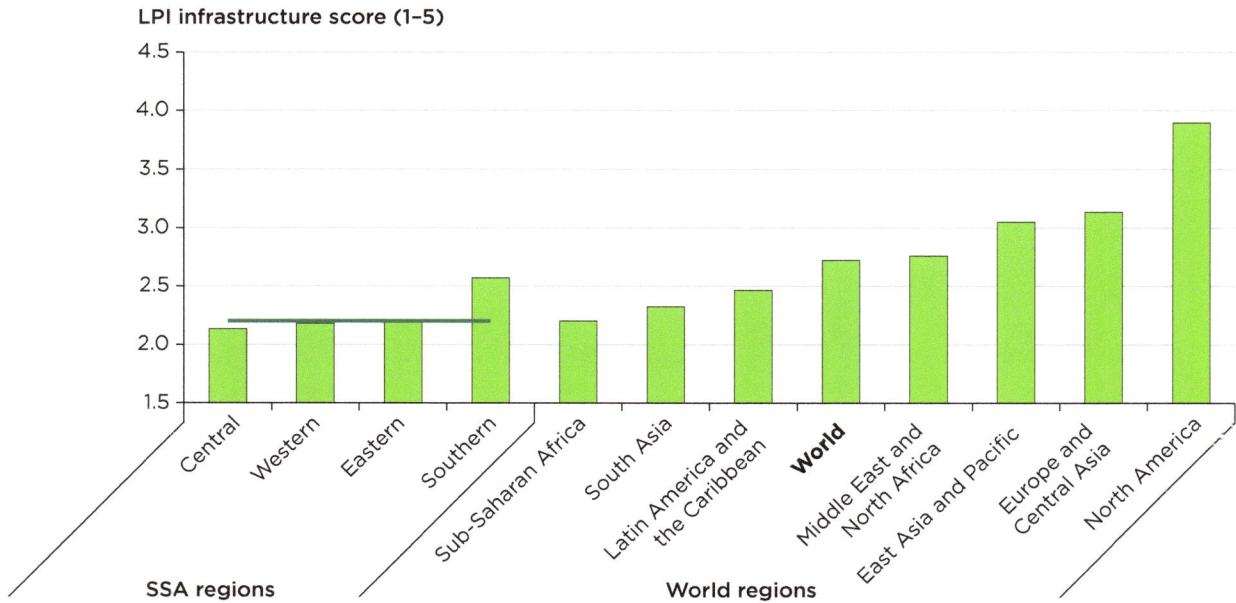

Source: Arvis et al. 2018.
Note: The dark green line is the average for Sub-Saharan Africa. LPI = Logistics Performance Index; SSA = Sub-Saharan Africa.

FIGURE 4.15 LPI score of perceived quality of transportation infrastructure, by region, 2018

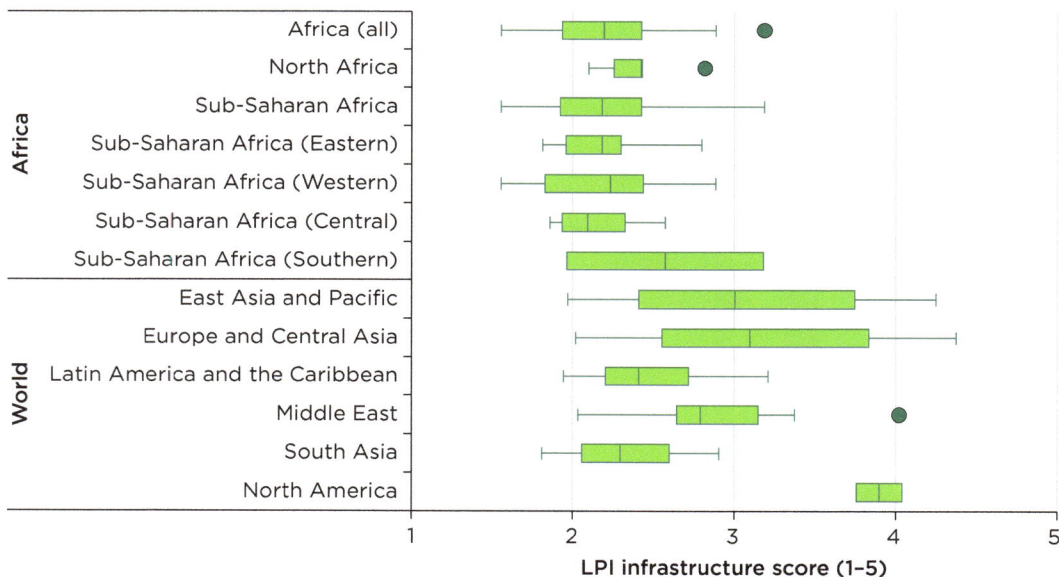

Source: Arvis et al. 2018.
Note: The box plots show the distribution of LPI scores per region. The vertical line within each box indicates the median. The dots represent outliers in the distribution of LPI infrastructure scores. LPI = Logistics Performance Index.

FIGURE 4.16 LPI score of perceived quality of transportation infrastructure in Africa, by country and subregion

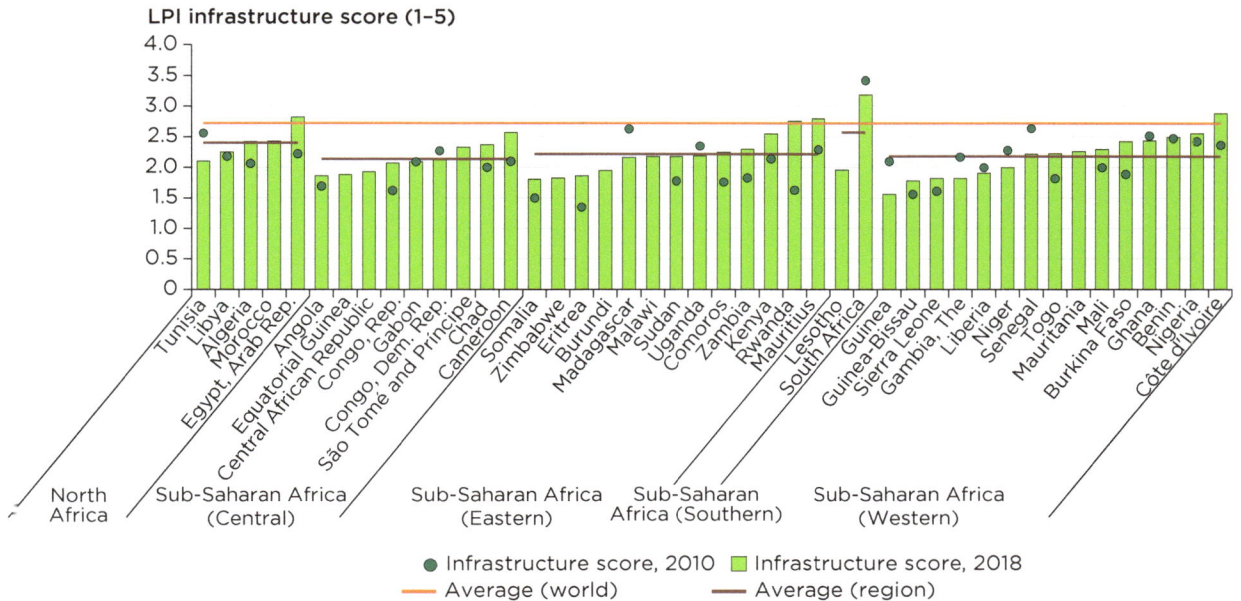

Source: Arvis et al. 2018.
Note: For some countries, 2010 data are not available. LPI = Logistics Performance Index.

LPI scores decline by 2018. Senegal experienced the largest decline with a score of –0.6, followed by Niger (–0.5), Guinea (–0.4), Madagascar (–0.3), and Tunisia (–0.3). On a more positive note, several countries in the region have improved LPI scores. They include Burkina Faso (0.39), Eritrea (0.39), Côte d'Ivoire (0.55), Somalia (0.87), and Rwanda (0.93).

Although poor roads increase the cost of transporting goods over long distances, other factors may have more significance, including long waiting times at borders and ports. Whereas almost every world region registered improvement in trade facilitation over the period 2006–18, Sub-Saharan Africa remains among the worst performers in ease of trading across borders.[17] These figures indicate that investment in reducing border and port delays is necessary to complement other transportation infrastructure investments.

To quantify the extent of sea and land border delays for African countries, the analysis for this chapter uses a series of indicators to create country pair land border frictions and country sea border frictions. First, it uses World Bank Ease of Doing Business indicators for country-level information on the ease of crossing land or sea borders by measuring the number of documents required to trade, the number of days to cross the border, and the related costs to export and import.[18] Second, ships face delays at ports that are calibrated using the median number of days for container ships at ports from UN Trade and Development data on the time vessels spend in port.[19] Finally, the analysis combines these data to calculate country pair land border and maritime gateway frictions.[20]

In order to reduce border delays, several countries have recently implemented One-Stop Border Posts (OSBPs) to enable goods, people, and vehicles to stop in a single facility in which they undergo necessary controls to exit one state and enter the adjoining state. The analysis includes such facilities using maps and status information from the Program for Infrastructure Development in Africa (PIDA) and various sources such as World Bank reports and the 2016 *One-Stop Border Post Sourcebook* on Africa's current OSBPs and those under construction and planned (AUDA-NEPAD and JICA 2022; World Bank 2020a). It assumes that land border delays are reduced by half when a functioning OSBP allows trucks to stop at only one facility.

Figure 4.17 and table 4.3 summarize the key findings of this analysis. First, average land border delays in Africa are 90 hours for borders without OSBPs and 50 hours for borders with OSBPs. Figure 4.17 shows the distribution of these delays for all land borders from delays below 10 hours to those above 250 hours. The smallest land border delays mostly occur in Northern Sub-Saharan Africa and between certain countries such as Botswana and Namibia, Mozambique and South Africa, and Kenya and Tanzania (table 4.3). The longest delays occur mostly in Central Africa between the Central African Republic and the Democratic Republic of Congo, and in Eastern Africa among Eritrea, South Sudan, and Sudan (table 4.3).

FIGURE 4.17 Distribution of land border delays in Africa, before and after new investments

Number of borders

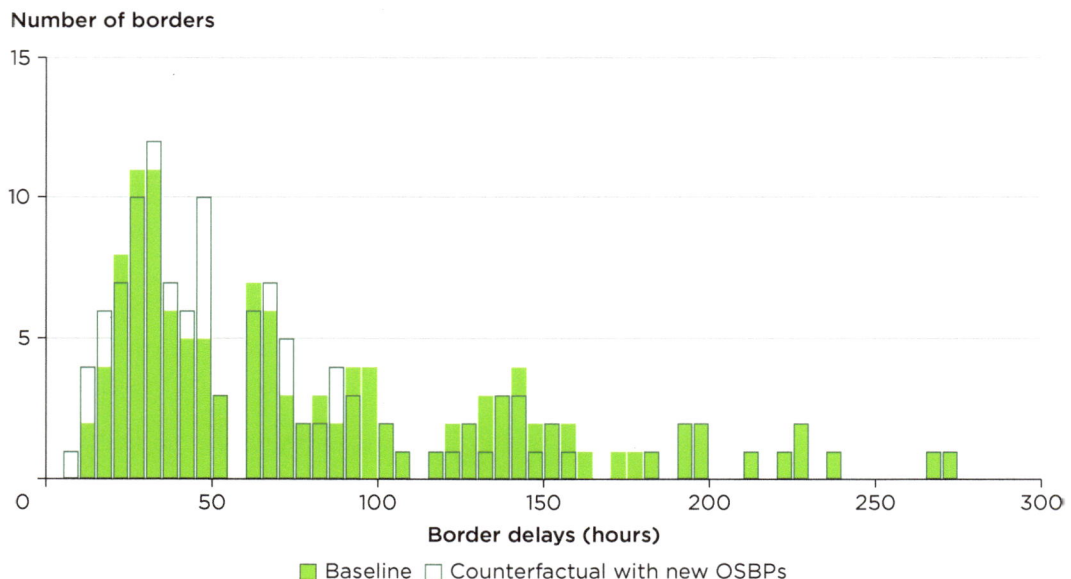

Source: Fontagné, Lebrand, et al. 2023.
Note: OSBPs = One-Stop Border Posts.

TABLE 4.3 Land border delays in hours, top-10 versus bottom-10 performers

a. Shortest delays

Economy A	Economy B	Number of hours
Botswana	Namibia	10
Morocco	Western Sahara	12
Israel	West Bank and Gaza	15
Mozambique	South Africa	15.4
Egypt, Arab Rep.	West Bank and Gaza	18
Jordan	West Bank and Gaza	19.3
Kenya	Tanzania	20
Libya	Tunisia	21
Egypt, Arab Rep.	Israel	21
Mauritania	Western Sahara	21.5

b. Longest delays

Economy A	Economy B	Number of hours
Congo, Dem. Rep.	Zambia	194
Central African Republic	Congo, Dem. Rep.	196
Ethiopia	South Sudan	197
Djibouti	Eritrea	211.8
Congo, Dem. Rep.	South Sudan	220
Eritrea	Ethiopia	226.8
Central African Republic	Chad	228
Saudi Arabia	Yemen, Rep.	236
Central African Republic	South Sudan	268
Eritrea	Sudan	271.3

Source: World Bank, Trading Across Borders indicators, https://archive.doingbusiness.org/en/data /exploretopics/trading-across-borders.
Note: Land border delays are nondirectional; the delays from economy A to economy B are assumed to be the same as between economy B and economy A.

Analysis

Addressing the challenges that hinder integration and growth in Africa is crucial to seizing the opportunities offered by deepening trade agreements and improving infrastructure. The first step in finding solutions is to understand the causes of these challenges, such as limited deep trade agreements and poor transportation infrastructure. African countries can unlock their full potential for growth and development by addressing these challenges and implementing effective trade and transportation reforms.

Challenges:

- Limited trade agreements involving African countries fall into the "deep" category, suggesting the need to promote deepening trade agreements in Africa to foster trade integration. According to Fontagné, Rocha, et al. (2023), "deep" agreements typically involve coordination on anti-dumping, competition, government procurement, and trade facilitation.

- Poor transportation infrastructure—including roads, border delays, and inefficient ports—contributes to prohibitive transportation times for goods, creating trade frictions that limit integration: it takes an average of 17 days for intra-African shipments to reach their destination.

- Underperformance is largely due to significant barriers to trade facilitation, including the need to reduce border and port delays and streamline customs procedures: the average time spent waiting at the border to import or export in Africa is 3.5 days.

Opportunities:

- Promoting the deepening of trade agreements in Africa can increase trade integration on the continent and create new growth opportunities. As noted by Goldberg and Reed (2022), without international integration, residents of low- and lower-middle-income countries lack the market size needed for sustained poverty reduction.

- Improving transportation infrastructure through initiatives such as the PIDA projects can have a significant impact on the reduction of transit times and improve the connectivity and integration prospects for countries in Africa, which could help reduce intra-African transit times by an estimated 20 percent.

- African countries can increase their global exports and GDP by signing a deep trade agreement linking all African countries and by implementing trade and transportation reforms: the combination of policy and infrastructure reforms could increase GDP by 2.27 percent compared with the baseline.

This section analyzes how trade and infrastructure reforms can improve trade integration and welfare in Africa. It relies on new research (Fontagné, Lebrand, et al. 2023) that explores the link between trade, trade agreements, and infrastructure improvements in a general equilibrium context. The analysis will proceed in three steps: first, characterize trade agreements in Africa and assess the trade costs associated with different levels of depth of regional trade agreements (RTAs); second, use Geographic Information System (GIS) analysis to compute shipping times for African countries with each other and with the rest of the world; and, third, rely on counterfactual analysis to provide a quantitative assessment of the trade and welfare impacts of trade and infrastructure reforms. To sharpen the focus of the potential effects of these reforms on integration, the analysis centers on trade in manufacturing and agricultural goods and abstracts from trade in mineral products.

Trade agreements

As a first step, the analysis groups the RTAs on the basis of their depth and then estimates structurally the trade impact of the different types of PTAs. This approach makes it possible to recover bilateral trade costs from econometric estimation. These costs can then be used in the simulations. Specifically, following work by Fontagné, Rocha, et al. (2023), this section uses clustering methods to define statistically significant groupings of trade agreements based on their content. The analysis relies on an exhaustive description of the provisions included in RTAs based on the World Bank Deep Trade Agreements database (Mattoo, Rocha, and Ruta 2020). It uses information on all policy areas (except tariffs) encompassing objectives, substantive commitments and enforcement procedures present in legal texts, and available annexes of the 278 RTAs in force and notified to the WTO up to 2017.

The clustering analysis allows for identification of three "clusters" of RTAs (figure 4.18 reports the position of the 278 agreements over the cluster space).[21] Intuitively, these three groups represent families of trade agreements that are similar in terms of their content in the sense that the distance between observations within each group of RTAs is minimized, and the distance between groups is maximized. Using these groupings of RTAs allows for estimation of the trade impact of each category. Here again, the analysis lets the data speak and uses a gravity model to estimate the mean impact of belonging to an RTA positioned in a certain cluster. The three groups have a (statistically) different impact on trade, which allows classification of these groups as "deep," "medium," and "shallow" in decreasing order of trade impact.

This analysis results in three preliminary conclusions: (1) as shown in figure 4.18, the separation between clusters is clear-cut with very few agreements at the "border" of their partition; (2) agreements in Cluster #1—the "deep" RTAs that are associated to stronger trade effects—appear to stand apart from the rest of the sample; and, most important, (3) all but two RTAs involving African countries are in either the "medium" or the "shallow" category, which suggests that promoting the deepening of trade agreements in Africa is necessary to boost trade integration on the continent.

FIGURE 4.18 Position of African regional trade agreements in the cluster space

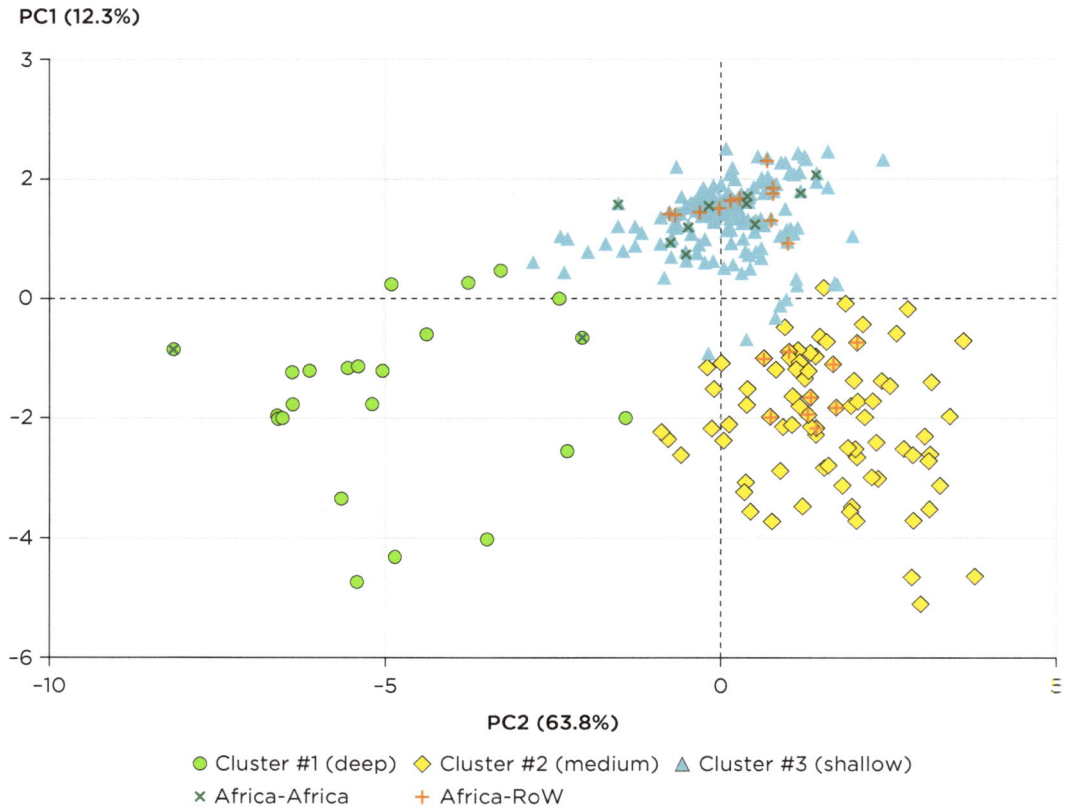

PC1 (12.3%)

PC2 (63.8%)

○ Cluster #1 (deep) ◇ Cluster #2 (medium) ▲ Cluster #3 (shallow)
× Africa-Africa + Africa-RoW

Source: Fontagné, Rocha, et al. 2023.
Note: Spatial representation of the three clusters (deep, medium, and shallow). Each point represents a trade agreement. The deeper the agreement, the stronger the trade effects. X-axis and y-axis values are defined using the first two principal components of the 18 features used by the clustering algorithm, centered on zero. PC = principal component; RoW = rest of world.

Transportation infrastructure

Transportation times to move goods across countries become prohibitive when roads are in poor condition, delays at the border are long, and ports are inefficient. The second step is to use GIS analysis to compute shipping times for African countries with each other and with the rest of the world, and to estimate changes in shipping times associated with transportation reforms.

As a starting point, the analysis relies on the current network of roads for Africa[22] and ports across the world, and employs a shortest-path algorithm to estimate current shipping times between every country pair. GIS software allows precise mapping of the current transportation network. From this reference point, the network is then enriched with the planned infrastructure improvements that can be linked to PIDA.[23]

Map 4.4 shows the different road types included in the primary road network in Africa, the location of ports, and currently functioning OSBPs reducing border delays. It also shows new investment in roads, ports, and border posts, as listed in the PIDA database. Comparing the pre- and post-PIDA scenarios allows quantification of the changes in shipment times resulting from new and improved transportation infrastructure projects.[24]

MAP 4.4 Existing transportation network in Africa and new investments in roads, ports, and border posts, 2022

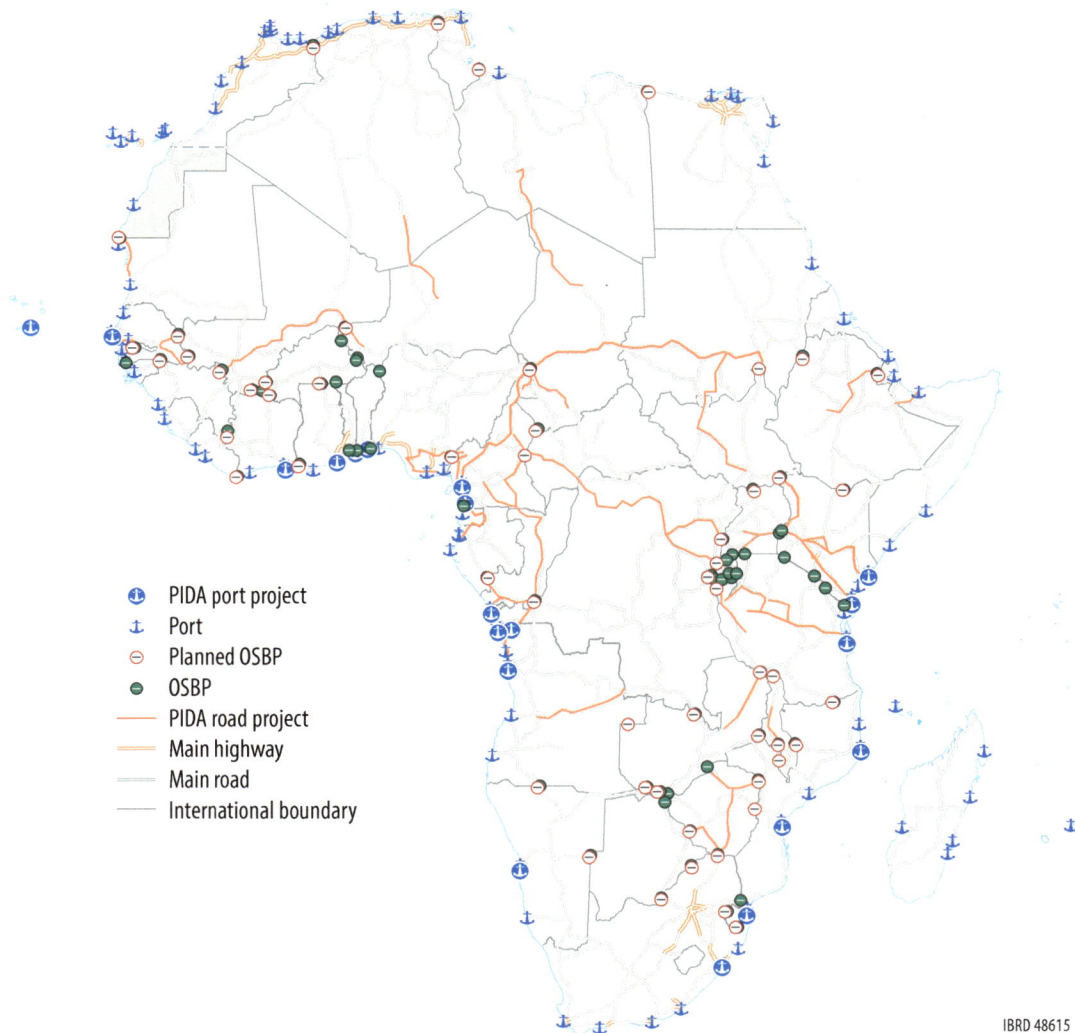

IBRD 48615 | JANUARY 2025

Source: Fontagné, Lebrand, et al. 2023.
Note: OSBP = One-Stop Border Post; PIDA = Program for Infrastructure Development in Africa.

The analysis shows that—by increasing the number of road and port connections and by improving the speed and processing times for improved road segments, borders, and ports—PIDA projects can contribute to a significant decrease in shipping times between a large number of city pairs within Africa as well as between Africa and other countries. New OSBPs will reduce average land border delays between African countries from 3.5 days to 2.9 days overall. Among the countries that will benefit from large reductions in land border times are Burkina Faso, Cameroon, the Democratic Republic of Congo, the Republic of Congo, Kenya, Malawi, Mozambique, Rwanda, South Sudan, Tanzania, and Uganda (figure 4.19). New border and port improvements at maritime gateways will reduce average sea border delays from and to Sub-Saharan African coastal countries by 16 percent on average, with larger gains in ports with the longest delays. The countries that will benefit from reductions in sea border times are Angola, Benin, the Democratic Republic of Congo, the Republic of Congo, Côte d'Ivoire, Kenya, Mozambique, Namibia, Senegal, Togo, and Tanzania (figure 4.20).

FIGURE 4.19 **Average land border delay, by country, baseline and counterfactual**

Average land border delay (days)

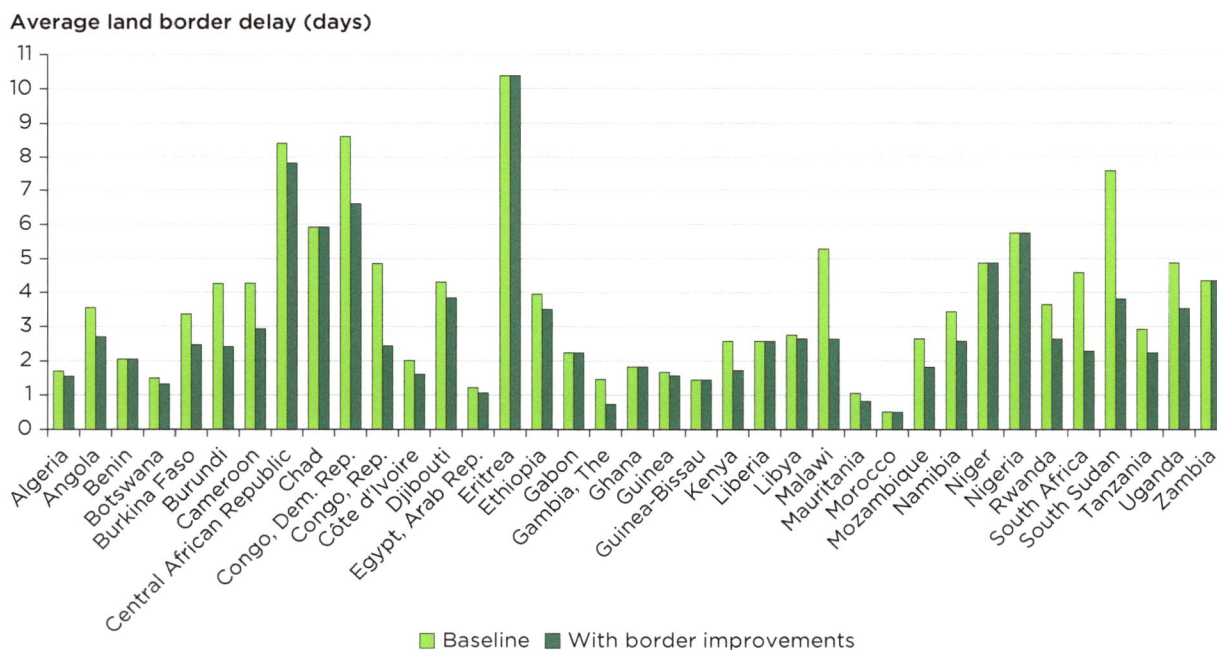

☐ Baseline ☐ With border improvements

Source: World Bank, Ease of Doing Business indicators, https://archive.doingbusiness.org/en/rankings.
Note: The graph shows for each African country the average land border delays per country before (the baseline scenario) and after (the counterfactual scenario). Border improvements come from reduced border delays due to new One-Stop Border Posts as shown in map 4.4. Border delays are calculated using border delays from the World Bank Trading Across Borders database on delays at the border for each country. For more details, refer to Fontagné, Lebrand, et al. (2023).

FIGURE 4.20 Average sea border delay, by country, baseline and counterfactual

Average sea border delay (days)

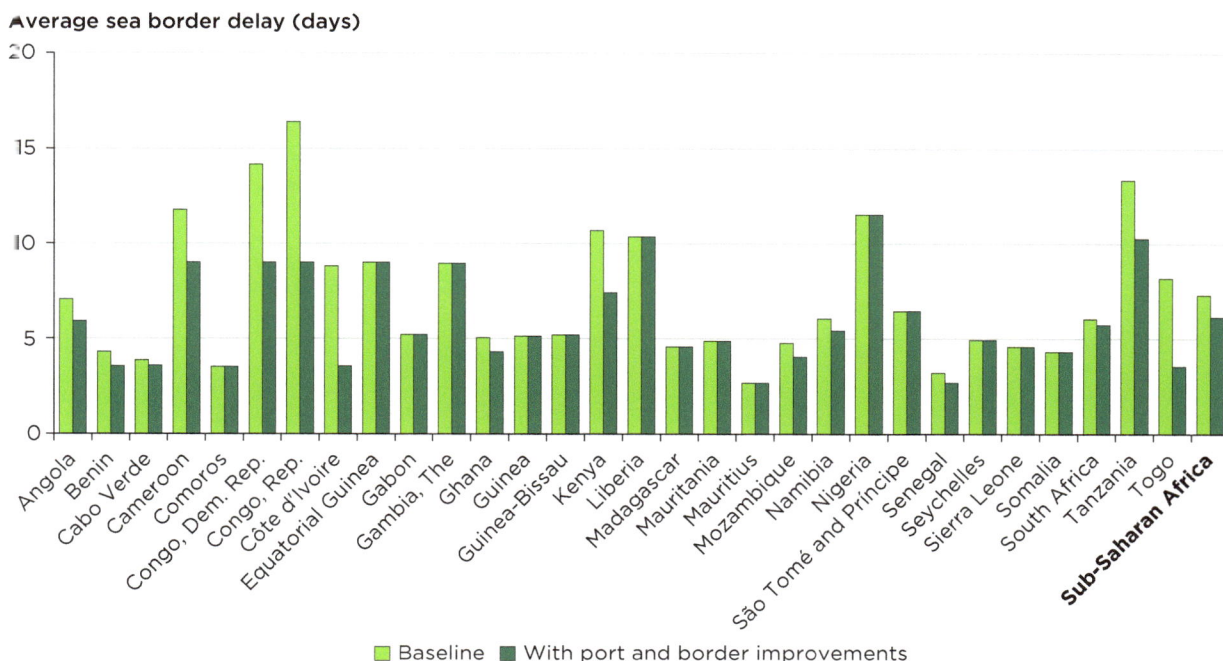

Baseline ■ With port and border improvements

Sources: UN Trade and Development (UNCTAD) data on port calls; World Bank, Doing Business indicators, https://archive.doingbusiness.org/en/rankings.
Note: The graph shows for each coastal African country the average sea border delays per country before (the baseline scenario) and after (the counterfactual scenario). Border improvements come from reduced border delays assumed from new investments in port infrastructure. Border delays are calculated using border delays at maritime gateways from the World Bank's Trading Across Borders database and UNCTAD data for port calls. For more details, refer to Fontagné, Lebrand, et al. (2023).

Table 4.4 shows the change in shipping times under four scenarios: (1) implementing only the road transportation projects from map 4.4; (2) implementing both the road and port transportation projects; (3) implementing the road transportation projects and reducing the land border times; and (4) implementing all PIDA projects reducing road travel times, border delays, and port processing times. Overall, the average transportation times for all pairs of countries will decrease by 0.4 percent in the first scenario, by 7 percent in the second, by 6 percent in the third, and by 11 percent in the last and most complete scenario. The large drop in average transportation time associated with the new OSBPs indicates the importance of border delays for connectivity in Africa and highlights the complementarity between transportation infrastructure and trade facilitation reforms.

TABLE 4.4 Change in transportation times between African countries and rest of world, by scenario

Percent

Scenario	Average change in transportation times to Africa	Average change in transportation times to rest of world, not including Africa	Average change in transportation times to the world
1 Road improvements only	−1	−0.2	−0.4
2 Road improvements and new ports	−10	−6	−7
3 Road improvements and new OSBPs	−14	−3	−6
4 Road improvements, new OSBPs, and port investments	−20	−7	−11

Source: World Bank staff calculations.

Note: The table provides average change of transportation times weighted by city population over all possible trips starting or ending in an African country, from the baseline scenario to one of the four counterfactuals as described in Fontagné, Lebrand, et al. (2023). The times used are computed assuming a preference for maritime transportation. OSBP = One-Stop Border Post.

Effects of trade and transportation reforms

The last step of the analysis relies on a general equilibrium model to quantify the trade and welfare impacts of counterfactual scenarios of trade and transportation reforms.[25] Specifically, it investigates three scenarios: (1) the signing of a deep trade agreement linking all African countries, such as the AfCFTA; (2) the completion of the PIDA transportation infrastructure and border posts projects; and (3) the combination of these two trade and infrastructure/trade facilitation reforms. This quantification exercise helps to identify priorities for reform to improve connectivity and integration prospects for countries in Africa.

Table 4.5 presents the key results of the counterfactual analysis. Columns (1) and (2) show that signing a deep trade agreement linking all African countries without removing important gaps in terms of infrastructure and large trade facilitation bottlenecks would lead to an increase in trade integration and GDP, but that these gains would be limited. In the new equilibrium, average exports from African countries would be 3.41 percent higher than in the baseline scenario. Trade within Africa would receive the biggest boost, with average growth of 34.68 percent per year, whereas GDP would grow by 0.64 percent per year.[26] Consistent with the view that Africa has significant transportation infrastructure and trade facilitation impediments, infrastructure and connectivity reforms would have a more significant impact. Specifically, columns (3) and (4) show that trade would increase by 9.61 percent (and up to 39.98 percent for intra-African trade), and that GDP would increase by 1.46 percent per year compared with the baseline scenario.

The results presented so far consider the simultaneous implementation of road, port, and border post improvements, but it is possible to quantify the expected benefits for each one separately. Road infrastructure improvements alone were found to increase GDP by an average of 0.09 percent. When these improvements were implemented in conjunction with reduced port delays, the increase in GDP rises to 0.39 percent. According to the PIDA, the estimated investment in transportation projects is US$25.4 billion. Given the estimated GDP impact, road development could generate a cumulative return of 3.35 percent for the African continent (sum of GDP gains for the countries in the sample).

Complementing road development with port improvement projects yields a return of 14.5 percent for the continent. These results are consistent with microeconomic estimates and reflect the typical internal rate of return for physical infrastructure. The combined implementation of roads, ports, and OSBPs accounts for most of the estimated gains (1.46 percent of GDP). In a context of debt distress and high interest rates, border improvement projects appear particularly attractive from a cost-benefit perspective, underscoring the integral role of effective border management in promoting trade and economic integration across Africa.

Finally, columns (5) and (6) show the complementarity of trade and transportation reforms in Africa. A combination of deeper trade agreements, improvements in transportation infrastructure, and trade facilitation reforms would lead to an increase in African countries' world exports of 14.80 percent (and up to 88.2 percent for intra-African exports), and an increase in GDP of 2.27 percent, all annual changes from the baseline scenario.[27]

Although all African countries show positive trade and welfare effects from trade and transportation reforms, these gains are not uniformly distributed. Countries like the Central African Republic, Malawi, and Zimbabwe have the largest percentage improvements in trade. These landlocked countries would benefit significantly from the reduction of trade frictions, particularly at the border. Countries like Burkina Faso, Cameroon, and the Democratic Republic of Congo would largely benefit from new trade facilitation programs increasing their market access to large neighboring countries. Others, such as Côte d'Ivoire, the Democratic Republic of Congo, Tanzania, and Togo, benefit from new port infrastructure reducing delays for maritime routes to the rest of the world. Finally, a planned road corridor between Cameroon and Gabon as shown in map 4.4 would also largely benefit Gabon by increasing its market access to neighboring countries. For those countries, new transportation and border infrastructure that reduces the currently high transportation times would magnify the gains from better trade integration. The combination of trade reforms and infrastructure improvements is emerging as a powerful strategy to promote economic growth and integration within Africa.

TABLE 4.5 General equilibrium effects of improving connectivity and deepening integration in Africa under three scenarios

Percent

Country	Intra-African exports	Scenario 1: Deepening trade agreements (1) Δ Export total	Scenario 1: Deepening trade agreements (1) Δ Intra-African exports	(2) Δ GDP	Scenario 2: Transportation and trade facilitation (3) Δ Export total	Scenario 2: Transportation and trade facilitation (3) Δ Intra-African exports	(4) Δ GDP	Scenario 3: Combined trade and transportation reform (5) Δ Export total	Scenario 3: Combined trade and transportation reform (5) Δ Intra-African exports	(6) Δ GDP
Algeria	5.32	1.77	47.94	0.28	11.10	58.63	1.76	14.42	133.50	2.22
Botswana	15.70	1.33	33.98	7.34	2.86	44.03	10.36	4.70	90.59	19.56
Burkina Faso	27.44	11.99	35.02	0.67	38.38	74.92	1.99	56.00	131.20	3.02
Burundi	16.75	14.27	40.77	0.28	43.22	45.84	1.45	66.42	106.59	1.89
Cabo Verde	8.82	4.26	61.56	0.26	2.55	12.97	0.17	6.86	79.51	0.46
Cameroon	3.62	1.91	32.31	0.23	9.47	54.09	1.89	11.63	96.82	2.14
Congo, Dem. Rep.	17.02	3.67	50.76	2.70	8.43	32.58	6.24	12.91	98.46	10.12
Côte d'Ivoire	7.25	1.87	26.33	0.32	15.20	46.62	2.17	18.74	81.67	2.58
Egypt, Arab Rep.	11.84	2.61	34.34	0.32	7.36	105.74	1.01	13.30	177.53	1.67
Eswatini	86.81	12.33	17.09	9.96	2.94	4.18	1.24	15.15	20.70	11.01
Ethiopia	3.79	1.24	19.70	0.06	8.92	44.14	0.36	10.64	70.11	0.43
Ghana	8.89	2.44	44.65	0.38	5.12	19.08	0.90	7.90	64.86	1.27
Kenya	27.16	9.36	33.97	0.44	24.83	16.79	1.70	38.71	56.03	2.21
Lesotho	39.69	6.99	32.70	9.45	-0.16	1.13	-0.51	7.09	33.90	8.75
Madagascar	7.69	3.62	43.69	0.46	0.74	17.24	0.09	4.60	66.63	0.57

(continued)

TABLE 4.5 General equilibrium effects of improving connectivity and deepening integration in Africa under three scenarios *(continued)*

Percent

Country	Intra-African exports	Scenario 1: Deepening trade agreements			Scenario 2: Transportation and trade facilitation			Scenario 3: Combined trade and transportation reform		
		(1) Δ Export total	Δ Intra-African exports	(2) Δ GDP	(3) Δ Export total	Δ Intra-African exports	(4) Δ GDP	(5) Δ Export total	Δ Intra-African exports	(6) Δ GDP
Malawi	31.40	10.53	28.68	0.88	17.07	45.25	1.36	31.95	87.96	2.68
Mauritius	15.70	3.70	33.79	1.13	-0.03	2.97	-0.02	3.70	36.22	1.07
Morocco	4.08	1.19	42.72	0.34	2.09	50.01	0.61	3.97	112.10	1.15
Mozambique	14.18	5.88	44.02	2.54	2.20	4.28	0.55	8.01	47.05	3.03
Namibia	28.60	2.84	25.72	7.42	3.43	18.15	7.10	6.55	48.40	15.96
Niger	14.74	3.47	8.59	0.22	1.59	34.96	4.51	9.51	51.64	4.73
Nigeria	11.27	2.10	34.59	0.18	13.59	23.61	1.38	17.65	64.67	1.49
Rwanda	14.23	18.34	59.26	0.85	36.46	33.91	1.50	61.22	107.96	2.73
Senegal	17.50	6.46	38.32	0.56	13.98	68.10	1.48	24.73	130.59	2.26
South Africa	21.76	4.38	24.90	0.68	3.89	17.00	0.57	9.37	46.74	1.35
Tanzania	40.24	10.21	30.45	0.85	20.83	21.71	2.78	33.30	55.72	3.65
Tunisia	6.79	1.78	47.97	0.78	3.05	65.92	1.36	5.91	141.07	2.66
Uganda	44.72	15.40	38.64	1.39	14.49	4.16	1.72	32.16	44.56	3.29
Zambia	17.07	6.93	35.83	2.34	14.14	47.02	4.86	22.33	98.70	8.43
Zimbabwe	67.28	5.96	17.24	9.92	10.02	25.70	15.76	16.08	42.46	28.97
Weighted average	**14.10**	**3.41**	**34.68**	**0.64**	**9.61**	**39.98**	**1.46**	**14.80**	**88.18**	**2.27**

Source: Fontagne, Lebrand, et al. 2023.

Policies

For decades, economics has emphasized that high trade costs adversely affect international trade, growth, and development opportunities (Goldberg and Reed 2020; World Bank 2009). Over the past 20 years, the international trade landscape has changed significantly, and the understanding of the determinants of trade costs has improved. Consequently, the regional integration agenda in Africa has been given new impetus with the emergence of new policy approaches and research.

This chapter documents Africa's trade landscape, quantifies the gains from further trade integration, and provides guidance on policy choices. The following key messages and policy recommendations emerge from the analysis:

- *Combine transportation infrastructure investment and trade reform.* The two have a strong complementarity that justifies simultaneous action. African countries can boost economic development and ensure that marginalized communities benefit from this progress by prioritizing investments in transportation infrastructure and implementing trade reforms.

- *Pursue deep integration.* Doing so involves combining tariff reforms with improving trade facilitation to reduce border delays, and implementing behind-the-border domestic regulatory reforms. Deep integration will allow African economies to become better integrated with each other, to benefit from economies of scale at the continental level, and to become more efficient in producing goods.

- *Focus on specific policy instruments and priority actions.* These efforts can include sectoral policies, institutional reforms, and targeted interventions that address the challenges and capitalize on the opportunities identified in this chapter. Examples include removing nontariff barriers, streamlining border procedures, and modernizing transportation infrastructure.

- *Promote open regionalism.* Improving infrastructure, reforming trade facilitation, and deepening nondiscriminatory trade agreements will allow African economies to continue opening up to the rest of the world, further supporting economic growth and promoting more inclusive and sustainable regional integration.

In conclusion, by considering these general policy recommendations and by focusing on specific policy instruments and priority actions, African countries could address the challenges posed by high trade costs and seize the opportunities associated with regional integration. In doing so, Africa can unleash its economic potential and gradually assert itself as an influential player in the global economy. Such an approach can help promote inclusive productivity growth and the pursuit of development goals of economic efficiency, social inclusion, and environmental sustainability.

Annex 4A. Additional figures and tables

FIGURE 4A.1 Sub-Saharan Africa's exports, by subregion and product, 2002–19

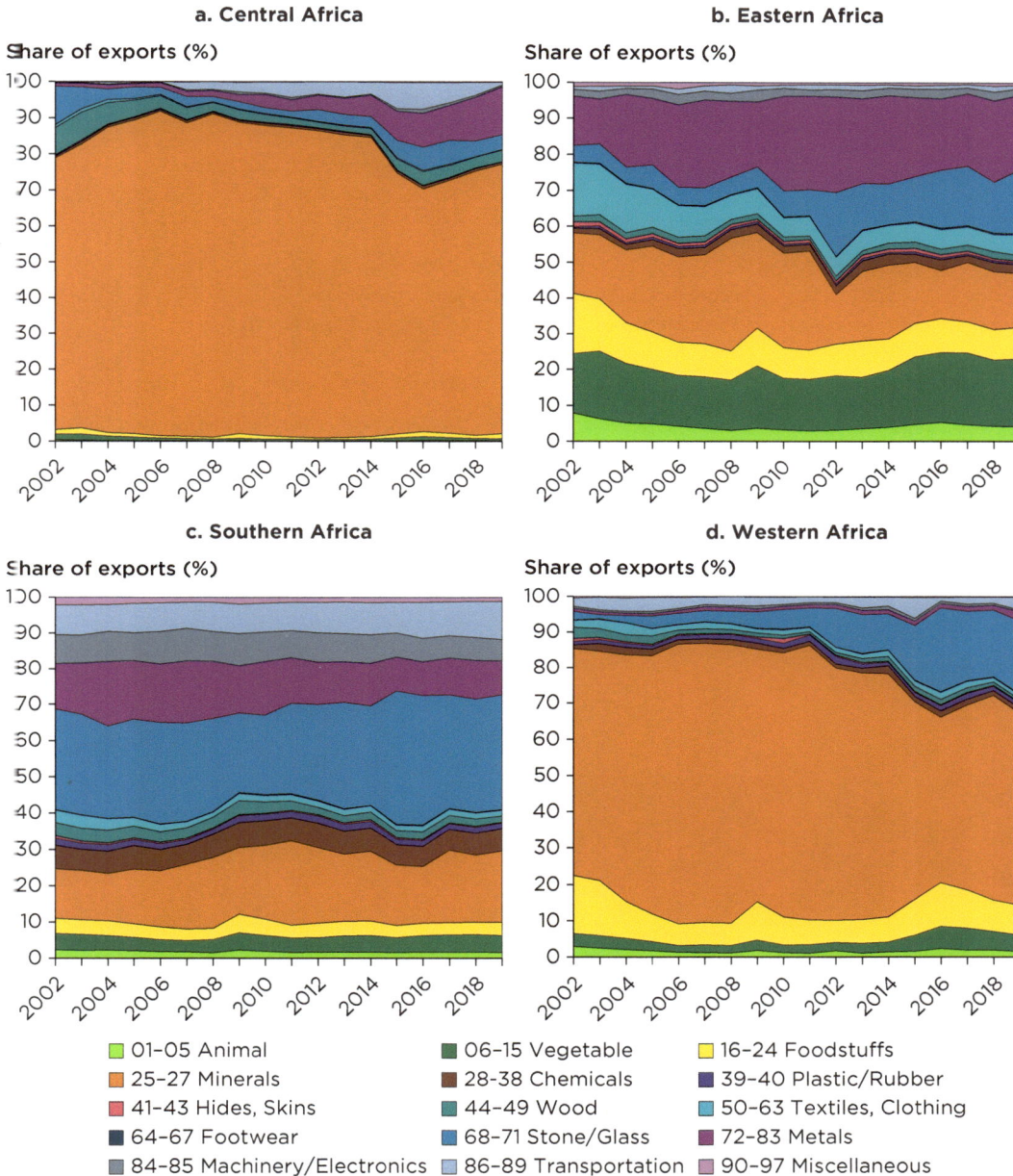

a. Central Africa
Share of exports (%)

b. Eastern Africa
Share of exports (%)

c. Southern Africa
Share of exports (%)

d. Western Africa
Share of exports (%)

Legend:
- 01–05 Animal
- 06–15 Vegetable
- 16–24 Foodstuffs
- 25–27 Minerals
- 28-38 Chemicals
- 39–40 Plastic/Rubber
- 41–43 Hides, Skins
- 44–49 Wood
- 50–63 Textiles, Clothing
- 64–67 Footwear
- 68–71 Stone/Glass
- 72–83 Metals
- 84–85 Machinery/Electronics
- 86–89 Transportation
- 90–97 Miscellaneous

Source: CEPII BACI International Trade database, https://www.cepii.fr/CEPII/en/bdd_modele/bdd _modele_item.asp?id=37.

FIGURE 4A.2 Sub-Saharan Africa's exports and imports, by destination and origin, 2002–19

a. Exports, by destination

Value (current US$)

b. Imports, by origin

Value (current US$)

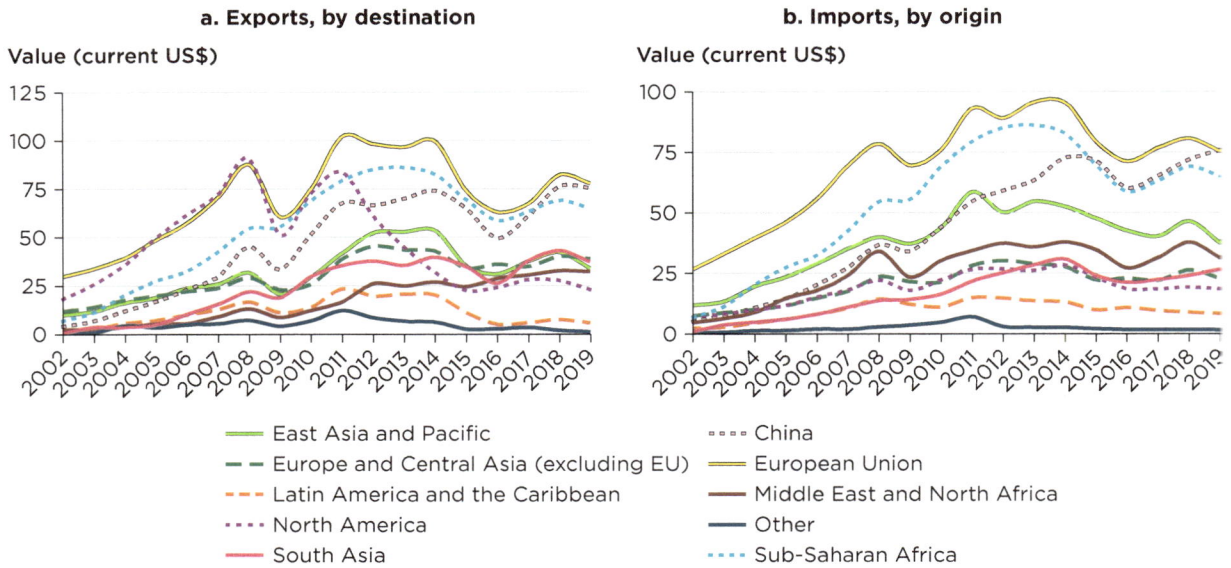

- ——— East Asia and Pacific
- – – – Europe and Central Asia (excluding EU)
- – – – Latin America and the Caribbean
- · · · · North America
- ——— South Asia
- · · · · China
- ——— European Union
- ——— Middle East and North Africa
- ——— Other
- · · · · Sub-Saharan Africa

Source: CEPII BACI International Trade database, https://www.cepii.fr/CEPII/en/bdd_modele/bdd_modele_item .asp?id=37.
Note: EU = European Union.

FIGURE 4A.3 Sub-Saharan Africa's intraregional trade, by corridor, 2002–19

Share of intraregional trade (%)

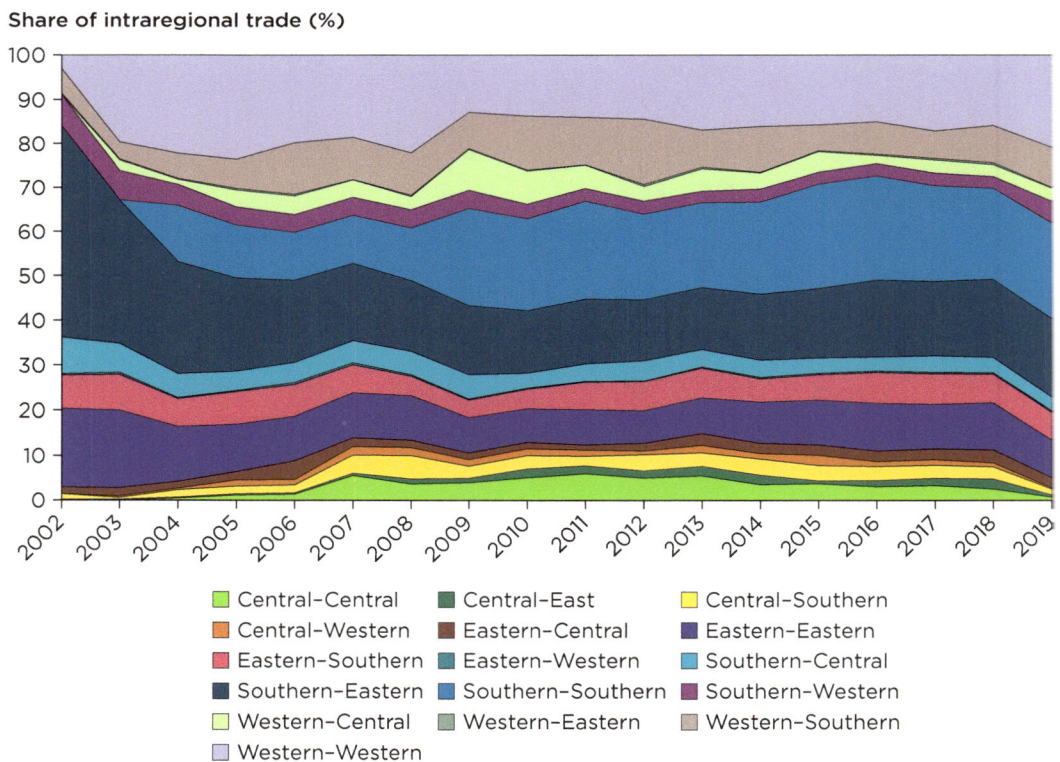

- ■ Central–Central
- ■ Central–East
- ■ Central–Southern
- ■ Central–Western
- ■ Eastern–Central
- ■ Eastern–Eastern
- ■ Eastern–Southern
- ■ Eastern–Western
- ■ Southern–Central
- ■ Southern–Eastern
- ■ Southern–Southern
- ■ Southern–Western
- ■ Western–Central
- ■ Western–Eastern
- ■ Western–Southern
- ■ Western–Western

Source: CEPII BACI International Trade database, https://www.cepii.fr/CEPII/en/bdd_modele/bdd _modele_item.asp?id=37.

TABLE 4A.1 Fifty "thickest" and "thinnest" bilateral borders worldwide, 2015–18 average

a. Thickest bilateral borders

Economy pair	Percent ad valorem	FTA
Niger-Chad	479	No
Lao PDR–Myanmar	479	Yes
Algeria-Mali	429	No
Chad-Nigeria	418	No
Central African Republic–Congo, Dem. Rep.	322	No
China-Afghanistan	293	No
Algeria-Niger	268	No
Uzbekistan-Afghanistan	261	No
Brazil-Suriname	256	No
Liberia-Sierra Leone	254	Yes
Angola-Zambia	251	Yes
Mauritania-Algeria	250	No
Myanmar-Bangladesh	244	No
Iraq-Türkiye	236	No
Tanzania–Congo, Dem. Rep.	218	Yes
Nepal-China	218	No
Côte d'Ivoire–Guinea	212	Yes
Central African Republic-Chad	210	Yes
Sudan-Uganda	207	No
Macao SAR, China–China	201	Yes
Nigeria-Benin	198	Yes
Nigeria-Cameroon	196	No
Tanzania-Rwanda	196	Yes
Ethiopia-Sudan	196	No
Iran, Islamic Rep.–Iraq	190	No
Brazil-Guyana	189	No
Israel–Egypt, Arab Rep.	188	No
Benin–Burkina Faso	188	Yes
Kenya-Ethiopia	184	Yes
Mexico-Belize	184	No
Tajikistan-China	183	No

(continued)

TABLE 4A.1 Fifty "thickest" and "thinnest" bilateral borders worldwide, 2015–18 average *(continued)*

a. Thickest bilateral borders *(continued)*

Economy pair	Percent ad valorem	FTA
Jordan-Iraq	183	Yes
Angola–Congo, Dem. Rep.	182	Yes
Côte d'Ivoire–Liberia	178	Yes
Tanzania-Mozambique	175	Yes
Tanzania-Burundi	175	Yes
Burundi–Congo, Dem. Rep.	174	Yes
Iran, Islamic Rep.–Pakistan	174	No
Tajikistan-Afghanistan	172	No
Indonesia-Timor-Leste	171	No
Uganda–Congo, Dem. Rep.	170	Yes
Cambodia–Lao PDR	169	Yes
Guinea-Sierra Leone	168	Yes
Cameroon-Chad	164	Yes
Armenia–Iran, Islamic Rep.	164	No
Pakistan-India	159	Yes
Jordan-Israel	158	No
Oman–Yemen, Rep.	155	Yes
Rwanda-Burundi	154	Yes
Mauritania-Mali	153	No

b. Thinnest bilateral borders

Economy pair	Percent ad valorem	FTA
Czech Republic–Poland	11	Yes
Czech Republic–Germany	11	Yes
China–Hong Kong SAR, China	12	Yes
Belgium-France	18	Yes
Austria–Czech Republic	19	Yes
Croatia-Slovenia	20	Yes
Belgium-Germany	22	Yes
Costa Rica-Panama	24	Yes
Spain-Portugal	27	Yes

(continued)

TABLE 4A.1 Fifty "thickest" and "thinnest" bilateral borders worldwide, 2015–18 average *(continued)*

b. Thinnest bilateral borders *(continued)*

Economy pair	Percent ad valorem	FTA
Germany-Poland	29	Yes
Belgium-Luxembourg	29	Yes
Austria-Germany	30	Yes
Lithuania-Poland	30	Yes
Latvia–Russian Federation	31	No
Belarus-Lithuania	31	No
Canada–United States	31	Yes
Mexico–United States	32	Yes
Austria-Slovenia	32	Yes
Bulgaria–North Macedonia	33	Yes
Germany-France	34	Yes
Switzerland-Germany	34	Yes
Bosnia and Herzegovina–Croatia	35	Yes
Spain-France	35	Yes
Bulgaria-Romania	36	Yes
Bulgaria-Greece	36	Yes
Namibia-South Africa	36	Yes
Norway-Sweden	38	Yes
Belarus–Russian Federation	38	Yes
United Arab Emirates–Oman	41	Yes
France-Italy	42	Yes
Italy-Slovenia	42	Yes
Belarus-Ukraine	42	Yes
Finland-Sweden	44	Yes
Colombia-Panama	44	Yes
Belarus-Latvia	44	No
Malaysia-Thailand	45	Yes
Austria-Switzerland	45	Yes
Botswana–South Africa	46	Yes
Switzerland-France	46	Yes
Lithuania–Russian Federation	47	No
Switzerland-Italy	47	Yes

(continued)

TABLE 4A.1 Fifty "thickest" and "thinnest" bilateral borders worldwide, 2015–18 average *(continued)*

b. Thinnest bilateral borders *(continued)*

Economy pair	Percent ad valorem	FTA
Eswatini–South Africa	48	Yes
Germany-Denmark	48	Yes
South Africa–Zimbabwe	48	Yes
United Kingdom–Ireland	49	Yes
Poland-Ukraine	50	Yes
Greece–North Macedonia	50	Yes
Lesotho–South Africa	50	Yes
Lao PDR–Thailand	51	Yes
Bulgaria-Türkiye	52	Yes

Sources: Calculations based on ESCAP-World Bank Trade Cost Database 2018, https://www.unescac
.org/resources/escap-world-bank-trade-cost-database. Data on FTAs come from the World Bank's
Deep Trade Agreements database (Mattoo, Rocha, and Ruta 2020).
Note: FTA = free trade agreement.

TABLE 4A.2 Cross-border trade costs within Sub-Saharan Africa, 2000 and 2018

Country X	Country Y	Trade cost, 2000	Trade cost, 2018	Change in trade costs, 2000–18 (%)
Namibia	South Africa	326	36	−89
Mozambique	Zambia	307	120	−61
Namibia	Zambia	179	74	−59
Sudan	Uganda	488	207	−58
Ethiopia (excludes Eritrea)	Sudan	404	196	−51
Mali	Niger	235	117	−50
Burkina Faso	Togo	150	77	−49
Guinea	Senegal	217	122	−44
Niger	Nigeria	227	132	−42
Malawi	Zambia	111	66	−41
Burkina Faso	Mali	160	96	−40
Tanzania	Zambia	147	92	−37
Burundi	Tanzania	272	175	−36

(continued)

Country X	Country Y	Trade cost, 2000	Trade cost, 2018	Change in trade costs, 2000–18 (%)
Burkina Faso	Ghana	132	87	−34
Zambia	Zimbabwe	81	55	−32
Rwanda	Uganda	163	112	−31
Botswana	Zambia	117	82	−30
Mauritania	Senegal	210	146	−30
Guinea	Liberia	190	143	−25
Benin	Togo	133	100	−25
Mozambique	South Africa	95	72	−24
Burkina Faso	Niger	136	104	−24
Angola	Zambia	320	251	−22
Cameroon	Equatorial Guinea	170	133	−22
Malawi	Tanzania	155	123	−21
South Africa	Zimbabwe	59	48	−19
Burundi	Rwanda	187	154	−18
Cameroon	Nigeria	232	196	−16
Tanzania	Uganda	168	145	−14
Botswana	Namibia	99	87	−12
Benin	Burkina Faso	213	188	−12
Burkina Faso	Côte d'Ivoire	78	70	−10
Ethiopia (excludes Eritrea)	Kenya	203	184	−9
Liberia	Sierra Leone	275	254	−8
Mozambique	Malawi	121	113	−7
Central African Republic	Cameroon	147	138	−6
Mozambique	Eswatini	137	133	−3
Kenya	Uganda	83	82	−1
Benin	Nigeria	200	198	−1
Mozambique	Zimbabwe	92	92	0
Mali	Senegal	74	75	1
Gambia, The	Senegal	122	129	6
Guinea	Sierra Leone	158	168	6

(continued)

TABLE 4A.2 Cross-border trade costs within Sub-Saharan Africa, 2000 and 2018 *(continued)*

Country X	Country Y	Trade cost, 2000	Trade cost, 2018	Change in trade costs, 2000–18 (%)
Ghana	Togo	89	95	7
Kenya	Tanzania	97	106	9
Cameroon	Chad	150	164	9
Côte d'Ivoire	Ghana	96	109	14
Côte d'Ivoire	Guinea	185	212	15
Benin	Niger	125	146	17
Rwanda	Tanzania	167	196	17
Central African Republic	Chad	177	210	19
Niger	Chad	372	479	29
Nigeria	Chad	319	418	31
Côte d'Ivoire	Mali	55	74	35
Côte d'Ivoire	Liberia	132	178	35
Angola	Namibia	88	128	45
Botswana	Zimbabwe	51	107	110

Source: Calculations based on ESCAP-World Bank Trade Cost Database, https://www.unescap.org/resources/escap-world-bank-trade-cost-database. Trade costs are in ad valorem equivalents.

TABLE 4A.3 Trade-weighted average tariffs, imports and exports, by country
Percent

Country	Imports		Exports	
	MFN rate	Applied tariff	MFN rate	Applied tariff
Algeria	12.6	8.9	1.4	0.6
Angola	—	—	0.2	0.1
Benin	12.5	11.2	6.5	0.6
Botswana	5.7	0.6	3.2	2.2
Burkina Faso	9.6	6.9	2.4	0.9
Burundi	13.1	7.2	1.9	0.9
Cabo Verde	12.2	12.2	12.0	0.5
Cameroon	14.2	14.1	2.8	0.6
Central African Republic	17.5	16.4	1.8	0.5

(continued)

TABLE 4A.3 Trade-weighted average tariffs, imports and exports, by country *(continued)*

Percent

Country	Imports		Exports	
	MFN rate	Applied tariff	MFN rate	Applied tariff
Chad	—	—	0.4	0.2
Comoros	—	—	12.0	0.7
Congo, Rep.	—	—	0.9	0.8
Côte d'Ivoire	—	—	5.3	2.0
Djibouti	—	—	1.8	1.3
Egypt, Arab Rep.	11.5	6.6	5.8	1.9
Equatorial Guinea	—	—	1.2	0.9
Eritrea	—	—	0.6	0.0
Eswatini	—	—	16.0	5.1
Ethiopia	—	—	7.2	3.0
Gabon	—	—	0.7	0.6
Gambia, The	—	—	8.2	0.6
Ghana	10.7	10.4	3.2	1.7
Guinea	—	—	2.5	2.3
Guinea-Bissau	—	—	20.0	19.0
Kenya	—	—	11.0	2.5
Lesotho	—	—	14.0	0.6
Liberia	—	—	1.5	0.3
Libya	—	—	0.4	0.3
Madagascar	7.8	6.5	7.6	0.4
Malawi	—	—	18.0	7.3
Mali	10.4	6.1	1.0	0.1
Mauritania	8.7	8.7	4.5	2.3
Mauritius	1.0	0.8	16.0	0.9
Morocco	10.8	3.8	8.7	1.8
Mozambique	—	—	6.2	1.9
Namibia	7.5	0.9	6.2	2.3
Niger	10.8	8.2	2.1	0.1
Nigeria	8.6	8.5	1.0	0.8

(continued)

TABLE 4A.3 Trade-weighted average tariffs, imports and exports, by country *(continued)*

Percent

Country	Imports		Exports	
	MFN rate	Applied tariff	MFN rate	Applied tariff
Rwanda	14.7	8.8	1.6	0.9
São Tomé and Príncipe	—	—	8.7	1.2
Senegal	9.4	8.7	14.0	1.7
Seychelles	—	—	1.0	0.5
Sierra Leone	—	—	2.5	1.9
Somalia	—	—	4.1	2.1
South Africa	6.5	4.4	0.1	0.0
Sudan	—	—	0.9	0.5
Tanzania	10.4	8.8	6.8	0.6
Togo	11.0	9.5	5.0	0.9
Tunisia	11.9	4.0	7.0	2.0
Uganda	10.5	8.1	7.7	1.8
Zambia	—	—	3.7	0.9
Zimbabwe	12.0	6.0	14.0	8.3
Africa	**10.0**	**6.4**	**4.0**	**1.5**

Sources: Mattoo, Rocha, and Ruta 2020; World Bank, Deep Trade Agreements database, https://datatopics.worldbank.org/dta/table.html.
Note: MFN = most favored nation; — = not available.

TABLE 4A.4 List of African trade agreements considered

Agreement	Year entered into force	Intra-Africa	Coverage ratio (%)
Agadir Agreement	2007	No	3.6
Common Market for Eastern and Southern Africa (COMESA)	1994	Yes	19.1
EFTA—Egypt, Arab Rep.	2007	No	18.4
EFTA—Morocco	1999	No	16.2
EFTA—Southern African Customs Union (SACU)	2008	No	13.4
EFTA—Tunisia	2005	No	17.8
EU—Algeria	2005	No	16.4

(continued)

TABLE 4A.4 List of African trade agreements considered *(continued)*

Agreement	Year entered into force	Intra-Africa	Coverage ratio (%)
EU—Cameroon	2009	No	13.8
EU—Côte d'Ivoire	2009	No	10.6
EU—Eastern and Southern Africa States Interim EPA	2012	No	9.8
EU—Egypt, Arab Rep.	2004	No	16.2
EU—Morocco	2000	No	15.3
EU—South Africa	2000	No	15.8
EU—Tunisia	1998	No	15.6
East African Community (EAC)	2000	Yes	12.3
East African Community (EAC)—Accession of Burundi and Rwanda	2007	Yes	4.2
Economic Community of West African States (ECOWAS)	1993	Yes	11.4
Economic and Monetary Community of Central Africa (CEMAC)	1999	Yes	6.1
Egypt, Arab Rep.—Türkiye	2007	No	11.2
Global System of Trade Preferences among Developing Countries (GSTP)	1989	No	1.5
Mauritius—Pakistan	2007	No	6.2
Pan-Arab Free Trade Area (PAFTA)	1998	No	1.3
Southern African Customs Union (SACU)	2004	Yes	2.9
Southern African Development Community (SADC)	2000	Yes	10.2
Southern African Development Community (SADC)—Accession of Seychelles	2015	Yes	5.2
Türkiye—Mauritius	2013	No	7.7
Türkiye—Morocco	2006	No	11.1
Türkiye—Tunisia	2005	No	11.5
United States—Morocco	2006	No	30.5
West African Economic and Monetary Union (WAEMU)	2000	Yes	6.7

Sources: Mattoo, Rocha, and Ruta 2020; World Bank, Deep Trade Agreements database, https://datatopics .worldbank.org/dta/table.html.

Note: Coverage ratio refers to the share of provisions contained in a given agreement relative to the maximum number of provisions. EFTA = European Free Trade Association; EPA = Economic Partnership Agreement; EU = European Union.

Notes

1. ESCAP–World Bank Trade Cost Database, https://www.unescap.org/resources/escap-world-bank-trade-cost-database.

2. The borders with the highest ad valorem equivalents in Africa are Niger-Chad with an ad valorem equivalent of 479, Algeria-Mali with 429, Chad-Nigeria with 418, the Central African Republic–Democratic Republic of Congo with 322, Algeria-Niger with 268, and Liberia–Sierra Leone with 254. These figures are the tariff-like costs of crossing each of these borders; the methodology for the calculation of these figures is described in the "Border Thickness and Trade Costs" section. Refer to annex table 4A.1 for a detailed list of the 50 borders with the highest ad valorem equivalents in the world.

3. Sub-Saharan Africa's exports grew faster than the world average between 2000 and 2010 (measured in current US dollars): 13.1 percent compared with 9.2 percent. This growth resulted in an increase in the region's share of global exports. The momentum slowed, however, between 2010 and 2019. Whereas global exports grew at an average rate of 3.6 percent during that period, Sub-Saharan Africa's export growth stagnated at a rate of −0.2 percent. For more details on Africa's export dynamics, refer to the "Summary" section.

4. The general equilibrium model of trade used for quantification is based on a structural gravity approach. However, structural gravity is not the only existing tool for solving quantitative models of trade: other prominent examples include computable general equilibrium models and models using Exact Hat Algebra. Bekkers (2019) provides evidence of the equivalence between the different approaches, provided that the baseline trade shares entering the models are identical. In this regard, Yotov et al. (2016) suggest that structural gravity models may be more robust to measurement errors in trade flows because they require the "baseline" to be calibrated to the shares predicted by a gravity equation.

5. As noted in chapter 9, Africa exports mostly commodities—that is, low-value-added products—to Asia. To increase the domestic value-added content of exports, African countries need to develop the capacity to process key export commodities locally before exporting them to Asia.

6. Note, however, that this statistic likely underestimates the true extent of intraregional trade because of the large volumes of informal cross-border trade not captured by official statistics. Calculations that exclude the exports of natural resources also find a greater extent of intraregional trade (Mold and Chowdhury 2021).

7. Although no further disaggregation is available for this category, the bulk of it is likely associated with trade-related services, which are relatively traditional.

8. Countries in the commodity group of the 2020 *World Development Report* taxonomy have a small share of manufacturing in total domestic value added (less than 60 percent) and limited backward GVC integration (defined as the share of imports embodied in manufacturing exports in a country's total exports). By contrast, countries specializing in limited manufacturing GVCs engage in some manufacturing exports in addition to commodity exports and exhibit medium backward GVC integration.

9. GVC firms are defined as those that engage in both exporting and importing activities.

10. In this definition, bilateral trade costs include all possible sources of frictions, including intangible sources. Therefore, they are much larger than actual monetary expenditures incurred in international trade, such as transportation costs or tariffs. Because of these costs, border thickness persists even in single markets, such as the European Union.

11. Annex table 4A.1 shows that less than half (24) of the country pairs with the thickest borders have a free trade agreement, whereas almost all of the country pairs with the thinnest borders have one (46 out of 50).

12. Trade costs are geometrically averaged over a window of four years. Geometric mean is also applied to regional averages.

13. The analysis provided using the deep agreements data set is based on commitments that are included in agreements and does not consider implementation.

14. The language in a PTA is considered "enforceable" if it is sufficiently precise from a legal point of view and if the agreement for a specific policy area foresees a dispute settlement mechanism to resolve disagreement.

15. Deep trade agreements signed after 2000 include United States–Morocco (2006), European Free Trade Association–Egypt, Arab Rep. (2007), European Free Trade Association–Tunisia (2005), EU-Algeria (2005), and EU-Egypt (2004).

16. The Global System of Trade Preferences among Developing Countries (GSTP), EU-Tunisia, Pan-Arab Free Trade Area (PAFTA), and European Free Trade Association–Morocco.

17. World Bank, Ease of Doing Business rankings, https://archive.doingbusiness.org/en/rankings.

18. The analysis is restricted to time delays for importing and exporting for the latest year available. For each country, the analysis defines both land and sea border delays if the country is coastal but only land border delays if the country is landlocked. Because data are reported only for the most used gateway per country, which for costal countries is generally a port, the analysis assumes that unobserved land border times are a fraction of reported sea border times. When only sea border delays are available in the data, the analysis assumes that land border delays are equal to a fourth of sea border delays, checking that this assumption is more or less in line with other cases when both land and sea border delays are available. In addition, the analysis compared the obtained delays with data from external documents to ensure that this coefficient is acceptable.

19. For data, refer to UN Trade and Development, "UNCTADstat Data centre," https://unctadstat .unctad.org/wds/TableViewer/tableView.aspx?ReportId=170027. The aggregated figures are derived from the fusion of automatic identification system information with port mapping intelligence by MarineTraffic (marinetraffic.com), covering ships of 1,000 gross tons. The data used are the median time that vessels spent within port limits (in days). The present analysis works with the median time, although the average time that vessels spend in port is longer for practically all countries and markets, because of statistical outliers (ships that spend weeks or months in a port, for example for repairs). The statistical distribution of time spent in ports has a "long tail." The global average time ships spent in port in 2020 was 42.3 hours, compared with 24.0 hours median time.

20. The analysis finally cross-checks the assumed border delays with observed delays from diverse external sources to validate the assumptions.

21. The coordinates represent the first two principal components extracted from the 18 features used in the clustering algorithm.

22. The road network for Africa comes from OpenStreetMap.

23. Assumptions regarding the average speed for different transportation modes as well as data for the processing time when reaching a port or when crossing borders are used (for details, refer to Fontagné, Lebrand, et al. 2023). The analysis prioritizes road transportation because the rail network in Africa consists of several disconnected components with heterogeneous market sizes

that make them difficult to compare with each other. In addition, the inclusion of multimodal transportation would also necessitate the introduction of intermodal elasticities, which require extremely detailed data to be estimated correctly.

24. The analysis focuses on road and maritime links for Africa abstracting from rail and air connectivity; other land transportation times in the rest of the world focused on rail are sourced from de Soyres et al. (2019), which allows simplification of the network analysis. Two main reasons justify this approach. First, most PIDA transportation projects consist of road and maritime infrastructure. Second, most international trade travels by sea and by rail, but road is by far the main transportation mode for trade between Sub-Saharan African countries. The nodes of the network in the global database, which serve as both origin and destination in the analysis, are all cities with populations greater than 500,000 as well as the two most populous cities in each country (data permitting).

25. For a detailed description of the model and the advantages and disadvantages of this approach, refer to Fontagné, Rocha, et al. (2023).

26. Trade between African countries and the rest of the world would remain substantially unaltered, on average, although some countries would experience trade diversion because a deeper regional agreement reduces frictions to intra-African trade relatively more than frictions on trade with the rest of the world.

27. The analysis can observe only formal trade, because informal trade avoids customs. Assuming that the data show only part of the trade between African countries, but that the output is correctly measured, informal trade leads to less trade openness (or a larger domestic market): in the calculation of general economic equilibrium effects, this could dampen the effects on international trade, which can then be read as a lower bound on the true effect. Furthermore, assuming that informal trade between African countries is partly due to trade frictions (and especially border difficulties), increasing infrastructure connectivity and trade facilitation measures may also have the indirect effect of reducing informal trade.

References

Arvis, Jean-François, Lauri Ojala, Christina Wiederer, Ben Shepherd, Anasuya Raj, Karlygash Dairabayeva, and Tuomas Kiiski. 2018. "Connecting to Compete: Trade Logistics in the Global Economy—The Logistics Performance Index and Its Indicators." World Bank, Washington, DC.

AUDA (African Union Development Agency)-NEPAD and JICA (Japan International Cooperation Agency). 2022. *One-Stop Border Post Sourcebook*. 3rd ed. Johannesburg, South Africa: AUDA-NEPAD and JICA.

Bekkers, Eddy. 2019. "The Welfare Effects of Trade Policy Experiments in Quantitative Trade Models: The Role of Solution Methods and Baseline Calibration." WTO Staff Working Paper ERSD-2019-02, Economic Research and Statistics Division, World Trade Organization, Geneva.

Coulibaly, Souleymane, Woubet Kassa, and Albert Zeufack. 2022. *Africa in the New Trade Environment: Market Access in Troubled Times*. Washington, DC: World Bank.

De Soyres, François, Alen Mulabdic, Siobhan Murray, Nadia Rocha, and Michele Ruta. 2019. "How Much Will the Belt and Road Initiative Reduce Trade Costs?" *International Economics* 159 (Q3): 151–64.

Fontagné, Lionel, Mathilde Lebrand, Siobhan Murray, Michele Ruta, and Gianluca Santoni. 2023. "Trade and Transport Integration in Africa." Policy Research Working Paper WPS10609, World Bank, Washington, DC.

Fontagné, Lionel, Nadia Rocha, Michele Ruta, and Gianluca Santoni. 2023. *The Economic Impact of Deepening Trade Agreements*. Washington, DC: World Bank. https://doi.org/10.1093/wber/lhad005.

Goldberg, Pinelopi Koujianou, and Tristan Reed. 2020. "Income Distribution, International Integration and Sustained Poverty Reduction." Policy Research Working Paper 9342, World Bank, Washington, DC.

Goldberg, Pinelopi Koujianou, and Tristan Reed. 2022. "Demand-Side Constraints in Development: The Role of Market Size, Trade, and (In)Equality." NBER Working Paper 27286, National Bureau of Economic Research, Cambridge, MA.

Hofmann, Claudia, Alberto Osnago, and Michele Ruta. 2017. "Horizontal Depth: A New Database on the Content of Preferential Trade Agreements." Policy Research Working Paper 7981, World Bank, Washington, DC.

Mattoo, Aaditya, Alen Mulabdic, and Michele Ruta. 2017. "Trade Creation and Trade Diversion in Deep Agreements." Policy Research Working Paper 8206, World Bank, Washington, DC.

Mattoo, Aaditya, Nadia Rocha, and Michele Ruta. 2020. *Handbook of Deep Trade Agreements*. Washington, DC: World Bank. https://openknowledge.worldbank.org/handle/10986/34055.

Mold, Andrew, and Samiha Chowdhury. 2021. "Why the Extent of Intra-African Trade Is Much Higher than Commonly Believed—And What This Means for the AfCFTA." Brookings Commentary, May 19, 2021. https://www.brookings.edu/articles/why-the-extent-of-intra-african-trade-is-much-higher-than-commonly-believed-and-what-this-means-for-the-afcfta/.

World Bank. 2009. *World Development Report 2009: Reshaping Economic Geography*. Washington, DC: World Bank. https://openknowledge.worldbank.org/handle/10986/5991.

World Bank. 2020a. *The African Continental Free Trade Area: Economic and Distributional Effects*. Washington, DC: World Bank. https://openknowledge.worldbank.org/handle/10986/34139.

World Bank. 2020b. *World Development Report 2020: Trading for Development in the Age of Global Value Chains*. Washington, DC: World Bank.

World Bank. 2021. "High Trade Costs: Causes and Remedies." Chapter 3 in *Global Economic Prospects*. Washington, DC: World Bank.

Yotov, Yoto V., Roberta Piermartini, José-Antonio Monteiro, and Mario Larch. 2016. *An Advanced Guide to Trade Policy Analysis: The Structural Gravity Model*. Geneva: World Trade Organization.

CHAPTER 5

Private Sector Investments

Leila Aghabarari, Ricardo David De Castro Martins, Justice Tei Mensah, Vincent Palmade, and Volker Treichel

Summary

Productive private investment is the engine of sustainable economic growth, yet it continues to lag in Africa. Cross-cutting constraints to productive private investments have been well documented, including political and macro instability and poor governance and business environment; however, sector-specific constraints have received less attention. Twenty-seven recent Country Private Sector Diagnostics (CPSDs) for Africa showed the collective importance of these sector-specific constraints, especially in light of the challenges and opportunities presented by the new megatrends (climate change and digital economy). This chapter discusses how these new megatrends affect the investment landscape in Africa. It then reviews the state of the private sector in Africa together with a brief overview of the well-documented cross-cutting constraints to productive private investments in Africa. A subsequent section provides policy insights, based on country examples from Africa and beyond, on how countries have overcome these cross-cutting and sector-specific constraints (government and market failures) in key sectors, distinguishing between sectors driving growth, such as mining, agribusiness, manufacturing, digital services, and tourism, and sectors enabling growth, such as transportation, energy, education, and finance. Finally, the chapter reviews institutional approaches that are followed by countries to successfully implement such policies.

Climate change, combined with rapid demographic growth and high levels of poverty, exacerbates Africa's food security challenge. Global trends, however, also bring new opportunities for Africa to achieve sustainable and inclusive private sector–led growth. Africa is well positioned to attract green private investments by leveraging its sources of renewable energy—carbon sink (forests) and critical minerals—as part of the global answer to climate change. In turn, access to green energy combined with rapidly improving (digital) infrastructure and skills position Africa to become competitive in a growing number of sectors. Increased competitiveness together with a rapidly growing population and the creation of the African Continental Free Trade Area will make Africa one of the largest and fastest-growing markets for private investors.

This chapter includes contributions by Bene Wende Anicet Kabre, Jean Michel Marchat, and Ibrahim Okumu.

Capitalizing on these opportunities will require a three-pronged policy strategy. In addition to resolving well-known cross-cutting constraints, countries will need key sector-specific reforms and proactive measures to attract strategic investors and support small and medium enterprises. A growing number of African countries are implementing such strategies in a growing number of sectors: Botswana in mining (leveraging its good governance); Ghana in light manufacturing (leveraging the highly efficient Tema port public-private partnership); Kenya in high-value agribusiness (through strategic alliances between smallholders and exporters supported by the government and development partners); Mauritius and Rwanda in high-end tourism (also through strong public-private sector collaboration); Morocco in high-value manufacturing (leveraging vocational training public-private partnerships); Nigeria in digital services (leveraging continuous reforms of its telecommunications sector); and Senegal in solar energy (following a successful international competition).

To replicate and scale up these successes across a broad number of critical sectors, African countries will need to rely on reform delivery teams following examples of the countries that have had the most success, including, in Africa, Botswana, Cabo Verde, Rwanda, and Togo. These countries relied on dedicated elite reform teams, connected to the top of government, that steered the reform process, coordinated and mobilized development partners, and engaged with the private sector and civil society. African countries will also need to drive and leverage economic integration between themselves and the rest of the world (the African Continental Free Trade Area, the World Trade Organization, and deep free trade agreements with key partners).

Context

Envisioning private sector development in Africa through 2050 will require consideration of several global megatrends. Factors like demographic shifts, the mounting challenges of climate change, evolving security challenges, and transformative digital technological advances are reshaping the continent's investment landscape. These megatrends, despite presenting unique challenges, also offer major opportunities for Africa.

For instance, although making it imperative to create more and better jobs for youth, Africa's rapid working-age population growth also offers the continent the prospect of becoming the source of a vast and competitive labor force as well as one of the largest and fastest-growing markets in the world. The population in Africa is expected to explode from 1.3 billion in 2020 to 2.5 billion by 2050 and to reach 4.3 billion by 2100. Consequently, Africa's share of the global population will likely increase from 17 percent in 2020 to 26 percent in 2050 and 39 percent in 2100 (figure 5.1). Ensuring that this vast labor force increase turns into a competitive advantage will require continued improvement of the education sector coupled with the provision of private sector–led technical skills as discussed in the "Analysis" section.

Increasing urbanization also presents both a challenge and an opportunity. Since 1990, the number of cities in Africa has more than doubled in number, from 3,300 to 7,600, and their

FIGURE 5.1 **Share of world population, by region, 2020 and projected for 2050 and 2100**

Share of world population (%)

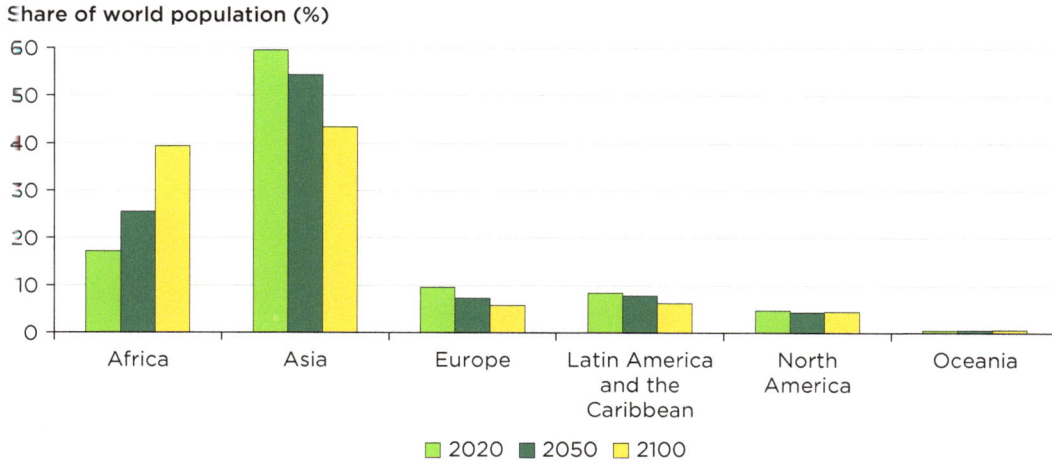

Source: United Nations Population Division 2022.
Note: Data are projections based on medium-variant fertility. Africa includes Western Asia.

cumulative population has increased by 500 million people. Africa's urbanization still has a long way to go—with a 42 percent urbanization rate, Africa is the second least urbanized region in the world, not far ahead of South Asia with 36 percent (UN DESA 2018). The predicted population explosion coupled with continued rural-urban migration (Behrens and Robert-Nicoud 2014) will put increasing strain on cities and continue to fuel the low-productivity urban informal economy, unless policies are put in place to enable productive urbanization, including effective planning, zoning, titling, and taxing of land together with macro reforms to enable mortgages. With the right policies, urbanization can be a major source of jobs and productivity growth through economies of agglomeration (Ahlburg 1996), providing several hundred million people with better jobs and improved access to services and infrastructure, with positive spillovers from urbanization spreading to rural areas in proximity to cities (OECD, ECA, and AfDB 2022)—refer also to the discussion of the housing construction sector in the "Analysis" section.

Africa's vast natural resources—green assets in particular—can be either a curse or a blessing (Collier 2015). If not well managed, exploitation of natural resources can lead to missed opportunities, Dutch disease, corruption, environmental and social harm, and even conflict. The "Analysis" section later in the chapter discusses the policies required to ensure sustainable and inclusive management of the mining sector. Poorly managed urbanization and exploitation of Africa's natural resources would exacerbate the negative impact of climate change on the continent. Wetland encroachments lead to a higher frequency of flooding, even during typical rainy seasons, because of the increase in impervious areas from human developments; the loss of forest cover causes heavier rains, floods, and heat waves. Map 5.1 shows various levels of climate-related risk exposure across Africa. These trends, paired with escalating unpredictable weather

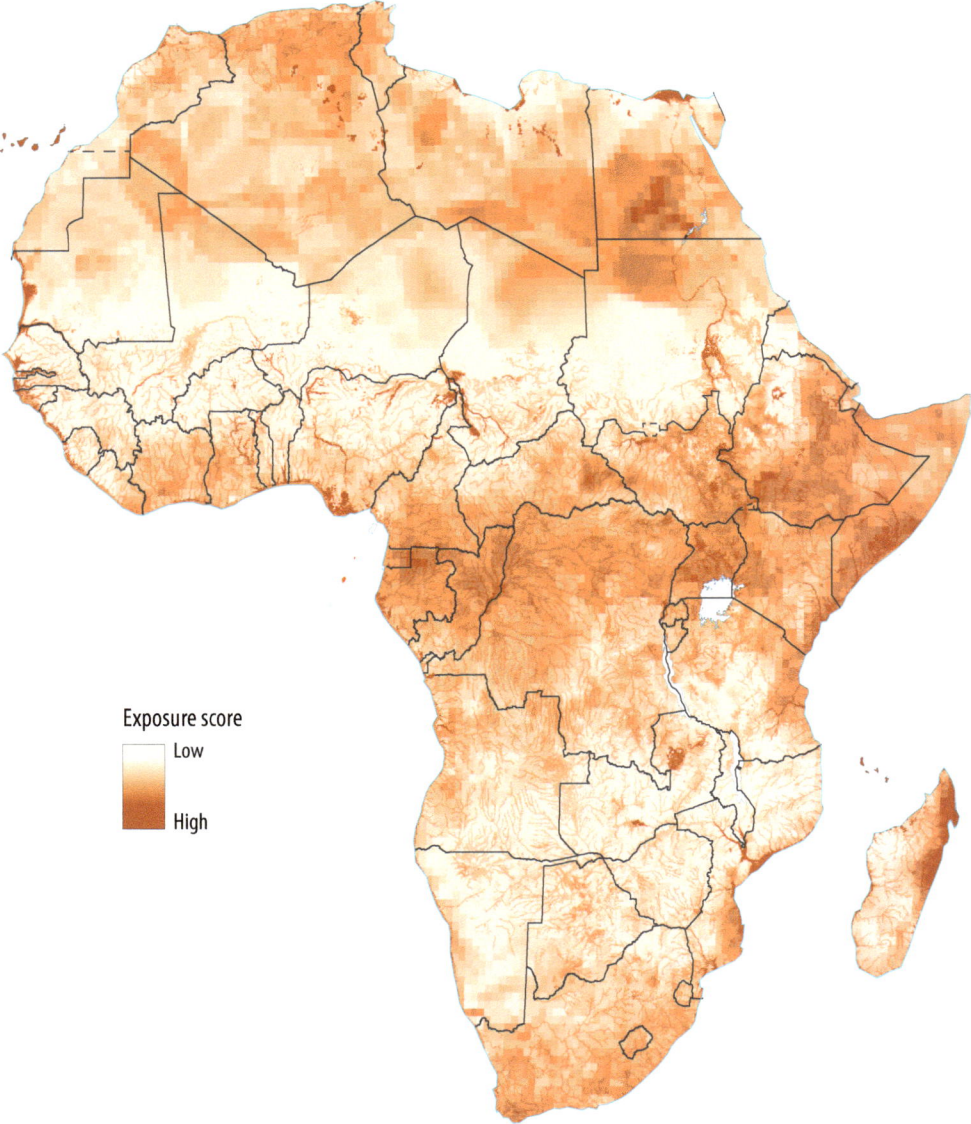

MAP 5.1 Heat map of climate vulnerability in Africa

Exposure score
Low
High

IBRD 48609 | JANUARY 2025

Source: Busby, Smith, and Krishnan 2014.

Patterns, also drive up the costs of business and insurance—particularly in agriculture, which is 95 percent rain-fed in Sub-Saharan Africa. The economic impacts of climate-induced damages are anticipated to be 10 percent higher in Africa compared with the next most exposed region, India, and more than double that of the other regions (AfDB 2011).

Security would become an increasing challenge in the absence of improved policies to manage urbanization, natural resources, and climate change. Map 5.2 shows the

MAP 5.2 Africa's deadliest armed conflicts, by type

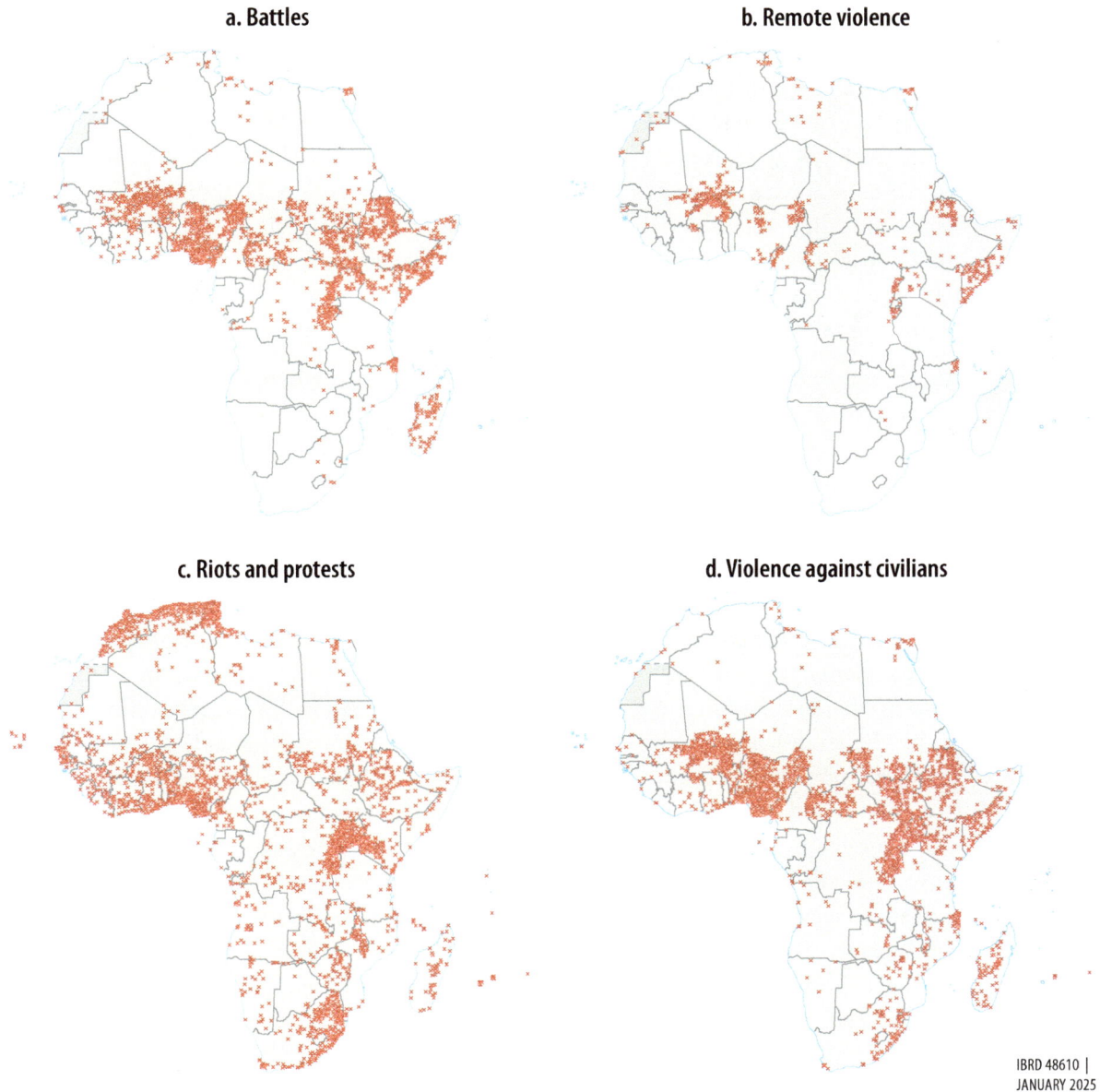

a. Battles

b. Remote violence

c. Riots and protests

d. Violence against civilians

IBRD 48610 | JANUARY 2025

Source: Armed Conflict Location & Event Data Project (ACLED), https://www.acleddata.com/.

prevalence of conflicts across Africa, often fueled by a sense of government neglect and marginalization (Damboeck et al. 2020). A weak state and military capacity frequently give rise to terrorism, which often spills over to neighboring countries (Collier 2015). In addition to increasing the cost and risk of doing business, insecurity undermines human capital development because of the disruption of school years, destruction of schools, and loss of quality of education; thus, insecurity further disincentivizes private sector investment because of low productivity and shortages of skilled labor.

Digital technology can act as either a barrier or a springboard for Africa's private sector–led growth. First, digital technology can increase within-firm productivity through adoption of technologies such as smartphones, digital transactions, and digital management solutions (Cusolito, Lederman, and Peña 2020). Digitalization also offers Africa an opportunity to reduce the fixed cost of exporting, such as through traceability solutions leveraging blockchains. Africa's private sector is currently characterized by low uptake of digital technology—only 25 percent of firms in Africa that have access to digital technology searched for suppliers using digital technology, and only 10 percent used e-commerce solutions (Zeufack et al. 2020). Furthermore, 900 million people in Africa are still not connected to the internet, and even those who are connected have limited use (Denis 2021). The "Analysis" section discusses the policies required to promote access to and use of digital services (subsections on digitalized services and digital infrastructure).

Africa stands at the crossroads of unparalleled challenges and opportunities. Megatrends such as demographic explosion, climate change, insecurity, and digital technology have the potential to both enhance and undermine Africa's private sector capacity and productivity (figure 5.2). This chapter explores the opportunities and reviews examples of policy solutions to overcome the constraints to private investment across Africa's main economic sectors.

Whereas the cross-cutting constraints to productive private investments have been well documented in Africa (political and macro instability, poor governance, and business environment), less attention has been given to the equally important sector-specific constraints identified in the 27 CPSDs recently completed in Africa, especially in light of the challenges and opportunities brought up by the new megatrends discussed earlier in this chapter. This section aims to provide policy insights, based on country examples from Africa and beyond, on how the cross-cutting and sector-specific constraints (government and market failures) have been overcome in key sectors—distinguishing between sectors that drive growth—such as mining, agribusiness, manufacturing, digitalized services, and tourism—and sectors that enable growth—such as transportation, energy, education, and finance. It also discusses the institutional approaches adopted by successful countries to implement such policies across and within a critical mass of sectors.

FIGURE 5.2 Megatrends, disruptions and challenges, and private sector opportunities in Africa

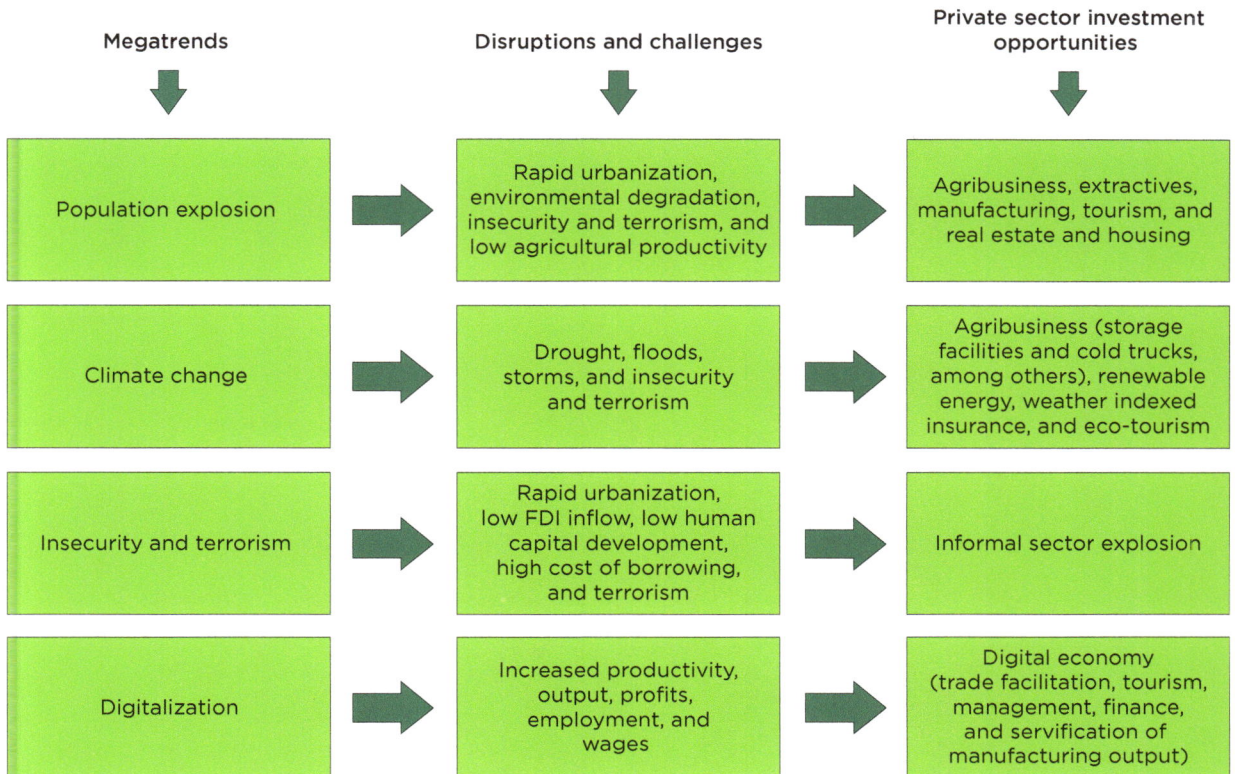

Megatrends	Disruptions and challenges	Private sector investment opportunities
Population explosion	Rapid urbanization, environmental degradation, insecurity and terrorism, and low agricultural productivity	Agribusiness, extractives, manufacturing, tourism, and real estate and housing
Climate change	Drought, floods, storms, and insecurity and terrorism	Agribusiness (storage facilities and cold trucks, among others), renewable energy, weather indexed insurance, and eco-tourism
Insecurity and terrorism	Rapid urbanization, low FDI inflow, low human capital development, high cost of borrowing, and terrorism	Informal sector explosion
Digitalization	Increased productivity, output, profits, employment, and wages	Digital economy (trade facilitation, tourism, management, finance, and servification of manufacturing output)

Source: World Bank.
Note: FDI = foreign direct investment.

Following a discussion of the state of the private sector and the familiar cross-cutting constraints to private investments, the chapter focuses on the sectoral level to highlight sector-specific opportunities, constraints, and possible solutions. Historically, broad reports have focused on either macro/cross-cutting or micro/firm-level constraints but not on a critical mass of mezzo/sector-level analysis. The recently completed CPSDs in 27 African countries enable us to fill this gap. CPSDs distinguish between three types of sectors: export locomotives that drive growth, urban-domestic sectors where most jobs are created, and enabling sectors in which performance affects all other sectors (figure 5.3). Figure 5.4 illustrates the framework integrating sector (vertical) with policy (horizontal) dimensions to enable prioritization of cross-cutting and sector-specific policy reforms, and table 5.1 shows the sector coverage of CPSDs across all African countries.

FIGURE 5.3 Jobs and economic transformation through a sector lens

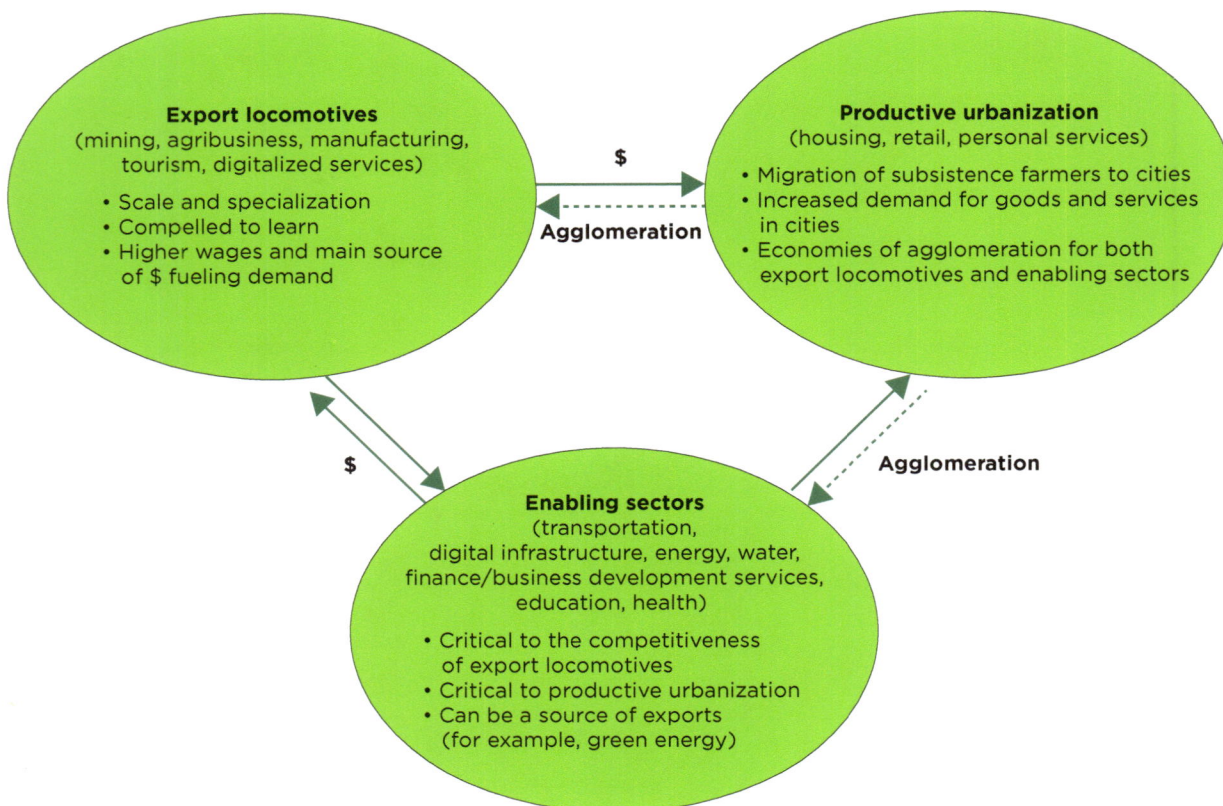

Export locomotives
(mining, agribusiness, manufacturing, tourism, digitalized services)
- Scale and specialization
- Compelled to learn
- Higher wages and main source of $ fueling demand

$ — Agglomeration

Productive urbanization
(housing, retail, personal services)
- Migration of subsistence farmers to cities
- Increased demand for goods and services in cities
- Economies of agglomeration for both export locomotives and enabling sectors

$ — Agglomeration

Enabling sectors
(transportation, digital infrastructure, energy, water, finance/business development services, education, health)
- Critical to the competitiveness of export locomotives
- Critical to productive urbanization
- Can be a source of exports (for example, green energy)

Source: World Bank.

Facts

The private sector in Africa is dominated by micro and small firms, and persistent high levels of informality. The service and manufacturing sectors in Africa have a large concentration of firms in the lower end of the size distribution, with a relatively low share of firms in the upper and middle segments of the size distribution (Abreha et al. 2022). These small, mainly informal, firms account for a large share of total nonagricultural employment. Specifically, the informal economy accounts for 59 percent of total nonagricultural employment in Africa, compared with 49 percent in Asia and Pacific, 15 percent in Europe and Central Asia, and 26 percent in the Americas (ILO 2018). These statistics highlight the importance of informal firms—private sector actors—in African economies, despite their persistent low levels of productivity. Research indicates that policy distortions such as labor regulations, export surrender requirements, and size-dependent tax policies contribute to the persistence of informality in the region (Bachas, Gadenne, and Jensen 2020). Informality not only adversely affects productivity but also limits the region's participation in global value chains. Currently, Africa's participation in global value chains is largely concentrated in the export of primary goods—minerals, crude oil, cocoa, cotton, and coffee—and imports

FIGURE 5.4 Diversified enablers and drivers of jobs and economic transformation

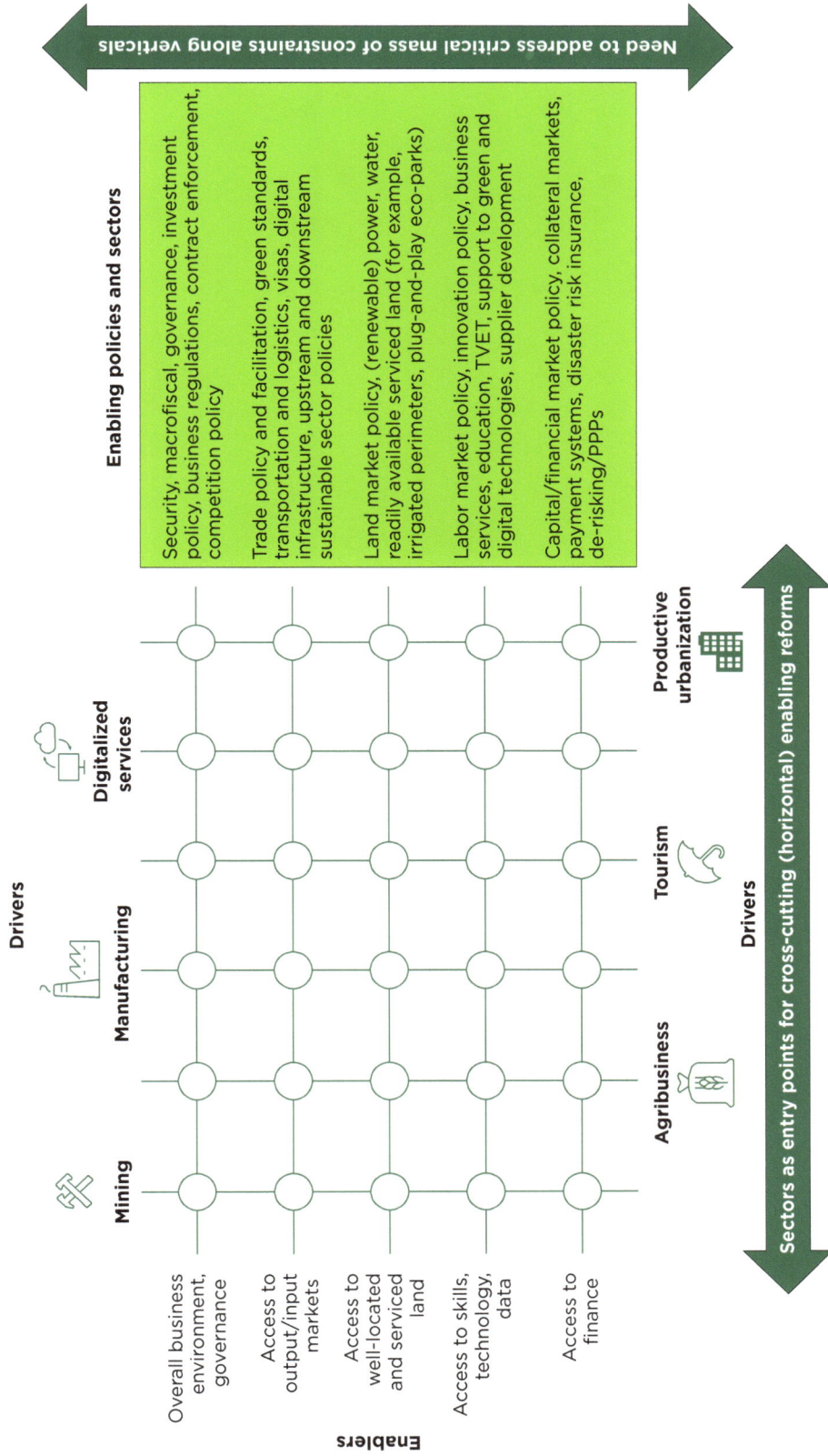

Need to address critical mass of constraints along verticals

Enabling policies and sectors

Security, macrofiscal, governance, investment policy, business regulations, contract enforcement, competition policy

Trade policy and facilitation, green standards, transportation and logistics, visas, digital infrastructure, upstream and downstream sustainable sector policies

Land market policy, (renewable) power, water, readily available serviced land (for example, irrigated perimeters, plug-and-play eco-parks)

Labor market policy, innovation policy, business services, education, TVET, support to green and digital technologies, supplier development

Capital/financial market policy, collateral markets, payment systems, disaster risk insurance, de-risking/PPPs

Drivers

	Mining	Manufacturing	Digitalized services			Productive urbanization

Enablers

- Overall business environment, governance
- Access to output/input markets
- Access to well-located and serviced land
- Access to skills, technology, data
- Access to finance

Drivers

Agribusiness — Tourism — Productive urbanization

Sectors as entry points for cross-cutting (horizontal) enabling reforms

Source: World Bank.
Note: PPPs = public-private partnerships; TVET = technical and vocational education and training.

TABLE 5.1 Sector coverage of Country Private Sector Diagnostics in Africa

Country	Drivers of growth						Enablers of growth						
	Mining	Agribusiness	Manufacturing	Tourism	Traded digital services	Productive urbanization	Transportation	Digital infrastructure	Energy	Water	Education/ skills	Finance/ business development services	Health
Angola	No	No	No	No	No	No	Yes	Yes	Yes	No	Yes	No	Yes
Benin	No	Yes	No	Yes	No	No	No	No	No	No	Yes	Yes	No
Botswana	No	No	No	Yes	No	No	No	No	Yes	Yes	No	No	No
Burkina Faso	Yes	Yes	No	No	No	No	Yes	Yes	Yes	No	Yes	No	No
Burundi	No	Yes	No	No	No	No	No	No	No	No	No	Yes	No
Cameroon	No	No	No	No	No	Yes	Yes	Yes	Yes	No	No	Yes	No
Chad	No	No	No	No	No	No	No	Yes	Yes	Yes	No	Yes	No
Côte d'Ivoire	No	Yes	No	No	No	No	Yes	Yes	No	No	Yes	Yes	No
Congo, Dem. Rep.	Yes	Yes	Yes	No	Yes	Yes	Yes	Yes	Yes	Yes	Yes	Yes	Yes
Egypt, Arab Rep.	No	Yes	Yes	No	Yes	No	No	No	No	No	Yes	No	Yes
Eswatini	No	Yes	Yes	No	No	No	No	No	No	No	Yes	Yes	No
Ethiopia	No	No	No	No	No	No	Yes	Yes	Yes	No	Yes	Yes	Yes
Ghana	No	Yes	No	No	Yes	No	No	Yes	No	No	Yes	No	No
Guinea	Yes	Yes	No	No	No	Yes	Yes	Yes	Yes	No	No	Yes	No
Kenya	No	Yes	Yes	No	No	Yes	Yes	Yes	Yes	No	No	Yes	Yes
Madagascar	No	Yes	Yes	Yes	No	No	No	No	No	No	Yes	Yes	No
Malawi	No	Yes	No	No	No	No	No	Yes	Yes	No	No	No	No
Mali	No	No	No	No	No	No	Yes	Yes	Yes	No	No	Yes	No
Morocco	No	No	Yes	No	No	No	No	Yes	No	No	Yes	Yes	No
Mozambique	No	Yes	No	Yes	No	Yes	No	Yes	Yes	No	No	Yes	No
Namibia	No	No	No	No	No	Yes	No	Yes	No	Yes	No	No	No
Nigeria	Yes	Yes	Yes	No	No	No	No	No	No	No	Yes	Yes	No
Rwanda	No	Yes	No	No	No	Yes	No	No	No	No	No	No	No
Senegal	No	Yes	No	No	No	No	No	Yes	Yes	No	No	Yes	No
South Africa	No	Yes	Yes	No	Yes	No	Yes	No	Yes	Yes	Yes	No	No
Togo	No	No	No	No	No	No	No	Yes	Yes	No	No	Yes	No
Uganda	No	Yes	No	No	No	Yes	No	No	Yes	No	No	No	No

Source: World Bank.

of manufactured products. Exports from manufacturing remain relatively low, despite emerging islands of excellence such as the case of light manufacturing in Ethiopia. Informality is both a symptom and a driver of low productivity in Africa.

Low levels of private sector investment

Sub-Saharan Africa has relatively low investment by the private sector compared with comparator regions such as East Asia and Pacific, and South Asia. Private investments as a share of gross domestic product (GDP) in Africa increased from an average of 8.5 percent in the 1990s to 9.2 percent in the 2000s and 9.5 percent in the 2010s, compared with the global average of 14.3 percent for the period 1990–2019 (figure 5.5). Meanwhile, the level of private investments in the East Asia and Pacific and the South Asia regions is about twice the level of Africa. Within the African continent, the top performers in average private investments as a percent of GDP over the last two decades include the Seychelles (31 percent), Morocco (24 percent), and Zambia (20 percent). The lowest levels of private investments as a percent of GDP were recorded in Libya (3.0 percent), Eritrea (3.0 percent), and Guinea-Bissau (1.4 percent). The situation was worsened by the COVID-19 pandemic, which led to a sharp decline in investments globally, despite a recovery in 2021.

FIGURE 5.5 **Trends in private investments, by world region, 1990–2019**

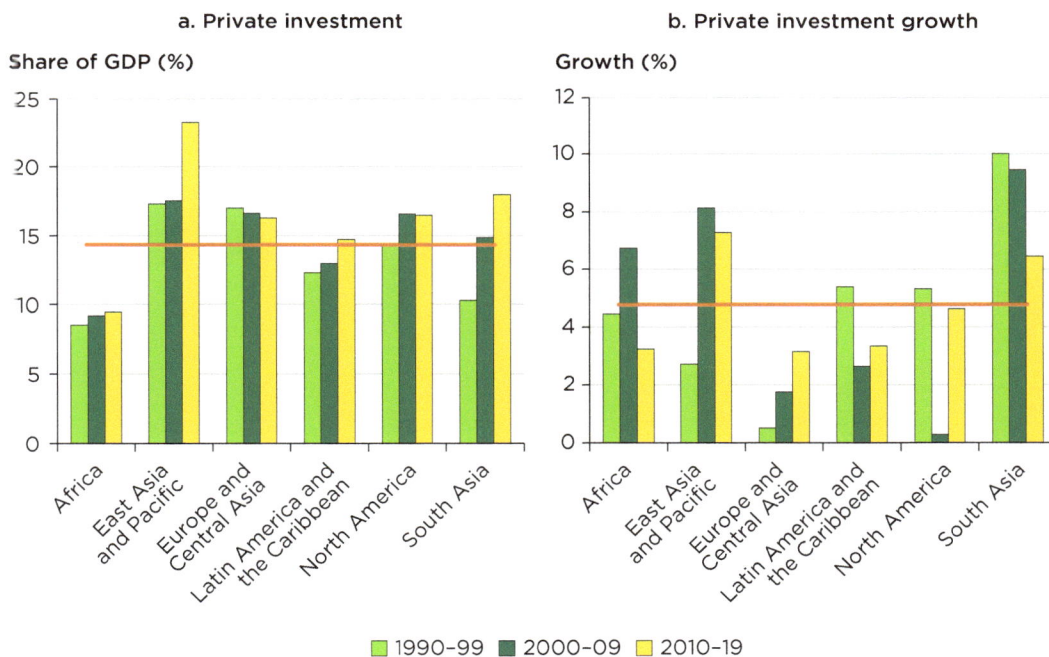

a. Private investment

b. Private investment growth

Legend: 1990–99, 2000–09, 2010–19

Source: Based on data from International Monetary Fund, Investment and Capital Stock Dataset, https://data.imf.org/?sk=1ce8a55f-cfa7-4bc0-bce2-256ee65ac0e4.
Note: The figure reflects private investment (gross fixed capital formation) in billions of constant 2017 international dollars. The horizontal line in panels a and b depicts the global average gross fixed capital formation and growth between 1990 and 2019.

A major contributing factor to the low levels of private investments in Africa has been the region's inability to attract significant foreign direct investment (FDI) outside the mining sector. Africa accounted for just 3 percent of total global FDI inflows between 2000 and 2022.[1] Figure 5.6 shows the trends in the share of global FDI inflows to Africa, Asia, and Latin America the Caribbean, as well as the total FDI receipts to Africa (right axis). Whereas Asia consistently witnessed an increase in the share of total FDI receipts, Africa's share increased marginally from 0.8 percent (US$17.6 billion) in 2000 to 3.5 percent (US$44.9 billion) in 2022.

A large share of FDI to the Africa region, especially Sub-Saharan Africa, occurs in the extractive sector. Between 2003 and 2022, the extractive sector (coal, oil, and gas; metals; and minerals) accounted for 39.2 percent of total (greenfield) FDI flows to Africa (figure 5.7). Real estate (construction and real estate services) and electricity (renewable energy) sectors accounted for 14 percent and 13 percent, respectively, of total FDI during the period. Manufacturing, however, has relatively low FDI compared with services. FDI into services accounts for more than 62 percent of nonextractive energy and construction-related FDI. Going forward, Africa will need to strengthen its efforts to attract FDI to boost private sector investments, particularly in the nonextractive and construction-related sectors of the economy. Doing so will involve, among other things, increasing the quality of infrastructure in the region and improving

FIGURE 5.6 **Trends in foreign direct investment inflows, by world region, 2000–22**

Share of global FDI inflows (%)   FDI (constant 2022 US$, billion)

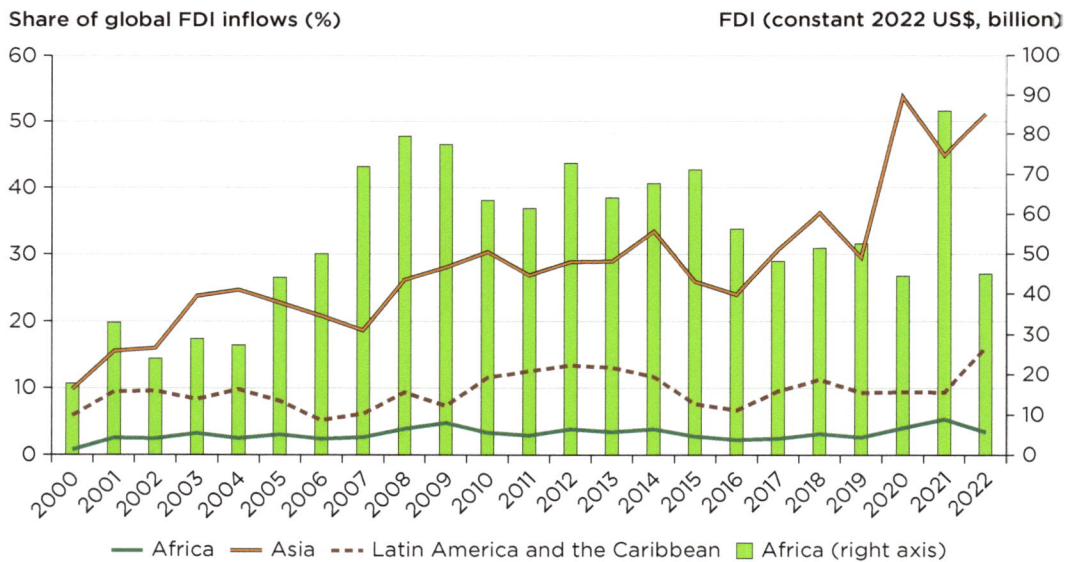

Legend: ▬ Africa ▬ Asia - - - Latin America and the Caribbean ▉ Africa (right axis)

Source: Based on data from UN Trade and Development, https://unctad.org/data-visualization /global-foreign-direct-investment-flows-over-last-30-years.
Note: Regions are defined according to groupings in the original source. FDI = foreign direct investment.

FIGURE 5.7 Foreign direct investment flows to Africa, by sector, 2003–22

Share of total FDI (%)

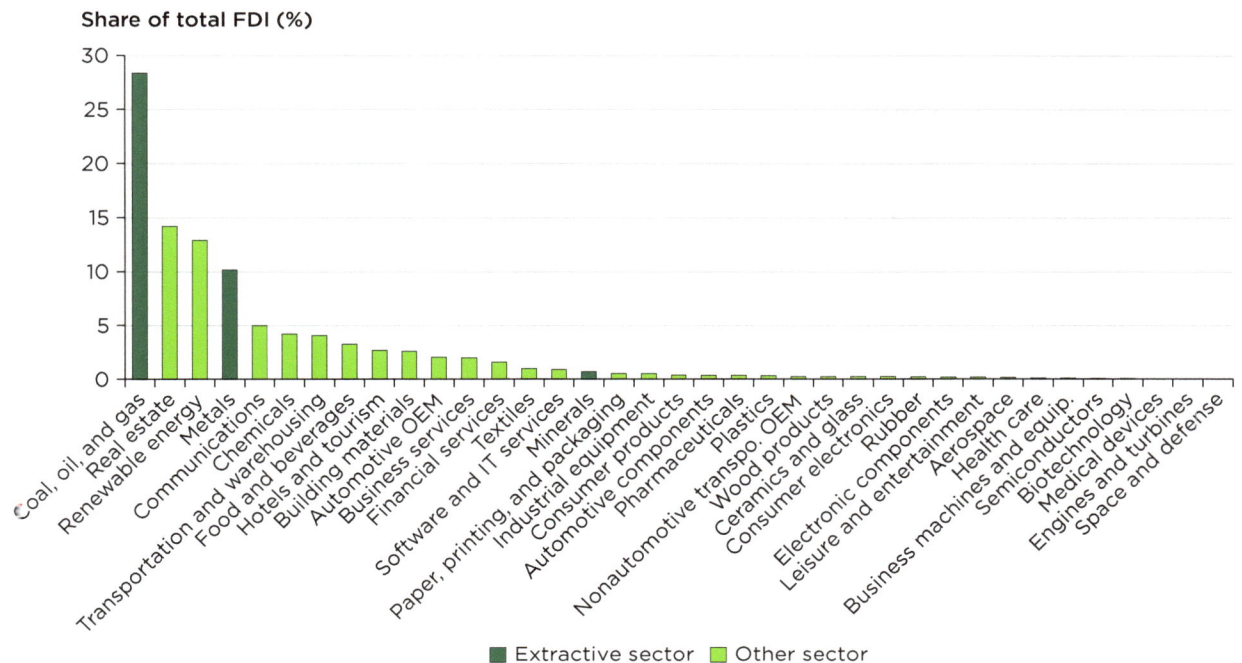

■ Extractive sector ■ Other sector

Source: Based on data from the fDi Markets database, https://fdimarkets.com/.
Note: The figure represents the percent of total foreign direct investment (in constant US dollars, million) accounted for by each sector. FDI = foreign direct investment; IT = information technology; OEM = original equipment manufacturer.

the governance landscape. Mensah and Traore (2023), for instance, show that access to quality infrastructure such as high-speed internet connectivity is associated with an increase in FDI into the service sector—particularly finance, technology, retail, and health services subsectors. They also show that access to complementary infrastructure, such as electricity and road connectivity, is crucial to amplify the impact of internet connectivity. In sum, the findings underscore the importance investors place on the quality of infrastructure in destination markets when making investment decisions.

Overview of constraints to private sector investments in Africa

Constraints to private investments in Africa, especially those that are cross-cutting, are well-known and have been documented by the World Bank Country Policy and Institutional Assessment (CPIA), which annually tracks the performance of low-income countries. Figure 5.8 shows that low-income countries in Sub-Saharan Africa did not improve their CPIA scores on structural policies over the last 10 years. Macroeconomic and governance scores have also deteriorated over the past decade (World Bank 2023c, 16).

FIGURE 5.8 Structural policies scores, Sub-Saharan Africa versus non-Sub-Saharan Africa, 2012–22

Structural policies score

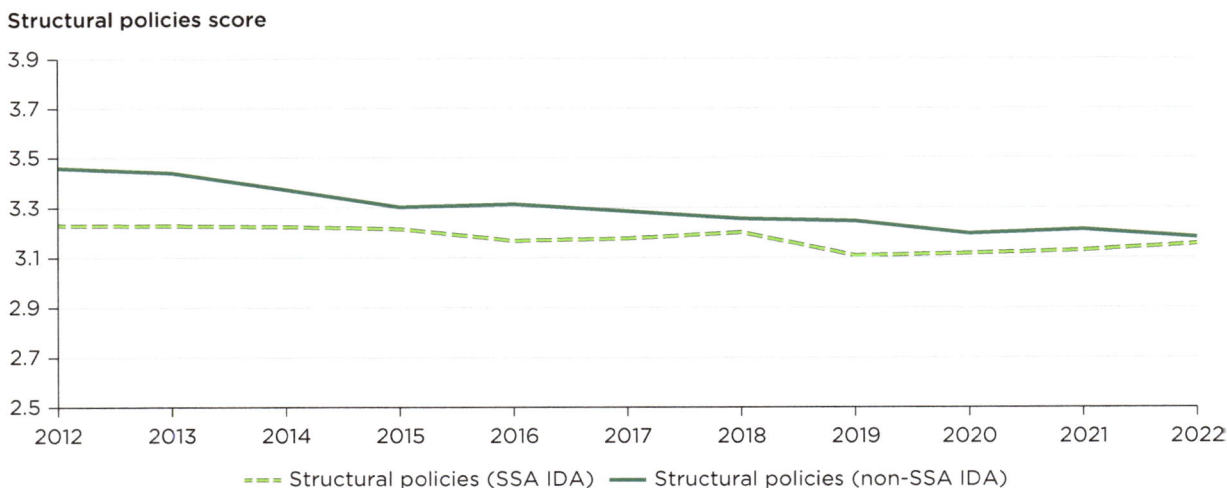

Source: Based on data from World Bank 2023c.
Note: Scores range from 1 to 6 (6 being the maximum good score). IDA = International Development Association; SSA = Sub-Saharan Africa.

In summary, Africa faces the following constraints to private sector investment:

- *Conflicts and political and macroeconomic instability.* Following a decline in the 2000s, the number of countries in conflict has risen in the 2020s. COVID-19 created a challenge to macroeconomic stability.

- *Governance and rule-of-law issues.* These issues led to policy uncertainty and unsecured property rights.

- *Insufficient public resources (domestic resource mobilization) to invest in public goods (infrastructure and skills) required for crowding in private investments.* The share of fiscal revenues remains steadfastly low in most of Africa, significantly below the 15 percent of GDP minimum threshold considered adequate.

- *Inadequate planning, prioritization, design, and implementation of public goods.* These challenges arise because of issues with the framework for public investment management and public-private partnerships (PPPs). Most PPPs are done through single-source unsolicited proposals.

- *Issues with tax, trade, investment, and competition policies.* The small formal sector carries much of the tax burden. Import tariffs remain high in some key countries, such as Nigeria, and customs procedures remain problematic in most countries. Competition policy frameworks are absent or weak.

- *Regulatory red tape, including business registration and business licensing and inspections*. Despite significant improvements, African countries remain at the bottom of the Ease of Doing Business rankings.

- *Issues with the way governments regulate factor markets (labor, capital, and land)*. Labor market regulations often lack flexibility, as in Ethiopia, South Africa, and the West Africa subregion. Land market policies struggle to combine traditional collective rights with individual property rights, and capital markets and access to finance remain limited because of macroeconomic instability and the high risks of doing business.

- *Issues with the way governments intervene and regulate in product markets*, differentiating between natural monopolies (infrastructure sectors) and competitive and contestable sectors (traded goods and services).

Figure 5.9, based on an analysis of 11 African countries, shows that the state has kept a strong presence in all sectors, including competitive and contestable sectors where its presence is more difficult to justify. Firms with at least 10 percent state participation have domestic revenues that average 20 percent of GDP in these African countries compared with the global average of 16 percent (World Bank 2023b). Nearly half of firms with state participation operate in competitive markets such as manufacturing, wholesale and

FIGURE 5.9 **Share of businesses of the state and revenue, by sector, 1990s–2010s**

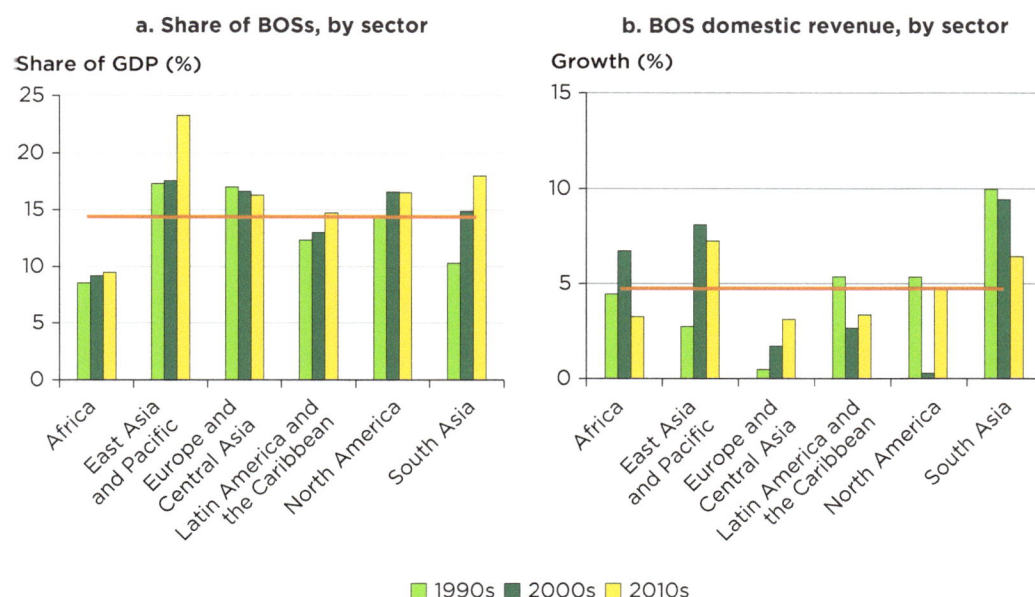

a. Share of BOSs, by sector

b. BOS domestic revenue, by sector

■ 1990s ■ 2000s ■ 2010s

Source: Based on 2023 data from World Bank, Business of the State database, https://www.worldbank.org/en/publication/business-of-the-state.
Note: The horizontal line in each panel depicts the global average. BOSs = businesses of the state.

trade, construction, accommodation, and hotels. Although state participation in contestable and competitive markets is not in and of itself suboptimal, policy distortions such as subsidies and market rules and regulations that give undue advantage to these businesses of the state over their private competitors can lead to suboptimal outcomes.

This last category of sector-specific constraints, collectively, may have the most significance for private investment in Africa, especially when considering their collective negative impact on public finances and the climate (for example, bailing out of state-owned enterprises (SOEs) and nontargeted subsidies to carbon-based energy and fertilizers). These constraints, however, have received relatively less attention than other constraints in the broad literature. Table 5.2 shows Africa's "policy heat map," distinguishing by types of policies and sectors and showing the critical and underappreciated importance of product (sector-specific) and land market policy issues.

Analysis

There are examples of policies that have been successful in Africa and beyond to overcome a critical mass of cross-cutting and sector-specific constraints to generate private investments. This section distinguishes between sectors that drive growth (traded goods and services as well as natural resources) and sectors that enable growth (infrastructure, human capital, and finance). These brief sector discussions are illustrative and not exhaustive; rather, they are meant to convey the importance of adopting a sector perspective to identify and resolve sector-specific market and government failures and to specify and motivate cross-cutting policy reforms (table 5.2).

TABLE 5.2 Africa's policy heat map

Policy issue	Sector								
	Mining	Agri-business	Manu-facturing	Tourism	Digital	Housing	Infra-structure	Skills	Finance
Macro	L	S	S	S	S	I	S	L	I
Tax	I	S	S	L	L	L	L	L	L
Trade	L	S	I	L	L	L	L	L	L
Product	I	I	S	S	L	S	I	S	S
Land	S	I	S	I	L	I	S	L	S
Labor	L	L	L	L	S	L	L	I	S
Capital	L	S	S	S	L	I	L	L	I

Source: World Bank.
Note: I = important; L = less important; S = somewhat important. Macro = macroeconomic.

Sectors driving growth

As shown in figures 5.3 and 5.4, the drivers of economic transformation and jobs are exports and (productive) urbanization. Exports can be categorized into five broad sectors: mining, agribusiness, manufacturing, tourism, and digitalized services. Urbanization is best seen through a construction sector lens.

Mining

Mining (including oil and gas) has been, for better or worse, a key source of foreign exchange for Africa. Africa now faces a global "gold rush" toward the rich mineral endowments that will drive the global energy transition (map 5.3). The challenge and opportunity ahead are to make these minerals rapidly available to the global economy and leverage them to generate revenues and support infrastructure and industrial development, without taking damaging economic, environmental, or social shortcuts. This is a tall order given the history of mismanagement of mining resources in many African countries.

Africa is home to

- About 30 percent of the world's mineral reserves and over 60 percent of the world's best solar resources;

- The world's largest reserves of cobalt (56 percent), diamonds, platinum group metals (more than 90 percent), and uranium;

- 6 percent of global reserves of copper, 25 percent of bauxite, 21 percent of graphite, 46 percent of manganese, 35 percent of chrome, and 79 percent of phosphate rock;

- 8 percent of the world's natural gas and 12 percent of oil reserves; and

- 40 percent of the world's gold reserves.

Principles of good practice mining policies should include the following steps: conducting geological surveys (in partnership with the private sector); planning exploitation (prioritizing quick wins that have limited social and environmental impacts); auctioning licenses based on a world-class mining code; collecting proceeds transparently (as per the Extractive Industries Transparency Initiative); and investing the proceeds wisely (public goods and rainy-day funds). Policies should consider ensuring peaceful and synergetic coexistence of large-scale and artisanal mining; creating opportunities to develop links with domestic suppliers; increasing value added, leveraging sources of green energy and avoiding expensive old-school industrial policy mistakes; and leveraging the infrastructure needed for mining to the benefit of other sectors.

Examples of good practice mining policies include the following:

- *Botswana's Diamond Trading Company*. With a strong commitment to mining revenue transparency and prudent management of mineral resources, the

MAP 5.3 **Africa is endowed with rich mineral resources critical to the global energy transition**

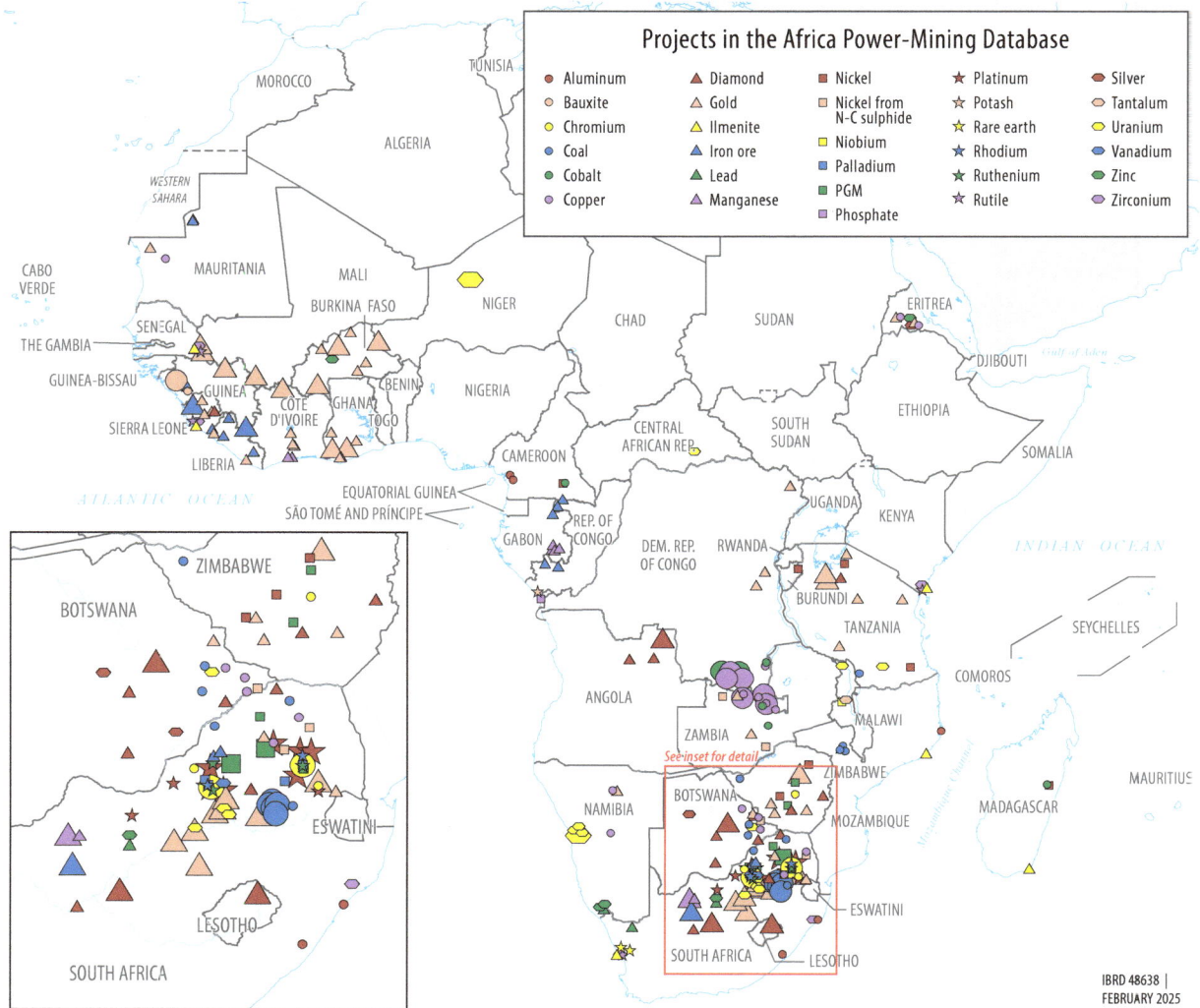

Projects in the Africa Power-Mining Database

- Aluminum
- Bauxite
- Chromium
- Coal
- Cobalt
- Copper
- Diamond
- Gold
- Ilmenite
- Iron ore
- Lead
- Manganese
- Nickel
- Nickel from N-C sulphide
- Niobium
- Palladium
- PGM
- Phosphate
- Platinum
- Potash
- Rare earth
- Rhodium
- Ruthenium
- Rutile
- Silver
- Tantalum
- Uranium
- Vanadium
- Zinc
- Zirconium

IBRD 48638 | FEBRUARY 2025

Sources: Bureau de Recherches Géologiques et Minières; World Bank, Africa Power-Mining Database, https://datacatalog.worldbank.org/int/search/dataset/0040272.

Note: Larger symbols indicate an aggregate of four mines located within 100 kilometers of each other. PGM = platinum group metals.

government of Botswana partnered with the De Beers Group to establish the Diamond Trading Company Botswana. This partnership ensures that a significant portion of the diamond value chain remains within the country. Additionally, Botswana's strict adherence to environmental regulations and comprehensive community engagement efforts have contributed to sustainable and responsible mining practices. Botswana's good governance in the mining sector can be traced back to its first president, who gave up the mining rights of his own tribe through the historic Mines and Minerals Act of 1967 to the benefit of the national government, inspiring other traditional chiefs to follow (Criscuolo and Palmade 2008).

- *Madagascar's Integrated Growth Poles Project.* With financing from the World Bank, Madagascar converted the mining Port of Ehoala to a multipurpose port. The US$145 million project, completed in July 2009 on time and under budget, has become a cornerstone for expanding the regional economy. In turn, it helped with crowding in a US$1.2 billion investment by the international mining company Rio Tinto (World Bank 2014). The government of Madagascar and Rio Tinto are now working together to rehabilitate a 109-kilometer section of National Road 13. This successful precedent paves the way for Madagascar to draw benefits from its 1.2 billion tons of graphite reserve, a sought-after mineral used in battery construction.

Agribusiness

Agribusiness is critical from both a food security and a growth perspective. Climate change, strong population growth, and geopolitical crises have raised serious food security challenges, especially in the Sahel and Horn of Africa regions. Agriculture productivity remains low and imports high. Nevertheless, Africa's large and untapped agribusiness—large water reserves and vast arable land—should enable it to meet the needs of its populations and develop high-value exports. Doing so will require developing rural infrastructure and storage to improve access to markets, investing in irrigation (only 5 percent of farming uses irrigation) to fight climate change, and improving seeds and farming techniques to improve productivity.

Building better food systems requires tackling multiple supply-side distortions that impede the development of robust and efficient agrifood value chains, generate harmful externalities, and waste critical resources such as water and energy. In many countries the bulk of the support for agriculture is delivered in a regressive and highly distortionary manner, creating disincentives for producers to be efficient, sustainable, or climate-friendly while crowding out the provision of public goods in partnership with the private sector. The resulting market distortions also often disincentivize private investment. Large input subsidies encourage climate-damaging and nonsustainable farming practices—excessive use of carbon-based fertilizers, overpumping groundwater with cheap or free electricity, inefficient use of underpriced water, or monocultural production systems of targeted output—and discourage production in areas that generate smaller environmental externalities. Policies thus need to transition from providing nontargeted, expensive, and climate-damaging subsidies to investing scarce fiscal resources on key public goods in partnership with the private sector (agricultural research to develop high-performing, drought-resistant seeds; extension services; solar-powered drip irrigation; cold chains; and laboratory and certification services). Policies should also be put in place to facilitate the transition from traditional and collective land property rights to secured and individual land property rights to increase farmers' incentives to invest in their land and facilitate investments by world-class firms, making sure the latter benefits local farmers and communities (land-lease payments and out-grower schemes).

Examples of good practice agribusiness policies include the following:

- *Kenya's world-class horticulture farms.* Horticulture in Kenya has grown 20 percent each year over the past two decades and now represents the country's third-largest source of foreign income. This growth was enabled by world-class logistics, as with the Port of Mombasa and Kenya Airways, and leading firms that worked with local farmers. For example, Kenya is now the fifth-largest flower exporter, with flowers transiting from Kenyan farms to global auctions in under 72 hours. The industry boasts 5,000 flower farms employing 100,000 workers, predominantly young women, indirectly supporting about 2 million livelihoods. Horticulture firms have started expanding to other African countries, such as Vegpro in Ghana.

- *Ghana's Savannah Accelerated Development Authority.* The government of Ghana partnered with development partners and leading private investors in 2013 to launch the Savannah Accelerated Development Authority, targeting 45,000 hectares of underused land. The initial phase established 400 hectares of irrigated farmland, directly involving 175 out-growers, and included knowledge transfer and infrastructure development. Ghana has also facilitated leading investors to access land (for example, Vegpro) with the support of the United States Agency for International Development and the World Bank.

- *Senegal's horticultural exports.* These exports increased from 24,000 tons in 2007 to 90,000 tons in 2016 (IFC 2020b, 49). There also, growth was enabled by improving trade facilitation and logistics and facilitating access to land for world-class foreign investors. For instance, Les Grands Domaines du Sénégal and Société de Conserves Alimentaires du Sénégal are well-known nontraditional product exporters in horticulture.

Manufacturing

Following a long decline since 1981, the share of manufacturing value added in Africa has grown from 10 percent of GDP in 2011 to around 12 percent of GDP in 2022 (figure 5.10). Africa's growing domestic markets have provided a strong foundation for manufacturing growth in subsectors such as construction materials and agroprocessing. Improved trade logistics and abundant labor also lay the foundations for Africa to become competitive in labor-intensive manufacturing, and the combination of abundant natural resources and renewable energy potential should create opportunities to export resource-based, energy-intensive products, such as wood and metal products.

Competitiveness in manufacturing hinges on several key factors: access to world-class transportation logistics for exporting products and importing inputs; reliable and affordable energy, particularly green energy; a skilled labor force; and a conducive and predictable enabling business environment. Private investors in manufacturing also require seamless access to well-located and well-serviced industrial land. Given that most domestic small and medium enterprises (SMEs) lack the financial capacity to

FIGURE 5.10 Manufacturing value added as a share of GDP, Africa, 1981–2022

Share of GDP (%)

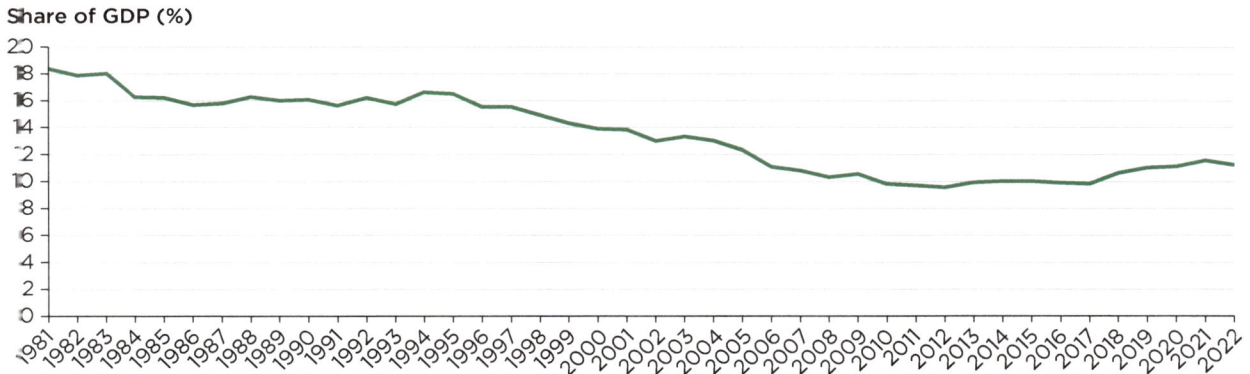

Source: Based on data from World Bank, World Development Indicators, https://data.worldbank.org/indicator/.

purchase land and construct their own facilities, access to "plug-and-play" facilities is crucial. Manufacturing policies should steer clear of undue protectionism and subsidies designed for infant industries, because these types of policies often result in noncompetitive sectors that rely on prolonged protections and subsidies. For investors, the quality of trade logistics, energy, industrial land, labor, and a stable business environment are far more significant than costly fiscal incentives. The provision of these public goods would also benefit a wide range of other industries.

Examples of good practice manufacturing policies include the following:

- *China's plug-and-play industrial zones.* As part of its vast industrial zone program, China developed hundreds of "plug-and-play" industrial zones for SMEs. Developed by local governments (under competitive pressure) in partnership with the private sector, these zones are intended to simplify the setup process for companies by providing essential services and amenities. The zones provide prebuilt infrastructure and ready-to-use facilities for business. They also provide affordable housing for workers near the plants, enabling (migrant) workers to save on (unsafe) housing and transportation time and costs. Such savings can represent up to 80 percent of a worker's salary. Finally, such zones include administrative centers to reduce red tape, and technology centers to help SMEs access technology and link up with lead firms and high-value markets. This approach greatly facilitated the growth of export-oriented SMEs and the migration of hundreds of millions of women subsistence farmers from the Western Provinces. These zones have helped SMEs grow into substantial enterprises, thus closing the "missing middle gap" in SME finance seen elsewhere.

- *Ethiopia's light manufacturing exports.* Ethiopia combined low labor costs, industrial zones, and improved trade logistics (railway connection to the efficient Port of Djibouti) to attract a critical mass of export-oriented FDI in labor-intensive manufacturing industries (apparel and shoe manufacturers). As shown in figure 5.11, this approach enabled Ethiopia to follow the same growth trajectory as Viet Nam when that country was at the same stage of its spectacular light manufacturing export journey.

FIGURE 5.11 Jobs created in industrial parks, Ethiopia and selected high-performing comparators

Number of jobs created

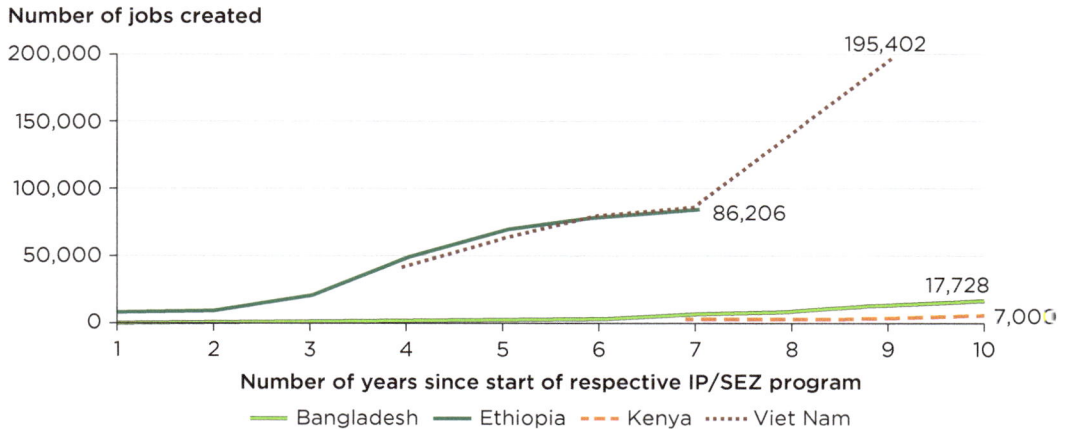

Sources: Bangladesh Export Processing Zones Authority, https://www.bepza.gov.bd; Ethiopia Industrial Parks Development Corporation, https://ipdc.gov.et; Kenya Export Processing Zones Authority, https://epzakenya.com; Farole 2011; trade data from the World Bank, International Monetary Fund, and www.macrotrends.net.
Note: IP = industrial park; SEZ = special economic zone.

- *Ghana's emerging potential in apparel.* Consider the case of Dignity DTRT (Do The Right Thing) Apparel. In less than a decade, the company grew from 50 to more than 5,000 employees, 70 percent of whom are women from low-income households. Two factors drove this success: its location near the efficient Port of Tema, one of the largest International Finance Corporation (IFC) investees in Africa, and significant and early investments by Dignity to develop high-quality human resources and systems.

- *Morocco's high-value manufacturing.* Experience from Morocco shows that building skills in PPPs complements world-class logistics and industrial zones to build competitiveness in high-value manufacturing sectors such as automotive and aerospace. Morocco is developing a successful PPP model for vocational training. For example, the Institut des Métiers de l'Aéronautique, under the Groupement des Industries Marocaines Aéronautiques et Spatiales (GIMAS), has a twinning arrangement with a French aerospace training center and is equipped with state-of-the-art equipment. Through GIMAS, the management maintains close ties to aerospace companies operating in the country. The six- to nine-month training courses are tailored to the specific needs and standards of individual companies, with participants selected through an admission test and paid a stipend during the training. This approach is based on the alternate model in which about 50 percent of training takes place on the job. More than 95 percent of those who complete the training find a job in the industry.

Tourism

Tourism is one of the largest and fastest-growing sectors of the global economy. In 2019, it accounted for US$1.8 trillion (8 percent of the global economy)[2] and is a major source of foreign exchange and jobs. Africa accounted for 5 percent of global tourism in 2022.[3] In 2018, Eastern and Southern Africa generated US$29 billion from tourism, whereas Western and Central Africa earned US$7 billion. Africa's tourism industry holds significant untapped potential, particularly in cultural and eco-tourism. The sector not only boosts SMEs and women-led businesses but also catalyzes burgeoning trends like eco-tourism and digital nomadism.

Achieving competitiveness and promoting productive private investments in tourism requires policies that provide a critical mass of enabling conditions on both the demand side and the supply side. Such conditions vary depending on the tourism segment (sea and sun tourism, eco-tourism, business tourism, digital nomads, and early retirees). Enablers on the demand side include physical security, including the capacity to deal with health emergencies; physical connectivity such as visas, including for digital nomads and early retirees, and competitive means of transportation; and digital connectivity to book in advance, to pay, and for digital nomads. On the supply side, enablers include the capacity to own or lease property, also relevant for digital nomads and early retirees; credible certification, for example, for diving instructors; resilient and green infrastructure; access to skills and finance, especially for SMEs; and policies that ensure local communities are involved in and benefit from tourism. This approach may initially target the most desirable and feasible segments and locations, particularly to attract strategic first movers. Even with a focused and strategic policy, however, it is essential to ensure that the benefits are widespread, including the positive demonstration effects that can inspire broader industry growth. Tourism can and should be used as a wedge to improve many of the enabling policies and sectors that will benefit the whole economy, including security, connectivity, land markets, and language skills.

Examples of good practice tourism policies include the following (Benin, Mali, and Uganda—although not discussed here—also demonstrate good practices):

- *Mauritius's Bel Ombre Nature Reserve.* Stretching over 2,500 hectares, the reserve showcases the island's rich biodiversity while promoting responsible travel. Bel Ombre uses local experts to guide visitors and, through training and employment, integrates the local community. In addition to offering eco-conscious experiences, Bel Ombre engages in conservation initiatives such as habitat restoration, species protection, and reforestation projects. In an era when discerning tourists not only prefer but often demand sustainable travel, the success story of the Bel Ombre Nature Reserve showcases how destinations can thrive by prioritizing both nature and community.

- *Rwanda's expanded eco-tourism.* Although the country's tourism ecosystem was predominantly tethered to gorilla trekking in the Virunga National Park, efforts have been intensified to expand and diversify the sector, positioning the country as a premier eco-tourism destination. Kigali has increasingly become a hub for business tourism that draws global audiences with modern facilities for meetings, incentives, conferences, and exhibitions. The Rwanda Development Board has played an instrumental role in enhancing the country's tourism blueprint. Its strategic initiatives focus on invigorating tourism in emerging destinations such as Akagera National Park, Karongi, and the Nyungwe Forest, providing tourists with a range of experiences from savannah safaris to pristine rainforest treks. By establishing robust regulatory standards and grading systems the Development Board aims to ensure that tourism remains sustainable and benefits local communities. Rwanda is introducing a new policy to open up national parks and game reserves for private investment, aiming to enhance tourist attractions.

- *Thailand's expanded visa options for tourism.* Broadening, enhancing, and deepening its attractiveness for tourists, Thailand provides visa exemptions for more than 60 countries, allowing stays from 14 to 90 days. Additionally, 21 countries benefit from a visa on arrival. The Multiple Entry Tourist Visa is valid for a six-month period with options for extensions. In response to challenges, Thailand has occasionally waived visa fees and introduced the Special Tourist Visa during the COVID-19 pandemic, granting stays of up to 270 days. The Thailand Elite Visa caters to affluent travelers, offering stays from 5 to 20 years.

Digitalized services

The proliferation of digital connectivity has spurred a global demand for services such as e-commerce, telemedicine, and e-learning, including in Africa, where a growing urban and middle-class population is driving demand for services provided by platforms such as Jumia and Ananse for online shopping, and iROKOtv for streaming. Additionally, global leaders such as Netflix, Spotify, and YouTube are investing in African content, enhancing the regional industry's global presence and facilitating diverse entertainment and learning opportunities and revenue streams. This rising demand, aligned with enhanced access to digital infrastructure, fosters a conducive environment for digital entrepreneurship in Africa, especially in the technology sector (Houngbonon, Mensah, and Traore 2022; Mensah and Traore 2023). Young entrepreneurs are leveraging this digital upheaval to establish start-ups offering varied services for mobile payments and e-logistics. For instance, Zeepay provides an integrative digital service connecting diverse digital assets to varied transaction needs, and Jobberman and Kobo360 are revolutionizing employment and e-logistics spaces, respectively.[4] Digitalized services offer a wealth of opportunities for Africa: improved performance of existing value chains, exports of digitalized services and content, and imports at much lower cost for high-value services in business, education, and health.

Investments in digital infrastructure, skills development, and entrepreneurial incubation are essential to optimize this upward trajectory and will require coordinated intersectoral policy initiatives. The Digital Economy for Africa Initiative[5] sets out five foundational pillars for the digital economy: digital infrastructure, digital financial services, digital public platforms, digital businesses, and digital skills. The section on enabling sectors discusses digital infrastructure, financial services, and digital businesses. Digital public platforms are potential launchpads for exporters of both goods and digitalized services. Thus, governments should facilitate their entry or growth and promote access to them, while ensuring fair and open competition between them. To succeed, digital businesses need an ecosystem that encourages entrepreneurship and innovation, and provides access to (global) leading-edge knowledge, protection of intellectual property rights, and (venture) capital.

Examples of good practice digital services policies include the following:

- *Labor-intensive artificial intelligence in Kenya.* Sama, established in Nairobi with headquarters in San Francisco, provides business process outsourcing services to big technology companies in Silicon Valley, including Google, Microsoft, NASA, Precision AI, and Qualcomm. The company employs mostly women for training for artificial intelligence (Lee 2018). The company processes millions of images manually. In addition to a pool of low-cost labor in Kenya, access to digital infrastructure such as high-speed internet is a key reason for the company's location in Nairobi.

- *Legal services arbitrage in Nigeria.* Taking advantage of improved digital connectivity and quality tertiary education, a woman entrepreneur from Kano has built a successful business placing (virtually) legal graduates from Nigerian universities in US law firms in California. The graduates earn twice as much money as their peers working in Nigeria, and the US firms have access to high-quality young professionals at a fraction of the cost of their American peers.[6]

- *African creativity exported through digital platforms.* Young African entrepreneurs are leveraging the YouTube platform to showcase their talents and build businesses. Africa's 3 percent global share of creative goods exports (Lusigi 2023) is expected to grow with African movies and music exports on the rise. African movies have become commonplace on Netflix, and major global platforms such as Boomplay and Spotify stream African music—Afrobeats and Amapiano. African "vloggers" have established a presence on YouTube, TikTok, and other social media platforms. With more than 1.4 million subscribers on YouTube, Wode Maya,[7] a Ghanaian vlogger, is on a mission to change the narrative on Africa, showing his global audience places on the continent that are not present in mainstream media, and sharing positive stories on Africa. The increasing popularity of this trend has led to the establishment of the #YouTubeBlack Voices Fund to promote and develop African content creators and to take advantage of the new "digital gold mine" (Ducard 2021).

Construction

As illustrated in figure 5.4, productive urbanization is one of the key drivers of economic transformation, bolstering the export economy through the benefits of agglomeration economies. Also, domestic urban sectors such as housing, retail, and personal services account for a large and growing share of employment as economies grow and urbanize. Among the domestic urban sectors, housing construction is one of the largest and represents the challenges faced by such sectors, particularly the large share of informal and low-productivity employment. As the housing crisis in Africa intensifies each year, with countries such as Burkina Faso and Kenya facing deficits of more than 200,000 housing units each, it has led to a significant expansion of slum dwellings that house about 50 percent of the urban population in Africa (CAHF 2021).[8]

Well-functioning land and capital markets are the key to a productive and growing housing construction sector. Developers need fair and secured access to large tracts of land to reap the economies of scale needed for low-cost quality housing schemes, and home buyers and investors need secured land property titles to access financing through mortgages. Well-functioning land markets require (local) government to conduct good and enforced planning and zoning as well as secured and efficient titling and registration. The planning and zoning need to reconcile the need to accommodate rapid urbanization with the need to protect natural resources and traditional rights. Governments need also to enable development of the necessary urban infrastructure financed by the related increase in land value (for example, through land privatization, auctions, or property taxes). Secured land property titles are a cornerstone of the formalization and rehabilitation of slums. Performance-based building codes are increasingly important to promote safe, resilient, and green housing. Macroeconomic stability and access to long-term sources of financing are, together with secured property titles, the key to affordable mortgage financing.

Examples of good practice housing construction policies include the following:

- *Mali's Agence de Cessions Immobilières*. Set up in 1992 to enhance transparency in land markets, the agency operates through a self-financed model, whereby it acquires and develops land—following due process and fair compensation—which it then auctions to private developers. Private developers and buyers could obtain bank financing because banks fully recognized the value of these titles. The agency auctioned 10,892 plots in Bamako between 1995 and 2004 (Farvacque-Vitkovic et al. 2007).

- *Singapore's urban marvel*. Singapore's success has its roots deeply embedded in strategic planning and the adoption of cutting-edge technology. Two primary instruments of this success have been the Land Acquisition Act and the Building Information Modelling (BIM).[9] The Land Acquisition Act allowed the government to purchase private land for critical developments, fostering a balance between individual landownership and the broader public interest. This legislative move deterred private speculative land hoarding and promoted systematic urban growth, with equitable compensation mechanisms in place. The BIM revolutionized the private construction sector by introducing digital advancements to building projects and streamlining designs for efficiency, cost-effectiveness, and sustainability. The mandatory BIM e-submissions for major projects helped private developers identify and rectify construction discrepancies early, resulting in considerable financial savings and expedited project timelines. As Singapore's Building and Construction Authority intensifies BIM implementation, the private construction industry in Singapore is positioned to leverage emerging technologies such as virtual and augmented reality, underscoring the city-state's private sector–led innovative approach.

Sectors enabling growth

As shown in figure 5.3 earlier in the chapter, seven "enabling" sectors influence the performance of all other sectors: transportation, digital infrastructure, energy, water, finance/business development services, education, and health. In addition to being enabling, these sectors can be a source of exports, and thus can also drive growth. The following subsections discuss each sector in turn.

Transportation

Efficient transportation infrastructures from roads to airports are key for sustainable development and for boosting economic growth, trade, and agriculture. As urbanization accelerates, effective public transportation mitigates congestion and improves urban life. Sustainable transportation is crucial for climate action, and enhanced connectivity promotes regional initiatives, such as the African Continental Free Trade Area, and boosts access to education and health care. Despite its importance, the sector has significant challenges related to deficient infrastructure, regulatory issues, conflicting stakeholders, and ineffective incentives. According to the World Development Indicators, the perceived quality of trade and transportation infrastructure in Africa is generally low, with only a few countries (Côte d'Ivoire, Rwanda, and South Africa) above the global average.

Principles of good practice transportation policies include identifying critical existing and future bottlenecks, conducting prefeasibility studies for crowding in private investments through a transparent and competitive PPP process, and establishing strong and independent regulators for ports, air transportation, rail, and roads.

Examples of good practice transportation policies include the following:

- *Ghana's Port of Tema.* An example of a successful PPP (supported by IFC), the port boasts a 1.4-kilometer quay with four deep berths and is equipped with sophisticated container handling gantry cranes and terminal operating systems. It can accommodate some of the world's largest cargo ships. The port has a capacity of 22,000 20-foot equivalent units, up from 5,000 20-foot equivalent units of the original port. A second expansion is now under way (APM Terminals 2023).

- *Côte d'Ivoire's transportation PPPs.* Côte d'Ivoire was one of the first countries in West Africa to effectively use PPPs in the transportation sector with the concession of railway, airport, and bridge infrastructure. Over the last five years, the government and the private sector have invested more than US$2 billion to upgrade and rehabilitate the transportation infrastructure, after more than a decade of underinvestment caused by the prolonged political crisis (IFC 2020a, 75).

Digital infrastructure

The rapid development of Africa's digital infrastructure has already enabled and boosted investments in sectors such as finance, technology, retail, and health, and led to job creation (Hjort and Poulsen 2019; Mensah and Traore 2023). Overall usage remains low, however: 25 percent of Africa's population did not have access to the internet in 2021, and the remaining 75 percent were often subject to high costs and slow speed (World Bank 2023a).

Principles of good practice digital infrastructure policies include conducting transparent and competitive spectrum auctions, such as the reallocation of unused and underutilized spectrums held by public entities, to enhance competition and generate government revenue. Countries should also promote infrastructure sharing and ensure equal access to backbone infrastructure; privatize and reform dominant SOEs; facilitate rights of way and coordination for the deployment of new digital infrastructure; eliminate restrictive practices, such as the limited use of Unstructured Supplementary Service Data platforms by mobile network operators (MNOs), which hinder smaller players from providing value-added services like digital financial services or mobile money; implement mobile number portability to allow users to switch networks while retaining their numbers; and enforce significant market power regulations to prevent large incumbent MNOs from abusing their dominance to stifle competition. Additionally, establishing universal service funds obliges telecom companies to contribute to expanding digital technology access in rural areas. Finally, a strong, independent regulator is essential to foster investment, competition, the adoption of new technologies, and broad access to digital services.

Examples of good practice digital infrastructure policies include the following:

Private sector innovation to reduce the cost of fiber-optic networks. Ghana, Liberia, Togo,[10] and Uganda enabled and promoted infrastructure sharing that opened the door to innovative private firms. CSquared specializes in the deployment of open-access fiber-optic internet, making it available to local MNOs and internet service providers (ISPs). Given the relatively high cost of deploying fiber networks, having one company serve MNOs and ISPs, as opposed to each deploying their own fiber infrastructure, offers significant savings. With investments from Google, IFC,[11] and Mitsui, CSquared provides services to more than 25 ISPs and MNOs with more than 1,200 towers.

- In Ghana, CSquared has built 840 kilometers of fiber network in Accra, Kumasia, and Tema.

- In Monrovia, Liberia, CSquared has more than 180 kilometers of metro fiber network and provides internet services to all ISPs, MNOs, and government departments in the country.

- In Uganda, the company operates 800 kilometers of fiber network in Entebbe and Kampala.

Energy

The energy sector in Africa plays a pivotal role in economic development and is essential for the continent's transition to a greener and more sustainable future. A significant portion of Africa's population still lacks access to electricity. The energy sector has been plagued by inefficiencies and is a significant drain on government budgets. A competitive and reliable energy sector is not only critical to industrial activities, but it also facilitates improved health care, education, and communication systems. Africa has the opportunity to leverage its abundant renewable energy resources to reform the sector, meet its energy needs, and make the sector a driver, not a constraint, to the competitiveness of (green) manufacturing.

Countries should prioritize reforming transmission and distribution to make energy policies financially viable, including governance reforms to ensure proper collection of fees and tariffs reflecting cost. These reforms are a prerequisite to reducing the risk premium requested by private independent power producers selling to the grid. Procuring renewable energy independent power producers through a competitive and transparent process should follow a careful evaluation and prioritization of both current and future energy needs. This approach should enable and promote renewable energy, particularly by focusing on major emitters and value chains at risk of noncompliance with requirements from key export markets and global buyers. Key actions include enabling Direct Power Purchase Agreements, establishing competitive wheeling tariffs, reforming building codes to support rooftop solar installations, promoting green financing, and supporting the development of Energy Service Company markets.

Examples of good practice energy policies include the following:

- *Large private investments in renewable energy in the Arab Republic of Egypt.* The 200-megawatt Kom Ombo solar power plant, owned by ACWA Power of Saudi Arabia, submitted the lowest bid in what was the first solar photovoltaic tender in Egypt. The plant is expected to serve 130,000 households. Private sector participation in the Kom Ombo project resulted from successful policy dialogue with the Ministry of Electricity and Renewable Energy and the Egyptian Electricity Transmission Company. Technical assistance programs were co-funded by the European Bank for Reconstruction and Development and the Green Climate Fund to support the transmission company in administering competitive renewable energy tenders. Importantly, broader energy sector reforms undertaken by Egypt and supported by the African Development Bank in recent years have strengthened the enabling environment to scale up private sector involvement. A total of US$112 billion of FDI was announced in Egypt in 2022, mostly for large-scale renewables projects (hydrogen and wind) by companies from Australia, France, India, the United Arab Emirates, and the United Kingdom (World Bank 2021, 42).

- *Scaling solar in Senegal.* As a result of an international PPP competition, nearly 540,000 people in Senegal will get access to clean and affordable power. This follows the launch of two solar photovoltaic plants, financed by IFC, the European Investment Bank, and Proparco, under the World Bank Group's Scaling Solar program. The two plants located in western Senegal have a total capacity of 60 megawatts of alternating current. They will provide energy at tariffs of €0.04 per kilowatt-hour—one of the lowest prices for electricity in Sub-Saharan Africa—and will help avoid 89,000 tons of carbon dioxide emissions per year (IFC 2021).

Water

Rapid population growth, climate change, and geopolitical crises have combined to make lack of water an acute problem in Africa, especially in the Sahel and Horn of Africa. Increasing episodes of drought have led to low water levels in hydro dams and low recharge rates of boreholes and other groundwater sources, resulting in water outages. Unregulated destruction of forests from activities such as mining, agriculture, and settlements also threatens the future of the water supply (Naadi and Lansah 2021).

Water utilities in the region face severe challenges when it comes to performance and financial sustainability. In many countries in the region, water infrastructure (pipelines) has a limited geographic footprint, often concentrated in large cities. Lack of regular maintenance and ageing infrastructure often lead to leaks and system breakdowns, and frequent water interruptions. Theft is another challenge facing the sector. These factors hinder revenue recovery of water utilities in the region. For many utilities in the region, revenue from water sales cannot cover operating costs, thereby leading to low investments in the sector. Nonrevenue water, that is, water produced that remains unaccounted for, accounts for nearly 38 percent of the total water produced in several countries in the region (figure 5.12).

Good practice water policies will involve identifying priority areas facing current and future water shortages by assessing existing water reserves and projected needs, and conducting prefeasibility studies to address these shortages through both supply- and

FIGURE 5.12 Nonrevenue water, selected utilities and countries

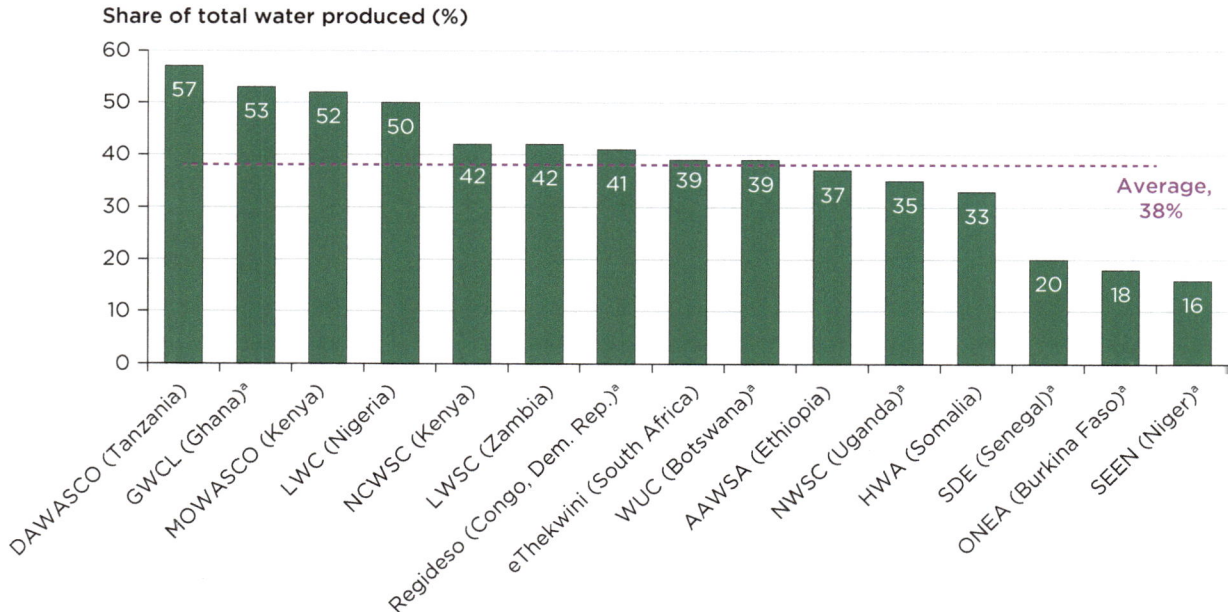

Share of total water produced (%)

Source: IFC 2022.
Note: Nonrevenue water is water produced that remains unaccounted for.
a. Denotes a national utility.

demand-side policy measures. These measures should include reforming nontargeted water subsidies, formalizing the management of critical water resources that are currently exploited informally, renegotiating water treaties with neighboring countries, promoting water usage efficiency (for example, drip irrigation), implementing recycling initiatives, and developing policies that enable and encourage private sector participation in the water sector (such as through competitive and transparent PPPs). For instance, performance-based contracts (PBCs) that engage private firms to manage formerly state-owned water utilities have proven to be an effective strategy. Additionally, establishing a strong and independent water regulatory authority is crucial to ensure the sustainable management and governance of water resources.

Examples of good practice water policies include the following:

- *Opportunity to develop irrigation PPPs in Chad.* Chad has the potential to irrigate 5.6 million hectares of farmland, a significant improvement over the 7,000 hectares currently irrigated. Private sector actors could invest in modernizing existing infrastructure or in new infrastructure in selected areas. They could oversee operations, with development partners undertaking technical, financial, and legal due diligence and facilitating PPP-type transactions. There is also great potential for PPP-type interventions such as management contracts in water supply and sanitation, such as the development of boreholes, drinking water supply systems in rural areas, and solar pumping technology in urban areas (IFC 2023a, 54).

- *Reducing water losses in South Africa.* In South Africa, the municipality in charge of water supply to the Evaton and Sebokeng townships launched a PBC with a private firm to address off-peak pressure in its water supply system. The firm invested US$500,000 to reduce water losses by 50 million cubic meters over a five-year period and saved 14,250 megawatts of energy per year, with a positive return on investment in less than two years.

- *Increasing revenue in Brazil.* In Brazil, a PBC in São Paulo led to US$72 million in revenue of which 75 percent accrued to the water utility, and an additional US$43 million accrued from bad debts for the water utility over three years (Kingdom, Liemberger, and Marin 2006).

Education and skills development

The key to unlocking Africa's potential is education and skills development that pave the way for robust socioeconomic advancement. This sector empowers the vast youth demographic with crucial knowledge and competencies, enabling them to address contemporary global challenges. A quality education system not only amplifies individual capacities but also seeds innovation, nurtures a competitive workforce, and fosters resilience in the face of modern-day adversities. Investment in human capital is a cornerstone for sustained economic progress and competitiveness. Beyond breaking the chains of poverty, education ushers in a realm of personal and professional opportunities, fostering civic participation, upholding democratic tenets, and fortifying social unity.

Good practice education policies will involve removing outright entry barriers to the private sector and leveling the playing field between public and private schools, for instance, by supporting and certifying informal private providers. In addition, countries should enable and promote PPPs, particularly in technical and vocational training; measure and publicize educational outcomes; establish credible certification mechanisms to ensure quality; and reform the primary education curriculum to enhance foundational skills such as reading, writing, problem-solving, teamwork, communication, English proficiency, and digital and financial literacy. In terms of private sector involvement, policies should encourage and promote innovative business models that leverage new technologies, including online learning and education technology, and should support the provision of lifelong learning by the private sector, including through employers. On the public sector side, countries need to increase public resources allocated to education—a critical public good—through enhanced domestic revenue mobilization and better coordination with development partners, and should improve the effectiveness of public investments by enhancing the governance of public schools and universities, refining public procurement practices, and optimizing the targeting of resources.

Examples of good practice education policies include the following:

- *Formalizing informal private education providers in Kenya.* The Kenya Ministry of Education, Science and Technology adopted the Alternative Provision of Basic Education and Training policy in 2009 to recognize nonformal schools and set up a framework to bring them into the formal system. In September 2015, the ministry released guidelines for schools under the provision, which included guidance on standards and procedures for registering these institutions and the minimum standards of quality education (IFC 2017, 30).

- *Expanding access to education in Morocco.* The country has made strides in expanding access to education and enhancing skills development (box 5.1). With a focus on promoting bilingual education, vocational training, and supporting education in rural areas, this approach can serve as a model for other African nations.

BOX 5.1

Vocational training in Morocco: Enhancing skills through public-private partnerships

Vocational training—a blend of public, private, and public-private partnership (PPP) initiatives—serves as a pivotal bridge for future instruction. The training is segmented into four levels based on education and continuing education aimed at refining employee skills to sync with market evolutions, thereby bolstering productivity. Although private technical and vocational education and training (TVET) providers are more numerous, nearly 80 percent of enrollments are in public institutions. Most private TVET providers tend to offer initial training for subjects such as hairdressing, marketing, and information and communication technology. The institutes of

(continued)

Health

Africa has made significant progress in improving health over the past two decades. Healthy life expectancy has improved from 46 years in 2000 to 56 years in 2019. Since 2000, under-five mortality has declined by 35 percent, and maternal mortality has declined by 28 percent. Progress has slowed in the past decade, however, given the numerous challenges related to health care access, infrastructure, and disease burden. Africa faces a double burden of communicable diseases, such as malaria, HIV/AIDS, and tuberculosis, and noncommunicable diseases such as diabetes and cardiovascular conditions. Over the past 20 years, out-of-pocket expenditures across most African countries have increased, pushing families into poverty. The COVID-19 pandemic highlighted the importance of a well-prepared and robust health sector to respond effectively to health crises. Climate change, in the form of weather-related health emergencies (heat waves) and increased transmission of communicable disease, will exacerbate Africa's health challenges. Engaging with and investing in private sector health care will be key to augment the capacity of the health sector. The private sector, including the vast informal health care sector, already plays a significant role in Africa's health sector, including medical equipment, pharmaceuticals, health care service delivery, and health care financing.

Good practice health policies will need to remove outright entry barriers to the private sector and level the playing field between private and public sectors by supporting and certifying informal private providers, enabling and promoting PPPs, especially in specialized care, and measuring and publicizing outcomes. They should also establish credible accreditation mechanisms to ensure quality; promote the adoption of groundbreaking medicines, early diagnostics, and advanced medical practices; encourage innovative business models that leverage new technologies, such as online diagnostics and consultations; support the development of private health insurance in coordination with public insurance schemes; increase public resources allocated to health as a critical public good through enhanced domestic revenue mobilization and improved coordination of development partners; and improve the effectiveness of public investments by strengthening the governance of public providers, refining public procurement processes, and better targeting PPPs.

Examples of good practice health policies include the following:

- *Angola's rebuilt health system.* After years of conflict, the country has rebuilt its health system with some dramatic results: life expectancy has increased from 42 years in 1990 to 62 years in 2016. Large geographic disparities persist, however, particularly for low-income and rural populations. Demand for health care is expected to increase, creating opportunities for private sector growth in health care delivery, telemedicine, and pharmaceuticals. Building off previous PPPs in health care and instituting regulatory and institutional health care reforms promise even greater private sector engagement.

- *Ethiopia's improved health outcomes.* In Ethiopia, infant mortality has decreased by 50 percent, from 97 deaths per 1,000 live births in 2000 to 48 deaths per 1,000 live births in 2016. Many health facilities still do not have basic amenities, and large disparities exist in the quality and availability of services. The government of Ethiopia seeks to improve access to essential health service and quality of care by giving a greater role to the private sector. As part of its Health Sector Transformation Plan II, Ethiopia has made PPPs a strategic priority for the delivery of health services and pharmaceuticals.

- *Kenya's growing private sector health care.* Kenya's health care system comprises the public sector, faith-based organizations, and the private sector. Although the public sector accounts for the largest part of the health sector, approximately 42 percent of health care is delivered privately. The Kenyan private sector continues to grow, commanding about 50 percent of all goods, services, products, and technologies. Kenya is also home to one of the fastest-growing pharmaceutical sectors in the region.

- *Leveling the playing field for health care in South Africa.* South Africa's health system is divided along socioeconomic lines with private health care covering about 16 percent of the population and the public sector covering the rest. A key driver of South Africa's health disparities is fragmentation of health financing, with the poor and rich using separate revenue collection and pooling mechanisms. South Africa's National Health Insurance Act of 2023 aims to pool public revenue and create a single framework for public funding and purchasing of health care services to reduce out-of-pocket costs and improve the quality of care for low-income South Africans.

- *Private investments in vaccine production in Rwanda.* In September 2021, IFC and the Rwanda Development Board signed an agreement to develop vaccine manufacturing capacity in Rwanda. IFC will support Rwanda to conduct feasibility studies of the technical and policy frameworks needed to establish a world-class vaccine manufacturing supply chain in Rwanda. The partnership will support Rwanda's association with BioNTech, a leading biotechnology company, and the kENUP Foundation to explore an end-to-end manufacturing capability for mRNA vaccines. Other pharmaceutical production facilities are expected to be co-located with BioNTech in the Kigali Special Economic Zone. Africa depends on other countries for 99 percent of its vaccine supply. The African Union and the Africa Centers for Disease Control and Prevention aim to have 60 percent of Africa's routine vaccines produced locally by 2040. The Africa Centers for Disease Control and Prevention have identified Rwanda (along with Senegal and South Africa) as potential regional vaccine manufacturing hubs in Africa.

Finance/business development services

The African financial sector, integral to the continent's evolving economic landscape, is undergoing significant adaptation in response to global megatrends, playing a crucial role in fostering sustainable development. With its current focus on enhancing financial stability and inclusion and mobilizing resources for key sectors such as infrastructure and renewable energy, the sector is positioned as a vital catalyst for attracting substantive private sector investments. This evolution, marked by embracing new financial technologies and innovative financing models, underscores the sector's commitment to meeting the diverse and expanding market needs, crucial for equitable economic participation and reducing poverty across the continent.

Private credit as a percentage of GDP in Sub-Saharan Africa averaged only 37 percent in 2022, significantly lower than the average in all other regions (figure 5.13, panel a). This ratio has had a slight downward trend, and there is a low penetration of commercial bank credit, with only 35 borrowers per 1,000 adults on average in Sub-Saharan Africa. Significantly increasing private credit will require reducing budget deficits because government borrowing has been crowding out private credits, and high inflation has led to high interest rates and the near absence of long-term lending. It will also require improving collateral markets by securing property rights and facilitating new entrants to enhance competition. Unlike private credit, Africa has leveraged new technologies to expand financial inclusion, with 55 percent of adults having bank accounts in 2021 (figure 5.13, panel b).

Access to finance. The high cost of credit and lack of collateral represent significant challenges for SMEs to access credit. According to the World Development Indicators, the cost of financial intermediation in Africa is high, with average interest rates at about 14.2 percent between 2012 and 2021, with several countries experiencing rates above 20 percent. Collateral requirements also pose a significant barrier to accessing finance for SMEs in Africa. These businesses often struggle to meet the stringent collateral demands set by financial institutions. This challenge is exacerbated by the lower valuation of assets owned by SMEs because of unsecured property rights, particularly in rural or underdeveloped areas. Consequently, many SMEs cannot secure the necessary funding to grow their businesses. High nominal rates and lack of secured property rights have also prevented mortgage finance, a key driver of productive urbanization, as noted in the earlier discussion on the construction sector.

Partial credit guarantees and credit lines. Alternative financing mechanisms have been set up to compensate for higher risk and lack of long-term financing. For example, the IMPACT project in Nigeria guarantees up to 60 percent of losses on SME loans (box 5.2).

FIGURE 5.13 Private credit and financial inclusion, by world region

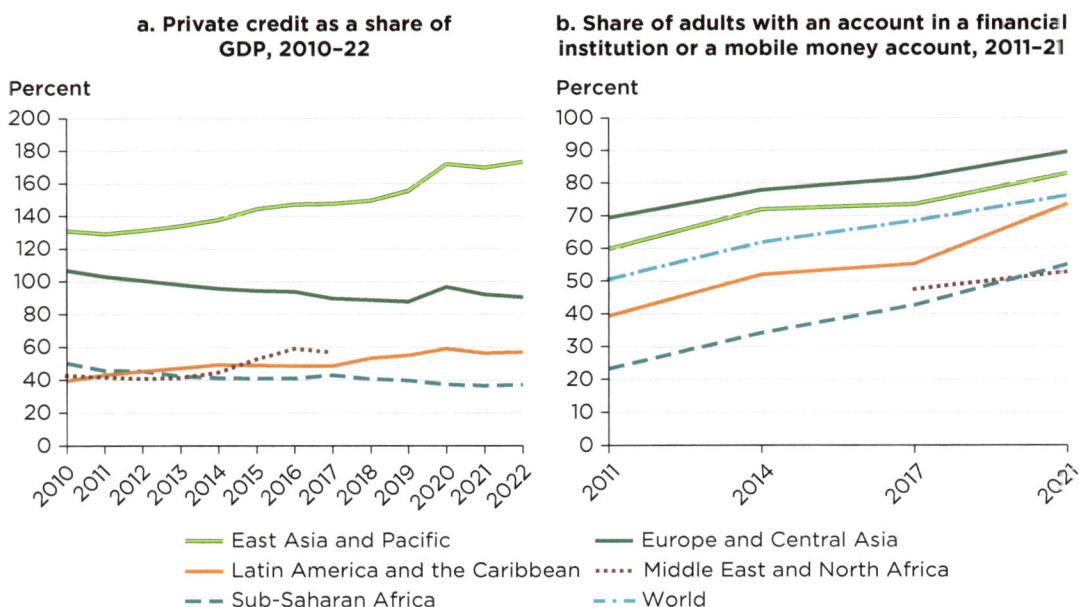

a. Private credit as a share of GDP, 2010–22

Percent

b. Share of adults with an account in a financial institution or a mobile money account, 2011–21

Percent

East Asia and Pacific
Europe and Central Asia
Latin America and the Caribbean
Middle East and North Africa
Sub-Saharan Africa
World

Sources: Global Financial Development Database, https://www.worldbank.org/en/publication/gfdr/data/global-financial-development-database; World Bank, World Development Indicators, https://data.worldbank.org/indicator/.

BOX 5.2

Using partial credit guarantees to stimulate MSME financing in Nigeria

Partial credit guarantees (PCGs), like those developed by the Development Bank of Nigeria's subsidiary Impact Credit Guarantee Limited, are essential to encourage banks to finance micro, small, and medium enterprises (MSMEs), especially in the challenging post-COVID-19 economic environment. Impact Credit Guarantee Limited's PCG aligns with international practices and offers up to 60 percent guarantees on MSME loans by eligible financial institutions. These institutions pay risk-adjusted fees to maintain the financial sustainability of the PCGs. Importantly, the use of PCGs is not disclosed to final beneficiaries, minimizing moral hazard. Claims can be filed after 180 days of loan delinquency, ensuring efficient processing and payouts within 45 days. Recognizing PCGs as a tool for mitigating risk can further incentivize banks to lend to MSMEs by reducing the risk-weighted assets calculation, considering the covered portion as collateral, and accepting guarantee coverage in lieu of provisioning for impaired loans.

Blended finance. Another instrument that can significantly increase access to finance for SMEs in Africa, blended finance leverages a mix of public and private funds to de-risk investments, making them more attractive to private sector actors. This approach is particularly effective in mobilizing capital for SMEs, which often have challenges accessing traditional banking services because of high collateral requirements and interest rates. By combining development finance, philanthropic contributions, and private capital, blended finance lowers the risk and cost of investing in SMEs, thus enhancing their ability to secure the necessary funding for growth and innovation. This method is instrumental in bridging the financing gap for SMEs, fostering economic development, and promoting sustainable growth in the African continent.

A prime example of blended finance in Africa is the 2023 IFC partnership with Orange Bank Africa to increase digital lending for small businesses in West Africa (IFC 2023b). This collaboration provides loans and microloans online to thousands of businesses, including those in rural and underserved areas. The IFC will offer a risk-sharing facility to help the bank scale its digital lending to micro, small, and medium enterprises in Côte d'Ivoire, Senegal, and other West African countries. This facility guarantees 50 percent of a portfolio of eligible short-term loans up to US$30 million, enabling the bank to provide an estimated 300,000 additional loans by 2025. This innovative risk-sharing facility, the first by IFC designed specifically for digital loans, expands financial inclusion by allowing borrowers to apply from anywhere. The IFC's support, backed by the International Development Association's Private Sector Window, also targets underserved segments such as women-owned businesses, young entrepreneurs, and creative industries, and supports mobile money agents and merchants accepting digital payments.

Green finance. With its vast green assets, Africa is well-positioned to attract significant amounts of green financing. Financial sector policies, such as climate-related disclosure requirements, taxonomies, and standards for sustainable financial instruments and products, should actively incentivize the transition to and financing of a low-carbon economy. They should also cover climate adaptation, a core issue for African countries (box 5.3).

BOX 5.3

Scaling up climate finance in Rwanda

Rwanda has pioneered a new strategy for climate investments through its one-stop center for green investment, Ireme Invest. This investment facility, established by the Rwanda Green Fund in collaboration with the Development Bank of Rwanda, received support from the Agence française de développement and the European Investment Bank under the International Monetary Fund's Resilience and Sustainability Facility framework. With a commitment to augment climate financing through budget backing, technical aid, and extended low-cost loans, this venture anticipates funding projects worth about €400 million, with private investors contributing €130 million in equity, underscoring the initiative's role as a catalyst. As the project portfolio grows, the government is ready to increase the equity of the Development Bank of Rwanda.

Source: IMF 2023.

BOX 5.4
Agrifinance and insurance in Nigeria

In Nigeria, innovative agrifinance programs that combine credit access with agricultural training and market access have significantly bolstered farmers' productivity and financial standing, enhancing their access to further financing. A substantial gap persists, however, in the provision of these tailored financial and insurance services, particularly for smallholder farmers and emerging agribusinesses. This gap represents a prime opportunity for private sector investment. By funding pioneering agrifinance models and microinsurance products, private investors can play a pivotal role in mitigating agricultural risks and catalyzing growth within this vital sector. Such investment not only meets a critical market need but also holds the potential for significant economic impact in bolstering Africa's agricultural sector.

Nigeria is also an example of the transformative impact of venture capital in Africa. Nigeria has witnessed a surge in tech-driven start-ups, particularly in cities like Abuja and Lagos. Fintech, agritech, healthtech, and e-commerce are some of the sectors that have received significant investment. Companies such as Flutterwave, a payments technology company, and Andela, which trains and employs software developers for businesses around the world, have raised substantial amounts from venture capital. The growth of Nigeria's technology ecosystem can be attributed in part to venture capital firms such as the Africa-focused TLcom Capital and global entities including Y Combinator that have actively invested in the region. Their investments have not only facilitated business growth but also spurred job creation and innovation, establishing Nigeria as a significant tech hub in Africa. Moreover, the success stories from Nigeria have further attracted international attention, pulling more investors into the African venture space.

Source: Savoy 2022.

Agrifinance and insurance are increasingly recognized as crucial to address the financing challenges faced by the agricultural sector in Africa. Agrifinance offers specialized financial products to farmers and agribusinesses that facilitate investments in necessary resources such as equipment and seeds. Concurrently and as discussed in the earlier agribusiness subsection, insurance services, especially for crops and livestock, mitigate farming risks exacerbated by climate change, creating a safer lending environment for both financial institutions and farmers. These tools collectively enhance the financial stability and creditworthiness of agricultural SMEs, fostering their growth and economic contribution. Examples of success in this area include agrifinance and insurance in Nigeria (box 5.4).

Digital financial services. Digital financial services in Africa are revolutionizing the financial landscape, breaking traditional barriers, and expanding access to banking and credit. With innovations such as mobile money platforms and peer-to-peer lending, these services are enhancing financial inclusion, particularly for underserved communities. This digital transformation, illustrated by success stories such as Mobile Money Service

(M-PESA), is facilitating convenient and efficient financial transactions across the continent. The rapid growth of financial technology (fintech) in Africa offers unparalleled consumer convenience and represents vast potential for private investment in a market eager for tailored financial solutions. This digital shift represents a significant step toward economic growth and financial empowerment in Africa.

The successes and even the failures across countries provide invaluable insights for potential investors. Governments across Africa increasingly recognize the importance of fostering a supportive regulatory environment for fintech innovation, including by establishing clear regulatory frameworks, promoting open banking standards, and encouraging collaboration between fintech and traditional financial institutions. In particular, ensuring mobile money interoperability allows for seamless transfer of mobile financial services between providers, as well as between these providers and banks (GSMA 2020).

Africa's financial integration with the global economy is advancing rapidly, driven by significant improvements in international payment systems and innovations in cross-border payments, notably in the electronic payments sector. This transformation is streamlining remittances, enhancing economic connections, and facilitating trade and investment flows, both within Africa and internationally. The Pan-African Payment and Settlement System, launched by the African Union, is a notable development that simplifies remittance processes and cuts costs, crucial in a continent that received US$42 billion in remittances in 2021. With digital payments constituting only 5–7 percent of all transactions, compared with much higher rates in other regions, this sector has vast potential for growth, and already generated significant revenue in 2020. This digital shift is crucial to boosting financial inclusion and economic growth, and attracting private investments in Africa.

In Africa, the landscape of digital financial services showcases a variety of innovative examples. Prominent among these are MNOs such as Mobile Telephone Network Mobile Money, Orange Money, and Tigo Money, collectively serving millions across numerous countries. MNO-led partnerships such as M-Shwari in Kenya combine banking and telecommunication services, offering consumer loans and deposits. World Bank–led partnerships, such as Equitel in Kenya, demonstrate the potential to extend beyond traditional banking services. As a mobile virtual network operator, Equitel offers a wide range of services, including mobile money, airtime top-ups, data bundles, Short Message Service, and international calls. This comprehensive approach allows banks to integrate more deeply into customers' daily lives, providing convenience and fostering financial inclusion. Additionally, banking apps such as FNB in South Africa cater to smartphone users, and fintech solutions such as Nigeria's Paga demonstrate significant customer growth, evolving into full-fledged payment companies. These diverse models are pivotal to enhancing financial access and convenience across the continent.

Blockchain in finance in Africa is gaining traction as an innovative solution to traditional financial challenges. This technology offers transparent and secure transactions, facilitating more efficient and reliable trade across various sectors. With blockchain, smallholder farmers and businesses can access crucial financial services that enhance their productivity and market reach. The success of these programs not only showcases blockchain's applicability in agriculture but also signals its broader potential to revolutionize value chain finance across the continent. Initiatives such as the Ethereum Foundation's crop insurance for Kenyan farmers demonstrate the potential of blockchain to provide targeted financial services. Etherisc, a proponent of Blockchain Climate Risk Crop Insurance from the 2019 Global Innovation Lab for Finance, uses blockchain technology to revolutionize agricultural insurance in Kenya. By providing 7,000 Kenyan farmers with parametric crop protection, Etherisc leverages the capabilities of Chainlink on the Avalanche[12] blockchain. This innovative approach offers a more efficient, transparent, and reliable method of insuring crops against climate risks, showcasing the transformative potential of blockchain to enhance agricultural finance and risk management in Africa.

Policies

The policy recommendations stemming from this chapter fall into two broad categories. The first one relates to necessary specific policy changes following a three-pronged strategy. The second one relates to the institutional and governance arrangements necessary for improving the government's capacity to address priority market and government failures on an ongoing basis.

A three-pronged policy strategy for crowding in private investments

The previous section laid out good practice policy principles with examples for African countries to generate private investments in key sectors, ranging from large transformative FDI to innovative domestic start-ups. The picture that emerges supports a three-pronged policy strategy that focuses on the following components:

1. *Go back to improving policy fundamentals.* Africa needs to reverse the downward trend on its Country Policy and Institutional Assessment scores by aiming for improvements in fundamentals (figure 5.14).

   - Political stability and good governance, including transparency, accountability, and inclusive decision-making.

   - Sustained macroeconomic stability that requires a monetary and exchange rate policy framework to maintain external balances and price stability, with adequate safeguards against internal or external shocks. Fiscal policy plays a crucial role in supporting macroeconomic stability and ensuring the adequate provision of public goods, which involves several key actions: (1) implementing prudent debt management strategies that account for contingent liabilities, (2) establishing fair, efficient, and progressive tax systems to boost domestic revenue generation, and (3) enhancing the quality of public expenditures. Countries can achieve these objectives by improving the targeting of subsidies, starting with those on carbon-based energy and fertilizers, reforming or privatizing SOEs that impose a financial

FIGURE 5.14 Country platforms to steer the three-pronged policy strategy

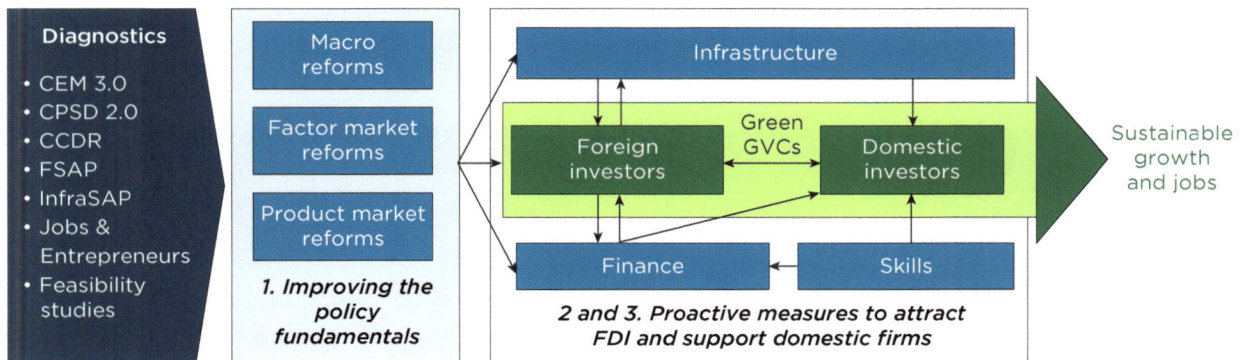

Diagnostics
- CEM 3.0
- CPSD 2.0
- CCDR
- FSAP
- InfraSAP
- Jobs & Entrepreneurs
- Feasibility studies

Macro reforms

Factor market reforms

Product market reforms

1. Improving the policy fundamentals

Infrastructure

Green GVCs

Foreign investors

Domestic investors

Finance

Skills

Sustainable growth and jobs

2 and 3. Proactive measures to attract FDI and support domestic firms

- **Strengthened reform delivery** (for example, priority reform diagnosed with private sector and partners; reform delivery teams; monitoring of reform implementation, impact evaluation)
- **Increased mobilization of development partners** (for example, coordinated budget support, investment lending, and technical assistance)
- **Improved foreign investor mobilization** (for example, identifying opportunities; investor outreach; de-risking)
- **Enhanced support to SMEs and entrepreneurs** (for example, access to [green] finance and skills)
- **Increased economic integration** (for example, leveraging AfCFTA, WTO, deep free trade agreements)

Source: World Bank.
Note: AfCFTA = African Continental Free Trade Area; CCDR = Country Climate and Development Report; CEM = Country Economic Memorandum; CPSD = Country Private Sector Diagnostic; FDI = foreign direct investment; FSAP = Financial Sector Assessment Program; GVCs = global value chains; InfraSAP = Infrastructure Sector Assessment Program; SMEs = small and medium enterprises; WTO = World Trade Organization.

burden on the budget, and better prioritizing support for public goods by leveraging the private sector, such as through competitive PPP processes.

- Low and harmonized tariffs with efficient customs that leverage new technologies and free trade agreements that can also be triggers for difficult domestic reforms, for example World Trade Organization accession, deep free trade agreements with the European Union or the United States, and the African Continental Free Trade Area.

- A world-class business regulatory environment with low entry barriers for foreign and domestic investors in most sectors, a solid and enforced legal framework to address anticompetitive conduct by firms, open procurement, streamlined licensing and inspections, and state interventions in goods markets limited to regulations to smooth out market imperfections.

- Independent regulators for natural monopoly sectors regulating and monitoring prices and quality of services to ensure productive delivery and avoid excess profits.

- Resilient and competitive financial sector with a level playing field for all types of actors and an efficient payment system, which can be achieved through a strong and independent regulator, ensuring adequate capitalization and supervision across the industry.

- Flexible labor markets for hiring and firing decisions, including for skilled expatriates. Attention should be given to flexibility in working hours, facilities to promote women's employment (for example, childcare facilities), and safe housing and transportation.

- Flexible and secured land markets with simple and reliable procedures to register property that protect the rights of communities, enable a productive and sustainable exploitation of Africa's rich natural resources, and enable the use of property as loan collateral (mortgages).

2. *Establish conditions to attract strategic first movers that face higher costs and risks, especially if all the fundamentals are not in place.* Special attention to these investors is justified by their capacity to markedly improve the performance of existing value chains or develop new high-value ones. They can also play a key role in providing access to markets, technology, and finance to domestic firms as suppliers. Such support should be provided through a transparent and, if possible, competitive process, focusing on the provision of public goods rather than privileges.

3. *Support small local firms.* This approach can be justified in Africa to address market and government failures that make it difficult for such firms to access markets, land, skills, and finance. Such support may include

- Supplier development programs with strategic first movers;

- Export promotion and certification bodies that, by reducing the fixed cost of exporting, facilitate SME access to high-value export markets;

- Plug-and-play industrial buildings that SMEs can rent, instead of having to invest large amounts of time and money developing their own facilities;

- Partial credit guarantees and lines of credit to facilitate access to long-term finance to SMEs, including to reduce carbon emissions and improve resilience (green finance); and

- Matching grants to promote access to business development services.

Reform delivery teams

Countries that have achieved strong and sustained private sector–led growth typically relied on a small, dedicated multiskilled reform team connected to the top of government. These teams were responsible for formulating and updating the reform strategy, monitoring the progress of reform implementation, helping remove implementation bottlenecks, and coordinating and mobilizing key stakeholders (development partners, private sector and civil society) (figure 5.14). Examples from outside Africa include the following:

- Dubai's Executive Office prepared and steered implementation of the main policy and investment decisions of the Ruler of Dubai.

- Georgia's deputy prime minister led the country's impressive reform program with a small cabinet of former bankers, consultants, and lawyers.

- Singapore's Economic Development Board was used to develop the infrastructure and policy framework required to attract world-class FDI.

Examples from Africa include the following:

- Botswana's Economic Planning Unit of 1965 started with two economists and drove the country's spectacular economic development. Botswana was the poorest country in the world in 1966 with only 22 university graduates and 12 kilometers of paved roads.

- Cabo Verde's equally impressive economic development established in 1975 relied on a small reform team of three returnee advisers around the prime minister, who also acted as the minister of planning and development assistance.

- Rwanda's Development Board was inspired by Singapore's Economic Development Board and led Rwanda's reforms and mobilization of foreign private investors.

African countries will also need to drive and leverage economic integration between themselves and the rest of the world through, for example, the African Continental Free Trade Area, the World Trade Organization, and deep free trade agreements with key partners.

Notes

1. Based on FDI data from UN Trade and Development (UNCTAD), "Global Foreign Direct Investment Flows over the Last 30 Years," https://unctad.org/data-visualization/global-foreign-direct-investment-flows-over-last-30-years.

2. World Travel & Tourism Council, https://wttc.org/research/economic-impact#:~:text=In%20 2022%2C%20the%20Travel%20%26%20Tourism,%2C%20only%2014.1%25%20below%202019.

3. UN Tourism, "Global and regional tourism performance," https://www.unwto.org/tourism-data/global-and-regional-tourism-performance.

4. Zeepay is a Ghanaian-owned financial technology company that provides digital payment services. It connects digital assets such as mobile money wallets, cards, ATMs, bank accounts, and digital tokens to international money transfer operators, payments, subscriptions, international airtime, and refugee payments. Jobberman is a Nigerian job portal that connects job seekers with companies. It is the largest job placement website in Sub-Saharan Africa. Kobo360 is a digital logistics platform that connects cargo owners with truck owners. The company is headquartered in Lagos and has a physical presence in six African countries.

5. World Bank, "The Digital Economy for Africa Initiative," https://www.worldbank.org/en/programs/all-africa-digital-transformation.

6. Interview in 2019 with Amal Hassan, founder and chief executive officer of Outsource Global.

7. For more information, refer to Wode Maya's YouTube channel, https://www.youtube.com/@WODEMAYA.

8. Approximately 50,000 in The Gambia, 200,000 in Burkina Faso, 320,000 in Benin, 322,000 in Senegal, 1 million in Algeria, 1.5 million in Zambia, and 2 million each in Ghana and Kenya (CAHF 2021).

9. Building Information Modelling is the management of information through the life cycle of a built asset, from initial design to construction, maintenance, and finally decommissioning, using digital modeling.

10. The 2021 Togo law mandates integrating fiber-optic networks into new infrastructure projects to broaden broadband access.

11. The International Finance Corporation website shows the many projects it supports: https://pressroom.ifc.org/all/pages/PressDetail.aspx?ID=25942.

12. Avalanche is a blockchain platform designed for high throughput, low latency, and sustainability, making it ideal for decentralized applications and financial solutions.

References

Abreha, K. G., X. Cirera, E. Davies, R. N. Fattal Jaef, and H. B. Maemir. 2022. "Deconstructing the Missing Middle: Informality and Growth of Firms in Sub-Saharan Africa." Policy Research Working Paper 10233, World Bank, Washington, DC. http://hdl.handle.net/10986/38324.

AfDB (African Development Bank). 2011. "The Cost of Adaptation to Climate Change in Africa." Abidjan, AfDB.

Ahlburg, D. A. 1996. "Population Growth and Poverty." In *The Impact of Population Growth on Well-Being in Developing Countries*, edited by D. A. Ahlburg, A. C. Kelley, and K. O. Mason, 219–58. Population Economics. Berlin: Springer.

APM Terminals. 2023. "Second Phase of Tema Port Expansion Dubbed 'New Era in Ghana's Maritime History.'" News release, November 17, 2023. https://www.apmterminals.com/en/news/news-releases/2023/231117-tema-expansion.

Bachas, P., L. Gadenne, and A. Jensen. 2020. "Informality, Consumption Taxes, and Redistribution." Policy Research Working Paper 9267, World Bank, Washington, DC.

Behrens, K., and F. Robert-Nicoud. 2014. "Survival of the Fittest in Cities: Urbanization and Inequality Get Access Arrow." *Economic Journal* 124: 1371–400.

Busby, J. W., T. G. Smith, and N. Krishnan. 2014. "Climate Security Vulnerability in Africa Mapping 3.0." *Political Geography* 43 (November): 51–67.

CAHF (Centre for Affordable Housing Finance in Africa). 2021. *2021 Housing Finance Yearbook*. Johannesburg: CAHF.

Collier, P. 2015. "Security Threats Facing Africa and Its Capacity to Respond: Challenges and Opportunities." *PRISM* 5 (2): 30–41.

Criscuolo, A., and V. Palmade. 2008. *Reform Teams*. Public Policy for the Private Sector Note 318. Washington, DC: World Bank.

Cusolito, A. P., D. Lederman, and J. Peña. 2020. "The Effects of Digital-Technology Adoption on Productivity and Factor Demand: Firm-Level Evidence from Developing Countries." Policy Research Working Paper 9333, World Bank, Washington, DC.

Damboeck, J., N. Perrin, B. Burckhart, and A. Rahim. 2020. "Together We Are Stronger: Supporting a Regional Dialogue on the Lake Chad Region." *Nasikiliza* (blog), February 13, 2020. https://blogs.worldbank.org/nasikiliza/together-we-are-stronger-supporting-regional-dialogue-lake-chad-region.

Denis, B. 2021. "The Rise of Africa's Digital Economy: The European Investment Bank's Activities to Support Africa's Transition to a Digital Economy." EIB Staff paper, European Investment Bank, Luxembourg. https://www.eib.org/attachments/thematic/study_the_rise_of_africa_s_digital_economy_en.pdf.

Ducard, M. 2021. "Investing in Black Artists, Creators and Stories." *YouTubeBlack Voices* (blog), January 12, 2021. https://blog.youtube/creator-and-artist-stories/investing-black-artists-creators -and-stories/.

Farole, Thomas. 2011. *Special Economic Zones in Africa : Comparing Performance and Learning from Global Experience*. Directions in Development. Washington, DC: World Bank.

Farvacque-Vitkovic, C., A. Casalis, M. Diop, and C. Eghoff. 2007. "Development of the Cities of Mali—Challenges and Priorities." Africa Region Working Paper 104a, World Bank, Washington, DC. https://citeseerx.ist.psu.edu/document?repid=rep1&type=pdf&doi=ea3597b58d8aafa6bd21 d21eb515c6485a7b383b.

GSMA. 2020. "Tracking the Journey towards Mobile Money Interoperability—Emerging Evidence from Six Markets: Tanzania, Pakistan, Madagascar, Ghana, Jordan, and Uganda." GSM Association. https:// www.gsma.com/solutions-and-impact/connectivity-for-good/mobile-for-development/wp-content /uploads/2020/06/GSMA_Tracking-the-journey-towards-mobile-money-interoperability-1.pdf.

Hjort, J., and J. Poulsen. 2019. "The Arrival of Fast Internet and Employment in Africa." *American Economic Review* 109 (3): 1032–79.

Houngbonon, G. V., J. T. Mensah, and N. Traore. 2022. "The Impact of Internet Access on Innovation and Entrepreneurship in Africa." Policy Research Working Paper 9945, World Bank, Washington, DC.

IFC (International Finance Corporation). 2017. "Creating Markets in Ghana." Country Private Sector Diagnostic, IFC, Washington, DC. https://www.ifc.org/content/dam/ifc/doc/mgrt/cpsd-creating -markets-in-ghana-nov-2017-v1.pdf.

IFC (International Finance Corporation). 2020a. "Creating Markets in Côte d'Ivoire: Mobilizing the Private Sector in Support of Economic Transformation in Côte d'Ivoire." Country Private Sector Diagnostic, IFC, Washington, DC.

IFC (International Finance Corporation). 2020b. "Creating Markets in Senegal: Sustaining Growth in an Uncertain Environment." Country Private Sector Diagnostic, IFC, Washington, DC.

IFC (International Finance Corporation). 2021. "Scaling Solar: Two PV Plants Bring Clean Energy to More than 500,000 in Senegal." Press release, June 1, 2021. https://www.ifc.org/en/pressroom /2021/scaling-solar-two-pv-plants-bring-clean-energy-to-more-than-500000-in-senegal.

IFC (International Finance Corporation). 2022. "Creating Markets in Botswana—A Diamond in the Rough: Toward a New Strategy for Diversification and Private Sector Growth." Country Private Sector Diagnostic, IFC, Washington, DC.

IFC (International Finance Corporation). 2023a. "Creating Markets in Chad: Mobilizing Private Investment for Inclusive Growth." Country Private Sector Diagnostic, IFC, Washington, DC.

IFC (International Finance Corporation). 2023b. "IFC Partners with Orange Bank Africa to Increase Digital Lending for Small Businesses in West Africa." Press release, July 4, 2023. https://www.ifc .org/en/pressroom/2023/ifc-partners-with-orange-bank-africa-to-increase-digital-lending-for -small-businesses-in-west-africa.

ILO (International Labour Organization). 2018. *Women and Men in the Informal Economy: A Statistical Picture*. 3rd ed. Geneva: ILO.

IMF (International Monetary Fund). 2023. "Rwanda, Team Europe and Partners Pioneer an Additional EUR 300 Million Financing to Crowd In Private Investment and Build Climate Resilience Following Resilience and Sustainability Facility Arrangement with the International Monetary Fund." Press Release No 23/224, June 22. https://www.eib.org/en/press/all/2023-237-team -europe-and-partners-pioneer-an-additional-eur-300m-financing-to-crowd-in-private -investment-and-build-climate-resilience-following-resilience-and-sustainability-facility -arrangement-with-the-international-mon.

Kingdom, B., R. Liemberger, and P. Marin. 2006. "The Challenge of Reducing Non-Revenue Water in Developing Countries—How the Private Sector Can Help: A Look at Performance-Based Service Contracting." Water Supply and Sanitation Sector Board Discussion Paper No. 8, World Bank, Washington, DC. https://openknowledge.worldbank.org/handle/10986/17238.

Lee, D. 2018. "Why Big Tech Pays Poor Kenyans to Teach Self-Driving Cars." *BBC*, November 2, 2018. https://www.bbc.com/news/technology-46055595.

Lusigi, A. 2023. "Accelerating Creativity and Innovation in Africa." *UNDP Ghana* (blog), April 21, 2023. https://www.undp.org/ghana/blog/accelerating-creativity-and-innovation-africa.

Mensah, J. T., and N. Traore. 2023. "Infrastructure Quality and FDI Inflows: Evidence from the Arrival of High-Speed Internet in Africa." Policy Research Working Paper 9946, World Bank, Washington, DC.

Naadi, T., and S. Lansah. 2021. "The Illegal Gold Mines Killing Rivers and Livelihoods in Ghana." *BBC*, August 10, 2021. https://www.bbc.com/news/av/world-africa-58119653.

OECD (Organisation for Economic Co-operation and Development), ECA (United Nations Economic Commission for Africa), and AfDB (African Development Bank). 2022. *Africa's Urbanisation Dynamics 2022: The Economic Power of Africa's Cities*. West African Studies. Paris: OECD Publishing.

Savoy, C. M. 2022. "Access to Finance for Smallholder Farmers." CSIS Commentary, December 7, 2022. https://www.csis.org/analysis/access-finance-smallholder-farmers.

UN DESA (United Nations Department of Economic and Social Affairs). 2018. *World Urbanization Prospects: The 2018 Revision*. ST/ESA/SER.A/420. New York: United Nations.

United Nations Population Division. 2022. *World Population Prospects*. New York: United Nations.

USAID (United States Agency for International Development). 2019. *Feed the Future: Nigeria Agribusiness Investment Activity*. Quarterly Progress Report (April 1–June 30, 2019). Washington, DC: USAID.

World Bank. 2014. "World Bank Supports Improved Social Service Delivery and Boosting Jobs Creation in Madagascar." Press release, December 18. https://www.worldbank.org/en/news/press-release/2014/12/18/world-bank-improved-social-service-delivery-boosting-jobs-creation-madagascar.

World Bank. 2017–23. *Country Private Sector Diagnostics (Including Guidance Notes)*. Washington, DC: World Bank.

World Bank. 2018. *Global Financial Development Report 2017/2018: Bankers without Borders*. Washington, DC: World Bank.

World Bank. 2021. "G20 Compact with Africa. Compact Monitoring Report. Africa Advisory Group Meeting." October. https://thedocs.worldbank.org/en/doc/aa3857aca02ec44306b7386314803731-0630032024/original/CwA-Monitoring-Report-October-2021.pdf.

World Bank. 2023a. "Accelerating the Use of Digital Technologies Is Key to Creating Productive Jobs and Boosting Economic Growth in Africa." Press release, March 13, 2023. https://www.worldbank.org/en/news/press-release/2023/03/13/accelerating-the-use-of-digital-technologies-is-key-to-creating-productive-jobs-and-boosting-economic-growth-in-africa.

World Bank. 2023b. *The Business of the State*. Washington, DC: World Bank.

World Bank. 2023c. "CPIA Africa: Assessing Africa's Policies and Institutions." Country Policy and Institutional Assessment, September 2023, World Bank, Washington, DC. https://documents1.worldbank.org/curated/en/099634410132333843/pdf/IDU02411084a0fdbd0462b0b4b1065aad2bcad42.pdf.

Zeufack, A. G., C. Calderon, G. Kambou, M. Kubota, C. Cantu Canales, and V. Korman. 2020. "Africa's Pulse, No. 22" (October). World Bank, Washington, DC.

CHAPTER 6

Industrialization

Kaleb Abreha, Woubet Kassa, and Pierre Nguimkeu

Summary

This chapter reviews the experiences and prospects of industrialization in Sub-Saharan Africa and pinpoints areas of policy focus to promote industrial development and its contribution to the economy. It summarizes the extent of industrialization in the region in terms of employment generation, value added contribution, productivity growth, and structural transformation since 2000. It then assesses the challenges and opportunities for successful industrialization by considering recent megatrends such as emerging technologies, evolving regional and global value chains (GVCs), and growing populations. Additionally, it provides policy directions based on broader principles (rather than detailed policy prescriptions) by distilling insights from the experiences of successful industrial policies and empirical research on industrialization and economic transformation.

Sub-Saharan African countries face ongoing and emerging trends that present new opportunities and pose challenges for successful industrialization. Over the past two decades, not only has the interconnectedness of countries grown but global production has also featured major spatial and task fragmentation across countries. Multinational enterprises, buoyed by declines in trading costs and an improved global policy environment, have increasingly extended their production processes beyond national boundaries, enlarging global production networks or GVCs. More recently, major technological developments, especially digital technologies, have started shaping the modes of production with significant implications for the prospects of productivity growth, job creation and displacement, and reshoring. These technologies have also created heterogeneity in modes of production across countries within the same industries so that the productivity and employment gains from manufacturing mainly depend on modes of production rather than sectoral specialization. Last, Sub-Saharan African countries have a large and growing youth population, which comes with the advantages of a large domestic market and the disadvantage of a serious resource burden to improve human capital. Overall, these trends may permit countries in the region to exploit the opportunities of GVCs, leapfrog to transformative industries, and reap the demographic dividend. At the same time, Sub-Saharan African countries face challenges in their industrialization endeavors because of a shortage of skilled workers, a risk of underinvestment in human capital, the digital divide, relatively high labor costs given the level of income, and heavy reliance on extractive industries with limited industrial upgrading.

Industrialization requires proactive prioritization and coordination of policies to address the microeconomic factors that determine firms' and industries' competitiveness, and the macroeconomic and institutional qualities that enable structural transformation. The mere availability of cheap labor and the existence of free trade do not build a globally competitive manufacturing sector. Three dimensions are critical for the success of industrialization drives in the region: economywide policy actions to create a business environment that maintains macroeconomic stability, fosters investment, and boosts productivity; industry-specific policy actions to exploit existing comparative advantages and create new ones; and policies to build firm and industry capabilities.

Context

Achieving industrialization—the reallocation of resources to industry, mainly manufacturing—can be a slow, risky, and costly process. Building a strong and efficient industrial capacity is also beset by a range of market failures such as missing markets, asymmetric information, externalities, problems of coordination, unpredictable learning sequences, deficient capital markets, and the absence of supporting institutions and skills. Given the complexities of the industrialization process, the type of policy actions taken and how they are managed matter for the pace and success of industrialization.

The performance of the industrial sector, particularly manufacturing, has been limited. In Sub-Saharan Africa, industry's contributions to employment and value added were about 12 percent and 27 percent in 2021 compared with 10 percent and 28 percent in 2000, respectively. As for manufacturing, shares of value added were 12 percent in 2021, substantially lower than the 24 percent in the East Asia and Pacific countries. In terms of employment, based on a select sample of countries for which manufacturing value added and employment data are available, employment shares increased from 7.0 percent in 2000 to 8.4 percent in 2018.

Despite a limited contribution to value added and jobs in Sub-Saharan Africa, with the right policy support, manufacturing can become the engine of economic growth and convergence in per capita income and productivity. Although manufacturing jobs are of better quality compared with informal services sector jobs, few high-quality manufacturing jobs pay living wages and provide better working conditions. The dominance of primary goods in the region's exports and the region's stronger forward links to GVCs indicate the potential for significant income and job growth from upgrading to knowledge-intensive products and high-skill tasks. Positioning the region to achieve industrial competitiveness will require leveraging the opportunities and mitigating the challenges of emerging regional and global trends in trade, technology, demography, and geopolitics. Specifically, policy interventions should prioritize creating a business environment with lower market frictions and higher contestability, building up firm and industry capabilities, and joining and strengthening value chain links to facilitate technology transfer and upgrading.

Facts

This section assesses the region's industrialization over the past two decades, focusing on employment, value added contribution, productivity, and structural transformation. It also explores challenges and opportunities driven by megatrends like emerging technologies, shifting value chains, and population growth.

Industrial patterns

Industry accounts for a rather low share of total employment and value added. Over the past two decades, industry—comprising manufacturing, mining and quarrying, construction, and public utilities (electricity, gas, and water)—has the lowest share of value added contribution of all regions, with the exception of South Asia (figure 6.1). The sector provides a source of employment for only a small fraction of the labor force. It hires only about 10–15 percent of the total employment in the region, considerably lower than the pattern observed in other regions. Within the industrial sector, manufacturing displays weaker performance compared with other developing regions such as Asia, Latin America, and North Africa. The relative contribution of manufacturing to value added and employment has been flat or declining over time. Still, the region's manufacturing workforce grew by 140 percent from a total of 8.9 million in 2000 to 21.3 million in 2018.[1]

Additionally, industrialization patterns vary significantly across countries and subregions, making it difficult to identify a single pattern as a defining feature of industrialization in the region. In 2021, the share of industry employment in total employment varied, and it was significantly smaller than the share in East Asia and Pacific countries (figure 6.2). By comparison, figure 6.3 shows that value added shares were higher than employment shares yet were still smaller than the value added contribution of the sector in East Asia and Pacific. Resource-rich countries such as Angola and Gabon are exceptions, suggesting that mining is the primary source of value added in the sector. Manufacturing also displays the same characteristics, with substantial heterogeneity across countries and significant underperformance compared with benchmark countries in the East Asia and Pacific region (figure 6.4).[2]

FIGURE 6.1 Industrial sector contributions to value added and employment, by world region, 2000–21

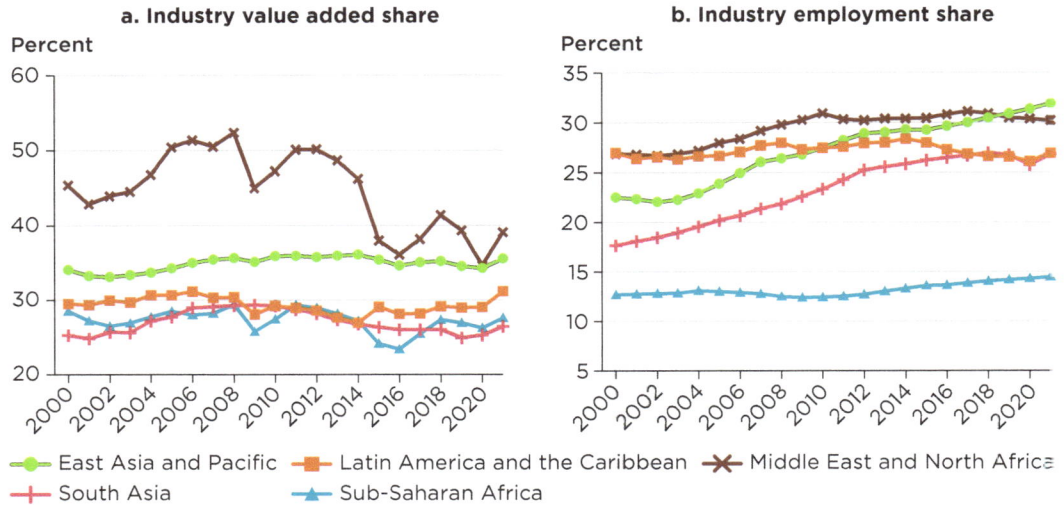

a. Industry value added share

b. Industry employment share

Legend:
- East Asia and Pacific
- Latin America and the Caribbean
- Middle East and North Africa
- South Asia
- Sub-Saharan Africa

Source: World Bank, World Development Indicators, https://data.worldbank.org/indicator/.
Note: Industry comprises mining and quarrying, manufacturing, construction, and public utilities (electricity, gas, and water).

Notwithstanding the poor performance of the sector, the region shows no strong evidence of premature deindustrialization. Although deindustrialization eventually occurs with the successful transformation of economies, it is important that the industrialization process does not end prematurely—that is, at a lower level of income. The rapid growth in the development and adoption of advanced manufacturing technologies have given rise to arguments that the prospects of manufacturing in the region are not bright and that the region may have already experienced premature deindustrialization. Manufacturing shares have started declining at rather lower levels of income. In the example of employment, however, the share of manufacturing employment has increased with the level of income (figure 6.5). Despite low levels of manufacturing employment in Sub-Saharan Africa in relation to other regions, a positive trend suggests a recovery in the most recent decade (Kruse et al. 2023; Nguimkeu and Zeufack 2019; te Velde et al. 2018), but with some disparities by subregion. Central and Western Africa have flat shares of manufacturing, whereas East Africa's shares are rising as the income levels of these countries grow (Nguimkeu and Zeufack 2019). Southern Africa is the only subregion that exhibits features of premature deindustrialization. Even there, the share of manufacturing peaks at relatively higher levels of income, often considered ambitious for many in the region.

FIGURE 6.2 Industry employment, Sub-Saharan Africa versus East Asia and Pacific, 2021

Share of total employment (%)

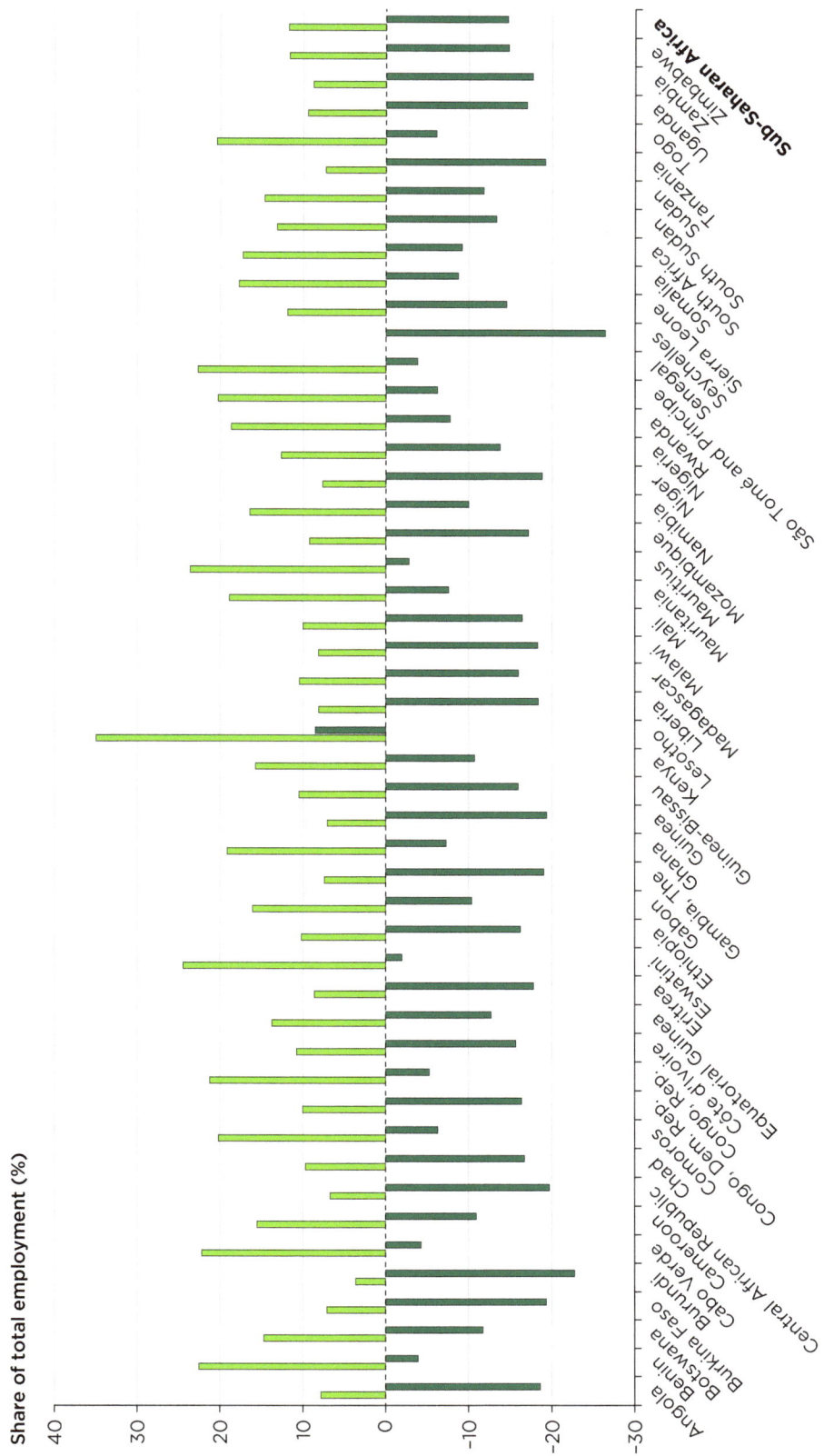

Source: World Bank, World Development Indicators, https://data.worldbank.org/indicator/.

Legend: Industry employment ☐ Industry employment compared with East Asia and Pacific (%)

FIGURE 6.3 Industry value added, Sub-Saharan Africa versus East Asia and Pacific, 2021

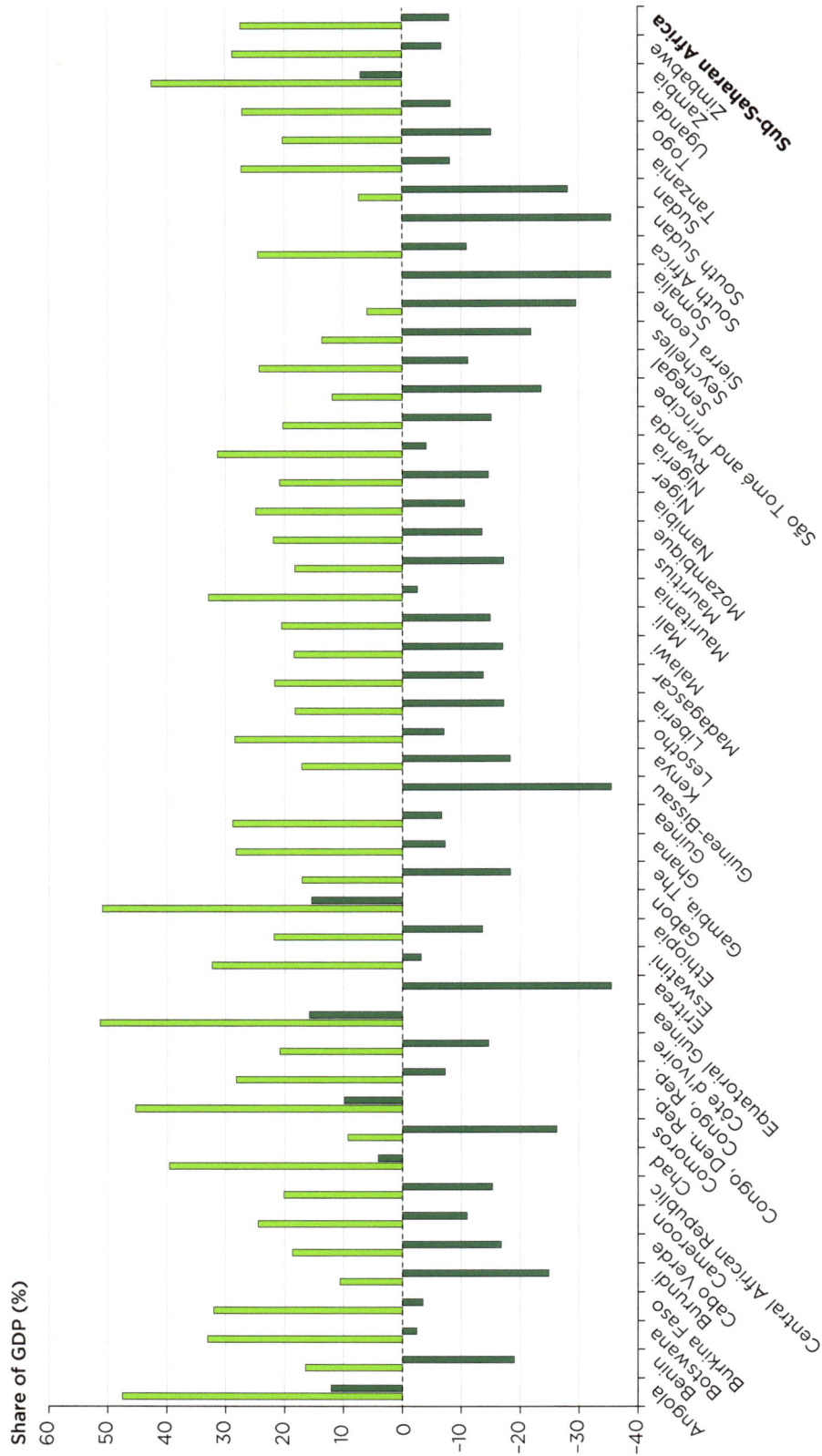

Share of GDP (%)

Countries (top to bottom): Sub-Saharan Africa, Zimbabwe, Zambia, Uganda, Togo, Tanzania, Sudan, South Sudan, South Africa, Somalia, Sierra Leone, Seychelles, Senegal, São Tomé and Príncipe, Rwanda, Nigeria, Niger, Namibia, Mozambique, Mauritius, Mauritania, Mali, Malawi, Madagascar, Liberia, Lesotho, Kenya, Guinea-Bissau, Guinea, Ghana, Gambia, The, Gabon, Ethiopia, Eswatini, Eritrea, Equatorial Guinea, Côte d'Ivoire, Congo, Rep., Congo, Dem. Rep., Comoros, Chad, Central African Republic, Cameroon, Cabo Verde, Burundi, Burkina Faso, Botswana, Benin, Angola

■ Industry value added   ■ Industry value added compared with East Asia and Pacific (pp)

Source: World Bank, World Development Indicators, https://data.worldbank.org/indicator/.

Note: pp = percentage point.

FIGURE 6.4 Manufacturing value added, Sub-Saharan Africa versus East Asia and Pacific, 2021

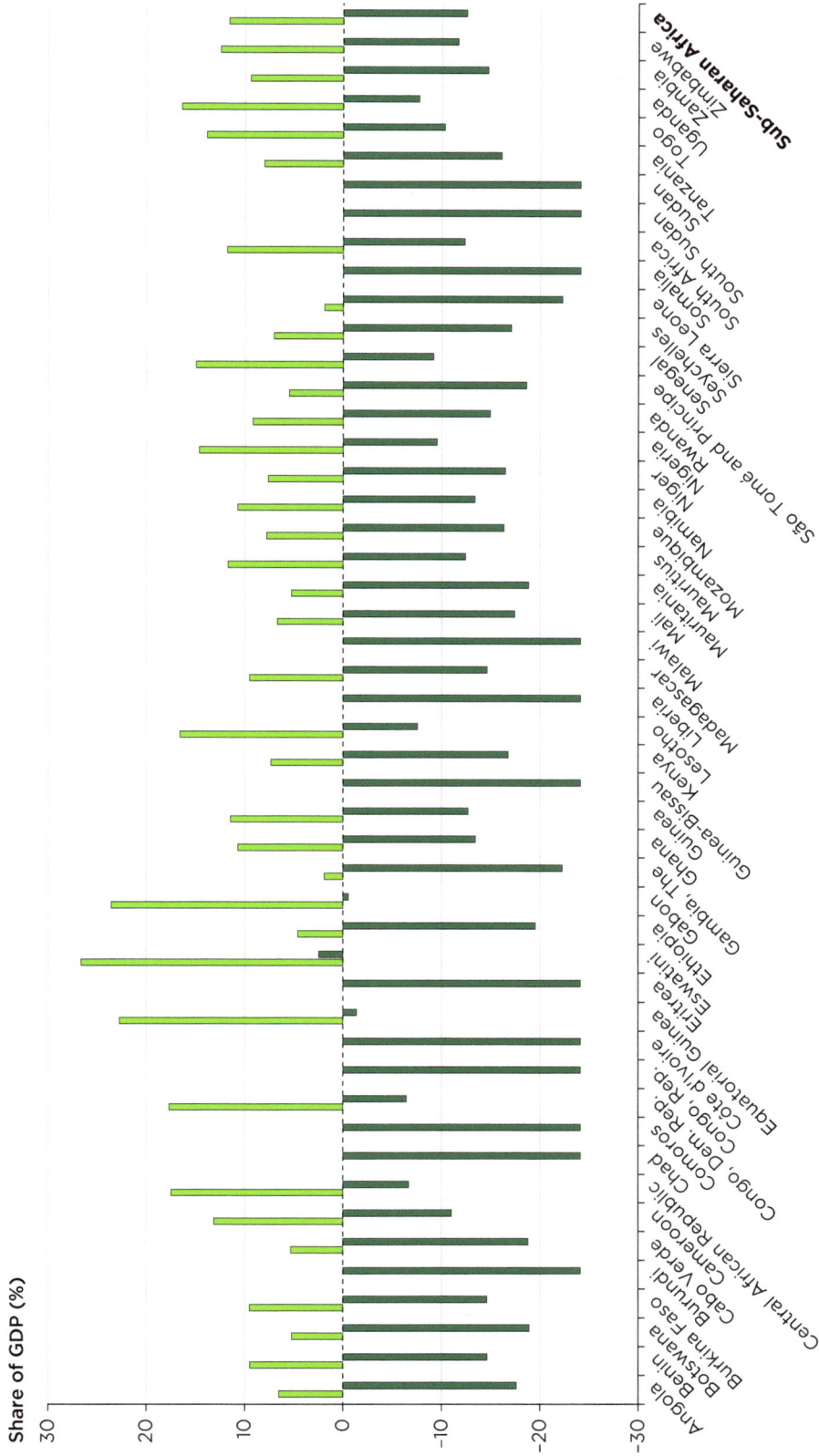

Share of GDP (%)

Manufacturing value added ■ Manufacturing value added compared with East Asia and Pacific (pp)

Source: World Bank, World Development Indicators, https://data.worldbank.org/indicator/.

Note: pp = percentage point.

FIGURE 6.5 Manufacturing employment and value added shares, by country income level, 2000–18

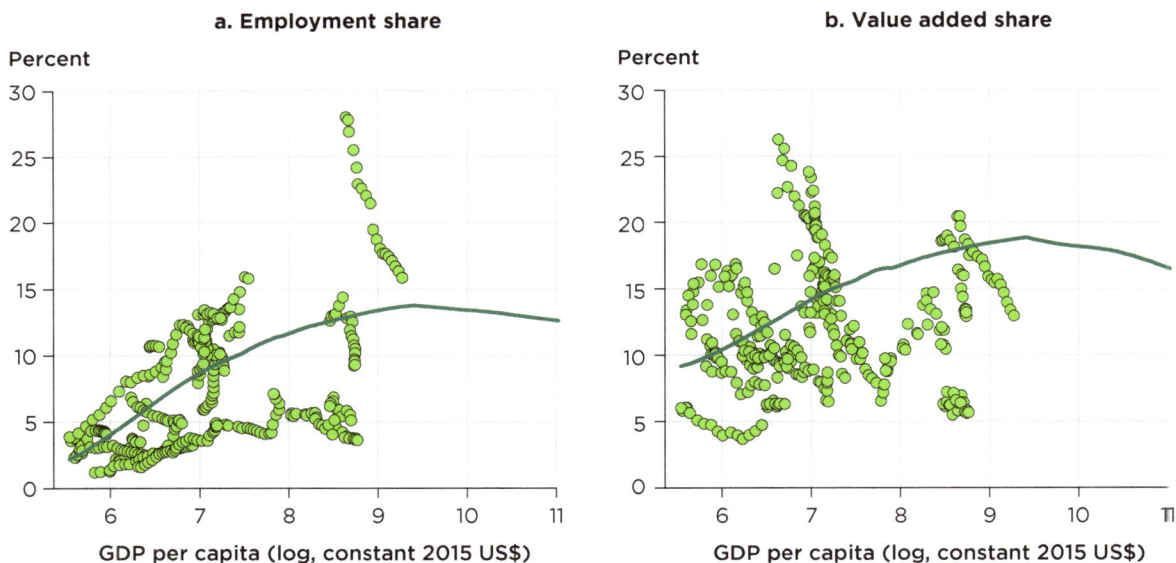

a. Employment share

b. Value added share

Sources: Based on data for the years 2000–18 from the Groningen Growth and Development Centre/United Nations University World Institute for Development Economics Research Economic Transformation Database, https://www.wider.unu.edu/database/etd-economic-transformation-database/, and World Bank, World Development Indicators, https://data.worldbank.org/indicator/.
Note: Each dot is a Sub-Saharan Africa country-year.

Additionally, the manufacturing sector of resource-rich countries, on average, underperforms compared with that of non-resource-rich countries, and countries' landlockedness stifles manufacturing development (figure 6.6). Resource-rich countries have a lower employment contribution of manufacturing compared with their non-resource-rich counterparts, after controlling for population size. Regarding shares of value added, no discernible difference is noted between the resource groups. Still, non-resource-rich countries perform better in terms of value added. Integration into the global economy in trade and investment is central to countries' industrialization endeavors because of the benefits that come with economic openness, such as access to cheaper or high-quality inputs and a larger customer base for goods and services, transfer of technology, and promotion and access to international capital markets. Geography, especially landlockedness, is a key constraint faced by several Sub-Saharan African countries.[3]

Although the sector has not had strong performance, manufacturing remains integral to the structural transformation of the region. A few countries have experienced success in light manufacturing in their industrialization efforts. Special economic zones (SEZs) offer a case in point. Despite the late adoption of SEZs in Sub-Saharan African countries, they have proliferated recently, and the region has attracted more foreign SEZ developers and investors, especially since 2006 (Zeng 2020). The region had 237

FIGURE 6.6 Manufacturing employment and value added shares, by country resource endowment and geography

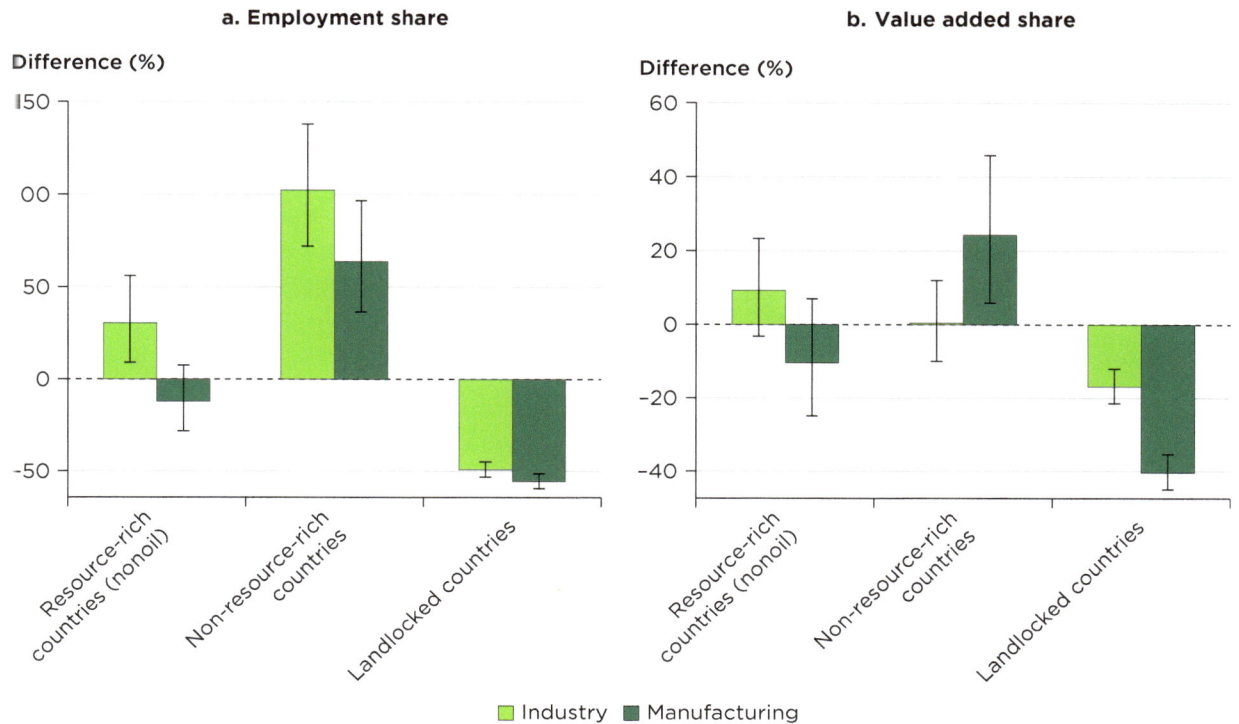

a. Employment share

Difference (%)

b. Value added share

Difference (%)

☐ Industry ■ Manufacturing

Sources: Based on data for the years 2000–18 from the Groningen Growth and Development Centre/United Nations University World Institute for Development Economics Research Economic Transformation Database, and World Bank, World Development Indicators, https://data.worldbank.org/indicator/.
Note: The panels show percentage differences in manufacturing employment and value added shares by comparing resource-rich countries relative to non-resource-rich countries, and landlocked relative to coastal Sub-Saharan African countries. Population size and year fixed effects are used as controls.

SEZs in 2020 compared with 155 in 2006 (UNCTAD 2021). Such rapid growth in the establishment of SEZs has occurred despite the recent financial crisis and deceleration in trade and foreign direct investment (FDI). In 2019, SEZs created a substantial number of direct jobs: 200,000 (Ethiopia), 110,000 (South Africa), 60,000 (Kenya), 45,000 (Tanzania), 30,000 (Ghana), 15,000 (Togo), 13,000 (Rwanda), 5,000 (Angola), and 4,500 (Senegal) (UNCTAD 2021).[4] Beyond job creation, SEZs are also sources of export earnings. For example, in 2018, export processing zones in Kenya generated an annual sales turnover of about US$650 million, with about 90 percent from export sales. In 2017, export processing zones accounted for 94 percent of the US$340 million in apparel exports to the United States and significantly contributed to Kenya's record as one of the best-performing countries to use the African Growth and Opportunity Act scheme (UNCTAD 2019).

Manufacturing and trade openness

Sub-Saharan Africa has registered fast growth in export and import trade over the past two decades; however, this growth has been accompanied by a decline in the ratio of trade to gross domestic product and the contribution of manufacturing exports in merchandise exports, albeit with some improvement in the latter. The region plays a small role in global trade. The share of Sub-Saharan African countries in global production and merchandise trade is about 3 percent, but these countries have started experiencing faster growth in recent years (Coulibaly et al. 2022). At the same time, countries in the region have comparably high degrees of trade openness (figure 6.7). Despite the region's trade openness, manufacturing exports constitute less than 40 percent of merchandise exports, a share only slightly higher than in South Asia.

FIGURE 6.7 Trade openness and goods composition of trade, selected world regions, 2000–21

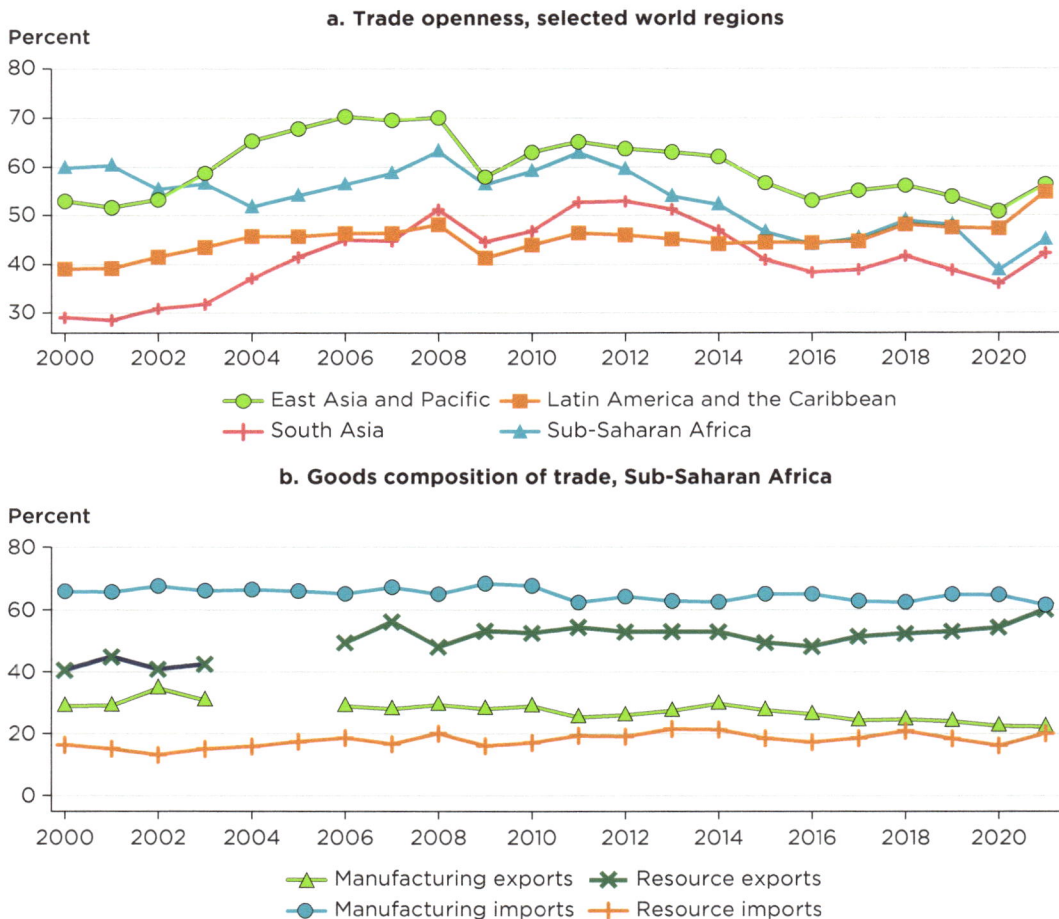

a. Trade openness, selected world regions

b. Goods composition of trade, Sub-Saharan Africa

Source: World Bank, World Development Indicators, https://data.worldbank.org/indicator/.

Countries in Sub-Saharan Africa have weak links along GVCs, with a small share in global value-added trade. The first form of GVC integration, backward participation, captures the foreign value-added content of gross exports. The second, forward integration, shows the value of domestic value added reexported by other countries. Overall GVC integration is the sum of backward and forward integrations. The degree of backward integration is higher in manufacturing compared with the whole economy, yet it is weaker compared with other regions. By contrast, Sub-Saharan African countries have stronger forward integration, particularly in nonmanufacturing sectors (figure 6.8), suggesting an association between higher forward links and exports of natural resources. Within manufacturing, resource-rich countries tend to have GVC integration primarily through forward links, whereas non-resource-rich countries have stronger backward integration (figure 6.9).

FIGURE 6.8 **GVC integration, 2000–15**

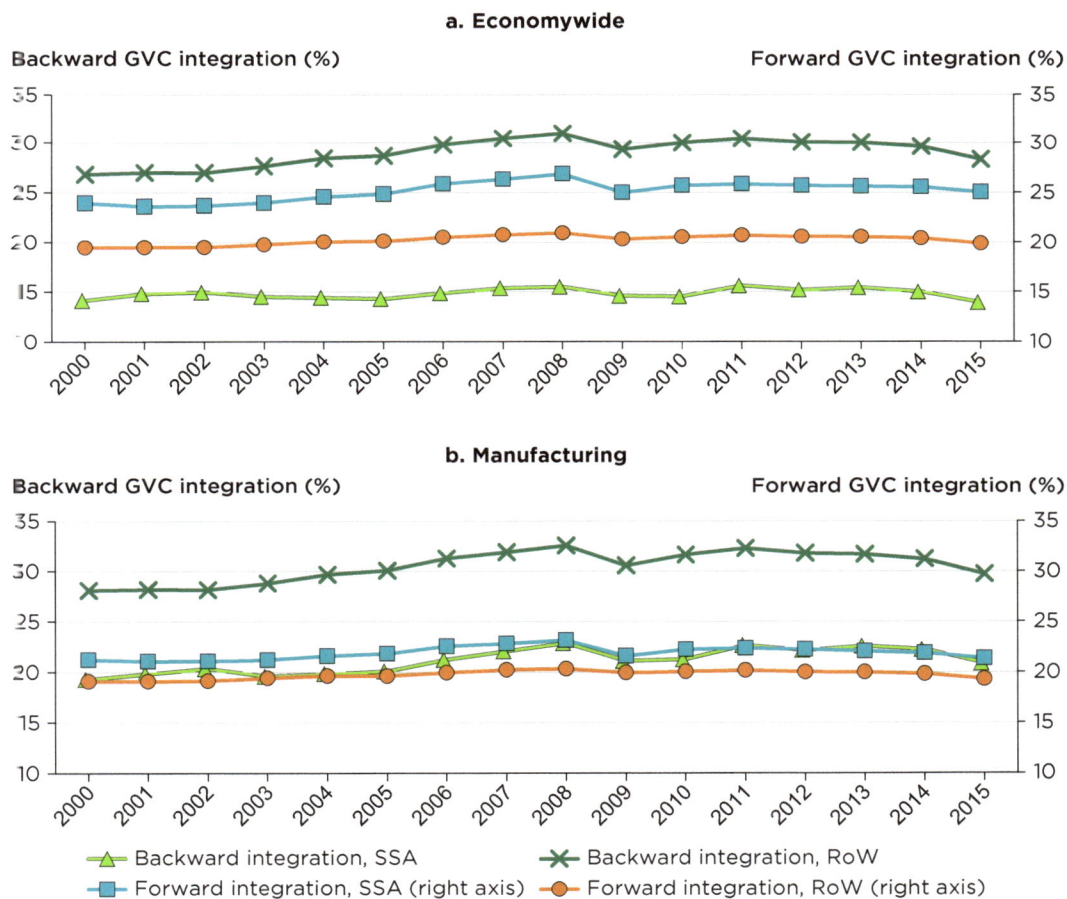

a. Economywide

b. Manufacturing

Sources: Casella et al. 2019; World Bank 2020.
Note: Backward integration captures the foreign value-added content of gross exports; forward integration shows the value of domestic value added reexported by other countries. GVC = global value chain; RoW = rest of world; SSA = Sub-Saharan Africa.

FIGURE 6.9 Manufacturing GVC integration, 2015

GVC integration (%)

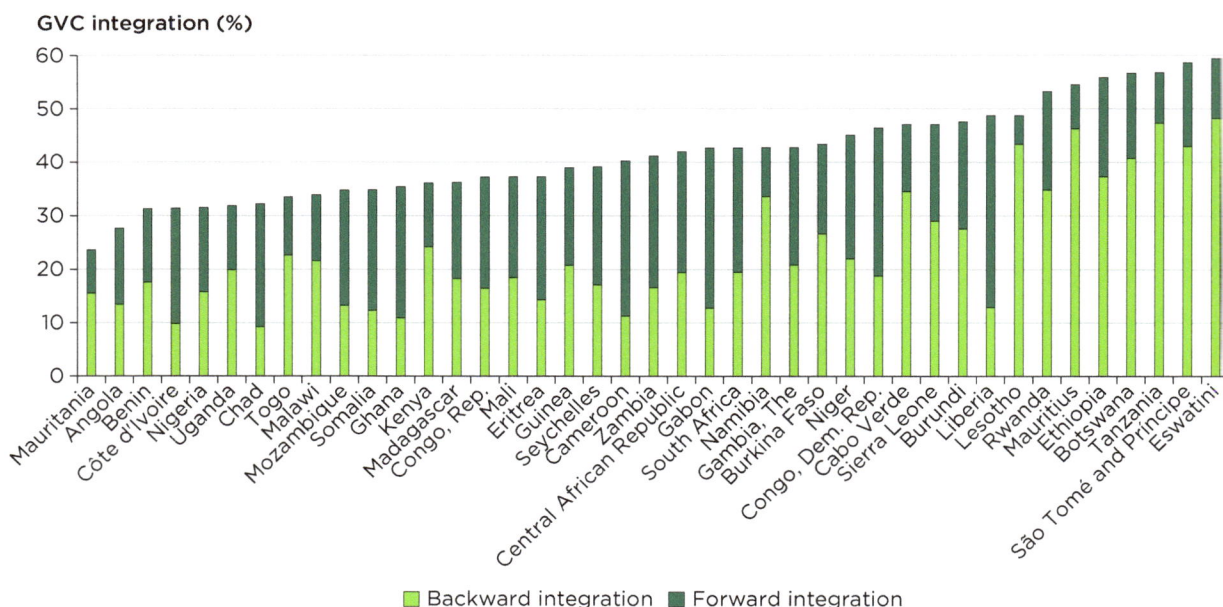

■ Backward integration ■ Forward integration

Sources: Casella et al. 2019; World Bank 2020.
Note: Backward integration captures the foreign value-added content of gross exports; forward integration shows the value of domestic value added reexported by other countries. GVC = global value chain.

A strong, positive relationship exists between GVC participation and manufacturing productivity and job growth. Countries with high GVC participation rates exhibit higher labor productivity levels and faster job growth. Higher GVC participation (at both the 25th and the 75th percentiles) is associated with a much higher productivity gain (figure 6.10). An increase in the GVC participation rate from the 25th to the 75th percentile is associated with a 1.5-percentage-point increase in labor productivity growth (Pahl and Timmer 2020). GVC integration overall is associated with higher productivity growth in the long run for all countries, but the effect is stronger through backward participation and for countries that are more integrated into GVCs. Furthermore, GVC participation has created jobs in manufacturing, but with a stronger effect in agriculture and services. Pahl et al. (2019) looked at job creation within the GVCs of final goods from 2000 to 2014. Their analysis reveals the creation of about 1.4 million jobs in Ethiopia, with 691,000 in agriculture, 482,000 in services, and 150,000 in manufacturing. In Kenya, 624,000 jobs were generated, including 471,000 in agriculture, 96,000 in services, and 64,000 in manufacturing, but other industries lost about 8,000 jobs. Senegal experienced a loss of 211,000 jobs, including 78,000 in agriculture, but manufacturing added 3,000 jobs. In contrast, South Africa faced a significant decline, losing 584,000 jobs, with 318,000 in agriculture and 184,000 in manufacturing.

21st-Century Africa

FIGURE 6.10 GVC participation and manufacturing productivity growth

a. GVC integration rate above and below the 25th percentile

b. GVC integration rate at the 75th percentile

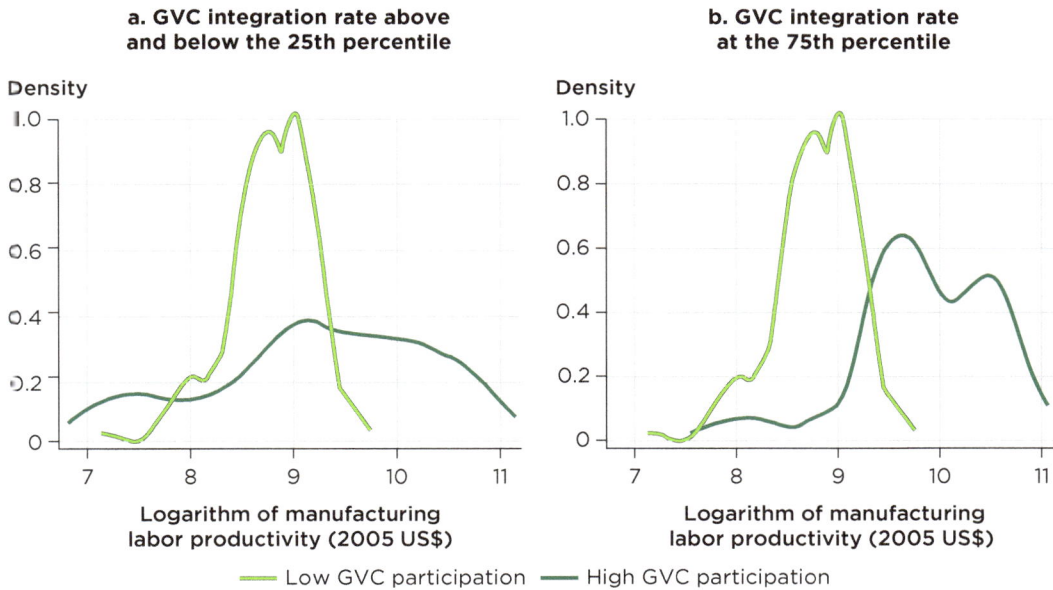

Low GVC participation — High GVC participation

Sources: Based on Casella et al. 2019 and the Groningen Growth and Development Centre expanded Africa Sector Database, https://www.rug.nl/ggdc/structuralchange/previous-sector-database/africa-sector-database?lang=en.

Note: In panel a, high GVC participation comprises linkage rates above the 25th percentile, and low GVC participation comprises linkage rates equal to and below that threshold. Panel b compares productivity at linkage rates at the 75th percentile and above (high GVC participation) with those at the 25th percentile and below (low GVC participation). GVC = global value chain.

Countries with relatively low levels of labor productivity have stronger productivity gains. Being further from the productivity frontier, Sub-Saharan African countries can potentially make significant gains in productivity growth by integrating into GVCs. For the least productive countries, the estimated impact of increasing the GVC participation rate from the 25th to the 75th percentile is an increase in labor productivity growth of 2.6 percentage points. Moreover, GVC participation is generally positively associated with employment growth, albeit with differences across industries in terms of the strength of this relationship: the estimated correlation coefficients range from 0.23 in the apparel and textile industry to as high as 0.59 in the transportation equipment and wood and paper industries (Abreha et al. 2021). This positive relationship occurs mostly through backward links, suggesting that access to more variety and higher-quality inputs promotes upgrading that leads to the expansion of the production scale and subsequent creation of more and better jobs. Forward integration also creates jobs, but they are likely to be lower paid and with limited opportunity for upgrading.

Countries in Sub-Saharan Africa still have viable options for job growth by integrating into manufacturing GVCs to offset the decline in labor requirements in GVC production. The end markets for manufacturing value added in GVCs vary widely across countries.

A feature common to all countries in the region, however, is the growing importance of the European Union and home markets—the domestic economy—as end markets for manufacturing value added in GVCs. In 2014, 12.9 percent of Ethiopia's manufacturing value added in GVCs ended up in the European Union market, 4.2 percent in the US market, 4.7 percent in the Chinese market, and 59.3 percent in domestic demand. Kenya and Senegal depend significantly on domestic final demand, which accounted for 78.2 percent and 66.7 percent of their value added in GVCs, respectively. Although the domestic market share is relatively small, manufacturing value added in GVCs is still important in South Africa. Of the country's value added in GVCs, 47.2 percent ends up in domestic demand and 13.0 percent goes to the European Union (figure 6.11). Thus, enhancing job creation by increasing the share of manufacturing value added in GVCs requires expanding external market access and leveraging home markets. In this strategy, entering and improving the region's shares in fast-growing end markets such as China, the European Union, and North America are as important as leveraging domestic demand.

FIGURE 6.11 End markets for manufacturing GVC value added, Sub-Saharan Africa and benchmark countries, 2014

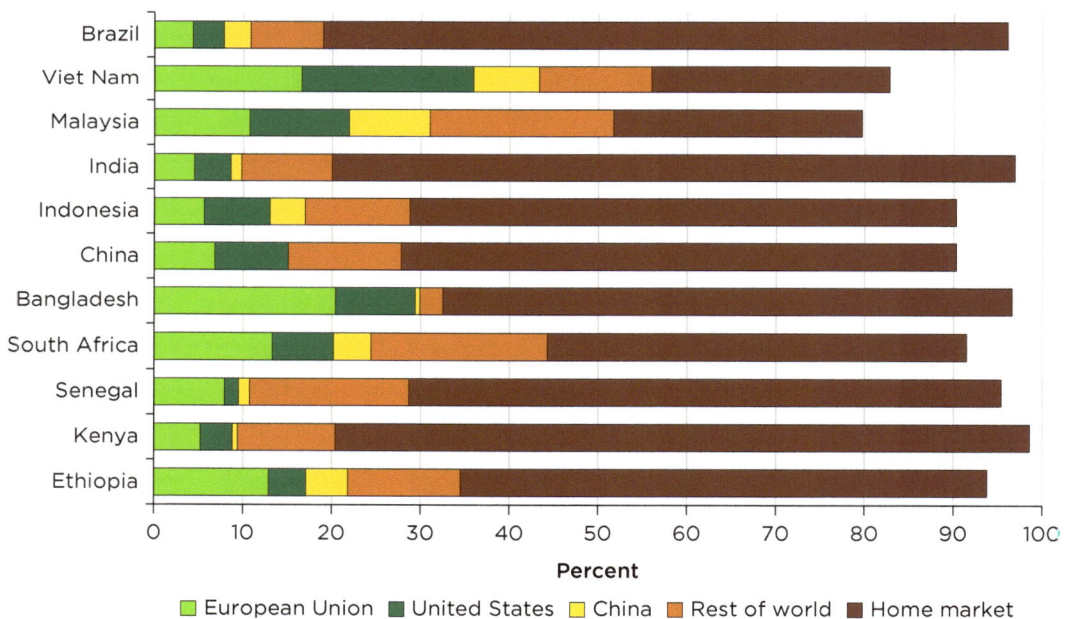

Legend: ■ European Union ■ United States ☐ China ■ Rest of world ■ Home market

X-axis: Percent (0 to 100)

Countries (top to bottom): Brazil, Viet Nam, Malaysia, India, Indonesia, China, Bangladesh, South Africa, Senegal, Kenya, Ethiopia

Source: Based on Pahl et al. 2019.
Note: "European Union" is the 28 member countries of the European Union as of 2014, plus Switzerland; United States includes the United States and Canada. The figure does not include the shares to East Asia (Japan, the Republic of Korea, and Taiwan, China) and Other emerging (Brazil, India, Indonesia, Mexico, the Russian Federation, and Türkiye), but those shares are included in the original estimation so that bars add up to 100, except for rounding. GVC = global value chain.

Manufacturing, job creation, and economic transformation

Strong productivity growth has not always accompanied the reallocation of resources from agriculture to industry, mainly manufacturing, highlighting the unsuccessful structural change in many Sub-Saharan African countries. Studies show that rapid urbanization and growth in the services economy have contributed to low and declining productivity growth (McMillan and Rodrik 2011), despite the reallocation of workers to market service activities (de Vries, Timmer, and de Vries 2013) and the lack of labor reallocation to high-productivity sectors in West Africa (Haile 2018). Recent growth accelerations in Sub-Saharan Africa are characterized by increasing productivity in agriculture, a declining share of the labor force employed in agriculture, and declining productivity in modern sectors such as manufacturing (Diao et al. 2021). These trends are also exacerbated by the pervasiveness of informality in the region (Abreha et al. 2022). In this respect, the manufacturing sector has not absorbed the large labor force released from agriculture, and has therefore played a limited role in reducing or reversing resource movement from agriculture to the informal, low-productivity services sector.

The rapid expansion of the manufacturing workforce in a few Sub-Saharan African countries has occurred at about the same time that they have experienced productivity growth. Cheap labor in the region has spurred substantial job growth, especially among new and young firms;[5] however, signs of high or rising labor costs in Sub-Saharan African countries underscore the crucial role of manufacturing productivity growth. The advantage that the manufacturing sector in these economies has had by hiring additional workers at roughly constant wage rates has been eroding, for example, the dynamics of wages in Ethiopian manufacturing. Some evidence also shows that labor costs in Sub-Saharan Africa are already high compared with countries in Asia (Gelb et al. 2020). Thus, boosting productivity growth is key to promoting job creation and manufacturing development. The productivity gains can be achieved through product and process innovations, technology adoption, and better management practices and organizational structure. Simultaneously, better resources and market relocation toward more productive firms will raise productivity. The latter channel possesses a large potential given the considerable cross-sector and inter- and intraindustry misallocation due to market distortions.[6] Addressing these misallocations has the potential to raise productivity and propel job creation.[7]

Looking ahead

Despite a narrow industrial base and slow industrialization in Sub-Saharan African countries, these countries have scope for large-scale industrialization through the implementation of industrial policy tools. Failure has often characterized the efforts of developing economies before their successful industrialization. These failures underscore the new set of challenges that countries in the region need to overcome.

In this respect, it is necessary to be cautious not to interpret these industrialization failures as dead ends. Several factors, such as resource endowments, shape the prospects for industrialization, and prospects depend critically on the capacity to exploit existing comparative advantages while developing capabilities to compete in high-skill and knowledge-intensive industries. Industrial policy should target building those capabilities while accounting for country-specific characteristics and emerging megatrends such as digitalization, emerging GVCs, and rapid population growth. It should also adopt strategies that strengthen regional integration, promote economic diversification, and facilitate the adoption of digital technologies in manufacturing, all of which will enable the industrial sector to be more resilient against major shocks such as a pandemic, conflicts, and geopolitical tensions.

Analysis

As the region seeks to accelerate its industrial development, it faces both challenges and opportunities: the dynamics of global trade and the integration of African economies into international trade and GVCs; technological advancements, particularly in digitalization; and the growing and youthful population.

Trade and GVCs

Sub-Saharan African countries must strengthen intraregional trade with concerted efforts to harmonize trade-related regulations and customs controls, reduce tariff and nontariff barriers, and improve infrastructures and connectivity to lower logistics costs. Strengthening regional integration between African countries is critical to scale up supply capacity, build regional value chains, and succeed in global markets. Countries can do so by taking more concrete steps to realize the African Continental Free Trade Area (AfCFTA). The establishment of AfCFTA presents opportunities to boost intra-African trade, reinforce the complementarities of production and exports, and create employment while mitigating the risks of global shocks. The success of AfCFTA requires greater regional integration, which entails improving physical integration, such as cross-border energy and transportation infrastructure; institutional cooperation, such as harmonizing customs, regulations, procedures, and business registration systems; and digital integration, such as harmonizing digital financial systems, laws for digital activities, and shared regulatory technology such as identity verification.

An encouraging example of interconnectivity comes from Angola, where the government projects that by 2025 it will have made progress on achieving cost-reflective tariffs that will reduce the energy sector's reliance on subsidies and encourage outside investment in the sector. In addition, although currently a nonoperating member of the Southern African Power Pool, Angola has plans to connect to the pool through Namibia, with joint construction of the Baynes Hydroelectric Power Station, as well as connecting to the north with the Democratic Republic of Congo through the Grand Inga Dam project.

This regional cooperation in power projects could substantially reduce costs, increase cross-border energy trading, and mitigate energy supply risks. Another example is Kenya's new Standard Gauge Railway from Mombasa to Nairobi in 2013, with an expected extension to Uganda, Rwanda, and the Democratic Republic of Congo. Kenya has also broken ground on construction of a new port at Lamu to serve the northern parts of the country, South Sudan, and Ethiopian outlets to the sea.

In general, small pockets of intensive intraregional integration exist throughout the continent where countries tend to trade significant shares of their GDP with neighbors; such pockets can provide a substantial source of spillovers at the subregional level. For instance, West African states such as Burkina Faso, Ghana, and Mali are large destination markets for exports worth more than 1 percent of GDP for some of their trading partners. Trade is significantly concentrated within subregions in Sub-Saharan Africa, but very little trade takes place between the subregions.

These patterns of integration reflect not only geographic proximity catalyzed by subregional trade agreements and lower nontariff barriers within subregions but also infrastructure and connectivity constraints between regions. The missing trade between these subregions therefore holds the greatest potential for further integration, and the AfCFTA agreement signed by countries from across the continent could play a major role in achieving it. Given that lower tariff rates are positively associated with GVC participation, and that lower tariffs on imports of capital goods are even more conducive to value chain participation (Abudu and Nguimkeu 2019; Slany 2019), a successful regional integration would imply reducing tariffs among member countries across the region and covering policy areas such as trade facilitation measures that cut red tape and simplify customs procedures.

Notwithstanding Sub-Saharan Africa's relatively minor role in global trade, a notable trend is the increasing relocation of labor- and resource-intensive tasks from advanced and emerging economies to the region. This phenomenon is fostering employment opportunities and facilitating knowledge transfer within Africa. It is a strategic choice for firms to relocate segments of their production value chains to countries where labor costs are lower or other competitive cost advantages exist. Light manufacturing, particularly the labor-intensive production of textiles and apparel, serves as a prime exemplar of industries in which African countries possess a natural comparative advantage and are poised to benefit from these shifts in GVCs. Although Africa's share of the volume of trade in manufactures remains marginal, it is important to recognize that participation rates across manufacturing GVCs exhibit significant heterogeneity among countries within the region. This variation is attributable to a confluence of factors, including but not limited to resource endowments and other country-specific characteristics that play a pivotal role in determining participation and upgrading within GVCs.

Some Sub-Saharan African countries have already attracted the attention of giant firms from industrialized countries, gaining footholds in oil refining, garments and textiles, agriculture processing, automobiles, and pharmaceuticals. For instance, under its TRANSFORM 2025+ brand strategy, the German automobile manufacturer Volkswagen has been building assembly plants in Ghana and Nigeria and developing skills in Ethiopia's labor force. It has also been developing vehicle assembly operations in Kenya and Rwanda, and looking at new upcoming markets (Koigi 2019). The US world energy leader General Electric, which has operated in Nigeria for four decades, plans to invest an additional US$1 billion to further strengthen its manufacturing and product services—power generation and oil and gas exploration and production—as well as to source local supplies and provide employee training in the surrounding communities. This investment is expected to create more than 2,300 manufacturing jobs in the local economy.[8] European multinational clothing companies—including Ireland's Primark, Sweden's H&M, and the United Kingdom's Tesco—already source much of their garment materials from countries such as Ethiopia (Juárez 2020). Even luxury producers such as New York's Beyond Good chocolate have recently expanded their workforce in Madagascar, thus acknowledging opportunities for small-scale production in Africa.

GVCs can create an avenue through which African countries can industrialize and generate employment and productivity growth. Participation in GVCs may allow suppliers in African countries to meet standards and regulations that allow access to rich country markets; it may permit exports and imports under privileged tariff treatment for intrafirm trade; or it may facilitate the use of network technology that would not otherwise be available (Newfarmer, Page, and Tarp 2019). Trade policy could therefore play an essential role in driving participation in manufacturing GVCs by enhancing preferential access to the export markets of developed economies, mainly Asia, the European Union, and the United States.

Access to these markets would have implications for manufacturing GVC participation, particularly in livestock exports, textiles, and apparel exports, in addition to the potential in processing of agricultural products and natural resources before export. For example, Kenya's flower industry has emerged as one of the largest in the world: the country is now a lead exporter of cut rose flowers to the European Union, with a market share of about 38 percent. About 65 percent of Kenya's exported flowers are sold in international markets through Dutch auctions to France, Germany, Japan, the Russian Federation, the United Kingdom, and the United States. The flower sector provides direct employment opportunities to about half a million people, mostly women, and indirectly supports more than 5 million livelihoods in Kenya. The global cut flower market, valued at US$36.4 billion in 2022, is projected to reach US$45.5 billion by 2027.[9] The bulk of cut flower processing occurs in Kenya, and smallholder farmers in the flower industry tend to profit more than those in the tea and coffee sectors. Kenya's cut-flower industry maintains this competitive momentum thanks to the adoption of efficient production methods (the country's heavy investments in greenhouses, machinery, and irrigation systems), cold storage facilities, and self-regulation with production standards benchmarked to international best practices.

Another example is the high productivity from transhumant livestock rearing in the Sahel region, which, according to Inter-réseaux (2015), is higher than ranching productivity in the United States. This finding highlights a high and still underexploited potential for the animal production and livestock processing industry. A country such as Côte d'Ivoire can emerge as the regional hub for livestock processing and exports in the Sahel. Doing so would, however, require more public investment in processing and packaging infrastructure and policies to stimulate regional trade in animal products. Moreover, to build a successful value chain for livestock processing, Côte d'Ivoire would need to coordinate with neighboring countries such as Burkina Faso and Mali, the main exporters of live cattle to Côte d'Ivoire, to set uniform health and safety standards across the value chain.

With low-cost labor, Sub-Saharan African countries can attract and retain GVC-related jobs, but these jobs should not come at the expense of fair trade, fair wages, and a better work environment. An important consequence of GVC-dominated trade is that, in a world in which production is allocated to the location with the lowest cost, countries that try to industrialize through import-substitution policies behind high tariff walls are unlikely ever to reduce their costs sufficiently to be competitive on global markets. The rise of GVCs has contributed to a reduction in the role of manufacturing, and the "smile curve" across production stages has substantially deepened over time (Baldwin 2016).

Equally important is the quality of jobs that would be created by strengthening GVC links. A GVC will make limited contributions to job creation and growth if the country cannot capture a significant share of the value added created in the chain. Fortunately, some African countries are making substantial efforts to ensure that more value added created in the chains accrues to their countries. In Botswana and Zambia, governments took steps to ensure that working conditions, royalties, and taxes from the diamond and copper mining industries, respectively, significantly contribute to their respective domestic economies in revenues and quality of jobs. With the discovery of large gas reserves in Mozambique, the government looked at ways of retaining some of the benefits within the country, and similar initiatives are apparent in the oil value chain in Equatorial Guinea and Gabon. However, the weak link of Sub-Saharan African countries to high-value-added activities in manufacturing GVCs is partly due to a less skilled labor force. Cognitive and noncognitive skills—including management and communication skills, information and communication technology (ICT) skills, and readiness to learn and think creatively—have been identified as critical factors in a country's capacity to thrive in GVCs (Grundke et al. 2017). Therefore, effective engagement in GVCs and upgrading within GVCs would require policy makers to align their industrial and trade policies with education policies and programs, and with training and reskilling programs to reinforce and build their workers' skills.

Trade policy shocks, emerging geopolitical trends in advanced economies, and the COVID-19 pandemic have raised concerns and uncertainty about the future of international trade and prompted a rethinking of GVCs, especially in manufacturing. Such shocks, occurring mainly since mid-2018, have affected Sub-Saharan African countries, with export growth declining across all subregions and country groups, both resource-rich and non-resource-rich. That decline resulted especially because of large contractions in major African economies driven by their reliance on export commodities with prices that have crashed in recent years. Although Africa's exports remain highly concentrated in resource-intensive products, such as petroleum, minerals, metals, and primary goods, a few countries, notably Kenya, Tanzania, and Uganda, have done relatively well in diversifying their export portfolios (Usman and Landry 2021).

By adopting de-risking strategies, African countries can build more sustainable economies that are resilient in the face of global shocks. Policy options include the following:

- *Further diversifying and strengthening strategic sectors such as food and health.* Africa is uniquely positioned to further leverage its rich agricultural resources by improving infrastructure and efficiency and agroprocessing capacity.

- *Improving coordination and collaboration between countries on surveillance and epidemic intelligence.* Enormous benefits can be gained from better sharing of data related to health risks, vulnerabilities, and outcomes. Data sharing can facilitate timely response, robust research, and, overall, better-informed policy outcomes. It implies creating channels of coordination for countries to learn from each other to produce regional models and share national insights. The case of the Ebola epidemic in West Africa, which was beaten by the Nigerian government, confirms that stopping a global health shock requires resilient health systems with trained personnel and, more important, risk information and risk communication systems, logistics and supply chain structures, financing mechanisms, and solid health governance as seen in Nigeria.

- *Strengthening digital infrastructure and adopting more digital technologies for manufacturing productions.* Sectors with a high level of digitalization have proven to be more resilient to global shocks. Greater digitalization implies strengthening the education system, especially the training and learning related to digital skills.

Technical challenges and digitalization

Digitalization will give a more prominent role to the intangible segments of the manufacturing process in Sub-Saharan Africa, providing new opportunities for industrialization. Benefits of digital technologies—complementary benefits, efficiency gains, and innovation gains—may improve the growth of the industrial sector. Intangible segments of the manufacturing process include design and research and development, marketing, logistics, and distribution, segments traditionally consigned to developed countries (World Bank 2017). Digitalization will affect these patterns of industrialization by allowing market-related data to reduce the costs of product innovation and design, thus driving an overall shift in emphasis from mass production to greater customization. Organizations such as a South African original equipment manufacturer have already moved from mass production to mass customization. Digital manufacturing provides on-demand parts to companies, creating agile product development at those companies and enabling them to offer much more personalized choices to their customers.

Digitalization provides new opportunities for industrialization if Sub-Saharan African countries can leverage data on market demand for design and production decisions—including, for instance, adopting new manufacturing technologies such as computer-aided design and manufacture, and giving intangibles (such as research and development, design, market research and branding, blueprints, software, and databases) a more prominent role along value chains. An example of digital innovation powering Africa's manufacturing sector is Nigeria's long-haul e-logistics platform Kobo360, a solution that connects manufacturers and cargo owners with truck operators, to move their goods seamlessly across the continent using an Uber-like app.[10] The company uses data analytics and artificial intelligence to reduce inefficiencies in last-mile delivery, provide transparency and visibility, reduce communication gaps within the entire ecosystem, optimize pick-ups and deliveries, and improve routes in real time. Kobo360 is already functioning in Nigeria and Togo and is expanding in several other African countries including Benin, Burkina Faso, Côte d'Ivoire, Ghana, Kenya, and Uganda.

Digital technologies could also promote high-tech start-up firms by providing platforms for small-scale manufacturers to deploy advanced technologies such as additive manufacturing (three-dimensional printing) and robotics. Advances in these areas could create new opportunities for manufacturing growth in Africa and leapfrog traditional industries. The technology could possibly make manufacturing easier and more accessible to the many artisans, small businesses, and informal entrepreneurs that form the core of most African economies. Increasing uptake of this technology, together with other robotics to transform the region's manufacturing sector, will require investments in producing tech entrepreneurs and in the continentwide rollout of the Internet of Things.

Examples of leapfrogging are growing in African countries, including Kenya's leap from landline telephones to mobile phones, increasing access to millions without the need for government investment in the expensive traditional landline infrastructure. The Third Eye project in Mozambique has used low-cost drones to help small-scale farmers improve crop production by 41 percent and reduce water use by 9 percent. In Rwanda, the government has partnered with a robotics company, Zipline, to address maternal mortality by using drones to deliver blood to medical facilities, overcoming the absence of road infrastructure and reducing the time to procure blood from 4 hours to 15 minutes (UNCTAD 2018). In addition to supporting the birth and growth of emerging entrepreneurs, promoting innovation in small-scale manufacturing is necessary for industrial upgrading, even in traditional labor-intensive sectors. The recent rise in the number of tech start-ups and tech hubs, and growth in the tech ecosystem, increasing by 41 percent between 2016 and 2018, reflects efforts already made in this direction. The volume of funding raised by tech start-ups across the continent has also soared, with tech start-ups attracting about US$334.5 million in investment in 2018 (GSMA 2018).

Despite the potential for leapfrogging associated with rapid digitalization and automation, there are growing concerns about deindustrialization in the region, partly driven by technological advancements in manufacturing. It is therefore critical to stress that leapfrogging from low-productivity primary sector activities to higher-value-added services should not be perceived as an outright dismissal of the key role that the industrial sector should play in the development process of African economies. Industrialization in Africa should be a pillar from the inception to the end of the structural transformation process, because it will help gradually shift production factors to more productive uses while increasing knowledge and skills and creating stable good-paying jobs.

To harness digitalization for industrialization, Sub-Saharan African countries should address key challenges, namely limited digitalization and its lower productivity impact. Leveraging the benefits of digitalization to achieve industrial development depends on the extent of digitalization in the region and countries' capabilities to boost productivity and competitiveness. To solve the challenges of low digitalization (the digital divide) and the low impact of digitalization on manufacturing labor productivity, African countries need to invest in internet connectivity and digital skills. Africa suffers from the digital divide because of the limited expansion of ICT, which attenuates the associated gains in productivity, jobs, and competitiveness, and therefore restricts widespread adoption of ICT in manufacturing.

Good examples already exist of African firms investing in technology, such as Funkidz in Kenya, and A to Z Textile Mills Ltd in Tanzania. Other examples from Kenya include the energy sector—which was the first to launch pay-as-you-go services—and the National Energy Strategy—which has, over the past decade, also used least-cost geospatial electrification planning to plan for energy access and the diffusion of solar power across the country. Promoting greater investment in technology would involve creating an ecosystem for boosting digital manufacturing; targeted skills development, with a focus on science, technology, engineering, and mathematics (STEM), and technical and vocational education and training; effective public-private partnerships in digital development and educational curricula; and technology and innovation hubs (such as the iHub in Kenya and the Kumasi Hive in Ghana) that are well embedded in the domestic economy.

Besides the necessary digital infrastructure, increasing the use of digital technologies requires complementary investments in physical infrastructure, for example electricity and transportation and logistics, and supporting institutional infrastructure such as regulations. Unfortunately, many countries still face issues related to the quality of mobile connections and telecommunications infrastructure as well as the risks of a worsened broadband internet access divide between urban and rural areas, primary and secondary cities, and within cities. Manyika et al. (2013) evaluated the ICT readiness of countries according to their national ICT strategy, business environment, infrastructure, financial capital, and ICT skills base. They show that most countries in the region are not ready to exploit the opportunities offered by the internet. The challenge is even more pronounced when considering the ICT skills base. Thus, African countries should invest not only in building and expanding digital infrastructure but also in developing complementary digital skills. That is, they need to build capacity and business ecosystems to absorb and use technology and improve skills through dynamic education policy and training programs, particularly in STEM, and technical and technical and vocational education and training. Such improvements also imply the need to enforce targeted reforms in ICT sector regulation that would enable firm and industry capabilities to facilitate adoption of digital technologies, providing incentives for digital entrepreneurship and promoting the widespread adoption of digital technologies in public services. Other dimensions of basic supporting institutional infrastructure should also be developed in many Sub-Saharan African countries.

Rapid growth of the labor force

The region's youth population and high prevalence of unemployment, underemployment, and informal employment, especially in urban areas, may constitute the much-needed labor supply for industrial development. Sub-Saharan Africa has the fastest-growing population and the youngest population in the world; more than 70 percent of the region's population is below age 30, with the region's youth population projected to represent 42 percent of the global population below age 30 by 2030, and to double by 2050. This youth population is largely unemployed or working in low-productivity sectors such as agriculture and informal household enterprises.

Labor-intensive manufacturing production could play a role in job growth, income expansion, and industrial intensification. A larger share of the labor force in the manufacturing sector in African countries is employed in less knowledge-intensive industries, with notable growth in employment shares in these industries. In Côte d'Ivoire, the four least knowledge-intensive industries (food and beverages, textiles and apparel, wood and paper, and metal products) together absorbed 83.8 percent of the formal manufacturing labor force. The four industries absorbed 88.0 percent of manufacturing workers in Malawi, 81.1 percent in Cameroon, 80.6 percent in Kenya, 78.6 percent in Ghana, 65.9 percent in Senegal, 56.5 percent in South Africa, and 49.9 percent in Ethiopia (Abreha et al. 2021). Thus, although population growth may lead to an increased demand for food, it may help the manufacturing sector to adopt increasing returns to scale technology. Whether an improvement of agricultural technology or an increase of population is beneficial to the manufacturing sector depends on the elasticity of demand for agricultural goods. Achieving industrialization requires both a sufficiently large market size from the demand side and a sufficiently large supply of technologies from the supply side.

Unlike other regions, which benefited from the demographic dividend by combining a rapid demographic transition with export-oriented policies that increased the demand for labor (Canning, Raja, and Yazbeck 2015), Sub-Saharan Africa has yet to fully realize its demographic potential. Rapid population growth, combined with extremely low productivity in traditional sectors, has led to a wave of urbanization at unprecedentedly low levels of average per capita income. In addition, if the size of a youth cohort affects its educational attainment—for example, a larger youth cohort receives fewer resources and schooling—this poorer accumulation of human capital may adversely affect its productivity when the cohort enters the labor force. Furthermore, an increase in the aggregate size of the labor force can reduce the amount of available land and capital stock per worker, thereby lowering productivity. In the long run, more investment can correct the shortage of capital, although this is not the case with land. The best possible outcomes will therefore result from economic policies that expand the demand for labor coupled with policies that support a healthy, skilled workforce that can attract investments that create jobs.

Although Africa's demographic growth can help to deliver more and higher-quality workers, the continent will achieve full economic benefits only with a strong demand for labor that also ensures productive employment for the workforce. This means attracting investments in both traditional and knowledge-intensive manufacturing industries. Some encouraging signs include a rise in FDI in recent years that compensates to some extent for weak domestic savings. Not all FDI is the same, however, in creating jobs. Some FDI may support the growth of extractive industries in ways that do not absorb the increase in labor supply. Thus, policies to attract FDI should be properly targeted to encourage investments that create high-productivity jobs that absorb the youth bulge. Trade policy could also play an essential role.

Policies

If Africa is set to trace the growth and industrialization path initially taken by the United Kingdom, followed by Japan and the United States and, more recently, many East Asia and Pacific economies, it will need to adapt lessons from the past to the changing nature of international production systems (GVCs), international trade, climate change, and other emerging challenges. Although the broad principles guiding policy toward industrialization are rather similar, successful policy frameworks are predominantly country specific. Considering the heterogeneity in resource endowment size, stage of development, and drivers of growth in Sub-Saharan African countries, no one-size-fits-all policy framework exists but some common requirements do.

They include institutional innovations in policy making and implementation, state building, high levels of investment, capability building to raise productivity in selected industries, and continuous learning by doing. They also require a strong state capacity to implement policies and marshal required resources, and policy independence to embark on new and risky endeavors with sufficient room to experiment and fail. Success requires strong synergies across multiple sets of policies in building skills, promoting market contestability, easing labor market rigidity, improving trade facilitation, developing physical infrastructure, pursuing special industries, providing easy access to credit, and ensuring sufficient policy space to experiment on policies on a large scale.

As mentioned earlier in this chapter, industrialization requires proactive prioritization and coordination of policies that address the microeconomic factors that determine the competitiveness of firms and industries and the macroeconomic and institutional qualities that enable structural transformation. Three dimensions are critical for the success of industrialization drives in the region:

1. Economywide policy actions that create a business environment that maintains macroeconomic stability, fosters investment, and boosts productivity

2. Industry-specific policy actions that exploit existing comparative advantages and create new ones

3. Policies to build firm and industry capabilities.

Policies for the first dimension are broad and aimed at supporting the growth and productivity of all sectors of the economy; they are not exclusive to manufacturing. These policies largely reflect a commitment to build competitiveness across the entire spectrum of the economy, reinforcing the learning capacity of private and public enterprises; facilitate the birth and growth of firms; and address economywide inefficiencies and misallocation that restrict firm growth and entry and exit necessary to raise aggregate productivity. Political stability, peace, and a well-functioning legal and contractual enforcement mechanism are essential aspects of this overall policy environment. The second dimension includes industry-specific policies that focus on priority areas for sustained and strong industrial development. They often involve lots of experimenting and learning while building specific industrial capabilities. Policies for the third dimension emphasize firm and industry capabilities that are central not only to the emergence and development of industries but also to maintaining long-term competitiveness.

Creating an environment that fosters competition, investment, and productivity

Creating a favorable business environment requires compatible, complementary, and credible policy actions in different areas of the economy. Evidence shows that Sub-Saharan African firms bear prohibitive costs because of poor infrastructure, low levels of skills and regulatory burdens, and poorly functioning institutions. In a survey of 40 Sub-Saharan African countries between 2006 and 2019, the biggest obstacles firms face in running their operations are poor access to finance, poor access to electricity, lack of skills, political instability, tax administration, and corruption (World Bank 2020). Results vary across countries in the region: for some, access to finance is the most critical challenge; for others, corruption in getting permits and taxes is a serious obstacle. Policy in this respect needs to identify the key constraints firms face in their operations from entry and registration, getting construction permits, access to electricity, access to credit, protecting property, enforcing contracts, and trading across borders. Limited resources and capacity make it infeasible to address these economywide and often pervasive challenges, and to invest in the required infrastructure in the short- and medium-term.

Because they are restricted to a more attainable geographic boundary and limited industrial priorities, special economic zones (SEZs) can effectively address the complex policy, regulatory, and infrastructure challenges. SEZs have been found effective in promoting industrialization, boosting exports, attracting FDI, facilitating transfer of technology, and serving as experimental labs to test out new and innovative policies. SEZs exist in many countries in East Asia and Pacific and in Sub-Saharan Africa, including in Ethiopia, Kenya, Mauritius, and Rwanda. One of the key lessons from decades of SEZ development, particularly in export processing zones, is that zones cannot and should not be viewed as a substitute for a country's larger trade and investment reform efforts. They are, however, an important instrument in the national economic and industrial development agenda aimed at industrialization, through the provision of incentives, streamlined procedures, and custom-built infrastructure. Box 6.1 highlights good practice for SEZs.

BOX 6.1
Good practice for special economic zones

To act as a catalyst for structural transformation, special economic zones (SEZs) need to be linked to key elements of infrastructure (like ports, railways, and highways) with good trade logistics and customs services; match well to local resources that leverage the nation's or province's comparative advantages, such as agroprocessing or textiles; form part of the global value chain; focus not only on exports but also on the domestic market; and have an effective system to run the operations and management of SEZs. In more detail, good practice for SEZs includes the following:

- *Effective legal, regulatory, commercial, professional, logistics (such as warehousing, transshipment) and other integrated government services.* Competent bureaucracies are a scarce resource in most developing countries, but most countries do have (or can build) pockets of bureaucratic competence (Rodrik 2004). These services are key not only for the success of industrialization but also as a key source of employment and income.

(continued)

- *Effective delivery of integrated government and business services and infrastructure.* Cumbersome procedures and controls, inadequate administrative structures or too many bodies involved in administration, and weak coordination between private developers and governments in infrastructure provision and management often cause SEZs to fail. Many of the early failures in Africa—including in Côte d'Ivoire, the Democratic Republic of Congo, Liberia, Namibia, and Senegal—are associated with excessive bureaucracy involving multiple institutions, especially customs; long delays in obtaining permits; elevated costs of operations (energy, water, communications); and rigid and constraining labor regulations. SEZs in other African countries such as Kenya, Madagascar, and Mauritius registered relative success with integrated government and business services and infrastructures.

- *Strategic location (in relation to other industries, access to ports, or related infrastructure) and the development and management of day-to-day operations.* Key reasons for failure have been poor site locations and poor SEZ design, entailing heavy capital expenditures with weak links to the rest of the economy. There is a risk that SEZ firms are generally import-dependent enclaves that take part in segmented, global production chains, frequently exporting under outward processing relief types of mechanisms. In Viet Nam, for example, many zones sat vacant because local and national authorities could not provide road or other infrastructure connections to the site. Maximizing the benefits of SEZs depends on the extent to which they are integrated with their host economies. Zones that operate as enclaves suppress the static and dynamic economic impacts of zone development; however, those impacts are multiplied when SEZs are accompanied by countrywide economic policy and structural reforms that enhance the competitiveness of domestic enterprises and facilitate the development of backward and forward linkages.

- *Alignment with overall national development strategy and robust support and commitment from the highest levels of political leadership.* A range of countries including China, Ireland, the Republic of Korea, and Malaysia used zones to facilitate a broader export orientation, build firm and industry capability in technology transfers, and improve the overall business environment by extending best-practice policy. When integrated in a broader national strategy, zones often garnered strong political support, which contributed to their success.

- *Specialized facilities that cater to the unique needs of targeted industries.* Such specialization allows for streamlined services relevant to a particular industry. A focus on a few priority industries contributes to success.

Sources: Adapted from Akinci and Crittle 2008; Rodrik 2004; Zeng 2016.

In addition, because of the difficulty of building economywide reforms and the required investments, countries need to build an ecosystem of government agencies, trade associations, and industrial ecosystems that simplify business processes, logistics, and other services within and outside SEZs; that coordinate private-public exchanges; and that serve as watchdogs against capture and rent-seeking. To build an industrial ecosystem that supports industrialization, the Ethiopian government set up new agencies and revitalized old ones to provide more effective state support to priority industries. The agencies include the Ethiopian Investment Commission, the Industrial Parks Development Corporation, the Ethiopian Industrial Inputs Development Enterprise, the Ethiopian Textile Industry Development Institute, and the Leather Industry Development Institute. Some were set up solely to support selected industries such as leather and textile.

Furthermore, the state's policy process is at least as important as the policies and the agencies themselves. The role of policy is integral to facilitating private sector development given that Sub-Saharan African countries are latecomers to industrialization and have poorly developed markets. There are apparent risks that policies will add distortions or perpetuate rent-seeking behaviors rather than fixing them. The state policy process needs to craft and implement policies efficiently and effectively, including setting clear and robust frameworks to identify where, when, and how to undertake policy actions (Rodrik 2004). When it comes to industrial policy, Rodrik (2004) notes that detailing the *process* is more important than detailing the *outcome*. The process should be devoid of self-imposed constraints regarding predefined roles for the state and the private sector; rather, the process should emphasize continuous experimentation, risk-taking, and local learning. It should also include clear benchmarks for success and failure to avoid entrenched failures (Rodrik 2004). The risk of capture and misappropriation of such preferences, including access to credit, land, markets, and fiscal incentives, could be higher without these benchmarks.

Industry-specific policies, building along global value chains

Sub-Saharan African countries need to focus on strategic industries that promote their respective competitiveness in the global economy. Industrializing along GVCs— whereby countries would initially pursue the development of industries and sectors with existing comparative advantages, and slowly transition and evolve into related but more complex industries, thus pursuing dynamic comparative advantage—should be at the core of industrial policy packages. One defining experience of the now high-income economies, old and new, is the continuous pursuit of upgrading to high-value and more complex production activities. GVCs have created opportunities for countries to kick-start industrialization by initially specializing in lower-value- added tasks in which countries have a comparative advantage, while actively investing in activities that culminate in building a comparative advantage in higher- value-added tasks. Given that many African countries already have higher GVC participation, policies need to refocus investments on building up along existing value chain links while raising productivity. Figure 6.12 highlights a few of the industrial policy frameworks and policy entry points that promote integration into regional and global value chains, reduce market distortions, and advance industrial upgrading along GVCs.

FIGURE 6.12 Industrial policy framework: Integrate, compete, upgrade, and build capabilities

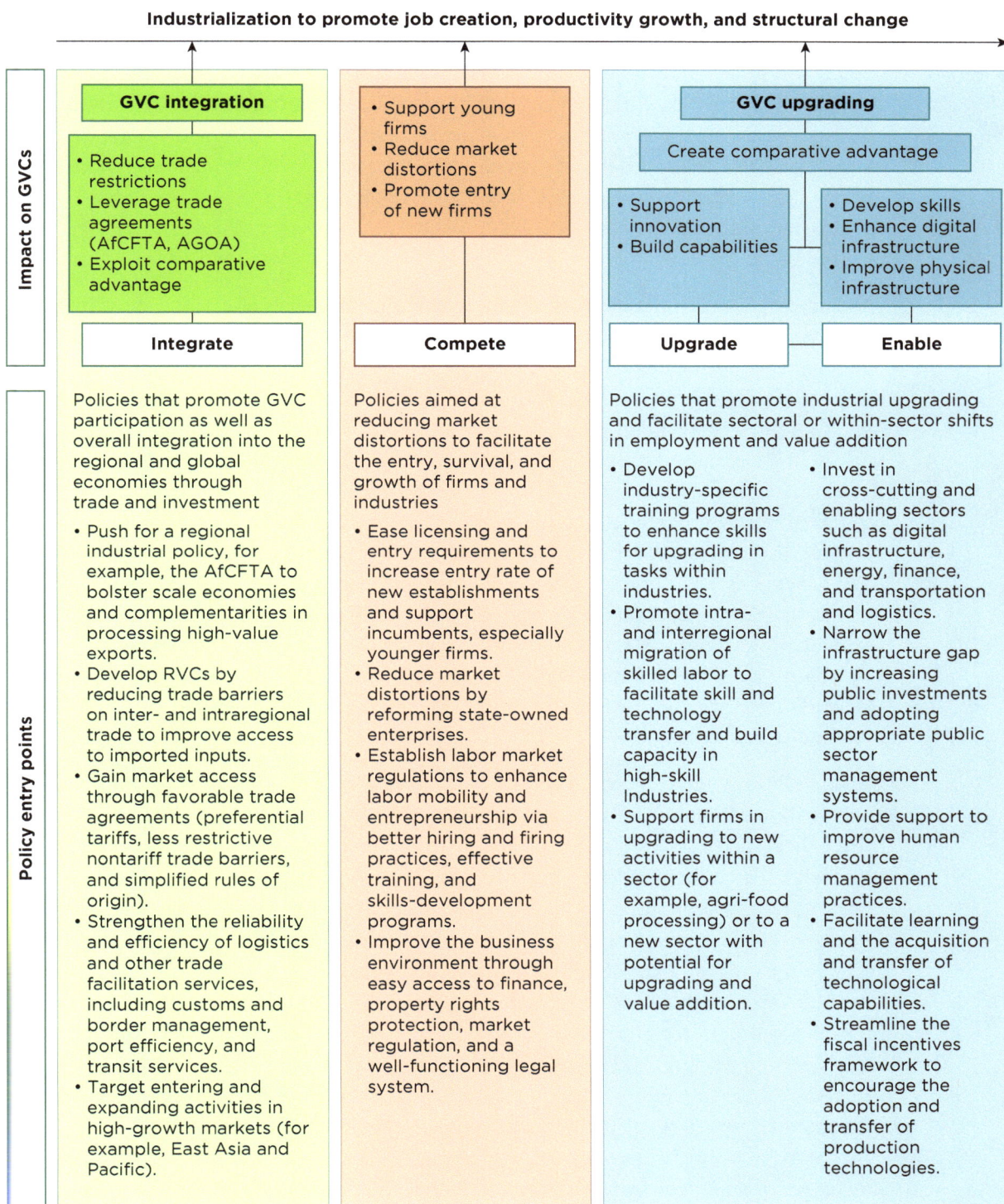

Industrialization to promote job creation, productivity growth, and structural change

Impact on GVCs

GVC integration

- Reduce trade restrictions
- Leverage trade agreements (AfCFTA, AGOA)
- Exploit comparative advantage

Integrate

- Support young firms
- Reduce market distortions
- Promote entry of new firms

Compete

GVC upgrading

Create comparative advantage

- Support innovation
- Build capabilities

- Develop skills
- Enhance digital infrastructure
- Improve physical infrastructure

Upgrade | **Enable**

Policy entry points

Policies that promote GVC participation as well as overall integration into the regional and global economies through trade and investment

- Push for a regional industrial policy, for example, the AfCFTA to bolster scale economies and complementarities in processing high-value exports.
- Develop RVCs by reducing trade barriers on inter- and intraregional trade to improve access to imported inputs.
- Gain market access through favorable trade agreements (preferential tariffs, less restrictive nontariff trade barriers, and simplified rules of origin).
- Strengthen the reliability and efficiency of logistics and other trade facilitation services, including customs and border management, port efficiency, and transit services.
- Target entering and expanding activities in high-growth markets (for example, East Asia and Pacific).

Policies aimed at reducing market distortions to facilitate the entry, survival, and growth of firms and industries

- Ease licensing and entry requirements to increase entry rate of new establishments and support incumbents, especially younger firms.
- Reduce market distortions by reforming state-owned enterprises.
- Establish labor market regulations to enhance labor mobility and entrepreneurship via better hiring and firing practices, effective training, and skills-development programs.
- Improve the business environment through easy access to finance, property rights protection, market regulation, and a well-functioning legal system.

Policies that promote industrial upgrading and facilitate sectoral or within-sector shifts in employment and value addition

- Develop industry-specific training programs to enhance skills for upgrading in tasks within industries.
- Promote intra- and interregional migration of skilled labor to facilitate skill and technology transfer and build capacity in high-skill Industries.
- Support firms in upgrading to new activities within a sector (for example, agri-food processing) or to a new sector with potential for upgrading and value addition.

- Invest in cross-cutting and enabling sectors such as digital infrastructure, energy, finance, and transportation and logistics.
- Narrow the infrastructure gap by increasing public investments and adopting appropriate public sector management systems.
- Provide support to improve human resource management practices.
- Facilitate learning and the acquisition and transfer of technological capabilities.
- Streamline the fiscal incentives framework to encourage the adoption and transfer of production technologies.

Source: Adapted from Abreha et al. 2021.
Note: AfCFTA = African Continental Free Trade Area; AGOA = African Growth and Opportunity Act; GVC = global value chain; RVC = regional value chain.

In many Sub-Saharan African countries, building up along existing value chain links means attracting large-scale investments in labor- and resource-intensive manufacturing. Continuous learning and industrial upgrading are essential so that production processes evolve along with changing comparative advantage. In this regard, the state's role can take different forms, including providing conditional incentives, addressing coordination failures, improving the working of market institutions, strengthening relevant skills, and providing complementary inputs such as finance and other services geared to the specific industry. The details of these policies depend on the relative endowment of labor, skills, and natural resources, and the priority industries.

Industrialization requires significant investment in resources and policy coordination with these efforts geared to specific industries. The key driver of industrialization is private investment, but success requires complementary investments to improve business services, infrastructure, skills, and institutional capabilities. There is also a need to build strategic complementarity between private and public investments, which can be achieved only through deliberate policy coordination. Experiences from the East Asia and Pacific region show that extensive investments in infrastructure, human capital, and institution building are essential. Financing and capacity constraints, however, make it unreasonable to expect countries to do it all. There is a need for concerted efforts in selective investments to support the development of high-growth industries that align with the comparative advantage of economies in the region. China and Viet Nam are examples of countries where broad reforms in governance and human capital were behind each country's manufacturing prowess (McMillan, Rodrik, and Verduzco-Gallo 2014) because they prioritized selected manufacturing industries.

These policies should focus on selected industries based on forward-looking comparative advantage and, at the same time, invest in the fundamental infrastructure required to attract investment and promote trade in these priority industries. Since the late 1990s and early 2000s, Ethiopia has been one of the fastest-growing economies in the world, in part because of the country's Industrial Development Strategy that identified priority sectors: textile and garment, leather and leather products, other agroprocessing industries, construction (cement), and later the flower industry. The strategy supported these industries with extensive incentive schemes for capacity building, infrastructure investments (including logistics), and preferential access to credit, land, and other programs. It gave preference to exporting firms and industries with one exception: the cement industry, an import-substituting industry, was considered central to the construction sector because of its strategic importance to economic activity. The flower, textile, and cement industries registered remarkable growth. The leather industry had limited success, but the lessons from the experience influenced subsequent iterations of the industry and further refined its links to the rich endowment of livestock with export demands.

These policies need to have an outward orientation, in terms of both integration to GVCs and expansion of production for exports because they promote productivity growth, job creation, and income gains, and facilitate technology transfer. Although an outward orientation facilitated technology transfer from advanced economies, large markets that absorbed the increasing production of manufacturing goods allowed for reduced costs and improved competitiveness from economies of scale. Efforts to support selective comparative advantage–based export promotion through providing attractive incentive schemes, improving trade logistics, providing information about external markets, and pursuing trade agreements are essential for success. Other complementary policies including exchange rate policies, investing in industrial clusters and export processing zones, and reducing trade costs both behind borders and at the border are essential. Box 6.2 elaborates on outward orientation and trade policy frameworks to support industrialization.

BOX 6.2

Outward orientation: Export promotion and lessons from Asia

Reducing antiexport bias of trade policies. Trade policies that provide preferential access to credit, foreign exchange, land, and infrastructure to import substituting firms may introduce an antiexport bias. Such bias has often restricted the entry of new and potentially more efficient firms, and has harbored inefficiency in large state-owned and state-affiliated enterprises. Lack of a clear path to exporting could restrict productivity and the emergence and growth of potentially more productive firms that would then export and contribute further to promoting aggregate productivity. Import substitution strategies may backfire by restricting imports of key intermediate inputs essential for exports. Although politically appealing, these policies often result in large domestic firms with limited prospects to improve productivity and that often shelter inefficiency. Policies need to make the jump to introduce conditional requirements for these firms to transition to exporting through a mix of trade, export promotion, creating and developing links with multinationals, and other targeted policies. Reducing the antiexport bias incorporates policies that would bias support to firms that export or are more likely to export rather than to firms producing exclusively for the domestic market.

Enforcing export discipline. Investments or policies to support selected firms and industries should be geared to firms that export, but with strict discipline. This support should be accompanied by the threat of withdrawal if a firm fails to export in the allotted time. Economies such as Japan, the Republic of Korea, and Taiwan, China, adopted strict measures to reward exporters with cheap credit, technology acquisition, support in trade facilitation, and, in some cases, protections from import competition; and they withdrew support from firms that failed to export in the given time frame.

Building a system of firm and industry capabilities

Industrialization is primarily a process of capacity building in firms and industries. Although fundamental factors such as infrastructure, human capital savings, and investment are essential for industrialization success, they are less likely to succeed if not accompanied by the development of very specific firm and industry capabilities, including, for example, capabilities to acquire, adopt, and diffuse production technologies. Latecomer firms, like latecomer countries, should accelerate the adoption of production technologies and invest in uptake and capability-building efforts in technology adoption and product upgrading. In many African countries, firms build technological capabilities through learning focused on acquiring, adapting, and modifying imported technologies, rather than through novel innovations at the technology frontier. Industrialization relies on the transfer of new technologies, in most cases, imported from abroad. Effective transfer of technologies and learning depends on an effectively functioning and strategic interaction with FDI or, in some cases, joint ventures with local firms. Thus, policy instruments that govern this transfer of technologies from FDI, associated licensing requirements, technical requirements to absorb and implement such technologies, and capacity in relevant skills and machinery should form part of the industrial policy architecture.

Much of the poor technology capability emerges from a simplistic view of technology as either hardware or software that could be imported and plugged in. Technology transfer, however, requires a complex and multidimensional system with an intricate network of institutions, skills, permitting markets, factories, deliberate measures that link FDI inflows with technology transfer agreements, and academic and research and development institutions. Building technological capabilities starts with the accumulation of basic production and management capabilities, followed by the replication of more sophisticated innovations, and finally, generation of new products, processes, and inventions. Looking at figure 6.13, many firms and industries in Sub-Saharan Africa would be in Stage 1, where the priorities are investing in building managerial and organizational capabilities and developing industry-relevant STEM skills and basic infrastructure that eases restrictions on physical, human, and knowledge capital accumulation.

Governments should adopt a hierarchy of policies at the national, industry, and firm levels because these policies are not only simple aggregations at each level; rather, they require a distinct approach to building technological capabilities at each stage. It is imperative to leverage links between the private sector and universities and research institutes to develop specific types of skills and human capital relevant to priority industries. In economies that industrialized—such as Germany; Hong Kong SAR, China; Singapore, and Taiwan, China—universities were considered bedrocks of skills formation and centers of advanced training institutions linked to the industrial strategies of each economy. This link also required investing in targeted skill-building programs to address the human capital needs of emerging industries. Chile's success as the second-largest producer of salmon is mainly due to the government's active engagement in disseminating new salmon farming technology, because technological adaptation was central in scaling up the quasi-artisan salmon production system and the selective skill development programs in the salmon industry (box 6.3).

FIGURE 6.13 **Prioritization of policies along the capabilities escalator**

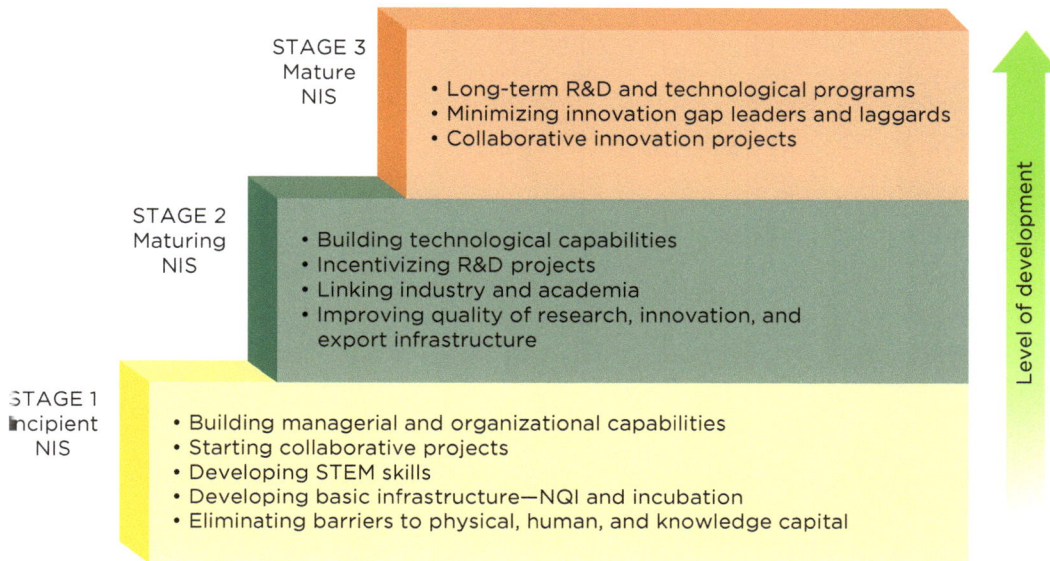

STAGE 3
Mature
NIS
- Long-term R&D and technological programs
- Minimizing innovation gap leaders and laggards
- Collaborative innovation projects

STAGE 2
Maturing
NIS
- Building technological capabilities
- Incentivizing R&D projects
- Linking industry and academia
- Improving quality of research, innovation, and export infrastructure

STAGE 1
Incipient
NIS
- Building managerial and organizational capabilities
- Starting collaborative projects
- Developing STEM skills
- Developing basic infrastructure—NQI and incubation
- Eliminating barriers to physical, human, and knowledge capital

Level of development

Source: Cirera and Maloney 2017.
Note: NIS = National Innovation System; NQI = national quality infrastructure; R&D = research and development; STEM = science, technology, engineering, and mathematics.

BOX 6.3

Case study from Chile: Acquiring, adapting, and disseminating technologies in the salmon industry

The remarkable success of the salmon industry in Chile provides a unique model for the institutions and mechanisms adopted to acquire and diffuse technologies across a range of large and small salmon producers. Such a collective learning process would not have been possible without a set of networks and links among key local authorities, domestic firms, and foreign partners that facilitated the process of acquiring, adapting, and disseminating new technologies. Although the technical requirements imposed by salmon production forced the industry to generate the necessary human capacities and networks needed to manage a complex system, the existence of local support institutions that work closely with industry and universities played a major role. Most of the technology developed involved these three core players that form part of Chile's national innovation system.

(continued)

Case study from Chile: Acquiring, adapting, and disseminating technologies in the salmon industry *(continued)*

The country set up several agencies to focus on acquiring, experimenting with, and diffusing technologies, including Fundación Chile, Secretaría Regional de Planificación y Coordinación, and CORFO. Fundación Chile contributed to the development and consolidation of aquaculture by continuously searching for appropriate foreign technologies and new fish-farming opportunities and providing technical assistance to local producers. It supported the specialization in American training centers of Chilean professionals in the various aquaculture and, through a producers' association (SalmonChile), enabled producers to gain access to international markets, establishing production and product standards for Chilean salmon and developing the "quality seal" that is now adopted by its members as a tool to promote salmon exports.

The Instituto Tecnológico del Salmón provides training in quality control and issues certificates on waste treatment practices of firms in the industry: members of SalmonChile are required to comply with standards. SalmonChile helps firms in the industry to upgrade their production, processing, and waste management standards, among others, so they may obtain certification from the Instituto Tecnológico del Salmón. These efforts played an important role in ensuring that the industry met international standards and developed in a sustainable manner.

Initially, success of the salmon industry relied on natural resource endowment, cheap labor, and import and adaptation of foreign technology. In order to achieve sustained exports and increase the value added of exports, however, Chile needed to develop technological capabilities to absorb, adapt, and master the transferred technologies and develop even more advanced technologies. To maintain and reinforce this competitive advantage, Chile further fine-tuned its production to reduce costs, invested in marketing and design, and introduced other measures to improve the regulatory environment and facilitated networks between international leaders, producers' associations, technology development institutions, and industry.

Source: Adapted from UNCTAD 2006.

Notes

1. The World Bank's World Development Indicators database does not separately report manufacturing employment shares. For the purposes of comparison, the analysis uses the Groningen Growth and Development Centre/United Nations University World Institute for Development Economics Research Economic Transformation Database. The database covers a sample of economies: Asia (Bangladesh; Cambodia; China; Hong Kong SAR, China; India; Indonesia; Israel; Japan; Republic of Korea; the Lao People's Democratic Republic; Malaysia; Myanmar; Nepal; Pakistan; the Philippines; Singapore; Sri Lanka; Thailand; Türkiye; and Viet Nam); Latin America (Argentina, Bolivia, Brazil, Chile, Colombia, Costa Rica, Ecuador, Mexico, and Peru); North Africa (the Arab Republic of Egypt, Morocco, and Tunisia); and Sub-Saharan Africa (Botswana, Burkina Faso, Cameroon, Ethiopia, Ghana, Kenya, Lesotho, Malawi, Mauritius, Mozambique, Namibia, Nigeria, Rwanda, Senegal, South Africa, Tanzania, Uganda, and Zambia).

2. Based on data from the Economic Transformation Database, which provides manufacturing value added and employment for a sample of Sub-Saharan African countries, significant differences also occur across the countries in the sample. In 2018, manufacturing value added shares were 17.3 percent (Senegal), 16.0 percent (Lesotho), 15.1 percent (Cameroon), 6.5 percent (Zambia), 6.3 percent (Rwanda), and 5.7 percent (Botswana). Correspondingly, the manufacturing employment shares were 15.9 percent (Mauritius), 15.8 percent (Ghana), 14.3 percent (Kenya), 13.1 percent (Lesotho), 3.6 percent (Botswana), 3.2 percent (Tanzania), and 2.0 percent (Mozambique).

3. The sample of landlocked countries includes Botswana, Burkina Faso, Ethiopia, Lesotho, Malawi, Rwanda, Uganda, and Zambia.

4. In Ethiopia, for example, the textile and leather industry has been on the priority list for government policy support since 2003, but it has not performed to expectation until recently. Building industrial parks that meet international standards has enabled Ethiopia to attract significant FDI, generating foreign earnings and creating jobs, particularly for female workers in apparel and textile industries (Gebreeyesus 2016; Oqubay and Kefale 2020; Zeng 2020).

5. For instance, in formal manufacturing sectors of Côte d'Ivoire and Ethiopia, there were 24,000 and 128,000 new jobs during the 2003–14 and 1996–2016 periods, respectively. These employment opportunities occurred mainly because of new establishments (Abreha et al. 2019).

6. Atkin and Khandelwal (2019) distinguish between market-level distortions and firm and sectoral distortions. The former affect all firms in operation and encompass factors in the input markets, domestic market frictions, and information and knowledge asymmetries. The latter refer to factors that led to distortions, affecting firms and sectors to varying extents.

7. A Ugandan study highlights the misallocation issues in Sub-Saharan African manufacturing (Dennis et al. 2016). Between 2002 and 2009, Ugandan firms experienced a 13 percent annual growth in labor productivity thanks to enhanced technical efficiency within firms and the movement of labor and capital across industries. About 20 percent of the growth resulted from the shift of labor to more productive sectors. Additionally, reallocating labor across firms explained 55 percent to 90 percent of industry-level growth (Dennis et al. 2016).

8. EPICOS, "GE International Operations (Nig.) Limited," https://www.epicos.com/company/13710 /ge-international-operations-nig-limited.

9. Markets and Markets, "Cut Flowers Market," https://www.marketsandmarkets.com/Market -Reports/cut-flowers-market-18187231.html.

10. For more information on the platform, refer to Kobo's website, https://www.kobo360.com.

References

Abreha, K., X. Cirera, E. Davies, R. Fattal-Jaef, and H. Maemir. 2022. "Deconstructing the Missing Middle: Informality and Growth of Firms in Sub-Saharan Africa." Policy Research Working Paper 10233, World Bank, Washington, DC.

Abreha, K., P. Jones, E. Lartey, T. Mengistae, and A. Zeufack. 2019. "Manufacturing Job Growth in Africa: What Is Driving It? The Cases of Côte d'Ivoire and Ethiopia." World Bank, Washington, DC.

Abreha, K., W. Kassa, E. Lartey, T. Mengistae, S. Owusu, and A. Zeufack. 2021. *Industrialization in Sub-Saharan Africa: Seizing Opportunities in Global Value Chains*. Africa Development Forum. Washington, DC: World Bank.

Abudu, D., and P. Nguimkeu. 2019. *Public Policy and Country Integration to Manufacturing Global Value Chains: The Roles of Trade, Labor Market Regulation and Tax Incentives*. Washington, DC: World Bank.

Akinci, G., and J. Crittle. 2008. "Special Economic Zones: Performance, Lessons Learned, and Implications for Zone Development." Foreign Investment Advisory Services (FIAS) Occasional Paper, World Bank, Washington, DC.

Atkin, D., and A. Khandelwal. 2019. "How Distortions Alter the Impacts of International Trade in Developing Countries." NBER Working Paper 26230, National Bureau of Economic Research, Cambridge, MA.

Baldwin, R. 2016. "The World Trade Organization and the Future of Multilateralism." *Journal of Economic Perspectives* 30: 95–116.

Canning, D., S. Raja, and A. S. Yazbeck, eds. 2015. *Africa's Demographic Transition: Dividend or Disaster?* Africa Development Forum Series. Washington, DC: World Bank.

Casella, B., R. Bolwijn, D. Moran, and K. Kanemoto. 2019. "Improving the Analysis of Global Value Chains: The UNCTAD-Eora Database." *Transnational Corporations* 26 (3): 115–42.

Cirera, X., and W. F. Maloney. 2017. *The Innovation Paradox: Developing-Country Capabilities and the Unrealized Promise of Technological Catch-Up.* Washington, DC: World Bank.

Coulibaly, S., W. Kassa, A. G. Zeufack, and A. Mattoo. 2022. *Africa in the New Trade Environment: Market Access in Troubled Times.* Washington, DC: World Bank.

De Vries, G., M. Timmer, and K. de Vries. 2013. "Structural Transformation in Africa: Static Gains, Dynamic Losses." *Journal of Development Studies* 51 (6): 674–88.

Dennis, A. C. K., T. A. Mengistae, Y. Yoshino, and A. G. Zeufack. 2016. "Sources of Productivity Growth in Uganda: The Role of Interindustry and Intra-Industry Misallocation in the 2000s." Policy Research Working Paper 7909, World Bank, Washington, DC.

Diao, X., M. Ellis, M. Margaret, and D. Rodrik. 2021. "Africa's Manufacturing Puzzle: Evidence from Tanzanian and Ethiopian Firms." NBER Working Paper 28344, National Bureau of Economic Research, Cambridge, MA.

Gebreeyesus, M. 2016. "Industrial Policy and Development in Ethiopia." In *Manufacturing Transformation: Comparative Studies of Industrial Development in Africa and Emerging Asia*, edited by Carol Newman, John Page, John Rand, Abebe Shimeles, Måns Söderbom, and Finn Tarp, 27–49. Oxford, UK: Oxford University Press.

Gelb, A., V. Ramachandran, C. J. Meyer, D. Wadhwa, and K. Navis. 2020. "Can Sub-Saharan Africa Be a Manufacturing Destination? Labor Costs, Price Levels, and the Role of Industrial Policy." *Journal of Industry, Competition and Trade* 20: 333–57.

Grundke, R., S. Jamet, M. Kalamova, F. Keslair, and M. Squicciarini. 2017. "Skills and Global Value Chains: A Characterisation." OECD Science, Technology and Industry Working Papers 2017/05, OECD Publishing, Paris.

GSMA. 2018. *Connected Society: State of Mobile Internet Connectivity.* London: GSM Association.

Haile, F. 2018. "Structural Change in West Africa: A Tale of Gain and Loss." Policy Research Working Paper 8336, World Bank, Washington, DC.

Inter-réseaux. 2015. "Pastoral Livestock Farming in Sahel and West Africa: 5 Preconceptions Put to the Test." Brochure, Inter-réseaux, Nogent-sur-Marne, France. https://www.inter-reseaux.org /wp-content/uploads/int-17-broch-pastoralismeuk-bd.pdf.

Juárez, C. 2020. "Ethiopa, the Next Front of Sourcing in the Light of the Coronavirus Crisis. *MDS*, March 9, 2020. https://www.themds.com/companies/ethiopia-the-next-front-of-sourcing-in-the -light-of-the-coronavirus-crisis.html.

Loigi, B. 2019. "Volkswagen Signs Agreement with Ethiopia to Develop Auto Industry in the Country." *Africa Business Communities*, January 29, 2019. https://africabusinesscommunities.com/news /volkswagen-signs-agreement-with-ethiopia-government-to-develop-automotive-industry-in-the -country/.

Kruse, H., E. Mensah, K. Sen, and G. de Vries. 2023. "A Manufacturing (Re)Naissance? Industrialization in the Developing World." *IMF Economic Review* 71: 439–73.

Manyika, J., M. Chui, J. Bughin, R. Dobbs, P. Bisson, and A. Marrs. 2013. "Disruptive Technologies: Advances that Will Transform Life, Business, and the Global Economy." McKinsey Global Institute.

McMillan, M., and D. Rodrik. 2011. "Globalization, Structural Change, and Economic Growth." In *Making Globalization Socially Sustainable*, edited by M. Bachetta and M. Jansen, 49–84. Geneva: International Labor Organization and World Trade Organization.

McMillan, M., D. Rodrik, and I. Verduzco-Gallo. 2014. "Globalization, Structural Change, and Productivity Growth, with an Update on Africa." *World Development* 63: 11–32.

Newfarmer, R., J. Page, and F. Tarp, eds. 2019. *Industries without Smokestacks: Industrialization in Africa Reconsidered*. WIDER Studies in Development Economics. Oxford, UK: Oxford University Press.

Nguimkeu, P., and A. G. Zeufack. 2019. "Manufacturing in Structural Change in Africa." Policy Research Working Paper 8992, World Bank, Washington, DC.

Oqubay, A., and D. Kefale. 2020. "A Strategic Approach to Industrial Hubs: Learnings in Ethiopia." In *The Oxford Handbook of Industrial Hubs and Economic Development*, edited by A. Oqubay and J. Lin, 876–913. Oxford, UK: Oxford University Press.

Pahl, S., and M. P. Timmer. 2020. "Do Global Value Chains Enhance Economic Upgrading? A Long View." *Journal of Development Studies* 56 (9): 1683–705.

Pahl, S., M. P. Timmer, R. Gouma, and P. J. Woltjer. 2019. "Jobs in Global Value Chains: New Evidence for Four African Countries in International Perspective." Policy Research Working Paper 8953, World Bank, Washington, DC.

Rodrik, D. 2004. "Industrial Policy for the Twenty-First Century." HKS Working Paper RWP04-047, Harvard Kennedy School, Cambridge, MA.

Slany, A. 2019. "The Role of Trade Policies in Building Regional Value Chains: Some Preliminary Evidence from Africa." *South African Journal of Economics* 87 (3): 326–53.

Te Velde, D., N. Balchin, K. Banga, and S. Hoque. 2018. "Manufacturing in Africa: Factors for Success." Paper prepared for the Second African Transformation Forum, Accra, Ghana (ATF2018).

UNCTAD (United Nations Trade and Development). 2006. *A Case Study of the Salmon Industry in Chile*. Geneva: United Nations.

UNCTAD (United Nations Trade and Development). 2018. "Leapfrogging: Look before You Leap." UNCTAD Policy Brief No 17, United Nations, Geneva.

UNCTAD (United Nations Trade and Development). 2019. *World Investment Report 2019: Special Economic Zones*. UNCTAD/WIR/2019. Geneva: United Nations.

UNCTAD (United Nations Trade and Development). 2021. *Handbook on Special Economic Zones in Africa: Towards Economic Diversification across the Continent*. Geneva: United Nations.

Usman, Z., and D. Landry. 2021. "Economic Diversification in Africa: How and Why It Matters." Carnegie Endowment for International Peace Working Paper, Carnegie Endowment for International Peace, Washington, DC.

World Bank. 2017 *Building Tomorrow's Africa Today: West Africa Digital Entrepreneurship Program.* An Initiative of the Digital Economy for Africa (DE4A). Washington, DC: World Bank.

World Bank. 2020. *World Development Report 2020: Trading for Development in the Age of Global Value Chains.* Washington, DC: World Bank.

Zeng, D. Z. 2016. "Special Economic Zones: Lessons from the Global Experience." PEDL Synthesis Paper Series 1, Private Enterprise Development in Low Income Countries, Centre for Economic Policy Research, Commonwealth and Development Office, UK.

Zeng, D. Z. 2020. "Special Economic Zones in Sub-Saharan Africa: What Drives Their Mixed Performance?" In *The Oxford Handbook of Industrial Hubs and Economic Development*, edited by A. Oqubay and J. Lin, 1008–23. Oxford, UK: Oxford University Press.

CHAPTER 7

Human Capital

Montserrat Pallares-Miralles, Yevgeniya Savchenko, and Anita Schwarz

Summary

Africa is projected to host almost 40 percent of the world's workforce by 2100, with approximately 2 million Africans joining the labor force each month. One of the main obstacles for Africa to unlock its full potential is the low level of skills relevant for the labor markets of the 21st century, which makes investment in human capital the top priority for Africa to claim the 21st century. The continent should take a holistic life-cycle approach to forming human capital to ensure that African youth build relevant skills for 21st-century labor markets and for job creation.

Since the beginning of the century, Africa has made significant progress in improving human capital outcomes along multiple dimensions:

- *Health*. Africa has reduced under-five child mortality by 22 percent, increased immunization by 21 percentage points, and reduced stunting by 27 percent.

- *Education*. The out-of-school population at the primary education level has decreased by more than 50 percent, with gender parity virtually achieved; and the continent has seen a more than 25 percent reduction at the lower-secondary level. Enrollment at the tertiary level has doubled.

- *Social protection*. Approximately 22 countries have developed social registries to support the most vulnerable populations; none of these programs existed before 2000.

Despite significant progress, however, the continent faces many challenges to ensure a skilled labor force to claim the 21st century. For example, a child born in Africa in 2020 will achieve, on average, only 40 percent of their potential human capital, clearly not sufficient to take advantage of the increasingly urgent need for skilled labor. More than 30 percent of children are malnourished, and 536 mothers die for every 100,000 live births. An astonishing 86 percent of 10-year-olds cannot read or understand a simple paragraph. Only about 42 percent of girls are enrolled in secondary schools. The skills

---

This chapter includes contributions by Emir Sfaxi, Venkatesh Sundararaman, and Quentin Wodon.

that youth are getting are not relevant for the labor markets, creating a shortage of skilled labor, especially in the fields of science, technology, engineering, and mathematics (STEM) and in sectors requiring digital skills.

Ensuring that Africa takes advantage of the demographic transition in the era of polycrisis will require getting all children off to the right start with access to quality education, strengthening the skills development system for building market-relevant 21st-century skills for employment and job creation, and strengthening skills development in governance and financing by partnering with the private sector.

Context

Unlike other parts of the world, Africa has a vast and growing population. Currently home to 14 percent of the world's working-age population, by 2100, Africa is projected to have 39 percent, representing more than a third of the workforce of the entire world (figure 7.1). This growth is a double-edged sword: If the continent can develop a skilled labor force, it will not only have higher growth but also become a driver of world growth. If it cannot, a growing population of unemployed people living in chronic poverty will likely exacerbate fragility in the region, limiting the amount of growth that can take place. Given the critical role that developing a skilled labor force plays in Africa's ability to claim the 21st century, this chapter focuses on the foundations necessary to build the human capital needed for a skilled labor force, the progress made thus far despite some brief backtracking during COVID-19, and what needs to be done to make rapid progress.

FIGURE 7.1 **Percentage of the world's working-age population, Africa versus rest of world, 2022 and 2100**

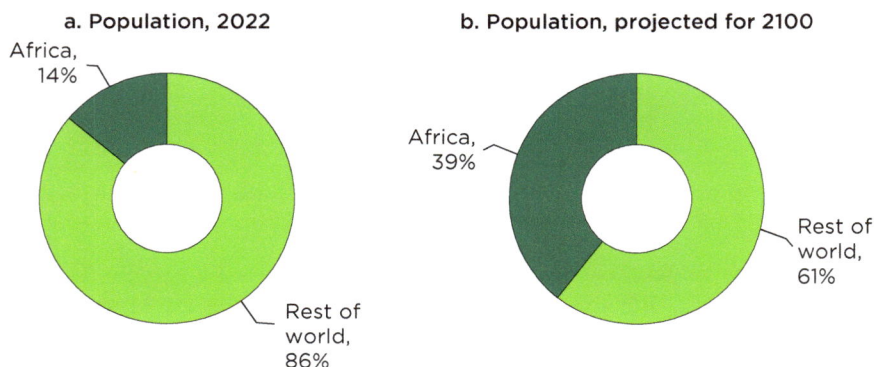

Source: Based on 2022 data from the United Nations Department of Economic and Social Affairs, World Population Prospects.
Note: In the figure, Africa includes the entire continent.

Going forward, general world population growth is expected to mirror growth in the working-age population, such that Africa, which now represents 15 percent of the world's entire population, will by 2100 represent 38 percent. Although Africa is somewhat poorer than the rest of the world, its consumption will clearly rise as a share of world consumption compared with current levels. Not only will industry potentially move to Africa to take advantage of the abundant labor resources but local industry and services will also need to respond to a greater number of consumers in the African market by locating close to final consumers and reflecting their preferences—but only if the appropriately skilled labor force exists.

Skilled African migrants could contribute labor that service industries around the world require. With remittances, these migrants could ensure that the next generation can receive the schooling and skills it needs, or could even help with reskilling existing workers to become more productive. More migration will likely take place within Africa as well, with workers from middle-income countries migrating to higher-income countries, and potentially replaced by workers from rural areas of middle- and lower-income countries. Whereas industrialization in Africa will depend on the level of skills, meeting infrastructure challenges, and stability, the migration potential will depend almost exclusively on the development of a skilled labor force. Clearly, a skilled labor force would provide many growth opportunities locally and globally, and the lack of one will severely limit those opportunities.

Facts

In order for Africa to skill its labor force, it will need various policies, programs, and measures for building and protecting human capital across the life cycle. Despite progress in building human capital since 2000, many African countries still have a long way to go as evidenced by the Human Capital Index (HCI), which looks at the human capital accumulation in each country based on health and education outcomes. Each person in Africa currently achieves only 40 percent of their potential human capital, on average, clearly not sufficient to take advantage of the increasingly urgent needs for skilled labor.[1]

Figure 7.2 shows the HCI for many countries in Africa in 2020. At the low end of the spectrum, a child born in the Central African Republic just before the COVID-19 pandemic will be 29 percent as productive upon reaching adulthood as a child who benefited from complete access to education and health services. This score is lower than the average for the Sub-Saharan Africa region (40 percent) and low relative to other low-income countries (38 percent). At the other end, a child born in the Seychelles just before the COVID-19 pandemic will be 63 percent as productive in adulthood as a child with complete access to education and health services. Although higher than the average for the Sub-Saharan Africa region, the Seychelles' score is still lower than the average for high-income countries (71 percent). A significant number of countries in Africa are characterized by fragility, conflict, and violence, which makes advances in the HCI particularly challenging.[2]

FIGURE 7.2 Human Capital Index, 2020

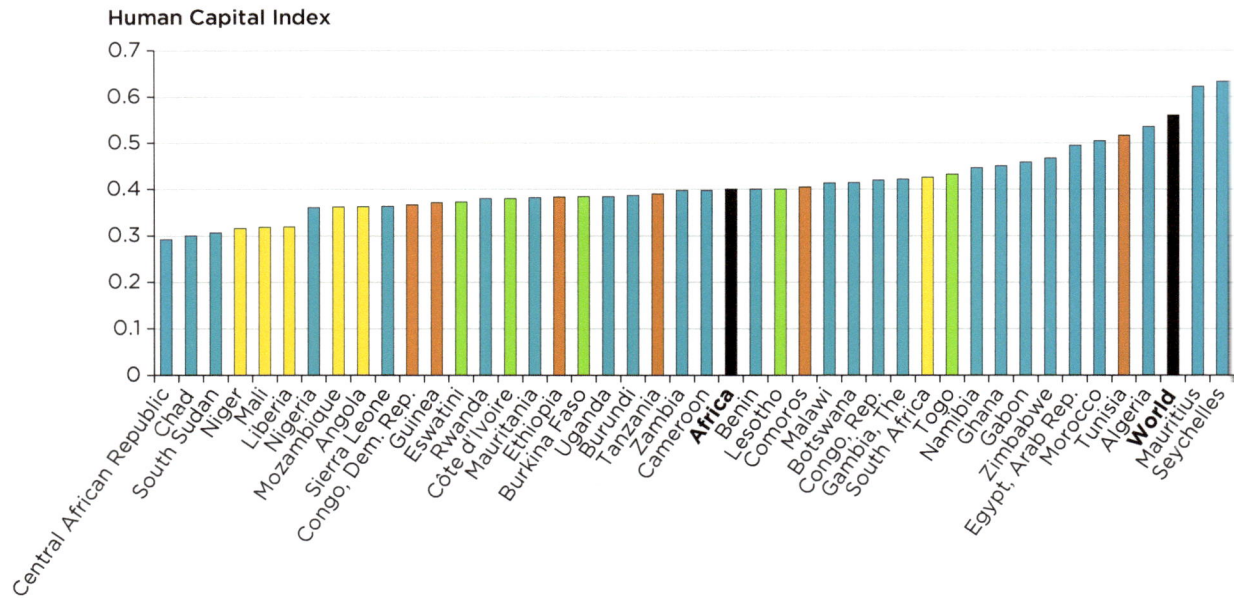

Human Capital Index

Source: World Bank, World Development Indicators, https://data.worldbank.org/indicator/.
Note: Black bars show averages for Africa and the world, green bars show countries where the Human Capital Index (HCI) has rapidly increased when compared with other countries during the last 10 years, orange bars show countries where the HCI has decreased, yellow bars show countries where the HCI increased very slowly, and blue bars indicate that previous data were not available to determine the growth experienced by the country over the period.

At the Africa Heads of State Human Capital Summit, held in Tanzania in July 2023, 43 heads of state signed the Dar es Salaam Declaration and recognized "…that priorities on investing in and protecting human capital will be critical to rebuilding a high-productivity, inclusive, and more resilient economy."[3] Figure 7.3 presents a simple framework that describes human capital accumulation across the life cycle and around which this chapter is organized.

Getting children off to the right start. Children must arrive at school age ready to learn. Components in this part of the life cycle include addressing childhood diseases through increased immunization and parental education. Reducing maternal mortality rates[4] will not only result in healthier children at birth but also ensure that mothers are there to provide nutrition and promote early childhood development. Malnutrition in young children, frequently attributable to household poverty, adversely affects brain development, limiting the capacity to learn and be productive throughout life. It also increases mortality directly and indirectly by making children more vulnerable to disease. Preventing malnutrition of children through parental education and cash transfers to poor families with young children can help address some of the nutrition issues. Preprimary programs can also promote readiness for learning.

FIGURE 7.3 Life cycle of accumulating human capital and building skills

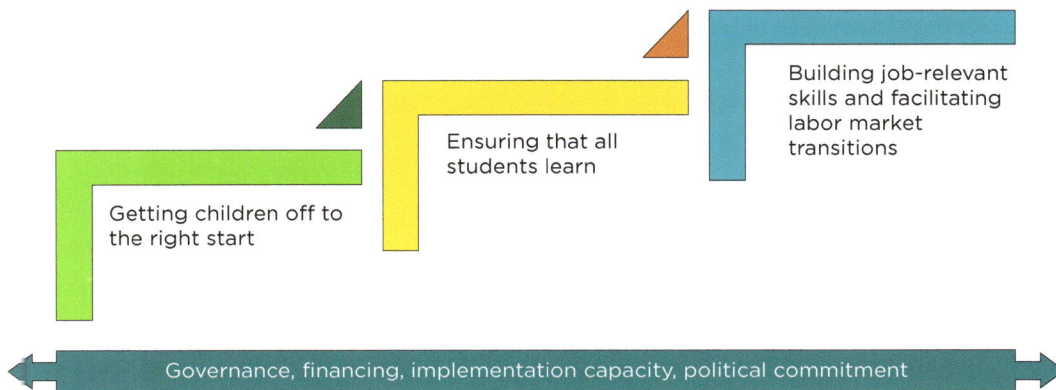

Getting children off to the right start

Ensuring that all students learn

Building job-relevant skills and facilitating labor market transitions

Governance, financing, implementation capacity, political commitment

Source: World Bank.

Ensuring that all students learn. Children who reach primary-school age need to attend school and be fed enough to learn. Reducing or eliminating school fees or providing conditional cash transfers to poor families with school-age children can facilitate school attendance. School feeding programs can not only encourage parents to send their children to school but can also ensure adequate nutrition so that students can focus on their learning. Children also need instruction at the appropriate level by well-prepared teachers, incorporating digital tools that can facilitate learning at the appropriate level and acquisition of digital skills even at a young age (refer to chapter 8 on digitalization).[5]

Learning needs to continue beyond primary school. Whereas primary education provides the foundational skills needed to move to higher levels, secondary education is critically important for honing these skills into what can be useful to potential employers. Improving the skill level of the labor force will require increasing attendance and learning in secondary schools. Because children of secondary school age could be earning money for the family, cash transfers to poor families of these children may help keep adolescents in school. Cash transfers not only alleviate the cost of schooling itself but can also bring income to households that might otherwise depend on adolescent earnings (World Bank 2021, 2023a); however, cash transfers cannot provide the safe school environment necessary to promote secondary education, particularly for girls, or counteract traditional and cultural practices that advocate against educating girls.

For girls, education at the secondary level also allows for education in reproductive health, thereby lowering the rate of teen pregnancies. Teen pregnancies are more likely to result in underweight babies because of poorer maternal health care and inadequate attention to their young children's health and education by less educated parents. Despite the higher payoffs to girls remaining in school, girls are less likely to continue at the secondary level. Social norms discourage education for girls at this level in some countries, and, as noted in the previous paragraph, schools often do not meet the needs of girls: appropriate sanitary facilities, protection from gender-based violence by teachers and male classmates, and safe roads and transportation to school.

Building job-relevant skills and facilitating labor market transitions. Developing the skilled labor force requires ensuring that youth have the specific skills that employers need and can find employment. A recent paper by Jedwab et al. (2023) suggests that skills acquired at work can be as important or more so than skills acquired at school. Policies to support skill building include expanding technical and vocational education, entrepreneurial training, apprenticeships, and youth employment programs, particularly those focused on young women and adolescent girls. Focusing on skills for the future, including digital skills and those appropriate for the green economy, will also help ensure that youth learn the skills relevant for employers.

The COVID-19 pandemic caused some setback in human capital accumulation because of school closures, difficulties with remote learning, and limited access to health facilities. Fortunately for most African countries, however, they had shorter school closures than elsewhere in the world, and the limited access to health facilities was also of short duration. Despite direct loss of life from COVID-19 and some type of impact on all of those younger than 24—because of fewer births in hospitals and clinics, school closures, and limited youth employment opportunities—services have returned to prepandemic levels. COVID-19 also indirectly affected governments: those with high levels of indebtedness have had to face much tighter fiscal constraints for spending on education, health, and social protection transfers that facilitate human capital accumulation. Furthermore, the disproportionate impacts of climate change on African countries necessitates expenditure and government attention to issues like droughts, climate migration, mudslides, climate-related diseases, and food shortages.

Analysis

This section looks at progress made on human capital indicators since the late 1990s, suggesting movement along the strategic path outlined in the previous section.

Getting children off to the right start

Adverse events experienced while a child is in utero and in the first five years of life can result in significant loss of human capital and can disrupt economic development. A first summary indicator of whether children are arriving to school ready to learn is the probability of an infant born in 2021 not surviving to age five, expressed as the number of child deaths per 1,000 newborns. The better-performing countries appear on the right in figure 7.4, and countries with high under-five mortality rates appear on the left. On average in Sub-Saharan Africa, the number of expected under-five deaths per 1,000 newborns fell from 128 in 1998 to 100 in 2021, a reduction of 22 percent. Countries shown with green bars had a reduction of at least 33 percent. Countries with notable

FIGURE 7.4 Projected under-five mortality rate for children born in 2021, by country

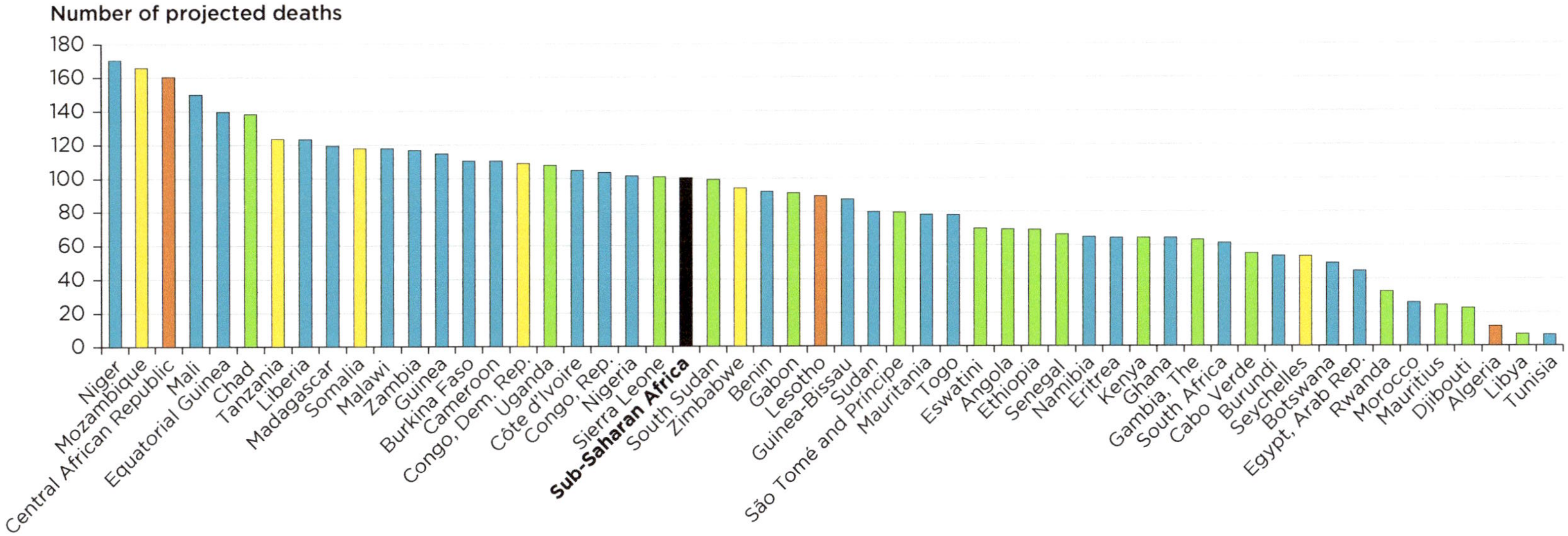

Number of projected deaths

Source: Estimates developed by the United Nations Inter-agency Group for Child Mortality Estimation (United Nations Children's Fund, United Nations Department of Economic and Social Affairs Population Division, World Bank, World Health Organization).

Note: The under-five mortality rate refers to the number of deaths of children under age five per 1,000 live births. Green bars signify that the country achieved a positive change over a period of roughly 10–20 years, yellow bars signify that the change was less than 50 percent of the Sub-Saharan Africa average, orange bars signify that the rate worsened from the earlier period, blue bars indicate that previous data were not available to determine the growth experienced by the country over the period, and the black bar shows the Sub-Saharan Africa average.

declines in the under-five mortality rate include Angola (68 percent decline); Ethiopia (53 percent); The Gambia (51 percent); Cabo Verde (48 percent); and Kenya (45 percent). Algeria, the Central African Republic, and Lesotho had notable reversals with the probability of under-five death rising by 4 percent in Algeria, 9 percent in the Central African Republic, and 13 percent in Lesotho between 1998 and 2021. Finally, a number of countries such as the Democratic Republic of Congo, Mozambique, the Seychelles, Somalia, Tanzania, and Zimbabwe showed little change from the 1998 values. The Dar es Salaam Declaration commits to reducing under-five mortality to 25 per 1,000 live births by 2030, suggesting that most countries have a long way to go to meet this target.

The projected child mortality rates shown in figure 7.4 present a summary; they do not provide particular insight into the policy measures, such as immunization, that might lead to more positive outcomes. Immunization rates rose between 1998 and 2021 in most countries in Sub-Saharan Africa. Figure 7.5 shows the percentage of children between the ages of 12 and 23 months who have received a full course of diphtheria, pertussis, and tetanus (DPT) vaccine, a standard childhood vaccination. The average rate of DPT vaccination across Sub-Saharan Africa increased for this age group from 49 percent in 1998 to 71 percent in 2021. Burkina Faso recorded the largest improvement, with the immunization rate increasing sixfold; Mauritania, where it quadrupled, followed by the Democratic Republic of Congo, where it tripled, and by the Republic of Congo and by Niger, where it almost tripled. Other countries saw large drops: in Equatorial Guinea, the immunization rate fell 35 percent; in Guinea, it fell 16 percent; and Botswana, Eswatini, The Gambia, Malawi, Mozambique, and the Seychelles had smaller drops. Many of these infants were born during the height of the COVID-19 pandemic, which might have affected their access to health services and immunization. Modest growth in some countries on the right-hand side of figure 7.5, which already had high immunization rates, might be expected; however, for those on the left-hand side, the lack of progress is more troublesome. The Dar es Salaam Declaration commits to achieving a 90 percent immunization rate by 2030, which currently only about 40 percent of the countries have achieved.

Malnutrition also strongly affects early childhood health, survival rates, and ability to learn. Severe malnutrition can result in stunted growth for the child. Stunting is defined here as the percentage of children under the age of five with height more than two standard deviations below the median height for their age based on international data. The percentage of stunting fell 27 percent between 2000 and 2022 across the region (figure 7.6), with substantial improvements in many countries. Algeria, Ghana, and São Tomé and Príncipe recorded improvements of more than 60 percent; and the Comoros and Equatorial Guinea improved by almost 60 percent. Unfortunately, stunting increased in two countries, more than doubling in Libya and increasing by 15 percent in Eritrea (orange bars in figure 7.6). Burundi, the Central African Republic, Niger, and Sudan achieved only minor progress (yellow bars in figure 7.6). Importantly, many of the countries currently on the right-hand side of the figure would have been on

FIGURE 7.5 Percentage of children ages 12–23 months immunized against diphtheria, pertussis, and tetanus, by country, 2021

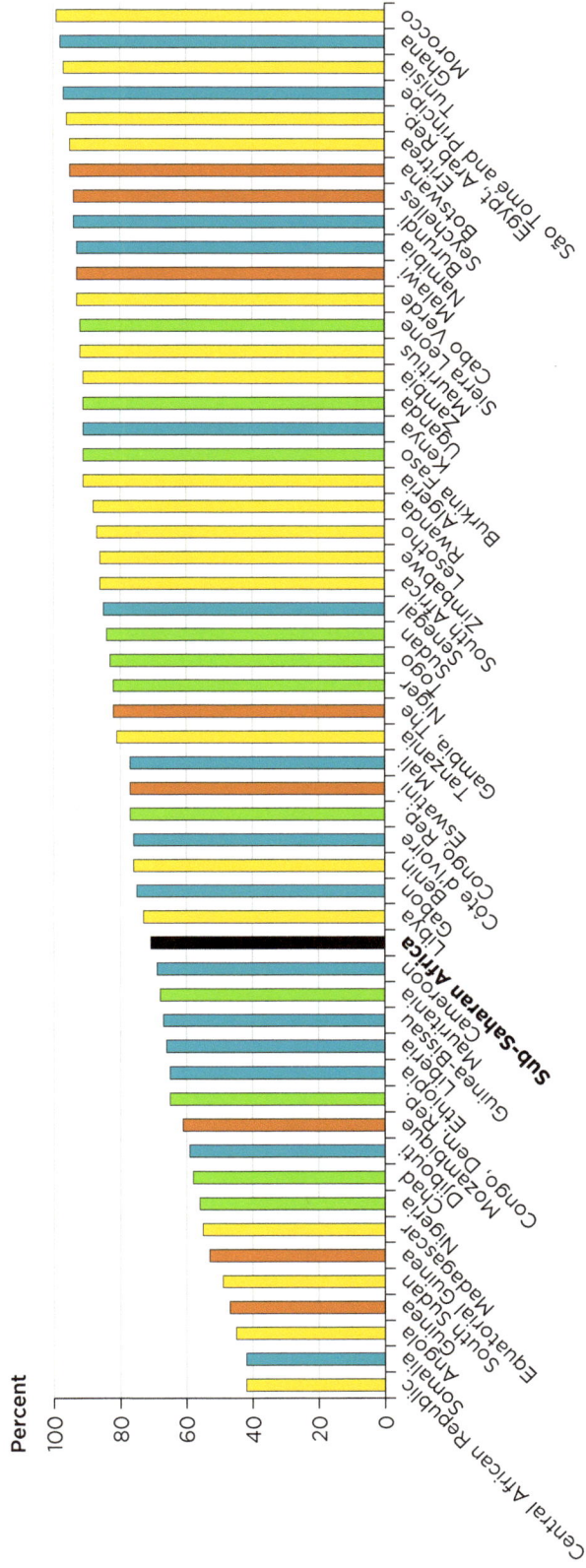

Sources: United Nations Children's Fund and World Health Organization databases.

Note: Green bars signify that the country achieved a positive change more than 50 percent higher than the change in the Sub-Saharan Africa average over a period of roughly 10–20 years, yellow bars signify that the change was less than 50 percent of the Sub-Saharan Africa average, orange bars signify that the rate worsened from the earlier period, blue bars indicate that previous data were not available to determine the growth experienced by the country over the period, and the black bar shows the Sub-Saharan Africa average.

FIGURE 7.6 Stunting rate, by country, 2022

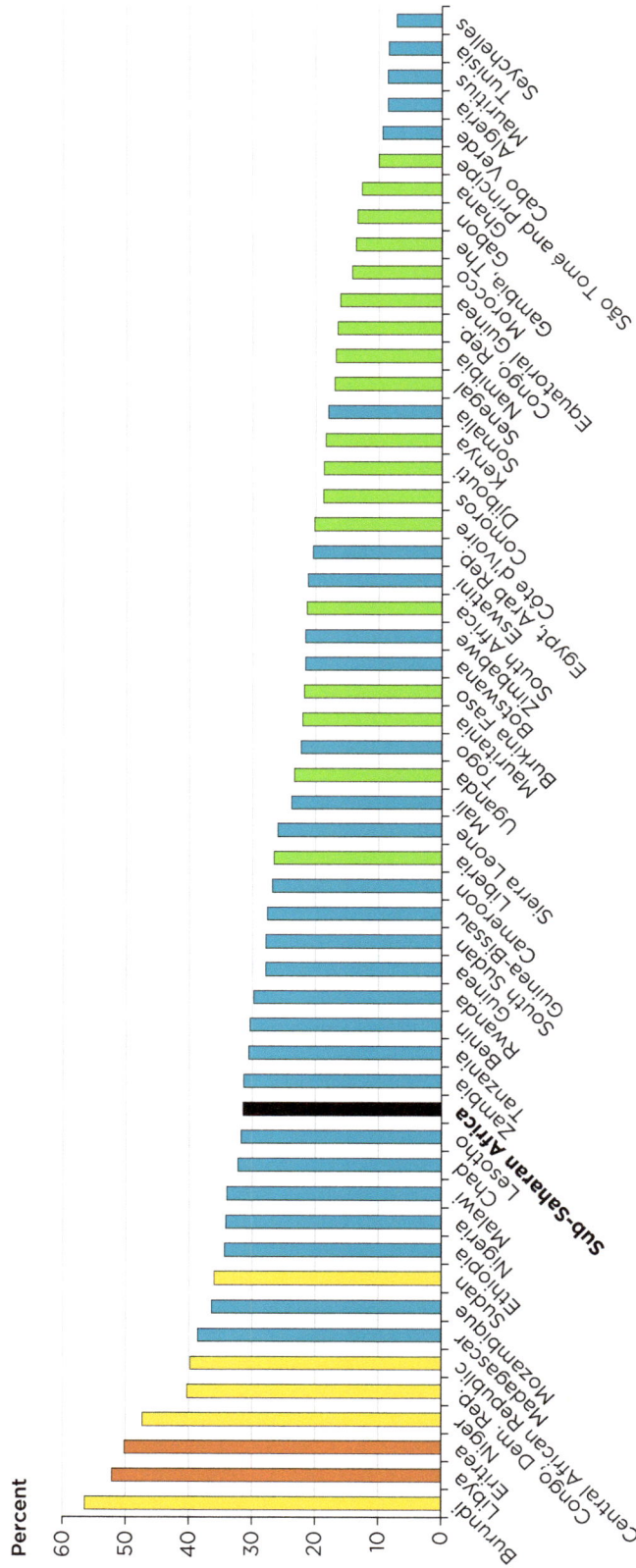

Percent

Sources: United Nations Children's Fund, World Health Organization, and World Bank Group joint child malnutrition estimates.

Note: Stunting refers to children under the age of five whose height is two standard deviations below the median height for their age. Green bars signify that the country achieved a positive change more than 50 percent higher than the change in the Sub-Saharan Africa average over a period of roughly 10–20 years, yellow bars signify that the change was less than 50 percent of the Sub-Saharan Africa average, orange bars signify that the rate worsened from the earlier period, blue bars indicate that previous data were not available to determine the growth experienced by the country over the period, and the black bar shows the Sub-Saharan Africa average.

the left-hand side in 2000. The Dar es Salaam Declaration commits countries to reducing stunting by 40 percent by 2030, which will require additional focus on nutrition, despite the progress already made.

Attendance in preprimary education is a strong predictor of successful learning when students reach school age. Because data on preprimary attendance as a percentage of the population one year before the official age of beginning primary school are not collected annually, figure 7.7 reports on fewer countries than other figures in the chapter. Preprimary attendance rates for countries with both an earlier data point and a more recent one show increased attendance of 45 percent. The best performers include Ethiopia, where preprimary attendance tripled; Burundi, Rwanda, and Uganda, where preprimary attendance more than doubled; and Madagascar, where preprimary attendance almost doubled (green bars in figure 7.7). Attendance rates fell in Chad by almost 33 percent and in Mauritania by about 15 percent (orange bars in figure 7.7). Cameroon, the Arab Republic of Egypt, Malawi, Namibia, Togo, and Zimbabwe saw only limited progress (yellow bars in figure 7.7). As in figure 7.6, the best performers (right-hand side of the figure) also generally made the most progress. Although the increase in preprimary attendance represents an improvement, the push to expand coverage for large numbers of children has exhausted the ability of the educational system to provide adequate teaching resources for these students, resulting potentially in a drop in the quality of the education.

FIGURE 7.7 **Adjusted preprimary net attendance rate, by country, various years**

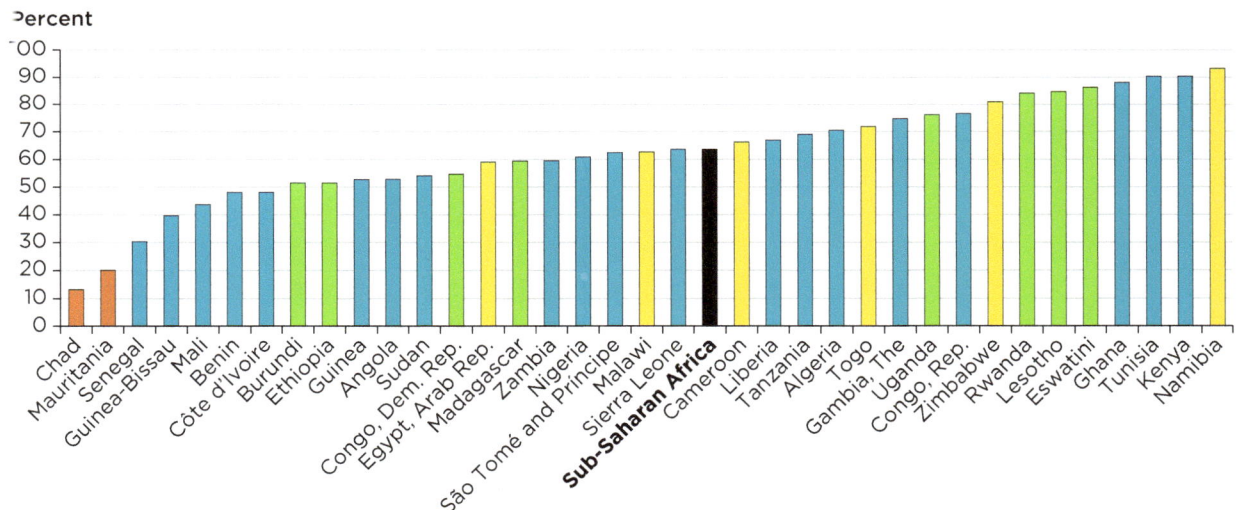

Source: World Bank, Education Statistics, 2020, https://datacatalog.worldbank.org/int/search/dataset/0038480 /education-statistics.
Note: The adjusted preprimary net attendance rate refers to the rate of children attending preprimary as a percentage of the population of children one year younger than the official entry age for primary school. Green bars signify that the country achieved a positive change more than 50 percent higher than the change in the Sub-Saharan Africa average over a period of roughly 10–20 years, yellow bars signify that the change was less than 50 percent of the Sub-Saharan Africa average, orange bars signify that the rate worsened from the earlier period, blue bars indicate that previous data were not available to determine the growth experienced by the country over the period, and the black bar shows the Sub-Saharan Africa average.

Cash transfers to poor families with young children play an important role in improving the health and nutrition of children as well as in helping them attend school, including preprimary. Cash transfers provide money that the family can use to improve the nutrition of pregnant and nursing mothers and young children, and to pay for school fees and school supplies for preprimary students. In some cases, cash transfers are conditional on children's immunization or attendance in preprimary programs. Cash transfer programs have expanded significantly in Africa since 2000 (World Bank 2018). An impact analysis suggests that families spend 75 percent of their cash transfer on increased consumption, including better and more food for the family, with no increase in tobacco or alcohol consumption (Ralston, Andrews, and Hsiao 2017).

Social safety net programs are increasingly leveraged to promote investments in human capital, especially for children, with a view to reducing the intergenerational transmission of poverty. Programs have demonstrated positive impacts on child health and education. They can promote the adoption of good practices related to nutrition, early childhood development, hygiene, education, health care, and so on. They can also stimulate the use of targeted basic services by encouraging (or demanding) health care visits, growth-monitoring sessions, or school attendance. Conditionalities, the mechanisms used to promote behavior or use of services, range from requirements to participate in promotion sessions; to conform with a particular behavior, without verification of compliance; or to conform to particular behaviors, with some verification of compliance (with or without sanctions for noncompliance).

At least 22 countries in Africa now have programs that use some mechanism to promote human capital investments. Examples include Burkin-Naong-Sa Ya, a program in Burkina Faso that requires participation in social and behavioral change communication activities related to nutrition and early childhood development; Mauritania Tekavoul (national social transfer program) requires participation in sessions of social promotion, with a focus on early childhood development, education, health, and civil registration; and the Niger social safety net project, which requires participation in social and behavioral change and communication activities related to nutrition and early childhood development. A safety net program in Togo conditions a bonus transfer on attendance at information sessions as a top-up to its main unconditional cash transfer for pregnant women and mothers of children under the age of two. Sessions often cover themes of prenatal and postnatal care, nutrition, early childhood development, child health, education, civil registration, and hygiene. Some country programs make participation in these sessions compulsory (Mauritania), whereas others simply encourage participation (Sierra Leone). Evaluations show that, even in the absence of active monitoring, sessions tend to have very high attendance rates. In Niger, for instance, 95 percent of beneficiaries attend the sessions, even without rigorous verification.

A long-term evaluation of South Africa's Child Support Grant program shows that a grant to benefit infants from birth to age two raises the likelihood that the children's growth will be monitored and that height-for-age scores will improve (depending on the educational attainment of the mothers). Niger's Social Safety Net project demonstrates that measures focused on accompanying behavior can lead to changes in nutrition practices related to exclusive breastfeeding and complementary feeding, which contribute to improving food security among children.

Tighter financing following recent global and regional crises makes it especially important to target interventions at households that can benefit the most in terms of building human capital. Social registries containing details of beneficiary households, households requesting assistance, vulnerable households, or even all households are often used to more efficiently target households that can best benefit from a particular type of intervention. Twenty-two countries in Sub-Saharan Africa have developed social registries to identify households for various types of interventions, including those beyond cash transfers. The Dar es Salaam Declaration committed all signing countries to establish social registries by 2030. Figure 7.8 shows the extent to which social registries already exist in Africa; none of these registries existed before 2000.

Interventions that have improved early childhood development include behavioral change communication, encouraging improvements to child and maternal health and nutrition and child development, micronutrient or food supplementation, caregiver education or support, and early childhood education at preschools or childcare centers (Lufumpa et al. 2023). As mentioned in the previous section, reducing maternal mortality rates will ensure that mothers are there to provide nutrition and promote early childhood development. Although maternal death declined in the Africa region by a third between 2000 and 2020, it remains high—at 536 deaths per 100,000 live births in 2020—and some countries have even seen an increase (figure 7.9).

FIGURE 7.8 **Social registries, by share of population covered, Africa, 2023**

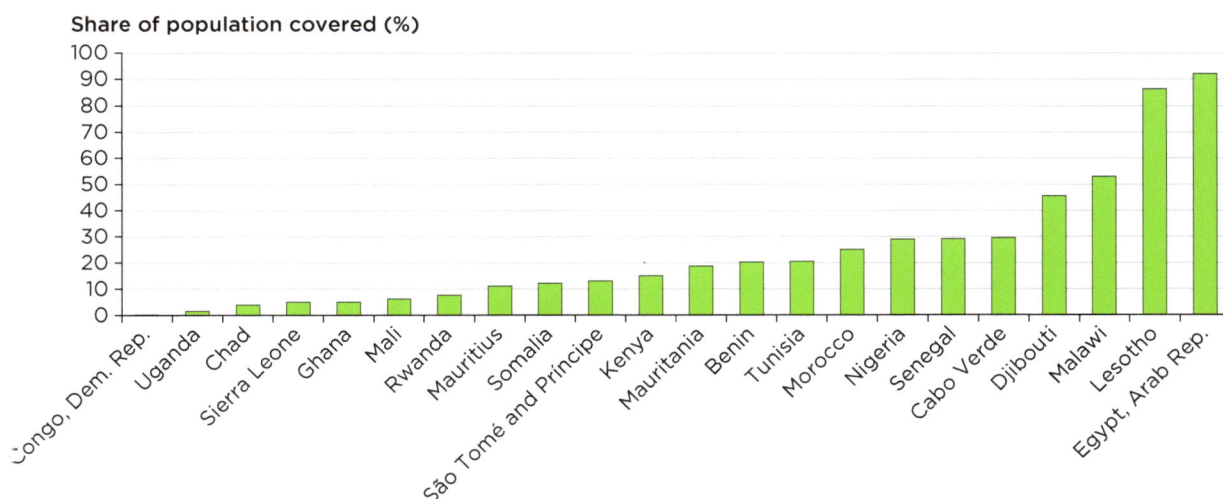

Share of population covered (%)

Source: Based on 2023 data from World Bank, Social Protection Delivery Systems Global Solutions Group, https://www.worldbank.org/en/topic/socialprotectionandjobs/publication/sourcebook-on-the-foundations-of-social-protection-delivery-systems.

FIGURE 7.9 Maternal mortality rates, modeled estimate, by country, 2020

Number of maternal deaths per 100,000 live births

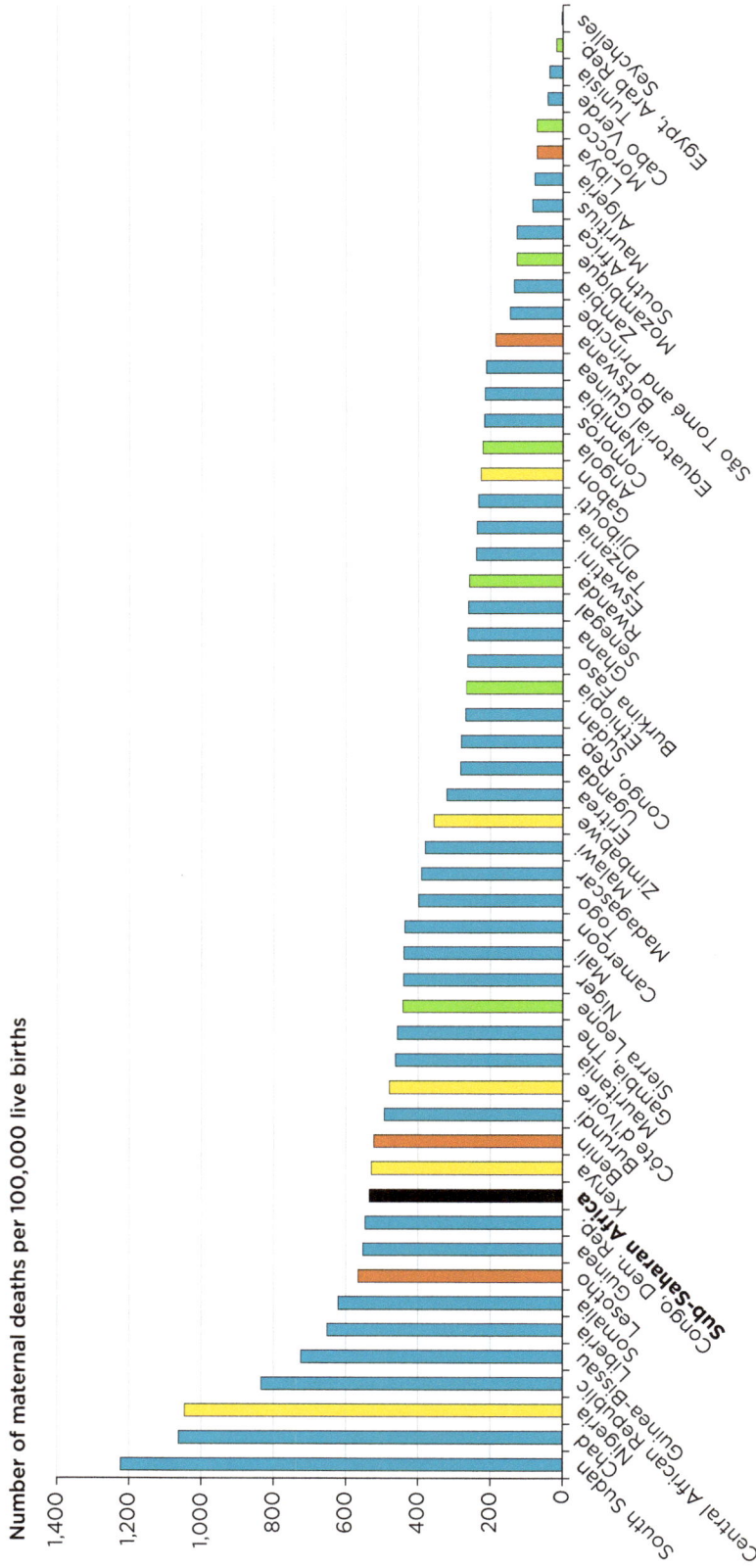

Source: World Bank, World Development Indicators, 2016–21, https://data.worldbank.org/indicator/.

Note: Green bars signify that the country achieved a positive change more than 50 percent higher than the change in the Sub-Saharan Africa average over a period of roughly 10–20 years, yellow bars signify that the change was less than 50 percent of the Sub-Saharan Africa average, orange bars signify that the rate worsened from the earlier period, blue bars indicate that previous data were not available to determine the growth experienced by the country over the period, and the black bar shows the Sub-Saharan Africa average.

Ensuring that all students learn

Since the beginning of the 21st century, much of Africa has made huge progress in getting children of primary school age into school. Many African countries have made primary education free, which encourages school enrollment. Figure 7.10 shows the percentage of primary-school-age children not in school in 46 countries.[6] Although the percentage fell by more than 50 percent on average across Sub-Saharan Africa, 16 countries still have significantly higher out-of-school rates for primary-school-age children than the African average of 19 percent. The nine countries for which data were not available might also have higher out-of-school rates. By contrast, 14 countries achieved reductions more than 50 percent higher than the average reduction. The best performers include Algeria, Lesotho, Madagascar, Morocco, Mozambique, Togo, and Zimbabwe, which each managed to reduce the percentage of primary-school-age children out of school by more than 90 percent. Cabo Verde, Mauritius, and the Seychelles, which already had some of the lowest out-of-school rates in Africa, experienced slight increases; but Nigeria had a notable increase, with large numbers of children out of school. Countries with minimal improvement or stagnation include Botswana, Eritrea, Eswatini, and South Africa. The percentage of primary-school-age girls out of school, indicated by the green dots in figure 7.10, is typically, but not always, higher than for all students.

Nevertheless, ensuring that children learn requires more than attendance; children need to stay in school and actually learn. One indicator of children remaining in school is the number of children matriculating in the last primary grade as a percentage of children of the age appropriate to that grade level. This indicator is not a perfect measure, however, because schools may move children up to the next grade level regardless of their achievement, meaning that less learning occurs than the indicator suggests. Additionally, the existence of repeaters among matriculating students may result in shares of matriculating students higher than 100 percent of the appropriate age. Nevertheless, this percentage does provide some indication of whether the children are remaining in school through primary education.

Available data for 46 African countries, almost all with a data point around the year 2000 and one after 2013, indicate that the average rate of matriculation in the last primary grade rose from 54 percent to 69 percent in Sub-Saharan Africa (figure 7.11). Of the 46 countries, 21 showed substantial improvement, including Mozambique, Niger, and Rwanda, where the last primary grade matriculation rate more than tripled, and Burkina Faso, Burundi, Djibouti, and Ethiopia, where the rate more than doubled. Some backtracking occurred in other countries, such as Cabo Verde, where the rate fell 18 percent; Liberia, where the rate fell 9 percent; Uganda, where it fell 13 percent; and Mauritius, where it fell 4 percent. The decreases in Cabo Verde and Mauritius may reflect the existence of fewer repeaters, which represents progress even though it results in a lower number.

FIGURE 7.10 Out-of-school rates for primary-school-age students, by country, most recent year after 2013

Share of primary-school-age children out of school (%)

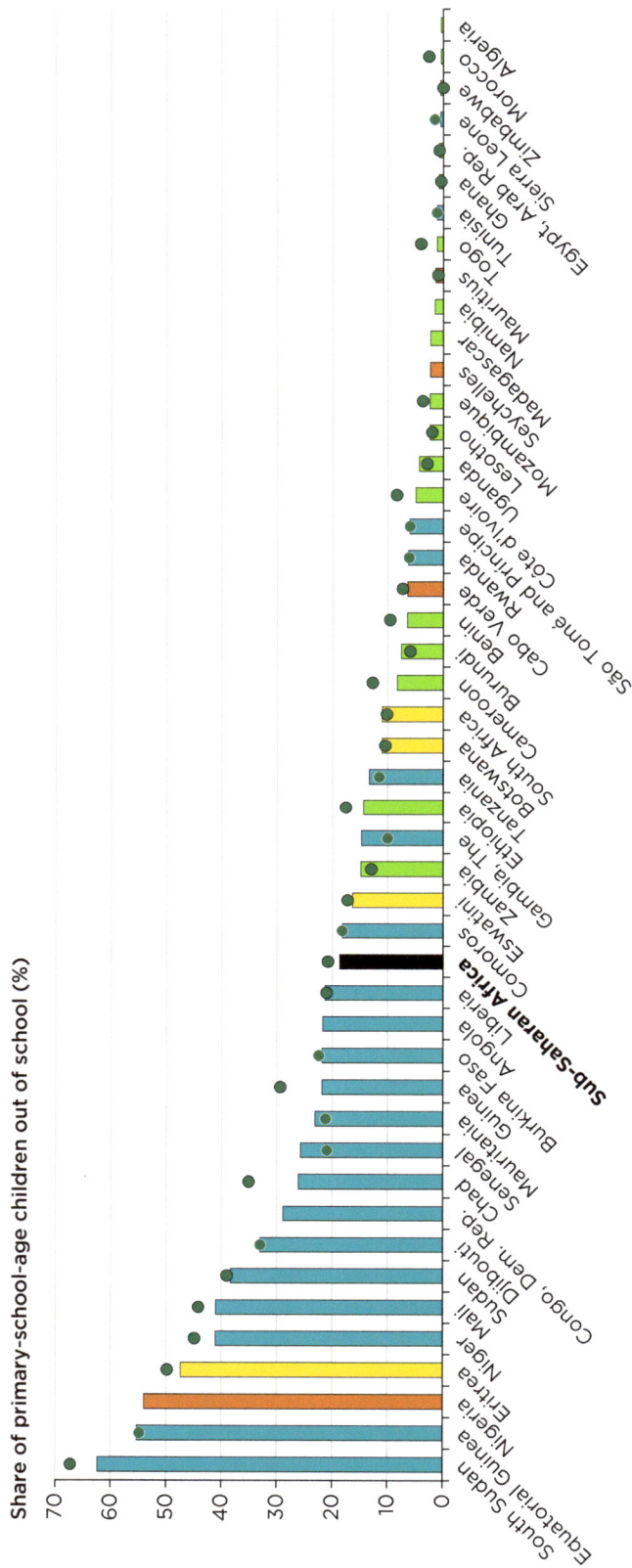

Source: World Bank, Education Statistics, 2020, https://datacatalog.worldbank.org/int/search/dataset/0038480/education-statistics.

Note: Green bars signify that the country achieved a positive change more than 50 percent higher than the change in the Sub-Saharan Africa average over a period of roughly 10–20 years, yellow bars signify that the change was less than 50 percent of the Sub-Saharan Africa average, orange bars signify that the rate worsened from the earlier period, blue bars indicate that previous data were not available to determine the growth experienced by the country over the period, and the black bar shows the Sub-Saharan Africa average. The green dots show the percentage of primary-school-age girls out of school; this data point was not available for all countries shown in the figure.

FIGURE 7.11 Primary school matriculation rates, by country, most recent year after 2013

Matriculation rate (%)

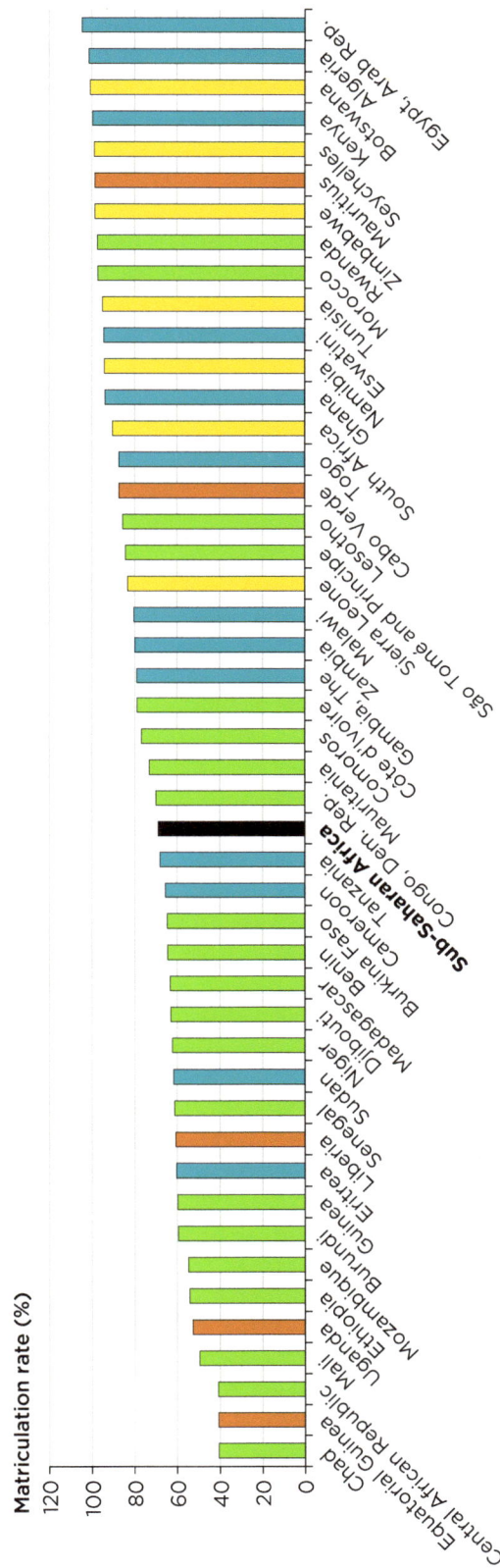

Source: World Bank, Education Statistics, 2020, https://datacatalog.worldbank.org/int/search/dataset/0038480/education-statistics.
Note: The primary school matriculation rate refers to the number of children matriculating at the highest primary grade level as a percentage of children at the appropriate age for that level. Green bars signify that the country achieved a positive change over a period of roughly 10–20 years, yellow bars signify that the change was less than 50 percent of the Sub-Saharan Africa average over a period of roughly 10–20 years, yellow bars signify that the change was less than 50 percent of the Sub-Saharan Africa average, orange bars signify that the rate worsened from the earlier period, blue bars indicate that previous data were not available to determine the growth experienced by the country over the period, and the black bar shows the Sub-Saharan Africa average. The existence of repeaters among matriculating students may result in shares of matriculating students higher than 100 percent.

Despite the progress that countries have made in having children attend and remain in school (refer to box 7.1), learning outcomes do not necessarily show similar progress. A few countries have undertaken internationally recognized learning assessments to provide a measure of learning poverty, defined as the percentage of 10-year-olds in a country who cannot read and understand a simple paragraph. Although tests differ and are sometimes given in fourth grade and sometimes in sixth grade and for different years—making the measure not entirely comparable across countries—data available for 27 countries still show a dishearteningly high level of learning poverty (figure 7.12). Only 5 of the 27 countries saw significant improvement, with Benin leading.

BOX 7.1

Strong progress in education over the past 20 years

With the fastest-growing population in the world, Sub-Saharan Africa is expected to host more than 700 million children under age 15 by 2050.[a] Although education represents a key to unleashing the youth potential and claiming demographic benefits, Sub-Saharan Africa faces several challenges. The region has an alarming number of children (over 100 million) between the ages of 6 and 18 years out of school.[b] Furthermore, 86 percent of 10-year-olds cannot read and understand a simple paragraph and live in learning poverty.[c] Despite progress by countries in closing the gender gap in primary education, disparities still exist at the secondary level, with gross enrollment rates for girls at 42 percent and for boys at 46 percent.[d]

Nevertheless, Sub-Saharan Africa has made significant progress in educating children since 2000. With the introduction of free primary education, countries in the region have seen 100 million more children enrolled. One of the latest examples is the Democratic Republic of Congo, which introduced its Free Primary Education Policy in 2019, leading to more than 4 million additional child enrollments in primary school between 2019 and 2024 (World Bank 2024). Furthermore, many countries in the region have introduced free secondary education to accommodate the increasing numbers of students coming from the primary stream (Zambia is the latest, in 2022), with a particular focus on improving girls' participation in secondary education (Nigeria and Tanzania).

Sub-Saharan African countries have been also working on improving the quality of education to ensure that children who come to school learn. For example, after introducing free primary education in 2003 and achieving universal primary education, Kenya also achieved substantial improvements in literacy outcomes at scale, reducing the share of nonreaders at grade 2 (English) from 38 percent (2015) to 14 percent (2019). To improve the quality of education, countries are focusing on systemic reforms to tackle key constraints such as strengthening teacher management, recruitment, and deployment. Examples include

- Merit-based teacher recruitment reforms in Cameroon and Senegal;
- Performance-oriented teacher management in Kenya;
- Structured pedagogy to support teachers in The Gambia, Ghana, and Senegal;

(continued)

- Rolling out textbook reforms to improve quality and availability, and reducing costs in Cameroon, Kenya, and Mozambique;

- Using mother-tongue as a language of instruction in early grades in the Central African Republic, Chad, and the Democratic Republic of Congo;

- Using technology to support teachers and improve classroom practices in Kenya, Nigeria (Edo State), and Rwanda; and

- Improving participation in secondary education by providing scholarships; shifting socio-cultural norms; improving water, sanitation, and hygiene facilities; and providing safe spaces for girls in Angola, the Democratic Republic of Congo, Niger, Nigeria, and Tanzania.

a. United Nations Department of Economic and Social Affairs, Population Division, World Population Prospects, 2022.

b. World Bank, World Development Indicators, 2022.

c. World Bank, Learning Poverty Global Database, 2022.

d. World Bank Education Statistics, 2020.

FIGURE 7.12 **Percentage of 10-year-olds unable to read and understand a simple paragraph, by country**

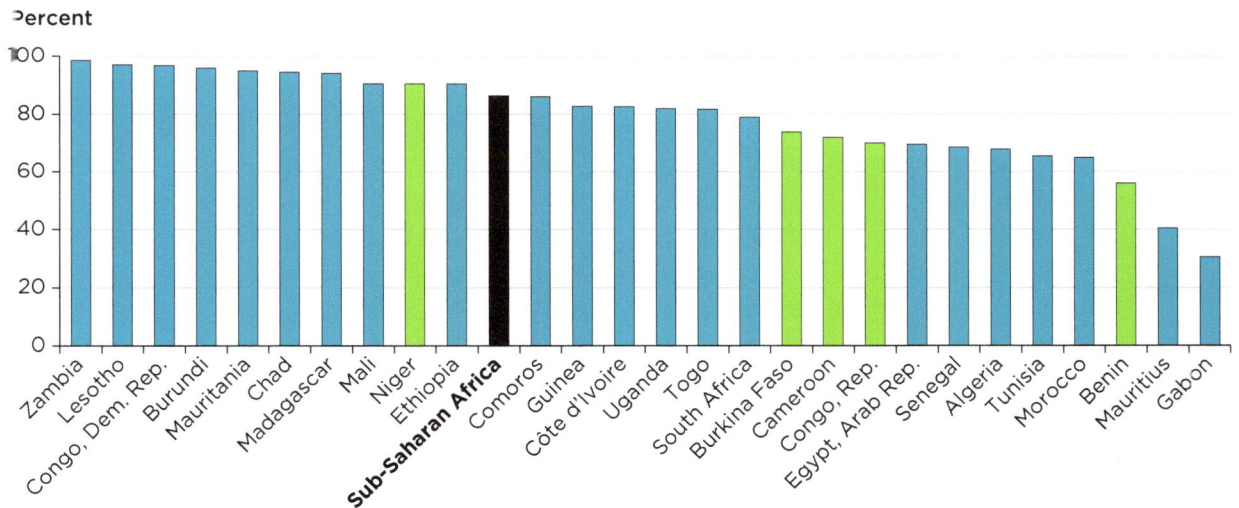

Source: World Bank, Learning Poverty Global Database 2022, https://www.worldbank.org/en/topic/education /publication/state-of-global-learning-poverty.

Note: Learning poverty refers to the percentage of 10-year-olds unable to read and understand a simple paragraph. Green bars signify improvement in learning poverty reduction, blue bars indicate that no data were available to estimate the change between 2015 and 2019, and the black bar shows the average for Sub-Saharan Africa.

Factors accounting for this learning poverty include the quality of the teaching, the access to quality educational materials, and the tendency to promote children to the next level regardless of their proficiency. Benin is showing the most significant improvement with a drop in those unable to read and understand a simple paragraph falling from 78 percent to 56 percent between 2014 and 2019. Rapid progress is possible but requires concerted effort.

In addition to cash transfer programs that now exist all over Africa,[7] school feeding programs have an impact on nutrition and school attendance for school-age children. The role of school feeding interventions is often evaluated by comparing the effects of school canteens and take-home rations. For instance, in Uganda, a food for education program led to a 9.3 percent expansion in school attendance in the afternoons but had little impact on attendance in the morning session. In upper-primary school (grades 6 and 7), take-home rations led to significant increases in both morning and afternoon attendance, averaging 17–18 percent, including a 30 percent rise in morning attendance among girls. In a Burkina Faso school canteens and take-home rations program, school feeding raised attendance among girls by 5 percent, with a flypaper effect (that is, the benefit stuck to the girls' households) whereby take-home rations enhanced anthropometric measures among beneficiaries' younger siblings ages one to five. Weight for age increased by 0.38 standard deviation, and weight for height by 0.33 standard deviation.

Whereas primary school sets the basic foundations for learning, it is in secondary school that adolescents begin to gain skills that will be useful in the workplace. The average percentage of out-of-school lower-secondary-school-age adolescents among Sub-Saharan African countries (37 percent) is almost double that of out-of-school primary-school-age children (19 percent), reflecting the many challenges to continued attendance. As noted earlier, adolescents can earn income for the household or take on more substantial household responsibilities, which often takes them out of the classroom. In more rural areas, the greater distance to secondary schools may require travel or boarding, which add to both the direct costs of schooling and the indirect costs of being unavailable to provide income and assistance to the household. Many African countries have eliminated school fees at the primary level, but almost all still have school fees at the secondary level. Entrance to secondary schools also requires passing exams, with exam fees that are quite steep relative to income for many households. Because adolescent girls also often reach puberty during lower-secondary-school ages, access to safe bathroom facilities and protection against gender-based violence are important factors if they are to attend school. Girls can be vulnerable to gender-based violence during travel to and from school, and at school where most teachers at the secondary level are male.

Figure 7.13 shows the out-of-school rate for lower-secondary-school-age adolescents across Africa, with the dots showing the rate for girls.[8] Only 34 countries had data points from within the last 10 years, and the figure shows the most recent. The average

FIGURE 7.13 Out-of-school rates for lower-secondary-school-age adolescents, by country, various years around 2018

Share of lower-secondary-school-age adolescents out of school (%)

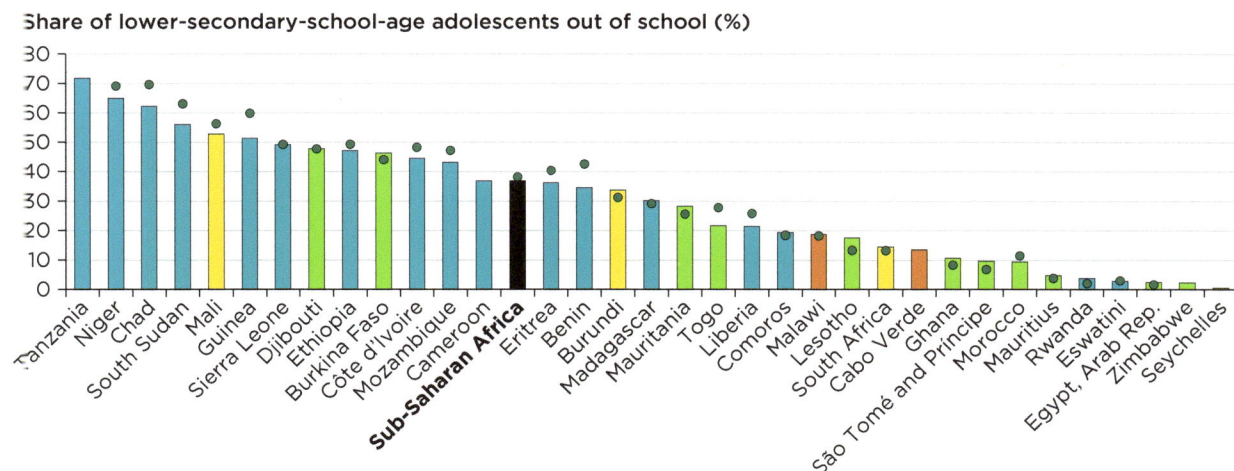

Source: World Bank, Education Statistics, 2020, https://datacatalog.worldbank.org/int/search/dataset/0038480 /education-statistics.

Note: Green bars signify that the country achieved a positive change more than 50 percent higher than the change in the Sub-Saharan Africa average over a period of roughly 10–20 years, yellow bars signify that the change was less than 50 percent of the Sub-Saharan Africa average, orange bars signify that the rate worsened from the earlier period, blue bars indicate that previous data were not available to determine the growth experienced by the country over the period, and the black bar shows the Sub-Saharan Africa average. The green dots show the percentage of girls out of school; this data point was not available for all countries shown in the figure.

out-of-school rate for lower-secondary-age adolescents has fallen by almost 25 percent in Sub-Saharan Africa. The best performers include Egypt and the Seychelles, with rates falling by more than 80 percent; and Ghana, Morocco, São Tomé and Príncipe, and Zimbabwe, where it fell by more than 67 percent. Despite some backtracking in Cabo Verde, where the out-of-school rates rose from 0.8 percent to 13 percent, and in Malawi, where the rates rose from 8 percent to 19 percent, both countries still have rates below the Sub-Saharan Africa average. As with younger age groups, most countries have a higher percentage of girls out of school than of overall adolescents.

Despite the importance of the percentage of out-of-school adolescents at lower-secondary-school age, completing or getting close to completing lower-secondary school indicates persistence at staying in school and potentially something about the learning that has taken place, particularly if schools do not regularly promote children from one grade to another on the basis of age. Between 2000 and 2019, the percentage of adolescents matriculating in the highest level of lower-secondary school as a percentage of age-appropriate adolescents rose by almost two-thirds. Of the 46 countries for which data are available, 19 showed improvements of more than 150 percent of the growth in the Sub-Saharan Africa average (figure 7.14). Best performers include Burkina Faso and Mozambique, where enrollment in the last grade of lower secondary increased more than sixfold, and Tanzania, where it more than quadrupled.

FIGURE 7.14 Lower-secondary school matriculation rates, by country, 2020 or closest available year

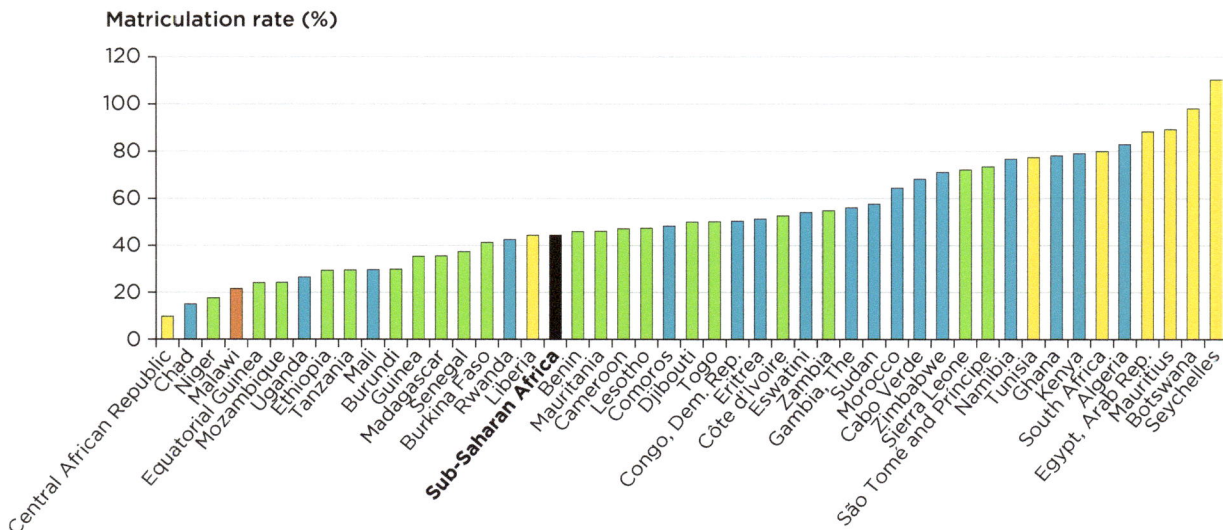

Matriculation rate (%)

Source: World Bank, Education Statistics, 2020, https://datacatalog.worldbank.org/int/search/dataset/0038480/education-statistics.

Note: The lower-secondary school matriculation rate refers to the number of adolescents matriculating at the highest grade level of lower-secondary school as a percentage of adolescents at the appropriate age for that level. Green bars signify that the country achieved a positive change more than 50 percent higher than the change in the Sub-Saharan Africa average over a period of roughly 10–20 years, yellow bars signify that the change was less than 50 percent of the Sub-Saharan Africa average, the orange bar signifies that the rate worsened from the earlier period, blue bars indicate that previous data were not available to determine the growth experienced by the country over the period, and the black bar shows the Sub-Saharan Africa average. The matriculation rate compares the number of students enrolled in the highest grade level of lower-secondary school to the number of adolescents in the official age group for that level. This rate can exceed 100 percent because it includes students who are older or younger than the official age range. Contributing factors include students repeating grades and those returning to school after dropping out, potentially at an older age.

Note that increases can result from automatic promotion and older repeaters who complete the last grade level of lower secondary. Numbers can also rise when a larger share of the population migrates to urban areas where schooling is more available. Aside from the Central African Republic and Liberia, slow growth occurred mainly in countries with already-high levels of matriculation, making this trend less worrisome.

Cash transfer programs that are conditional on school attendance have a significant positive impact on enrollment and attendance, with a 60 percent improvement in the odds of enrollment when conditionality is explicitly monitored and implemented. Unconditional cash transfers also have a positive, but smaller, impact. Improvements in school attendance are also consistent with other positive impacts detected in consumption expenditure related to education—such as the purchase of shoes, uniforms, and blankets—the lack of which presents a key barrier to enrollment and attendance, especially in secondary school. For example, cash transfers reportedly resulted in education-related expenditure increases of 23 percent in the Kenya GiveDirectly program and 16 percent in the Lesotho Child Grants Program and the Malawi Social Cash Transfer Program (World Bank 2018).

Building job-relevant skills and facilitating labor market transitions

Moving to upper-secondary school is even more important to employment than previous schooling. In Africa, however, even more adolescents are out of school at the upper-secondary level than at the lower-secondary level. All of the elements that discourage students from attending lower-secondary school are even stronger at the upper-secondary level. When asked why they dropped out after primary school, about two-thirds, on average, of girls in Burkina Faso, Chad, Mali, Mauritania, and Niger said it was because of pregnancy or marriage. Even higher percentages of adolescent girls reported beginning, but then dropping out of, secondary school because of pregnancy or marriage, with particularly high rates of potential students out of school in Niger and Tanzania (World Bank 2021). Although the same percentages may not apply all over Africa, these data provide a sense of the challenges to building a skilled labor force. Between 2000 and 2019, the average number of out-of-school upper-secondary-school-age adolescents in Sub-Saharan Africa fell only from 68 percent to 56 percent. Among the 35 countries with available data, the best performers on reducing out-of-school rates were São Tomé and Príncipe and the Seychelles, where the out-of-school rate for upper secondary age fell by more than two-thirds (figure 7.15). As in earlier school levels, the percentage of female adolescents out of school is in most cases higher than the overall percentage.

FIGURE 7.15 Out-of-school rates for upper-secondary-school-age students, by country, various years around 2018

Share of upper-secondary-school-age adolescents out of school (%)

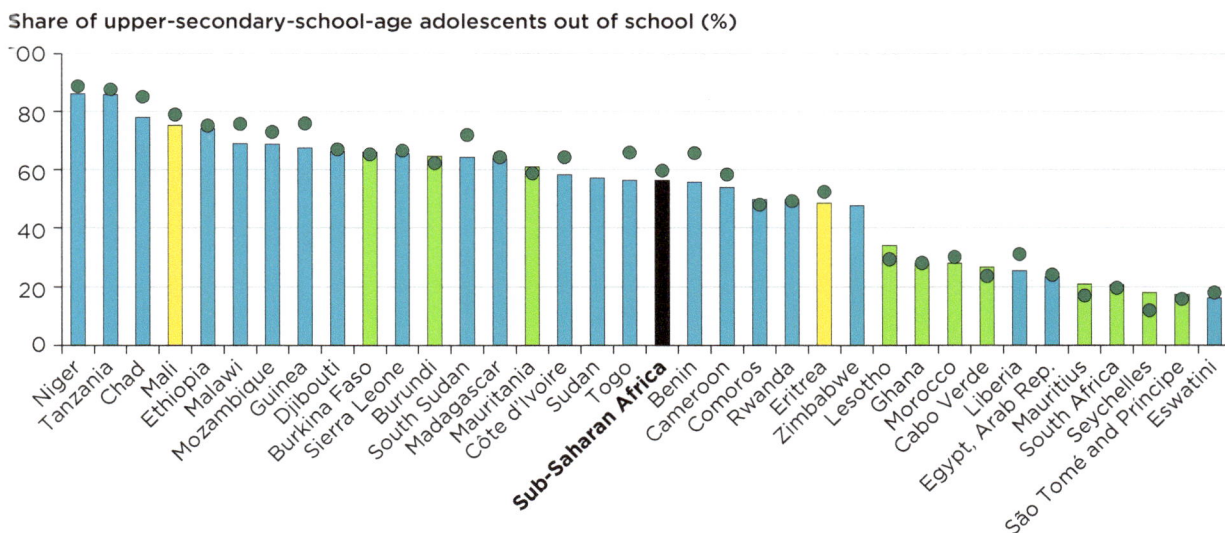

Source: World Bank, Education Statistics, 2020, https://datacatalog.worldbank.org/int/search/dataset/0038480 /education-statistics.

Note: Green bars signify that the country achieved a positive change more than 50 percent higher than the change in the Sub-Saharan Africa average over a period of roughly 10–20 years, yellow bars signify that the change was less than 50 percent of the Sub-Saharan Africa average, blue bars indicate that previous data were not available to determine the growth experienced by the country over the period, and the black bar shows the Sub-Saharan Africa average. The green dots show the percentage of adolescent girls out of school; this data point was not available for all countries shown in the figure.

Data are available on secondary school completion rates for 37 countries, but this indicator does not measure learning outcomes. On average, the reporting countries doubled the rate of secondary school completion over the past 10–20 years, albeit from low initial levels. Best performers include Togo, where the secondary school completion rate rose from less than 1 percent to 21 percent; Ghana, where it rose almost eightfold; Sierra Leone, where it rose more than fivefold; and Côte d'Ivoire, Rwanda, and Sudan, where it more than tripled (figure 7.16). Even countries at the low end of the scale achieved substantial progress. The rate fell only in Egypt, but by more than a third. The Gambia, Guinea-Bissau, Madagascar, Malawi, Nigeria, and São Tomé and Príncipe saw modest growth.

As noted earlier, teenage pregnancies are a major factor preventing girls from completing secondary education. The girls are often asked to leave school at a certain stage in their pregnancies and, even if legally permitted to return, are often not welcomed back by their classmates and teachers after the child is born. In addition, most girls are discouraged from going back to school as their household responsibilities increase: along with responsibilities they had before giving birth, they now have the care of a baby in addition to their schoolwork if they do go back to school. This negative impact also extends to the next generation. Often unaware that they are pregnant until late in their pregnancies, teenage mothers are less likely than older mothers to have received good prenatal care. Teenage mothers are also typically less equipped to care for their children, financially, nutritionally, and behaviorally, and less able to help them become ready for learning.

FIGURE 7.16 Secondary school completion rate, by country, 2020

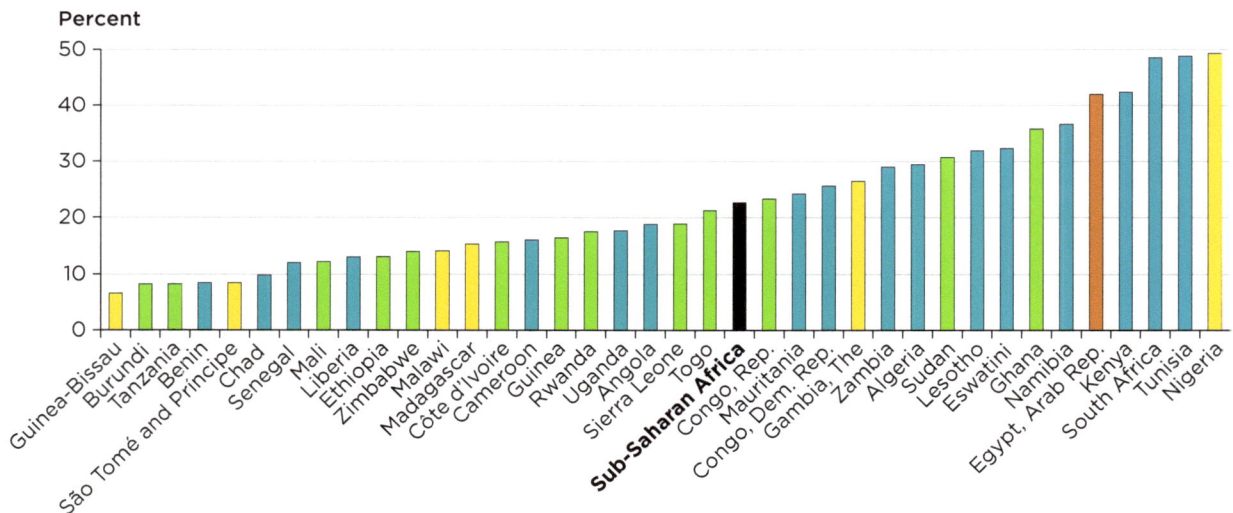

Source: World Bank, Education Statistics, 2020, https://datacatalog.worldbank.org/int/search/dataset/0038480/education-statistics.
Note: Green bars signify that the country achieved a positive change more than 50 percent higher than the change in the Sub-Saharan Africa average over a period of roughly 10–20 years, yellow bars signify that the change was less than 50 percent of the Sub-Saharan Africa average, the orange bar signifies that the rate worsened from the earlier period, blue bars indicate that previous data were not available to determine the growth experienced by the country over the period, and the black bar shows the Sub-Saharan Africa average.

Figure 7.17 shows the number of births per 1,000 women ages 15–19 for selected countries in Sub-Saharan Africa. From 2000 to 2021, the overall average number of births fell from 128 per 1,000 adolescent girls to 100, a 22 percent decline. Burundi, Cabo Verde, the Comoros, Eswatini, Ethiopia, The Gambia, Kenya, Libya, Mauritius, São Tomé and Príncipe, Senegal, Sierra Leone, South Sudan, and Uganda saw even greater declines. By contrast, adolescent fertility actually rose in Algeria, the Central African Republic, and Lesotho; and Mozambique, the Seychelles, Somalia, South Africa, Tanzania, and Zimbabwe recorded little change. Measures to lower adolescent fertility rates include reproductive education and access to safe and effective contraception. The Dar es Salaam Declaration committed to reducing teenage pregnancies by half by 2030.

Many countries in the region have seen increased gross enrollment rates of women in secondary education.[9] On average in Sub-Saharan Africa, gross school female enrollment in secondary education (lower and upper combined) increased from 26 percent in 2000 to 44 percent in 2020, although with great variation across the region (figure 7.18). South Africa (106 percent), Mauritius (98 percent), São Tomé and Príncipe (95 percent), and Cabo Verde (92 percent) had the highest secondary enrollment rates in 2020; in the same year, the Central African Republic (14), Chad (14), Niger (21), and Uganda (23) had the lowest. Countries with green bars experienced a substantial increase of female enrollment from 2016 to 2020: Burkina Faso from 35 to 41 percent, Côte d'Ivoire from 38 to 56 percent, Mauritania from 15 to 39 percent, Mozambique from 26 to 38 percent, and Rwanda from 39 to 49 percent. Enrollment decreased during the same period in Cabo Verde (98 to 92 percent), Mauritius (98 to 96 percent), the Seychelles (87 to 82 percent), and South Africa (109 to 106 percent).

Tertiary education

The Africa Heads of State Human Capital Summit placed high importance on tertiary education, with a commitment to aim for a gross enrollment ratio of 20 percent. For Africa as a whole, the rate of tertiary enrollment as a percentage of the appropriate-age population has more than doubled since the beginning of the century (figure 7.19; refer also to box 7.2, which highlights successful interventions). Best performers include Angola and Ethiopia, both of which started the century with enrollment of less than 1 percent of the relevant population; the Republic of Congo and Guinea both more than quadrupled their enrollment. Mali, Nigeria, Tanzania, Uganda, and Zimbabwe saw only modest increases, whereas Egypt and Sierra Leone saw declines.

In terms of women's participation in tertiary education, the gross female enrollment rate increased in Sub-Saharan Africa on average, from 3.7 percent in 2000 to 8.7 percent in 2020. Once again, however, great variation occurs across the region (figure 7.20), with the highest enrollment rates in Algeria (66 percent), Mauritius (52 percent), Tunisia (43 percent), and Morocco (41 percent). The lowest rates in the same year occurred in South Sudan (0.3 percent), Malawi (1.2 percent), Eritrea (2.7 percent), and Niger (2.8 percent); however, Malawi increased enrollment from 0.7 percent to 1.2 percent in only four years (2014–18).

FIGURE 7.17 Adolescent fertility rate, by country, 2021

Number of births per 1,000 women ages 15–19

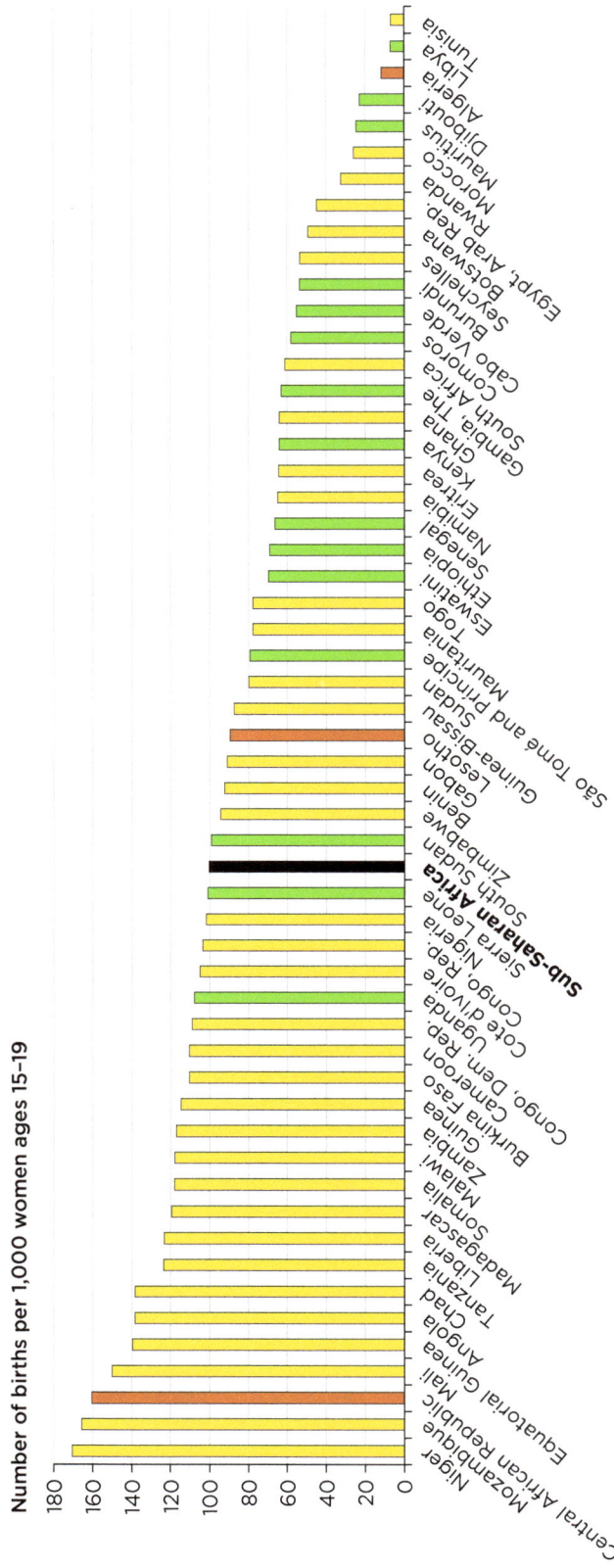

Source: United Nations Population Division, World Population Prospects, https://data.worldbank.org/indicator/SP.ADO.TFRT.

Note: The adolescent fertility rate reflects the number of births per 1,000 women ages 15–19. Green bars signify that the country achieved a positive change more than 50 percent higher than the change in the Sub-Saharan Africa average over a period of roughly 10–20 years, yellow bars signify that the change was less than 50 percent of the Sub-Saharan Africa average, orange bars signify that the rate worsened from the earlier period, and the black bar shows the Sub-Saharan Africa average.

FIGURE 7.18 Gross female secondary school enrollment, by country, most recent year, 2016–20

Female enrollment as share of age-appropriate female population (%)

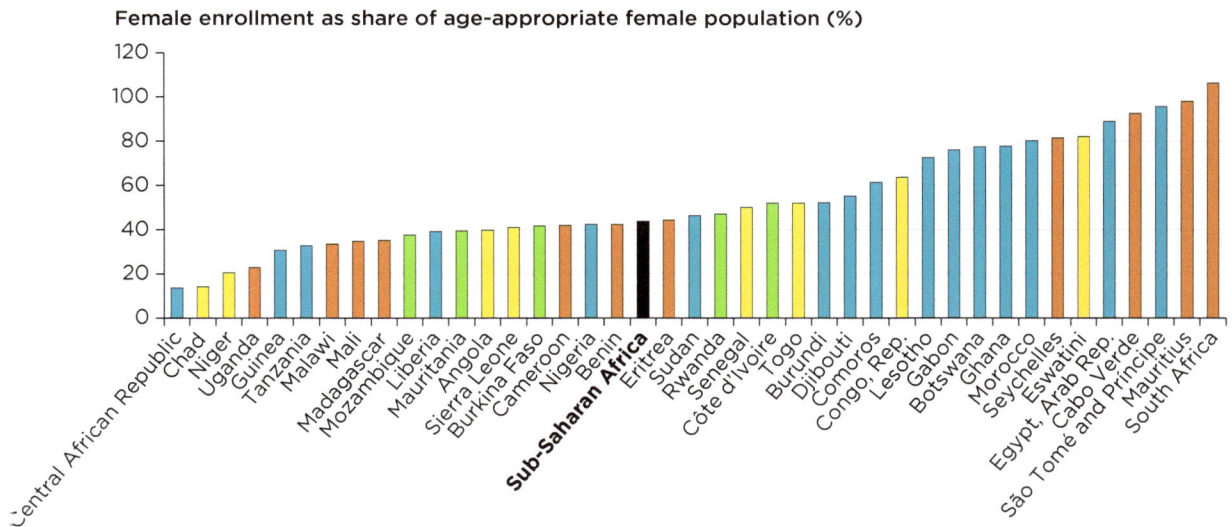

Source: United Nations Educational, Scientific, and Cultural Organization, Institute for Statistics, https://uis.unesco.org/.
Note: Gross female secondary school enrollment refers to the number of women enrolled as a percentage of the number of age-appropriate women. Green bars signify that the country achieved a positive change more than 50 percent higher than the change in the Sub-Saharan Africa average over a period of roughly 10–20 years, yellow bars signify that the change was less than 50 percent of the Sub-Saharan Africa average, orange bars signify that the rate worsened from the earlier period, blue bars indicate that previous data were not available to determine the growth experienced by the country over the period, and the black bar shows the Sub-Saharan Africa average. Gross enrollment rate can exceed 100 percent because it includes students who are older or younger than the official age range. Contributing factors include students repeating grades and those returning to school after dropping out, potentially at an older age.

FIGURE 7.19 Gross tertiary school enrollment, by country, 2018 or latest year

Enrollment as share of age-appropriate population (%)

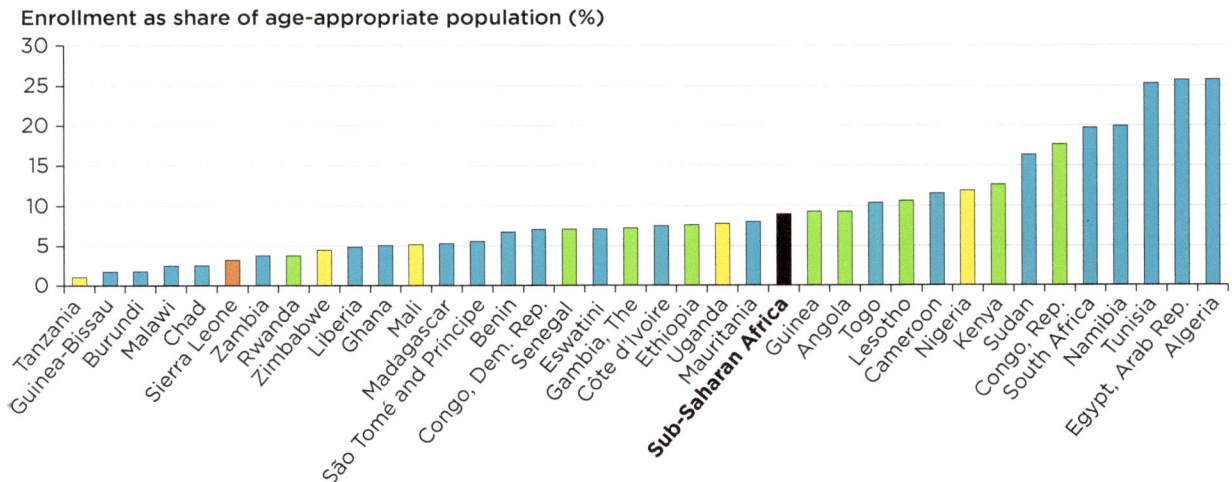

Source: World Bank, Education Statistics, 2020, https://datacatalog.worldbank.org/int/search/dataset/0038480 /education-statistics.
Note: Gross tertiary enrollment refers to the number of students enrolled as a percentage of the number of the age-appropriate population. Green bars signify that the country achieved a positive change more than 50 percent higher than the change in the Sub-Saharan Africa average over a period of roughly 10–20 years, yellow bars signify that the change was less than 50 percent of the Sub-Saharan Africa average, the orange bar signifies that the rate worsened from the earlier period, blue bars indicate that previous data were not available to determine the growth experienced by the country over the period, and the black bar shows the Sub-Saharan Africa average.

BOX 7.2
Positive impacts from the Africa Centers of Excellence program in higher education

Africa's 15- to 24-year-old youth population, one of the continent's greatest assets, could devolve into one of its greatest challenges if it does not urgently prioritize the education, skills, and jobs prospects for this demographic. Globally, Africa has the youngest population and, by 2050, is projected to have 35 percent of the global youth population. Despite progress in improving access to tertiary education, Sub-Saharan Africa has the lowest gross enrollment rate in tertiary education and the smallest share in global scientific and technological research output compared with other regions. Specifically, although Sub-Saharan Africa's average gross tertiary enrollment rate increased from about 3.0 percent in 1990 to 9.4 percent in 2021, it remained significantly lower compared with 27.3 percent in South Asia, 41.0 percent in the Middle East and North Africa, and 84.2 percent in North America. Countries across Africa are prioritizing the science, technology, engineering, and mathematics (STEM) agenda in their policies and strategies, but implementation has been slow. Further, women continue to be underrepresented in STEM programs and careers, especially in those related to engineering and information and communication technology (ICT).

Several national and regional interventions are helping governments in Sub-Saharan Africa make progress in improving the region's tertiary education sector. The World Bank–supported regional Africa Centers of Excellence program in higher education, initiated in 2014, has so far supported 20 Sub-Saharan African governments in funding more than 80 centers to train the next generation of Africa's highly skilled workforce through postgraduate degree programs, upskilling or reskilling the existing workforce through professional short courses, and improving STEM research outputs across fields such as health, agriculture, ICT, energy, sustainable mining, environment, STEM education, and water. As of August 2023, the centers had trained more than 70,000 students (27 percent are women), published more than 8,500 peer-reviewed journal articles, raised more than US$170 million in external revenue, and obtained international accreditation for 116 academic degree programs. Enrollment and retention of female students continue to improve through a strong program-level financial incentive structure and various center-level initiatives such as STEM-focused outreach initiatives in secondary schools, hosting targeted webinars, implementing sexual harassment policies, providing competitive maternity leave packages, and offering preferential housing for female students with families.

Through their quality research, centers have made a remarkable impact on addressing some of the region's pressing development challenges. Many have gone further in advancing their research-to-market efforts by providing entrepreneurship training to both students and faculty, improving the technology transfer capabilities of their host universities, setting up incubation centers, and providing seeding grants for promising innovations. Health-focused centers in Ghana, Nigeria, and Tanzania contributed significantly to mass testing, genomic sequencing, and monitoring of the COVID-19 virus in the region. Agriculture-focused centers in Ghana, Kenya, and Nigeria have helped curb food insecurity by developing and sharing with farmers crop varieties that are more resistant to climate change, pests, and diseases. Centers in Rwanda and Senegal that focus on ICT are using advanced digital technologies (artificial intelligence and Internet of Things) to enhance e-health, e-agriculture, and e-transportation, and to assess and predict pollution. A fisheries center in Malawi

(continued)

BOX 7.2

Positive impacts from the Africa Centers of Excellence program in higher education (continued)

is developing a rapid test kit for early detection, surveillance, and prevention of disease outbreaks in fish. A coastal resilience center in Ghana is helping to build capacity in the region's coastal countries to address challenges related to the blue economy and climate change.

The Africa Centers of Excellence program has demonstrated that Africa does not lack talent or the acumen to deliver on STEM research and innovations, but rather, in most cases, it lacks critical opportunities (strategic financing and technical assistance) to help its young people develop their skills. To turn the tide and ensure a demographic dividend in an increasingly digital and green world will require a sustained level of investments across the learning life cycle of African children and youth.

FIGURE 7.20 **Gross female tertiary school enrollment, by country, most recent year, 2016–20**

Female enrollment as share of age-appropriate female population (%)

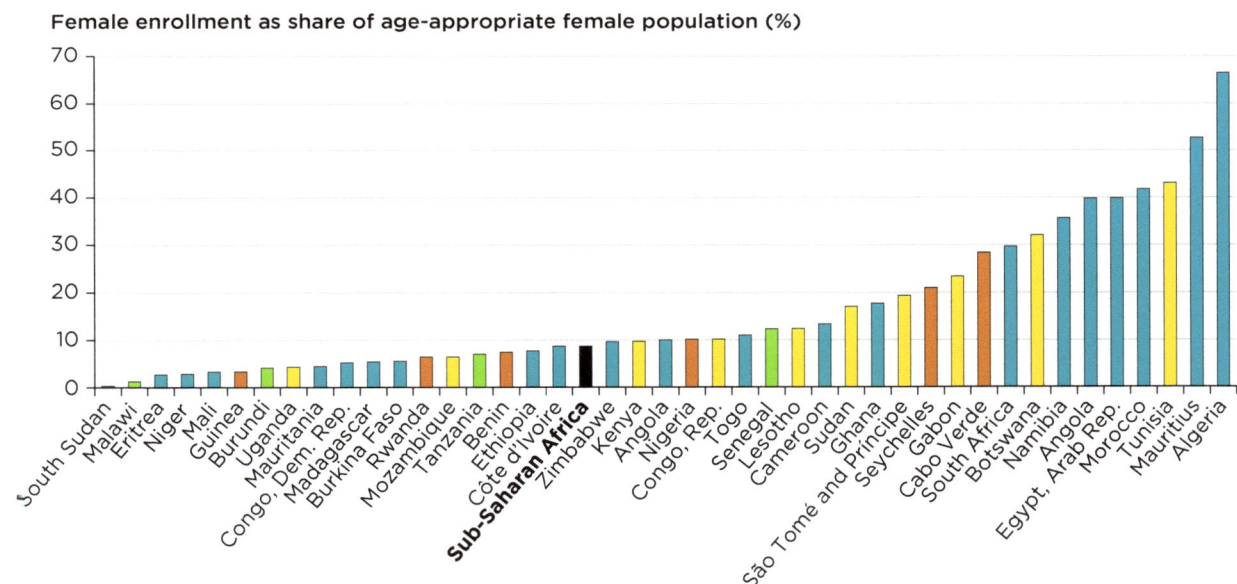

Source: United Nations Educational, Scientific, and Cultural Organization, Institute for Statistics, https://uis.unesco.org/.
Note: Gross female tertiary school enrollment refers to the number of women enrolled as a percentage of the number of age-appropriate women. Green bars signify that the country achieved a positive change more than 50 percent higher than the change in the Sub-Saharan Africa average over a period of roughly 10–20 years, yellow bars signify that the change was less than 50 percent of the Sub-Saharan Africa average, orange bars signify that the rate worsened from the earlier period, blue bars indicate that previous data were not available to determine the growth experienced by the country over the period, and the black bar shows the Sub-Saharan Africa average.

Burundi, Tanzania, and Senegal increased enrollment rates by more than 50 percent, with Tanzania almost tripling its female enrollment from 2.4 to 7.1 percent in only two years, and Senegal almost doubling it from 8.1 percent in 2016 to 14.9 percent in 2021. Other countries saw female enrollment rates slightly decrease; however, in some of these countries with available data, rates increased again in 2021. For instance, female tertiary enrollment in Guinea was 5.4 percent in 2017, 3.3 percent in 2020, and 4.2 percent in 2021; in the Seychelles, it increased from 20.9 percent in 2020 to 27.5 percent in 2021. The Dar es Salaam Declaration committed to increasing access of secondary and tertiary education to at least 20 million additional adolescent girls on the African continent by 2030.

Building skills beyond school

As noted previously, a significant portion of skills building occurs on the job rather than in the classroom. It is crucially important for youth coming out of education to build on their school-acquired learning through jobs before their learning begins to deteriorate. The African continent currently has limited skills building of this type, with a high proportion of young people ages 15–24 not in employment, education, or training, or NEET (figure 7.21). Although data on the proportion of NEET youth are less frequently collected and exist for only 32 African countries, existing data are sufficient to highlight two troubling trends: the large number of NEET youths and rising NEET rates, even in countries that have experienced substantial growth, such as Ghana. These trends can be

FIGURE 7.21 Youth NEET rates, by country, 2018 or most recent year

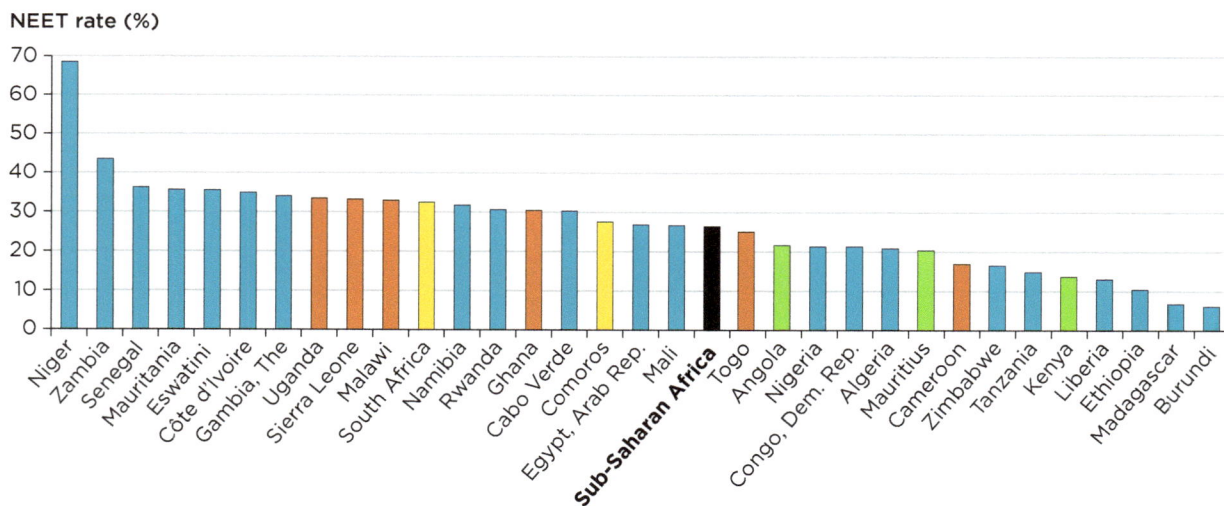

NEET rate (%)

Source: World Bank, Education Statistics, 2020, https://datacatalog.worldbank.org/int/search/dataset/0038480/education-statistics.
Note: The youth NEET rate refers to the proportion of young people ages 15–24 who are not in employment, education, or training. Green bars signify that the country achieved a positive change more than 50 percent higher than the change in the Sub-Saharan Africa average over a period of roughly 10–20 years, yellow bars signify that the change was less than 50 percent of the Sub-Saharan Africa average, orange bars signify that the rate worsened from the earlier period, blue bars indicate that previous data were not available to determine the growth experienced by the country over the period, and the black bar shows the Sub-Saharan Africa average.

attributed to the limited number of jobs and tertiary education and training opportunities coupled with a bulging youth population. Despite improvement in NEET rates in Angola, Kenya, and Mauritius, rates worsened notably in Cameroon, Ghana, Malawi, Togo, and Uganda and saw relatively little change in the Comoros and South Africa.

Many African countries note not only a mismatch between skills supply and demand but also a shortage of workers with a general level of education (World Bank 2023b). Employers identify the lack of an adequately educated labor force as a major constraint to firms' growth and development. Figure 7.22 shows adult literacy rates for many countries in Africa for 2021 (or the most recent year after 2016), highlighting the variation across countries. In Mali, for instance, only 30 percent of adults are literate; by contrast, in South Africa, 95 percent of adults are literate. Since the early 2000s, some countries have experienced rapid literacy increases—such as Côte d'Ivoire (from 48 percent to 89 percent) and The Gambia (from 36 percent to 58 percent)—when compared with other countries. Others have experienced decreases, with a significant decrease in the Central African Republic (from about 50 percent in the early 2000s to 36 percent) and slight decreases in Sudan (from 61 percent to 60 percent), Chad (from 28 percent to 26 percent), and the Comoros, from 68 percent to 61 percent).

African labor markets have an acute shortage of skilled labor across the whole spectrum but have a particular need for science and technology technicians and professionals, nurses and doctors, and skilled labor with hard technical skills needed for construction, energy, agroprocessing, and service industries. Digital skills, including basic skills such as web research and basic software use, are in high demand together with more advanced skills such as digital marketing and artificial intelligence (IFC 2020). Digital skills are particularly important in linking informal sector entrepreneurs with markets for their products and in expanding these markets (Ng'weno and Porteous 2018). The Dar es Salaam Declaration commits countries to provide training for digital skills for an additional 19 million by 2030. Developing skills for green economies is gaining momentum across the continent, for example in Botswana (greening the mining sector), the Democratic Republic of Congo (forest management), Namibia (skills for green energy production), and South Africa (renewables).

Efforts to align skills development with job creation to spur economic growth go beyond the education sector and require private sector participation and employer engagement in design and delivery of skills programs, public-private partnerships, and a whole-of-government approach. Apprenticeships and skills building should be coupled with practical on-the-job training, networking opportunities, mentorship, and career advice. In addition to job-specific skills, the World Economic Forum (2023) emphasizes that workers must be agile in order to adapt to a rapidly changing world with (1) adaptable skills so employees can respond to the unfamiliar and unexpected; (2) a growth mindset to enable creative thinking and an ability to engage in lifelong learning when needed; (3) innovative thinking that allows employees to analyze information to establish facts

FIGURE 7.22 Adult literacy rates, by country, 2021 or most recent year after 2016

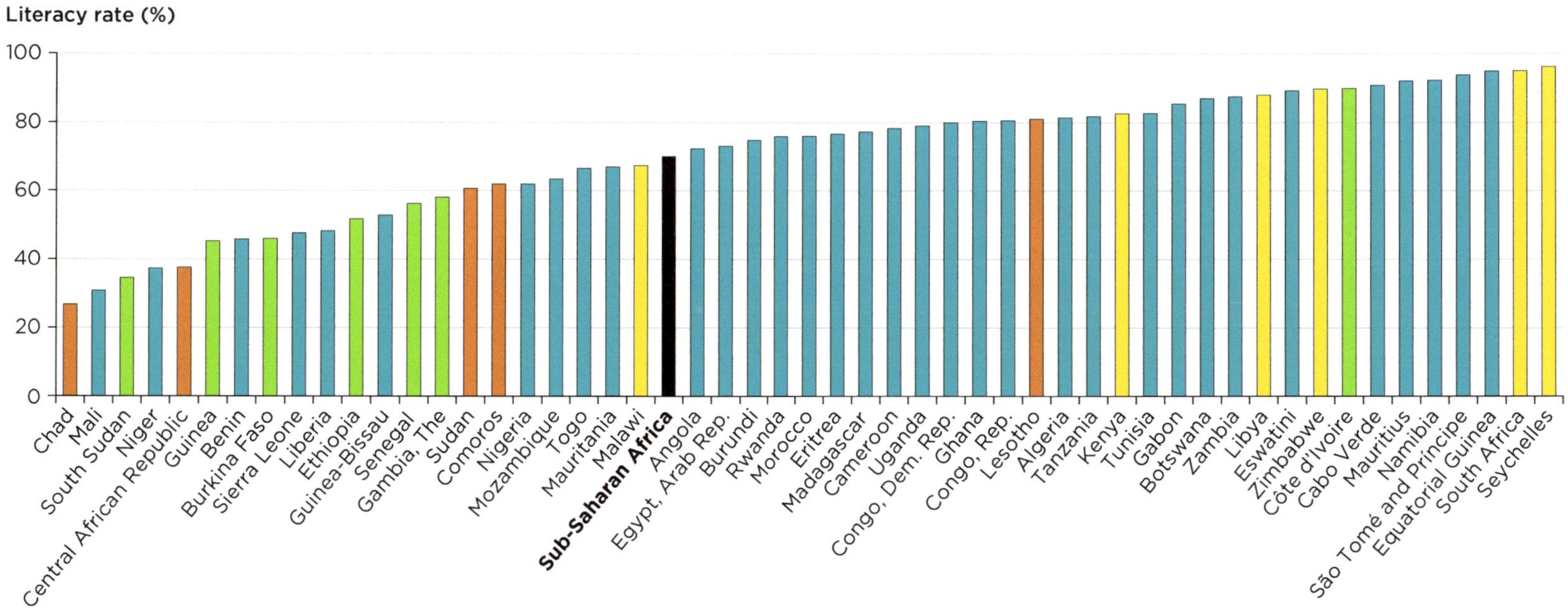

Literacy rate (%)

Source: World Bank, World Development Indicators, https://data.worldbank.org/indicator/.

Note: Green bars signify that the country achieved a positive change more than 50 percent higher than the change in the Sub-Saharan Africa average over a period of roughly 10–20 years, yellow bars signify that the change was less than 50 percent of the Sub-Saharan Africa average, orange bars signify that the rate worsened from the earlier period, blue bars indicate that previous data were not available to determine the growth experienced by the country over the period, and the black bar shows the Sub-Saharan Africa average.

and solve problems; (4) leadership potential to inspire colleagues with values of integrity, hard work, and excellence; and (5) emotional intelligence that allows team members to work well in teams, using empathy and good listening skills to anticipate and respond to customers' needs. The large percentage of employment growth in Africa occurring in the services sector makes the soft skills emphasized under emotional intelligence increasingly important.

There has been a growing focus on how large cash grants, typically blended with labor market initiatives and skills training, can lead to enhanced employment opportunities among select groups, including youth. Unlike traditional safety net interventions, the core objective of these cash grant programs is to create employment. Although some of these interventions have been pilot programs, and others may not scale up easily, the following examples suggest the potential positive impact of interventions like these.

- The Kenya Digital Public Works for Urban Resilience Project trained 282 vulnerable youth in basic digital skills and provided them with mobile phones, drones, and laptops. With these tools, they created Geographic Information System data on roads, buildings, and points of interest.

- The Kenya Youth Employment and Opportunities Project provided 300,000 out-of-work youth with training in life skills, core business skills, and job-specific skills. The project also provided business grants and soft skills and business development services. Of the total participants who received training, 77 percent found jobs; 93 percent of those who received grants set up businesses.

- The Nigeria Youth Employment and Social Support Operation provided training in life skills, sector-specific skills, and entrepreneurship skills—all in areas with employer demand. In addition, participants received six-month internships and a starter pack of tools, equipment, and, when appropriate, links to microcredit. Seventy-two percent of beneficiaries ended up either employed or in self-employment.

- The Yokk Koom Koom Project in Senegal targeted extremely poor safety net beneficiaries. They received training in life skills and microentrepreneurship. In addition, they received a productive grant equal to US$250 and were enrolled in weekly savings groups, which resulted in creation of 12,000 viable microenterprises, with business revenue increasing 24 percent and savings increasing 125 percent in three months.

- The Youth Opportunities Program in Uganda supplies a one-time grant of about US$382 per member to groups of youths, which has led to increases in business assets (57 percent), work hours (17 percent), and earnings (38 percent). Many members also formally registered their enterprises and hired labor.

The evidence suggests that these programs can work particularly if they involve components that tackle a range of vulnerabilities, rather than focusing on just one. (Refer also to box 7.3 for a discussion of the potential of global skills partnerships.)

The potential promise of expanding global skills partnerships

To address labor shortages for particular types of skills in some countries and an excess supply of labor in others, a number of global skills partnerships have sprung up. The destination country, which has high demand for a particular skill, generally underwrites part or all of the training in the home country, and may provide language training. Typically, not all trainees end up migrating, which leaves the home country with a more highly skilled labor force. Those who do migrate can send remittances back to the home country while supplying labor to the destination country. If managed well, the partnership can be a win-win for both the home and destination countries.

The most well-known example is in the Philippines. In this case, however, the Technical Education and Skills Development Authority of the Philippines focuses on occupations in high demand domestically and globally, such as nursing, and provides training to more than 800,000 graduates per year. The government provides predeparture orientation programs to inform migrants of the risks and benefits of migration, labor rights, safety measures, and information specific to the destination. The Department of Migrant Workers supports migrants and their families before departure, while abroad, and on return. Although funded domestically, the training and assistance result in a high volume of both migrants and remittances.

Three newer projects include agreements between Australia and Pacific Island countries for automotive repair, manufacturing, construction and electrical, tourism and hospitality, and health and community services; between Belgium and Morocco in the information and communication technology sector; and between Germany and Kosovo in the construction sector. The Australia Pacific Training Coalition was established in 2007 with campuses in Fiji, Papua New Guinea, Samoa, the Solomon Islands, Timor-Leste, and Vanuatu. The government of Australia heavily subsidizes the course fees. Despite an overall employment rate of 84 percent, the program has placed only 3 percent of its graduates in Australia and New Zealand. The Belgium-Morocco partnership, begun in March 2019, has not yet placed its trainees in Belgium; however, as of March 2021, it had placed 41 percent of its trainees in Morocco, although this time frame included the COVID-19 years.

Still in their early days and with many kinks to be worked out in the development of such agreements, they present a promising way to train workers in middle- and low-income countries with skills that are relevant both domestically and abroad.

Even with immediate improvement in learning and skills-building prospects, children born today will not enter the labor force until the middle of the century and would not represent a substantial portion of the African labor force for 20 or 30 years beyond that. Some efforts will need to focus on achieving greater literacy and numeracy among today's working-age population, particularly among younger adults. Enhacing access to this education will require developing pedagogy specifically for adults on the use of technology and mobile phones. These programs need to occur concurrently with the push to get children, adolescents, and youth to remain in school and to gain employment. Fortunately, programs can be mutually reinforcing: literate parents can help children with schoolwork, and children can help their parents with literacy and numeracy.[10]

Policies

The figures throughout the chapter show the wide differences in achievement across Africa. Thus, recommendations for moving forward must take account of the heterogeneity among African countries. The good news is that it is possible to make significant improvements in a relatively short period of 10–20 years. Countries that have prioritized resources in a particular area of skill and human capital development have made remarkable progress, as shown in the following examples:

- Child mortality fell by approximately 50 percent in Cabo Verde, Ethiopia, and The Gambia.

- Stunting decreased by more than 60 percent in Algeria, Ghana, and São Tomé and Príncipe.

- Infant immunization rates more than tripled in Burkina Faso, the Democratic Republic of Congo, and Mauritania.

- Preprimary school attendance more than doubled in Burundi and Ethiopia.

- The percentage of primary-school-age children out of school dropped by more than 95 percent in Algeria, Ghana, Morocco, and Zimbabwe.

- The percentage of lower-secondary school-age students out of school dropped by 80 percent in Egypt and the Seychelles.

- The number of upper-secondary school-age students out of school dropped by more than 50 percent in Ghana, São Tomé and Príncipe, and the Seychelles.

- The number of teenage pregnancies dropped by more than 45 percent in Cabo Verde, Ethiopia, The Gambia, Kenya, and Libya.

- The percentage of youth NEET dropped by more than 40 percent in Kenya and Mauritius.

Understandably, countries may not have the resources or the bandwidth to focus on improvements in all areas at once. Recommendations need to be as heterogenous as the countries and can be organized around the life cycle and country context. The overall policy recommendations are summarized around the following themes.

Getting children off to the right start:

- Make sure that children are prepared to learn.

- Reduce malnutrition.

- Focus on early childhood development.

Ensuring that all students learn:

- Expand learning opportunities by increasing access to and transforming learning spaces; reducing costs of education, especially for the poor and girls; shift socio-cultural norms around girls' education; ensure safe and inclusive learning environments; and increase the availability, accessibility, and resilience of schools.

- Improve teaching and learning by transforming the teaching profession with a focus on better training, recruitment, and deployment practices; support teaching with structured pedagogy; provide learning resources and edtech tools; teach at the right level in the language that children understand; and foster a culture of regular learning assessments.

Building job-relevant skills for all:

- Dismantle the barriers to skills acquisition through equitable access to remedial programs and boot camps; diversify student financing options; expand access to flexible, lower-cost, and high-quality skilling options; invest in expanding access to and improving quality and relevance of higher education programs, with a focus on STEM; and leverage the private sector.

- Manage delivery for quality and relevance of skills, including developing job-oriented and entrepreneurship skills with industry participation, harnessing digital technologies, promoting innovative pedagogies, investing in targeted research and development, and leveraging regional approaches.

- Strengthen the governance of skills provision, including reforming traditional apprenticeships, formalizing employers' roles in skills provision, enhancing quality frameworks to diversify learning pathways, and facilitating mobility.

Strengthening skills system governance and financing:

- Elevate skills development priorities above line ministries, adopt a whole-of-government approach to skills development, and partner with the private sector and leverage its financing for sustainable skills development.

- Plan and allocate funding to achieve the goals of skills development and tightening public financial management for efficient use of budgets.

- Generate timely data, and use them for evidence-based policy making.

For the most part, countries shown on the left-hand side of each of the figures need to focus on the basics, making sure that young children are prepared to learn, that they can attend school all the way through upper-secondary school, and that they are actually learning. Countries in the middle of the figures already provide skilling opportunities to a significant portion of the youth but might need to focus on those who might be left out: children from poorer families, girls, and children in rural areas (refer to box 7.4). Countries on the right-hand side of the graphs largely have the foundational skills in place but now need to focus on the quality of education. They should emphasize specific skills, such as soft skills and strong information and communication skills, once students have mastered the foundational skills. Programs should guide students toward STEM fields, providing apprenticeships and entrepreneurial skills that will help them find and create jobs as they become adults.

BOX 7.4

Spotlight on disability and inclusion

Although Africa has made significant progress over the past three decades in providing students with access to quality education, millions of the most vulnerable and marginalized students are still left behind. Children with disabilities are among the most invisible, vulnerable, and marginalized groups. Globally, an estimated 1 billion people live with disabilities, or about 15 percent of the world's population; of these, between 93 million and 150 million are children under the age of 14 (WHO and World Bank 2011). In Africa, an estimated 6.4 percent of children in this age group have moderate to severe disabilities, and less than 10 percent of under-14 children with disabilities attend school. People with disabilities are less likely to have access to assistive devices, mobility aids, and support services, which could worsen exclusion (Rohwerder 2015). Social service delivery in refugee camps and humanitarian assistance programs may not be designed to include children with disabilities, lowering access to education (Rohwerder 2015).

Census data for 11 Sub-Saharan African countries show large disparities in educational outcomes for people with disabilities (Wodon et al. 2018). The gap in primary completion rates between children with and without disabilities has increased over time, reaching 13 percentage points for boys and 10 percentage points for girls. Data from the Programme d'Analyse des Systèmes Educatifs de la CONFEMEN (PASEC) in 2014 also show that primary school children identifying as having vision or hearing challenges performed worse on standardized literacy and numeracy tests in all but one (Chad) of 10 PASEC countries.[a]

Children with disabilities lag significantly behind children without disabilities in school enrollment, completion, and literacy rates. Learners with disabilities make up an estimated 15 percent of the out-of-school population. People with sensory, physical, or learning disabilities are 2.5 times more likely to have never attended school than their peers without disabilities (UNESCO 2020). Learners with disabilities living in low-income countries, especially in Sub-Saharan Africa, are more disadvantaged. Even before the COVID-19 pandemic, an estimated 50 percent of all young people with disabilities living in low-income countries were excluded from education (Education Commission 2016). Inequalities in school participation are even greater for children and young people with multiple or severe disabilities (UNICEF 2021).

Girls with disabilities are seen to have a double burden of marginalization: gender and disability (Nguyen 2020). In Burkina Faso, Mali, and Niger, they are less likely to receive an education or to be employed, and are at greater risk of abuse, including sexual violence, compared with all other groups (boys with or without disabilities, and girls without disabilities).

(continued)

Spotlight on disability and inclusion *(continued)*

Although a significant proportion of the population in Sub-Saharan Africa has some form of disability, disability prevalence data are scarce and patchy. Some West and Central African countries such as Burkina Faso, Cameroon, The Gambia, and Ghana plan to or already invest in more robust data collection on children with disabilities; although Burkina Faso implemented its first census on children with disabilities in 2013, the data are still limited.

Recommendations for better inclusive education for learners with disabilities include the following:

- Increase the collection and availability of robust and reliable data for more informed and evidence-based decision-making. For example, ensure that data on disability are disaggregated by geographical area, age, gender, and enrollment status. Address the dearth of research on the educational needs and experiences of children with disabilities, which results from the lack of funding for data collection and disability-specific educational programming (UNESCO 2019).

- Provide better access to assistive technology and digital skills as enablers to education and work. For example, develop opportunities for digital skills training that improves the capabilities of youth with disabilities. On completion of these training opportunities, youth should receive appropriate accredited certification.

- Foster inclusive and accessible school infrastructure or classroom and school environments, and adopt universal design principles adopted for school construction. To promote inclusion, countries should identify infrastructure barriers that prevent children from accessing schools and systematically remove these barriers. It is important to amend construction standards to reflect universal design principles, as in South Sudan (UNICEF 2017). Improvements should extend beyond buildings, such as improving transportation to and from schools and supporting infrastructure.

a. The PASEC student assessment—administered in 10 francophone countries in West Africa (Benin, Burkina Faso, Burundi, Cameroon, Chad, Côte d'Ivoire, Niger, the Republic of Congo, Senegal, and Togo)—is designed to assess student abilities in mathematics and reading (French).

Notes

1. World Bank Africa Human Capital Project, https://www.worldbank.org/en/programs/africa-human-capital-plan.

2. Of the 37 countries globally that the World Bank considers characterized by fragility, conflict, and violence, more than half are on the African continent.

3. Dar es Salaam Declaration on Africa Heads of State Human Capital Summit, July 26, 2023, http://www.maelezo.go.tz/storage/app/uploads/public/64d/de5/c57/64dde5c57b473811726139.pdf.

4. According to the World Health Organization, maternal mortality refers to the death of a woman during pregnancy or within 42 days after abortion, irrespective of the duration and place of the pregnancy, from any cause related to or aggravated by the pregnancy or its management but not from accidental or unintentional causes (https://files.aho.afro.who.int/afahobckpcontainer/production/files/iAHO_Maternal_Mortality_Regional_Factsheet.pdf).

5. Africa needs better and more jobs for its growing population. The main message of chapter 8 is that broader use of productivity-enhancing technologies—both digital and analog—by enterprises can help generate such jobs, including for lower-skilled people.

6. Although figure 7.10 shows the percentage of children out of school in each country, it does not necessarily provide a clear picture of the percentage of school-age children in Africa who are out of school, because countries have different population sizes. The overall number of out-of-school children in Africa is strongly influenced by larger countries like the Democratic Republic of Congo and Nigeria, both of which have a large percentage of children not in school.

7. The number of programs has skyrocketed since the mid-2000s (although many programs remain limited in size), and all countries have now deployed safety net interventions as part of their core development program. This shift in social policy reflects the progressive evolution in the understanding of the role that social safety nets can play in the fight against poverty and vulnerability, and more generally in the human capital and growth agenda of much of the continent (World Bank 2018).

8. Two of the countries with the largest school-age populations, the Democratic Republic of Congo and Nigeria, did not have recent data available to include in figure 7.13.

9. The gross enrollment ratio for secondary school is calculated by dividing the number of students enrolled in secondary education regardless of age by the population of the age group which officially corresponds to secondary education, and multiplying by 100. The gross enrollment ratio for tertiary school is calculated by dividing the number of students enrolled in tertiary education regardless of age by the population of the age group which officially corresponds to tertiary education, and multiplying by 100. Data on education are collected by the United Nations Educational, Scientific, and Cultural Organization (UNESCO) Institute for Statistics from official responses to its annual education survey. All the data are mapped to the International Standard Classification of Education (ISCED) to ensure the comparability of education programs at the international level. The current version was formally adopted by UNESCO Member States in 2011. Population data are drawn from the United Nations Population Division. Using a single source for population data standardizes definitions, estimations, and interpolation methods, ensuring a consistent methodology across countries and minimizing potential enumeration problems in national censuses.

10. World Bank (2021) emphasizes the importance of establishing higher levels of adult literacy and the strategies for doing so.

References

Education Commission (International Commission on Financing Global Education Opportunity). 2016. "The Learning Generation: Investing in Education for a Changing World." Education Commission. https://report.educationcommission.org/wp-content/uploads/2016/09/Learning _Generation_Full_Report.pdf.

IFC (International Finance Corporation). 2020. *Digital Skills in Sub-Saharan Africa: Spotlight on Ghana*. Washington, DC: IFC.

Jedwab, R., P. Romer, A. M. Islam, and R. Samaniego. 2023. "Human Capital Accumulation at Work: Estimates for the World and Implications for Development." *American Economic Journal: Macroeconomics* 15 (3): 191–223.

Lufumpa, N., A. Hilger, O. Ng, and B. L. De La Brière. 2023. "Protecting Human Capital from the Impact of Early Life Shocks: Key Interventions for Lower-Middle-Income Countries." Sahel Adaptive Social Protection Program Policy Note 7, World Bank, Washington, DC.

Nguyen, X. T. 2020. "Whose Research Is It? Reflection on Participatory Research with Women and Girls with Disabilities in the Global South." *Jeunesse: Young People, Texts, Cultures* 12 (2): 129–53.

Ng'weno, A., and D. Porteous. 2018. "Let's Be Real: The Informal Sector and the Gig Economy Are the Future, and the Present, of Work in Africa." CGD Note, October 2018, Center for Global Development, Washington, DC.

Ralston, L., C. Andrews, and A. Hsiao. 2017. "The Impacts of Safety Nets in Africa: What Are We Learning?" Policy Research Working Paper 8255, World Bank, Washington, DC.

Rohwerder, B. 2015. "Disability Inclusion: Topic Guide." GSDRC, International Development Department, College of Social Sciences, University of Birmingham, Birmingham, UK.

UNESCO (United Nations Trade and Development). 2019. *On the Road to Inclusion: Highlights from the UNICEF and IIEP Technical Round Tables on Disability-Inclusive Education Sector Planning.* Paris: UNESCO.

UNESCO (United Nations Trade and Development). 2020. *Global Education Monitoring Report, 2020: Inclusion and Education. All Means All.* Paris: UNESCO.

UNICEF (United Nations Children's Fund). 2017. *UNICEF Annual Report 2017: Sudan.* New York: United Nations.

UNICEF (United Nations Children's Fund). 2021. *Seen, Counted, Included: Using Data to Shed Light on the Well-Being of Children with Disabilities.* New York: United Nations.

WHO (World Health Organization) and World Bank. 2011. *World Report on Disability.* Geneva: World Health Organization.

Wodon, Q. T., C. Male, C. E. Montenegro, and K. A. Nayihouba. 2018. *The Challenge of Inclusive Education in Sub-Saharan Africa.* The Price of Exclusion: Disability and Education. Washington, DC: World Bank.

World Bank. 2018. *The State of Social Safety Nets 2018.* Washington, DC: World Bank.

World Bank. 2021. *The Wealth of Today and Tomorrow.* Sahel Education White Paper. Washington, DC: World Bank.

World Bank. 2023a. "Sierra Leone Human Capital Review: Maximizing Human Potential for Resilience and Inclusive Development." Report No. AUS0003323, World Bank, Washington, DC.

World Bank. 2023b. *Western and Central Africa Education Strategy.* Washington, DC: World Bank.

World Bank. 2024. "Democratic Republic of Congo: Expanding and Equipping Primary School Classrooms for Better Learning Outcomes." Press release, February 26, 2024. https://www.worldbank.org/en/news/press-release/2024/02/28/democratic-republic-of-congo-afe-expanding-and-equipping-primary-school-classrooms-for-better-learning-outcomes.

World Economic Forum. 2023. *Future of Jobs Report.* WEF: Geneva.

CHAPTER 8

Digitalization

Izak Atiyas and Mark Dutz

Summary

African countries need better and more jobs for their growing populations. The main message of this chapter is that broader use of productivity-enhancing digital and analog technologies by all enterprises can help generate such jobs, including for lower-skilled people. Adaptation and adoption of better technologies can support Africa's vision of economic transformation with more inclusive job growth. However, neither adoption of better technologies nor their positive contribution to inclusive job growth is automatic. Without the effective implementation of additional policies and without more public and private investments in productive assets, digitalization may proceed at too slow a pace to generate the needed jobs. Further, unless policy actions are taken urgently, digitalization may overwhelmingly benefit those enterprises and workers who already have privileged access to more advanced technologies, hindering the goal of generating good jobs and incomes for all.

Increased internet availability over recent years has led to job creation and poverty reduction. In Nigeria and Tanzania, labor force participation causally increased by 3 and 8 percentage points, respectively, after three or more years of exposure to the internet relative to areas with no coverage, and poverty rates fell by 7 percentage points. Welfare impacts are higher among poorer and less educated households. At the enterprise level, the use of more sophisticated digital and complementary technologies is also associated with higher productivity and job growth, especially for informal firms.

Despite those benefits, too few enterprises are productively using digital technologies, and incomplete digitalization is widespread across Africa. Mobile internet availability has increased in recent years, but Africa's internet availability still lags other regions, compounded by a significant usage gap. Although 88 percent of people in Africa had third-generation (3G) mobile internet services available to them in 2022, only 23 percent used those services—amounting to an uptake gap of 74 percent as a share of those with internet availability, the highest gap in the world. Among firms using digital technologies such as business applications, most do not use them intensively: 62 percent of firms adopting digital technologies for productive purposes do not use their most advanced technology intensively but rely instead on less sophisticated and manual technologies; only one in three firms that adopt sophisticated digital technologies uses them intensively.

To realize the inclusive job growth benefits of digitalization, Africa needs to implement two sets of complementary policies:

1. *Affordable availability policies to ensure that all enterprises are able to pay for sufficiently high-quality digital technologies*. Availability policies must jointly address internet and complementary electricity affordability, quality internet availability, adequate data infrastructure, and availability of affordable complementary assets and technologies. Integrated regional connectivity and data markets could be indispensable over the coming years to facilitate the scalability of technologies across the continent, boosting positive network effects, economies of scale and scope, and competition benefits.

2. *Policies on attractiveness and capabilities to elicit willingness to use technologies for productive purposes*. They include technology policies, data policies and regulations, capability support programs, and national strategies. For use to be inclusive, technology entrepreneurs need to provide sophisticated yet simple-to-use and attractive apps on 3G, 4G, and 5G networks through touch-screen pictures, voice, and video in languages people speak to enable enterprises and households with their existing capabilities to want them, use them, and learn as they work. Africa needs to implement policies for technology entrepreneurs to redirect technologies to the level of skills that most people have—and thereby enable them to boost their skills and earnings over time.

Context

Digitalization refers to the representation, modification, and transmission of information through binary digits in ways that improve business and other daily processes. For digitalization, "claiming the 21st century" means a massive uptake of digital tools that are attractive to all people with the skills they have and that enable them to learn and to increase their earnings over time through better jobs. Attractive digital technologies (DTs)—supported by investments in capabilities and complementary infrastructure and other technologies—are tools that can help enable growth in good jobs through economywide productive use. DTs support the creation of more and better jobs by larger expanding firms, young and growing start-up entrepreneurs, and informal microenterprises willing and able to use them. The chapter leverages two reports on DTs that are informed by novel survey instruments measuring the use of technologies at the enterprise level, as well as other new empirical studies (Begazo, Blimpo, and Dutz 2023; Cruz 2024). It also includes new empirical analyses. This section presents a framework for assessing the impact of DTs on inclusive productivity growth and jobs. The framework is useful to highlight inclusive impacts on jobs through productivity enabled by digitalization.

This chapter emphasizes technological transformation driven by innovation and diffusion. The term "economic transformation" is defined as pathways to inclusive productivity growth, namely, better ways of doing things that generate more jobs and income, especially for low-income people, as opposed to productivity growth that generates more output without also generating more jobs or that generates jobs only for a small share of higher-income, higher-skilled people. Technological transformation as a pathway to more inclusive productivity growth occurs both through diffusion, when enterprises adopt and more intensively use better existing technologies, and through innovation, when enterprises create new technologies including by adapting existing technologies for local contexts with these technologies generating more jobs and income for low-income people as well.

Generating more jobs through the adoption of productivity-enhancing technologies, including for lower-skilled people, is not typically straightforward. In addition to profitable production and sales by new firms, it requires larger volumes of production and sales by existing firms that result from the cost reductions and quality improvements enabled by these technologies. These advances require competition in input and output markets for more efficient firms to expand and sufficient responsiveness of consumer demand to the lower prices stimulated by technologies and product competition. They also require adopted technologies to be sufficiently complementary with lower-skilled workers so that their jobs are not eliminated but rather enhanced into new tasks for which they can build the needed capabilities as they work. Generated and adopted technologies need to be jobs-enhancing and to increase people's marginal productivity, rather than jobs-replacing.[1]

Two complementary pathways to inclusive productivity growth—sectoral and spatial transformation—arise from improving the allocation of resources rather than from innovation and diffusion of technologies. *Sectoral transformation* is the reallocation of resources to more efficient, job-creating activities across firms and industries driven by market contestability. *Spatial transformation* is the reallocation of resources to more efficient job-creating locations driven through different types of spatial integration, including greater regional regulatory harmonization, deeper regional trade facilitated by regional digital platforms, better links between smaller and larger local and global firms in specific value chains, urbanization and associated agglomeration economies, and improved links across urban and rural and lagging regions. Although digitalization can also help support sectoral and spatial transformations as additional complementary pathways toward better jobs for more people, its main contribution is to support technological transformation.

The chapter's framework links availability of DTs and their use to inclusive job growth and poverty reduction impacts (figure 8.1). It includes five digital enablers of DT availability that facilitate use and impact of DTs: digital infrastructure, skills, businesses, finance, and public platforms. The framework begins with the figure's left column on availability of DTs. Affordable availability of broadband internet is a necessary condition

FIGURE 8.1 Conceptual framework on availability, use, and impacts of DTs

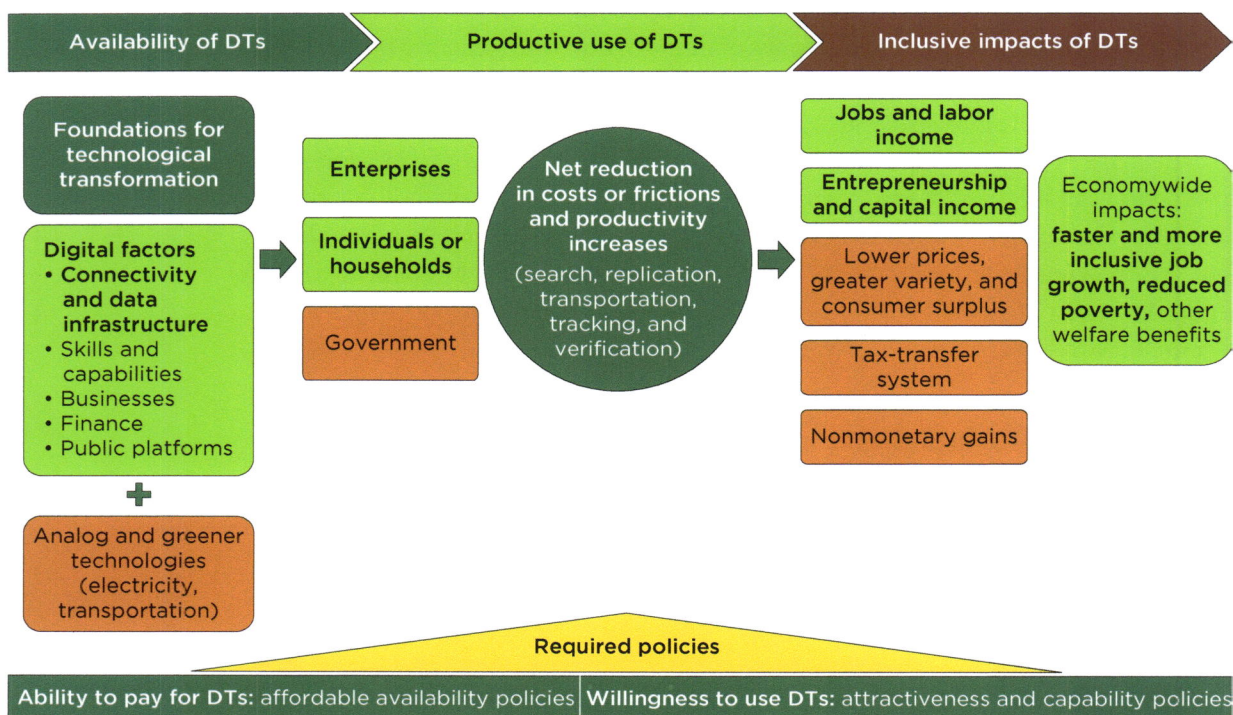

Source: Begazo, Blimpo, and Dutz 2023, figure 1.3.
Note: Bolded text indicates the primary focus of this chapter, emphasizing the production side of the economy.
DTs = digital technologies.

as an economywide enabler, without which none of the other more sophisticated DTs and complementary technologies that rely on internet can be accessed and used. Affordable availability also includes investments in analog complements: the Internet of Things requires not only internet but also analog "things," such as tractors and irrigation systems on which data sensors can be installed, electricity infrastructure to power internet and associated DTs, and transportation infrastructure to get inputs to farms and produced goods to markets.

The middle column of the figure is about adoption and productive use by enterprises, and by individuals and households as entrepreneurs, managers, and workers. Drivers of use by enterprises and individuals, on the supply side, are related to affordability, including of access technologies (smartphones, computers, and tablets) and electricity, and sufficient disposable income or access to finance to be able to pay. Adoption and use are facilitated by cost-reflective prices, stimulated by investments in new infrastructure-related technologies and competition for available digital infrastructure connections. On the demand side, drivers affecting willingness to use DTs include attractiveness to users, including available information about the DTs; relevance to the local context; ease of use, potentially linked to age, gender, language, and relevant local content;

various types of risk and uncertainty; trust; being part of valued networks such as having friends or other firms in one's ecosystem using similar DTs; and basic education and skills-related capabilities to use and extract value from DTs.

Finally, as highlighted in the figure's right column, the inclusive impacts of DTs depend on how intensively people use technologies that enhance productivity. Interactions with analog technologies and other complements as well as with the prevailing business environment also affect outcomes arising from DT use.

The framework centers on the distinguishing characteristic of DTs: their effect on reducing different types of economic costs or business-related frictions. The internet is a "general purpose technology" that reduces costs across the economy and allows better data-driven decision-making, which in turn can enable technological and broader economic transformation. DTs help reduce different types of costs for search, replication, transportation, tracking, and verification (Goldfarb and Tucker 2019), and thereby facilitate productive learning by enterprises, their entrepreneurs, managers, and workers. The framework clarifies how these cost reductions have effects across five channels: jobs and labor income arising from lower costs faced by enterprises and individuals as workers; entrepreneurship and capital income earned by owners of larger firms and household enterprises; consumer surplus arising from lower prices, higher quality, and wider variety; the tax-transfer system; and nonmonetary gains. As costs decline, the resulting shifts in economic behavior have implications for firms, households, and government. The cost-centric framework and its components highlight how DT uptake and use increase opportunities to access local and global product, labor, land, and financial markets by enterprises and individuals. The framework also clarifies that it is through the reduction of various costs that DT use facilitates business continuity when face-to-face or close-contact production of goods and services would otherwise be disrupted by COVID-19 or similar health risks.

The informal economy is a major source of income and job creation for most people in Africa and is therefore a special focus of this chapter. Many informal businesses are in wholesale and retail trade, and are also often owned or headed by women. A recent cross-country microenterprise survey found that women owned or headed 54 percent of such businesses, with high rates especially in Nigeria (59 percent), Ghana (58 percent), and Mozambique (50 percent) (Mothobi, Gillwald, and Aguera 2020). Self-employment is one of the major reasons why entrepreneurs start their own business (about 40 percent in all surveyed countries). Closing the digital gap is critical, especially among microenterprises where most poor, lower-skilled people work.

Because the formal private sector is still too small in most countries to absorb the existing stock of informal workers and the growing working-age population, working in the informal sector is probably the main pathway to generate incomes for most of the labor force in the short term. Generating increases in income will therefore require productivity upgrading within the informal sector. If the productivity of self-employed household enterprises and other microenterprises is improved through DTs and complementary technologies, it will lead to positive employment effects—more income, more job creation—reducing poverty and enabling shared prosperity. Understanding the uses of DTs among microenterprises, including youth and women entrepreneurs, and their association with productivity, sales, exports, and jobs, will aid effective policies to improve the availability of affordable digital infrastructure and increase firms' technological adaptation. Concurrently, a better understanding of the uses of DTs among larger formal enterprises is also important, because formal wage jobs in more productive new and growing formal firms offer the pathway to generate quantum leaps in higher sustainable incomes for all over the longer term.

By focusing on productive use and inclusive impacts, the conceptual framework highlights an important distinction between two views of digitalization. The traditional view of digitalization, largely a supply-side view, is to provide universal availability of digital infrastructure; however, this chapter's conceptual framework highlights the need to also focus on boosting productive use. The traditional emphasis on universal service of digital communications must move away from focusing on universal coverage of the fastest internet to targeting productive use that generates large inclusive jobs-related spillover effects. A more nuanced view of digitalization underscores the interdependency between demand and supply. Making DTs affordable and usable by lower-skilled people will require more flexible support policies that allow for trial and error to spur further innovations in an open, transparent, and predictable environment. Innovations are particularly needed in technologies that lower-skilled people find attractive, want to use, and that enable them to learn and boost their capabilities to generate higher earnings. This view of digitalization emphasizes the interdependency between demand and supply, because greater demand for productive use and the ability to pay for these services will enable investments in needed higher-quality DT services to be sufficiently profitable to move forward with the required urgency.

Facts

This section provides basic facts about the impact of digitalization on economic outcomes such as productivity, jobs, and welfare, and on access to and adoption of digital technologies.

Positive impacts of digitalization on jobs and welfare

The good news regarding the effects of digital infrastructure is that an increasing body of robust evidence shows that internet availability has had a causal inclusive impact on increasing jobs and reducing poverty in selected African countries over recent years. New evidence is available based on both household and enterprise data.

Faster internet in Sub-Saharan Africa was facilitated by the gradual arrival of submarine cables from Europe in the late 2000s and early 2010s that greatly increased the speed and capacity of terrestrial networks. For enterprises and households located in the vicinity of those terrestrial networks, the probability that an individual is employed increased by 6.9 percent and 13.2 percent, respectively, for countries in different samples—demographic and health surveys across eight Sub-Saharan African countries and Afrobarometer surveys across nine Sub-Saharan African countries—and by 3.1 percent in South Africa, relative to areas unconnected to submarine cables (Hjort and Poulsen 2019). Importantly, the increase in jobs in these areas did not occur because of job displacement in unconnected areas. These impacts attributable to faster internet are net positive job increases and sizable in magnitude. In terms of the skill content of jobs, faster internet adoption is skills-biased—that is, internet complements more skilled jobs, as shown in high-income countries.[2] In terms of educational attainment, even low-educated workers benefit, although workers who did not complete primary education were disadvantaged: the percentage change in the probability of employment was significantly positive in the range of 6 percent for workers with primary, secondary, and higher education levels, but not statistically significant for workers not having completed primary education. In terms of the mechanisms through which faster internet availability increases jobs, net firm entry explains part of the increase in jobs (about 23 percent in South Africa), including a large increase in firm entry and a decrease in firm exit of similar magnitude. Another component of the jobs increase appears to be due to increased productivity in existing manufacturing firms (in Ethiopia). Enterprises in Ghana, Kenya, Mauritania, Nigeria, Senegal, and Tanzania with access to faster internet export more, communicate with clients more, and train employees more, according to World Bank Enterprise Survey data. The productivity of lower-educated workers, those who completed only primary education, may have benefited from targeted on-the-job training by employers.

Two new empirical studies based on household data add to the rapidly growing positive evidence base by exploring the direct impact of mobile internet availability (3G or 4G coverage) on jobs and welfare (Bahia et al. 2020; Bahia et al. 2023). The studies take advantage of geospatial information on the rollout of mobile internet towers over time, combined with at least two rounds of household data over a period of six to seven years. Figure 8.2 summarizes the main jobs and welfare (consumption and poverty) results for Nigeria and Tanzania.

Internet availability had positive impacts on jobs and welfare in Nigeria. Labor force participation and wage employment increased by 3 and 1 percentage points, respectively, after three or more years of exposure in areas with internet availability, relative to those with no coverage. Total consumption increased by about 9 percent, whereas the proportion of households below the extreme poverty line declined by 7 percent after three years. Welfare results are higher among poorer and rural households. Job estimates for Tanzania are similarly significant. Working-age individuals living in areas with internet availability witnessed increases in labor force participation and wage employment of 8 and 4 percentage points, respectively, after three or more years of exposure. Total consumption per capita among households residing in areas with 3G availability was about 10 percent higher than in areas without coverage. Moreover, the proportion of households falling below the national basic need

FIGURE 8.2 **Impact of internet availability on job creation and household welfare, Nigeria and Tanzania**

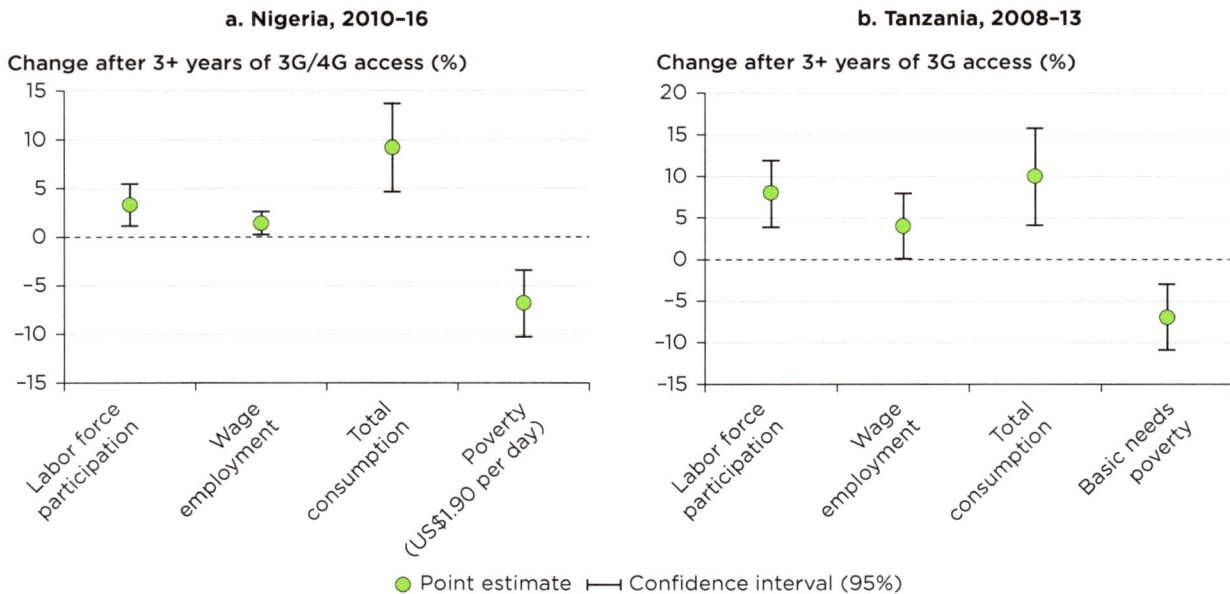

a. Nigeria, 2010–16   b. Tanzania, 2008–13

Change after 3+ years of 3G/4G access (%)   Change after 3+ years of 3G access (%)

Source: Begazo, Blimpo, and Dutz 2023, figure 1.5, based on Bahia et al. 2020 and Bahia et al. 2023.
Note: Difference-in-difference estimates with 95 percent confidence intervals. Each point represents the estimated impact of mobile internet coverage on labor and welfare outcomes. The reported effects on poverty in the graph are not comparable. For Nigeria, poverty status is defined using the international poverty line of US$1.90 per day. For Tanzania, the graph reports the impact of 3G coverage on basic needs poverty, derived using the cost of buying adequate daily nutrition per person plus the cost of some nonfood essentials. 3G (4G) = third (fourth) generation.

poverty line dropped by 7 percentage points. Welfare gains were higher among households headed by women, those with lower incomes, and those with less education (not having completed primary school).

At the enterprise level, new and compelling evidence indicates that innovation, as reflected in the use of more sophisticated DTs, is associated with higher average productivity levels and better jobs for more people. The studies are based on two different firm-level surveys, the Firm-level Adoption of Technology (FAT) survey and the Research ICT Africa (RIA) After Access Business survey.[3]

The FAT survey, restricted to enterprises with five or more employees, was initially available for Ghana, Kenya, Malawi, and Senegal, together with Brazil and Viet Nam as comparator countries (Cirera, Comin, and Cruz 2022). To measure DT use, the FAT survey links technologies to specific business functions. For each enterprise, it asks what technology the enterprise uses most intensively for each of its general business functions (GBFs). GBFs are tasks that all firms conduct, regardless of their main economic activity: business administration, including human resources, accounting, and financing; production planning; sourcing, including procurement and supply chain management; marketing, including product development; sales; payment; and quality control. The technologies used most intensively for each GBF are used to calculate an index score ranging from 1 to 5, where 1 reflects the most basic level of technology (invariably analog), 2 typically represents the simplest DT, and 5 refers to the most sophisticated frontier-level technology. Firms with a uniform technological sophistication index score of 1 do not use DTs intensively for any of their GBF tasks; they most frequently use hand-written processes for accounting, face-to-face conversations for marketing, and simple manual and visual inspection techniques for quality control. Firms with an index score of 2 use the simplest DTs such as the most basic Excel software on a computer for accounting, online chat (for example, on a pre-internet 2G phone version of WhatsApp) for marketing, and human inspection supported by a simple computer or digital phone for quality control. Firms with an index score of 5 use the most sophisticated enterprise resource planning or equivalent software, integrated with other back-office functions for accounting, big data analytics supported by machine learning algorithms for marketing, or sensor- and laser-based automated inspection systems for quality control.

The use of more sophisticated DTs and related technologies is associated with higher productivity country by country across Africa, especially for informal firms. At the country level, firms with higher average technological sophistication have higher levels of productivity on average, with varying degrees of responsiveness: formal firms with a one-point higher score in the technology adoption index for technologies for GBF tasks that the firm uses most intensively are associated with a higher level of labor productivity in Ghana (1.9), Kenya (1.2), Malawi (1.4), and Senegal (2.0) (figure 8.3, panel a). Interestingly, in Senegal, informal firms show a significantly higher association between technology use and productivity compared with formal firms: on average, informal firms have double the value added per worker from more sophisticated technology use than formal firms, 4.0 percent relative to 2.0 percent increase in labor productivity. On average, firms in Ghana, Malawi, and Senegal also have a higher productivity level associated with an increase in technological sophistication than firms in Brazil and Viet Nam.

Importantly, more intensive use of DTs is also associated both with more jobs and with more inclusive jobs. Formal firms with a one-point higher technology adoption score for technologies used most intensively for GBF tasks have a statistically significant higher number of workers in Ghana and Senegal (figure 8.3, panel b). In Ghana, this increase is higher on average than in Brazil and Viet Nam. Firms in Senegal are also more likely to see an expansion in the share of lower-skilled workers. Even if some new DTs may be labor-saving, firms in Senegal disproportionally increase the share of lower-skilled workers as they expand total jobs: firms with a one-point higher technology adoption score for technologies used most intensively for GBF tasks have a 7 percent lower share of high-skilled workers in total employment. These country-level findings of higher and more inclusive employment also hold for a larger cross-country sample of firms across Bangladesh, Brazil, Ghana, India, Kenya, the Republic of Korea, Senegal, and Viet Nam,

FIGURE 8.3 Association between the use of more sophisticated DTs and firm productivity and job growth, selected countries

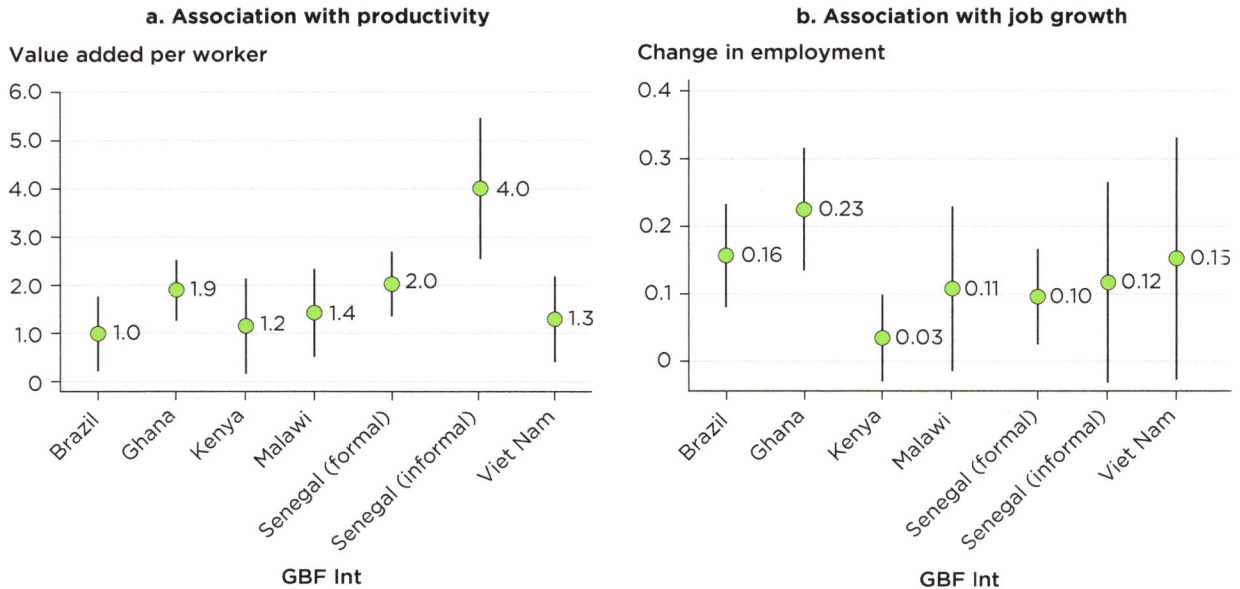

a. Association with productivity

Value added per worker

b. Association with job growth

Change in employment

GBF Int

GBF Int

Source: Begazo, Blimpo, and Dutz 2023, figure O.4, based on Cirera, Comin, and Cruz 2022.
Note: The figure shows a positive and statistically significant association between changes in the technology sophistication index, which averages the most intensively used technologies across GBFs (GBF Int) for each firm, and changes in productivity levels (panel a) and changes in employment levels (panel b). Data show associations for firms with a one-point higher level of the technology sophistication index after controlling for firm characteristics, such as firm size, formality status, sector, and region. The surveys were implemented during 2019–2ʳ. DTs = digital technologies; GBFs = general business functions.

where a one-point higher technology index for GBFs at the intensive margin is associated with an 8.9 percent higher number of workers on average and a 0.8-percentage-point lower share of high-skilled workers.

The RIA After Access Business survey, which focuses on microenterprises, yields a similar positive correlation between the use of more sophisticated DTs and higher levels of jobs. The median RIA enterprise is a self-employed household enterprise with no full-time employees, and most firms in the survey are informal. This sample covers Ghana, Kenya, Mozambique, Nigeria, Senegal, South Africa, and Tanzania. Findings show that a greater range of more sophisticated DT uses by microenterprises based on internet-enabled computers or smartphones (figure 8.4, light green bars) relative to DT uses based on only 2G phones (figure 8.4, dark green bars) are conditionally associated with higher job levels. Importantly, the findings show a positive progression in the number of more sophisticated DTs associated in turn with higher productivity, sales, and job levels. These more sophisticated DT uses are associated with and may enable greater-scale expansion, especially jobs.

FIGURE 8.4 Association between the use of more sophisticated DTs and microenterprise productivity, sales, and jobs

Conditional correlations

Use of DTs enabled by computers or smartphones
Use of DTs enabled by 2G (non-internet-enabled) mobile phones

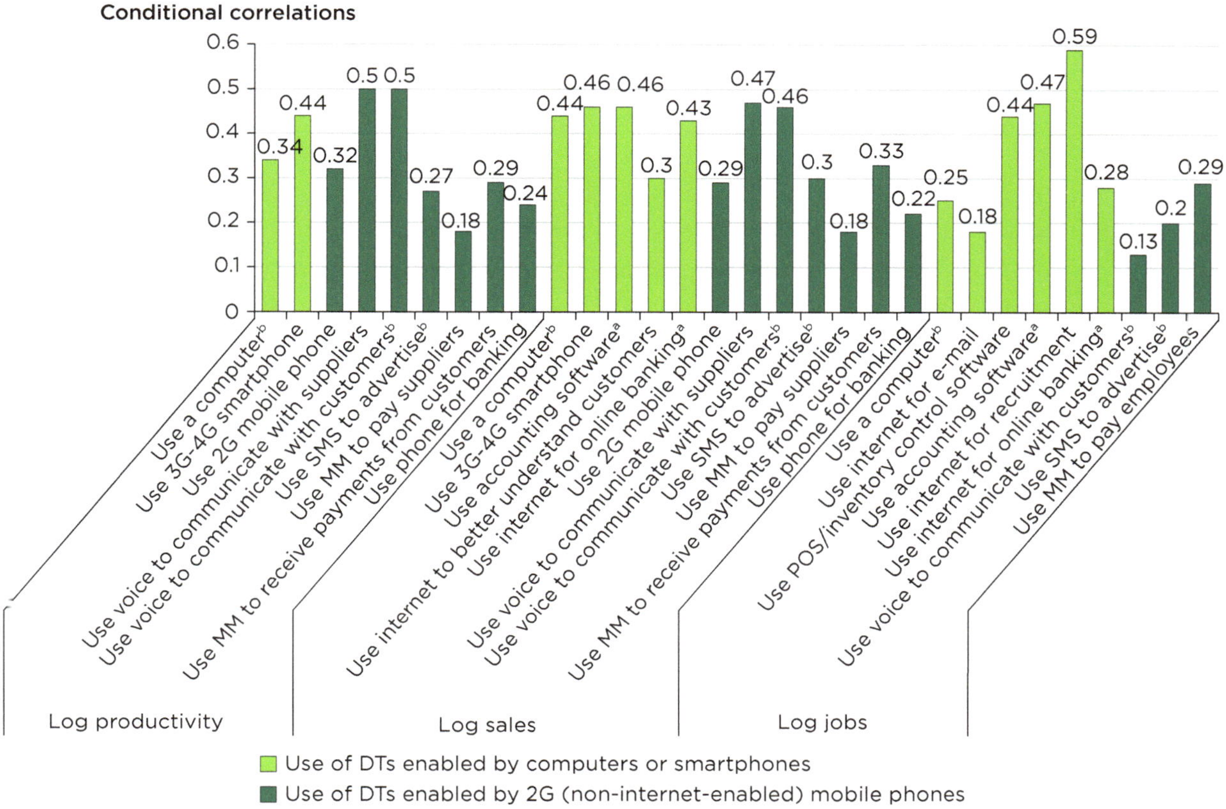

Source: Atiyas and Dutz 2023.

Note: Conditional correlates of productivity, sales, and jobs that are significant at least at the 5 percent level based on ordinary least squares with robust standard errors using unweighted data. Controls include manager age, schooling, and vocational training; firm age; having electricity and a loan; whether the owner is transformational (owners selecting themselves as entrepreneurs for the profit-making opportunity as opposed to a necessity or subsistence choice to supplement earnings or because there is no preferred wage job available); links with more sophisticated upstream suppliers or downstream customers; informal and urban/rural status; and sector. Data cover 3,325 firms across Ghana, Kenya, Mozambique, Nigeria, Senegal, South Africa, and Tanzania during 2017–18. Productivity is measured as value added (total sales minus raw materials and intermediate inputs plus water and electricity used in production) divided by the sum of full-time workers and the number of owners. The value of total sales or turnover reflects, as described in the questionnaire, "revenues money received by the business." Employment is the number of full-time employees plus owners. 2G (3G, 4G) = second (third, fourth) generation; DTs = digital technologies; MM = mobile money; POS = point of sale; SMS = Short Message Service.
a. Denotes variables that are statistically significant across both sales and jobs.
b. Denotes variables that are statistically significant across all three performance outcomes.

These findings of an association between the sophistication of DT use and largely informal microenterprise job performance explicitly control for whether the enterprise has ever had a loan, has access to electricity, is run by transformational entrepreneurs, or has links with more sophisticated upstream suppliers or downstream customers, among other available relevant variables.

Six internet-enabled and three non-internet-enabled DT uses are the only significant conditional correlates of higher job levels—in addition to the gender and age of the manager (being male and younger), the manager having had vocational training, the owner being a transformational entrepreneur, the enterprise having more sophisticated upstream and/or downstream links with suppliers and customers, and key enterprise characteristics, such as older and formal firms, and whether the firm has ever had a loan and has electricity. The manager's level of schooling is a significant positive conditional correlate of productivity, sales, and wages per worker, and whether the manager had vocational training is a significant positive conditional correlate of sales, profits, and jobs. On its own, using a smartphone is not conditionally associated in a statistically significant way with performance outcomes, but using a computer is, as is using the internet to find suppliers, to understand customers, and for online banking, and using accounting and inventory control/point-of-sale (POS) software. Importantly, use of DTs for these simple management functions is strongly associated with an increase in the number of jobs, relative to most other uses of DTs reported by microenterprises: the use of accounting and inventory control/POS software is associated with larger firm size—by roughly 1.6 people (0.47 and 0.44 log points, respectively)—than not using such software. This is a sizable increase, especially if extended over the very large number of microenterprises across Africa.

Underperformance, especially in uptake and intensive use

Countries in Sub-Saharan Africa have made significant progress in the past decade in terms of the share of their population covered by internet-enabled (3G and 4G) networks, yet they still lag most other developing country regions of the world (figure 8.5). For 3G networks, a major convergence has occurred in the last few years in all regions, although the most advanced regions (North America and East Asia and Pacific) have switched away from 3G network equipment availability toward the more profitable 4G networks in recent years. By 2023, 3G networks covered 98 percent of country populations averaged by region in Europe and Central Asia and 97 percent in the Middle East and North Africa, 90 percent in East Asia and Pacific, 89 percent in Sub-Saharan Africa, and 88 percent in South Asia. With regard to coverage of 4G networks, the Sub-Saharan African region has a starker lag in convergence. By 2023, North America and Europe and Central Asia had coverage above 97 percent; East Asia and Pacific, Latin America and the Caribbean, the Middle East and North Africa, and South Asia had coverage rates between 90 percent and 94 percent. By contrast, Sub-Saharan Africa had only 73 percent coverage. To summarize, faster mobile network availability in Sub-Saharan Africa has increased at a slower pace relative to the rest of the world and seriously lags.[4]

FIGURE 8.5 Availability of internet-enabled networks, by world region, 2010–23

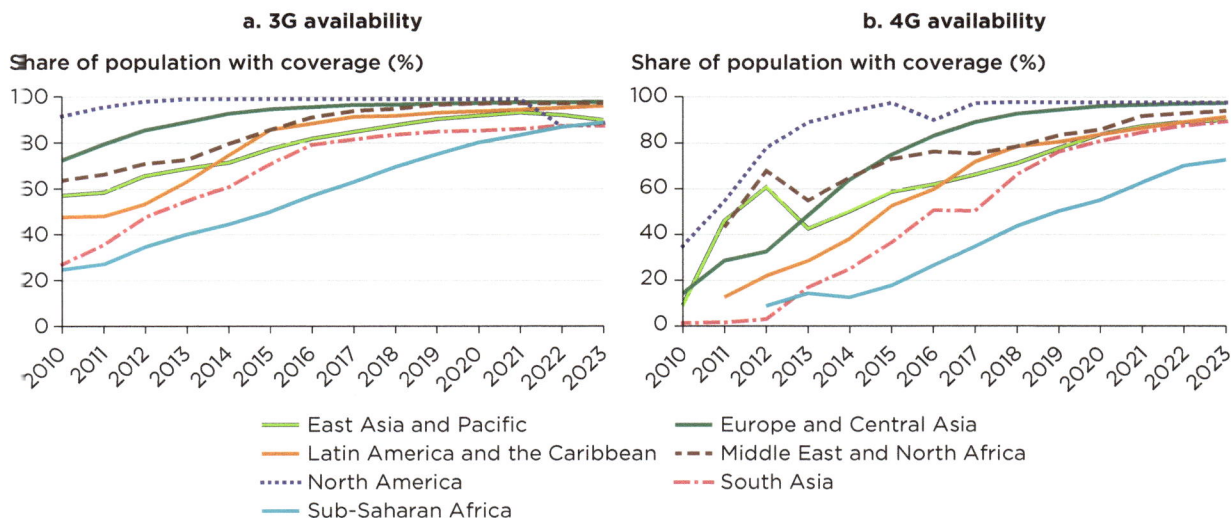

a. 3G availability
Share of population with coverage (%)

b. 4G availability
Share of population with coverage (%)

Legend:
- East Asia and Pacific
- Latin America and the Caribbean
- North America
- Sub-Saharan Africa
- Europe and Central Asia
- Middle East and North Africa
- South Asia

Source: GSMA Intelligence data set, Global System for Mobile Communications, https://www.gsmaintelligence.com/subscriptions-services/data/data-platform.
Note: Mobile internet availability (the percentage of population living in areas covered by 3G or 4G technology signals) is expressed as unweighted averages of countries in each region, as a share of total country populations. By giving equal importance to each country, heterogeneity across countries is highlighted. Regions are defined according to World Bank classifications. "North America" includes Bermuda, Canada, and the United States. 3G (4G) = third (fourth) generation.

As shown in figure 8.6, across country groupings within Africa, availability of internet-enabled 3G networks increased the most in North Africa and in nonfragile/non-resource-rich Sub-Saharan African countries ("Other SSA"), and the least in fragile and conflict-affected situations (FCS) in the region. Interestingly, availability of 3G networks for non-resource-rich, non-FCS countries in the region, at over 95 percent in 2023, surpasses the average level of countries in South Asia (88 percent). Average availability across North African countries was already at a relatively high level in 2010 (at 59 percent), so the increase over the past decade to 96 percent by 2023 was not as large. On the other hand, the average level of availability for FCS Sub-Saharan African countries only reached 84 percent for non-resource-rich FCS countries and 81 percent for resource-rich FCS countries by 2023.

A similar cross-regional lag exists with respect to the use of mobile internet. Even though Sub-Saharan African countries have made significant progress in increasing mobile internet subscriptions over the past decade, a large and increasing usage gap with other regions remains. Countries in the region have made progress in 3G+ mobile unique internet subscriptions over the past decade, reaching 24.3 percent of country populations averaged across Sub-Saharan Africa by the end of 2023 (figure 8.7). The gap between Sub-Saharan Africa and South Asia, however, has increased—from about 3.3 percentage points (7.6 percent in South Asia compared with 4.3 percent in Sub-Saharan Africa) in 2010 to 18 percentage points (42 percent compared with 24 percent, respectively) in 2023. Market penetration of unique mobile internet was well above 50 percent in all other regions by 2023, with a high of 79 percent in North America.

FIGURE 8.6 Availability of 3G networks, by country fragility and resource status, North and Sub-Saharan Africa, 2010–23

Share of population with coverage (%)

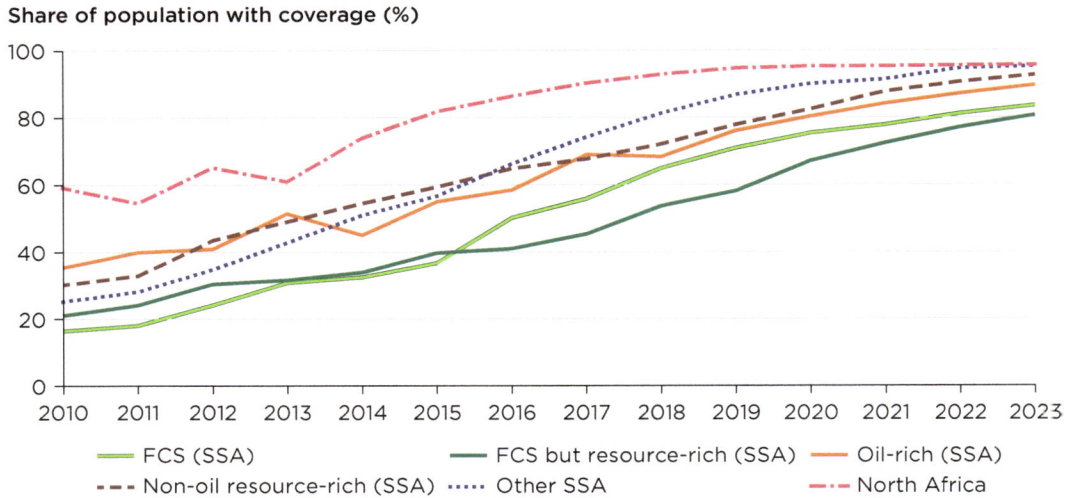

- FCS (SSA)
- FCS but resource-rich (SSA)
- Oil-rich (SSA)
- Non-oil resource-rich (SSA)
- Other SSA
- North Africa

Source: GSMA Intelligence data set, Global System for Mobile Communications, https://www .gsmaintelligence.com/subscriptions-services/data/data-platform.
Note: Mobile internet availability (the percentage of population living in areas covered by 3G technology signals) is expressed as unweighted averages of countries in each subregion, as a share of total country populations. 3G = third generation; FCS = fragile and conflict-affected situations; SSA = Sub-Saharan Africa.

FIGURE 8.7 Use of mobile internet, by world region, 2010–23

Share of population using mobile internet (%)

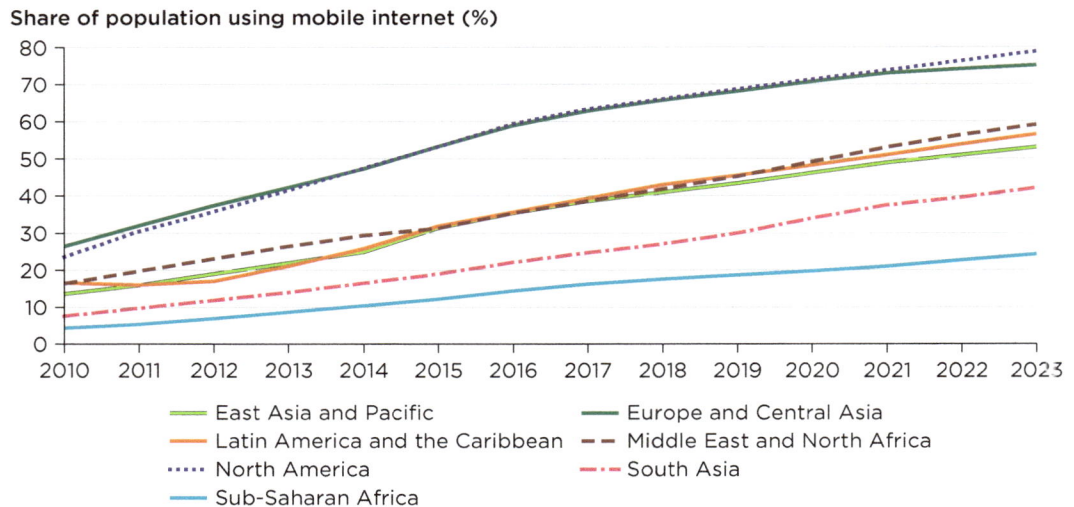

- East Asia and Pacific
- Europe and Central Asia
- Latin America and the Caribbean
- Middle East and North Africa
- North America
- South Asia
- Sub-Saharan Africa

Source: GSMA Intelligence data set, Global System for Mobile Communications, https://www .gsmaintelligence.com/subscriptions-services/data/data-platform.
Note: Usage (unique mobile internet subscribers) is expressed as unweighted averages of countries in each region, as a share of total country populations. By giving equal importance to each country, heterogeneity across countries is highlighted. There is a discontinuity in 2015 due to a methodological change, but general trends remain unaffected. Regions are defined according to World Bank classifications. "North America" comprises Bermuda, Canada, and the United States.

Across different country groupings within Africa, use of mobile internet increased the most in North Africa, followed by non-oil-resource-rich Sub-Saharan African countries, and non-resource-rich Sub-Saharan African countries, and increased the least in FCS countries (figure 8.8). Strikingly, use of mobile internet even for non-oil-resource-rich Sub-Saharan African countries in 2023, at 33 percent, remained significantly below the average level of countries in South Asia (42 percent), and even further below the average level of North African countries (50 percent). Unfortunately, the use of mobile internet for FCS countries reached only 15.7 percent for non-resource-rich FCS countries and 18.8 percent for resource-rich FCS countries by 2023.

FIGURE 8.8 Use of mobile internet, by country fragility and resource status, North and Sub-Saharan Africa, 2010–23

Share of population using mobile internet (%)

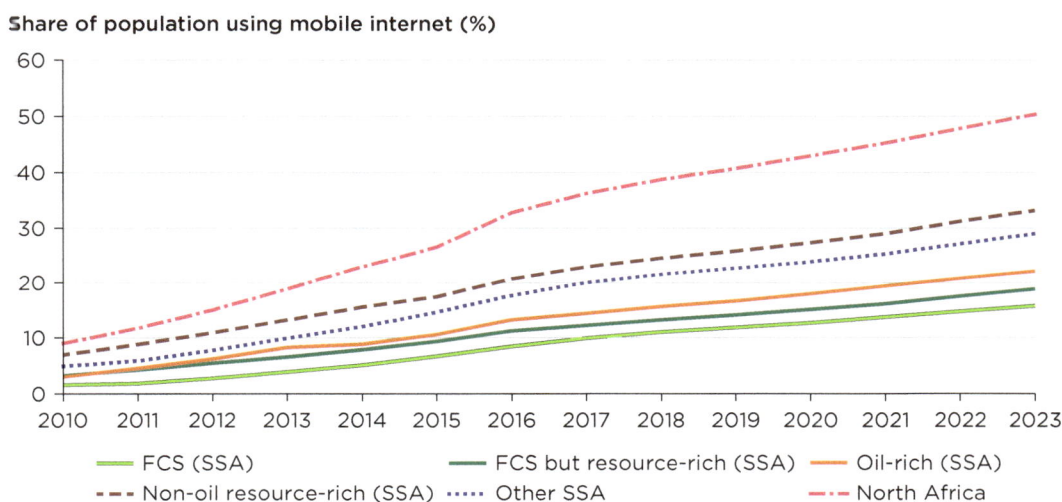

Source: GSMA Intelligence data set, Global System for Mobile Communications, https://www.gsmaintelligence.com/subscriptions-services/data/data-platform.
Note: Usage (unique mobile internet subscribers) is expressed as unweighted averages of countries in each region, as a share of total country populations. FCS = fragile and conflict-affected situations; SSA = Sub-Saharan Africa.

Alarmingly, uptake of mobile internet in Africa over time has occurred more slowly than increases in availability. Figure 8.9 shows the evolution of the "uptake gap," defined as the share of all people with internet availability who have not taken up internet use. The average uptake gap has decreased markedly in all regions over time except in Sub-Saharan Africa, falling to 11 percent and 23 percent in the North America and Europe and Central Asia regions, respectively. Whereas the uptake gap had fallen to 52 percent in South Asia and to 41 percent in the East Asia and Pacific and Latin America and the Caribbean regions, on average, by 2023, it remained stuck in the mid-70 percent range throughout the past decade in Sub-Saharan Africa and at 73 percent in 2023, the highest gap in the world. That almost three-quarters of Africa's people with 3G+ availability remain unconnected and without a subscription suggests that the physical availability of internet-enabled networks is not the main constraint to the use of mobile internet. Rather, it implies that, unless other constraints that prevent uptake are addressed, expansion of availability alone will not ensure the use of internet.

FIGURE 8.9 **Internet uptake gap, by world region, 2010–23**

Internet uptake gap (%)

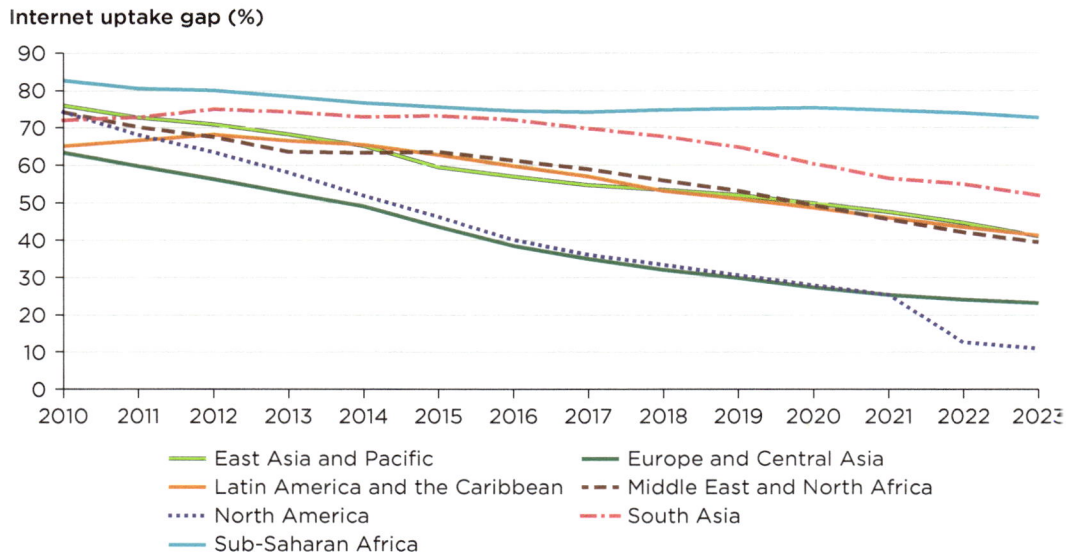

Legend:
- East Asia and Pacific
- Latin America and the Caribbean
- North America
- Sub-Saharan Africa
- Europe and Central Asia
- Middle East and North Africa
- South Asia

Source: GSMA Intelligence data set, Global System for Mobile Communications, https://www.gsmaintelligence.com/subscriptions-services/data/data-platform.
Note: Uptake gaps are defined as the share of all people with internet availability who have not taken up internet use. Uptake gaps are expressed as unweighted regional averages across countries (giving equal importance to each country highlights heterogeneity across countries). North America comprises Bermuda, Canada, and the United States.

As illustrated in figure 8.10, across country groupings within Africa, the largest uptake gaps occur in FCS countries in Sub-Saharan Africa, and the smallest in North Africa, followed by non-oil-resource-rich Sub-Saharan African countries. In 2023, non-resource-rich FCS countries had an uptake gap of 81 percent, and resource-rich FCS countries had a gap of 77 percent. Although it decreased from 90 percent in 2010, the continued uptake gap for non-resource-rich FCS countries implies that four out of five people in areas with internet availability are not using internet services. North Africa had the largest decline in the uptake gap over the past decade, with the smallest gap (47 percent), lower than South Asia (52 percent).

Incomplete digitalization is widespread among African firms. Besides the internet uptake gap, most firms do not use intensively technologies they have already adopted. Consider the following:

- Of firms adopting DTs for productive purposes, 62 percent do not use their most advanced technology intensively, rather relying on less sophisticated, including manual, technologies.

- Only one out of three firms that adopt sophisticated DTs uses them intensively.

- For firms with five or more workers, 14 percent have not adopted any form of mobile, computer, or internet connectivity in their businesses.

FIGURE 8.10 **Internet uptake gap, by country fragility and resource status, North and Sub-Saharan Africa, 2010–23**

Internet uptake gap (%)

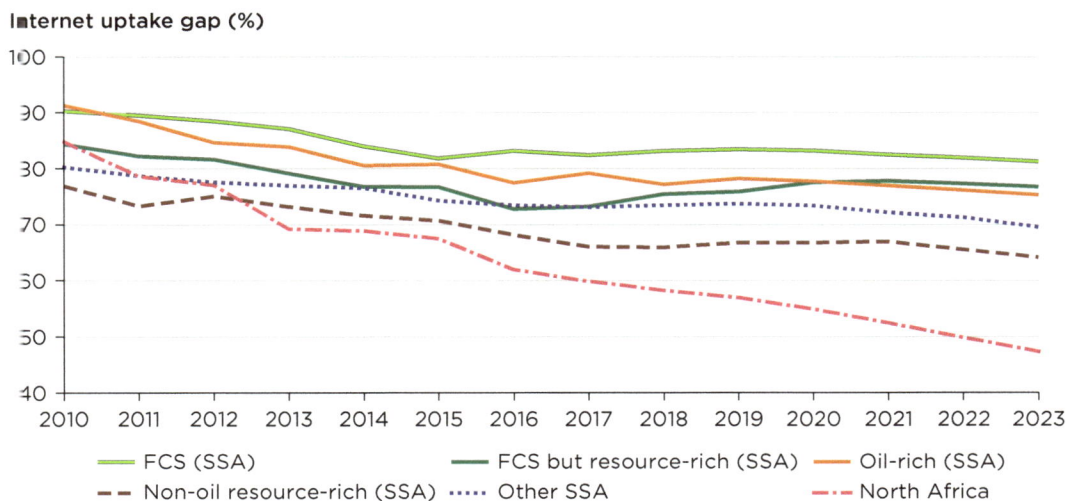

Legend:
- FCS (SSA)
- FCS but resource-rich (SSA)
- Oil-rich (SSA)
- Non-oil resource-rich (SSA)
- Other SSA
- North Africa

Source: GSMA Intelligence data set, Global System for Mobile Communications, https://www .gsmaintelligence.com/subscriptions-services/data/data-platform.
Note: Uptake gaps are defined as the share of all people with internet availability who have not taken up internet use. FCS = fragile and conflict-affected situations; SSA = Sub-Saharan Africa.

- Among small and microbusinesses, this gap is significantly larger, with less than 7 percent using computers.

- Of firms with access to digital devices or internet connectivity, 23 percent do not adopt DTs to perform day-to-day operations such as accounting, planning, sales, and payments.

- Only 36 percent of firms adopt a sophisticated DT—specialized software for business administration, operations, sales, or payment—to perform a specific business function.

- Among firms adopting business apps, a large share still relies exclusively or mostly on manual procedures for performing key tasks such as business administration, planning, sales, and payments, missing out on the performance benefits DTs can provide.

This dual challenge of low adoption rates and lack of intensive use describes different stages of "incomplete digitalization." These cases of incomplete digitalization are not driven by firms recently switching to DTs. On average, these firms have had sophisticated technologies for more than eight years but still rely intensively on less-sophisticated technologies (Cruz 2024).

A similar type of incomplete digitalization gap exists among microenterprises, for which uptake of digital-enabling technologies does not directly translate into adoption or use of productivity-enhancing business technologies. Among firms that have at least one mobile phone, one computer, or internet connectivity ("enabling technology," about 87 percent of respondents), less than half use a nonmanual technology in any of their business functions ("business technology," that is, a nonmanual technology for accounting, planning, managing supplies, marketing, sales, or payments).[5] A simple multinomial logit model capturing firms' choices between (1) no technology, (2) at least one enabling technology or at least one business technology, or (3) both an enabling technology and a business technology found that access to electricity, the level of owners' education, and the quality of suppliers and customers are associated with a lower probability of having no technology at all. In addition, the quality of suppliers and customers and having a loan are associated with having either an enabling technology or a business technology, whereas the level of owners' education and skills, and having a bank loan are associated with having both. These results suggest that having a bank loan is closely associated with having technology. Further, electricity is crucial for having any technology at all, and skills are important for having both at least one enabling and one business technology.

Analysis

This section presents an analysis of the state and drivers of adoption of digital technologies. It provides evidence of adoption gaps between enterprises of different sizes as well as by the gender and age of owners. It then provides a discussion of which factors or variables might explain the low levels of digitalization in Sub-Saharan Africa, even relative to countries with similar levels of income in other regions.

A large productive upside from greater DT use by enterprises, especially the smallest

Despite compelling evidence that DT use matters for enterprise productivity and job creation, a large technological gap persists across enterprises in Africa. In Ghana, Kenya, Malawi, and Senegal, African enterprises employing five or more full-time employees lag, on average, in the use of enablers, such as smartphones and computers, relative to available comparator countries (figure 8.11). Only 25 percent of small enterprises (with 5–19 employees) in Senegal, whether formal or informal, use smartphones, compared with more than 60 percent of small firms in Brazil and Viet Nam. Small enterprises across the African countries in the data set lag in computer use, ranging from 63 percent to 73 percent in Ghana,

FIGURE 8.11 Smartphone and computer use, by firm size, selected countries

Share of firms using technology (%)

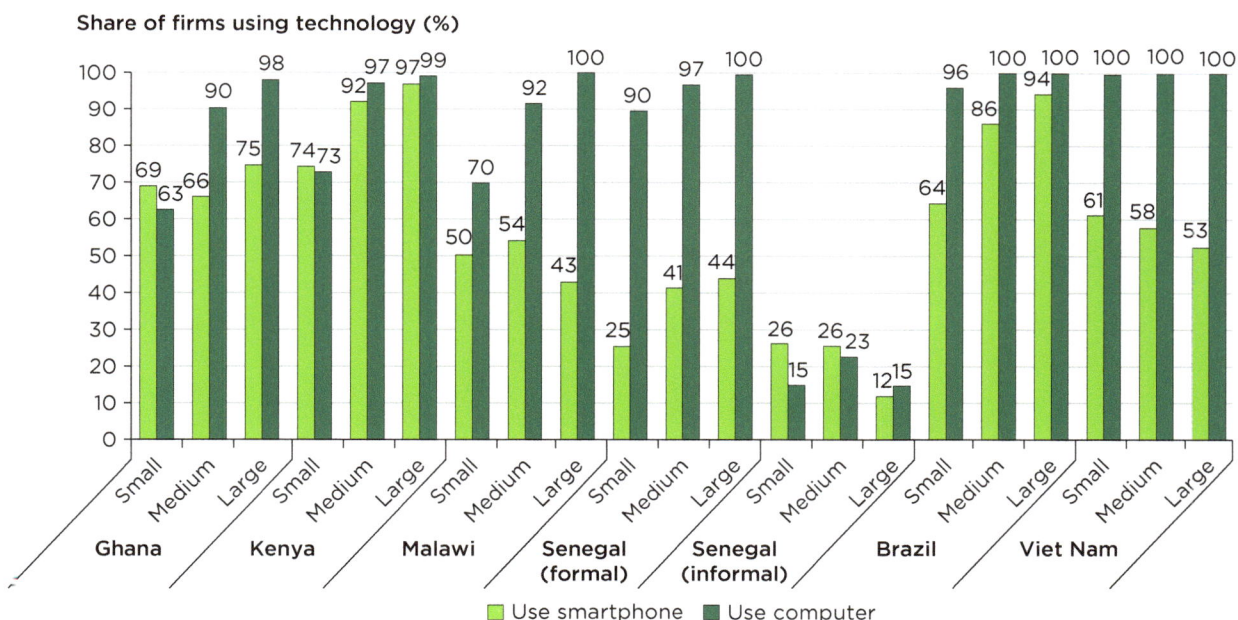

Use smartphone   Use computer

Source: Begazo, Blimpo, and Dutz 2023, figure 2.8, based on Cirera, Comin, and Cruz 2022.
Note: Data are based on 2019–21 Firm-level Adoption of Technology survey data. Analysis includes enterprises employing at least five full-time workers. "Large" firms have 100 or more employees; "medium" firms, 20–99 employees; and "small" firms, 5–19 employees. Senegal data are disaggregated into formal and informal firms, the latter being those without a formal accounting system according to SYSCOA (accounting standards of the West African Economic Union) or an alternate formal harmonized accounting system.

Kenya, and Malawi, as compared with 90 percent and higher among medium (20–99 employees) and large (100+ employees) African enterprises and among small enterprises in Brazil and Viet Nam. Only 15 percent of small and large informal enterprises in Senegal use computers.

Microenterprises lag even more in the use of DTs, with large digital divides (figure 8.12). Although only 7 percent of all microfirms use a smartphone, 3 percent of firms owned by older women use one. Computer use shows an even larger digital divide, with only 2 percent of firms owned by young women using one and four times more firms owned by younger men using one (8 percent). Less than 3 percent of microenterprises use inventory control/POS software. Enterprises owned by young men are consistently the largest users of internet-enabled DTs.

FIGURE 8.12 Use of DTs, by owner characteristics and type of technology

Share of firms using technology (%)

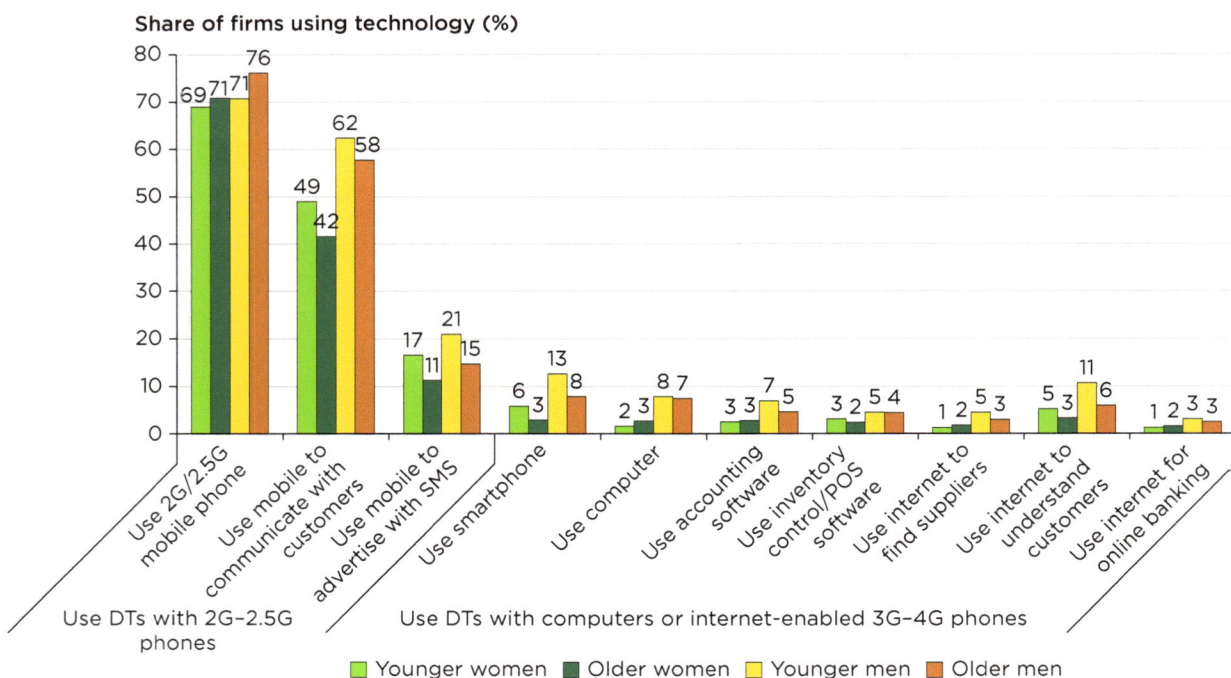

Younger women | **Older women** | **Younger men** | **Older men**

Source: Atiyas and Dutz 2023.
Note: Data are based on the Research ICT Africa After Access 2017–18 Business survey covering 2,174 enterprises across Ghana, Kenya, Mozambique, Nigeria, Rwanda, Senegal, South Africa, and Tanzania that responded to owner gender and age (youth = 30 years and younger) questions. The COVID-19 shock and attendant social distancing and lockdown measures implemented in many countries generated additional incentives for firms to adopt or increase the use of DTs, because DTs could enable firms to change work patterns more easily and better adjust at times when required social distancing limited face-to-face interactions. However, firm responses to the COVID-19 shock have been uneven, and digital divides across countries and types of firms have increased because of the pandemic. 2G (3G, 4G) = second (third, fourth) generation; DTs = digital technologies; POS = point of sale; SMS = Short Message Service.

The COVID-19 pandemic accelerated enterprise use of and investment in DTs but also increased digital divides. Although COVID-19-related restrictions expanded the use of DTs in firms across Africa, a lower share of African enterprises is investing in DTs than in other lower-income countries outside of Africa. Moreover, significant heterogeneity exists across African countries and enterprise size groups, with COVID-19 accelerating DT use in all countries but increasing divides between small and large enterprises (figure 8.13, panel a). More than four of five firms interviewed in Kenya and South Africa increased their use of DTs, whereas just over two of five small firms in Ghana and Tanzania increased DT use. Regarding new investments (figure 8.13, panel b), a significantly greater share of large firms than of small firms invested in new DTs: 66 percent of large firms invested in new DTs in Tanzania, but only 7 percent of small firms—a nearly 10-fold difference. In Kenya, 59 percent of large firms invested in new DTs compared with only 27 percent of small firms. These trends, if unaddressed, risk widening gaps in productivity, sales, and owner and worker incomes over time.

FIGURE 8.13 Use of DTs following COVID-19 pandemic, by firm size, selected countries

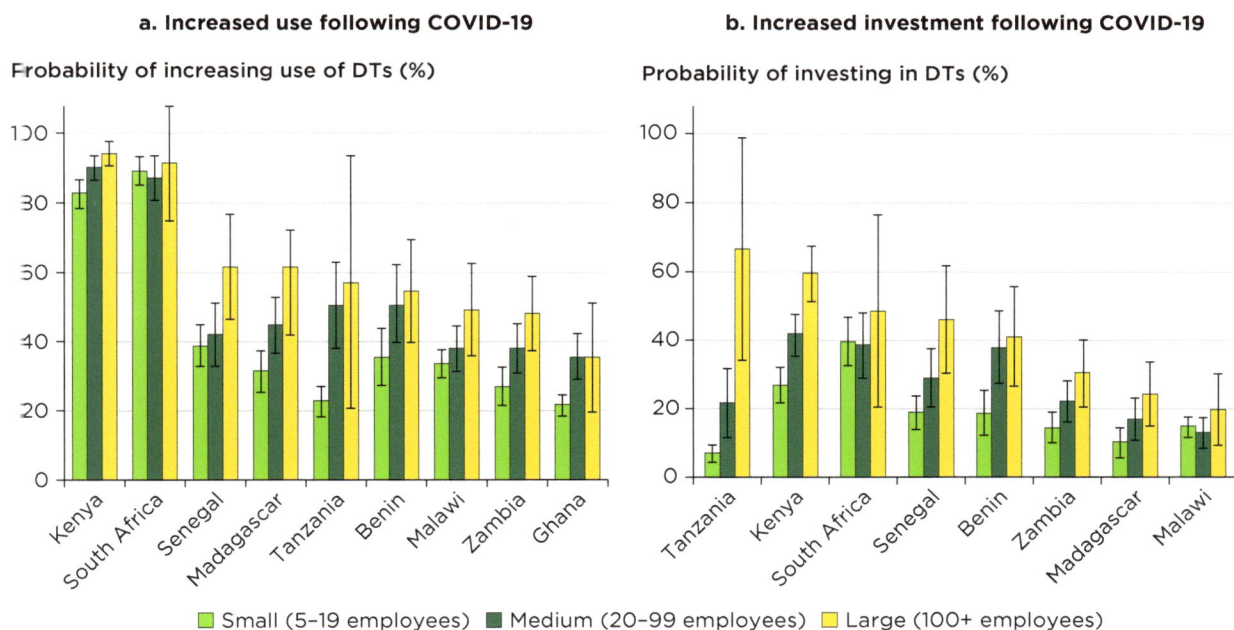

a. Increased use following COVID-19

Probability of increasing use of DTs (%)

b. Increased investment following COVID-19

Probability of investing in DTs (%)

Legend: ☐ Small (5–19 employees) ☐ Medium (20–99 employees) ☐ Large (100+ employees)

Source: Begazo, Blimpo, and Dutz 2023, figure 2.15, based on World Bank COVID-19 Business Pulse Survey 2021.
Note: Surveys of enterprises employing five or more full-time workers, implemented from September 2020 to February 2021. Number of observations: Benin (981), Ghana (979), Kenya (816), Madagascar (490), Malawi (789), Senegal (425), South Africa (363), Tanzania (457), and Zambia (507). Conditional average probabilities of starting or increasing the use of digital solutions (panel a) and investing in digital solutions (panel b), controlling for size, sector, and country. Panel a reflects responses to the question "Has this establishment started using or increased the use of internet, online social media, specialized apps, or digital platforms in response to COVID-19 outbreak?" Panel b shows responses to "Has this establishment invested in any new equipment, software or digital solution in response to COVID-19?" Size is based on values before the pandemic. All country weights are equal to one. Unweighted samples within countries. Error bars represent 95 percent confidence intervals. DTs = digital technologies.

Constraints impeding greater enterprise digitalization

The low availability and uptake of mobile internet across Sub-Saharan Africa could simply reflect that these countries are poorer. To explore whether this is the case, the analysis for this chapter includes some simple cross-country regressions for the period 2010–20 (table 8.1). The dependent variable is unique mobile internet uptake. In the first column, this variable is regressed on gross domestic product (GDP) per capita (in constant purchasing power parity), GDP per capita squared, and GDP per capita cubed (to allow for the possibility that the association between mobile internet uptake and per capita income may be nonlinear). The results show that over this period income alone explains a little more than half of the variation in mobile internet uptake across countries and years. Thus, income is a key driver of mobile internet uptake. In the second column a dummy for Sub-Saharan Africa is added to the right-hand-side variables. The coefficient on that dummy variable is

TABLE 8.1 Regression analysis of mobile internet uptake and GDP per capita

Dependent variable: Unique mobile internet uptake	(1)	(2)
Sub-Saharan Africa = 1		−0.0560***
		(0.0199)
GDP per capita, constant PPP	0.0191***	0.0170***
	(0.00171)	(0.00201)
GDP per capita squared	−0.000235***	−0.000199***
	(4.23e-05)	(4.47e-05)
GDP per capita cubed	8.70e-07***	7.13e-07***
	(2.33e-07)	(2.35e-07)
Constant	0.103***	0.139***
	(0.0108)	(0.0198)
Observations	2,084	2,084
R-squared	0.514	0.522

Sources: Original calculations based on data from GSMA Intelligence data set, https://www
.gsmaintelligence.com, and World Bank, World Development Indicators, https://data.worldbank.org
/indicator/.
Note: The dependent variable is unique mobile internet uptake from GSMA. Income is measured by
per capita GDP at constant PPP international prices, from the World Bank World Development
Indicators. The period is 2010–20. Errors are clustered around countries. Robust standard errors in
parentheses. PPP = purchasing power parity.
*$p < 0.1$ **$p = 0.05$ ***$p < 0.01$

negative and statistically highly significant, suggesting that, controlling for income, mobile internet uptake is about 5.6 percentage points lower than in the rest of the world. Thus, although income is a key driver, income alone does not explain the gap in mobile internet uptake between Sub-Saharan Africa and the rest of the world.

Table 8.2 presents an overview of where the region stands with respect to some of the key variables that studies have shown to drive the adoption of mobile internet. The first panel shows that Sub-Saharan Africa suffers from a large gap in capabilities. Capabilities, such as years of schooling and literacy, determine the extent to which people can use the internet productively; thus they are major determinants of attractiveness. The capabilities gap is especially important when few internet applications exist that are appropriate for productive use by low-skilled users. Learning-adjusted years of schooling is only 5.0 years in Sub-Saharan Africa compared with 6.5 years in South Asia and 8.3 years in East Asia and Pacific. Sub-Saharan Africa has much lower rates of adult literacy, especially among young adults, than do other regions: the average literacy rate among young people is only 81 percent in Sub-Saharan Africa as compared with 91 percent in South Asia, the region with the second-lowest rate of youth literacy. All other regions have rates higher than 98 percent.

TABLE 8.2 Correlates of mobile internet adoption, by key driver and world region

Driver	East Asia and Pacific	Latin America and the Caribbean	Middle East and North Africa	South Asia	Sub-Saharan Africa
Capabilities					
Learning-adjusted years of schooling[a]	8.3	7.8	7.6	6.5	5.0
Adult literacy (%)[b]	94.1	94.4	92.0	74.8	69.2
Youth literacy (ages 15–24) (%)[b]	98.3	98.4	98.5	91.1	80.5
Affordability[c]					
Mobile data and voice high-usage package (US$)	23.3	26.9	13.7	4.7	10.2
Mobile data and voice low-usage package (US$)	16.7	23.5	9.3	3.4	6.2
Mobile data and voice high-usage package (% of GNI)	4.8	6.4	2.7	3.4	12.1
Mobile data and voice low-usage package (% of GNI)	3.1	4.4	1.8	2.5	6.9
Regulatory policy					
ITU Index of overall ICT regulation, 2022	65.3	73.4	64.6	67.7	70.7
Mobile termination rate, 2020 (TeleG, US$)	0.027	0.013	0.010	0.002	0.018
HHI, 2020 (calculated from TeleG market shares of subscribers)	0.50	0.45	0.43	0.37	0.49
Complementary assets: Electricity					
Electricity access, rural (%)[b]	92.9	97.7	93.7	97.8	34.6
Electricity access, urban (2021–22) (%)[b]	97.5	99.4	98.6	99.7	79.5
Electricity access, overall (%)[b]	94.3	97.6	95.3	97.9	54.1
Informality					
Share of informal in total employment (%)[d]	58.3	57.3	57.5	78.8	81.9
E-government					
Online service index[e]	0.53	0.54	0.55	0.55	0.36
E-participation index[e]	0.48	0.40	0.41	0.38	0.26

Sources: World Bank calculations based on indicated data sources.
Note: GNI = gross national income; HHI = Herfindahl-Hirschman Index; ICT = information and communication technology; ITU = International Telecommunication Union.
a. Human Capital Index data set, 2020.
b. World Bank, World Development Indicators, 2021–22.
c. International Telecommunication Union, 2023.
d. International Labour Organization, 2022.
e. UN DESA 2022.

The second panel of table 8.2 shows that affordability is a major problem as well. As seen in the first two rows, Sub-Saharan Africa does not have a very high absolute level of tariffs compared with other regions, except for South Asia. The third and fourth rows in that panel, however, show that the costs of mobile data and voice packages are on the order of between 7 percent and 12 percent of gross national income (GNI), whereas this ratio is lower than 6 percent in other regions. It also shows that high usage tariffs are relatively less affordable in Sub-Saharan Africa than those in other regions.

The third panel of table 8.2 provides data on regulatory policy. The first row shows the average of an index of overall regulation prepared by the International Telecommunication Union. According to that measure, Sub-Saharan Africa does not appear to perform badly; in fact, the index in the region is higher than in the East Asia and Pacific, Middle East and North Africa, and South Asia regions. Based on a de jure assessment of the existence of relevant laws and regulations, the ITU index does not consider the extent to which these laws and regulations are effectively enforced. The next two variables better capture the degree to which regulatory authorities adopt a pro-competition stance. The first indicator is the average mobile termination rate—the tariff that mobile operators charge to their competitors when a subscriber of a competitor calls a subscriber of the receiving or the terminating operator. The higher the mobile termination rate, the easier it is for incumbents to prevent the entry and expansion of smaller competitors. Sub-Saharan Africa has higher mobile termination rates than other regions except for East Asia and Pacific. The Herfindahl-Hirschman Index (HHI) is the sum of squared market shares of mobile operators. A high HHI amounts to a more concentrated market and generally reflects a lower degree of competition. Sub-Saharan Africa has quite a high HHI; however, with the exception of South Asia, so do other regions.

The next panel shows the extent of electricity access. Electricity is necessary to charge mobile handsets and is also a key driver of digital inclusion (Houngbonon, Le Quentrec, and Rubrichi 2021). The table shows that in Sub-Saharan Africa almost half of the population does not have access to electricity, whereas electricity access is above 90 percent in the rest of the world's regions. The problem is especially acute in rural areas, where only 35 percent of the Sub-Saharan African population has access to electricity.

Informality, shown in the fifth panel of table 8.2, is often found to be associated with lower uptake of DTs, which could be because informal firms have less access to finance. Informality can also be associated with lower levels of the capabilities that are correlated with adoption and use of DTs. The table shows an extremely high share of informal jobs in total employment in Sub-Saharan Africa (82 percent), followed by South Asia (79 percent).

The lowest panel in table 8.2 provides regional summaries of two indexes of e-government services compiled for the United Nations E-Government Survey (UN DESA 2022). The online service index is based on data collected from an independent online assessment, conducted by the United Nations Department of Economic and Social Affairs. It assesses the national online presence of United Nations member countries, complemented by a country-level survey.[6] The e-participation index, a subindex of the online service index, captures the use of online services to facilitate provision of information by governments to citizens ("e-information sharing"), interaction with stakeholders ("e-consultation"), and engagement in decision-making processes (UN DESA 2022). Higher index values could reflect an effort by governments to expand government services and higher levels of citizen participation through digital media and therefore could support wider uptake.[7] The data presented show that both indexes are lower in Sub-Saharan Africa relative to other regions.

To further explore what non-income constraints may be the most important drivers of mobile internet adoption, table 8.3 presents how these drivers differ across Sub-Saharan African countries and non-Sub-Saharan African countries with similar levels of per capita income in 2023. The table shows that the two sets of countries have very similar average per capita income but an almost 15 percentage point difference in mobile internet uptake (21 percent versus 36 percent). The largest differences in other variables that could explain lower levels of internet adoption in Sub-Saharan Africa are electricity access and capabilities. Electricity access is on average almost 50 percent higher in non-Sub-Saharan African countries, and learning-adjusted years of schooling are 27 percent higher. It is plausible that lower levels of electricity access and lower levels of education could be the main factors for lower uptake across the population. Poor countries in Sub-Saharan Africa do not lag that far behind poor countries in other regions on most other indicators, and actually perform visibly better on many, such as affordability, regulatory policy, and online e-government services. Both sets of countries have a very high share of informal employment, but the share is higher in Sub-Saharan Africa, presumably creating higher financial and legal barriers to productive use of DTs.

TABLE 8.3 Non-income drivers of mobile internet adoption, Sub-Saharan Africa and comparators

Driver	Sub-Saharan Africa	Non-Sub-Saharan Africa
Per capita GDP (current US$)[a]	1,619	1,697
Unique mobile internet uptake (%)[b]	21.3	36.2
Capabilities		
Learning-adjusted years of schooling[c]	5.2	6.6
Adult literacy (%)[d]	69.6	80.8
Youth literacy (ages 15–24) (%)[d]	81.5	94.9

(continued)

TABLE 8.3 Non-income drivers of mobile internet adoption, Sub-Saharan Africa and comparators (*continued*)

Driver	Sub-Saharan Africa	Non-Sub-Saharan Africa
Affordability[e]		
Mobile data and voice high-usage package (US$)	8.0	12.6
Mobile data and voice low-usage package (US$)	4.8	7.4
Mobile data and voice high-usage package (% of GNI)	6.6	7.8
Mobile data and voice low-usage package (% of GNI)	4.8	7.4
Regulatory policy		
ITU Index of overall ICT regulation, 2022	75.1	58.6
Mobile termination rate (TeleG, US$, 2020)	0.013	0.02
HHI (calculated from TeleG market shares of subscribers, 2020)	0.476	0.428
Complementary assets: Electricity		
Electricity access, rural (%)[d]	41.44	90.28
Electricity access, urban (2021–22) (%)[d]	89.01	94.56
Electricity access, overall (%)[d]	59.48	88.36
Informality		
Share of informal in total employment (%)[f]	89.07	77.05
E-government		
Online service index[g]	0.43	0.39
E-participation index[g]	0.30	0.30

Sources: World Bank calculations based on indicated data sources.
Note: Averages of key drivers of matched SSA and non-SSA countries with similar per capita income levels. Samples include all countries with 2023 GDP per capita between $1,000 and $2,300 (current US$). SSA countries are Angola, Benin, Cameroon, the Comoros, Ethiopia, Ghana, Guinea, Kenya, Mauritania, Nigeria, Rwanda, Senegal, Sudan, Tanzania, Togo, Uganda, Zambia, and Zimbabwe. Non-SSA countries are Cambodia, Haiti, Kiribati, the Kyrgyz Republic, the Lao People's Democratic Republic, Myanmar, Nepal, Pakistan, the Solomon Islands, Tajikistan, and Timor-Leste. GNI = gross national income; HHI = Herfindahl-Hirschman Index; ICT = information and communication technology; ITU = International Telecommunication Union; SSA = Sub-Saharan Africa.
a. *World Bank, World Development Indicators, 2023.*
b. *GSMA, 2023.*
c. *Human Capital Index data set, 2020.*
d. *World Bank, World Development Indicators, 2021–22.*
e. *International Telecommunication Union, 2023.*
f. *International Labour Organization, 2022.*
g. *UN DESA 2022.*

The key DT-related issue for African enterprises is low productive use. The main factors affecting enterprise use of smartphones and computers, and of more sophisticated DTs that rely on these access technologies, are linked to the ability to pay for them and the willingness to use them (figure 8.14). These factors are relatively similar across larger enterprises (with five or more workers) and microenterprises.

FIGURE 8.14 Correlates of the main drivers of DT use, larger firms and microfirms

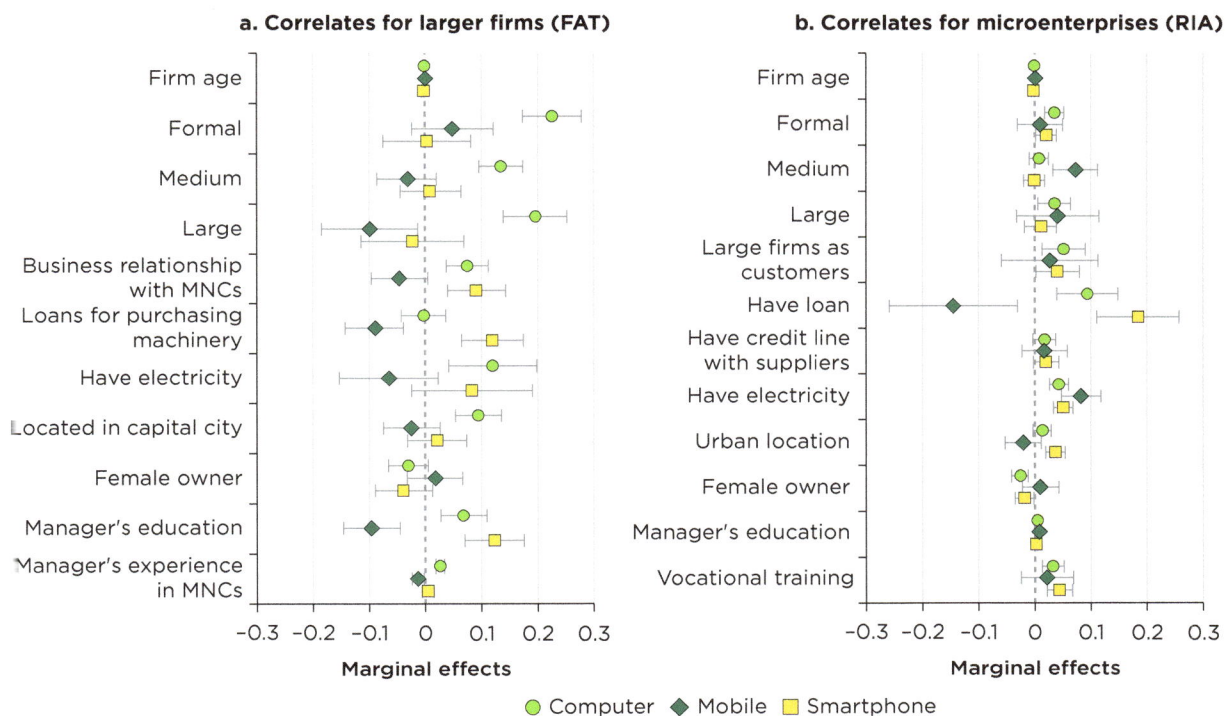

a. Correlates for larger firms (FAT)

b. Correlates for microenterprises (RIA)

● Computer ◆ Mobile ■ Smartphone

Source: Begazo, Blimpo, and Dutz 2023, figure 2.18, based on Cirera, Comin, and Cruz 2022 and Atiyas and Dutz 2023.
Note: Reported results are marginal effects based on probit regressions on enterprise characteristics, controlling for country fixed effects. Smartphone adoption is modeled as a multinomial regression with enterprise choice of smartphone, 2G or 2.5G phone (without full internet functionality), or no phone. Computer adoption is modeled as a simple yes/no choice. FAT countries include Ghana, Kenya, and Senegal; RIA countries include Ghana, Kenya, Mozambique, Nigeria, Rwanda, Senegal, South Africa, and Tanzania. The findings are restricted to statistically significant conditional correlations and do not allow inferences to be made about causality. 2G = second generation; FAT = Firm-level Adoption of Technology (survey); MNCs = multinational corporations; RIA = Research ICT Africa (survey).

Ability to pay, or affordable availability, is linked to the price of quality internet services, access technologies, and apps relative to enterprise earnings, as well as to the level of access to financing to help pay for DTs. The average cost across African countries of the cheapest plan providing 1.5 gigabytes of high-speed internet data (greater than or equal to 256 kilobits per second) over 30 days, a package that covers a few hours of basic daily use, amounts to about one-third of the income of those who fall below the global extreme poverty line (40 percent of the African population). The average cost of 1.5 gigabytes as a share of GNI per capita in 2020 was 9.4 percent in Sub-Saharan Africa, and more than 20 percent in the Central African Republic, the Democratic Republic of Congo, Guinea-Bissau, and Malawi.[8] Compared to other regions, data plans for small and medium enterprises are also more costly in Africa, speeds lower, and data allocations more limiting, including lower allocations in mobile plans or lack of unmetered offers in fixed internet plans. In at least 11 Sub-Saharan African countries, operators do not have a standard offering that grants at least 25 megabits per second of download speed, the approximate speed needed for light web browsing and email for up to five workers, and operating a POS terminal. In 10 Sub-Saharan African countries, no packages with unlimited data allowance were available (Vergara-Cobos 2021). This lack of availability affects the kind of content and DTs that can be offered online and limits consumer experience (for business and individuals), preventing demand from being pulled by online digital services, as it should.

Ability to pay is also linked to complementary infrastructure, especially the affordable availability of reliable electricity, as well as transportation and logistics services (proxied by whether the enterprise is in an urban or rural location). Affordability is proxied by whether larger firms have loans to purchase machinery and equipment, and whether microfirms have a loan; information is also available on whether microfirms have a credit line with suppliers, which could be an indicator of their creditworthiness. Access to finance, as reflected by having a loan, is one of the largest correlates of use. Larger firms that have a loan are 12 percent more likely to use smartphones and 9 percent less likely to use a 2G phone. Microenterprises that have a loan are 18 percent more likely to use smartphones and nearly 15 percent less likely to use a 2G phone; they are also over 9 percent more likely to use a computer. Having electricity and being in an urban location are associated with computer use for larger firms, and with smartphone use for microenterprises.

Willingness to use DTs is linked to capabilities: people's skill levels and technological capabilities to enable enterprises to use DTs productively and extract value from them, and attractiveness related to both the availability of information about DTs and whether they meet the productive needs of users, including internet at sufficiently high speeds without interruptions of data transmission. Skills, especially the manager's education level in the case of larger firms and vocational training in the case of microenterprises, are strongly associated with both smartphone and computer use. Enterprise technological capabilities are proxied by firm size, firm age, formality status, and sector of industrial activity:

- Firms with five or more workers and larger microfirms are more likely to use computers.

- Firms with five or more workers and microfirms that have been in operation longer are less likely to use a smartphone than younger firms.

- Formal firms with five or more workers and formal microfirms are more likely to use computers.

The sector of enterprise activity also plays a role: firms with five or more workers in manufacturing, wholesale and retail trade, and other services are more likely to use a smartphone than those in agriculture. Attractiveness of DTs, likely driven by the need to adopt specific DTs when larger firms have business relationships with multinational companies and when microenterprises have large firms as customers, is also strongly associated with both smartphone and computer use. Interestingly, among the reasons microenterprises reported for not using the internet, 7 out of 10 nonusers cited lack of attractiveness (Atiyas and Dutz 2023).[9]

Data from the RIA survey also suggest that e-government services in the region do not play a key role in promoting uptake, possibly reflecting a lag in the provision of such services. Table 8.4 shows that, in all countries, many enterprises that use mobile money do not use it to pay taxes. Furthermore, the use of the internet to obtain information from government organizations or to interact with government organizations is much lower than the ratio of microenterprises that have access to the internet. The only exception is Rwanda, which, along with India and Ecuador, is highlighted as a country with strong e-government services (UN DESA 2022, 21).

Finally, specific elements of the business environment (linked to access to markets and competition-related incentives to take advantage of that access) and socioeconomic factors (such as whether social norms and rules make ownership of access devices difficult for women) also affect use. The only available socioeconomic variable is whether the enterprise is female owned. For larger firms (with five or more workers), the relationships between female ownership and smartphone and computer use are not statistically significant. Presumably, for larger enterprises, with owners typically removed from day-to-day management, the owner's gender is not as relevant to technology adoption decisions. Among microenterprises, however, female-owned firms are less likely to use both a smartphone and a computer. Because most of these microfirms are owned and managed by self-employed individuals with no full-time paid employees, this digital divide may reflect prevailing social norms and rules that make ownership of access devices relatively more difficult for women.

TABLE 8.4 Microenterprise use of digital media to access government services, selected countries, 2017

Percent

Country	Use mobile money	Use mobile money to pay tax	Use internet for business purposes	Access internet through a mobile phone	Use internet to obtain information from government organizations	Use internet to interact with government organizations
Ghana	40.1	1.4	6.4	3.2	1.0	0.4
Kenya	63.0	8.4	5.8	4.0	0.7	0.5
Mozambique	22.6	0.7	1.9	1.2	0.0	0.0
Nigeria	3.5	0.4	5.6	3.4	1.1	1.1
Rwanda	48.5	13.7	3.9	0.0	2.3	1.0
Senegal	34.2	3.5	18.0	16.2	3.1	1.4
South Africa	8.7	0.3	23.5	13.0	4.3	3.8
Tanzania	15.2	1.2	4.4	4.4	0.8	0.4
Overall average	**28.4**	**3.4**	**8.6**	**5.8**	**1.6**	**1.0**

Source: Research ICT Africa after Access Business Survey 2017–18.
Note: ICT = information and communication technology.

Policies

Supporting inclusive productivity growth requires a rethinking of digitalization policies across the continent. So far, digital policy making in Africa has focused on only a subset of needed policies. Policies for inclusive impacts from DTs must move from supporting internet availability to actively supporting uptake and productive use for more and better jobs for all. This move requires two sets of complementary and mutually reinforcing policies. Policies must address both potential users' ability to pay for DTs and their willingness to use them. Policies must also manage the downside, including the potential for increasing digital divides, especially affecting low-income people displaced by the adoption of newer technologies and unable to adjust and adapt. Artificial intelligence (AI) and the associated collection of large data sets present additional risks that must be managed, including the potential for misuse by business (data integrity, privacy and protection, cybersecurity, and consumer protection) and government (surveillance and misinformation). On balance, the net benefits of AI are uncertain, particularly important in an international context of lagging regulations. Mitigating these risks and leveraging the full potential of AI will require sound regional regulations addressing the risks from AI, along with possibly mandated private actions such as the use of decision rules that are stable under manipulation.[10]

Africa's future should embrace the adoption of jobs-enhancing technologies in general, and DTs in particular. Policies should support cloud computing, AI, and robotics in ways that enhance the learning and earning potential of each country's workforce. The expected positive impacts can, however, materialize only if governments, enterprises, and households are willing to jointly support bold policy actions that create an appropriate enabling environment.

Policies to ensure availability and affordability of DTs

Ensuring potential users' ability to pay for DTs will require affordable availability policies. Availability policies must jointly address internet affordability, additional quality internet availability, adequate data infrastructure, and availability of affordable complementary assets and technologies.

Internet affordability policies encompass effective pro-competition regulations to reduce investment costs and price-cost margins. They include pro-competition rules on licensing and regulation of operators that are dominant in their markets, infrastructure access and sharing, and spectrum availability and use, ideally through more integrated continental markets. Additional regulations to help drive down operational costs also contribute to affordability. They include rules on network sharing, access to essential infrastructure controlled by state-owned enterprises (SOEs), operation of open-access fiber networks, and progressive elimination of excise taxes.

Additional quality internet availability policies include support for better internet quality everywhere and for availability in areas that are not commercially viable. These two sets of infrastructure supply-side policies need demand-side interventions as complements. They include targeted subsidies or vouchers[11] and social tariffs to support greater demand from lower-income groups. Financing will be needed through earmarked funds, obligations on operators, and universal service funds. Jointly these demand-side incentives should help to boost use and commercial viability in unmet areas and enable investments to improve service quality.

Adequate data infrastructure policies are needed for affordable availability of data infrastructure and physical infrastructure. Such policies include pro-competition rules for upgrading internet exchange points that can grow into regional data centers and for cloud computing facilities to help drive down data costs and eventually user prices. Effective regional integration for cross-border digital connectivity and data markets is critical to gain economies of scale and to expand and upgrade data infrastructure.

Availability of affordable complementary assets and technology policies are needed to support affordable access to complementary analog technologies. These assets and technologies include improvement of electricity, transportation, and agricultural (tractors and irrigation) systems that enhance the income-generating potential of DT use and strengthen potential users' ability to pay in the medium term.

Finally, renewed and more forceful implementation of all of these policies is required. The most important problem in effectively addressing affordable availability of DTs is that market structures across infrastructure and digital services products do not yet enable enough competition in Africa. Markets are excessively concentrated (figure 8.15). Monopolies and duopolies still exist in many countries, including in key bottleneck markets such as international connectivity. SOEs remain important across these markets and have the potential to thwart competition. Moreover, vertical integration of dominant firms creates risks to competition: 53 firms in 36 countries have at least 40 percent market share in mobile retail or fiber backbone and are vertically integrated into two other segments (Begazo, Blimpo, and Dutz 2023). A big part of the problem is that implementation of pro-competition rules is weak, including on licensing and radioelectric spectrum, dominant operators, access to essential infrastructure controlled by SOEs or dominant private operators, and operation of open-access fiber networks.

FIGURE 8.15 Market structures across infrastructure and digital services impede competition needed to lower costs and price-cost margins

Market structure variable	Upstream infrastructure layer		Middle infrastructure layer		Downstream infrastructure layer		Mobile money	Digital services	
	International connectivity (submarine cables, gateways)	Passive infrastructure (towers)	Fixed wholesale (fiber backbone)	Mobile wholesale (roaming, MVNO, sharing)	Fixed retail	Mobile retail		Data and cloud services	Digital platforms
Concentration (HHI)[a]									
Eastern and Southern Africa	orange	orange	orange	yellow	orange	orange	orange	brown	5,000+ digital firms headquartered in Africa
Western and Central Africa	orange	orange	orange	orange	orange	orange	orange	yellow	—
North Africa	orange	orange	orange	orange	orange	orange	orange	brown	—
Market structure[b]									
Monopolies	orange	yellow	yellow	21 countries allowing for MVNO but no entry	orange	yellow	yellow	brown	—
Duopolies	orange	orange	orange	—	yellow	orange	yellow	brown	—
New entry (2017–20)[c]									
All Africa	brown	yellow	brown	orange	yellow	yellow	—	—	brown
State presence (majority, minority)[d]									
SOE	orange	orange	orange	brown	yellow	orange	yellow	brown	—
SLE	yellow	yellow	brown	brown	yellow	yellow	yellow	brown	—

Sources: Begazo, Blimpo, and Dutz 2023, figure 4.8; World Bank, Africa Digital Market Players Database (internal), 2021, built on data from numerous sources, including TeleGeography, Global System for Mobile Communications Association, Africa Bandwidth Maps, Afterfibre.org, Policytracker, TowerXchange, PeeringDB, and Xalam Analytics.

Note: Brown circles represent higher risk to competition, on average; orange circles, medium risk; and yellow circles, lower risk. The sample covers 54 African countries for mobile retail, 38 for fixed retail, 52 for fiber backbone, 26 for telecommunications towers, 35 for submarine cables, 25 for data centers, and 15 for mobile money. HHI = Herfindahl-Hirschman index (market concentration measure); MVNO = mobile virtual network operator; SLE = state as minority shareholder; SOE = majority or fully state-owned enterprise; — = not available.

a. A market with HHI of less than 1,500 is considered to have a competitive market structure, HHI of 1,500–2,500 is moderately concentrated, and HHI of 2,500 or greater is highly concentrated.

b. Yellow = less than 5 percent of countries are monopolies/duopolies; orange = 5–20 percent of countries are monopolies/duopolies; brown = above 20 percent of countries are monopolies/duopolies.

c. Brown = new entry in less than 5 percent of countries; orange = new entry in 5–20 percent of countries; yellow = new entry in more than 20 percent of countries.

d. Yellow – SOE presence in less than 10 percent of countries; orange = SOE presence in 10–50 percent of countries; brown = SOE presence in more than 50 percent of countries.

Creating a single continental market for both connectivity and data is perhaps the most important policy direction for boosting competition and investments for affordable availability of DTs. It will require harmonization and compatibility of national policy and regulatory frameworks, with national and subregional policies all focused on promoting competition within and across markets. Integrated regional connectivity and data markets, in turn, can facilitate the scalability of DTs across the continent, boosting positive network effects, economies of scale and scope, and competition benefits. Digital regional integration for telecommunications services is occurring in selected pockets in Africa.[12] The convergence of national regulatory frameworks is more limited regarding licensing, spectrum policy, or subsidies for digital connectivity. The long-term goal of a truly integrated market would allow for (1) spectrum auctions to cut across countries (as in the United States across states); (2) harmonized regulation to control dominant operators, boost expansion of high-speed internet, and enable start-ups and enterprises to easily switch data centers and cloud computing providers within the region (as in the European Union); and (3) logistics and transportation digital platforms to operate seamlessly across borders. It would be a remarkable achievement if Africa could show the rest of the world the substantial benefits of full continental integration.

Policies that elicit willingness to use DTs

For DTs to elicit sufficient willingness to use them for productive purposes will require policies on attractiveness and capabilities. These types of policies use incentives, offered on both the demand and supply side, and have been greatly underemphasized to date, left largely to pilot approaches or small-scale interventions. They are essential to address the increasing gap between availability and use.

Policies to elicit greater willingness to use DTs must include the following:

- *Technology policies* are essential to redirect technology development toward generating and scaling up skills-appropriate DTs. To enable enterprises and households to use DTs and learn as they work, Africa must provide sophisticated, inclusive, and attractive apps in languages that local people speak.

- *Data policies and regulations* are needed to enable and safeguard data use and reuse. Policies are needed to ensure appropriate levels of trust in sharing data to facilitate the development of more attractive apps and greater use of DTs. These policies range from clear rules on data protection and cybersecurity, consumer protection, and e-commerce to policies for data sharing between government and business and across enterprises.

- *Capability support programs* that enhance the productive use of available DTs must be institutionalized for micro, small, and medium enterprises (MSMEs) as well as for households. These programs include business advisory services, technology information and upgrading services, and manager and worker skills training, together with longer-term investments in high-quality secondary and tertiary education.

- *National strategies* are essential to support familiarity with and use of DTs to support higher earnings. Depending on the local context, national strategies could include investments in common access facilities; demonstrations at internet cafes, local schools, or community centers; and other mechanisms to foster familiarity of use and to illustrate the productive potential of DTs for households and microenterprises.

Perhaps most important, enhancing the attractiveness of DTs requires the effective execution of technology policies to redirect technology development toward generating and scaling up skills-appropriate DTs. Rodrik and Stantcheva (2021, 832) argue: "As a matter of logic, the gap between skills and technology can be closed in one of two ways: either by increasing education to match the demands of new technologies, or by redirecting innovation to match the skills of the current (and prospective) labor force. The second strategy, which gets practically no attention in policy discussions, is worth taking seriously." A critical added benefit of designing skills-appropriate DTs for lower-skilled people that enable learning as people work is that it transforms what would be a one-time productivity increase, namely adoption of a new DT, into dynamic growth in productivity, with people continuously boosting the productivity of their tasks or moving to higher-skilled tasks as they develop new skills over time (box 8.1).

BOX 8.1
Examples of skills-appropriate technologies

Africa should redirect technologies, including technologies based on artificial intelligence (AI), to the level of skills that most African people have. When technologies create new uses for people and enhance learning, they expand the ways that people can contribute to production and increase their marginal productivity (Björkegren 2023). New technologies do not automatically bring widespread prosperity, however: whether they do or not reflects an economic, social, and political choice (Acemoglu and Johnson 2023). Many digital technologies (DTs) have the potential to be adapted and redirected as skills-appropriate technologies. DTs can enhance human abilities rather than excessively automating them, because specific DTs can incorporate images on tactile screens, voice-activated commands, and instructional videos—in any local language dialect—in ways that are particularly appropriate to facilitate learning. Existing DTs can also be modified and simplified to become intuitive, easy-to-use applications that ideally require no prior digital skills to use, to empower lower-skilled workers to perform higher-skill tasks and learn as they work.

In principle, the recording, tracking, and verification features of DTs can enable rural farmers and other local producers who possess valuable localized data to upload these data. The data can then be aggregated in ways that enhance their value and that allow workers to be remunerated and benefit fairly and equitably from these data flows across input, production, and logistics markets. A similar approach is possible from tagged data indicating where, how, and by whom food and other products were produced, to the extent that these data are valued by end-use consumers. In finance, AI can enable workers who lack traditional forms of collateral to gain access to credit and insurance services by demonstrating over time the ability both to make small purchases and

(continued)

Examples of skills-appropriate technologies *(continued)*

to put aside small savings within their budget. Specific DTs also can enable workers who lack the ability to do basic arithmetic to accept payments for goods and services rendered, as done successfully with Uber-type mobility apps. In health care, AI tools can enhance diagnostic and treatment capabilities of nurses, physicians' aides, and other medical technicians, allowing lower-skilled practitioners to perform tasks traditionally undertaken by physicians with many more years of professional education (Acemoglu and Restrepo 2020).

In education, AI can augment the capabilities of teachers, rather than replacing them. A recent experiment with an AI chatbot designed to assist teachers in Sierra Leone with professional development to improve their instruction yields highly encouraging results. In early implementation across 122 schools, 193 teachers used the system for lesson planning, classroom management, and subject matter. A subset of teachers used the system intensively. Although many teachers eventually found it natural to use a conversational interface over an existing chat app, getting to that point required training and overcoming obstacles. The results suggest that the usefulness of such apps may not be immediately obvious and may take time and experimentation to realize. The experience also suggests that AI tools can be useful for low-resourced schools, although implementation will look different from that in the wealthiest schools (Choi et al. 2023). More broadly, the experience suggests that policy support and concessional finance, together with experimentation, will be required to understand how best to promote the design, adoption, and scaling of new skills-appropriate apps by technology entrepreneurs for the low-income, low-capabilities context of most African owners and workers.

Policies that incentivize the generation of more attractive DTs for the jobs-related needs of lower-income African countries need to build on complementary policies that address availability, affordability, attractiveness, and capabilities of existing DTs. The creation and profitable commercialization of new skills-appropriate DTs requires a business environment that sufficiently rewards start-up entrepreneurs, global buyers, and input provider corporations to design local solutions that allow them to aggregate the relatively small-value purchases (dictated by ability to pay) of disparate low-income users. In turn, these potential users need to find the DTs sufficiently attractive and be able to afford the costs of digital connectivity and the underlying smartphones, tablet computers, or other access technologies.[13]

Possible prerequisites for local start-up entrepreneurs, as well as global corporations, to build viable business models and invest in designing such new skills-appropriate DTs include public investments in public data systems and open data policies. Public data systems, including in partnerships with private companies, could make available a set of common resource public goods such as spatial mapping, including digital addresses for all geographic locations, geotagging of land records, and local weather mapping. The availability of such public goods, accessible through user fees, seems to be the preferred alternative over individual investments by competing corporations for spatial digital mapping of the areas where they operate, because such individual investments create private rights for these data and prevent access by all entrepreneurs and other users seeking to add value to these data.

The generation and adoption of these new DTs will require supply- and demand-side support across enterprises and households. This support includes financing instruments such as targeted partial credit guarantees on the entrepreneurship supply side, and information demonstrations, matching grants, and vouchers on the demand side. Figure 8.16 summarizes the range of policy instruments typically used to support technology generation and adaptation, as well as diffusion and adoption. These policy instruments mainly apply to MSMEs, including household enterprises, because the largest enterprises typically develop such services in-house. The most common instrument to support firms in the productive use of DTs is business advisory services. Such services support the types of general business functions that are the focus of many DTs, including general enterprise management capabilities and more specific marketing, sales, and e-commerce platforms. Together with technology extension services and technology centers that support sector-specific business functions, such as weeding and storage for agriculture and input testing and packaging for food processing firms, they typically provide both services and financial support. Supporting both the generation and adoption of technology often requires additional financing instruments. Public financial support is needed where there are positive externalities and existing financial markets on their own do not provide the needed resources. On the technology adoption side, financing the acquisition of required skills is needed. On the innovation side, financing is required to generate and test new technologies that constitute adaptations of available technologies to local contexts with significant positive social spillovers.

With availability and wider use of digital tools that are easy to use for people with lower levels of skills, digital skills requirements may end up not presenting a fundamental barrier to DT use by lower-skilled people. Of the two complementary approaches to address skills-related challenges in the use of DTs, simplifying apps so that lower-skilled people can use them and learn as they do is likely a lower-cost and more effective strategy than investing significant resources in digital skills training. With higher levels of skills across the population as people learn from the use of attractive tools for productive use, larger enterprises will also be able to adopt better technologies, source more efficiently produced local inputs, expand production, and profitably sell to more prosperous local, regional, and global markets, thereby generating more good jobs. For this approach to be feasible, it is essential that the small number of digital entrepreneurs who design and scale these digital tools have benefited from top-level training in the world's best learning environments for digital programming.

FIGURE 8.16 Policy instruments used to support generation, adoption, and transfer of technologies

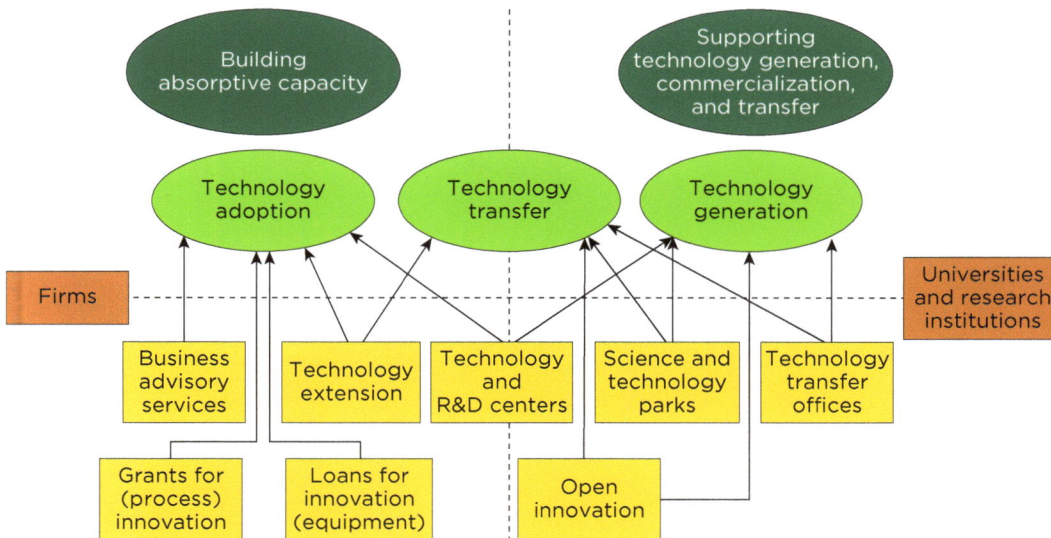

Source: Cirera et al. 2020, figure 4.5.
Note: In addition to grants for soft technologies and subsidized loans for hard technologies (equipment), public financing support may also be required to help address other barriers related to capabilities, attractiveness, and affordability-related drivers of digital technology use, as well as for new technology generation (including altering the direction of technology change)—either combined with business advisory services, technology extension services, and technology center services, or separately. R&D = research and development.

Sequencing

Sub-Saharan Africa lags behind other regions in terms of adoption and use of DTs and their application to basic business functions. Closing the gap will require policies and regulations in complementary areas. This chapter has underlined that simply expanding coverage will not generate widespread adoption and productive use of DTs. Given limited resources, implementation will take time. It is therefore imperative to sequence measures according to country characteristics.

Sub-Saharan African countries display a large heterogeneity with respect to both coverage and uptake (figure 8.17). Several countries have 3G coverage below 70 percent, namely Burkina Faso, Burundi, the Central African Republic, Chad, the Democratic Republic of Congo, Equatorial Guinea, and South Sudan. For these countries, 4G coverage is below 40 percent (except for Burkina Faso, where 4G coverage is 62 percent). Expanding the network is a priority for this group of countries, suggesting that they would especially benefit from competition rules, cost-reducing regulations, and cross-border agreements that enable access to larger markets. For these same countries, however, unique mobile internet uptake varies between 7 percent and 21 percent, so these countries already suffer from large uptake gaps. Thus, because network expansion by itself will not result in higher uptake, these countries also need to quickly design and implement measures that address willingness to pay.

FIGURE 8.17 3G coverage and unique mobile internet uptake, Sub-Saharan Africa, 2022

3G coverage (%)

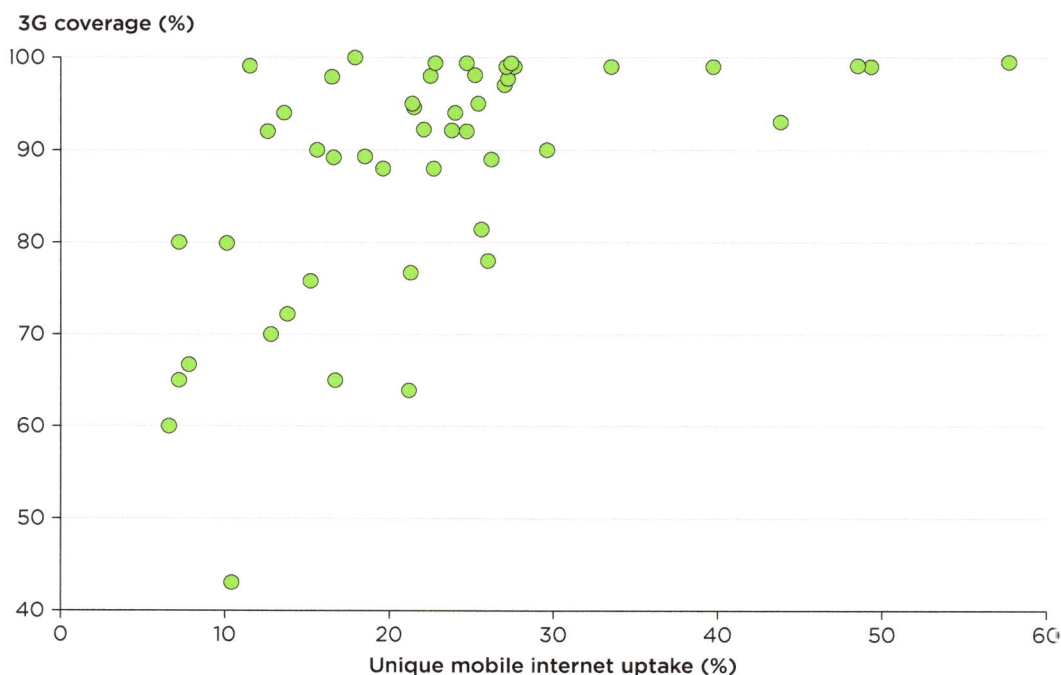

Source: Global System for Mobile Association.
Note: 3G = third generation.

For a large number of countries (30 out of 49 for which GSMA data are available for 2022), 3G network coverage is already above 90 percent. For 4G coverage, 12 countries have coverage above 90 percent, and another 4 countries have between 80 percent and 90 percent coverage. For these countries, the short-term focus should be on reducing the uptake gap. Further network expansion should be implemented only when policies to enhance willingness to pay have shown an impact by increasing uptake.

Expansion of productive use of DTs critically hinges on increased access to electricity for almost all countries in Sub-Saharan Africa. Total electricity access is above 80 percent only for eight countries (seven countries for access to electricity in rural areas). More than half of countries in the region have electricity access below 60 percent, lower than, for example 3G network coverage. These numbers clearly show that, even though electricity access is available at radio access network sites, a significant number of households living around these sites do not have electricity. In fact, access to electricity typically reflects not only a supply-side problem but also low willingness to pay, just like access to DTs (Blimpo and Cosgrove-Davies 2019), and will require similar policies to enhance willingness to pay.

Notes

1. Refer to, among others, Trajtenberg (2019), who emphasizes the need to design policies to minimize the detrimental effects of artificial intelligence (AI) and enhance its positive ones, including (1) education and skills development, with a focus on developing analytical, creative, interpersonal, and emotional skills relevant for an AI-based economy, and (2) changing the direction of technical change to support "human-enhancing innovations" that magnify and enhance sensory, motoric, and other such human capabilities instead of "human-replacing innovations" that replace human intervention and often leave for humans mostly repetitive, nonlearning jobs.

2. A key mechanism that likely underlies the inclusive jobs outcome of skills-biased internet availability is the output expansion effect highlighted by Dutz, Almeida, and Packard (2018) in Latin American countries. In separate complementary empirical studies on Argentina, Brazil, Chile, Colombia, and Mexico summarized therein, low-skilled workers also benefit from the more intensive use of the internet because firm productivity and output increase sufficiently to overcome the substitution of lower-skilled workers for higher-skilled workers at initial output levels.

3. DataFirst, RIA ICT Access Survey 2017–2018, https://www.datafirst.uct.ac.za/dataportal/index .php/catalog/765/related_materials.

4. For many countries, data on 4G coverage contain missing values in the earlier years of the sample period although the share of missing values declines over time. The ratio of missing values is especially high for Sub-Saharan African countries (in 2015 only half of the countries in the region had nonmissing values). If missing values correspond to very low coverage ratios, then average coverage ratios for the region in the earlier years may be exaggerated on the upside and, in reality, may be even lower.

5. These findings are based on data covering 2,303 microenterprises from Ethiopia, Nigeria, South Africa, and Uganda collected in 2022 (refer to Atiyas et al., forthcoming).

6. The survey questionnaire assesses several features related to online service delivery, including whole-of-government approaches, open government data, e-participation, multichannel service delivery, mobile services, uptake and digital divides, and innovative partnerships using information and communication technology.

7. The causal effect of e-government on uptake is not as well established as other drivers presented in table 8.2. A strong conditional correlation exists, however, between e-government indexes. For example, a simple regression of unique mobile uptake individually on the online service index and the e-participation index (controlling for GDP per capita, its square, and its cube) yields highly significant coefficients.

8. International Telecommunication Union, DataHub, "Indicator Catalogue," https://datahub.itu.int /indicators/.

9. By indicating "no need" as the major reason they do not use the internet, microenterprises could be indicating that (1) no apps are available that are useful to them in their local language that meet their productive needs; (2) their general skill level does not enable them to understand how they could productively use available apps; or (3) the available quality of service is so poor (with no or limited download availability of useful information when it is needed) that it is not useful to them.

10. By explicitly modeling incentives to manipulate, decision rules can be devised that are stable under manipulation. A large field experiment in Kenya stress-tested this approach. When implemented, decision rules estimated with such a strategy-robust approach outperform those based on standard machine-learning approaches (refer to Björkegren, Blumenstock, and Knight 2023).

11. Refer to Björkegren and Karaca (2022), who analyze a program in Rwanda that subsidized the equivalent of 8 percent of the stock of mobile phones. Subsidized handsets overwhelmingly stayed in rural areas: 85 percent of accounts receiving subsidized handsets mostly use a rural tower, suggesting effectiveness of the targeting. More generally, the effect of a subsidy depends on whether people are close to the margin of adopting (in which case small, dispersed interventions can tip the network), or if clusters of people are far from the margin (in which case larger, clustered interventions are likely to be more successful). A combination of empirical models of networks and reasoning about the structure of spillovers can inform the design most appropriate for a particular type of good.

12. For example, the East Africa One Network Area has facilitated roaming in this region. The initiative was launched in January 2015; to date, Kenya, Rwanda, South Sudan, and Uganda have capped international mobile roaming tariffs, and Tanzania confirmed its participation. The Economic Community of West African States launched a similar initiative, but implementation has been more limited.

13. The positive lessons from renewable energy illustrate the possibility of a sizable redirection of technological change, if supported by subsidies, a measurement framework, and changes in social norms and societal pressure. Acemoglu (2023) provides suggestive evidence that equilibrium distortions in the direction of technology can be substantial in the context of industrial automation, health care, and energy, and that correcting these distortions could have sizable welfare benefits.

References

Acemoglu, Daron. 2023. "Distorted Innovation: Does the Market Get the Direction of Technology Right?" *AEA Papers and Proceedings* 113: 1–28.

Acemoglu, Daron, and Samuel Johnson. 2023. *Power and Progress: Our Thousand-Year Struggle over Technology and Prosperity*. New York: Public Affairs.

Acemoglu, Daron, and Pascual Restrepo. 2020. "The Wrong Kind of AI? Artificial Intelligence and the Future of Labor Demand." *Cambridge Journal of Regions, Economy and Society* 13 (1): 25–35.

Atiyas, Izak, Marcio Cruz, Mark A. Dutz, Justice Mensah, and Andrew Partridge. Forthcoming. "Incomplete Digitalization among Microenterprises in Africa." Working paper.

Atiyas, Izak, and Mark A. Dutz. 2023. "Digital Technology Uses among Microenterprises: Why Is Productive Use So Low across Sub-Saharan Africa?" Policy Research Working Paper 10280, World Bank, Washington, DC.

Bahia, Kalvin, Pau Castells, Genaro Cruz, Takaaki Masaki, Xavier Pedrós, Tobias Pfutze, Carlos Rodríguez-Castelán, and Hernan Winkler. 2020. "The Welfare Effects of Mobile Broadband Internet: Evidence from Nigeria." Policy Research Working Paper 9230, World Bank, Washington, DC.

Bahia, Kalvin, Pau Castells, Genaro Cruz, Takaaki Masaki, Carlos Rodríguez-Castelán, and Viviane Sanfelice. 2023. "Mobile Broadband, Poverty and Labor Outcomes in Tanzania." *World Bank Economic Review* 37 (2): 235–56.

Begazo, Tania, Moussa Blimpo, and Mark A. Dutz. 2023. *Digital Africa: Technological Transformation for Jobs*. Washington, DC: World Bank. https://openknowledge.worldbank.org/entities/publication/7bc68e4b-c73d-42bd-8c71-4e96b2ec03dd.

Björkegren, Daniel. 2023. "Artificial Intelligence for the Poor: How to Harness the Power of AI in the Developing World." *Foreign Affairs*, August 9, 2023. https://www.foreignaffairs.com/world/artificial-intelligence-poor.

Björkegren, Daniel, Joshua Blumenstock, and Samsun Knight. 2023. *Training Machine Learning to Anticipate Manipulation*. New York: Center for Development Economics and Policy, Columbia University.

Björkegren, Daniel, and Burak Ceyhun Karaca. 2022. "Network Adoption Subsidies: A Digital Evaluation of a Rural Mobile Phone Program in Rwanda." *Journal of Development Economics* 154: 102762. https://doi.org/10.1016/j.jdeveco.2021.102762.

Blimpo, Moussa P., and Malcolm Cosgrove-Davies. 2019. *Electricity Access in Sub-Saharan Africa: Uptake, Reliability, and Complementary Factors for Economic Impact*. Africa Development Forum Series. Washington, DC: World Bank.

Choi, Jun Ho, Oliver Garrod, Paul Atherton, Andrew Joyce-Gibbons, Miriam Mason-Sesay, and Daniel Björkegren. 2023. "Are LLMs Useful in the Poorest Schools? The Teacher.AI in Sierra Leone." Cornell University, arXiv:2310.02982v2. https://arxiv.org/abs/2310.02982.

Cirera, Xavier, Diego Comin, and Marcio Cruz. 2022. *Bridging the Technological Divide: Technology Adoption by Firms in Developing Countries*. Washington, DC: World Bank.

Cirera, Xavier, Jaime Frías, Justin Hill, and Yanchao Li. 2020. *A Practitioner's Guide to Innovation Policy: Instruments to Build Firm Capabilities and Accelerate Technological Catch-Up in Developing Countries*. Washington, DC: World Bank.

Cruz, Marcio, ed. 2024. *Digital Opportunities in African Businesses*. Washington, DC: World Bank.

Dutz, Mark A., Rita K. Almeida, and Truman G. Packard. 2018. *The Jobs of Tomorrow: Technology, Productivity, and Prosperity in Latin America and the Caribbean*. Washington, DC: World Bank.

Goldfarb, Ari, and Catherine Tucker. 2019. "Digital Economics." *Journal of Economic Literature* 57 (1): 3–43.

Hjort, Jonas, and Jonas Poulsen. 2019. "The Arrival of Fast Internet and Employment in Africa." *American Economic Review* 109 (3): 1032–79.

Houngbonon, Georges V., Erwan Le Quentrec, and Stefania Rubrichi. 2021. "Access to Electricity and Digital Inclusion: Evidence from Mobile Call Detail Records." *Humanities and Social Sciences Communications* 8: 170.

Mothobi, Onkokame, Alison Gillwald, and Pablo Aguera. 2020. "A Demand Side View of Informality and Financial Inclusion." Research ICT Africa Policy Paper No. 9, Series 5: After Access, Research ICT Africa, Cape Town.

Rodrik, Dani, and Stefanie Stantcheva. 2021. "Fixing Capitalism's Good Jobs Problem." *Oxford Review of Economic Policy* 37 (4): 824–37.

Trajtenberg, M. 2019. "AI as the Next GPT: A Political-Economy Perspective." Chapter 6 in *The Economics of Artificial Intelligence: An Agenda*, edited by Ajay Agrawal, Joshua Gans, and Avi Goldfarb. Chicago: University of Chicago Press.

UN DESA (United Nations Department of Economic and Social Affairs). 2022. *E-Government Survey 2022: The Future of Digital Government*. New York: United Nations.

Vergara-Cobos, Estefania. 2021. "High Broadband Prices and Limited Offerings Constraining Data Use by SMEs." Unpublished background note, World Bank, Washington, DC.

CHAPTER 9

External Economic Partnerships

Abdoulkadre Ado and Josephine Ofori Adofo

Summary

The final chapter of this publication focuses on the dynamic of Africa's external economic cooperation with foreign economies, especially those of Asian and Western countries. The analysis examines how Africa can claim the 21st century by better mobilizing its increasing economic, human, and business ties with external partners. Through partnerships, Africa can realize an immense potential to improve trade, attract more strategic investments, achieve industrialization, and generate inclusive economic growth.

Based on the analysis, several key messages emerge regarding trends and the potential for economic growth:

- *Asia has become a top player in Africa's external economic cooperation, and this trend is expected to continue.* Despite the continued importance of Africa's trade with Western countries, trade with Asia has significantly increased and diversified, making a jump of more than 948 percent between 2001 and 2021.

- *China has eclipsed the United States on investments in Africa for new infrastructure and increased industrialization.* In 2006, US direct investments in Africa were five times higher than investments from China; however, on average, Chinese investments in Africa have been relatively increasing over the past 15 years. Investments from China have consistently been more than 900 percent higher than those from the United States every year from 2017 to 2021, reaching US$5 billion by the end of 2021.

- *Africa's next economic growth surge could occur through digitalization.* Affordable indigenous and foreign technologies in Africa have increased in many countries, which has helped businesses, generating additional exports worth billions of dollars in digitally deliverable services.

This chapter includes contributions by Hoyoung Kwon, Yujin Lee, Jinhwan Oh, and Jisun Song.

- *Joint ventures and diversified trade with international partners will support Africa to take advantage of economic digitalization and to climb the global value chain.* Africa must develop its manufacturing industries to generate trade surplus, including by transforming and exporting high-value-added products in key sectors such as agribusiness. Key to this development will be the expansion and sophistication of special economic zones and diversifying Africa's international trade and economic partners.

- *Entrepreneurship among African youth and members of African diasporas worldwide presents great potential for external cooperation.* Many successful African immigrants and their networks invest and act as bridges in business ventures and international partnerships between Africa and external investors. Africa also needs more inclusive policies that support promising women entrepreneurs across the continent.

The analysis also reveals important opportunities for African countries:

- *Sustainable energy supply.* International and cross-border partnerships to increase a sustainable energy supply can help address the rising demand for power and some of the lowest electrification rates in the world.

- *Urban infrastructure* remains a critical need on the continent. Experience from and partnerships with megacities in Asian and Western countries could provide relevant learning and coordination for urban infrastructure projects in Africa.

- *Digitalization and inclusive industrialization* carry significant potential for African trade, economic growth, and modernization in many sectors. External partnerships could support Africa to develop innovative ecosystems and affordable technologies and to modernize, digitalize, industrialize, and grow from technology and knowledge transfer. These efforts will support development of the manufacturing sector across Africa and create jobs and capabilities for inclusive industrialization.

- *Business ties and trade between Africa and the rest of the world* are strengthened by African diasporic entrepreneurs. Entrepreneurs can attract investors, contribute to skills transfer, bridge trade networks across continents, and achieve national development objectives.

- *Agribusiness* has enormous potential to boost local manufacturing industries, learning from external partners in manufacturing and promoting special economic zones.

Capitalizing on these trends and opportunities will require that African countries address certain challenges:

- *Difficulty attracting needed foreign investments.* Addressing this challenge will require a prioritization strategy regarding investments from Asia, the West, and other regions, as well as an improved institutional environment to ease business.

- *Debt sustainability*. The lack of transparency on loans and investments in African countries from some external funders presents a serious challenge to good governance and accountability in Africa.

- *Competition between Asian and Western countries*. This emerging challenge pushes African countries to choose one partner or the other. Africa should face this challenge with confidence and negotiate with all partners, traditional and nontraditional, for its strategic development.

The rest of this chapter elaborates on the opportunities and challenges in Africa's external economic cooperation, drawing lessons from success in various countries; analyzes positive outcomes and areas for improvement from megatrends of the past two decades between Africa and the rest of the world; and proposes policy considerations to position Africa as a prosperous, innovative, and major global economic power in the 21st century.

Context

The United Nations Sustainable Development Goals (SDGs) and the African Union's Agenda 2063 illustrate the critical role of partnerships for Africa to achieve inclusive growth. SDG 17 emphasizes the role of partnerships as key to achieving the development goals. The African Union's Agenda 2063 defines a goal of "Africa as a major partner in global affairs and peaceful co-existence."[1]

From a development perspective, economic and commercial partnerships among African countries and with non-African countries have the potential to accelerate trade integration and socioeconomic prosperity. For example, improved collaboration among countries through the African Continental Free Trade Area could reduce exchange barriers and trade costs on the continent by up to 14.3 percent (Songwe, Macleod, and Karingi 2021). Continental and global partnerships, however, require more trade diversification, both in terms of partners and in terms of products being traded, especially toward higher-value-added exports from Africa to international markets. According to the 2023 *Sustainable Development Goals Report*, the share of exports in global trade for the least developed countries has revolved around only 1 percent since 2011 (United Nations 2023). For this pattern to improve, African economies need better-quality investments, from both local and foreign investors, to enable industrialization that would contribute to improving the continent's international trade balance. Also, opportunities to catalyze inclusive development in Africa should be explored, including mobilizing digitalization while addressing sustainability issues through the adoption of pertinent new technologies.

African countries and continental and global trade

These sectoral improvements coupled with improved human capital and better governance could boost productivity nationally and across the continent, and the overall development of Africa. These improvements would mean not just more trade but better trade with top trade partners such as China, the European Union, or the United States and better joint ventures with partner organizations from emerging countries such as India, Saudi Arabia, and Türkiye. In fact, major economies such as India and the Republic of Korea have signaled that their collaboration model with Africa will increasingly focus on health care, pharmaceutical innovations, capacity building, and technology transfer through digitalization (Karingi and Naliaka 2022; WHO 2019, 2020). Such opportunities for collaboration between Africa and external partners represent ways the continent could benefit from experience from other parts of the world in the areas of sustainable funding, shared experience regarding development, and sociotechnical innovation for inclusive growth.

To better understand Africa's potential for more effective economic partnerships, it is important to acknowledge the increasing importance of Asian countries, especially China, as economic partners in Africa; the rise of inclusive digitalization; the need to boost pan-African free trade; and the significance of green growth and climate resilience on the continent. It is critical for Africa to harness the opportunities presented by such megatrends to create inclusive growth and prosperity for the continent.

Over the past 20 years, statistics have shown a change in the economic dynamics of the African continent. Two decades ago, Africa's trade was mostly with Europe and the United States.[2] Now, most African economies have an Asian or other non-Western economy as their main trade partner. In fact, 2023 data from United Nations Trade & Development (UNCTAD) show that 30 countries in Africa had an Asian or non-Western country as their top trade partner in 2020 and that this number rose to 33 countries in 2021.[3] The top trade partners among these 33 countries include China (16 countries), the United Arab Emirates (9 countries), India (6 countries), Bangladesh (1), and Oman (1).

The beginning of the 21st century was characterized by an Africa-Asia cooperation strengthened through bilateral and multilateral cooperation platforms.[4] Meanwhile, Africa continues its traditional economic cooperation with Western countries such as France, Germany, and the United States. As a region of increasing and significant interest for Asia, Europe, and North America, Africa is in a favorable position to redefine its external economic cooperation during this 21st century.

This dynamic presents Africa with both opportunities and challenges, particularly regarding economic and human development. Although Western countries continue to serve as a model for Africa's aspiration for advanced and high-quality development, successes in other emerging economies are informing African choices in development policies and partnership negotiations in areas such as strategic trade and investments, joint ventures, diversification, and cooperation with external partners worldwide (Ado et al. 2025). This dynamic also raises an important question: *How can Africa leverage its cooperation with global partners to effectively promote inclusive productivity growth considering the potential in many sectors on the continent?* The current analysis focuses on the economic and human capital development realities and trends. It identifies opportunities and challenges for African development through more effective engagements with external partners.

African countries and their top trade partners

In recent years, Africa has intensified economic relations with countries such as China, India, and the United Arab Emirates, making them the top trade partners of most African countries. Also, the past two decades have seen an increase in foreign investments and development assistance for Africa. China and India are now the top economic partners of many African countries, with China; Hong Kong SAR, China; India; and Singapore also among top sources of foreign direct investments (FDI) on the continent. Meanwhile, countries such as China, Japan, Korea, and Saudi Arabia provide among the most significant development assistance in Africa, even compared with Western traditional assistance.

In 2000, only three African countries had an Asian or non-Western country as top trade partner: Benin had India, the Democratic Republic of Congo had China, and the Seychelles had Saudi Arabia. By 2021, however, 60 percent of Africa (or 33 African countries) had an Asian or non-Western country as top trade partner. In 2000, France, the United Kingdom, and the United States represented 44 percent of Africa's top trade partners among the 43 countries for which data were available. By 2021, China, India, and the United Arab Emirates represented more than 57 percent of Africa's top trade partners, with France, the United Kingdom, and the United States representing less than 6 percent. Figure 9.1 shows the significant shift in top trade partners for Africa, with the shift indicating how important Asia has become for African countries. The changing trade patterns also indicate that Africa now represents a significant region for external partners and international businesses.

For Africa to claim the 21st century, the continent needs to take a more significant part in global trade and to capture more revenue from the global value chain. That is, external trade with other regions needs to continue growing in quantity and in value toward a sustained surplus for Africa's trade balance in relation to the rest of the world. Over the past two decades, Africa has had massive imports of high-value-added manufactured goods and exports of low-value-added commodities. Better economic cooperation with foreign partners can contribute positively to changing this dynamic.

Claiming the 21st century also means that high-quality investments from Western and non-Western countries should be based on a more strategic prioritization of sectors and segments along the global value chain. Ultimately, Africa should be manufacturing

FIGURE 9.1 Africa's leading trade partners, 2000 versus 2021

Number of African countries as trading partner

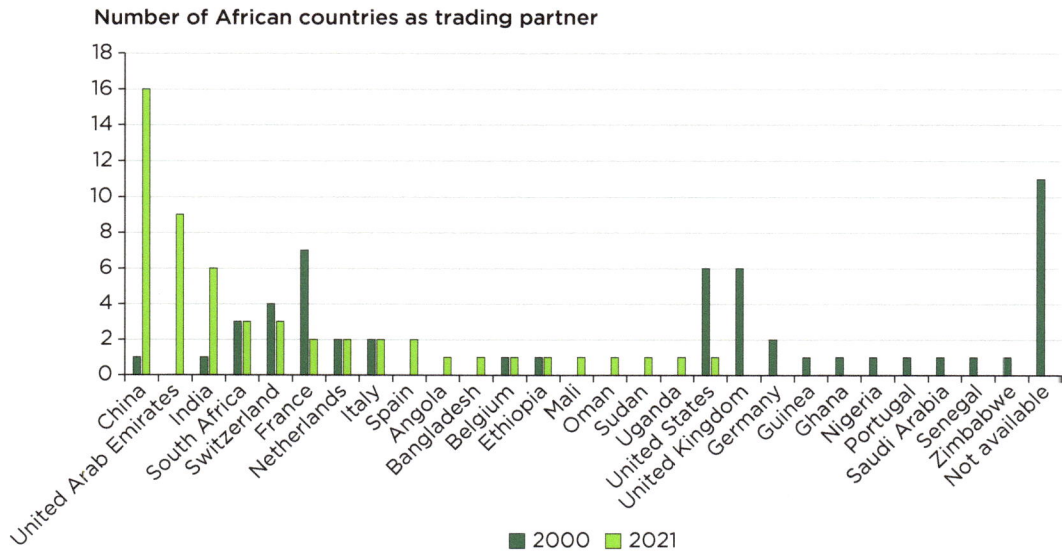

Source: World Bank, based on 2023 data from United Nations Trade & Development, UNCTADstat Data Centre, https://unctadstat.unctad.org/datacentre/.

many of the products it currently imports, but such manufacturing should take place in African countries that have comparative advantages in terms of natural and mineral resources, human capital, and other critical factors of production. Thus, when strategizing to attract foreign investments, including from Asia, the continent must base its 21st-century strategy on the logic of value addition, rather than on the logic of simply producing more raw materials and commodity exports. To do so, Africa will need to define the areas where it can leverage external partnerships more effectively for qualitative economic and human development, and long-term trade surplus, and to encourage strategic investments that lead to sustainable inclusive growth.

Although many African countries continue to rank among the top performers in economic growth despite the slowdown caused by COVID-19, this closing chapter elaborates on ways more countries in Africa could nurture the growth momentum through better economic cooperation and trade diversification with other world regions, including with Asia, which is also going through a vibrant economic transformation and is Africa's current top trade partner.

Facts

This section looks at Africa's relationship with Asia and with the West from both an economic and a human development perspective. It highlights quantitative facts for the main aspects of economic ties and partnerships between Africa and the rest of the world over the past 20 years and identifies the megatrends and areas of mutual significance for Africa and its external partners.

Highlights

Over the past two decades, ties between Africa and the rest of the world (advanced and emerging economies) have seen major shifts in trade, investments, economic cooperation, human capital, and development assistance.

What has gone right:

- *Improved and diversified trade with Asia, especially exports to Asia.* Africa's trade with Western countries continues to be very important (Africa's exports to Germany increased 159 percent in the past 20 years); however, trade between Africa and Asia has significantly improved and diversified, especially in terms of exports to Asia, reaching an increase of more than 948 percent between 2001 and 2021. Africa's shift to Asian countries as top trade partners—moving from 3 African countries in 2000 to 33 countries in 2021—mitigates trade dependency risks in relation to Western and non-Western countries. In 2021, Africa's exports to Asia were 572 percent more than Africa's exports to the United States. Africa's exports to the United Arab Emirates also jumped significantly—by 4,000 percent from 2001 to 2021.

- *A significant shift to China as a top trade partner.* By 2021, Chinese investments in Africa were five times more than US investments. On average, Chinese investments in Africa have been relatively increasing over the past 15 years and have consistently been more than 900 percent higher than those from the United States each year between 2017 and 2021, reaching US$5 billion at the end of 2021. A significant part of foreign investments in Africa went into the construction sector for the development of new infrastructure and into the mining sector. Also, strong economic growth in Asian countries, especially China and India, created many positive spillovers in trade and investment opportunities for both oil-rich and resource-rich African countries. These investments have created jobs in Africa.

- *Increased digitalization in African countries, helping businesses and generating additional exports worth billions of dollars in digitally deliverable services.* Between 2005 and 2014, the Central Africa subregion consistently ranked highest in the proportion of digitally deliverable services. From 2015 to 2020, Western Africa was the highest performer, but Southern Africa claimed the lead on trade digitalization in 2021, at 57 percent in digitally deliverable services.

- *Expanded external partnerships with increased opportunities for African entrepreneurship.* The number of Africans studying in Asian or other non-Western countries increased by 297 percent from 2000 to 2017. Although most African students continue to choose Western Europe and North America as leading destinations for study, the larger number of Africans studying in other areas is significant. These student movements have resulted in a significant increase in the number of successful African immigrant entrepreneurs in Western and non-Western countries, particularly in China, the European Union, Saudi Arabia, the United Arab Emirates, and the United States. Many of these successful African immigrants invest and act as bridges in business ventures and in international partnerships between Africa and external investors.

- *Emergence of new official development assistance (ODA) partners.* Asian and Western development assistance is significant for Africa and has contributed to capacity building. Emerging non-Western partners such as Saudi Arabia have joined the top traditional partners such as Germany and the United States. Saudi Arabia ranked third after the United States and Germany in net ODA to Africa, with more than US$5 billion in 2022, more than France with US$4.3 billion that same year. Loans were more prevalent than grants in funding infrastructure in Africa.

What has gone wrong:

- *Decreasing US investments and trade in Africa, and low Asian ODA.* In 2006, US direct investments in Africa were five times higher than investments from China. Since then, Africa's exports to the United States decreased from a peak of US$110 billion in 2008 to US$34.8 billion in 2021, a level below Africa's exports to India, which accounted for US$42.5 billion in 2021. Moreover, in recent years, investments from the United States have decreased significantly. US investments in Africa represented 14.3 percent of global investments in Africa in 2006, but that number fell to nearly 0 percent in 2021. At the same time, Asian ODA is still very low compared with traditional Western partners, restricting the impact of such assistance to small projects or isolated locations rather than affecting regional integration and continental development.

- *Persistence of commodity-based trade with Asia, which has not enhanced Africa's position on the global value chain.* Africa ships raw materials to Asia and imports expensive merchandise made in Asia. In 2021, Africa's imports from China alone were US$121.8 billion, which increased the continent's unfavorable trade balance and deficits in relation to Asia. This pattern has not significantly improved Africa's position on the global value chain despite increased investments from Asia. Although a significant part of Asian investments in Africa went into minerals, oil, and gas projects, they did not necessarily transform the extracted raw materials and resources in Africa to add local value before export to global markets.

- *Slow pace of digitalization.* Despite the significant potential in many sectors to take advantage of affordable digital resources to support businesses and improve digitally deliverable trade services, the Eastern and North Africa subregions are not yet using their full digital potential, performing below the Sub-Saharan average of 25 percent of the region's total trade in services from 2005 to 2021. By contrast, South Asia's average, for instance, stood at 64 percent of its total trade in services over the same period.

To maximize the potential of Africa's external partnerships, it is important for Africa to continue to improve trade through high-value-added exports to Asian and Western countries, and to attract high-quality foreign investments that will contribute to key sectors such as manufacturing and agriculture to achieve sustainable industrialization, local value addition, and inclusive productivity growth. Digitalization is also crucial to increase business prosperity and Africa's international trade. African diasporic entrepreneurs could also act as a significant source of trade networks between Africa and the rest of the world. Meanwhile, development assistance from both Asian and Western partners could be channeled to support Africa's strategic development choices on larger scales.

The Africa-Asia and Africa-West trade dynamics

Africa's trading partners have changed significantly over the past two decades, but the commodity-based model for trade has remained the same. In 2001, Asia represented only US$22.3 billion in Africa's global exports, whereas Africa exported nearly the same amount to just the United States. By 2021, Africa's exports to the United States had risen 56 percent to US$34.8 billion, and Africa's exports to Asia increased almost 935 percent to US$233 billion. At the country level, China has surpassed the United States as Africa's biggest trading partner. In 2001, Africa's exports to the United States were worth six times that of China. By 2021, Africa's total exports to China were 270 percent of its exports to the United States.

Figure 9.2 illustrates the changes in Africa's exports over the period 2001–21. For instance, exports to the United States decreased from a record of US$110 billion in 2008 to US$34.8 billion in 2021, a level below Africa's 2021 exports to India of US$42.5 billion. Meanwhile, Africa's exports to Germany increased from US$8.5 billion in 2001 to US$22 billion in 2021, a jump of 159 percent over 20 years. Although not shown in the figure, Africa's exports to the United Arab Emirates also experienced a significant jump of nearly 4,000 percent from 2001 to 2021.

In terms of imports, Asian countries now represent a significant share of Africa's trade, with China as the leading source of imports for the continent. In 2001, Africa imported US$10.2 billion from Germany but only US$5 billion from China. By 2021, Africa's imports from China had grown to US$121.8 billion, four times more than imports from Germany. In 2001, Africa imported US$3 billion from the United States and US$33 billion from Asia. By 2021, Africa's imports from Asia were 3,650 percent more than Africa's imports from the United States and 834 percent more than Africa's imports from Germany. With regard to other major trade partners, Africa's imports in 2021 from China were worth 120 percent of Africa's imports from Australia, France, Germany, the United Kingdom, and the United States combined (figure 9.3), reflecting a major change in the trade pattern since 2001, when Africa's imports from France alone were worth 289 percent of imports from China.

FIGURE 9.2 Africa's exports to individual major economies, 2001–21

Exports (US$, million)

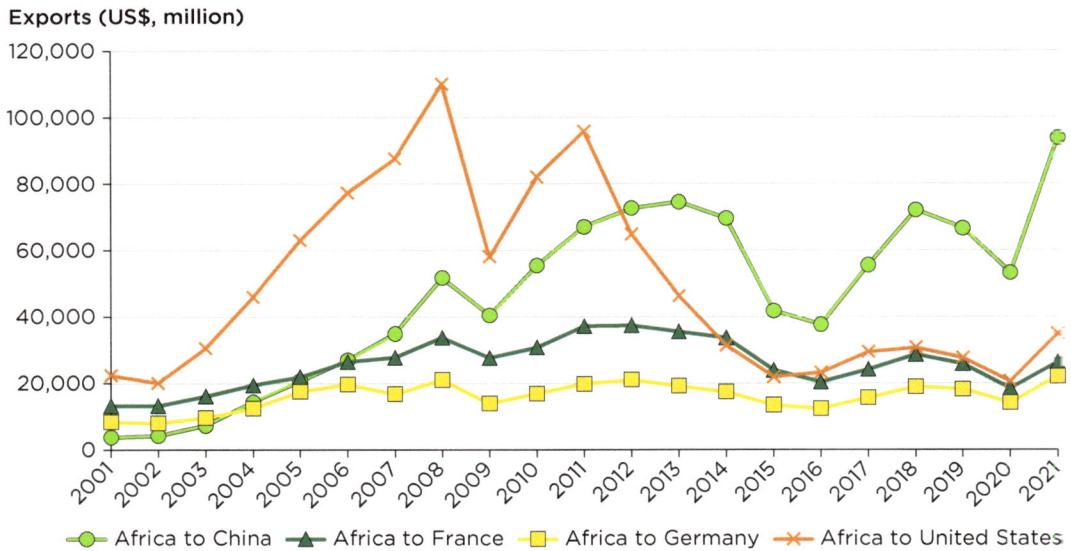

Source: World Bank, based on 2023 data from United Nations Trade & Development, UNCTADstat Data Centre, https://unctadstat.unctad.org/datacentre/.

FIGURE 9.3 Africa's imports from individual major economies, 2001–21

Imports (US$, million)

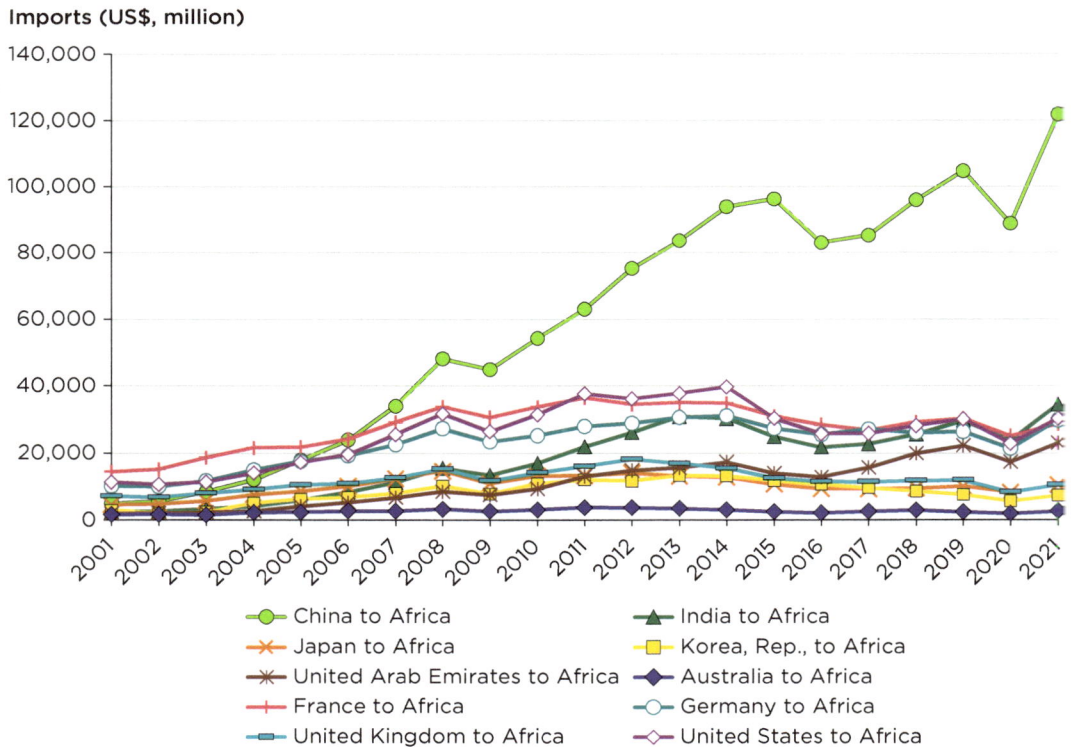

Source: World Bank, based on 2023 data from United Nations Trade & Development, UNCTADstat Data Centre, https://unctadstat.unctad.org/datacentre/.

For many Asian countries, Africa's imports have remained relatively stable over the past two decades; a massive jump from China is the exception. Also, statistics show that, although COVID-19 caused a decrease in trade volumes between Africa and Asia, the post-COVID-19 trend has started increasing again toward more trade, both in exports and imports, for individual countries as well as for groups of African and Asian countries.

Although the volume of trade between Africa and other countries, particularly those outside the West, has risen, the nature of products traded by Africa has remained consistent: commodities still dominate most of what many Sub-Saharan African countries export to Asia. Many countries in Africa continue to export only raw materials to Asia and import processed food and other manufactured products especially from China, India, and the United Arab Emirates. Despite some stagnation, the proportion of exports of primary or secondary goods over time has not changed significantly, and primary goods still make up most exports. From 2000 to 2019, on average, 81 percent of Sub-Saharan Africa's exports were primary commodities, whereas only 19 percent were goods manufactured in Africa. Exports of minerals from Sub-Saharan Africa went up 3 percentage points to 10.1 percent, but exports of manufactured goods decreased from 20.5 percent to 17.7 percent. Africa has considerable potential to grow and expand its manufacturing sector, which was relatively underdeveloped as of 2019, contributing only about 18 percent to the continent's economy.

Oil-rich countries such as the Republic of Congo and Nigeria continue to export mainly oil and petroleum products, which represent more than 98 percent of exports to their Asian and non-Western top trade partners. For mineral-rich countries such as Botswana and Guinea, exports to Asia are nearly 100 percent dominated by diamonds and aluminum, respectively. For Burundi, 97 percent of exports to the United Arab Emirates were gold and chemicals. For Benin, rice represented 74 percent of imports from India. In Botswana, 82 percent of imports from the United Arab Emirates were, interestingly, diamonds and electronics. Table 9.1 shows the strong diversity of products shipped from Africa to Asian partners: aluminum, cashews, chemicals, coffee, copper, cotton, diamonds, flours, fruits, gas, gold, iron, leather, manganese, meat, metals, minerals, nuts, oil, petroleum, seeds, stones, wood, and zinc.

Some products have continued to dominate exports from particular African countries to China, Indonesia, and Malaysia.

- *Exports to China.* South Africa's exports to China of iron by-products represent nearly 25 percent of its total exports, a proportion that has remained quite steady in recent years. South Africa's exports of iron increased by 4 percentage points from 2002 to 2020. Meanwhile most of Senegal's exports to China remained groundnuts, a shift from the mollusk prevalence that characterized the early 2000s.

TABLE 9.1 Top products exported and imported between Africa and Asia, 2019

African country	Top trade partner	Main export(s) to top trade partner			Main import(s) from top trade partner		
		Product(s)	Share of exports to partner (%)	US$, billion	Product(s)	Share of imports from partner (%)	US$, billion
Benin	India	Nuts, cashews, wood, cotton	72.0	0.06	Rice	74.0	0.30
Botswana	United Arab Emirates	Diamonds	99.0	1.00	Diamonds, electronics	81.8	0.03
Burundi	United Arab Emirates	Gold, chemicals	97.2	0.09	Oil, vehicles, cloth	58.3	0.04
Cameroon	China	Oil, gas, wood	92.0	0.94	Footwear, motorcycles, pesticide, cotton	12.3	0.21
Congo, Rep.	China	Oil, wood, copper	98.1	5.8	Fabrics, clothing, footwear, paper	15.9	0.07
Eritrea	China	Copper, zinc	99.0	0.21	Tires, machines, electronics	36.0	0.02
Ethiopia	China	Oil, seeds, fruits, nuts, leather, coffee	89.8	0.31	Lamps, clothing, fabrics, oil	19.8	0.46
Gabon	China	Oil, manganese, wood	98.5	4.60	Railways, tires, fish, ceramics, machines	18.1	0.07
Ghana	China	Oil, manganese, wood	96.0	2.40	Iron, footwear, pesticide, hair	12.3	0.61
Guinea	China	Aluminum	99.0	2.50	Footwear, ships, machines, vehicles, electronics	17.9	0.31
Mauritania	China	Iron, copper, flours	93.9	0.88	Fabrics, tea, footwear	32.0	0.33
Namibia	China	Chemicals, copper, zinc, meat	90.1	0.47	Iron, electronics, electricals	14.8	0.03
Nigeria	India	Petroleum	98.0	8.14	Appliances, motorcycles	57.8	3.33

(continued)

TABLE 9.1 Top products exported and imported between Africa and Asia, 2019 (*continued*)

African country	Top trade partner	Main export(s) to top trade partner			Main import(s) from top trade partner		
		Product(s)	Share of exports to partner (%)	US$, billion	Product(s)	Share of imports from partner (%)	US$, billion
Rwanda	United Arab Emirates	Gold, stones, diamonds, minerals	94.6	0.33	Oil, machines, electricals	57.3	0.14
Seychelles	United Arab Emirates	Oil	98.0	0.30	Oil	71.0	0.23
Sierra Leone	China	Wood, chemicals, metals	99.1	0.20	Rice, electronics, iron, footwear, tomato paste	27.6	0.09

Source: United Nations Trade & Development, UNCTADstat Data Centre, 2023 data, https://unctadstat.unctad.org /datacentre/.

Note: The shares of exports and imports show the shares of the country's total exports or imports to each specific trade partner. For example, 98 percent of Nigeria's exports to India is petroleum.

- *Exports to Indonesia.* In 2010, cotton dominated Tanzania's exports to Indonesia (94 percent); however, in 2019, the most-exported Tanzanian products to Indonesia were raw groundnuts (32 percent). For Madagascar, the dominant exported product changed from essential oils (78 percent) in 2010 to cloves (68 percent) in 2019.

- *Exports to Malaysia.* For Côte d'Ivoire, cocoa beans represented 46 percent of the country's total exports to Malaysia in 2002, a percentage that remained steady until 2020, when the rate dropped slightly to 43 percent and natural rubber became the export leader at 53 percent. Meanwhile, Ghana also exported mostly cocoa beans to Malaysia, although the percentage dropped from 94 percent in 2002 to 73 percent in 2019.

Sub-Saharan Africa has seen a significant change in regional sources for imports and destinations for exports in relation to Asia and North America. In fact, the East Asia and Pacific and South Asia regions have become Sub-Saharan Africa's top trade partners, with more than three times the volume of trade for exports and imports in relation to other major regions such as North America. In 2000, Sub-Saharan Africa's exports to North America represented more than 140 percent of exports to the East Asia and Pacific region. By 2020, however, Sub-Saharan Africa's exports to the region represented more than 60 percent of exports to North America, a trade share increase of 144 percent to the East Asia and Pacific region compared with a trade share decrease of 267 percent in relation to North America.

Western and Asian investments in Africa

The investment landscape in Africa has also changed considerably over the past two decades. Although the West remains a significant investor in Africa, current FDI flows to Africa are mostly dominated by China and other emerging economies, which continue to expand internationally into all regions of Africa. India and Singapore have increased their FDI to Africa, and India, the Russian Federation, and Türkiye have increased trade with Africa (Sun 2020). China and Russia have major investment initiatives targeting Africa: The 2018 Forum on China-Africa Cooperation announced a US$60 billion finance package. The 2019 Russia-Africa Summit and Economic Forum led to 50 agreements for a total of more than US$10 billion, mainly in infrastructure and natural resource development projects (UNCTAD 2020b).

Investments from the United States have decreased, whereas those from China have increased over the past 15 years. In 2006, US direct investments in Africa were five times higher than investments from China; however, by 2021, Chinese investments in Africa were five times more than investments from the United States (figure 9.4). For each year between 2017 and 2021, on average, Chinese investments in Africa have been more than 900 percent higher than those from the United States, reaching US$5 billion at the end of 2021. US investments in Africa represented 14.3 percent of global investments in Africa in 2006, but that ratio fell to almost 0 percent in 2021.

FIGURE 9.4 **Financial flows into Africa, 2006–21**

FDI in Africa (US$, billion)

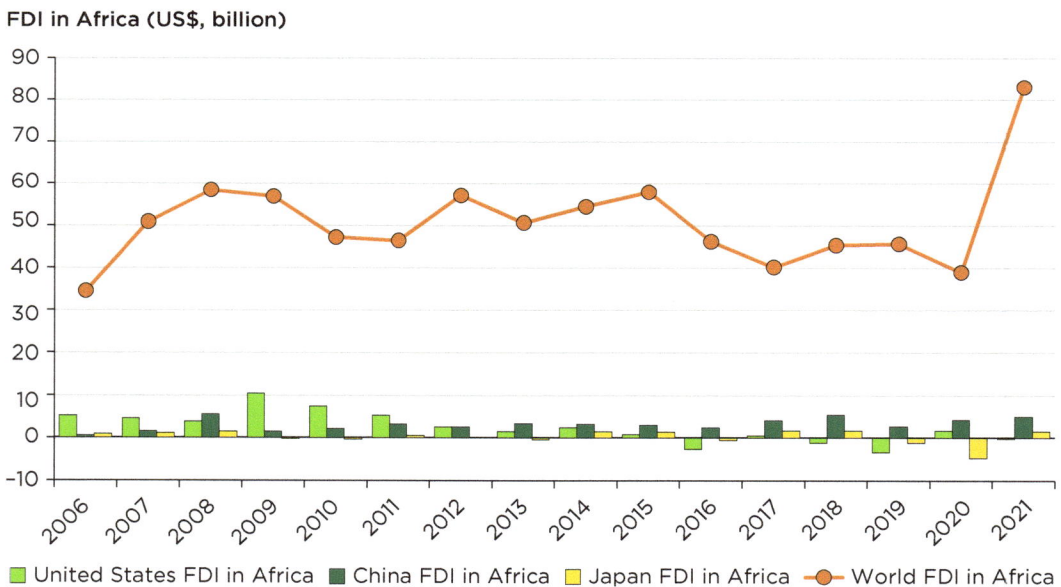

■ United States FDI in Africa ■ China FDI in Africa ■ Japan FDI in Africa ●— World FDI in Africa

Source: World Bank, based on data from the Japan External Trade Organization, 2023; United Nations Trade & Development, UNCTADstat Data Centre, 2023; Ministry of Commerce of China, 2023; and the US Bureau of Economic Analysis, 2023.
Note: A negative value means that Africa experienced more divestments than investments during that year from that specific country. FDI = foreign direct investment.

21st-Century Africa

Meanwhile, Japanese investments in Africa also stayed relatively low during that period, ranging from US$1 billion in 2006 to US$2 billion in 2021.

As FDI from major Asian countries such as China has increasingly dominated the financial landscape, contracts awarded by African entities (both private and public) are increasingly offered to Asian corporations. In recent years, Asian companies have gained an increasing number of contracts in Africa relative to Western companies. Other non-Western countries such as Saudi Arabia and the United Arab Emirates have also significantly invested across Africa. During the recent 2023 Saudi-Africa Summit, Saudi Arabia announced anticipated investments of more than US$25 billion in Africa (Argaam 2023).

All five subregional groupings in Africa[5] have received significant levels of FDI over the past two decades, but some have attracted more than others. In 2021, the Southern Africa subregion received more than US$41 billion in foreign investments, three times more than the next recipient, Western Africa, with $13.8 billion. The total amount of investments received individually by each of three subregions—Eastern, Southern, and Western Africa—in 2021 represents more than all investments (US$10.4 billion) in Africa in 2000. Overall, African subregions combined have received significant foreign investments in recent years, totaling more than US$924 billion over a 21-year period, an increase of 700 percent from 2000 to 2021.

In 2000, the top 10 African recipients of global FDI (originating from all foreign countries worldwide) attracted only US$2 billion in investments. In 2021, the top 10 recipients managed to attract US$30 billion in foreign investments, but with significant differences between the top five and the second group of five recipients of FDI. The top five (the Arab Republic of Egypt, Nigeria, Morocco, Mozambique, and Ghana) received US$343 billion, or 142 percent more FDI than the second group of recipients (Ethiopia, Algeria, Sudan, the Republic of Congo, and the Democratic Republic of Congo) with US$142 billion. That is, for the period 2000–21, the top five recipients of FDI received more than a third of total global investments in Africa.

Meanwhile, for the 2003–19 period, 15 African countries each received at least US$1 billion in investments from China (figure 9.5). During that period, investments from China to Egypt represented only 1 percent of total foreign investments in Egypt (US$1.2 billion). For the same period, the proportion was 38 percent in Zimbabwe, 24 percent in Mauritius, 19 percent in Zambia, and only 8 percent in Ethiopia. In those 16 years, South Africa accounted for 28 percent of total investments received by the other top 14 countries combined.

Along with China, top sources of foreign investments in Africa include the United Kingdom and the United States; however, Chinese investments have increased, whereas UK and US investments have held steady or decreased. From 2005 to 2014, China invested only US$0.25 for each dollar invested by the United States in Africa. Over the next several years, from 2015 to 2021, China's investment increased to

FIGURE 9.5 Top 15 recipients of Chinese FDI in Africa, 2003–19

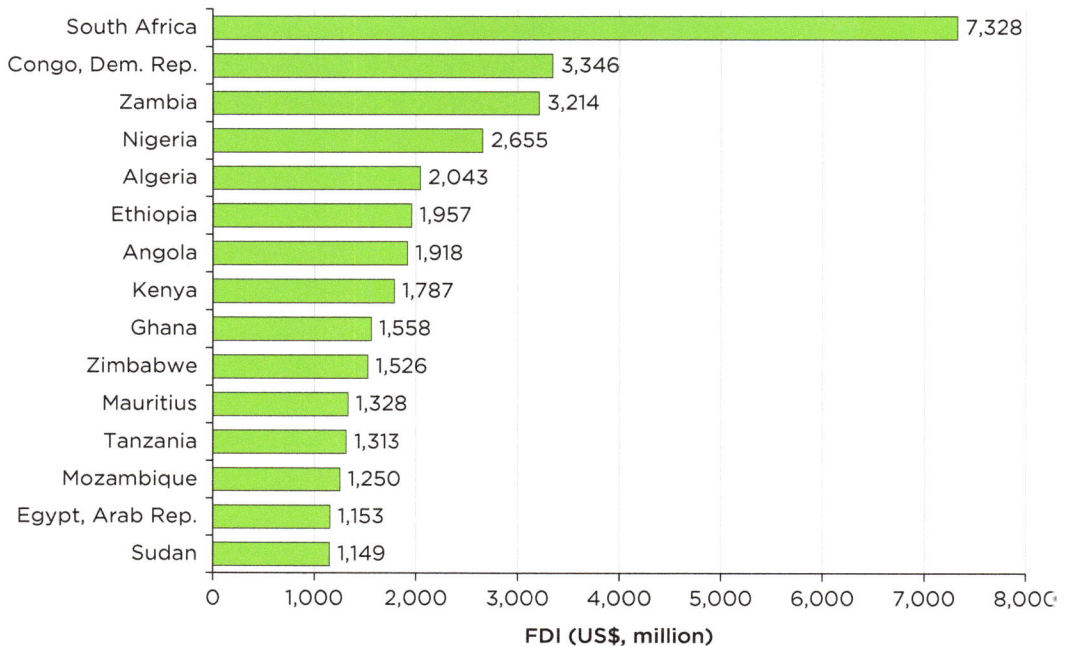

Country	FDI (US$, million)
South Africa	7,328
Congo, Dem. Rep.	3,346
Zambia	3,214
Nigeria	2,655
Algeria	2,043
Ethiopia	1,957
Angola	1,918
Kenya	1,787
Ghana	1,558
Zimbabwe	1,526
Mauritius	1,328
Tanzania	1,313
Mozambique	1,250
Egypt, Arab Rep.	1,153
Sudan	1,149

Source: World Bank, based on data from the Ministry of Commerce of China and the China Africa Research Initiative at the Johns Hopkins University School of Advanced International Studies. *Note:* FDI = foreign direct investment.

US$0.89 for each dollar invested by the United States in Africa. In 2021, China held about US$44 billion worth of FDI stock in Africa (an increase of 2,100 percent since 2005), mainly in four sectors (figure 9.6). In comparison, US FDI stocks increased only 96 percent, meaning that the United States had less than twice its amount of FDI stock on the continent in 2021 (US$45 billion) compared with 2005 (US$23 billion). Meanwhile, the United Kingdom's FDI position has remained slightly steady at US$55 billion in 2021, an increase of US$3 billion compared with the 2012 level of US$52 billion.

Digitalization and Africa's foreign trade

From 2005 to 2021, Africa and Asia made some progress in digitalizing their economies by creating and adopting new technologies in national and international business. The pace of digitalization in Africa is slow, however, compared with that in Asian countries. In the Southern Asia region,[6] India and Pakistan have made particularly notable progress, with more than half of their trade now in digitally deliverable services. This region can serve as an example and a source for Africa to upgrade its use of technologies and increase trade in digital services.

FIGURE 9.6 **China's FDI stock in Africa, by main sector, 2013–21**

FDI (US$, million)

Source: World Bank, based on 2023 data from the Ministry of Commerce of China and the China Africa Research Initiative at the Johns Hopkins University School of Advanced International Studies.
Note: FDI = foreign direct investment.

There have been some notable differences in the proportion of digitally deliverable services between Africa and Asia, and within Africa. For the period 2005–21, Eastern and Northern Africa had the lowest average proportion of digitally deliverable services at 17 percent and 19 percent, respectively, representing 266 percent less than Southern Asia's average of 64 percent for the same period. The Eastern and Northern Africa subregions also performed below the Sub-Saharan average of 25 percent from 2005 to 2021. Although the Western Africa subregion made significant progress in digitalization from 2016 to 2021, most African subregions still lag Asian superpowers such as Japan and Singapore (each had 57 percent in 2019).

Regional differences within Africa for digitally deliverable services in international trade have evolved since 2005. For instance, from 2005 to 2014, the Central Africa subregion consistently ranked highest in the proportion of digitally deliverable services, averaging 34.5 percent, but was overtaken by Western Africa, which improved from 26 percent in 2014 to 48 percent in 2021. Ghana had a notable 57-percentage-point increase, from 23 percent in 2014 to 80 percent in 2021, the highest among all Western African countries. In 2021, Guinea-Bissau was the second-best performer with 66 percent of international trade in digitally deliverable services, followed by Mali (40 percent) and Togo (39 percent). Benin, Sierra Leone, and The Gambia lagged at 9 percent, 7 percent, and 5 percent, respectively. In 2021, Southern Africa, with 57 percent, claimed the lead. On average, Central, Southern, and Western Africa performed above the Sub-Saharan Africa average from 2005 to 2021.

From a value perspective, however, Ghana still dominates in performance, which is not surprising given its booming service and entertainment industries (TV shows and movie production). Ghana had US$7.3 billion in digitally deliverable services in 2021. In Western Africa, Nigeria has the second-highest amount of digitally deliverable services in international trade, at more than US$1 billion in 2021. However, the percentage of digitally deliverable services in Nigeria's overall trade is still among the lowest in the region, despite the nation's position as a leading economy in Africa. Thus, the potential for higher exports through digitally deliverable services appears significant for these digitalizing African economies.

Export of digitally deliverable services

Ghana is the top performer in the export of digitally deliverable services with nearly twice the total amount of the combined exports of seven other Western African countries. Between 2010 and 2021, Ghana exported US$43.7 billion through digital services compared with a total of US$22.4 billion for Benin, Burkina Faso, Côte d'Ivoire, Mali, Nigeria, Senegal, and Togo combined. On an annual average between 2014 and 2021, Ghana exported 271 percent of what the other seven countries combined exported even though Ghana's gross domestic product (GDP) represented only 11 percent of the total GDP of those countries. In 2021, Ghana had a ratio of digitally deliverable trade services to GDP of 9 percent; by contrast, Nigeria and Côte d'Ivoire, the largest and second-largest economies in West Africa, respectively, each had a ratio of only 0.3 percent.

From 2010 to 2021, Ghana and the other seven countries each had a minimum total of US$1 billion in exports of digitally deliverable services, attesting to the potential of creative industries, including entertainment, to contribute to inclusive development, productivity, and economic growth in Africa. Making the most of this potential, however, presents a challenge. For example, despite increasing demand for African movies and music online in foreign countries, and the significant potential for internationalization (Ado and Diamouténé 2023), many African countries lack a digital trade strategy to take advantage of such interesting opportunities.

According to 2017 trade data from UNCTAD, five African countries (Guinea-Bissau, Malawi, Niger, Senegal, and Sierra Leone) and three Asian and non-Western countries (India, Israel, and Kuwait) were among the world's top 10 economies by share of information and communication technology (ICT) services in total services exports.[7] The African Union and the United Nations Economic Commission for Africa, furthermore, stressed the importance of creating an African information highway to develop ICT and cooperate with member states as well as with UNCTAD; the United Nations Educational, Scientific, and Cultural Organization (UNESCO); and the World Bank to facilitate a more digitalized society and economy (African Union 2020). The resulting Digital Transformation Strategy for Africa (2020–30) emphasizes the immense potential of the digital era to meet the SDGs and the goals of Agenda 2063.

Many projects initiated by Asian countries align with these development strategies and complement the long-term agendas of the continent. The tremendous momentum for African economies comes at a time when exports of services deliverable online (movies, music, insurance, business processes, or financial services) have grown annually by 7–8 percent over the past decade globally and amounted to more than US$2.7 trillion in 2017, five times greater than the total value of ICT services. In this dynamic, some African and Asian countries such as Ghana, India, and Singapore continue to capture a bigger trade share of digitally deliverable services. Developing economies in Asia accounted for the largest increase in the past 10 years, with a collective annual growth rate of 11 percent between 2005 and 2017. Meanwhile, in Western Africa, Sierra Leone ranked third worldwide in digitally deliverable services as a share of all services exports, with 75 percent of exports digitally deliverable. African Union member states have developed ICT policies, and mobile phones are becoming more available and affordable. Despite this encouraging dynamic, weak coordination and limited regulatory activity among the digital actors remain challenges for the continent.

Partnerships for education and entrepreneurship

Vocational education and skills-based training that enhance digital literacy can significantly improve the potential of African youth to engage more in digital opportunities (Ado 2023). Considering that young people ages 15–24 account for 20 percent of Africa's population, and that those under the age of 35 make up 75 percent of the population, Africa has an unparalleled incentive to encourage youth vocational training (UN DESA 2015). Several Asian scholarship programs for African youth and young professionals provide opportunities to develop digital literacy. Examples include the China-Africa Universities 20 + 20 Cooperation Plan, Japan's African Business Education Initiative for Youth (ABE Initiative), and Korea's Capacity Improvement and Advancement for Tomorrow and technical and vocational education and training programs.

African countries could learn from other regions' external partnerships. For instance, the ASEAN [Association of Southeast Asian Nations] International Mobility for Students program, launched in 2010 to promote student exchange and mobility among universities in member states, can serve as an inspiration for African countries. The program has trained more than 7,000 international students across 87 participating universities,[8] showing that partnerships among academic institutions and businesses in key sectors such as ICT have the potential to encourage entrepreneurship and facilitate innovation.

Female entrepreneurs contributed more than US$250 billion to African economies in 2016, representing 13 percent of the continent's GDP (Roland Berger 2018). Africa has the highest women's entrepreneurship ratio in the world, at 24 percent of African women, surpassing Latin America and the Caribbean (17 percent), North America (12 percent), Southeast Asia and Pacific (11 percent), the Middle East (9 percent), and

Europe and Central Asia (6 percent) (IFC 2023b). Thus, strengthening women's entrepreneurship in Africa through strong, valuable networks that support women entrepreneurs is critical for their success (Harvard University Center for African Studies 2020). Collaborative initiatives such as the African Women's Entrepreneurship Program, which offers funding and capacity building to African businesswomen, could boost female entrepreneurship on the continent.[9] Other encouraging partnership programs expected to have a significant impact on the continent include She Wins Africa, which aims to assist 400 promising women entrepreneurs in Africa through training, mentorship, and networking opportunities to start new businesses (IFC 2023a).

Partnerships for inclusive digitalization

The Better Than Cash Alliance, a United Nations–based global partnership, supports the transition from cash to digital payments.[10] Such a transition supports, among other things, inclusive growth by unlocking economic opportunity for the financially excluded and enabling a more efficient flow of resources in the economy. Kenya provides an example of how digital payments have created financial inclusivity across the East African subregion. Its mobile money platform Mobile Money Service (M-PESA) has revolutionized the digital payment landscape in Kenya and beyond. Thanks to such financial innovation, Kenya is currently one of the only countries to which individuals can send money from abroad with zero transfer fees. Continued efforts to search for innovative solutions will add momentum to Africa's development, especially when such financial innovations facilitate business transactions between Africa and the world.

According to the *African Economic Outlook 2018* (AfDB 2018), Africa will need investments of between US$4 billion and US$7 billion annually for the ICT sector to boost inclusive digitalization. Since 2015, China has increased its digital presence in Africa and continues to provide major funding to the ICT sector across the continent, with annual investments above US$1 billion. Zhongxing Telecommunications Equipment and Huawei, China's two largest telecommunication equipment manufacturers, have also become significant investors in ICT across Africa. With a commitment to inject US$60 billion into African economies between 2018 and 2021 to support infrastructure, including ICT, the government of China supports this increased presence.

These developments indicate the need for more collaboration—public-public, public-private, and private-private partnerships—to support the much-needed digital transformation of Africa. There are already cases of successful collaboration between African and foreign countries and organizations, particularly those from Asia and the West. Such collaborations include the Korea Telecom Corporation in Rwanda, which helped move more than 90 percent of the Rwandan population to fourth-generation (4G) long-term evolution services, and China's StarTimes in Nigeria, which supported the digital connection of 169 million people (83 percent of the country's population) since 2020, an increase of 8 percent from the previous year. Other countries could scale up such successful examples to build stronger digital economic capital across the continent.

Developing human capital: Africans studying abroad

Sub-Saharan Africa's Human Capital Index of 0.41[11]—half that of Central Asia's and lower than the world average of 0.57—highlights the need to improve education systems. The continent captures only 55 percent of its young human capital, compared with a global average of 65 percent (Doualeh 2021). Thus, African youth need to receive more quality education and training locally and in foreign countries. Africans who study in countries in Asia and North America are more likely to become entrepreneurs as they graduate and change their professional status in those countries. In recent years, entrepreneurship in the African diaspora has gained momentum, increasing the connection between Africa and the rest of the world, and making business ties more significant. Organizations such as the African Diaspora Network facilitate the strategic involvement of African expatriates in the development of Africa.[12]

The number of Africans going to Western countries to study has decreased, whereas the number of African students going to Asia and the Pacific has increased significantly, from 2,983 in 2000 to 11,851 in 2017, an increase of nearly 297 percent over 17 years.[13] The proportion of students going to Asian and other non-Western countries is still relatively small, but growing, especially in the case of African countries that have increased ties with emerging economies such as China, Saudi Arabia, and Türkiye. Although many of these countries have a higher total proportion of students bound for Asia and the Pacific than those bound for North America and Western Europe, for other African countries, Europe and North America remain the leading destinations. The three African countries with the highest cumulative proportion of Asia-bound students are Mauritius (31 percent), Somalia (19 percent), and Nigeria (16 percent)— refer to figure 9.7.

According to United Nations data collected by the World Bank in 2021, most African students heading to Western countries continue to choose countries in North America and Western Europe, with, for instance, 33,495 Nigerian students going to the United Kingdom and the United States, more than to the top-four Asian destinations for Nigerian students combined.[14] By contrast, 5,822 students from Egypt went to Türkiye, many more than the numbers going to the United Kingdom or the United States. Meanwhile, more Tanzanian students (1,223) went to India than to any Western destination. Students from the Democratic Republic of Congo landed in Canada and France (a total of 2,727 students), more than in any other destination.

FIGURE 9.7 **Student flows from Mauritius, Nigeria, and Somalia, by destination, 2000–17**

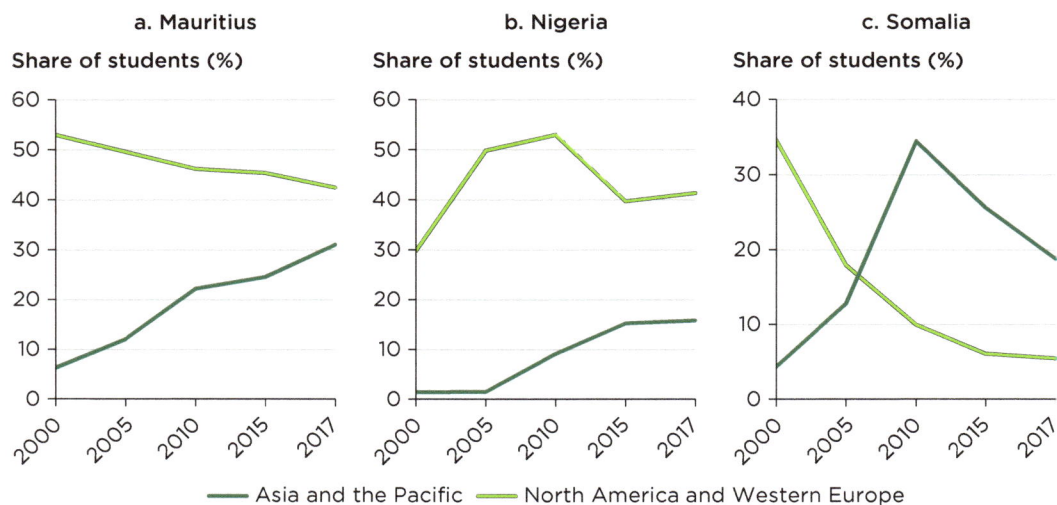

a. Mauritius

Share of students (%)

b. Nigeria

Share of students (%)

c. Somalia

Share of students (%)

— Asia and the Pacific — North America and Western Europe

Source: United Nations Educational, Scientific, and Cultural Organization, Institute for Statistics, "Other Policy Relevant Indicators—Education," https://databrowser.uis.unesco.org/browser /EDUCATION/UIS-EducationOPRI.
Note: Regional groupings following the original source.

Among Africa's most-populous countries, five (the Democratic Republic of Congo, Egypt, Ethiopia, Nigeria, and Tanzania) sent significant numbers of students to destinations in the West and in Asian and other non-Western countries. In 2017, the top-five countries receiving these students were Malaysia (7,202), Saudi Arabia (6,040), Türkiye (2,048), Qatar (1,772), and India (1,756). For 2019, refer to table 9.2. Data for China were not available.

Capacity-building initiatives

Entering the 21st century, Asian countries have developed capacity-building programs that invite scholars and government officials from Africa for opportunities to build partnerships, encourage cultural exchange, and promote knowledge transfer. The following paragraphs discuss examples from China, Japan, and Korea.

China. Africa's young population presents both an opportunity and a potential challenge for the continent. When well-managed, the healthy and well-educated youth population could drive Africa's inclusive development and accelerate innovation and entrepreneurship. In that sense, investments in social infrastructure such as health and education are crucial. Over the past two decades, China has developed significant international scholarship programs making it one of the most popular destinations for African students. The 2019–21 Forum on China-Africa Cooperation Beijing Action Plan included 50,000 government scholarships and 50,000 seminars and workshops for Africans.[15]

TABLE 9.2 Student flows from five populous African countries, by destination, 2019

Students' country of origin	Top Western destinations		Top non-Western destinations	
	Destination	Number of students	Destination	Number of students
Congo, Dem. Rep.	Canada	1,401	Russian Federation	259
	France	1,326	Türkiye	224
	United States	1,196	India	46
	Belgium	767	Japan	43
Egypt, Arab Rep.	Germany	6,049	Türkiye	5,822
	United States	3,657	Jordan	4,248
	United Kingdom	3,227	Saudi Arabia	3,369
	Ukraine	2,950	Russian Federation	2,252
Ethiopia	United States	2,271	India	901
	Germany	523	Türkiye	725
	Italy	414	Saudi Arabia	476
	Canada	309	Korea, Rep.	259
Nigeria	United Kingdom	21,241	Malaysia	3,564
	United States	12,254	Türkiye	3,174
	Canada	8,337	Australia	1,750
	Germany	4,350	India	1,334
Tanzania	United States	703	India	1,223
	United Kingdom	700	Türkiye	404
	Canada	504	Malaysia	379
	Germany	172	Saudi Arabia	239

Source: United Nations Educational, Scientific, and Cultural Organization, Global Flow of Tertiary-Level Students, 2021.

Japan. The country has been involved in education in Africa since before the 21st century. The first Tokyo International Conference on African Development (TICAD) was held in 1993 to strengthen Japan-Africa ties. In the 1990s, the Japan International Cooperation Agency began pursuing projects to expand access to basic education across Africa. More recent initiatives, such as the Japanese Grant Aid for Human Resource Development Scholarship, are also having a significant impact on the continent (Oh 2017). The Yokohama Action Plan, adopted at TICAD IV, identified four objectives for basic education: (1) improve access and the learning environment through school construction; (2) reform teacher training systems, train and retain more teachers; (3) improve school-based management with community participation; and (4) promote experience sharing among partners from Africa and Asia through culture- and gender-sensitive curricula.

Japan has also promoted public-private partnerships with Africa. The African Business Education Initiative for Youth (ABE Initiative) originally aimed to provide opportunities for 1,000 youths in Africa to study for a master's degree at Japanese universities and to gain practical experience with internships at Japanese companies. Participants stay in Japan for two years to complete a master's degree, followed by a six-month internship to gain practical skills. Since inauguration of the ABE Initiative in 2014, a total of 1,218 students have participated, exceeding the target of 1,000. In 2019, at TICAD VII, Japan launched the ABE Initiative 3.0, aiming to invite 3,000 African students by 2026. So far, the African students who benefited from the ABE Initiative have commented positively on their experiences. The training in Japan has opened new career opportunities for many participants and has enabled them to contribute to their home countries' development.

Korea. In collaboration with the World Bank, Korea supports the Partnership for Skills in Applied Sciences, Engineering, and Technology to develop science and technology capacity in Africa. The program offers regional scholarships and innovation funds, collaboration with Korean organizations, and support for improving governance and knowledge sharing. The Korea-Africa Foundation promotes partnership in politics, economy, and culture by enabling collaboration between the public and private sectors, strengthening exchange and cooperation with African countries to enhance understanding, and conducting trend analysis and research by country, region, and theme.

The Korea International Cooperation Agency (KOICA) launched Capacity Improvement & Advancement for Tomorrow, a global fellowship program that offers scholarships to government officials and policy makers from developing countries. The program offers a master's degree in subjects such as economics, trade, gender inclusivity, and urban development. Since its inauguration in 2012, the program has had more than 46,000 participants and has produced more than 3,400 master's graduates, many from Africa.[16] The KOICA scholarship program cooperates with leading Korean universities with programs such as the Ewha Womans University–KOICA Master's Program in International Studies. A sample survey of Africans trained abroad though these academic and professional partnerships between African and foreign governments indicates they have gained significant experience that contributes to local, national, and regional development in their areas of specialization.

In 2018, Korea set up triangular cooperation projects for vocational training between Korea and Cameroon, Côte d'Ivoire, Morocco, Senegal, and Tunisia. These African countries needed a specialized workforce in the manufacturing sector, especially related to the automotive field. Compared with programs initiated by China and Japan, Korean education projects in Africa are relatively new and smaller in scale, with room for improvement in African student outreach programs.

African entrepreneurship dynamism around the globe

In recent years, non-Western countries have hosted and produced an increasing number of African entrepreneurs. Africans have immigrated to China and countries in the Middle East (Saudi Arabia and the United Arab Emirates) to start new businesses and connect the African and Asian continents. Thanks to those entrepreneurs, trade has skyrocketed and more financial flows are taking place across the countries.

African entrepreneurs in China

During the period 2000–20, China attracted thousands of Africans for higher education and business opportunities. Of the many African graduates from Chinese universities, several of them chose to become entrepreneurs in China. The city of Guangzhou, nicknamed "Little Africa," hosts the highest number of African immigrants and entrepreneurs. An estimated 15,000 Africans, particularly from the Democratic Republic of Congo, Egypt, Mali, and Nigeria, live in the bustling city. More than 500,000 Africans travel annually to Guangzhou to buy Chinese products for export to Africa (Dotto 2019). Trade between Africa and Guangzhou increased from US$500 million per year in 1996 to US$3 billion per year in 2008, with exports from Guangzhou increasing nearly 10-fold from US$165 million in 1996 to US$2 billion in 2008 (Li, Ma, and Xue 2009).

As noted earlier, the number of African students in China has increased, mostly through Chinese scholarship programs. Thus, in addition to African students in China who transition into entrepreneurships, many Africans travel to China as new or established entrepreneurs, operating in a country that is culturally unique and in an institutional environment that is fundamentally different from their own. Members of the African diaspora living in China include small-scale entrepreneurs and professionals who work for multinational or international organizations. Guangzhou; Hong Kong SAR, China; and Yiwu are at the center of the African entrepreneurial community in China. Guangdong Province has a significant pool of dynamic African entrepreneurs who are connecting business opportunities between Africa and Asia (Ado, Chrysostome, and Su 2016). Despite progress in African entrepreneurship in China, the entrepreneurial ecosystem needs to be further developed to address various challenges faced by Africans in China (figure 9.8).

According to the government of China and UNESCO, China now hosts more than 100,000 people from the African diaspora, and the numbers keep climbing. Africans in

FIGURE 9.8 Expert ratings of entrepreneurial framework conditions, China, 2020

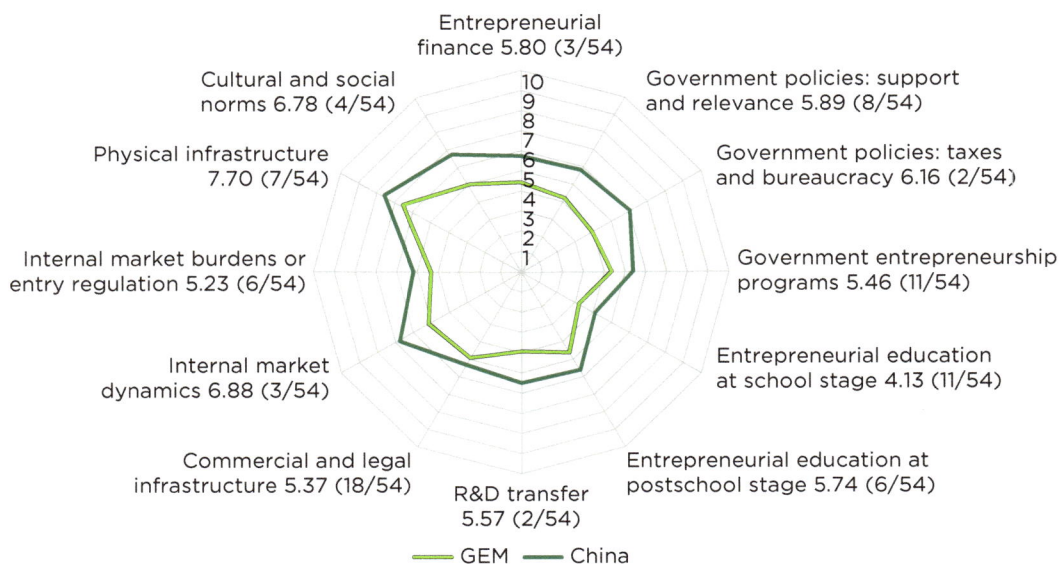

Source: Bosma et al. 2020.
Note: At least 36 national experts were rigorously selected from each of the 54 surveyed countries. Then the total average scores from all experts are used to form the basis of comparison for individual national conditions. Scale: 0 = very inadequate; 10 = very adequate. Rank out of 54 countries. GEM = Global Entrepreneurship Monitor; R&D = research and development.

China engage mostly in four types of business activities either independently or with local Chinese partners: sourcing of Chinese products for African buyers, warehousing of export products before shipment, consulting and translation and interpretation services between African and Chinese parties, and shipping brokerage for containers heading to African ports. More African entrepreneurs are needed to help export African products to China. This pull of China-based Africans, many of whom are seasoned immigrant entrepreneurs, can serve as a catalyst to increase economic activity and trade between Asia and Africa.

Many Africans who became successful entrepreneurs in China have returned to Africa to develop new ventures. According to a study by Marfaing and Thiel (2014), by far the most successful among African entrepreneurs in China are those who have established joint ventures in China to produce the goods that African buyers need. This is the case of some joint ventures in Guangzhou, where African partners raised the financial capital and Chinese partners provided the production sites and machinery. Some successful joint ventures in China even found investment opportunities to expand and diversify their businesses in Africa, including, for example, construction of a hotel and residential complex by a Perennial and Shangri-La joint venture that pledged more than US$250 million investment in Accra,

Ghana (Perennial 2015). An informal partnership between Chinese and Ghanaian entrepreneurs in the textile industry evolved into multiple additional businesses including new retail shops in Guangzhou and Yiwu, with nearly 250 jobs created by this partnership alone (Marfaing and Thiel 2014). The Chinese partner often takes care of local bureaucracy and cultural risks, whereas the African partner focuses on growing their foreign markets and investment diversification across Africa. Many African entrepreneurs in China plan to transfer their successful business models from China to Africa so that over time more manufacturing can take place in the African countries where the products are needed.

African entrepreneurs in the Middle East

Africans have increasingly migrated to the Middle East, attracted by opportunities for entrepreneurship. A study of several African countries finds that young people engaged in some form of entrepreneurial activity in record numbers in recent years, particularly in Hong Kong SAR, China; Saudi Arabia; and the United Arab Emirates (Bosma et al. 2020). The challenges young African entrepreneurs face in relation to Gulf Cooperation Council countries include unstable currencies, reluctant investors, difficulty in identifying the right joint venture partners, and significant data gaps between the two regions (Economist Intelligence Unit 2017); however, these challenges do not stop entrepreneurs from developing strategic plans to expand back into African countries. Although many Africans see the Middle East region as a major source of capital for start-ups, investors and businesses in the region are also sharing knowledge on operational and legal strategies with Africans, and the Gulf region is increasingly importing African products and services, particularly in the retail and food sectors.

According to Bosma et al. (2020), India, Korea, Madagascar, Qatar, Saudi Arabia, and the United Arab Emirates are among the countries with the highest early-stage entrepreneurial activity across Africa, Asia, and the Middle East (figure 9.9). Twenty percent of Madagascar's adult population owns individually established businesses, making it one of the most entrepreneurial ecosystems along with megacities such as Dubai; Guangzhou; Hong Kong SAR, China; and Mumbai. More interesting, in Madagascar, women's entrepreneurship is higher than men's (Bosma et al. 2020). Morocco and South Africa also have high rates of early-stage entrepreneurial activity.

When it comes to the age of entrepreneurs in the most entrepreneurial countries in Africa and Asia, the youngest entrepreneurs are still in Madagascar and the United Arab Emirates, with 18- to 24-year-olds representing more than 20 percent of entrepreneurs in each country. Youth in Africa and the Middle East are driving entrepreneurial initiatives in those top-performing countries.

FIGURE 9.9 Expert ratings of the entrepreneurial framework conditions, selected countries, 2020

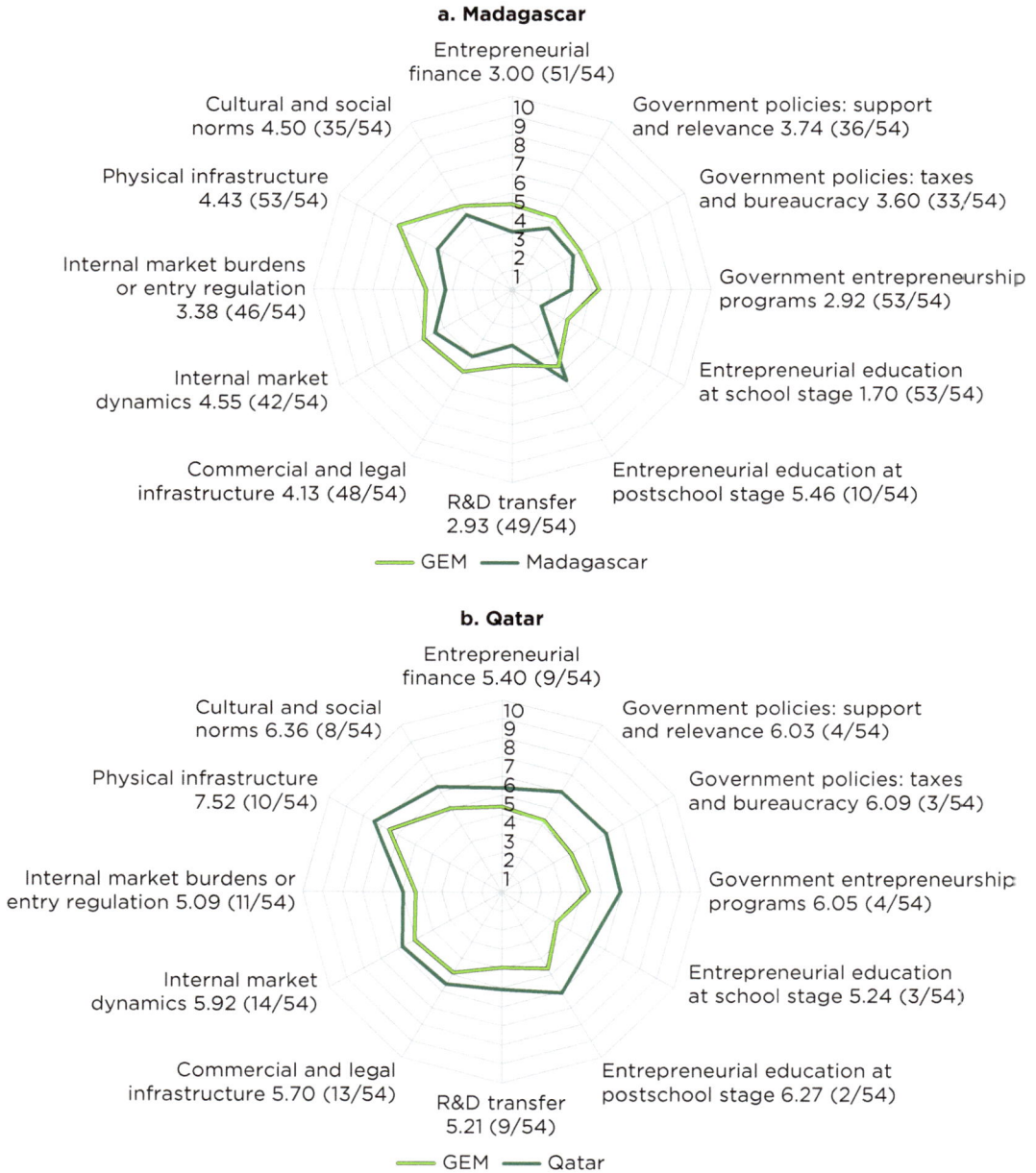

a. Madagascar

Entrepreneurial finance 3.00 (51/54)
Government policies: support and relevance 3.74 (36/54)
Cultural and social norms 4.50 (35/54)
Government policies: taxes and bureaucracy 3.60 (33/54)
Physical infrastructure 4.43 (53/54)
Government entrepreneurship programs 2.92 (53/54)
Internal market burdens or entry regulation 3.38 (46/54)
Entrepreneurial education at school stage 1.70 (53/54)
Internal market dynamics 4.55 (42/54)
Entrepreneurial education at postschool stage 5.46 (10/54)
Commercial and legal infrastructure 4.13 (48/54)
R&D transfer 2.93 (49/54)

GEM — Madagascar

b. Qatar

Entrepreneurial finance 5.40 (9/54)
Government policies: support and relevance 6.03 (4/54)
Cultural and social norms 6.36 (8/54)
Government policies: taxes and bureaucracy 6.09 (3/54)
Physical infrastructure 7.52 (10/54)
Government entrepreneurship programs 6.05 (4/54)
Internal market burdens or entry regulation 5.09 (11/54)
Entrepreneurial education at school stage 5.24 (3/54)
Internal market dynamics 5.92 (14/54)
Entrepreneurial education at postschool stage 6.27 (2/54)
Commercial and legal infrastructure 5.70 (13/54)
R&D transfer 5.21 (9/54)

GEM — Qatar

(continued)

FIGURE 9.9 Expert ratings of the entrepreneurial framework conditions, selected countries, 2020 (*continued*)

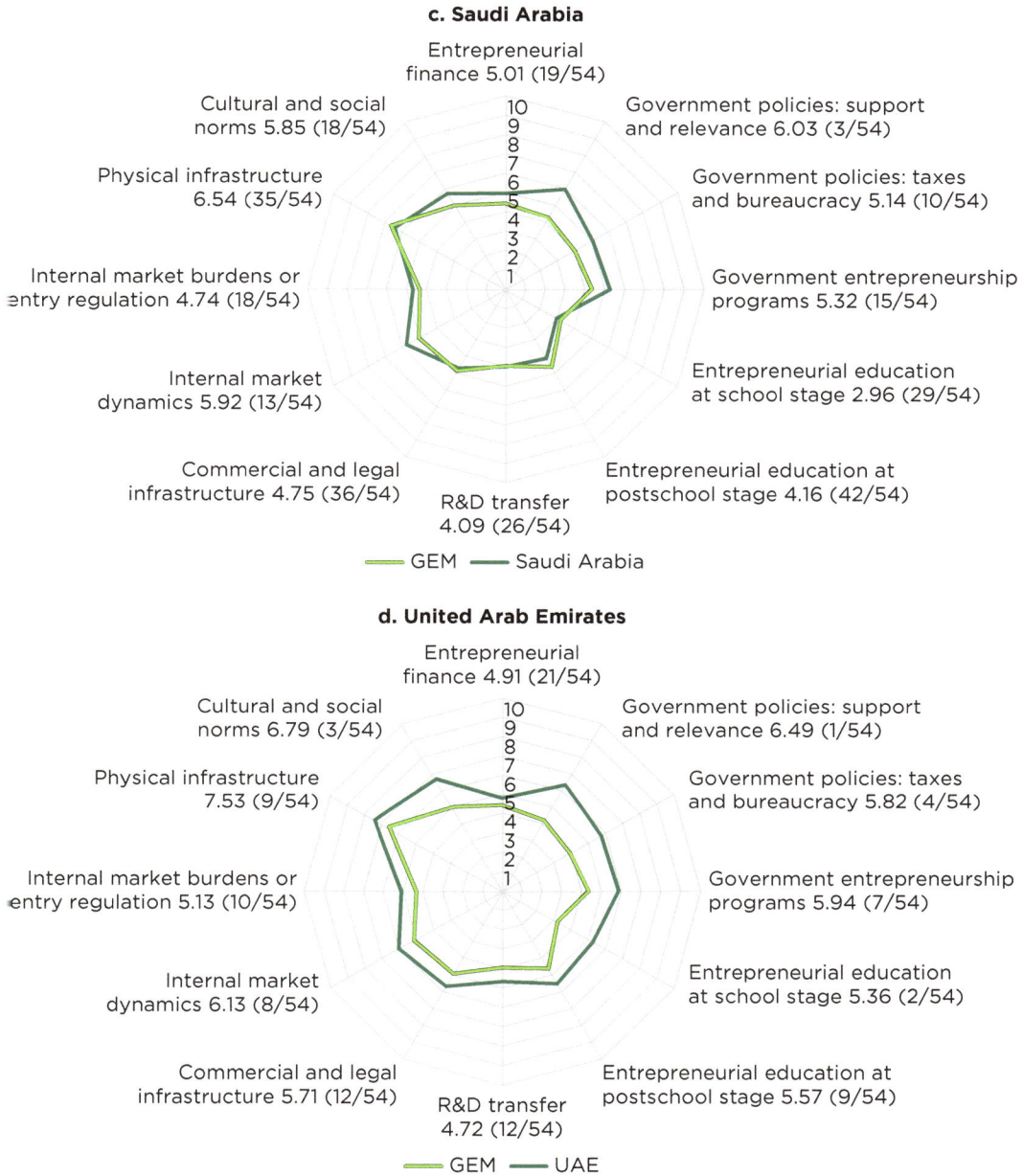

c. Saudi Arabia

Entrepreneurial finance 5.01 (19/54)
Government policies: support and relevance 6.03 (3/54)
Cultural and social norms 5.85 (18/54)
Government policies: taxes and bureaucracy 5.14 (10/54)
Physical infrastructure 6.54 (35/54)
Government entrepreneurship programs 5.32 (15/54)
Internal market burdens or entry regulation 4.74 (18/54)
Entrepreneurial education at school stage 2.96 (29/54)
Internal market dynamics 5.92 (13/54)
Entrepreneurial education at postschool stage 4.16 (42/54)
Commercial and legal infrastructure 4.75 (36/54)
R&D transfer 4.09 (26/54)

— GEM — Saudi Arabia

d. United Arab Emirates

Entrepreneurial finance 4.91 (21/54)
Government policies: support and relevance 6.49 (1/54)
Cultural and social norms 6.79 (3/54)
Government policies: taxes and bureaucracy 5.82 (4/54)
Physical infrastructure 7.53 (9/54)
Government entrepreneurship programs 5.94 (7/54)
Internal market burdens or entry regulation 5.13 (10/54)
Entrepreneurial education at school stage 5.36 (2/54)
Internal market dynamics 6.13 (8/54)
Entrepreneurial education at postschool stage 5.57 (9/54)
Commercial and legal infrastructure 5.71 (12/54)
R&D transfer 4.72 (12/54)

— GEM — UAE

Source: Bosma et al. 2020.
Note: At least 36 national experts were rigorously selected from each of the 54 surveyed countries. Then the total average scores from all experts are used to form the basis of comparison for individual national conditions. Scale: 0 = very inadequate; 10 = very adequate. Rank out of 54 countries. GEM = Global Entrepreneurship Monitor; R&D = research and development.

International development assistance and capacity-building cooperation

Western donors still represent the most significant source of development assistance for Africa, but development assistance from non-Western countries has increased since the beginning of the 21st century (figure 9.10), creating new partners. Africa must avoid simply transferring its dependence on Western aid to aid from non-Western countries, however. Ranging from the education sector to industrial capacity building in other economic sectors, countries such as China, Japan, Korea, and Saudi Arabia play an important role in supporting Africa's development, industrialization, and transition to a green economy.

FIGURE 9.10 Distribution of net ODA to Africa, selected source countries, 2000–22

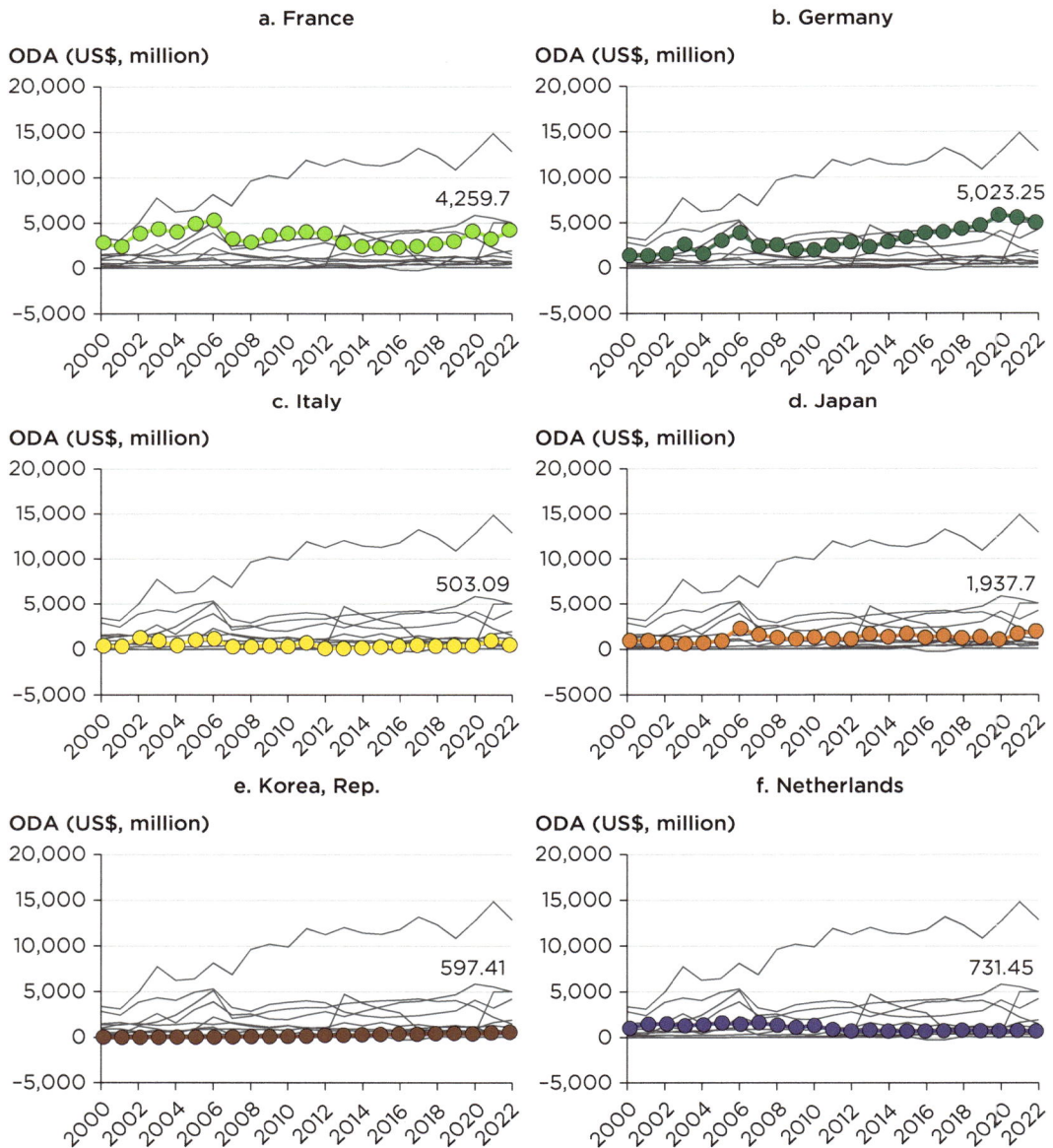

a. France

b. Germany

c. Italy

d. Japan

e. Korea, Rep.

f. Netherlands

(continued)

FIGURE 9.10 **Distribution of net ODA to Africa, selected source countries, 2000–22 (*continued*)**

g. Saudi Arabia

ODA (US$, million)

5,044.47

h. Sweden

ODA (US$, million)

1,119.63

i. Türkiye

ODA (US$, million)

59.72

j. United Arab Emirates

ODA (US$, million)

438.04

k. United Kingdom

ODA (US$, million)

1,508.88

l. United States

ODA (US$, million)

12,882.61

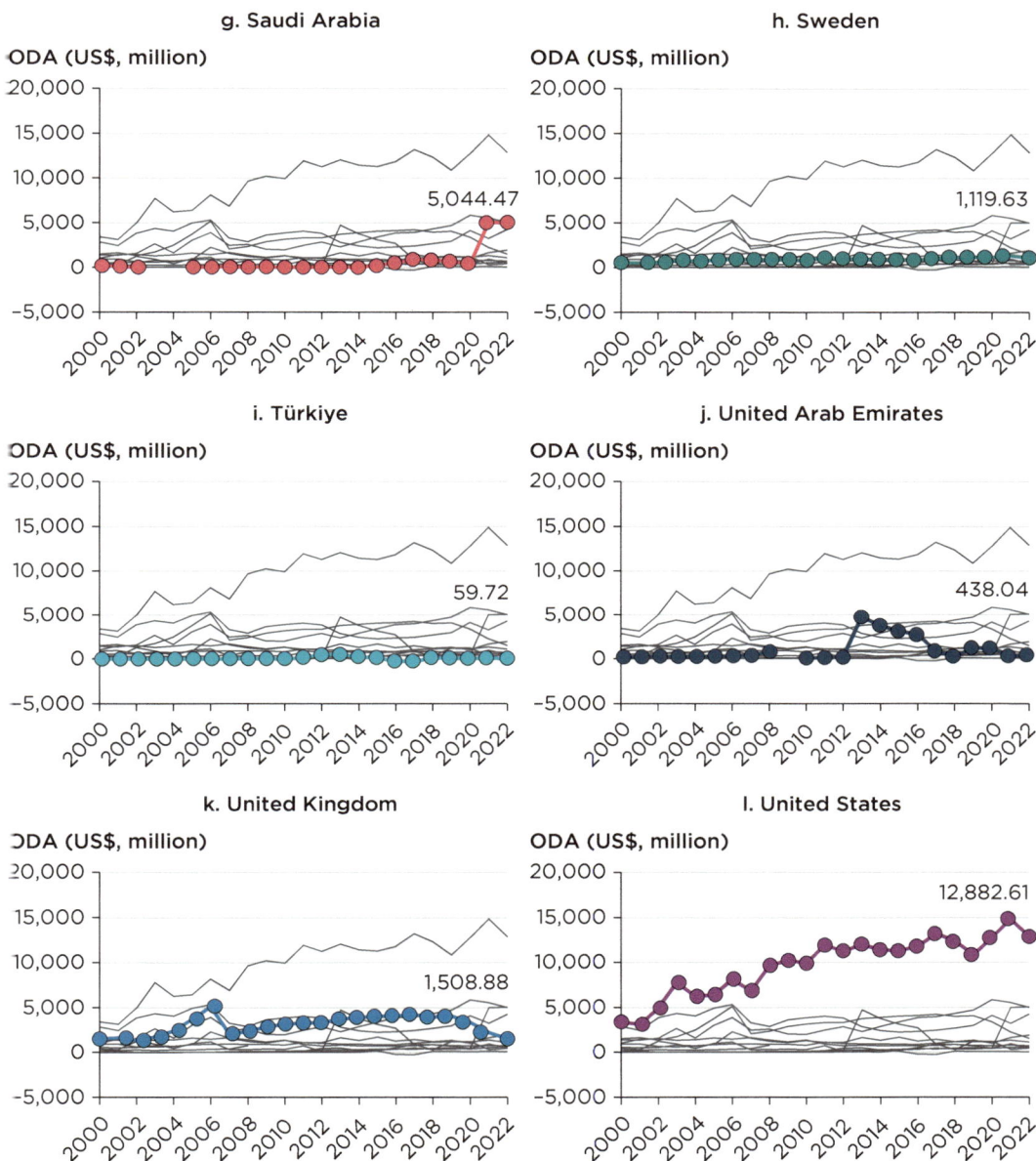

Source: Organisation for Economic Co-operation and Development Data Explorer, https://data
-explorer.oecd.org/ (accessed October 9, 2024).
Note: ODA = official development assistance.

Asia's aid differs from traditional Western aid in that it has high proportions of loans and a strong focus on economic infrastructure. Western aid has higher proportions of grants and, increasingly, budget support. European donors have shifted from project aid to general budget support in recent years, whereas Asian donors still spend most of their ODA on project-type interventions, especially in economic infrastructure projects. The United States, like the United Kingdom, has provided almost 100 percent of development aid as grants to Africa since 2002 (table 9.3). Other countries have divided their bilateral partnerships with African countries into a mix of grants and loans: France (49 percent loans), Japan (33 percent loans), and Korea (35 percent loans) as of 2019.

Regarding ODA to Africa's tertiary education sector, France and Germany are still the first and second leading sources of funding, with 31 percent and 18 percent, respectively. Saudi Arabia has emerged as a significant player since 2018, with an average share of 5 percent (Galán-Muros, Chacón, and Escribens 2022). It recently announced US$25 billion worth of new investments in Africa along with US$5 billion for development finance to Africa by 2030 and US$1 billion toward development initiatives across the continent over the next decade (Argaam 2023).

Most loans from China to Africa went to economic infrastructure—particularly for ICT, energy, water, and transportation—whereas grants went more toward social

TABLE 9.3 Evolution of loan and grant proportions of ODA to Africa, by donor, 2002–19

Donor country	ODA type	Proportion of ODA (%)				
		2002	2007	2012	2017	2019
France	Grants	88	92	76	52	49
	Loans	12	8	24	47	49
Germany	Grants	90	94	95	90	89
	Loans	10	5	4	8	10
Japan	Grants	89	94	100	71	67
	Loans	11	6	0	29	33
Korea, Rep.	Grants	100	60	45	55	65
	Loans	0	40	55	45	35
United Kingdom	Grants	100	100	100	100	100
	Loans	0	0	0	0	0
United States	Grants	97	100	100	100	100
	Loans	3	0	0	0	0

Source: Organisation for Economic Co-operation and Development, "Distribution of net ODA," https://www.oecd.org/en/data/indicators/distribution-of-net-oda.html#indicator-chart.
Note: ODA = official development assistance.

infrastructure. From 2000 to 2019, China committed more than US$153 billion to Africa through a total of 1,141 loan agreements. Of that amount, nearly 30 percent went to transportation infrastructure, 24 percent to power, and 12 percent to mining.[17] Loans from China to Africa were more significant than grants in funding infrastructure, representing on average 86 percent of total Chinese development assistance to African economic infrastructure between 2000 and 2014. By contrast, grants represented only 2.2 percent during that same period. For social infrastructure, loans accounted for 63.4 percent of assistance and grants for 33.5 percent.

After a look back at Africa's engagements with the world over the past two decades, the next section analyzes the current situation to identify opportunities and challenges in Africa's bilateral and multilateral cooperation with other continents, and particularly with Asia as the emerging top partner with Africa in many regards. The analysis will focus on strategic areas relevant to African development in this 21st century.

Analysis

The megatrends of the past 20 years present both opportunities and challenges for partnerships between Africa and the rest of the world. After outlining those opportunities and challenges, this analysis discusses avenues to achieve Africa's inclusive growth objectives and to fill its needs for infrastructure and expertise for sustainable industrialization across key sectors of the economy. It also provides examples of successful partnerships in those sectors, along with any challenges revealed by their experiences.

Opportunities

Increasing Africa's sustainable energy supply. The number of Africans without access to electricity surpassed 580 million in 2019. Nearly 50 percent of households have no access to electricity in about 67 percent of Africa. In 2000, Central, Eastern, and Southern Africa (excluding South Africa) had the lowest electrification rates on the continent at 15 percent, 10 percent, and 14 percent, respectively. Twenty years later and despite improvements, Central, Eastern, and Southern Africa still have the highest need of power in Africa, with current coverage at 24 percent, 47 percent, and 39 percent, respectively. Addressing these gaps and the rising demand for power in most African countries presents a major opportunity for Africa to foster global partnerships to fix this persistent economic need on the continent. Maximizing the impact of these efforts will require cross-border partnerships among Africa's subregional blocs.

Addressing the massive need for urban infrastructure. Rising urbanization across major cities in Africa and the necessity for regional and continental integration make urban infrastructure essential. Megacities in Western and Asian countries could be relevant partners for learning, defining, and coordinating urban infrastructure projects. As of 2019, Chinese funding went mostly to infrastructure projects, particularly in the transportation, shipping, and ports sectors (52.8 percent); energy and power (17.6 percent); real estate (14.3 percent, including industrial, commercial, and residential real estate); and mining (7.7 percent). Many African countries, however, need increased diversification of investments across other sectors such as manufacturing. For instance, Benin produced 714,714 tons of cotton in 2020 but transformed only 5 percent into more value-adding manufactured goods.

Increasing digitalization and inclusive industrialization. Among the projected 603 million new mobile subscribers by 2025 worldwide, 213 million will be from Africa and the Middle East. External partnerships could support Africa to develop innovative ecosystems and affordable technologies. Also, for Africa to modernize, digitalize, industrialize, and grow, it will need to benefit from technology and knowledge transfer because it still lacks many key technological capabilities. It can enable such transfer through new joint venture opportunities by collaborating with international partners willing to cooperate and share technology and knowledge. This collaboration will also support the development of the manufacturing sector across Africa and create jobs and capabilities for inclusive industrialization. Africa has such significant manufacturing potential that the massive human capital in Africa could unlock continental development.

Taking advantage of diasporic entrepreneurship. The number of African entrepreneurs outside of Africa represents an opportunity to create more business ties and trade between Africa and the rest of the world. These entrepreneurs are well-equipped to attract investors, contribute to skills transfer, bridge trade networks across continents, and achieve national development objectives. Some of the major development objectives in Africa, however, are achievable only through basket funding (global multistakeholder partnerships), especially in sectors such as health care and education.

Realizing the massive potential for agribusiness. Because African countries import significant amounts of manufactured food, African agribusiness is still lagging. Promoting more agribusinesses could boost local manufacturing industries, with those industries learning from external partners in terms of both manufacturing and the promotion of special economic zones. Rwanda exported nearly US$7 million worth of textiles and clothing in 2016, more than three times what the country exported in 2001. Meanwhile, leading cotton producers such as Benin should become textile leaders as well to capture more value.

Challenges

Attracting needed foreign investments that align with inclusive development objectives and priorities. Africa needs billions of investments in infrastructure each year to meet the current needs of the continent and provide opportunities for growth. It is important for Africa to develop a prioritization strategy regarding investments from the West, Asia, and other regions, and to improve its institutional environment to ease business. To attract the most transformative external investments to support integration and industrialization, Africa also needs to carefully position itself in China's Belt and Road Initiative (BRI), a global development strategy launched by the Chinese government in 2013 to enhance regional connectivity and economic cooperation.

Improving debt data and transparency. Debt sustainability has become an important issue in Africa, especially in the post-COVID-19 era; however, data on debt for many African countries are not fully and publicly disclosed. This lack of data about Africa and the lack of transparency on loans and investments from some external funders creates a serious challenge to good governance and accountability in Africa. Thus, boosting trade, investment, and inclusive development will require more transparency and strong governance in many African countries. Between 2010 and 2019, among all the economic governance indicators in Africa, only the infrastructure index made significant progress, moving from 30.6 percent to 43.4 percent.

Addressing competition between Asian and Western countries. This competition presents an emerging challenge for African countries, which are pushed to choose one partner or the other. Africa should face this challenge with confidence and negotiate with all partners, traditional and nontraditional, for its strategic development.

For Africa to maximize its potential for economic and human capital development, it must consider these critical opportunities and challenges. The recommendations for more effective international joint ventures, better special economic zones, high-quality investments, inclusive policies, and mobilizing African diasporas are particularly significant factors in moving Africa forward into the 21st century.

Sustainable energy development and the potential impact of foreign partners

According to projections, Africa is at the crossroads of energy opportunities and challenges (Africa Energy Chamber 2021). Africa's need for electricity will quadruple by 2040 (Lakmeerahan et al. 2020). With that higher demand, Africa has an excellent opportunity to increase the availability, sustainability, and efficiency of power sources, especially with renewable energy. Most projections about Africa's population show that it will keep growing fast in the 21st century and that 50 percent of the world's population growth by 2040 will comprise new Africans, thus setting Africa on course to be more populous than China or India. Meanwhile, population growth and heavy urbanization in Africa—with 500 million Africans becoming urbanized by 2040—is much higher than the growth seen in China in the two decades (1980s and 1990s) of its economic and energy boom. As China navigates its urbanization through efficient, inclusive, and sustainable strategies, following six recommendations for policy reforms highlighted in a comprehensive report (World Bank and DRC 2014), Africa could use similar strategies.

Africa's economic and energy future will depend on addressing the major gap between urbanization trends, population growth, and energy demand. Despite a doubling of the yearly increase of access to electricity from 9 million people between 2000 and 2013 to 20 million people between 2014 and 2019 in Africa, access remains a major challenge: in 2019, 580 million people still lacked access. Comparatively, in developing Asia, about 1.2 billion people gained access to electricity in the same period, improving from 67 percent electricity access in the region in 2000 to 96 percent in 2019. Despite noticeable progress, particularly in Ethiopia, Ghana, Kenya, Rwanda, and Senegal, most of the progress over the past decade in Africa occurred through grid connections plagued by unreliable power supply (Ofori Adofo 2020). In addition to challenges with reliability, most countries generally have low electricity consumption because of high electricity prices. In 2014, for example, electric power consumption in Sub-Saharan Africa was 487 kilowatt-hours per capita compared with 707 kilowatt-hours per capita in South Asia and 3,048 kilowatt-hours per capita in the East Asia and Pacific region (Blimpo and Cosgrove-Davies 2019).[18]

Although most African countries have improved access to electricity for their citizens, supply still falls short except in rare cases such as South Africa, where almost all people have access to electricity. South Africa represents opportunities to trade electricity with other lagging countries on the continent. In addition, the continent's natural comparative advantage in solar energy sources offer abundant opportunities to scale up renewable power sources and help African economies gain access to more reliable, affordable, and sustainable energy. For instance, off-grid systems are increasing through new solar home systems (IEA 2019). Asian and Western countries have the potential to play a key role in closing Africa's energy gap through investments, technology and knowledge transfer, and capacity building (Ado, Su, and Wanjiru 2017). To boost electricity production across the continent, African countries could leverage expertise from Asian giants (China and India) and the United States, which have primarily led solar photovoltaic innovation (UNCTAD 2021).

Several Asian and non-Western countries present promising opportunities for partnerships in sustainable energy development. For instance, China's government has financed several projects in renewable energy production including hydropower projects, wind farm projects, and solar photovoltaic projects. Chinese enterprises serve as both developers of power plants and suppliers of technological components, and have completed and continue to build projects designed to upgrade about 20,000 megawatts (MW) of power generation capacity, and more than 30,000 kilometers of transmission and transformation lines in Africa. Notable completed projects that have played a role in closing the energy gap include the Adama Wind Farm project in Ethiopia and the Bui Hydropower project in Ghana. In Ethiopia, China is heavily involved in constructing power plants and supplying electrical accessories to support the government's plan to increase power generation capacity from 2,178 MW to 10,000 MW (Oqubay 2019).

The Lekki Free Zone Development Company is a joint venture formed by the Lagos State Government, Lekki Worldwide Investments Limited, and a consortium of Chinese companies represented under the China-Africa Lekki Investment Limited as the majority shareholder. It was created to produce more made-in-Nigeria products and to move manufacturing activities up the value chain. Through the attraction of significant foreign investments, many of them from Asia, the Lekki Free Trade Zone (LFTZ) provides foreign companies a place to move their activities to increase performance, contribute to GDP growth, and develop local industrial operations while enjoying preferential tax and tariff treatment from the federal and local governments through the zone's special status. The LFTZ now has its own independent power production facility, has attracted multiple foreign companies (currently hosting 132 enterprises), and has induced the development or upgrade of infrastructure including roads, buildings, and new major real estate as well as urban development around the entire city of Lagos. The LFTZ encompasses an industrial district; a commercial logistical, trading, and warehousing district; and a residential district. A major challenge to this model is that Africans lack experience developing free trade zones.

Japan's Marubeni Corporation is a potential partner for Africa's international trade. The company is involved in financing, developing, and exporting energy and power, agribusiness products, infrastructure projects, and real estate opportunities. The company already has activities in South Africa, including through a development portfolio of power supply of more than 5,000 MW as well as investments in the Africa Innovation & Healthcare Fund (Marubeni Corporation 2022). The challenge here is to consider regional power needs to make investments and projects more efficient through economies of scale and bigger regional market sizes.

Other non-Western countries such as Türkiye have begun to play an increasing role in addressing Africa's energy dilemma, prompting new business models from Turkish companies. Although Türkiye already has an African presence, especially in the construction and infrastructure investment sectors, it has increasingly extended its presence into manufacturing as well. The country and its companies continue bidding to supply Africa with reliable energy. The Turkish firm Karpowership, operating in several African countries, helps address power shortages with pay-as-you-go options for energy needs. Karpowership generates and feeds power from its floating plant across coastal locations into national grids in many African countries such as The Gambia, Ghana, Senegal, and Sudan; nations such as Guinea-Bissau are already meeting nearly 100 percent of their energy through this Turkish company. The project aims to meet Africa's energy needs quickly and consistently, ranging from 36 MW to 470 MW capacity, with an innovative approach to power production and delivery across the African continent. A major challenge will be that Africa's landlocked countries may need to rely on coastal countries to share grids and energy across the continent.

Transportation infrastructure, urbanization, integration, and foreign partnerships

Investments in Africa have shifted over the past few years from extractives to infrastructure.[19] A significant amount of recent foreign investment in Africa, especially from Asia, has occurred in transportation, roads, railways, airports and ports, energy and power, and telecommunications infrastructure. Connecting African countries with railways, ports, and roads can improve connectivity, reduce shipping costs, and increase intra-African trade. Improving Africa's infrastructure calls for global investment partnerships to support these opportunities, especially within the context of massive projects such as China's BRI, and through the application of new international logistical concepts such as the physical internet (Ado et al. 2014).

China, for instance, was involved in more than 200 infrastructure projects as of 2019. Chinese companies have finalized and are constructing projects aimed at increasing and improving about 30,000 kilometers of highways, 2,000 kilometers of railways, and 85 million tons per year of port throughput capacity (Edinger and Labuschagne 2019). Thanks in part to international funding, African countries are promoting regional integration through transportation networks such as the Addis Ababa–Djibouti and the Lobito–Dar es Salaam railways. Moreover, in 2015, China signed a memorandum of understanding with the African Union to support construction of a new generation of transportation links between capital cities across the continent (Lopes 2018).

Africa currently has the fastest urbanization rate in the world, with cities such as Abidjan, Cairo, Lagos, and Nairobi expected to experience significant population increases over the next decades. This population growth trend in African megacities brings both opportunities and challenges in relation to housing, electricity, jobs, inclusiveness, traffic, and transit systems. Modern transit infrastructure developments are important for Africa because infrastructure deficit is one of the continent's major bottlenecks to development, even though the World Bank observes that Africa is now 40 percent urban with a GDP per capita of US$1,100, nearly three times less than Asia's at the same historic level of urbanization (Lall, Henderson, and Venables 2017). Africa must address these considerations collectively in order to contain its urbanization boom while industrializing.

Asian and other non-Western countries are playing an increasingly major role in developing urban transportation and transit systems. For instance, China claims more than 40 percent of Africa's infrastructure contracts, whereas other partners such as Europe and the United States claim only 34 percent and 7 percent, respectively. China's transportation infrastructure projects include the following:

• In Ethiopia, Chinese companies have been involved in roughly 60 percent of the country's road construction and are financing more than 2,000 kilometers of national rail and about 30 kilometers of Addis Ababa railway construction. Ethiopia obtained a commercial loan from China that included US$2.5 billion for the Ethiopia–Djibouti railway and US$500 million for light city railways in Addis Ababa (Cheru and Oqubay 2019).

- In Kenya, China has supported the 483-kilometer Mombasa-Nairobi Standard Gauge Railway, at a cost of US$3.8 billion, and the Lamu Port extension, which is expected to increase yearly throughput to 23.9 million tons in the upcoming decade.

- Tanzania's US$11 billion Port of Bagamoyo represents a collaboration between China, Oman, and Tanzania (Edinger and Labuschagne 2019; Sun 2017).

In addition to its investments in transportation infrastructure, China has increased its FDI in tech infrastructure over the past two decades with the Digital Silk Road, part of the BRI. Promising mobile industry growth in Sub-Saharan Africa is expected to generate 142 million new subscribers by 2025, the second-largest increase next to 247 million in Asia Pacific. Because of the low penetration rate of mobile phone subscribers (45 percent as of 2018), the Sub-Saharan African market is expected to have the most room for growth (GSMA 2020). Huawei, which has had a presence in markets such as South Africa since 1998, is expanding its presence in Africa. It now provides major ICT infrastructure in several African countries and has signed a memorandum of understanding with the UNESCO Regional Office for Eastern Africa to make digital skills and artificial intelligence capabilities accessible to everyone in Africa. As of 2016, Huawei is investing heavily in training young Africans, with seven training centers established in Angola, the Democratic Republic of Congo, Egypt, Kenya, Morocco, Nigeria, and South Africa, and training programs throughout the continent. In 2020, the company committed to a five-year, US$50 million investment to train 2 million ICT professionals globally through its Huawei ICT Academy Development Incentive Fund. As Africa becomes very dependent on Chinese ICT, the West has expressed concerns over Huawei's cybersecurity.

Korea's Intelligent Transport System (ITS) program merges ICT with major transportation infrastructure to comprehensively manage traffic, guaranteeing punctuality of bus arrival and providing a digitalized Hi-pass for collection of road tolls. The ITS program—shared with Kenya, to manage transit in Nairobi, and with Mozambique—has revealed the need for radical infrastructure upgrading of African roads that were initially built for small traffic. Five Kenyan government officials attended capacity-building workshops in Seoul to learn about Korea's ITS technology, institutions, and legislation that complement ITS and the problems faced by Korea's traffic management system. Experience-sharing initiatives by Korea have already resulted in completed projects in Asia through Korea's knowledge-sharing programs. Countries that have benefited from these programs include Cambodia, Mongolia, Myanmar, the Philippines, and Viet Nam.

Digitalization and internet connectivity upgrade and international cooperation

On the digital front, telecommunications companies that produce devices (for example, Huawei and Zhongxing Telecommunications Equipment in China, and

Samsung in Korea) and network operators (for example, Airtel in India and Etisalat in the United Arab Emirates) have made mobile devices that are available and affordable to African markets. Between 2005 and 2020, Chinese technology investments and contracts in Sub-Saharan Africa reached US$7.19 billion. Huawei and Zhongxing Telecommunications Equipment have created national fiber-optic communications networks and e-government platforms for more than 20 African countries and have constructed more than 40 3G networks in more than 30 African countries (Hruby 2021). The demand for communication devices and internet is expected to grow, given this affordability coupled with Africa's relatively youthful population. Africa, like other developing areas, must catch up on upgrading digital technologies and promoting the use, adoption, and adaptation of frontier technologies while extending access and mobilizing digital innovation to reduce inequities (UNCTAD 2021). The continent can leverage the presence of global tech companies to embark on a massive digital transformation. Embarking on this transformation journey will also provide countries with an opportunity to build better infrastructure to support the transformation. Improved transportation networks together with digital technologies can further attract foreign investors to the region and spur growth in other sectors. In this regard, countries such as Japan have financed and supported intellectual property development activities in Africa (WTO 2020); and Chinese, European, and US companies have partnered with Africans to make more businesses go digital.

StarTimes, a Chinese electronics and media company in Sub-Saharan Africa, offers digital terrestrial television and satellite television services to consumers and provides technologies to countries and broadcasters switching from analog to digital television. The company has entered into joint ventures to do business in several African countries, including the Democratic Republic of Congo, Ghana, Nigeria, and Tanzania. While bringing digital technologies to its African partners on the continent, the company also uses partners' knowledge of local markets and their extensive network and social capital. These joint ventures are particularly successful in conquering the TV subscription business and in enabling a fast upgrade of African TV operators to digital broadcasting. Joint ventures in Nigeria in the digital segment in particular have had a significant impact on the media and creative industries business across the nation. A challenge here is that some sectors in Africa are strictly regulated by governments and still dominated by state-owned companies.

Digitalization in Africa has the potential to introduce more value-added widely available services into African economies, including fast internet, 4G TV, closed-circuit TV, virtual private networks, and online payment systems that will improve well-being, inclusivity, and information security and accessibility. It can also develop African content in 4G TV and local economies by promoting African creative industries, including international digital marketing of fashion and cinematography. The wider availability of financial innovations in easy and fast electronic payments and the broader use of technologies in local companies can reduce business costs. More economies of scale across industries can contribute to solving competitiveness issues across African countries. Meanwhile, efforts by governments to boost demand for digital services and increased investment in human capital will expand the potential of digital infrastructure.

KT Corporation has cooperated with Rwanda's ICT-based economic growth through a public-private partnership with the government of Rwanda to broaden Rwanda's online services capacity and to install a wide range of high-speed broadband networks. The KT Rwanda Networks joint venture, launched in 2014 to provide 4G LTE services from Kigali, led to Africa's first nationwide 4G LTE network. Now more than 90 percent of the Rwandan population has 4G LTE services, and Rwanda has achieved the highest ICT growth rate in Africa. Improvements are needed, however, to address underused 4G network services and lack of digital skills in rural areas, affordability of digital equipment, and proper competition among companies.

Technology and knowledge development and global collaborations

In Africa, the presence of transnational firms can create knowledge and technology spillovers to the local economy (Chen 2020). Joint venture arrangements between foreign and local firms are another way to increase the capacity of local industries, generate local employment, and increase public-private knowledge and experience sharing. Examples include the following:

- In Angola, the Sonangol Sinopec International joint venture with China in the extractives sector led to new energy infrastructure and technology transfer (Madavo 2007).

- In Ethiopia, HydroChina, a company in charge of the Adama Wind Farm development, trained local engineers for operations and maintenance both on site and in Beijing (Chen 2020).

- In Madagascar, Hunan Agri, a Chinese agricultural company, opened an agrotechnology demonstration facility to teach local farmers how to grow a new type of rice. The company also provides learning and training materials in Malagasy to solidify knowledge transfer to the people (Zhang and Chi 2019).

A study of 29 partnerships between African and foreign companies identified the main opportunities pursued by Africans, many focusing on accessing foreign technologies to develop local manufacturing in the African countries hosting the joint ventures (Ado, Su, and Wanjiru 2017). The study included interviews with African staff involved in joint ventures in 12 African countries (Benin, Burundi, Cameroon, Chad, the Republic of Congo, Côte d'Ivoire, the Democratic Republic of Congo, Ghana, Niger, Nigeria, Rwanda, and Togo). Table 9.4 summarizes these interviews, focusing on objectives, success factors, and challenges reported by the interviewees.

TABLE 9.4 **Joint ventures and technology transfer to Africa**

Industry	Objectives of Africans	Success factors	Challenges
Aviation services	Access to foreign funding	Partner's willingness	Cultural or social conflicts
Construction	Access to foreign market	Cultural intelligence	Government instability
Manufacturing	Access to foreign technology	Cultural training	Knowledge hiding
Mining or refining	Build manufacturing capacity	Entrepreneurial mindset	Politicization of appointments
Power and energy	Add value to raw materials	Financial resources	Unclear hiring policies
Telecom or media	Value chain upgrade	Informality	
Textiles		Technological compatibility	
Water sanitation		Training in China	

Source: Direct interviews with African staff involved in joint ventures in Benin, Burundi, Cameroon, Chad, the Republic of Congo, Côte d'Ivoire, the Democratic Republic of Congo, Ghana, Niger, Nigeria, Rwanda, and Togo.

Some of this collaboration has helped African partners to start processing their products locally and then export them to Asia. One successful example is the SORAZ (Société de raffinage de Zinder) refinery in Niger—a joint venture between the government of Niger (40 percent owner) and the China National Petroleum Corporation (60 percent owner)—which now refines 20,000 barrels per day of crude oil before exporting it. Since beginning its operation in 2011, SORAZ has served as a means of not only transfering knowledge and technologies from China to Niger but also supporting Niger in moving up the global value chain by producing and exporting more value-adding products. Through its partnership with China, Niger has now become an oil producer and exporter of refined products. Output from the oil field was estimated at 1 million metric tons per year for a life span of about 40 years (IMF 2014). Recent statistics show an 818 percent increase in Niger's crude oil production, from 3,920 terajoules in 2011 to 35,973 in 2021.[20]

Nevertheless, joint ventures with foreign multinational companies involve challenges, including knowledge hiding and patent protection. The knowledge and technologies that Africans require to industrialize are mostly owned by foreign private companies, not necessarily by foreign governments or state-owned companies, making partnerships difficult when both companies are private and are direct competitors. Co-opetition— whereby two parties cooperate while still in competition—presents a real dilemma because many foreign companies do not want their strategic knowledge and technologies discovered by African partners who could become competitors. Making such partnerships work requires transparent negotiations to set the initial terms and outcome expectations in the partnership agreement.

The African diaspora's global entrepreneurship

Although governments cannot employ all of the 11 million young Africans projected to join the labor market each year until 2030 (ILO 2020; IMF 2018), Africa should find new opportunities for training African entrepreneurs, especially among its youth. As noted earlier in this chapter, increasing numbers of Africans have gone to Asian and other non-Western countries to study and do business, in addition to the many Africans who continue to go to Western countries. The experience of these Africans can serve as a catalyst for creating a more entrepreneurial mindset across Africa. Africans are increasingly doing business in countries like China, Saudi Arabia, and the United Arab Emirates. This new trend represents an opportunity to create a stronger network of African immigrants that can bridge business opportunities between Africa and foreign countries. The return of these African immigrants to Africa for entrepreneurial ventures after gaining business experience overseas offers opportunities for skills transfer.

Several partnerships support entrepreneurs in Africa, with successful examples including the Tony Elumelu Foundation Entrepreneurship Program and Asia's Alibaba Netpreneur Africa Training Program. Alibaba's Jack Ma recently identified '4 Es" for digital development in Africa: entrepreneurship, education, e-government, and e-infrastructure. The 2020 Africa's Business Heroes competition and the Jack Ma Foundation's Africa Netpreneur Prize Initiative identified the most promising entrepreneurs in Africa out of more than 10,000 applications from 50 African countries. After a two-stage selection process, the competition awarded US$1.5 million to be shared among the top 10 finalists.

Such entrepreneurial support initiatives between African and other internationally accomplished entrepreneurs can generate more new and young entrepreneurs in Africa. The many successful foreign entrepreneurs now looking to Africa as a place to grow their business can provide an opportunity for Africans to join forces for more youth entrepreneurship in Africa, including the Africans returning from other continents after gaining relevant experience. For example, in the case of Alpha CD Technologies in Burundi, an entrepreneur and managing director (from the African diaspora in China) convinced his Chinese partner to move from China to Burundi, bringing with him expertise and equipment to start a manufacturing business in Bujumbura. This Burundian businessman mobilized his experience of doing business in China and, with the help of his Chinese partner, opened a new factory in Bujumbura that manufactures high-quality furniture, made locally and sold both nationally and across East Africa. To encourage such moves, African countries will need strategies to incentivize returnee entrepreneurs from African diasporas.

Job creation, manufacturing, and global cooperation

As Africa's population continues to grow, its labor force provides an advantage to fuel an increasingly booming manufacturing industry across the continent. Several companies have relocated their activities from Asia, Europe, and the United States for the more affordable labor and attractive national investment policy frameworks in many African countries. Three shoe factories from Asia—Huajian and George Shoes from China, and New Wing from Hong Kong SAR, China—opened production lines in Ethiopia thanks in part to low labor costs and cheap raw materials such as leather. Huajian hired 2,000 Ethiopians at the end of 2012 and, by 2013, had 4,000 workers. Tooku Garments Company, a subsidiary of the Chinese garment company JDU Group, was established in 2012 in Tanzania, also taking advantage of low labor costs (Brautigam, Xiaoyang, and Xia 2018; Ozawa 2016). Even European and US companies have entered this interesting dynamic of African manufacturing. Volkswagen launched a car assembly plant in Rwanda, revealing its first locally assembled car in 2018. In Kenya, France's PSA Groupe revealed its first locally assembled car in 2019. Such recent developments add to a manufacturing boom across many industries and create more jobs for the African workforce. In fact, as the demand for vehicles continues to grow in Africa, manufacturing in this sector has the potential to contribute significantly to more inclusive growth and sustainable development, especially if these new vehicles are electric or use renewable energy sources. Countries such as the Democratic Republic of Congo and Morocco have the potential to become major engines of growth in manufacturing electric vehicle batteries and producing and storing renewable energy.

Africa imports four times more automobiles than it exports. With a growing population and increased purchasing power of the middle class, Africa represents an attractive investment destination for foreign companies to manufacture affordable cars on the continent. Consumer spending rose at an annual average rate of 10 percent over the past few years, and the Association of African Automotive Manufacturers expected new vehicle sales in Africa to reach 3 million in 2023 (Pandey and Wrede 2021). New vehicle sales increased by 32 percent in 2021 in Africa, with 1,131,249 new vehicles sold (AAAM 2022). To take advantage of increased competitiveness in the global market and integration in the global value chain, African and foreign investors could support domestic production of automobiles in countries such as Morocco and South Africa. These two countries, now the largest auto producers in Africa, still represent only about 1 percent of global production.

Cooperation with foreign companies in manufacturing will contribute to industrialization, particularly in promising sectors such as automobile industries. In addition to bringing foreign manufacturing to Africa, joint ventures have upgraded existing manufacturing in Africa. For instance, in Benin, where the textile sector contributes significantly to the economy, the government has initiated partnerships in the sector with Asian multinationals. The Beninese Textile Company (Compagnie Béninoise des Textiles, or CBT)—a joint venture between the Société des Industries

Textiles du Bénin (49 percent owner) and the China Textile Industrial Corporation for Foreign Economic and Technical Cooperation (51 percent owner)—is among the top producers of unbleached fabric in Africa. Initiated in 1998, CBT began operations in 2002, transforming cotton into unbleached fabric for both regional and global markets. Although CBT has allowed Benin to add value to its locally produced cotton, increase its production of unbleached fabric, and create jobs, the sector still faces challenges. For instance, Benin produced 714,714 tons of cotton in 2020 but transformed less than 5 percent into value-adding goods such as clothes and sheets. With sufficient support and well-executed manufacturing upgrades, companies like CBT could help the cotton sector add between 300,000 and 350,000 jobs in Benin by 2030.

In addition, the comparative advantage of many African countries in solar energy production offers an opportunity to increase the manufacturing of electric vehicles in Africa. For example, Chinese-German Gotion High-Tech committed in 2023 to investing US$6.4 billion in Morocco to build Africa's first electric vehicle battery plant (Metz 2024). Morocco serves as an example of sound renewable energy production policies that align with sustainable automobile industry development. The country aims to make renewable energy contribute 50 percent of its total electricity production by 2030.

Agriculture and agribusiness mindset and international partnerships

With half of the world's uncultivated arable land in Africa, agribusiness represents an economic opportunity to address persistent food insecurity. Many Africans still believe that agriculture is only for the poor and uneducated. Asian countries like China, however, have become economic powers by prioritizing the agriculture sector during a time comparable to Africa's current stage of development. Thus, Africa can adopt effective agricultural policies and even broadly partner with foreign partners to develop the agribusiness sector across the continent.

African countries are now mobilizing expertise from Asian countries to transform raw materials locally and climb value chains. For instance, SOSUMO (Société Sucrière du Moso), a company in Rutana province in southeast Burundi that grows sugar cane and produces and markets sugar, initially relied on foreign engineers and technicians to run the sugar production and improve productivity. Later, the company was able to develop a more strategic human resources plan and now relies mostly on local staff. In recent years, SOSUMO harvested nearly 220,000 tons of sugar cane per year from an area of 2,653 hectares and produced on average 25,000 tons of sugar each season.

Partnering with the National Agricultural Export Development Board of Rwanda, a Korean sericulture company, HEworks, announced in 2017 that it would make two investments in Rwanda's sericulture industry: US$5 million for silk farming development and capacity building of farmers, and US$5 million for a silk processing factory in Rwanda. The factory, located in Rwanda's Kigali Special Economic Zone, aims to generate US$50 million in silk exports annually. The firm's products target Asian markets including China, India, Japan, and Korea as well as the European market. According to World Bank data on the growing sericulture industry, Rwanda exported nearly US$41 million worth of textiles and clothing in 2021, more than 23 times what the country exported in 2001.[21] With global demand for silk projected to continue growing, Rwanda's national development strategy prioritizes the textile and garment industry as a potential engine of economic growth (Republic of Rwanda 2017). The government now focuses on identifying and developing priority value chains while attracting more significant private, foreign investments.

Attracting more foreign investment will require more strategic and holistic approaches to agribusiness development. Impact investing, improving digital capacity, and integrating ICT into business processes could generate high value for African exporters and economies. In this regard, the introduction of ITS can enhance road transportation systems and contribute to economies of scale through lower transportation costs and better operational efficiencies and innovation (Ying 1990). In East Africa, for instance, more companies are starting to use Global Positioning System technology to track product shipments and maximize fleet flexibility. This technology, coupled with improved road conditions through ITS, can create better business environments for precision agriculture, agribusiness, and manufacturing for trading nationally and internationally while capturing more value in the production chains.

Basket funding in Africa with global partners

Compared to traditional Western donors, ODA from Asian countries to Africa over the past decade has primarily taken the form of loans, causing a debt burden for the continent. For instance, China's increasing assistance and investment in infrastructure have occurred mostly through loans, and Japan and Korea have increased their loan portions over the past 20 years. In addition, the increased presence of Asian countries and the competitive nature of their policy frameworks results in fragmented aid, sometimes reducing its effectiveness. The lack of a reliable data source, particularly for Chinese funding, and poor selectivity, with funding not disbursed enough to countries with sound policies or those in serious need (the least-developed countries or fragile states), are other stumbling blocks. Mutualization of risk is one way to address such challenges.

Basket funding is a mechanism that pools funds from various sources—governments, donors, and the private sector—to ensure adequate resource allocation for programs. It represents an opportunity for synergy between Asian and Western partners, especially in health care and education programs in Africa (as discussed in the following paragraphs), and when partners share the same values and priorities for development. A central basket allocation of funds allows greater accountability and decentralization of services, and collaboration among multiple countries and institutions generates synergies and better results in Africa. Despite the opportunity basket funding represents, such funding can also increase a country's debt burden and can result in fragmented aid and dependence on one major donor. Moreover, an emphasis on results-based financing approaches will require countries to develop and implement new monitoring mechanisms.

Through Tanzania's Health Basket Fund (HBF), an initiative aligned with the country's Health Sector Strategic Plan and the SDGs, donors have been pooling funds and providing technical assistance to contribute to the well-being of Tanzanians since 2015. For instance, between 2016 and 2019, Korea contributed US$6 million. HBF aims to decentralize the health care system and provide services to local government in councils and districts where 80 percent of Tanzania's population resides. HBF's goals and primary outputs (delivery of primary health care services to mothers and children, and ensuring infrastructure and quality for primary health care services and their monitoring) align with the national development priorities, and the project is considered sustainable in that it uses Tanzania's health care systems to improve overall health care service. Although HBF has undergone few changes during the 20 years of implementation, donors have relatively high overall satisfaction, which is expected to continue.

Basket funding with new Asian donors can also help with effective implementation of education solutions in Africa. Such funding is highly relevant to national human capital development and contributes to more inclusive education. For instance, Tanzania's Education Programme for Results is based on three key pillars: diversify growth and enhance productivity, boost human capital and social inclusion, and make institutions efficient and accountable. The initiative arose out of Big Results Now, a 2013–16 program that adopted an approach of results-based aid and that identified education as one of the National Key Results Areas in Tanzania (Janus and Keijzer 2015). In 2015, the government of Tanzania implemented the new Fee-Free Basic Education Policy, which provides free education for the lower-secondary level. The Education Sector Development Plan 2016/17–2020/21 stressed the need for equal opportunity for inclusive and better-quality education, and improved education systems (Tanzania, Ministry of Education, Science, and Technology 2018). The plan aimed to provide inclusive education opportunities for marginalized communities such as political refugees, orphans, and vulnerable children. The Education Programme for Results had a satisfactory outcome for six years and led to significant enrollment and improvements in the quality of basic education (World Bank 2021). This relative performance prompted the funders to extend the closing date of the program by one year. This type of funding requires good budget and cost management and may lead to dependence on one major donor, such as the World Bank.

Attracting more foreign investments in Africa

As noted earlier, over the next decade through 2035, Africa is expected to require significant financing for infrastructure development, with financing needs estimated at US$150 billion per year to keep pace with current needs and growth opportunities

(Lakmeerahan et al. 2020). Although many foreign investors have postponed investments because of the persistent weak institutional environment for doing business, Western countries continue to invest in Africa. Asian and non-Western countries such as China, Japan, Korea, Saudi Arabia, Türkiye, and the United Arab Emirates have also become big sources of foreign investments, particularly in closing the infrastructure gap in Africa.

Foreign investments contribute to higher value added and to creating more jobs in key sectors with high economic potential—and the number of sectors with such potential is increasing. The Toyota Boshoku Corporation, a Japanese manufacturer of automotive seats and interior components, established its plant in South Africa in 2005. In 2022, the plant had an annual production capacity of 165,000 units and employed 1,137 people.[22] Such investments in manufacturing contribute to industrialization in key sectors of the economy while also creating jobs for Africans. Zanzibar's Water Authority has concluded several partnerships with organizations such as the Japan International Cooperation Agency (JICA) to boost access to clean water across the island through better management of capacity, infrastructure development, and effective maintenance. Meanwhile, other partnerships between Tanzania and JICA are in the making to attract more Japanese companies to the East African nation.[23]

Africa needs major foreign investments in many areas, including digitalization, power, and transportation. Foreign investments from Asia could help close a shortage of funding, especially at a time when Africa and other emerging powers such as Brazil, China, India, and Türkiye are in search of potential shared interests and strategic partnerships for the future (Ado and Osabutey 2018). Such investment needs are exacerbated by megaprojects such as the BRI, which is expected to connect infrastructure development across Africa. BRI investments rose from US$8.6 billion in 2013 to US$17.3 billion in 2022, with a high of US$40.1 billion in 2018, an increase of more than 368 percent over the period 2013–18 in the transportation infrastructure sector alone. Sub-Saharan Africa's share of Chinese investments and contracts in transportation infrastructure related to the BRI fell from 63 percent in 2013, the first year of the initiative, to 32 percent in 2020.

Overall, between 2005 and 2022, Chinese partners invested and executed contracts in the transportation sector alone worth more than US$100 billion.[24] Many foreign investments in Africa, however, still focus on commodities and low-value-adding goods. This situation needs to change, especially through better alignment of industrial policy and investment policy, as has occurred in countries such as Ethiopia and Rwanda. Countries can attract more foreign investments to improve manufacturing capacity building through better equipment, technologies, and transportation infrastructure by creating additional special economic zones that focus on attracting multinational firms and investors. This means designing policies and regulations that incentivize and convince foreign investors to come to Africa.

Chinese and US organizations are bridging trade and investment partnerships in Africa. The China-Africa Development Fund (China) and Prosper Africa (United States) are strategic business partners in increasing Africa's foreign trade and investment attractivity. The China-Africa Development Fund—with US$10 billion and five regional offices in Ethiopia, Ghana, Kenya, South Africa, and Zambia—has been involved in improving access to capital, technologies, and talent to support Africa's industrialization. Prosper Africa has already concluded more than 380 deals, including 130 deals in agribusiness, 83 in energy, 33 in consumer goods, 32 in health care, 32 in ICT, 26 in aerospace and defense, 25 in distribution and logistics, and 24 in environmental technology (Prosper Africa 2023). Such deals contribute to Africa's economic dynamism, but increasing competition among external actors in Africa limits synergies between foreign investors.

African countries' debt and Asian partners' transparency on loans

There is a growing debate about whether Africa is gaining easy access to loans from some Asian partners, particularly from countries such as China. Criticism for allegedly pursuing debt-trap diplomacy in Africa has sometimes come from the media, academia, and policy worlds. This narrative should be carefully questioned because the evidence behind this criticism is not yet strong (Brautigam 2020). One of the challenges in Africa-Asia partnerships is the availability and transparency of data on financial flows to Africa, including the amount of loans negotiated for and received from countries such as China. The data are not always clear, complete, or available at all. For instance, current data on Chinese loans to African countries vary from one source to another, with China and African countries sometimes reporting significantly different numbers and publishing limited data. Such discrepancies may arise because of differences between what Chinese partners want to make public and what African partners choose to publish. Data transparency informs better and more sustainable policies and ensures more reliable data for African countries' real debt levels in national and international accounts. Addressing this challenge requires serious governance improvements and ensuring that the loans African countries negotiate with foreign countries are channeled to critical industrial development needs and productive investments in Africa, rather than unproductive spending. Overall, the issue of debt service and debt sustainability and transparency in Africa in relation to certain foreign investors and partners is significant and should be addressed in a strategic manner.

African policies and governance challenges

For Africa to optimize its economic capital, countries need to improve their business environments as well as their good governance indicators on multiple fronts. Despite improved governance in Africa from 2010 to 2019, progress has slowed in recent years (Mo Ibrahim Foundation 2020), and the score on overall governance has stagnated across the continent. Although 20 countries slightly improved their performance in human development and foundations for economic opportunity, their performance in the rule of law and inclusion diminished. The trajectories of the main indexes on

TABLE 9.5 Variation in Economic Opportunity and Human Development Indexes

Economic Opportunity Index	Variation from 2010 to 2019	Human Development Index	Variation from 2010 to 2019
Overall governance	1.2	Overall governance	1.2
Public administration	0.1	Health	6.8
Business environment	1.7	Education	1.7
Infrastructure	12.8	Social protection	−0.3
		Sustainable environment	3.8

Source: Mo Ibrahim Foundation 2020.

economic and human capital for the past decade illustrate the growing imbalances that must be addressed to improve economic development and inclusive growth (table 9.5).

Competition between Asian and Western partners in Africa

Western countries have traditionally been major investors and trade and development partners for Africa, but African countries are becoming increasingly closer to Asia, often at the expense of Western traditional partners' long-standing privilege. This shift creates a challenge for African countries to align their development aspirations to embrace more cooperation with Asia (particularly with China), while not suffering economic isolation from Western countries and global institutions. In a recent speech on the 60th anniversary of the African Union, the chairperson of the African Union Commission noted an "...intensification of the hegemonic struggle between the big powers. In this international context of confrontation of divergent geopolitical interests, the will of each side threatens to transform Africa into a geostrategic battleground" (Mahamat 2023). Although not new, this competition between superpowers in Africa has increased over the past decade. For instance, just a few months after China pledged US$60 billion in financing for African economies during the 2018 Forum on China-Africa Cooperation, the United States created in 2019 its International Development Finance Corporation that pledged exactly US$60 billion in financing to Africa (Development Finance Corporation 2020). Such financing announcements, although welcomed by Africans, must not lead to an unhealthy economic rivalry between China and the United States in Africa; rather, African countries should pursue competitive development funding and deploy productive investments on the continent.

This superpower competition requires careful monitoring by Africans because the closer some African countries get to one superpower, the more pressure they receive from another. Besides China and the United States, the European Union and other actors also contribute to this Western competition with emerging powers such as China. Because all of these countries have different governance systems, the competition dynamic often translates into a competition on values, ideologies, and debates on democratic choices. Africa will have to navigate this challenge in the 21st century in order to enhance its cooperation with Asian and Western countries and maintain a healthy economic relationship with all relevant actors.

The next section offers policy recommendations for moving Africa's international cooperation forward, particularly to strengthen economic and human capital. It highlights major areas of improvement and of mutual interest for African and foreign partners while emphasizing the necessity among African countries to act in a coordinated and timely manner.

Policies

An analysis of the past 20 years of Africa's development path reveals many ways for the continent to strengthen its development cooperation with foreign partners through better economic partnerships. The objective is to move toward better external economic cooperation that leads to greater pan-African diversification, continental integration, and increased competitiveness. In the context of Africa's economic cooperation with Western countries such as Organisation for Economic Co-operation and Development nations, this objective means making ODA more effective. For instance, the Accra Agenda for Action advocates for improving the quality of development support and its impact based on key principles of ownership, inclusive partnerships, delivering results, and capacity development. Approaches such as program-based assistance and pooled funding with multiple partners will require sharing relevant technological and development experiences and promoting more development support that is based on improving Africa's international trade balance and value chain upgrade.

At the same time, domestic policy frameworks including better governance and institutional context can promote inclusive productivity growth in Africa through more effective economic cooperation with external partners both in the West and from other regions, particularly with significant trade partners such as Asia. The key policy actions that could move Africa forward include

- Establishing more effective joint ventures while increasing knowledge and technology transfer;

- Creating more well-regulated special economic zones and negotiating to attract better foreign investments, especially in infrastructure; and

- Trading more strategically with foreign economies through better industrialization and manufacturing.

Many of the analyses and recommendations made throughout this chapter also consider the experiences of developing and emerging regions when they were at similar stages of development as Africa today: Japan in the 1950s, Korea in the 1960s and 1970s, Malaysia and Thailand in the 1970s and 1980s, China in the 1980s and 1990s, and Cambodia and the Lao People's Democratic Republic in the 1990s and early 2000s. Reference to these historical development periods helps to draw lessons from exemplary practices and effective initiatives that could be considered in Africa for productivity growth and development strategies. Special focus is on African countries with strong institutional capacity and sound policies that have successfully achieved domestic reforms and attracted foreign investments.

Overall, the key areas for Africa's economic partnerships in terms of trade, human development, investments, governance, industrialization, climate and environment, digitalization, and productivity emphasize the need to engage in better cooperation with global partners by scaling up what has worked. Figure 9.11 summarizes the main recommendations for a better future of Africa's external economic cooperation.

FIGURE 9.11 **Policy recommendations for Africa's external partnerships**

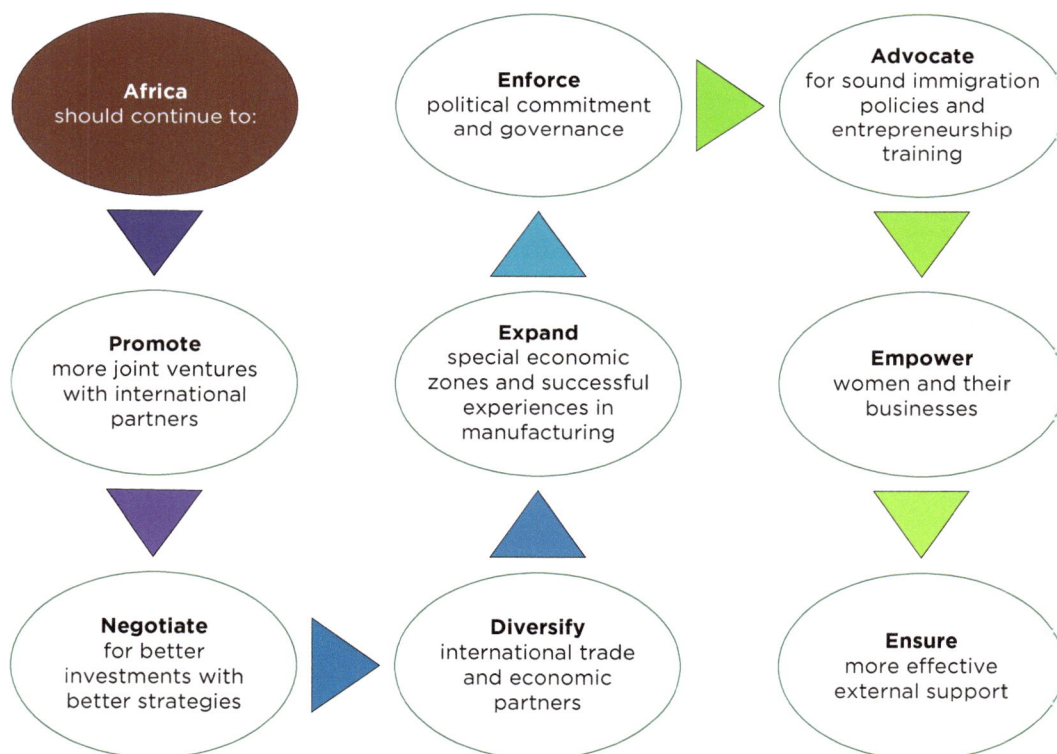

Source: World Bank.

Promote more joint ventures with international partners

Promoting international joint ventures across all sectors of the economy, and considering all opportunities for public-private partnerships between African and foreign organizations and companies, can help build and capitalize on Africa's much-needed economic capital. At the continent's current stage of development and with its need for technology and other crucial resources, joint ventures are Africa's best option for a win-win cooperation with international partners. Although Africa receives support from Asia in multiple forms, including through Asian private and state-owned enterprises operating in Africa, joint ventures offer the best opportunities for creating economic synergies whereby partners bring different skills and resources to exploit business opportunities otherwise unexploitable by a single company. Joint ventures also have the advantage of providing greater benefits for host countries such as through experience sharing and knowledge and technology transfer in key areas like digitalization, energy production, and infrastructure. To create more effective Africa-foreign joint ventures, African and foreign countries need to provide incentives to private and public organizations to encourage their engagement. As in China in the 1970s and later, joint ventures can be created in any sector (transportation, energy, digitalization, infrastructure, agriculture), making them fundamentally interesting, crucially relevant for African development, and significant and timely for a more key role of foreign investments in Africa. Joint ventures offer the following benefits:

- *Joint ventures can attract more foreign investments.* As such, they are key to facilitating the inflow of productive financial capital into African economies, especially in the context of special economic zones across the continent. Joint ventures tend to facilitate investments for foreign companies by providing them with local partners who know African markets and can help navigate country risks, local institutional environments, and related challenges.

- *Joint ventures can access more knowledge from foreign partners.* Joint ventures are known to be more beneficial to host countries in terms of experience sharing and knowledge transfer. African countries and foreign partners need to design incentives to encourage the creation of more joint ventures over other forms of entry modes. That is, while African countries and businesses pursue their strategic external economic cooperation agenda, they also need to promote and support joint ventures, particularly in areas where foreign companies have significant expertise such as in digitalization.

- *Joint ventures can move Africa up global value chains.* Because they often operate at the lower end of global value chains, most African enterprises do not add significant value to their products before marketing them internationally. This situation needs to change, and joint ventures are the right tool to upgrade African businesses to operate on the economic segment of higher-value-adding activities, thus increasing Africa's global competitiveness.

- *Joint ventures support digital infrastructure for innovation and entrepreneurship.* China currently controls more than 70 percent of Africa's 4G networks, mostly built by Huawei and Zhongxing Telecommunications Equipment (sometimes through joint ventures with local technological start-up companies such as Econet), with overall investments and contracts in Chinese technology in Sub-Saharan Africa worth more than US$7 billion between 2005 and 2020. Because mitigating project duplication requires better coordination among governments and organizations, joint ventures offer an opportunity for countries (both African and foreign) to create international synergy and complementarity. Digitalization requires better policies and regulations to address cybersecurity challenges in Africa. Additionally, capitalizing on Africa's large and increasing digitally savvy youth population will require creating more vocational education to incubate digitally enabled youth and train them in digital infrastructure to seize entrepreneurship opportunities.

Negotiate for better investments with better strategies

The rise of investment appetite from foreign partners (both Western and non-Western), particularly China, has the potential to promote inclusive productivity growth in Africa as long as African governments strategically negotiate for investments. Governments must choose investments that align with their long-term national and regional development goals. Prioritizing investments (by sector, region, and integration potential) will put African governments in a better position to negotiate for investments with strategic goals in mind. Governments need to employ effective negotiation strategies with external partners to agree from the outset on the terms and conditions that will be most beneficial to economic and social outcomes. According to Soule (2019), key negotiation aspects to consider for better deals in Africa's partnerships include the following:

- *Public involvement.* Governments must involve all key stakeholders in the negotiation process, including civil society, business executives, and relevant government agencies. Although doing so may lengthen the negotiation process, it has the advantage of ensuring a coherent, inclusive process devoid of corruption because all government agencies and other stakeholders are clear about the role of each agency in the negotiation process. It also ensures adherence with national regulations. A lack of coordination and coherence among government agents may cause the negotiation strategy to be ineffective.

- *A transparent process.* Negotiators must be empowered to avoid partisan interference, for instance by the executive branch, whose influence in the negotiation process may sometimes be politically motivated. Empowering civil servants for negotiations helps avoid the problem of the executive bypassing national regulations. On the contrary, transparent and legally valid interference can sometimes be advantageous if the goal is to improve on the negotiation style.

- *A trustworthy approach.* Keeping the public informed and engaged will help manage public perception about certain partners such as China, which is popular with many African heads of governments but less so among many ordinary Africans. This approach will help generate more constructive criticism than pure negativity from various stakeholders.

Diversify international trade and economic partners

As noted earlier in this chapter, Africa's trade strategy has centered mainly on exports of commodities, especially agricultural and primary products. To promote inclusive productivity growth, African countries should revise their trade strategies to include diversification of exports and expansion of local productive capacities and capabilities. Doing so will require a change from dependence on primary commodities that are vulnerable to price shocks to prioritizing value-added sectors and expanding the share of value-added products. Various strategies in this regard include the following:

- Simplify bilateral trade procedures and provisions that encourage direct investments in African manufacturing industries (Decreux and Spies 2012).

- Increase regional cooperation and trade diversification strategies through the African Continental Free Trade Area. Integration in regional and global value chains enabled countries such as China, Korea, Thailand, and Viet Nam to diversify and improve the quality of their exports. African countries could learn from such experiences and capitalize on trade with their partners to secure greater access to Asian and Western markets.

- Improve the competitiveness of African exports and expand the export capacity of industries through investments and technology gains (Songwe and Moyo 2012).

Expand special economic zones, build upon successful experiences, and manufacturing

Most resource-rich African countries continue to export mostly raw materials to European and non-Western countries, particularly to destinations such as China, France, Korea, and the United Arab Emirates. That is, Africa exports low-value commodities but imports finished products, mainly from Asia. Companies that invest in special economic zones (SEZs) have created waves of knowledge transfer and technological upgrade and partnerships with Asian companies, thus improving the African manufacturing industry and high-value-adding activities to capture more revenues on the global value chain. This kind of success in industrial development offers important lessons for African countries interested in developing their industries and overall economies.

At the beginning of the 21st century, Asian countries were at a similar stage of development as many African countries now. They transformed their economies by implementing sound economic policies aimed at promoting industrialization and inclusive economic development. Such policies included building national and regional development plans with a greater goal of industrialization, and effective industrial policies such as SEZs, infrastructure development, human capital development, rural development, and agricultural processing. To diversify their industrial sector, they developed SEZs to attract investments in manufacturing of automobiles, smartphones, solar panels, electronics, food, and garments. These countries achieved their success by also providing tax incentives to foreign investors and establishing SEZs near the border for better integration, providing examples for African countries that have ports for shipment or have neighboring countries with bigger economic capacity and markets for stronger integration into the global value chain. In the context of Latin America, research shows that sustainable development can occur in developing countries with the adoption of novel transformational approaches that support meaningful innovation and inclusive growth (De Fuentes and Peerally 2022). The industrial transformation of Africa's economy will certainly benefit from more effective SEZs on the continent.

Enforce political commitment and governance

African economies can enhance their external economic cooperation by implementing relevant economic policies and improving governance and the business environment. Governments must commit to creating strong and stable economic and political institutions. To do so, African governments must resolve conflicts that threaten political stability and foreign investments. In addition, Africa needs to strengthen its business environment by implementing business-friendly regulations that support social inclusivity, business prosperity, and sustainable development, such as by addressing regulatory barriers that hinder the competitiveness of the investment climate across the continent. Political stability, coupled with efficient business regulations and government support, will boost investor confidence and attract more foreign investments.

African countries must develop more consistent, reliable, and enduring regulatory frameworks and manage risks more effectively, including debt risk, loan transparency, and environmental and social impacts. They must strengthen and enforce existing regulations on environmental sustainability, labor standards, and doing business. Governments need to determine whether foreign investments meet fundamental environmental standards, because the bulk of infrastructure projects have significant environmental impacts. Ultimately, this can be achieved with transparent and rigorous environmental assessments for projects and ensuring that investors comply with regulations. Besides environmental standards, governments must also strengthen labor standards that govern local labor, wages, and working conditions. If done right, such improvements will make investors train and hire locals, and, consequently, create more jobs for Africa's growing population.

Advocate for sound immigration policies and entrepreneurship training

Africa must negotiate with partner countries to open their immigration policies more transparently to allow and encourage more African entrepreneurs to live and do business across partner countries legally and easily. For instance, in countries such as China and Japan, obtaining permanent resident status remains a challenge for many African entrepreneurs. These immigration-related challenges and entrepreneurship obstacles in Asia and other places such as North America and Western Europe need to be addressed in those countries at the national, provincial, and even local levels of major business cities. Such improvement could stimulate more economic activity between, for instance, Africa and Asian megacities specifically. Also, it is important to galvanize the entrepreneurial spirit of African students through training in entrepreneurship in African and foreign schools, such as by awarding more international scholarships in study areas that could catalyze more international entrepreneurship for members of African diasporas. In this regard, East Asian countries have initiated many capacity-building educational programs to invite scholars and government officials from Africa for opportunities to study, build partnerships, encourage cultural exchange, and promote skills transfer.

Empower women and their businesses

Supporting women-owned enterprises is crucial to inclusive economic development of Africa. With the increasing proportion of women entrepreneurs in Africa, in strategic areas such as agribusiness and cultural industries, realizing the potential of women entrepreneurs is critical. Entrepreneurship is a multifaceted area that requires not just business-related solutions, such as greater investment and inclusive business environment, but also increasing women's access to education, capital, and other resources while transforming social narratives on gender roles. In this regard, innovative training involving the use of technology to create internet-based platforms and mobile apps can enhance opportunities and peer-to-peer lending groups for women entrepreneurs across Africa. Increasing digitalization could enhance gender inclusivity across African entrepreneurial ecosystems.

Aspiration 6 of the African Union's Agenda 2063 calls for "an Africa, whose development is people-driven, relying on the potential of African people, especially its women and youth, and caring for children."[25] Realizing that aspiration will require promoting new initiatives that empower women entrepreneurs. Examples of such initiatives include the ShEquity Business Accelerator that provides funding and technical support to women-run scalable businesses in agribusiness, health care, technology, renewable energies, and fast-moving consumer goods; the Africa Technology Business Network; and the Accelerating Women-Owned Micro-Enterprises that supports female microentrepreneurs.

Ensure more effective external support

Africa's development can be achieved only through significant gains in the quality of its human capital. It is imperative, therefore, to upgrade people's education, skills, health, employment, and overall well-being. Economic cooperation with foreign partners offers significant potential to boost efforts to strengthen human capital in Africa. Such potential can be channeled through ODA to sectors such as education, entrepreneurship, health care, and overall capacity building in the fundamentals of infrastructure and industrialization for economic development. This approach needs to be customized for the African social and regional context.

Scholarship programs should be complemented with vocational training that teaches practical skills and digital literacy to Africans, especially in rural areas. These programs should link African trainees with employment and entrepreneurial opportunities both in Africa and overseas. For joint programs, basket funding provides not just opportunities for collective accountability but also room for synergies between all types of donors, especially because some donors cannot carry out individual projects alone. Basket funding has risen as an innovative financing method for improved harmonization among donors and as an opportunity for small donors to contribute to bigger goals. Basket funding programs ensure long-term sustainability of projects by creating internal transformations in governance and aligning project goals with national development agendas. Therefore, all donors are encouraged to pursue such collaborative support modalities.

Conclusion

Economic cooperation with external partners is crucial for Africa to claim the 21st century. To the extent that it benefits Africa's development, such cooperation should continue with both emerging and advanced economies. This chapter highlights the achievements, opportunities, and challenges in Africa's global cooperation. It offers key policy recommendations for Africa to catalyze economic cooperation globally that support inclusive growth, trade, continental integration, human development, investments, productivity, transition to green economy, digitalization, governance, and sustainable industrialization.

Notes

1. African Union, "Goals & Priority Areas of Agenda 2063," https://au.int/agenda2063/goals.
2. World Integrated Trade Solution, "World Trade Summary 2000 data," https://wits.worldbank.org/CountryProfile/en/Country/WLD/Year/2000/Summary.
3. UNCTAD, UNCTADstat Data Centre, "Merchandise: Total trade and share, annual," https://unctadstat.unctad.org/datacentre/dataviewer/US.TradeMerchTotal; UNCTAD, "Foreign direct investment: Inward and outward flows and stock, annual," https://unctadstat.unctad.org/datacentre/dataviewer/US.FdiFlowsStock.

4. These platforms include the Forum on China-Africa Cooperation; the Tokyo International Conference on African Development; the Africa Singapore Business Forum; the Korea-Africa Economic Cooperation Conference; summits on Asia-Africa cooperation, India-Africa, Japan-Africa, and Russian Federation–Africa; and the New Asian-African Strategic Partnership.

5. The subregions follow UNCTAD grouping of African countries as follows: Central Africa (Angola, Cameroon, the Central African Republic, Chad, the Democratic Republic of Congo, the Republic of Congo, Equatorial Guinea, Gabon, and São Tomé and Príncipe); Eastern Africa (Burundi, the Comoros, Djibouti, Eritrea, Ethiopia, Kenya, Madagascar, Malawi, Mauritius, Mozambique, Rwanda, the Seychelles, Somalia, South Sudan, Tanzania, Uganda, Zambia, and Zimbabwe); Northern Africa (Algeria, the Arab Republic of Egypt, Libya, Morocco, Tunisia, Sudan); Southern Africa (Botswana, Eswatini, Lesotho, Namibia, and South Africa); and Western Africa (Benin, Burkina Faso, Cabo Verde, Côte d'Ivoire, The Gambia, Ghana, Guinea, Guinea-Bissau, Liberia, Mali, Mauritania, Niger, Nigeria, Senegal, Sierra Leone, Togo).

6. This discussion uses the UNCTAD classification of Southern Asia, which comprises Afghanistan, Bangladesh, Bhutan, India, the Islamic Republic of Iran, Maldives, Nepal, Pakistan, and Sri Lanka.

7. UNCTADstat Data Centre, https://unctadstat.unctad.org/datacentre.

8. Southeast Asian Ministers of Education Organization Asian International Mobility for Students Programme, "Programme Milestones," https://aims-rihed.net/programme-history/.

9. For more information on the program, refer to US Department of State web page, "African Women's Entrepreneurship Program," https://www.state.gov/african-womens-entrepreneurship-program/.

10. For more information on the Better Than Cash Alliance, refer to https://www.betterthancash.org/about/members.

11. World Bank DataBank, "Human Capital Index (HCI) (scale 0–1) – Sub-Saharan Africa," https://data.worldbank.org/indicator/HD.HCI.OVRL?end=2020&locations=ZG&most_recent_year_desc=false&start=2020&view=bar&year=2020.

12. For more information on the African Diaspora Network, visit its website at https://africandiasporanetwork.org/mission-and-vision/.

13. United Nations Educational, Scientific, and Cultural Organization, Institute for Statistics, "Other Policy Relevant Indicators—Education," https://databrowser.uis.unesco.org/browser/EDUCATION/UIS-EducationOPRI/int-stud.

14. United Nations Educational, Scientific, and Cultural Organization, Institute for Statistics, "Other Policy Relevant Indicators—Education," https://databrowser.uis.unesco.org/browser/EDUCATION/UIS-EducationOPRI.

15. For more on the forum, visit http://www.focac.org/eng/zywx_1/zywj/201809/t20180912_7933578.htm.

16. KOICA, "What We Do," https://www.koica.go.kr/koica_en/3441/subview.do.

17. Boston University Global Policy Development Center, Chinese Loans to Africa Database, https://www.bu.edu/gdp/chinese-loans-to-africa-database/.

18. World Bank, DataBank, "Electric Power Consumption (kWh per capita)," https://data.worldbank.org/indicator/EG.USE.ELEC.KH.PC.

19. EY, "About the EY Attractiveness Program," https://www.ey.com/en_gl/foreign-direct-investment-surveys.

20. International Energy Agency, "Niger," https://www.iea.org/countries/niger/oil.

21. World Integrated Trade Solution, "Rwanda Textiles and Clothing Exports by Country and Region in US$ Thousands 2021," https://wits.worldbank.org/CountryProfile/en/Country/RWA/Year /2021/TradeFlow/Export/Partner/all/Product/50-63_TextCloth.

22. For more information on Toyota Boshoku South Africa, refer to the company's "About Us" page, https://www.toyota-boshoku.sa.com/company-overview.

23. Japan International Cooperation Agency, "Activities in Tanzania," https://www.jica.go.jp /Resource/tanzania/english/activities/partnership.html.

24. China Global Investment Tracker, https://www.aei.org/china-global-investment-tracker/.

25. African Union, "Our Aspirations for the Africa We Want," https://au.int/agenda2063/aspirations.

References

AAAM (African Association of Automotive Manufacturers). 2022. "African New Vehicle Sales Increase by 32%." News release, May 18, 2022. https://aaamafrica.com/news/f/african-new-vehicle-sales -increase-by-32%25.

Ado, A. 2023. *L'entrepreneuriat numérique durable au Bénin: opportunités, défis et stratégies.* Berlin: Humboldt Institut für Internet und Gesellschaft. https://www.hiig.de/wp-content/uploads /2023/02/Lentrepreneuriat-numerique-durable-au-Benin-Opportunites-defis-et-strategies.pdf.

Ado, A., E. Chrysostome, and Z. Su. 2016. "Examining Adaptation Strategies of Sub-Saharan African Immigrant Entrepreneurs in China: The Case of Guangdong." *Journal of Developmental Entrepreneurship* 21 (4): 1–25.

Ado, A., and M. I. Diamouténé. 2023. "Creative Industries' Entrepreneurial Success: Social Capital, Networks, and Internationalization Strategy." *Journal of Comparative International Management* 26 (2): 144–58. https://doi.org/10.55482/jcim.2023.33460.

Ado, A., and E. L. Osabutey. 2018. "Africa–China Cooperation: Potential Shared Interests and Strategic Partnerships?" *AIB Insights* 18 (4): 20–3.

Ado, A., E. L. Osabutey, P. Sinha, and O. Adeola. 2025. "Africa's International Trade Paradox, Technology Transfer, and Value Chain Upgrade." *Technological Forecasting and Social Change* 213 (April): 124014. https://doi.org/10.1016/j.techfore.2025.124014.

Ado, A., I. Ben Othmane, M. Matei, and B. Montreuil. 2014. "Towards Physical Internet Enabled Interconnected Humanitarian Logistics." *1st International Physical Internet Conference*, Vol. 30.

Ado, A., Z. Su, and R. Wanjiru. 2017. "Learning and Knowledge Transfer in Africa-China JVs: Interplay between Informalities, Culture, and Social Capital." *Journal of International Management* 23 (2): 166–79.

AfDB (African Development Bank Group). 2018. *African Economic Outlook 2018.* Abidjan, Côte d'Ivoire: AfDB.

Africa Energy Chamber. 2021. *Africa Energy Outlook 2021.* Johannesburg: Africa Energy Chamber. https://energychamber.org/wp-content/uploads/AEC_Outlook_2021.pdf.

African Union. 2020. *The Digital Transformation Strategy for Africa (2020–30).* Addis Ababa, Ethiopia: African Union. https://au.int/en/documents/20200518/digital-transformation-strategy-africa-2020 -2030.

Argaam. 2023. "Saudi Arabia Aims to Invest Over $25 Bln in Africa: Crown Prince." Argaam, October 11, 2023. https://www.argaam.com/en/article/articledetail/id/1683983#:~:text=In%20his%20 opening%20speech%2C%20Crown,billion%20to%20Africa%20until%202030.

Blimpo, M. P., and M. Cosgrove-Davies. 2019. *Electricity Access in Sub-Saharan Africa: Uptake, Reliability, and Complementary Factors for Economic Impact*. Africa Development Forum. Washington, DC: World Bank.

Bosma, N., S. Hill, A. Ionescu-Somers, D. Kelley, J. Levie, A. Tarnawa, and the Global Entrepreneurship Research Association. 2020. *Global Entrepreneurship Monitor 2019/2020 Global Report*. London: Global Entrepreneurship Research Association. https://www.gemconsortium.org/report/gem -2019-2020-global-report.

Brautigam, D. 2020. "A Critical Look at Chinese 'Debt-Trap Diplomacy': The Rise of a Meme." *Area Development and Policy* 5 (1): 1–14.

Brautigam, D., T. Xiaoyang, and Y. Xia. 2018. "What Kinds of Chinese 'Geese' Are Flying to Africa? Evidence from Chinese Manufacturing Firms." *Journal of African Economies* 27 (Suppl_1): i29– i51.

Chen, Y. 2020. "'Africa's China': Chinese Manufacturing Investments in Nigeria in the Post-Oil Boom Era and Channels for Technology Transfer." Working Paper 36, April 2020, China Africa Research Initiative, Johns Hopkins School of Advanced International Studies, Washington, DC.

Cheru, F., and A. Oqubay. 2019. "Catalyzing Africa-China Ties for Africa's Structural Transformation: Lessons from Ethiopia." Chapter 14 in *China-Africa and an Economic Transformation*, edited by A. Oqubay and J. Y. Lin. New York: Oxford University Press.

Decreux, Y., and J. Spies. 2012. "Africa's Trade Potential: Export Opportunities in Growth Markets." *International Trade Forum* 4: 14.

De Fuentes, C., and J. A. Peerally. 2022. "Transforming Innovation Systems for Sustainable Development Challenges: A Latin American Perspective." In *The Emerald Handbook of Entrepreneurship in Latin America*, edited by O. J. Montiel Méndez and A. A. Alvarado, 133–57. Leeds: Emerald Publishing Limited.

Development Finance Corporation. 2020. "U.S. International Development Finance Corporation Begins Operations." Press Release, January 2, 2020. https://www.dfc.gov/media/press-releases/us -international-development-finance-corporation-begins-operations.

Dotto, C. 2019. "'Little Africa' in China." *New Internationalist*, March 11, 2019. https://newint.org /features/2019/03/11/%E2%80%98little-africa%E2%80%99-china.

Doualeh, M. S. 2021. Statement by the Permanent Representative of Djibouti to the UN, "Human Capital and Building Forward Better after the COVID-19." United Nations Africa Dialogue Series, Public Policy Forum. https://www.un.org/osaa/sites/www.un.org.osaa/files/docs/pr_statement _and_input_osaa.pdf.

Economist Intelligence Unit. 2017. *Next-Generation Africa-GCC Business Ties in a Digital Economy*. Economist Intelligence Unit Limited. https://eiuperspectives.economist.com/economic -development/next-generation-africa-gcc-business-ties-digital-economy-0.

Edinger, H., and J. P. Labuschagne. 2019. "If You Want to Prosper, Consider Building Roads." Deloitte Insights, Deloitte University EMEA CVBA. https://www2.deloitte.com/content/dam/insights/us /articles/za22330_consider-building-roads/DI_If-you-want-to-prosper-consider-building-roads .pdf.

Galán-Muros, V., E. Chacón, and M. Escribens. 2022. *Exploring International Aid for Tertiary Education: Recent Developments and Current Trends*. Paris: UNESCO. https://unesdoc.unesco.org /ark:/48223/pf0000381747.

GSMA. 2020. *The Mobile Economy 2020*. GSM Association. https://www.gsma.com/mobileeconomy /wp-content/uploads/2020/03/GSMA_MobileEconomy2020_Global.pdf.

Harvard University Center for African Studies. 2020. "Concept Note: Women and the Changing Face of Entrepreneurship in Africa." Prepared for the Center for African Studies Conference, Harvard University, Cambridge, MA. https://africa.harvard.edu/files/african-studies/files/women_and _the_changing_face_of_entrepreneurship_in_africa_revised_concept_note.pdf.

Hruby, A. 2021. "The Digital Infrastructure Imperative in African Markets." *AfricaSource* (blog), April 8, 2021. https://www.atlanticcouncil.org/blogs/africasource/the-digital-infrastructure -imperative-in-african-markets/.

IEA (International Energy Agency). 2019. *Africa Energy Outlook 2019*. Paris: IEA. https://www.iea.org /reports/africa-energy-outlook-2019.

IFC (International Finance Corporation). 2023a. "IFC Launches Program to Empower Women-Led Startups in Sub-Saharan Africa." Press Release, June 5, 2023. https://pressroom.ifc.org/all/pages /PressDetail.aspx?ID=27578.

IFC (International Finance Corporation). 2023b. "SheWins Africa: Unlocking the Potential of Women-Led Startups in Africa." Brochure, IFC, Washington, DC. https://www.ifc.org/content/dam/ifc /doclink/2023/ifc-she-wins-africa-brochure.pdf.

ILO (International Labour Organization). 2020. *World Employment and Social Outlook: Trends 2020*. International Labour Office. Geneva: ILO. https://www.ilo.org/wcmsp5/groups/public /---dgreports/---dcomm/---publ/documents/publication/wcms_734455.pdf.

IMF (International Monetary Fund). 2014. *Niger: Second and Third Reviews Under the Extended Credit Facility Arrangement and Requests for Waivers of Nonobservance of Performance Criteria and for Extension of the Program Period and Arrangement, Rephasing of Disbursements, and Modification of Performance Criteria*. Washington, DC: IMF. https://www.elibrary.imf.org/view/journals /002/2014/168/article-A001-en.xml.

IMF (International Monetary Fund). 2018. *IMF Annual Report 2018: Building a Shared Future*. Washington, DC: IMF. https://www.imf.org/external/pubs/ft/ar/2018/eng/assets/pdf/imf-annual -report-2018.pdf.

Janus, H., and N. Keijzer. 2015. "Big Results Now? Emerging Lessons from Results-Based Aid in Tanzania." Discussion Paper 4/2015, German Development Institute/Deutsches Institut für Entwicklungspolitik (DIE), Bonn. https://www.idos-research.de/fileadmin/migratedNewsAssets /Files/DP_4.2015.pdf.

Karingi, S., and L. N. Naliaka. 2022. "The Future of India-Africa Relations: Opportunities Abound." *Brookings Commentary*, February 25, 2022. https://www.brookings.edu/articles/the-future -of-india-africa-relations-opportunities-abound/.

Lakmeerahan, K., Q. Manji, R. Nyairo, and H. Pöltner. 2020. "Solving Africa's Infrastructure Paradox." *McKinsey & Company Insights*, March 6, 2020. https://www.mckinsey.com/business-functions /operations/our-insights/solving-africas-infrastructure-paradox.

Lall, S. V., J. V. Henderson, and A. J. Venables. 2017. Africa's Cities: Opening Doors to the World. Washington, DC: World Bank. https://openknowledge.worldbank.org/entities/publication /88ece2e5-4bca-5f57-ad41-85ea3288e355.

Li, Z., L. J. C. Ma, and D. Xue. 2009. "An African Enclave in China: The Making of a New Transnational Urban Space." *Eurasian Geography and Economics* 50 (6): 699–719.

Lopes, C. 2018. *Africa in Transformation: Economic Development in the Age of Doubt*. London: Palgrave Macmillan.

Madavo, C. E. 2007. "China and Africa: Opportunities, Challenges and Forging a Way Forward." *Business and Public Administration Studies* 2 (3): 1.

Mahamat, M. F. 2023. "Speech for the Celebration of the 60th Anniversary of OAU/AU." May 25, 2023. https://au.int/en/speeches/20230525/speech-chairperson-celebration-60th-anniversary-oauau.

Marfaing, L., and A. Thiel. 2014. "'Agents of Translation': West African Entrepreneurs in China as Vectors of Social Change." Working Paper No. 4, Priority Program 448, German Research Foundation, Leipzig and Halle.

Marubeni Corporation. 2022. "Investing in Fund Focused on the Healthcare Sector in Africa." News release, August 22, 2022. https://www.marubeni.com/en/news/2022/release/00061.html.

Metz, S. 2024. "Chinese Firms Eye Morocco as Way to Cash In on US Electric Vehicle Subsidies." Associated Press, July 2, 2024. https://apnews.com/article/china-morocco-electric-vehicles -batteries-subsidies-ea055ee37c5da66d30a38df80e4d198e.

Mo Ibrahim Foundation. 2020. *Ibrahim Index of African Governance 2020: Report.* London: Mo Ibrahim Foundation.

Ofori Adofo, J. 2020. "Electrification, Power Outages and Employment." *Applied Economics and Finance* 7 (4): 147–59.

Oh, J. 2017. "Spread or Concentrated: Where Is South Korean Inbound Education Aid Aimed and Where Should It Be Directed? A Comparison with the Japanese Case." *Review of Urban and Regional Development Studies* 29 (2): 114–34.

Oqubay, A. 2019. "The Structure and Performance of the Ethiopian Manufacturing Sector." Chapter 36 in *The Oxford Handbook of the Ethiopian Economy*, edited by F. Cheru, C. Cramer, and A. Oqubay. Oxford, UK: Oxford University Press.

Ozawa, T. 2016. "The Next Great Industrial Transmigration: Relocating China's Factories to Sub-Saharan Africa, Flying-Geese Style? The 'Flying-Geese' Theory of Multinational Corporations and Structural Transformation." In *The Evolution of the World Economy*, 121–54. Cheltenham, UK: Edward Elgar Publishing.

Pandey, A., and I. Wrede. 2021. "German Car Industry Doubles Down on Africa." *DW In Focus*, January 7, 2021. https://www.dw.com/en/german-cars-auto-africa-vw/a-56156343.

Perennial. 2015. "Perennial Enters into 55–45 Joint Venture with Shangri-La to Develop an Over US$250 Million Integrated Mixed-Use Development in Accra, Ghana." Press Release. August 21, 2015. https://investor.perennialholdings.com/newsroom/20150821_070054_40S _UPR5H9DJM7VKUQC3.2.pdf.

Prosper Africa. 2023. "Top Sectors by Deal." https://www.prosperafrica.gov/results/.

Republic of Rwanda. 2017. *7 Years Government Programme: National Strategy for Transformation (NST 1) 2017–2024.* Government of Rwanda. https://www.greenpolicyplatform.org/sites/default /files/downloads/policy-database/NST1_7YGP_Final.pdf.

Roland Berger. 2018. "Recent Development Paradigms to Support Women's Empowerment." *Insights*, September 28, 2018. https://www.rolandberger.com/en/Insights/Publications/Africa-First -female-entrepreneurs-in-the-high-tech-sector-as-new-role-models.html.

Songwe, V., J. A. Macleod, and S. Karingi. 2021. "The African Continental Free Trade Area: A Historical Moment for Development in Africa." *Journal of African Trade* 8 (2): 12–23.

Songwe, V., and N. Moyo. 2012. "China-Africa Relations: Defining New Terms of Engagement." In *Foresight Africa: Top Priorities for the Continent in 2012*, edited by J. O. Adeoti, J. Agbor, M. Diene, R. Joseph, A. Kamau, S. N. Karingi, M. S. Kimenyi, et al., 3–5. Washington, DC: Brookings Institution. https://www.brookings.edu/wp-content/uploads/2016/06/01_foresight_africa_full _report.pdf.

Soule, F. 2019. "How to Negotiate Infrastructure Deals with China: Four Things African Governments Need to Get Right." *The Conversation*, January 3, 2019. https://theconversation.com/how-to -negotiate-infrastructure-deals-with-china-four-things-african-governments-need-to-get -right-109116.

Sun, Y. 2017. "China and the East Africa Railways: Beyond Full Industry Chain Export." *Commentary*, July 6, 2017. https://www.brookings.edu/articles/china-and-the-east-africa-railways -beyond-full-industry-chain-export/.

Sun, Y. 2020. "Unpacking the Engagement of Nontraditional Actors in Africa: China and Other Emerging Players." *Commentary*, January 14, 2020. Brookings. https://www.brookings.edu/blog /africa-in-focus/2020/01/14/unpacking-the-engagement-of-nontraditional-actors-in-africa-china -and-other-emerging-players/.

Tanzania, Ministry of Education, Science, and Technology. 2018. *Education Sector Development Plan (2016/17–2020/21)*. Government of Tanzania. https://www.globalpartnership.org/node/document /download?file=sites/default/files/2019-04-gpe-tanzania-esp.pdf.

UNCTAD (United Nations Trade & Development). 2020a. *Global Investment Trends Monitor, No. 36*. New York: United Nations. https://unctad.org/system/files/official-document/diaeiainf 2020d4_en.pdf.

UNCTAD (United Nations Trade & Development). 2020b. *World Investment Report 2020: International Production beyond the Pandemic*. New York: United Nations. https://unctad.org /webflyer/world-investment-report-2020.

UNCTAD (United Nations Trade & Development). 2021. *Technology and Innovation Report 2021: Catching Technological Waves: Innovation with Equity*. New York: United Nations. https://unctad .org/page/technology-and-innovation-report-2021.

UN DESA (United Nations Department of Economic and Social Affairs, Population Division). 2015. "Youth Population Trends and Sustainable Development." Population Fact Sheet 2015/1, United Nations, New York. https://www.un.org/development/desa/pd/content/youth-population -trends-and-sustainable-development.

United Nations. 2023. *Sustainable Development Goals Report: Special Edition*. New York: United Nations. https://unstats.un.org/sdgs/report/2023/The-Sustainable-Development-Goals -Report-2023.pdf.

WHO (World Health Organization). 2019. "Republic of Korea Launches Five-Country Health Security Initiative in West Africa, in Partnership with WHO." WHO Africa, September 10, 2019. https:// www.afro.who.int/news/republic-korea-launches-five-country-health-security-initiative -west-africa-partnership-who.

WHO (World Health Organization). 2020. "The Government of South Korea and WHO Extend Support Worth Ten Million Dollars towards Health System Strengthening for Improving Reproductive, Maternal, Child and Adolescent Health-Service Delivery in Five Districts in Busoga Sub-Region in Uganda." WHO Africa, July 16, 2020. https://www.afro.who.int/news/government -south-korea-and-who-extend-support-worth-ten-million-dollars-towards-health-system.

World Bank. 2021. "Restructuring Paper on a Proposed Program Restructuring of the Tanzania Education Program for Results. Report RES44224." World Bank, Washington, DC. https:// documents1.worldbank.org/curated/en/778981611361061674/pdf/Disclosable-Restructuring -Paper-TZ-Education-Program-for-Results-P147486.pdf.

World Bank and DRC (Development Research Center of the State Council, P.R. China). 2014. *Urban China: Toward Efficient Inclusive and Sustainable Urbanization*. Washington, DC: World Bank. https://hdl.handle.net/10986/18865.

WTO (World Trade Organization). 2020. *Trade Policy Review—Japan*. Report by the Secretariat, WT/TPR/S/397, WTO, Geneva. https://www.wto.org/english/tratop_e/tpr_e/s397_e.pdf.

Ying, J. S. 1990. "The Inefficiency of Regulating a Competitive Industry: Productivity Gains in Trucking Following Reform." *Review of Economics and Statistics* 72 (2): 191–201.

Zhang, D., and J. Chi. 2019. "Chinese Technology, Experts Help Madagascar Triple Rice Yield." *Global Times*, December 10, 2019. https://www.globaltimes.cn/content/1173002.shtml.

www.ingramcontent.com/pod-product-compliance
Lightning Source LLC
Chambersburg PA
CBHW041239020426
42333CB00002B/15